# Israel

**The complete guide, thoroughly up-to-date**

Packed with details that will make your trip

**The must-see sights, off and on the beaten path**

What to see, what to skip

**Mix-and-match vacation itineraries**

City strolls, countryside adventures

**Smart lodging and dining options**

Essential local do's and taboos

**Transportation tips, distances, and directions**

Key contacts, savvy travel tips

**When to go, what to pack**

Clear, accurate, easy-to-use maps

**Books to read**

Fodor's Travel Publications, Inc.
New York • Toronto • London • Sydney • Auckland
www.fodors.com

# Fodor's Israel

**EDITOR:** Christine Cipriani

**Area Editors:** Magda Abdou, Nora El Samahy, Judy Stacey Goldman, Lisa Perlman, Mike Rogoff
**Editorial Production:** Stacey Kulig
**Maps:** David Lindroth, Inc., *cartographer*; Steven K. Amsterdam, Bob Blake, *map editors*
**Design:** Fabrizio La Rocca, *creative director*; Guido Caroti, *associate art director*; Jolie Novak, *photo editor*
**Production/Manufacturing:** Mike Costa
**Cover Photograph:** Richard Nowitz
**Database Production:** Phebe Brown, Janet Foley, Mark Laroche, Victoria Lu, Andrea Pariser, Priti Tambi, Julie Tomasz, Martin Walsh, Lucy Wu, Alexander Zlotnick

## Copyright

## Special Sales

# CONTENTS

# Contents

## Maps

# ON THE ROAD WITH FODOR'S

WHEN I PLAN A VACATION, the first thing I do is cast around among my friends and colleagues to find someone who's just been where I'm going. That's because there's no substitute for a recommendation from a good friend who knows your tastes, your budget, and your circumstances, someone who's just been there. Unfortunately, such friends are few and far between. So it's nice to know that there's *Fodor's Israel*.

In the first place, this book won't stay home when you hit the road. It will accompany you every step of the way, steering you away from wrong turns and wrong choices and never expecting a thing in return. It includes a wonderful, full-color map from Rand McNally, the world's largest commercial mapmaker. Most important of all, it's written and assiduously updated by the kind of people you *would* hit up for travel tips if you knew them. They're as choosy as your pickiest friend, except they've probably seen a lot more of Israel. In these pages, they don't send you chasing down every town and sight in Israel but have instead selected the best ones, the ones that are worthy of your time and money. To make it easy for you to put it all together in the time you have, they've created short, medium, and long itineraries and, in cities, neighborhood walks that you can mix and match in a snap. Just tear out the map at the perforation, and join us on the road in Israel. Will this be the vacation of your dreams? We hope so.

## About Our Writers

Our success in helping to make your trip the best of all possible vacations is a credit to the hard work of our extraordinary writers and editors.

**Magda Abdou** became a Red Sea addict the first time she visited the Sinai and its coast in the late 1980s. Since then she has worked summers at hotels and diving companies, explored the desert, camped out under the stars, and made hundreds of dives among some of the most amazing marine life on the planet. She also writes on film and women's issues for the Cairo fashion magazine *Pose*.

**Nora El Samahy,** who corevised our Side Trips to the Sinai and Petra, has been on the go for the last six years, but will always consider Cairo home. Fortunately, her family and friends remain there, giving her a viable excuse to return often. Her affinity for the Sinai has grown even stronger since she learned to scuba dive. Now living in San Francisco, she is pursuing an acting career.

**Judy Stacey Goldman** was born in Montréal and has lived in Israel, where she is now a professional tour guide, for 26 years. She has coauthored three books about Jerusalem and Tel Aviv and is currently preparing a new book on Jerusalem. Her Fodor's territories include the Northern Coast, Western Galilee, Eilat, and the Negev.

**Lisa Perlman,** a native of Australia, wrote her way through Japan and France before moving to Israel in 1986. She specializes in environmental issues and is a former editor of the *Jerusalem Post*'s Tel Aviv weekly, *Metro*. Her work on this edition of *Fodor's Israel* includes Tel Aviv, the Upper Galilee and the Golan, and the Gold Guide.

**Mike Rogoff,** a professional tour guide and writer, has been exploring and studying the byways of Israel since he moved there from his native South Africa in 1970. His calling—to excite visitors of all persuasions about his new-old land—became a profession when he discovered that people would actually pay him for doing what he loved best. Mike lives in Jerusalem and is a recipient of the Israel government's Guide of the Year award. He has contributed to *Fodor's Israel* since 1985; look for his byline in the Jerusalem, Around Jerusalem, Lower Galilee, and Destination: Israel chapters.

## Connections

We're pleased that the American Society of Travel Agents continues to endorse Fodor's as its guidebook of choice. ASTA is the world's largest and most influential travel trade association, operating in more than 170 countries, with 27,000 members pledged to adhere to a strict code of ethics reflecting the Society's motto, "Integrity in Travel." ASTA shares Fodor's devotion to providing smart, honest travel information and advice to travelers, and we've long recommended that our readers—even those who have guidebooks and traveling friends—consult ASTA member agents for the experience and professionalism they bring to your vacation planning.

On Fodor's Web site (www.fodors.com), check out the new Resource Center, an online companion to the Gold Guide chapter of this book, complete with useful hot links to related sites. In our forums, you can also get lively advice from other travelers and more great tips from Fodor's experts worldwide.

## How to Use This Book

### Organization

Up front is the **Gold Guide,** an easy-to-use reference section arranged alphabetically by topic. Under each heading are tips and information to help you plan your trip to Israel, as well as the addresses and phone numbers of organizations and companies offering Israel-specific services and detailed information and publications.

The first chapter in the guide, **Destination: Israel,** helps get you in the mood for your trip. What's Where gets you oriented, Pleasures and Pastimes describes the activities and sights that make Israel unique, New and Noteworthy cues you in on trends and happenings, Fodor's Choice showcases our top picks, and Festivals and Seasonal Events alerts you to special events you'll want to seek out.

Chapters are arranged regionally, beginning with Jerusalem and its environs and Tel Aviv. The next three chapters cover Israel's northern coast and areas of the Galilee and the Golan. The book then moves south to Eilat and the Negev and concludes with side trips to the Sinai and Petra.

Each **city chapter** begins with an Exploring section, which is subdivided by neighborhood. Each subsection recommends a walking or driving tour and lists sights in alphabetical order. Each **regional chapter** is divided by geographical area; within each area, towns are covered in logical geographical order, and attractive stretches of road and minor points of interest between

them are indicated by the designation *En Route.* Throughout the book, *Off the Beaten Path* sights appear after the places from which they are most easily accessible. And within town sections, all restaurants and lodgings are grouped together.

To help you decide what to visit in the time you have, all chapters begin with **recommended itineraries.** You can mix and match those from several chapters to create a complete vacation. The **A to Z** section that ends each chapter covers getting there, getting around, and helpful contacts and resources.

At the end of the book you'll find a complete **Chronology** and suggestions for **Further Reading.** The former covers thousands of years of history in a few pages; the latter suggests both fiction and nonfiction to enrich your visit to Israel.

### Icons and Symbols

★   Our special recommendations
✕   Restaurant
🏠   Lodging establishment
✕🏠   Lodging establishment whose restaurant warrants a special trip
♻   Good for kids (rubber duck)
☞   Sends you to another section of the guide for more information
✉   Address
☎   Telephone number
☺   Opening and closing times
💰   Admission prices (those we give apply to adults; substantially reduced fees are almost always available for children, students, and senior citizens)

Numbers in white and black circles ③ ❸ that appear on the maps, in the margins, and within the tours correspond to one another.

### Dining and Lodging

The restaurants and lodgings we list are the cream of the crop in each price range. Price charts for Jerusalem and Tel Aviv appear in the Dining and Lodging sections of those chapters; price charts for all other regions appear in the Pleasures and Pastimes section following the chapter introduction.

### Hotel Facilities

We always list the facilities that are available—but we don't specify whether you'll be charged extra to use them: when pricing accommodations, always ask what's included. In addition, assume that all rooms have private baths unless noted otherwise. In addition, when you book a room, be sure to mention if you have a disability or are traveling with children, if you prefer a private bath or a certain type of bed, or if you have specific dietary needs or other concerns.

Assume that hotels operate on the **European Plan** (EP, with no meals) unless we specify that they use the **Continental Plan** (CP, with a Continental breakfast daily), **Modified American Plan** (MAP, with breakfast and dinner daily), or the **Full American Plan** (FAP, with all meals).

### Restaurant Reservations and Dress Codes

Reservations are always a good idea; we mention them only when they're essential or are not accepted. Book as far ahead as you can, and reconfirm as soon as you arrive. Unless otherwise noted, the restaurants listed are open daily for lunch and dinner. We mention dress only when men are required to wear a jacket or a jacket and tie. Look for details on local dining-out habits in the Dining section of Smart Travel Tips, and in the Pleasures and Pastimes section following each chapter introduction.

### Credit Cards

The following abbreviations are used: **AE**, American Express; **DC**, Diners Club; **MC**, MasterCard; and **V**, Visa.

## Don't Forget to Write

You can use this book in the confidence that all prices and opening times are based on information supplied to us at press time; Fodor's cannot accept responsibility for any errors. Time inevitably brings changes, so always confirm information when it matters—especially if you're making a detour to visit a specific place.

Were the restaurants we recommended as described? Did our hotel picks exceed your expectations? Did you find a museum we recommended a waste of time? Keeping a travel guide fresh and up-to-date is a big job, and we welcome your feedback, positive *and* negative. If you have complaints, we'll look into them and revise our entries when the facts warrant it. If you've discovered a special place that we haven't included, we'll pass the information along to our correspondents and have them check it out. So send us your thoughts via e-mail at editors@fodors.com (specifying the name of the book on the subject line) or on paper in care of the Israel editor at Fodor's, 201 East 50th Street, New York, NY 10022. In the meantime, have a wonderful trip!

Karen Cure
*Editorial Director*

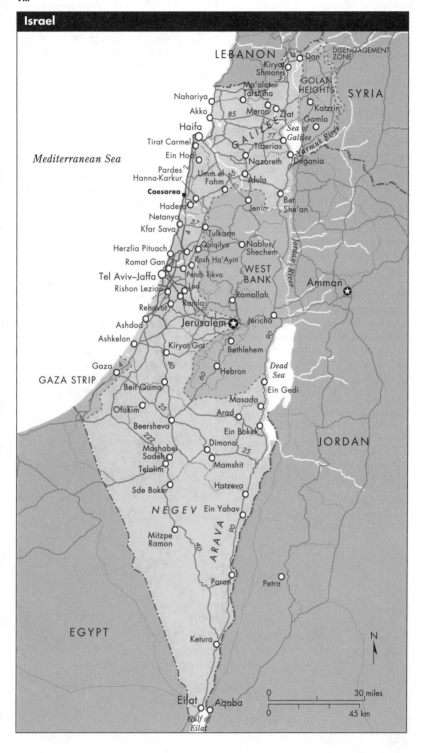

# Israel

Mediterranean Sea

LEBANON

SYRIA

GOLAN HEIGHTS

DISENGAGEMENT ZONE

Dan

Kiryat Shmona

Ma'alot Tarshiha

Nahariya

Akko

*85*

Meron

Zfat

Katzrin

Gamla

Haifa

Tirat Carmel

Ein Hod

*GALILEE*

Tiberias

*Sea of Galilee*

*77*

*Yarmuk River*

Pardes Hanna-Karkur

Umm el Fahm

*65*

Nazareth

Degania

**Caesarea**

Hadera

Afula

Netanya

Jenin

Bet She'an

Kfar Sava

*57*

Tulkarm

*4*

Qalqilya

Nablus/ Shechem

Herzlia Pituach

Rosh Ha'Ayin

*Jordan River*

Ramat Gan

Petah Tikva

WEST BANK

Amman

Tel Aviv–Jaffa

Lod

Rishon Lezion

Ramallah

Rehovot

Ramla

Ashdod

Jerusalem

Jericho

*90*

Ashkelon

Kiryat Gat

Bethlehem

Gaza

*40*

Hebron

*Dead Sea*

GAZA STRIP

Beit Qama

*60*

Ein Gedi

Ofakim

*25*

Masada

Arad

Beersheva

Ein Bokek

*222*

Dimona

Mashabei Sadeh

*25*

Telalim

Mamshit

Sde Boker

Hatzeva

*NEGEV*

Ein Yahav

Mitzpe Ramon

*40*

*ARAVA*

*90*

Paran

Petra

EGYPT

Ketura

N

Eilat

Aqaba

*Gulf of Eilat*

JORDAN

0        30 miles

0        45 km

# Geography of Israel

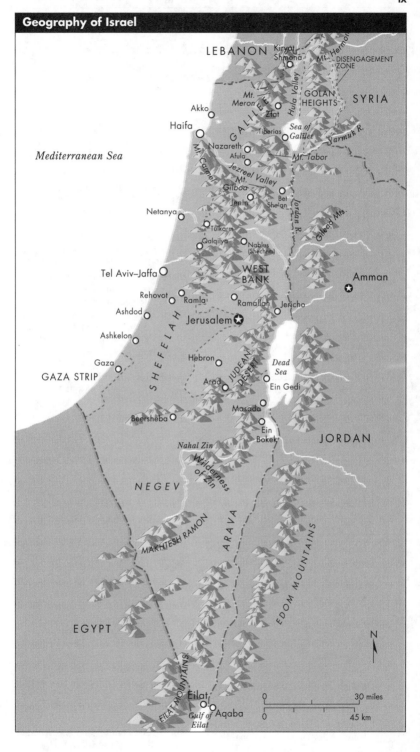

# SMART TRAVEL TIPS A TO Z

*Basic Information on Traveling in Israel, Savvy Tips to Make Your Trip a Breeze, and Companies and Organizations to Contact*

## AIR TRAVEL

### BOOKING YOUR FLIGHT

Price is just one factor to consider when booking a flight: frequency of service and even a carrier's safety record are often just as important. Major airlines offer the greatest number of departures. Smaller airlines—including regional and no-frills airlines—usually have a limited number of flights daily. On the other hand, so-called low-cost airlines usually are cheaper, and their fares impose fewer restrictions, such as advance-purchase requirements. As a group, low-cost carriers have the best safety record—about equal to those of major carriers.

When you book, **look for nonstop flights** and **remember that "direct" flights stop at least once.** Try to **avoid connecting flights,** which require a change of plane. Two airlines may jointly operate a connecting flight, so ask if your airline operates every segment—you may find that your preferred carrier flies you only part of the way. International flights on a country's flag carrier are almost always nonstop; U.S. airlines often fly direct.

**Ask your airline if it offers electronic ticketing,** which eliminates all paperwork. There's no ticket to pick up or misplace; you simply go directly to the gate and give the agent your confirmation number. There's no need to wait in line while precious minutes tick by.

### CARRIERS

When flying internationally, you must usually choose between a domestic carrier, the national flag carrier of the country you're visiting (El Al, in the case of Israel), and a foreign carrier from a third country. National flag carriers have the greatest number of nonstops; domestic carriers may have better connections to your home town and serve a greater number of gateway cities. Third-party carriers may have a price advantage.

➤ MAJOR AIRLINES: From the U.S.: **El Al Israel Airlines** (☎ 212/768–9200 or 800/223–6700). **Delta** (☎ 800/241–4141). **Tower** (☎ 718/553–8500 or 800/221–2500). **TWA** (☎ 800/892–4141). **World Airways** (☎ 800/967–5350). **CSA/Czech Airlines** (☎ 212/682–5833) has flights to Tel Aviv requiring an overnight stay in Prague, but the airline pays for two meals and accommodations. From Canada: **Air Canada** (☎ 800/776–3000 from the U.S., 800/268–7240 from Toronto, 800/361–8620 from Montréal, 800/663–3721 from Vancouver). **El Al Israel Airlines** (☎ 212/768–9200 or 800/223–6700; 514/875–8900 or 416/804–9779 in Canada).

➤ FROM THE U.K.: **British Airways** (☎ 0181/897–4000 or 0345/222–111 outside London). **El Al Israel Airlines** (☎ 0171/957–4100).

➤ DOMESTIC FLIGHTS: **Arkia Israeli Airlines** has flights from Jerusalem and Tel Aviv (Sde Dov Airport) to Eilat and Rosh Pina, and from Tel Aviv to Haifa, Masada (Bar Yehuda), Mitzpe Ramon, Gush Katif, and the Dead Sea (Ein Yahav). There is also service from Haifa to Jerusalem, Eilat, and the Dead Sea. Children fly for half price. Tour packages sometimes offer better deals on these flights. For reservations contact the Arkia reservations center (✉ Sde Dov Airport, Box 39301, Tel Aviv 61392, ☎ 1–800–444888, FAX 03/699–3134). There are Arkia offices in Jerusalem (✉ Clal Center, ☎ 02/625–5888, FAX 02/623–5758), Eilat (✉ Shalom Center, ☎ 07/638–4888, FAX 07/637–3370), and Haifa (✉ 80 Ha'atzmaut Blvd., ☎ 04/861–1606, FAX 04/866–3097), among other cities.

## CHECK IN & BOARDING

Airlines routinely overbook planes, assuming that not everyone with a ticket will show up, but sometimes everyone does. When that happens, airlines ask for volunteers to give up their seats. In return these volunteers usually get a certificate for a free flight and are rebooked on the next flight out. If there are not enough volunteers, the airline must choose who will be denied boarding. The first to get bumped are passengers who checked in late and those flying on discounted tickets, so **get to the gate and check in as early as possible,** especially during peak periods.

Although the trend on international flights is to drop reconfirmation requirements, many airlines still ask you to reconfirm each leg of your international itinerary. Failure to do so may result in your reservation being canceled.

Always **bring a government-issued photo ID to the airport.** You may be asked to show it before you're allowed to check in.

Note that **security checks on airlines flying to Israel are stringent.** Be prepared for what might sound like personal questions about your itinerary, packing habits, and desire to travel to Israel. Remember that the staff is concerned with protecting you, and be patient. Once you're in Israel, expect to have your handbags searched as a matter of course when you enter department stores, places of entertainment, museums, and public buildings. These checks are generally fast and courteous.

## CONSOLIDATORS

Consolidators buy tickets for scheduled international flights at reduced rates from the airlines, then sell them at prices that beat the best fare available directly from the airlines, usually without restrictions. Sometimes you can even get your money back if you need to return the ticket. Carefully read the fine print detailing penalties for changes and cancellations, and **confirm your consolidator reservation with the airline.**

➤ CONSOLIDATORS: Cheap Tickets (☎ 800/377–1000). Discount Travel Network (☎ 800/576–1600). Unitravel (☎ 800/325–2222). Up & Away Travel (☎ 212/889–2345). World Travel Network (☎ 800/409–6753).

## COURIERS

When you fly as a courier, you trade your checked-luggage space for a ticket deeply subsidized by a courier service. It's all perfectly legitimate, but there are restrictions: You can usually book your flight only a week or two in advance, your length of stay may be set for a certain number of days, and you probably won't be able to book a companion on the same flight.

## CUTTING COSTS

The least expensive airfares to Israel are priced for round-trip travel and usually must be purchased in advance. It's smart to **call a number of airlines, and when you're quoted a good price, book it on the spot**—the same fare may not be available the next day. Airlines generally allow you to change your return date for a fee. If you don't use your ticket, you can apply the cost toward the purchase of a new ticket, again for a small charge. However, most low-fare tickets are nonrefundable. To get the lowest airfare, **check different routings.** Compare prices of flights to and from different airports if your destination or home city has more than one gateway. Also price off-peak flights, which may be significantly less expensive.

Travel agents, especially those who specialize in finding the lowest fares (☞ Discounts & Deals, *below*), can be especially helpful when booking a plane ticket. When you're quoted a price, **ask your agent if the price is likely to get any lower.** Good agents know the seasonal fluctuations of airfares and can usually anticipate a sale or fare war. However, waiting can be risky: the fare could go *up* as seats become scarce, and you may wait so long that your preferred flight sells out. A wait-and-see strategy works best if your plans are flexible. If you must arrive and depart on certain dates, don't delay.

THE GOLD GUIDE / SMART TRAVEL TIPS

## ENJOYING THE FLIGHT

For better service, **fly smaller or regional carriers,** which often have higher passenger-satisfaction ratings. Sometimes you'll find leather seats, more legroom, and better food.

For more legroom, **request an emergency-aisle seat.** Don't sit in the row in front of the emergency aisle or in front of a bulkhead, where seats may not recline.

If you have special dietary needs, such as vegetarian, low-cholesterol, or kosher food, **ask for special meals when booking.**

When flying internationally, try to maintain a normal routine, to help fight jet lag. At night, **get some sleep.** By day, **eat light meals, drink water (not alcohol), and move around the cabin** to stretch your legs.

Many carriers have prohibited smoking on all of their international flights; others allow smoking only on certain routes or certain departures, so **contact your carrier regarding its smoking policy.**

## HOW TO COMPLAIN

If your baggage goes astray or your flight goes awry, complain right away. Most carriers require that you **file a claim immediately.**

➤ AIRLINE COMPLAINTS: U.S. Department of Transportation **Aviation Consumer Protection Division** (✉ C-75, Room 4107, Washington, DC 20590, ☎ 202/366–2220). **Federal Aviation Administration Consumer Hotline** (☎ 800/322–7873).

## AIRPORTS

The main airport is **Ben-Gurion International Airport,** which is about halfway between Jerusalem and Tel Aviv. Charter flights from the United States sometimes land at **Ovda Airport or Eilat Airport,** in southern Israel.

➤ AIRPORT INFORMATION: **Ben-Gurion International Airport** (☎ 03/971–0111). **Ovda Airport** (☎ 07/637–5880; operates from late September through May). **Eilat Airport** (☎ 07/636–3838 or 07/636–3813).

## BEACHES

Israel's Mediterranean coastline has many public beaches; most offer changing facilities and bathrooms for a modest fee. It's advisable to swim only in designated areas, where lifeguards are on duty. A flag system indicates how dangerous the waves and undertow are: a black flag means that conditions are rough, and swimming is not allowed; a red flag means moderate waves, swim with discretion; a white flag indicates a calm sea.

Women often sunbathe topless on the beaches in Eilat. At the other extreme, many beaches offer sections for women and men who prefer to bathe separately in the interest of modesty. Some Mediterranean beaches, and most beaches on the Dead Sea and the Sea of Galilee, are stony, so be sure to wear rubber beach shoes, especially amid the spiky coral reefs of the Red Sea.

## BIKE TRAVEL

### BIKES IN FLIGHT

Most airlines will accommodate bikes as luggage, provided they are dismantled and put into a box. Call to see if your airline sells bike boxes (about $5; bike bags are at least $100), although you can often pick them up free at bike shops. International travelers can sometimes substitute a bike for a piece of checked luggage for free; otherwise, it will cost about $100. Domestic and Canadian airlines charge $25–$50.

## BUS TRAVEL

You can get almost anywhere in Israel by bus, and the Central Bus Station is a fixture in most towns: ask for the *tahana merkazit.* The **Egged** bus cooperative handles all of the country's bus routes except those in metropolitan Tel Aviv, where the **Dan** company also operates. Rates are relatively low, and timetables are accurate. You do not need exact change on city buses. If you get on a bus at a highway stop, you can pay the driver. Keep in mind that public transportation generally stops for Shabbat (the Jewish sabbath, which lasts from late Friday afternoon to Saturday evening), although some lines run minibuses in Tel Aviv; and

Haifa, with a large Arab population, also has some Shabbat service. It's a good idea to reserve seats in advance on buses from the major cities to Eilat and the Dead Sea.

➤ BUS COMPANIES: **Dan** (☎ 03/639–4444). **Egged** (☎ 03/694–8888).

➤ INFORMATION: **Egged** (☎ 02/530–4704 in Jerusalem, 04/854–9250 in Haifa, 03/694–8888 in Tel Aviv, 06/694–0740 in Kiryat Shmona).

## DISCOUNT PASSES

Egged offers a variety of bus passes. The Israbus Pass, payable in shekels and available only at Egged Tours offices in Israel, allows tourists unlimited travel. A seven-day pass costs NIS 270 ($77); 14-day pass, NIS 430 ($123); 21-day pass, NIS 540 ($154). You must present your passport at the time of purchase. Within each city you can purchase a multiride ticket, or *kartisia* (10% reduction of bulk tickets of 10 or 20 rides), and monthly tickets (unlimited service within the month) at nearly any city bus station or on the bus. These are particularly good for children and senior citizens, who get large discounts.

## BUSINESS HOURS

For information on national and religious holidays in Israel and their effects on various businesses and services, *see* National and Religious Holidays *in* Chapter 1. The weekly observance of Shabbat (sabbath, from sundown Friday through sundown Saturday) has a different impact on different parts of the country: businesses in Jewish Israel close, but many nonkosher restaurants stay open.

Businesses are often open by 8:30 in Israel and shops a little later (9–10); neighborhood grocery stores usually open around 7. Some businesses still close for a two- or three-hour siesta between 1 and 4. Most stores do not close before 7 PM; supermarkets are often open later, and in large cities, there are all-night supermarkets. Arab-owned stores usually open at 8 and close in late afternoon.

## BANKS

Although hours can differ among banks, almost all open by 8:30. Most close from 12:30 to 4 and then re-open until 5:30 or even later. Banks are closed on Saturday except in Muslim areas, where they're closed Friday. In Christian areas they're open Saturday morning and closed Sunday.

## MUSEUMS & STORES

Museums don't have a fixed closing day, so although hours are usually 10–6, you'll want to confirm the schedule before you go. Stores are closed Friday afternoon; some restaurants and kiosks remain open. Some supermarkets are open Saturday night.

## CAMERAS & COMPUTERS

### EQUIPMENT PRECAUTIONS

Always **keep your film, tape, or computer disks out of the sun.** Carry an extra supply of batteries, and **be prepared to turn on your camera, camcorder, or laptop** to prove to security personnel that the device is real. Always **ask for hand inspection of film,** which gets clouded after successive exposure to airport X-ray machines, and **keep videotapes and computer disks away from metal detectors.**

### TRAVEL PHOTOGRAPHY

➤ PHOTO HELP: Kodak Information Center (☎ 800/242–2424). *Kodak Guide to Shooting Great Travel Pictures,* available in bookstores or from Fodor's Travel Publications (☎ 800/533–6478; $16.50 plus $4 shipping).

## CAR RENTAL

Rental rates in Israel start at around $68 a day and $450 a week for an economy car with unlimited mileage; some companies require a minimum of three weeks' rental in high season. There is no tax on car rentals in Israel.

➤ MAJOR AGENCIES: **Alamo** (☎ 800/522–9696, 0800/272–2000 in the U.K.). **Avis** (☎ 800/331–1084, 800/879–2847 in Canada, 008/225–533 in Australia). **Budget** (☎ 800/527–0700, 0800/181181 in the U.K.). **Dollar** (☎ 800/800–4000; 0990/565656 in the U.K., where it is known as Eurodollar). **Hertz** (☎ 800/654–3001, 800/263–0600 in Canada, 0345/555888 in the U.K.,

03/9222–2523 in Australia, 03/358–6777 in New Zealand). **National InterRent** (☎ 800/227–3876; 0345/222525 in the U.K., where it is known as Europcar InterRent).

## CUTTING COSTS

To get the best deal, **book through a travel agent who is willing to shop around.**

Also **ask your travel agent about a company's customer-service record.** How has the company responded to late plane arrivals and vehicle mishaps? Are there often lines at the rental counter? If you're traveling during a holiday period, does a confirmed reservation guarantee you a car?

Be sure to **look into wholesalers,** companies that do not own fleets but rent in bulk from those that do and often offer better rates than traditional car-rental operations. Prices are best during off-peak periods. Rentals booked through wholesalers must be paid for before you leave the United States.

➤ RENTAL WHOLESALERS: **Auto Europe** (☎ 207/842–2000 or 800/223–5555, FAX 800–235–6321). **Kemwel Holiday Autos** (☎ 914/835–5555 or 800/678–0678, FAX 914/835–5126).

## INSURANCE

When driving a rental car you are generally responsible for any damage to or loss of the vehicle. You also are liable for any property damage or personal injury that you may cause while driving. Before you rent, **see what coverage you already have** under the terms of your personal auto-insurance policy and credit cards.

## REQUIREMENTS

Your own driver's license is acceptable in Israel, but an International Driver's Permit is still a good idea; it's available from the American or Canadian Automobile Association, and, in the United Kingdom, from the Automobile Association or Royal Automobile Club. This international permit is universally recognized, so having one in your wallet is extra insurance against problems with the local authorities.

## SURCHARGES

Before you pick up a car in one city and leave it in another, **ask about drop-off charges or one-way service fees,** which can be substantial. Note, too, that some rental agencies charge extra if you return the car before the time specified in your contract. To avoid a hefty refueling fee, **fill the tank just before you turn in the car,** but be aware that gas stations near the rental outlet may overcharge.

## CAR TRAVEL

The Hebrew word for a native-born Israeli is *sabra,* which literally refers to a prickly cactus with sweet fruit inside. You'll meet the sweet Israeli if you get lost or have automotive difficulties—helping hands are quick to arrive—but behind the wheel, Israelis are prickly, very aggressive, and honk their horns far more than their Western counterparts. Try not to take it personally.

## AUTO CLUBS

➤ IN ISRAEL: The local representative of AAA and of the British AA in Israel is **Memsi** (☎ 03/564–1133 for visitor information in Tel Aviv; 02/625–0661 in Jerusalem).

➤ IN AUSTRALIA: **Australian Automobile Association** (☎ 06/247–7311).

➤ IN CANADA: **Canadian Automobile Association** (CAA; ☎ 613/247–0117).

➤ IN NEW ZEALAND: **New Zealand Automobile Association** (☎ 09/377–4660).

➤ IN THE U.K.: **Automobile Association** (AA; ☎ 0990/500–600), **Royal Automobile Club** (RAC; ☎ 0990/722–722 for membership, 0345/121–345 for insurance).

➤ IN THE U.S.: **American Automobile Association** (AAA; ☎ 800/564–6222).

## GASOLINE

Service stations are generally full-service. Many rental cars now take unleaded gas. At press time, a liter of high-octane gasoline cost about 90¢ ($3.60 a gallon). City gas stations stay open into the evening, and quite a few are open around the clock. Many close for Shabbat and religious holidays, though many highway gas stations stay open through holidays and late into the night as well.

## ROAD CONDITIONS

Israeli highways are basically in good shape, except in some rural areas. Try to avoid entering and leaving the main cities at rush hours (7:30 AM– 8:30 AM and 4 PM–6 PM), when roads are absolutely jammed. Roads are marked with international traffic symbols, but because signs are often in Hebrew only, it's smart to write down the road numbers before setting out. Good maps in English are available at bookstores and through the Israel Government Tourist Office (IGTO).

It's a good idea to carry extra water— both for yourself and for your car— while driving at any time of year. Every winter there are several days of flash flooding in the desert; if it's raining, try to find a police officer or call the IGTO to ask about road and weather conditions.

Israel is slowly assigning numbers to its roads and highways (north–south, even; east–west, odd), but most people still know them simply by the towns they connect: the Tiberias– Nazareth Road, for example. Inter- sections and turnoffs are similarly indicated, as in "the Eilat Junction." In addition, interurban signs for parks and historic sights are being changed from orange to brown.

## CHILDREN & TRAVEL

### CHILDREN IN ISRAEL

Israel welcomes young tourists, and baby supplies are readily available. Children travel at half price on do- mestic flights and on trains. Many tourist sights offer excellent educa- tional programs that children will enjoy. Remember that children dehy- drate faster than adults, so bring along a canteen for each child when you head out. Sunscreen and sun hats are also essential.

Be sure to plan ahead and **involve your youngsters** as you outline your trip. When packing, include things to keep them busy en route. On sightsee- ing days, try to schedule activities of special interest to your kids. If you're

renting a car don't forget to **arrange for a car seat** when you reserve.

### FLYING

If your children are two or older, **ask about children's airfares.** As a general rule, infants under two not occupying a seat fly at greatly reduced fares or even for free.

The adult baggage allowance gener- ally applies to children paying half or more of the adult fare. When book- ing, **ask about carry-on allowances for those traveling with infants.** For babies charged 10% of the adult fare, you are usually allowed one carry-on bag and a collapsible stroller, which may have to be checked. You may be limited to less if the flight is full.

Experts agree that it's a good idea to use safety seats aloft for children weighing less than 40 pounds. Air- lines, however, can set their own policies: U.S. carriers allow FAA- approved models but usually require that you buy a ticket, even if your child would otherwise ride free, since the seats must be strapped into regu- lar seats. Airline rules vary, so it's important to **check your airline's policy about using safety seats during takeoff and landing.** Safety seats cannot obstruct the movement of other passengers in the row, so get an appropriate seat assignment as early as possible.

When making your reservation, **request children's meals or a free- standing bassinet** if you need them; the latter are available only to those seated at the bulkhead, where there's enough legroom. Remember, however, that bulkhead seats may not have their own overhead bins, and there's no storage space in front of you— a major inconvenience.

### GROUP TRAVEL

When planning to take your kids on a tour, look for companies that special- ize in family travel.

➤ FAMILY-FRIENDLY TOUR OPERATORS: Families Welcome! (✉ 92 N. Main St., Ashland, OR 97520, ☎ 541/ 482–6121 or 800/326–0724, FAX 541/482–0660).

## HOTELS

Most hotels in Israel allow children under a certain age to stay in their parents' room at no extra charge, but others charge them as extra adults; be sure to **ask about the cutoff age for children's discounts.** Children's discounts are often less generous at kibbutz guest houses. Many hotels, especially in resorts such as Eilat, feature entertainment that appeals to children and activities such as arts and crafts or field trips.

The **Hilton** hotels in Jerusalem and Tel Aviv offer a family plan, an organized youth camp during the summer months, and/or an all-day children's program. The **Dan** hotels offer the Family Advantage plan and usually have recreation programs during vacations. **Ramada** hotels in Jerusalem and Tel Aviv also offer a family plan, as do the **Radisson Moriah** hotels in Jerusalem, Tel Aviv, the Dead Sea, Eilat, and Tiberias, which also have children's programs during school vacations.

➤ BEST CHOICES: **Hilton** (☎ 800/445–8667, 0181/780–1155 in the U.K.). **Dan** (☎ 212/752–6120, 0171/439–9893 in the U.K.) **Radisson Moriah** (☎ 800/221–0203).

## CONSUMER PROTECTION

Whether you're making travel arrangements before your trip or shopping at your destination, **pay with a major credit card** whenever possible. This way, you can cancel payment or get reimbursed if there's a problem, as long as you can provide documentation.

If you're doing business with a particular company for the first time, **contact your local Better Business Bureau and the attorney general's offices** in your state and the company's home state, as well. Have any complaints been filed?

Finally, if you're buying a package or tour, always **consider travel insurance** that includes default coverage (☞ Insurance, *below*).

➤ LOCAL BBBs: **Council of Better Business Bureaus** (✉ 4200 Wilson Blvd., Suite 800, Arlington, VA 22203, ☎ 703/276–0100, FAX 703/525–8277).

## CUSTOMS & DUTIES

When shopping, **keep receipts** for all of your purchases. Upon reentering the country, **be ready to show customs officials what you've bought.** If you feel a duty is incorrect, appeal the assessment. If you object to the way your clearance was handled, get the inspector's badge number. In either case, first ask to see a supervisor, and then write to the appropriate authorities, beginning with the port director at your point of entry.

### IN ISRAEL

Those over 17 may import into Israel duty-free: 250 cigarettes or 250 grams of tobacco products; 2 liters of wine and 1 liter of spirits; ¼ liter of eau de cologne or perfume; and gifts totaling no more than $200 in value. You may also import up to 1 kg of food products, but no fresh meats.

Israeli customs sometimes require a large deposit to bring expensive and/or professional-quality video and computer equipment into the country; this is to ensure that the equipment is not being imported for resale. The deposit is refundable in the original currency on departure and can be paid in cash, in traveler's checks, or by Visa credit card.

### IN AUSTRALIA

Australia residents who are 18 or older may bring back $A400 worth of souvenirs and gifts (including jewelry), 250 cigarettes or 250 grams of tobacco, and 1,125 ml of alcohol (including wine, beer, and spirits). Residents under 18 may bring back $A200 worth of goods.

➤ INFORMATION: **Australian Customs Service** (Regional Director, ✉ Box 8, Sydney, NSW 2001, ☎ 02/9213–2000, FAX 02/9213–4000).

### IN CANADA

Canada residents who have been out of Canada for at least seven days may bring in C$500 worth of goods duty-free. If you've been away less than seven days but more than 48 hours, the duty-free allowance drops to C$200; if your trip lasts 24–48 hours, the allowance is C$50. You may not pool allowances with family members. Goods claimed under the

C$500 exemption may follow you by mail; those claimed under the lesser exemptions must accompany you. Alcohol and tobacco products may be included in the seven-day and 48-hour exemptions but not in the 24-hour exemption. If you meet the age requirements of the province or territory through which you reenter Canada, you may bring in, duty-free, 1.14 liters (40 imperial ounces) of wine or liquor *or* 24 12-ounce cans or bottles of beer or ale. If you are 16 or older you may bring in, duty-free, 200 cigarettes and 50 cigars.

You may send an unlimited number of gifts worth up to C$60 each to Canada duty-free. Label the package UNSOLICITED GIFT—VALUE UNDER $60. Alcohol and tobacco are excluded.

➤ INFORMATION: **Revenue Canada** (✉ 2265 St. Laurent Blvd. S, Ottawa, Ontario K1G 4K3, ☎ 613/993–0534, 800/461–9999 in Canada).

### IN NEW ZEALAND

Homeward-bound New Zealand residents with goods to declare must present themselves for inspection. If you're 17 or older, you may bring back $700 worth of souvenirs and gifts. Your duty-free allowance also includes 4.5 liters of wine or beer; one 1,125-ml bottle of spirits; and either 200 cigarettes, 250 grams of tobacco, 50 cigars, or a combo of all three up to 250 grams.

➤ INFORMATION: **New Zealand Customs** (✉ Custom House, 50 Anzac Ave., Box 29, Auckland, New Zealand, ☎ 09/359–6655 or 09/309–2978).

### IN THE U.K.

From countries outside the EU, including Israel, you may import, duty-free, 200 cigarettes or 50 cigars; 1 liter of spirits or 2 liters of fortified or sparkling wine or liqueurs; 2 liters of still table wine; 60 milliliters of perfume; 250 milliliters of toilet water; plus £136 worth of other goods, including gifts and souvenirs.

➤ INFORMATION: **HM Customs and Excise** (Dorset House, Stamford St., London SE1 9NG, ☎ 0171/202–4227).

### IN THE U.S.

U.S. residents may bring home $400 worth of foreign goods duty-free if they've been out of the country for at least 48 hours (and if they haven't used the $400 allowance or any part of it in the past 30 days).

U.S. residents 21 and older may bring back 1 liter of alcohol duty-free. In addition, regardless of your age, you are allowed 200 cigarettes and 100 non-Cuban cigars. Antiques, which the U.S. Customs Service defines as objects more than 100 years old, enter duty-free, as do original works of art done entirely by hand, including paintings, drawings, and sculptures.

You may also send packages home duty-free: up to $200 worth of goods for personal use, with a limit of one parcel per addressee per day (and no alcohol or tobacco products or perfume worth more than $5); label the package PERSONAL USE, and attach a list of its contents and their retail value. Do not label the package UNSOLICITED GIFT, or your duty-free exemption will drop to $100. Mailed items do not affect your duty-free allowance on your return.

➤ INFORMATION: **U.S. Customs Service** (Inquiries, ✉ Box 7407, Washington, DC 20044, ☎ 202/927–6724; complaints, Office of Regulations and Rulings, ✉ 1301 Constitution Ave. NW, Washington, DC 20229; registration of equipment, Resource Management, ✉ 1301 Constitution Ave. NW, Washington DC 20229, ☎ 202/927–0540).

## DINING

Israel is not an essential stop on a gastronomic world tour, yet it serves up some of the world's tastiest food and most tantalizing aromas. This is, after all, the Middle East, where fresh grilled fish and plates of hummus and warmed pita bread are staples; but today you can also sample any national cuisine you want—Italian, Indian, Chinese, Turkish, Indonesian, Hungarian, even American. And whereas "kosher" once meant "uniform," kosher restaurants today have to compete with a growing number of nonkosher restaurants (which, among other differences, serve seafood, and milk and meat together), so the variety of kosher food is growing. Moreover, with street stalls and ice cream stores on every corner, you can be sure you won't go hungry in Israel.

In hotels, the day begins with a huge, buffet-style breakfast comprising a variety of breads and rolls, eggs, oatmeal, excellent yogurt, cheeses, vegetable and fish salads, and Western-style breakfast foods like corn flakes and granola. Every city and small town has modestly priced restaurants that open in mid-morning and serve soup, salad, and grilled meats. Many restaurants offer business-lunch specials or fixed-price menus, but à la carte menus are most common. A service charge (*sherut* in Hebrew) of 10%–15% is sometimes levied and should be noted separately on your bill.

When used in reference to food, the word Oriental (a translation of the Hebrew for "eastern") means Middle Eastern cuisine, not Asian cuisines such as Thai or Chinese.

Israelis do like Western-style fast food, such as hamburgers and pizza, but more traditional favorites are falafel served with salad and condiments in a pita pocket, *shwarma* (grilled meat), cheese, and *borekas* (phyllo turnovers filled with spinach, cheese, or potato). Many falafel stands have salad bars where you can fill the pita yourself. Supermarkets, particularly in the large cities, have long, eclectic counters of takeout food, with everything from fried eggplant to chocolate croissants.

## DISABILITIES & ACCESSIBILITY

### ACCESS IN ISRAEL

Facilities in Israel for people with disabilities still lag behind those of many other Western countries. Crowded, hilly streets and steps can make it difficult to get around without a companion, and adapted minibuses and rental cars are hard to come by. However, new hotels are required to provide facilities for guests with disabilities, and several tourist sights are making improvements.

➤ LOCAL RESOURCES: **Roof Association of Organizations of Persons with Disabilities** (✉ 55 Hamasger St., Tel Aviv 67217, ☎ 03/561–8557). **MILBAT—The Israeli Center for Technical Aids and Transportation** (✉ Tel Hashomer, Tel Aviv 52621, ☎ 03/530–3739). **ILAN—The Israeli Foundation for Handicapped Children** (✉ 9 Gordon St., Tel Aviv 63458, ☎ 03/524–8141).

To obtain a copy of "**Access in Israel**," a guide to accessible sights and accommodations in Israel, contact the **Pauline Hephaistos Survey Projects** (✉ 39 Bradley Gardens, West Ealing, London W13 8HE, England). The **Jerusalem Action Committee** (☎ 02/563–9839) offers advice on special problems.

### MAKING RESERVATIONS

When discussing accessibility with an operator or reservations agent, **ask hard questions.** Are there any stairs, inside *or* out? Are there grab bars next to the toilet *and* in the shower/tub? How wide is the doorway to the room? To the bathroom? For the most extensive facilities meeting the latest legal specifications, **opt for newer accommodations,** which are more likely to have been designed with access in mind. Older buildings or ships may have more limited facilities. Be sure to **discuss your needs before booking.**

### TRANSPORTATION

➤ COMPLAINTS: **Disability Rights Section** (✉ U.S. Department of Justice, Civil Rights Division, Box 66738, Washington, DC 20035–6738, ☎ 202/514–0301 or 800/514–0301, TTY 202/514–0383 or 800/514–0383; FAX 202/307–1198) for general complaints. **Aviation Consumer Protection Division** (☞ Air Travel, *above*) for airline-related problems. **Civil Rights Office** (U.S. Department of Transportation, Departmental Office of Civil Rights, S-30, 400 7th St. SW, Room 10215, Washington, DC, 20590, ☎ 202/366–4648, FAX 202/366–9371) for problems with surface transportation.

### TRAVEL AGENCIES & TOUR OPERATORS

As a whole, the travel industry has become more aware of the needs of travelers with disabilities. In the U.S., the Americans with Disabilities Act requires that travel firms serve the needs of all travelers. Note, though, that some agencies and operators specialize in making travel arrangements for individuals and groups with disabilities.

➤ TRAVELERS WITH MOBILITY PROBLEMS: **Access Adventures** (✉ 206 Chestnut Ridge Rd., Rochester, NY 14624, ☎ 716/889–9096), run by a former physical-rehabilitation counselor. **Accessible Journeys** (✉ 35 W. Sellers Ave., Ridley Park, PA 19078, ☎ 610/521–0339 or 800/846–4537, FAX 610/521–6959), for escorted tours exclusively for travelers with mobility impairments. **CareVacations** (✉ 5019 49th Ave., Suite 102, Leduc, Alberta T9E 6T5, ☎ 403/986–6404, 800/648–1116 in Canada) has group tours and is especially helpful with cruise vacations. **Flying Wheels Travel** (✉ 143 W. Bridge St., Box 382, Owatonna, MN 55060, ☎ 507/451–5005 or 800/535–6790, FAX 507/451–1685), a travel agency specializing in customized tours and itineraries worldwide. **Hinsdale Travel Service** (✉ 201 E. Ogden Ave., Suite 100, Hinsdale, IL 60521, ☎ 630/325–1335), a travel agency that benefits from the advice of wheelchair traveler Janice Perkins.

## DISCOUNTS & DEALS

Be a smart shopper and **compare all your options** before making any choice. A plane ticket bought with a promotional coupon may not be cheaper than the least expensive fare from a discount ticket agency. For large travel purchases, such as packages or tours, keep in mind that what you get is just as important as what you save. Just because something is cheap doesn't mean it's a bargain.

### CLUBS & COUPONS

Many companies sell discounts in the form of travel clubs and coupon books, but these cost money. You must use participating advertisers to get a deal, and only after you recoup the initial membership cost or book price do you begin to save. If you plan to use the club or coupons frequently, you may save considerably. Before signing up, find out what discounts you get for free.

➤ DISCOUNT CLUBS: **Entertainment Travel Editions** (✉ 2125 Butterfield Rd., Troy, MI 48084, ☎ 800/445–4137; $20–$51, depending on destination). **Great American Traveler** (✉ Box 27965, Salt Lake City, UT 84127, ☎ 801/974–3033 or 800/548–2812; $49.95 per year). **Moment's Notice Discount Travel Club** (✉ 7301 New Utrecht Ave., Brooklyn, NY 11204, ☎ 718/234–6295; $25 per year). **Privilege Card International** (✉ 237 E. Front St., Youngstown, OH 44503, ☎ 330/746–5211 or 800/236–9732; $74.95 per year). **Sears's Mature Outlook** (✉ Box 9390, Des Moines, IA 50306, ☎ 800/336–6330; $19.95 per year). **Travelers Advantage** (✉ CUC Travel Service, 3033 S. Parker Rd., Suite 1000, Aurora, CO 80014, ☎ 800/548–1116 or 800/648–4037; $59.95 per year). **Worldwide Discount Travel Club** (✉ 1674 Meridian Ave., Miami Beach, FL 33139, ☎ 305/534–2082; $50 per year family, $40 single).

### CREDIT CARD BENEFITS

When you use your credit card to make travel purchases, you may get free travel-accident insurance, collision-damage insurance, and medical or legal assistance, depending on the card and the bank that issued it. American Express, MasterCard, and Visa provide one or more of these services, so **get a copy of your credit card's travel-benefits policy.** If you are a member of an auto club, always **ask hotel and car-rental reservations agents about auto-club discounts.** Some clubs offer additional discounts on tours, cruises, and admission to attractions.

### DISCOUNT RESERVATIONS

To save money, **look into discount-reservation services** with toll-free numbers, which use their buying power to get a better price on hotels, airline tickets, even car rentals. When booking a room, always **call the hotel's local toll-free number** (if one is available) rather than the central reservations number—you'll often get a better price. Always ask about special packages or corporate rates.

When shopping for the best deal on hotels and car rentals, **look for guar-**

*THE GOLD GUIDE / SMART TRAVEL TIPS*

**anteed exchange rates,** which protect you against a falling dollar. With your rate locked in, you won't pay more, even if the price goes up in the local currency.

➤ AIRLINE TICKETS: ☎ **800/FLY-4-LESS.**

➤ HOTEL ROOMS: **Steigenberger Reservation Service** (☎ 800/223-5652).

## PACKAGE DEALS

Packages and guided tours can save you money, but don't confuse the two. When you buy a package, your travel remains independent, just as though you had planned and booked the trip yourself. Fly-drive packages, which combine airfare and car rental, are often a good deal.

## ELECTRICITY

To use your U.S.-purchased electric-powered equipment, **bring a converter and adapter.** The electrical current in Israel is 220 volts, 50 cycles alternating current (AC); wall outlets take Continental-type plugs, with two round prongs.

If your appliances are dual-voltage, you'll need only an adapter. Don't use 110-volt outlets, marked FOR SHAVERS ONLY, for high-wattage appliances such as blow-dryers. Most laptops operate equally well on 110 and 220 volts and so require only an adapter.

## ETIQUETTE & BEHAVIOR

"Etiquette" is not a key word in the Israeli vocabulary. In this highly informal society, there are many traditions but few rules. That said, both Jewish and Arabic cultures have their own social customs and strictures. Visitors (particularly women) to ultra-Orthodox Jewish quarters, such as B'nei Brak, near Tel Aviv, and the Jerusalem neighborhood Mea She'arim should wear modest dress. Local women keep their knees and elbows covered and do not wear pants; married women also keep their heads covered (keep a scarf handy). Tourists wandering the streets will feel more comfortable if they observe this dress code, and it becomes essential when you enter a synagogue or other important religious institution (again, women in particular, though head covering for men will also be appreciated). Very religious Jews, who wear black garb, do not shake hands or mingle socially with members of the opposite sex.

Guests in Muslim households insult their hosts if they decline a drink (strong coffee or a soft drink is usually offered). Muslims do not drink alcohol, so a gift of wine is inappropriate. Like religious Jews, Muslims do not eat pork. Remove your shoes upon entering a mosque; women should cover their hair. Note that shaking hands or picking up food with the left hand is considered impolite.

## GAY & LESBIAN TRAVEL

➤ GAY- AND LESBIAN-FRIENDLY TRAVEL AGENCIES: **Corniche Travel** (✉ 8721 Sunset Blvd., Suite 200, West Hollywood, CA 90069, ☎ 310/854-6000 or 800/429-8747, FAX 310/659-7441). **Islanders Kennedy Travel** (✉ 183 W. 10th St., New York, NY 10014, ☎ 212/242-3222 or 800/988-1181, FAX 212/929-8530). **Now Voyager** (✉ 4406 18th St., San Francisco, CA 94114, ☎ 415/626-1169 or 800/255-6951, FAX 415/626-8626). **Yellowbrick Road** (✉ 1500 W. Balmoral Ave., Chicago, IL 60640, ☎ 773/561-1800 or 800/642-2488, FAX 773/561-4497). **Skylink Travel and Tour** (✉ 3577 Moorland Ave., Santa Rosa, CA 95407, ☎ 707/585-8355 or 800/225-5759, FAX 707/584-5637), serving lesbian travelers.

➤ LOCAL RESOURCES: **Association for Gay Men, Lesbians and Bisexuals in Israel** (✉ 28 Nahmani St., Tel Aviv 65794, ☎ 03/620-4327). **Community of Lesbian Feminists** (✉ Box 22997, Tel Aviv 61228, ☎ 03/699-5606).

## HEALTH

It is safe to drink tap water and eat fresh produce after it's been washed, but take care when buying cooked products from outdoor food stands; the food may have been sitting unrefrigerated for a long time.

Israel gets very hot: a sun hat is a must, as is a canteen or bottled water (available even in the most remote places) to guard against dehydration.

## MEDICAL PLANS

No one plans to get sick while traveling, but it happens, so **consider signing up with a medical-assistance company.** Members get doctor referrals, emergency evacuation or repatriation, 24-hour telephone hot lines for medical consultation, cash for emergencies, and other personal and legal assistance. Coverage varies by plan, so **review the benefits of each carefully.**

➤ MEDICAL-ASSISTANCE COMPANIES: **International SOS Assistance** (✉ 8 Neshaminy Interplex, Suite 207, Trevose, PA 19053, ☎ 215/245–4707 or 800/523–6586, FAX 215/244–9617; ✉ 12 Chemin Riantbosson, 1217 Meyrin 1, Geneva, Switzerland, ☎ 4122/785–6464, FAX 4122/785–6424; ✉ 10 Anson Rd., 14-07/08 International Plaza, Singapore, 079903, ☎ 65/226–3936, FAX 65/226–3937).

## HOLIDAYS

*See* National and Religious Holidays *in* Chapter 1.

## INSURANCE

Travel insurance is the best way to **protect yourself against financial loss.** The most useful plan is a comprehensive policy that includes coverage for trip cancellation and interruption, default, trip delay, and medical expenses (with a waiver for preexisting conditions).

Without insurance, you will lose all or most of your money if you cancel your trip, regardless of the reason. Default insurance covers you if your tour operator, airline, or cruise line goes out of business. Trip-delay covers unforeseen expenses that you may incur due to bad weather or mechanical delays. It's important to compare the fine print regarding trip-delay coverage when comparing policies.

For overseas travel, one of the most important components of travel insurance is its medical coverage. Supplemental health insurance will pick up the cost of your medical bills should you get sick or injured while traveling. U.S. residents should note that Medicare generally does not cover health-care costs outside the United States, nor do many privately issued policies. Residents of the United Kingdom can buy an annual travel-insurance policy valid for most vacations taken during the year in which the coverage is purchased. If you are pregnant or have a preexisting condition, make sure you're covered. British citizens should buy extra medical coverage when traveling overseas, according to the Association of British Insurers. Australian travelers should buy travel insurance, including extra medical coverage, whenever they go abroad, according to the Insurance Council of Australia.

Always **buy travel insurance directly from the insurance company;** if you buy it from a cruise line, airline, or tour operator that goes out of business, you probably will not be covered for the agency or operator's default, a major risk. Before you make any purchase, **review your existing health and home-owner's policies** to find out whether they cover expenses incurred while traveling.

➤ TRAVEL INSURERS: In the U.S., **Access America** (✉ 6600 W. Broad St., Richmond, VA 23230, ☎ 804/285–3300 or 800/284–8300); **Travel Guard International** (✉ 1145 Clark St., Stevens Point, WI 54481, ☎ 715/345–0505 or 800/826–1300). In Canada, **Mutual of Omaha** (✉ Travel Division, 500 University Ave., Toronto, Ontario M5G 1V8, ☎ 416/598–4083, 800/268–8825 in Canada).

➤ INSURANCE INFORMATION: In the U.K., **Association of British Insurers** (✉ 51 Gresham St., London EC2V 7HQ, ☎ 0171/600–3333). In Australia, **Insurance Council of Australia** (☎ 613/9614–1077, FAX 613/9614–7924).

## LANGUAGE

Hebrew has a unique history: the language of the Bible was long dormant, used only for reading the Holy Scriptures and prayers, writing religious works and poetry, and as the Jewish lingua franca to communicate with Jews in other countries. The revival begun a century ago has given

Hebrew a whole new life. If Abraham, Isaac, and Jacob came back today, they'd have to take *ulpan* classes just like other new immigrants. English has also had an impact on Hebrew, to the extent that you'll hear not only official words like *bank, telefon,* and *lefaksess* (to fax) but also slang such as *ledaskess* (to discuss) and *heppening* (happening, event). Arabic is Israel's other official language, spoken by Arabs as well as many Jews (especially those with origins in Arab lands). Because Israel is a nation of immigrants, mistakes and various accents are tolerated cheerfully, and polyglot Israelis speak so many different languages that you might be able to try out French, Spanish, Italian, or Russian. All Israeli schoolchildren study English and speak it to varying degrees of fluency.

Israelis use a lot of hand gestures when they talk. A common gesture is to turn the palm outward and press the thumb and forefinger together to mean "wait a minute"; rest assured that this has no negative connotations. Just as harmless is the Israeli who says "I don't believe you" to express that something is unbelievably wonderful. Few Israelis differentiate between "bus stop" and "bus station" (because one Hebrew word covers both), so if you want the Central Bus Station, make sure you ask for it (*tahana merkazit*). Different systems of transliteration have produced widely inconsistent spellings: so is that Golan town Katzrin or Qazrin?

You can hear news in English on Reshet Alef, the "A" station of Kol Yisrael at 7 AM and 5 PM. There's an English news broadcast on TV Channel One (Ha'arutz Harishon) Sunday through Thursday at 6:15 PM, Friday at 4:30 PM, and Saturday at 5 PM. Movies are almost always shown in their original language, with Hebrew subtitles. You can pick up a copy of the daily newspapers, *Ha'aretz* and the *Jerusalem Post,* or the semimonthly news magazine *The Jerusalem Report* at most newsstands. *Ha'aretz* consists of translations from Israel's Hebrew daily and is sold together with the *International Herald Tribune,* providing local and international news in one package. Many stores carry a wide range of English titles.

## LODGING

Nearly all hotel rooms in Israel have private bathrooms with a combined shower and tub. A buffet breakfast, often sumptuous, is almost always included in the room rate (☞ *Dining, above*). The best hotels have a swimming pool, a health club, and tennis courts; and with rare exceptions in the major cities, most hotels have parking facilities. Although the government's star ratings of hotels have officially been abolished, people still speak of "five-star hotels" in reference to the top category.

### APARTMENT & VILLA RENTALS

If you want a home base that's roomy enough for a family and comes with cooking facilities, **consider a furnished rental.** These can save you money, especially if you're traveling with a large group. Home-exchange directories list rentals (often second homes owned by prospective house swappers), and some services search for a house or apartment for you (even a castle if that's your fancy) and handle the paperwork. Some send an illustrated catalog; others send photographs only of specific properties, sometimes at a charge. Up-front registration fees may apply.

➤ RENTAL AGENTS: **Europa-Let/Tropical Inn-Let** (✉ 92 N. Main St., Ashland, OR 97520, ☎ 541/482–5806 or 800/462–4486, ℻ 541/482–0660). **Hometours International** (✉ Box 11503, Knoxville, TN 37939, ☎ 423/690–8484 or 800/367–4668). **Property Rentals International** (✉ 1008 Mansfield Crossing Rd., Richmond, VA 23236, ☎ 804/378–6054 or 800/220–3332, ℻ 804/379–2073). **Rental Directories International** (✉ 2044 Rittenhouse Sq., Philadelphia, PA 19103, ☎ 215/985–4001, ℻ 215/985–0323). **Hideaways International** (✉ 767 Islington St., Portsmouth, NH 03801, ☎ 603/430–4433 or 800/843–4433, ℻ 603/430–4444; membership $99) is a club for travelers who arrange rentals among themselves.

### B&BS

Many of Israel's *kibbutzim* (communal settlements) have opened bed-and-breakfast lodgings in which a visitor rents a simple room and takes meals in the kibbutz dining room. Most kibbutzim have large lawns, swimming pools (usually open only in summer), and athletic facilities and offer lectures and tours of the settlement. Private home owners are also increasingly opening their doors to guests.

### CAMPING

Most Israeli campsites offer water, bathrooms, showers, first aid, telephones, and cabins for rent and often have mobile homes set on blocks. Some even have swimming pools or are near beaches. They are all guarded and lighted at night. Advance reservations are recommended for July, August, and Jewish holidays.

➤ INFORMATION: **Israel Government Tourist Office** (☞ Visitor Information, *below*).

### CHRISTIAN HOSPICES

Christian hospices (meaning hostelries, not facilities for the ill) provide lodging and sometimes meals; these are mainly in Jerusalem and the Galilee. Some are real bargains, while others are merely reasonable; facilities range from spare to luxurious. They give preference to pilgrimage groups, but almost all will accept secular travelers when space is available. A full list of hospices is available from the Israel Government Tourist Office.

### HOLIDAY VILLAGES

Holiday villages can range from the near primitive to quite luxurious but tend to be relatively inexpensive. Commonly they offer simple facilities, usually sleeping from four to six persons in a unit, with basic cooking facilities in each unit. Some villages have full kitchens and even TVs, and most have a grocery store on the grounds. The rooms vary from huts and trailers to little houses.

### HOSTELS

No matter how old you are, you can **save on lodging costs by staying in hostels.** Hostelling International (HI; formerly the International Youth Hostel Association), the umbrella group for a number of national youth-hostel associations, offers single-sex and dorm-style arrangements and, at many hostels, "couples" rooms and family accommodation in some 5,000 locations in more than 70 countries around the world. Open to travelers of all ages, membership in any HI national hostel association allows you to stay in HI-affiliated hostels at member rates (a one-year membership is about $25 for adults; hostels run about $10–$25 per night). Members also have priority if the hostel is full and are eligible for discounts around the world, even on rail and bus travel in some countries.

Youth hostels in Israel have improved in recent years and now compete with hotels and guest houses. Many of Israel's 31 hostels provide family rooms with private baths; most are air-conditioned; some have communal cooking facilities; and all provide meals. It's worth coming equipped with a valid HI membership card—otherwise, the attractive, modern hostels charge guest-house prices. Even without a card, however, hostels are a good deal.

➤ HOSTEL ORGANIZATIONS: **Hostelling International—American Youth Hostels** (✉ 733 15th St. NW, Suite 840, Washington, DC 20005, ☎ 202/783–6161, FAX 202/783–6171). **Hostelling International—Canada** (✉ 400-205 Catherine St., Ottawa, Ontario K2P 1C3, ☎ 613/237–7884, FAX 613/237–7868). **Youth Hostel Association of England and Wales** (✉ Trevelyan House, 8 St. Stephen's Hill, St. Albans, Hertfordshire AL1 2DY, ☎ 01727/855215 or 01727/845047, FAX 01727/844126; membership in the U.S. $25, in Canada C$26.75, in the U.K. £9.30). The **Israel Youth Hostel Association** (✉ Binyenei Ha'Ooma, Congress Center, Box 1075, Jerusalem 91009, ☎ 02/655–8420, FAX 02/655–8430; 36 Bnei Dan, Tel Aviv 61021, ☎ 03/544–1742, FAX 03/544–1030) offers several bargain travel packages.

### KIBBUTZ GUEST HOUSES

Kibbutz guest houses, popular in Israel for years, are similar to motels; guests are taken in as a source of extra income for the kibbutz and are not involved in its social life (with the possible exception of having meals in the communal dining room). Unlike motels, though, kibbutzes offer rustic, quiet settings and usually have pools and athletic activities.

➤ INFORMATION: **Kibbutz Hotels Chain** (✉ 90 Ben Yehuda St., Box 3193, Tel Aviv 61031, Israel, ☎ 03/524–6161, FAX 03/527–8088; ✉ 60 E. 42nd St., Suite 620, New York, NY 10165, ☎ 212/697–5116; ✉ Israel Hotel Reservation Center, 20 S. Van Brunt St., Englewood, NJ 07631, ☎ 201/816–0830 or 800/522–6401).

## MAIL

Israel's mail service has improved dramatically in recent years. The post office handles regular and express letters, sends and receives faxes, accepts bill payments, sells phone cards and parking cards, handles money transfers, and offers quick-delivery service. Nearly every neighborhood has a post office, identified by a racing deer on a red background, and English is almost always spoken. The main branches are usually open from 8 until 6 or 7, and small offices are usually open Sunday–Tuesday and Thursday 8–12:30 and 3:30–6, Wednesday 8–1:30, and Friday 8–noon. In Muslim cities and in Gaza the post office is closed Friday; in Christian towns it's closed Sunday; and in Jericho it's closed Saturday. You must bring identification if you want to send packages.

In most big cities, yellow mailboxes are for mail being sent within the same city; red boxes are for all other mail.

In mailing addresses, the abbreviation M.P. stands for Mobile Post (M.P. Gilboa, for example). You'll see this as part of the address in more rural areas.

### POSTAL RATES

A regular letter within Israel costs about 30¢. An air letter to the United States or Europe costs about 45¢. If you bring a letter to the post office before 10 AM, same-day delivery is guaranteed for about NIS 10.60 ($3) within the city, NIS 18 ($5.10) out of town. A letter of 20 grams or less to

Europe costs about NIS 1.80 (50¢), and postage is about NIS 2.20 (63¢) to the United States. An airmail postcard to anywhere in the world requires an NIS 1.40 (40¢) stamp. Mail abroad takes 5 to 10 days. The first page of a fax costs about NIS 6.80 ($2) within Israel, NIS 11.50 ($3.3) to the United States.

### RECEIVING MAIL

Tourists who want to receive mail at a local post office should have it addressed to "Poste Restante" along with the name of the town. Such mail will be held for pickup free of charge for up to three months. American Express offices in the major cities also receive and hold mail free for card members; for a list of foreign American Express offices, call 212/477–5700 in New York City or 800/525–4800.

## MONEY

### COSTS

Israel is a moderately priced country compared to Western Europe, but it's more expensive than many of its Mediterranean neighbors. Tourist costs, calculated in dollars, are little affected by inflation. Prices are much the same throughout the country. To save money, try the excellent prepared food from supermarkets (buy local brands), take public transportation, eat your main meal at lunch, eat inexpensive local foods such as falafel once a day, and stay at hotels with kitchen facilities and guest houses. Airfares are lowest in winter.

Sample prices: cup of coffee, $2; falafel, $1.80; beer at a bar, $3; canned soft drink, $1–$2; hamburger at a fast-food restaurant, $3; 2-km (1-mi) taxi ride, about $3.50; movie, $7.

### CREDIT & DEBIT CARDS

Should you use a credit card or a debit card when traveling? Both have benefits. A credit card allows you to delay payment and gives you certain rights as a consumer (☞ Consumer Protection, *above*). A debit card, also known as a check card, deducts funds directly from your checking account and helps you stay within your budget. When you want to rent a car, though, you may still need an old-fashioned credit card—although you can always *pay* for your car with a debit card, some agencies will only *reserve* a car with a debit card.

Otherwise, the two types of plastic are virtually the same. Both will get you cash advances at ATMs worldwide if your card is properly programmed with your personal identification number (PIN); both offer excellent, wholesale exchange rates; and both protect you against unauthorized use if the card is lost or stolen. Your liability is limited to $50, as long as you report the card missing.

➤ ATM LOCATIONS: **Cirrus** (☎ 800/424–7787). **Plus** (☎ 800/843–7587) for locations in the U.S. and Canada, or visit your local bank.

➤ REPORTING LOST CARDS: To report lost or stolen credit cards, call the following toll-free numbers: **American Express** (☎ 800/327–2177); **Diners Club** (☎ 800/234–6377); **Discover Card** (☎ 800/347–2683); **Master-Card** (☎ 800/307–7309); and **Visa** (☎ 800/847–2911).

## CURRENCY

Israel's monetary unit is the New Israel Shekel, abbreviated NIS. There are 100 agorot to the shekel. The silver-color one-shekel coin is about the size of an American dime, but thicker. Smaller-value bronze coins are the half-shekel and the 10-agorot coin (both of which are larger than the shekel), and the less-used 5-agorot coin. There is also a 5-shekel coin (silver in color), about the size of an American quarter, and a similar-size 10-shekel coin (bronze center, silver-color rim). Paper bills come in 20-, 50-, 100-, and 200-shekel denominations.

Israeli currency fluctuates against the U.S. dollar, so exact rates vary daily. At press time, the exchange rate was about 3.5 shekels to the dollar. Because of the frequent fluctuations, prices quoted throughout this book are listed both in shekels and in their approximate equivalent in U.S. dollars. Because paying bills at hotels, car-rental firms, and special tourist shops in foreign currency eliminates the value-added tax (VAT), price charts in the dining and lodging sections of the book are in U.S. dollars.

## EXCHANGING MONEY

For the most favorable rates, **change money at banks,** or at change points officially approved by the Bank of Israel (unlike the banks, these do not charge a commission). Although fees charged for ATM transactions may be higher abroad than at home, Cirrus and Plus exchange rates are excellent, because they're based on wholesale rates offered only by major banks. You won't do as well at exchange booths in airports, rail and bus stations, hotels, restaurants, or stores, although you may find their hours more convenient. To avoid lines at airport exchange booths, **get a bit of local currency before you leave home.**

➤ EXCHANGE SERVICES: **Chase Currency to Go** (☎ 800/935–9935; 935–9935 in NY, NJ, and CT). **International Currency Express** (☎ 888/842–0880 on the East Coast, 888/278–6628 on the West Coast). **Thomas Cook Currency Services** (☎ 800/287–7362 for telephone orders and retail locations).

## TRAVELER'S CHECKS

Do you need traveler's checks? It depends where you're headed. If you're going to rural areas and small towns, go with cash; traveler's checks are most widely accepted in cities. Lost or stolen checks can usually be replaced within 24 hours. To ensure a speedy refund, buy your own traveler's checks rather than let someone else pay for them—irregularities like this can cause delays. The person who bought the checks should make the call to request a refund.

## NATURE PARKS & RESERVES

For such a small, arid country, Israel has a good many parks and nature reserves. Obtain a full list of parks, including those with camping facilities, from the **Jewish National Fund,** which also runs summer camping programs for families (☎ 02/625–8210). For information on nature reserves and national parks, contact the **Israel Nature Parks Protection Authority,** which also offers a pass for unlimited entry to all nature reserves and national parks around the country for one month.

➤ INFORMATION: **Jewish National Fund** (JNF; ✉ Corner of Keren Kayemet and Keren Hayesod Sts., Box 283, Jerusalem 91002, ☎ 02/670–7411). **Israel Nature Parks Protection Authority** (✉ 78 Yirmiyahu St., Jerusalem 94467, ☎ 02/500–5444; ✉ 35 Jabo St., Ramat Gan 52511, ☎ 03/576–6888).

## OUTDOOR ACTIVITIES & SPORTS

### GOLF

Israel's only golf course, the **Caesarea Golf Club** (✉ Box 1010, Caesarea 38900, ☎ 06/636–1172), on the northern coast, is open seven days a week. Tourists can obtain special memberships, and the club rents all equipment.

### TENNIS

There are tennis centers throughout the country, with nominal court fees; reserve in advance. Ask for the **National Tennis Center** in your area (Central office: ✉ Box 51, Ramat Hasharon 47100, ☎ 03/645–6666).

### WATER SPORTS

Scuba diving and snorkeling are popular in Eilat and at various Mediterranean beaches. Information is available from the **Israeli Diving Federation** (✉ Box 3404, Tel Aviv 61033, ☎ 03/523–6436). Divers must present an advanced open-water license or a junior scuba license, or take a course. Windsurfing and waterskiing are offered at various beaches but not at hotels.

## PACKING

### LUGGAGE

The number of carry-on bags you can take with you is up to your airline; most allow two, but the limit is often reduced to one on certain flights. Gate agents will take excess baggage—including bags they deem oversize—from you as you board and add it to checked luggage. To avoid this situation, make sure that everything you carry on board will fit under your seat. Moreover, get to the gate early, and request a seat at the back of the plane; this way you'll probably board first; while the overhead bins are still empty. Since big, bulky baggage

attracts the attention of gate agents and flight attendants on a busy flight, make sure your carry-on is really a carry-on. An item that's long and narrow is more likely to go unnoticed than one that's wide and squarish.

Note that baggage allowances on international flights may be determined not by piece but by weight—generally 88 pounds (40 kilograms) in first class, 66 pounds (30 kilograms) in business class, and 44 pounds (20 kilograms) in economy.

Airline liability for baggage is limited to $1,250 per person on flights within the United States. On international flights it amounts to $9.07 per pound or $20 per kilogram for checked baggage (roughly $640 per 70-pound bag) and $400 per passenger for unchecked baggage. You can buy additional coverage at check-in for about $10 per $1,000 of coverage, but it excludes a rather extensive list of items, shown on your airline ticket.

Before departure, **itemize your bags' contents** and their worth, and label the bags with your name, address, and phone number. (If you use your home address, cover it so that potential thieves can't see it readily.) Inside each bag, **pack a copy of your itinerary**. At check-in, **make sure that each bag is correctly tagged** with the destination airport's three-letter code. If your bags arrive damaged or fail to arrive at all, file a written report with the airline before leaving the airport.

### PACKING LIST

Israel is a very casual country, where comfort comes first. Rarely will you need more than an afternoon dress or sports jacket to feel adequately dressed. Even posh restaurants do not require a jacket and tie. For touring in the hot summer months, wear cool, easy-care clothing. If you're coming between May and September, you won't need a coat, but you should bring a sun hat that completely shades your face and neck. Take one sweater for cool nights, particularly in the hilly areas and the desert. Also take long pants to protect your legs and a spare pair of walking shoes for adventure travel. A raincoat with a zip-out lining is ideal for October to April, when the weather can get cold enough for snow (and is as likely to be warm enough in the south for outdoor swimming). Rain boots may also be a useful accessory in winter. Pack a bathing suit for all seasons. Note that many religious sites forbid shorts and sleeveless shirts for both sexes; and women should bring modest dress for general touring in religious neighborhoods.

Along with the sun hat, take plenty of sunscreen, insect repellent, a water canteen, and sunglasses in summer.

In your carry-on luggage **take an extra pair of eyeglasses or contact lenses** and **enough of any medication you take** to last the entire trip. You may also want your doctor to write a spare prescription using the drug's generic name, since brand names may vary from country to country. **Never put prescription drugs or valuables in luggage to be checked.** To avoid customs delays, carry medications in their original packaging. And don't forget to copy down and carry addresses of offices that handle refunds of lost traveler's checks.

## PASSPORTS & VISAS

When traveling internationally, **carry a passport even if you don't need one** (it's always the best form of ID), and make **two photocopies of the data page** (one for someone at home and another for you, carried separately from your passport). If you lose your passport, promptly call the nearest embassy or consulate and the local police.

### ENTERING ISRAEL

U.S., Canadian, and U.K. citizens, even infants, need only a valid passport to enter Israel for stays of up to 90 days.

Israel issues three-month tourist visas free of charge at the point of entry when a valid passport is presented. At press time, there were still some countries (particularly in the Middle East) that refused to admit travelers whose passports carried an Israeli visa entry stamp, so if you're concerned about regional mobility, you can ask the customs officer at your point of entry to issue a tourist visa on a separate piece of paper; or you can apply for a second passport and include a letter with the application explaining that you need the passport for travel to Israel. Be advised that it is not unheard of for Israeli customs officers to stamp passports despite requests not to do so; if you plan to travel repeatedly between Israel and those Arab states still hostile to Israel, a second passport is advisable.

### PASSPORT OFFICES

The best time to apply for a passport or to renew is during the fall and winter. Before any trip, check your passport's expiration date, and renew it as soon as possible if necessary. (Some countries won't allow you to enter on a passport that's due to expire in six months or less.)

➤ AUSTRALIAN CITIZENS: **Australian Passport Office** (☎ 13/1232).

➤ CANADIAN CITIZENS: **Passport Office** (☎ 819/994–3500 or 800/567–6868).

➤ NEW ZEALAND CITIZENS: **New Zealand Passport Office** (☎ 04/494–0700 for information on how to apply, 0800/727–776 for information on applications already submitted).

➤ U.K. CITIZENS: **London Passport Office** (☎ 0990/21010), for fees and documentation requirements and to request an emergency passport.

➤ U.S. CITIZENS: **National Passport Information Center** (☎ 900/225–5674; calls are charged at 35¢ per minute for automated service, $1.05 per minute for operator service).

## SAFETY

Traveling throughout most of Israel is safe and comfortable; you'll see Jews and Arabs peacefully coexisting in the major cities. You should, of course, use common sense when driving or walking in isolated areas at night, yet you'll find that even the downtown areas of major cities are comfortable enough for solo walking at any hour.

Over the years, television and in print media have created confusion and consternation around political tensions in various parts of Israel. The Golan Heights are as safe as anywhere else in Israel. Jerusalem's Old City is thronged during the day and relatively empty at night, when almost everything there is closed. The Arab neighborhoods of East Jerusalem have become less hospitable of late, but the daytime wanderer should not encounter any problems. In the Palestinian autonomous areas, Bethlehem and Jericho are still often visited, though many travelers prefer to see them on an organized tour or with a guide who knows the area well. Changing political realities elsewhere in the West Bank—some parts of which have been transferred to the Palestinian Authority—have put many towns, like Hebron, outside tourist itineraries. Even public buses traveling in these areas have reinforced glass to protect them from stone-throwing. Do not drive your own car through these areas, and avoid the Gaza Strip entirely. There are standard security checks along the roads to the West Bank, but the routes are open except in periods of particular political tension.

## SENIOR-CITIZEN TRAVEL

To qualify for age-related discounts, **mention your senior-citizen status up front** when booking hotel reservations (not when checking out) and before you're seated in restaurants (not when paying the bill). Note that discounts may be limited to certain menus, days, or hours. When renting a car, **ask about promotional car-rental discounts,** which can be cheaper than senior-citizen rates.

➤ EDUCATIONAL PROGRAMS: Elderhostel (⊠ 75 Federal St., 3rd floor, Boston, MA 02110, ☎ 617/426–8056).

## SHOPPING

The Ministry of Tourism publishes a guide to shopping in Israel, with frequent updates on special discounts for tourists; this is available at Israel Government Tourist Offices (☞ Visitor Information, *below*).

Jewelry, gems, and locally cut diamonds are considered good buys in Israel. The large cities have many reputable jewelry outlets. Ethnic items such as embroidered skullcaps (*kippot,* or yarmulkes), tie-dyed scarves, spice boxes, blown glass, Hanukkah lights, and the like are popular gifts.

Israeli clothing is not cheap, but many travelers find its high-fashion designs appealing, particularly in bathing suits and leather goods. Tel Aviv is the fashion center.

Jerusalem is a good place to look for antiques and Judaica (Jewish religious items). The downtown area known as Arts and Crafts Lane, the Cardo in the Jewish Quarter of the Old City, and the neighborhood called Mea She'arim have a large selection. Christian objects are also plentiful in Jerusalem, especially in the Old City. If you're shopping in an outdoor market (except a food market), stall owners will expect you to bargain.

## STUDENT TRAVEL

➤ LOCAL RESOURCES: The **Israel Student Travel Association** (ISSTA; ⊠ 128 Ben Yehuda St., Tel Aviv 63401, ☎ 03/521–4444) has 12 branches, most of them on university campuses throughout Israel. Other main offices are in Tel Aviv (⊠ 50 Dizengoff St., 64332, ☎ 03/525–0037), Jerusalem (⊠ 31 Hanevi'im St., 95103, ☎ 02/625–7257), and Haifa (⊠ 29 Nordau St., 33121, ☎ 04/867–0222). ISSTA offers discounted tours, car rentals, hotels, and flights. Students from abroad often take advantage of ISSTA's international travel programs.

### TRAVEL AGENCIES

To save money, **look into deals available through student-oriented travel agencies.** You'll need a bona-fide student ID card to qualify. Members of international student groups are also eligible.

➤ STUDENT IDs & SERVICES: **Council on International Educational Exchange** (CIEE; ⊠ 205 E. 42nd St., 14th floor, New York, NY 10017, ☎ 212/822–2600 or 888/268–6245, FAX 212/822–2699), for mail orders only, in the United States. **Travel Cuts** (⊠ 187 College St., Toronto, Ontario M5T 1P7, ☎ 416/979–2406 or 800/667–2887) in Canada.

➤ STUDENT TOURS: **Contiki Holidays** (⊠ 300 Plaza Alicante, Suite 900, Garden Grove, CA 92840, ☎ 714/740–0808 or 800/266–8454, FAX 714/740–2034).

## TAXES

### VALUE-ADDED TAX (VAT)

A value-added tax (17% at press time) is charged on all purchases and transactions except tourists' hotel bills and car rentals paid in foreign currency (cash, traveler's checks, or foreign credit cards). Upon departure, you are entitled to a refund of this tax on purchases made in foreign currency of more than $50 on one invoice; but the refund is not mandatory, and not all stores are organized with VAT return forms. Stores so organized display TAXVAT signs and give 5% discounts. If you charge meals and other services to your room at a hotel and pay with foreign currency, there is no VAT; the refund does not apply. Keep your receipts and ask for a cash refund at Ben-Gurion Airport or Haifa Port (Bank Leumi has a special desk for this purpose in the duty-free area); if you leave from another departure point, the VAT refund will be sent to your home address. You are expected to be able to produce the items on which you claim a VAT refund, so allow time and space for this procedure when you plan your departure. The Ministry of Tourism distributes a useful booklet, "Made in Israel," free of charge at Ben-Gurion International Airport and at Israel Government Tourist Offices (☞ Visitor Information, *below*).

## TAXIS

Taxis are plentiful and relatively inexpensive, and they can be reached by phone. On the whole, drivers are cheerful. According to law, every driver must use the meter unless you hire him for the day or for a trip out of town, for which there are set rates. If you're pressed to take the cab at a set price, you can ask your hotel staff for an estimate of the cost of your journey. In such a case, agree on the price before you begin the journey and assume that the driver has built in a tip. In the event of a serious problem with the driver, report his cab number (on the illuminated plastic sign on the roof) or license-plate number to the Ministry of Tourism or the Ministry of Transport. Note that official rates are 25% higher after 9 PM and any time public transportation is not running (on Shabbat, for example).

Certain shared taxis or minivans run fixed routes, such as from Tel Aviv to Haifa or from the airport to Jerusalem; such a taxi is called a *sherut* (as opposed to a "special," the term used for a private cab). These have fixed rates, which are generally slightly more expensive than bus rates; and they leave whenever they're full. Some sheruts can be booked in advance.

### GUIDE-DRIVEN LIMOUSINES

Modern, air-conditioned limousines and minibuses driven by expert guides are often available at prices lower than those of taxis; these are a good value for a family or a group of five to seven. At press time, the cost was $281 per day (nine hours) for up to 3 passengers, $318 for 4 to 7 passengers, and $360 for 9–11 passengers. Rates are based on 200 km (120 mi) of travel a day, averaged out over the entire tour, and nine hours a day of touring. An additional $60–$80 per night (depending on location) is charged for the driver's expenses if he or she sleeps away from home. Half-day tours are also available.

➤ LIMO COMPANIES: **Eshkolot Tours** (✉ 36 Keren Hayesod St., Jerusalem, ☎ 02/563–5555 or 02/566–5555, ℻ 02/563–2101). **Superb Limousine Services,** Twelve Tribes' subsidiary at Ben-Gurion Airport (☎ 03/973–1780). **Twelve Tribes** (✉ 29 Hamered St., Tel Aviv, ☎ 03/510–1911, ℻ 03/510–1943).

## TELEPHONES

Israel's phone company is called Bezek. It still has a monopoly on regular services within the country, but it now has competitors for international calls and cellular phone services, often with significantly cheaper prices. Israel's phone system is now digital, so all phone numbers have seven digits. Double-check the number if you don't get an answer.

Toll-free numbers in Israel begin with either 177 or 1–800 (the latter is becoming the norm). When calling an out-of-town number within Israel, be sure to dial the zero that begins every area code.

## COUNTRY CODES

The country code for Israel is 972. When dialing an Israeli number from abroad, drop the initial 0 from the local area code.

## DIRECTORY & OPERATOR INFORMATION

Dial 144 for information. If the operator doesn't speak English or can't find your number, you can ask for a *mefakahat* (supervisor) to help you. Dial 188 for an international operator.

## INTERNATIONAL CALLS

You can make international calls using a telecard from a public phone. A call from Israel to most countries costs about 25¢ per minute. Large cities have central phone agencies—usually near or at main post offices—where you make your call and pay upon completion.

By dialing Israel's toll-free number (1–800 or 177) and the number of your long-distance service, you can link up directly to an operator in your home country. This service works from public phones without a telecard, and often from your hotel room (once you have an outside line).

AT&T, MCI, and Sprint international access codes make calling the United States relatively convenient, but you may find the local access number blocked in many hotel rooms. First ask the hotel operator to connect you. If the hotel operator balks, ask for an international operator, or dial the international operator yourself. One way to improve your odds of getting connected to your long-distance carrier is to travel with more than one company's calling card (a hotel may block Sprint, for example, but not MCI). If all else fails, call from a pay phone in the hotel lobby.

➤ ACCESS CODES: In the United States: **AT&T Direct** (☎ 800/435–0812). **MCI WorldPhone** (☎ 800/444–4141). **Sprint International Access** (☎ 800/877–4646).

## PUBLIC PHONES

Public phones operate with a magnetic telephone card (telecard), available in units of 20 (NIS 11, or $3) or 50 (NIS 24, or $7) and sold at post offices, many newsstands and kiosks, some hotel reception desks, and the occasional special vending machine. Competing phone companies also sell international phone cards. On public phones, the number you're dialing appears on a digital readout; to its right is the number of units remaining on your card.

## TIPPING

There are no hard-and-fast rules for tipping in Israel. Taxi drivers do not expect tips, but a gratuity for good service is in order. If you have negotiated a price, assume the tip has been built in. If a restaurant bill does not include service, 10% is expected—round up if the service was particularly good, down if it was dismal. Hotel bellboys should be tipped a lump sum of NIS 5–NIS 10 ($1.75–$3.50), not per bag. Tipping is customary for tour guides, tour-bus drivers, and chauffeurs. Bus groups normally tip their guide NIS 14–NIS 17 ($4–$5) per person per day, and half that for the driver. Private guides normally get tipped NIS 70–88 ($20–$25) a day from the whole party. Leave NIS 2 (60¢) for bathroom and coatroom attendants. A small tip is expected by both the person who washes your hair and the stylist—except if one of them owns the salon.

## TOUR OPERATORS

Buying a prepackaged tour or independent vacation can make your trip to Israel less expensive and less of a hassle: because everything is prearranged, you'll spend less time planning.

Operators that handle several hundred thousand travelers per year can use their purchasing power to give you a good price. Their high volume may also indicate financial stability. But some small companies provide more personalized service, and because they tend to specialize, they may also be more knowledgeable about a given area.

### BOOKING WITH AN AGENT

Travel agents are excellent resources. In fact, large operators accept bookings made only through travel agents. But it's a good idea to **collect bro-**

chures from several agencies, because some agents' suggestions may be influenced by relationships with tour and package firms that reward them for volume sales. If you have a special interest, **find an agent with expertise in that area**; ASTA (☞ Travel Agencies, *below*) has a database of specialists worldwide.

**Make sure your travel agent knows the accommodations** and other services he or she recommends. Ask about a hotel's location, room size, beds, and whether it has a pool, room service, or programs for children, if these affect you. Has your agent been there in person, or sent others you can contact?

Do some homework on your own, too. Local tourism boards can provide information about lesser-known and small-niche operators, some of which may sell only directly.

## BUYER BEWARE

Every year consumers are stranded or lose their money when tour operators—even very large ones with excellent reputations—go out of business. So **check out the operator.** Find out how long the company has been in business, and ask several travel agents about its reputation. If the package or tour you are considering is priced lower than in your wildest dreams, **be skeptical.** Try to **book with a company that has a consumer-protection program.** If the operator has such a program, you'll find information about it in the company's brochure. If the operator you are considering does not offer some kind of consumer protection, then ask for references from satisfied customers.

In the U.S., members of the National Tour Association and United States Tour Operators Association are required to set aside funds to cover your payments and travel arrangements in case the company defaults. It's also a good idea to choose a company that participates in the American Society of Travel Agent's Tour Operator Program. This gives you a forum if any disputes arise between you and your tour operator; ASTA will act as mediator.

➤ TOUR-OPERATOR RECOMMENDATIONS: **American Society of Travel Agents** (☞ Travel Agencies, *below*). **National Tour Association** (NTA; ✉ 546 E. Main St., Lexington, KY 40508, ☎ 606/226–4444 or 800/755–8687). **United States Tour Operators Association** (USTOA; ✉ 342 Madison Ave., Suite 1522, New York, NY 10173, ☎ 212/599–6599 or 800/468–7862, ℻ 212/599–6744).

## COSTS

The more your package or tour includes, the better you can predict the ultimate cost of your vacation. Make sure you know exactly what is covered, and **beware of hidden costs.** Are taxes, tips, and service charges included? Transfers and baggage handling? Entertainment and excursions? These can add up.

Prices for packages and tours are usually quoted per person, based on two sharing a room. If traveling solo, you may be required to pay the full double-occupancy rate. Some operators eliminate this surcharge if you agree to be matched with a roommate of the same sex, even if one is not found by departure time.

## GROUP TOURS

Among companies that sell tours to Israel, the following have proven reputations and offer plenty of options. The classifications below represent different price categories, and you'll probably encounter these terms when talking to a travel agent or tour operator. The key difference is usually in accommodations, which run from budget to better and better-yet to best.

➤ SUPER-DELUXE: **Abercrombie & Kent** (✉ 1520 Kensington Rd., Oak Brook, IL 60521-2141, ☎ 630/954–2944 or 800/323–7308, ℻ 630/954–3324). **Travcoa** (✉ Box 2630, 2350 S.E. Bristol St., Newport Beach, CA 92660, ☎ 714/476–2800 or 800/992–2003, ℻ 714/476–2538).

➤ DELUXE: **Globus** (✉ 5301 S. Federal Circle, Littleton, CO 80123-2980, ☎ 303/797–2800 or 800/221–0090, ℻ 303/347–2080). **Maupintour** (✉ 1515 St. Andrews Dr., Lawrence, KS 66047, ☎ 913/

843–1211 or 800/255–4266, FAX 913/843–8351).

➤ FIRST-CLASS: **Collette Tours** (✉ 162 Middle St., Pawtucket, RI 02860, ☎ 401/728–3805 or 800/340–5158, FAX 401/728–4745). **General Tours** (✉ 53 Summer St., Keene, NH 03431, ☎ 603/357–5033 or 800/221–2216, FAX 603/357–4548). **Insight International Tours** (✉ 745 Atlantic Ave., No. 720, Boston, MA 02111, ☎ 617/482–2000 or 800/582–8380, FAX 617/482–2884 or 800/622–5015). **Isram World of Travel** (✉ 630 3rd Ave., New York, NY 10117, ☎ 212/661–1193 or 800/223–7460, FAX 212/370–1477). **Trafalgar Tours** (✉ 11 E. 26th St., New York, NY 10010, ☎ 212/689–8977 or 800/854–0103, FAX 800/457–6644).

➤ BUDGET: **Cosmos** (☞ Globus, *above*).

## PACKAGES

Like group tours, independent vacation packages are available from major tour operators and airlines. The companies listed below offer vacation packages in a broad price range.

➤ AIR/HOTEL: **General Tours** (☞ Group Tours, *above*). **TWA Getaway Vacations** (☎ 800/438–2929).

➤ FROM THE U.K.: **Longwood Travel & Holidays** (✉ 182 Longwood Gardens, Ilford, Essex IG5 0EW, ☎ 0181/551–4494, FAX 0181/550–0086). **Pullman Holidays** (✉ 31 Belgrave Rd., London, SW1V 1RB, ☎ 0171/630–5111, FAX 0171/931–7016). **Superstar Holidays** (✉ 180 Oxford St., London, W1N 0EL, ☎ 0171/957–4300, FAX 0171/957–4399).

## THEME TRIPS

➤ ADVENTURE: **Himalayan Travel** (✉ 110 Prospect St., Stamford, CT 06901, ☎ 203/359–3711 or 800/225–2380, FAX 203/359–3669). **Wilderness Travel** (✉ 1102 Ninth St., Berkeley, CA 94710, ☎ 510/558–2488 or 800/368–2794).

➤ ARCHAEOLOGY: **Archaeological Tours** (✉ 271 Madison Ave., New York, NY 10016, ☎ 212/986–3054,

FAX 212/370–1561). **Crow Canyon Archaeological Center** (2339 Road K, Cortez CO 81321, ☎ 970/565–8975 or 800/422–8975, FAX 970/565–4859). **Smithsonian Study Tours and Seminars** (✉ 1100 Jefferson Dr. SW, Room 3045, MRC 702, Washington, DC 20560, ☎ 202/357–4700, FAX 202/633–9250).

➤ JUDAISM: **American Jewish Congress** (✉ 15 E. 84th St., New York, NY 10028, ☎ 212/879–4588 or 800/221–4694). **B'nai B'rith Center for Jewish Identity** (✉ 1640 Rhode Island Ave. NW, Washington, DC 20036, ☎ 202/857–6577 or 800/500–6533).

➤ LEARNING: **IST Cultural Tours** (✉ 225 W. 34th St., New York, NY 10122-0913, ☎ 212/563–1202 or 800/833–2111, FAX 212/594–6953). **Smithsonian Study Tours and Seminars** (☞ Archaeology, *above*).

➤ NATURAL HISTORY: **Society for the Protection of Nature in Israel (SPNI) Nature Trails** (✉ 89 5th Ave., Suite 800, New York, NY 10008, ☎ 212/645–8732 or 212/398–6750). **Victor Emanuel Nature Tours** (✉ Box 33008, Austin, TX 78764, ☎ 512/328–5221 or 800/328–8368, FAX 512/328–2919).

➤ SCUBA DIVING: **Rothschild Dive Safaris** (✉ 900 West End Ave., No. 1B, New York, NY 10025-3525, ☎ 800/359–0747, FAX 212/749–6172).

➤ SINGLES AND YOUNG ADULTS: **Contiki Holidays** (✉ 300 Plaza Alicante, No. 900, Garden Grove, CA 92640, ☎ 714/740–0808 or 800/266–8454, FAX 714/740–0818).

➤ WALKING/HIKING: **Wilderness Travel** (☞ Adventure, *above*).

## TRAIN TRAVEL

The train from Tel Aviv to Jerusalem is scheduled for a complete overhaul during 1999 and 2000, putting it out of service completely. This is no great setback for travelers, for although the ride is picturesque, service has traditionally been both infrequent and slow. Trains are much more frequent between Tel Aviv and Haifa, running almost hourly. Express trains take an hour to make the trip; local trains, about 1½ hours. The cost is NIS 19

($5.20). There are also trains to Nahariya for NIS 29 ($8.50), and to Beersheba for NIS 21 ($6). All train stations post up-to-date schedules in English.

➤ INFORMATION: ➤ INFORMATION: **Central Station** (also known as Arlosoroff) in Tel Aviv (☎ 03/577–4000).

## TRAVEL AGENCIES

A good travel agent puts your needs first. Look for an agency that has been in business at least five years, emphasizes customer service, and has someone on staff who specializes in your destination. In addition, **make sure the agency belongs to a professional trade organization,** such as ASTA in the United States. (If your travel agency is also acting as your tour operator, *see* Buyer Beware in Tour Operators, *above*).

➤ LOCAL AGENT REFERRALS: **American Society of Travel Agents** (ASTA, ☎ 800/965–2782 24-hr hot line, FAX 703/684–8319). **Association of British Travel Agents** (⊠ 55–57 Newman St., London W1P 4AH, ☎ 0171/637–2444, FAX 0171/637–0713). **Association of Canadian Travel Agents** (⊠ Suite 201, 1729 Bank St., Ottawa, Ontario K1V 7Z5, ☎ 613/521–0474, FAX 613/521–0805). **Australian Federation of Travel Agents** (☎ 02/9264–3299). **Travel Agents' Association of New Zealand** (☎ 04/499–0104).

## TRAVEL GEAR

Travel catalogs specialize in useful items, such as compact alarm clocks and travel irons, that can **save space when packing.** They also offer dual-voltage appliances, currency converters, and foreign-language phrase books.

➤ CATALOGS: **Magellan's** (☎ 800/962–4943, FAX 805/568–5406). **Orvis Travel** (☎ 800/541–3541, FAX 540/343–7053). **TravelSmith** (☎ 800/950–1600, FAX 800/950–1656).

## U.S. GOVERNMENT

Government agencies can be an excellent source of inexpensive travel information; **inquire about government publications** when planning your trip.

➤ ADVISORIES: **U.S. Department of State** (⊠ Overseas Citizens Services Office, Room 4811 N.S., Washington, DC 20520; ☎ 202/647–5225 or FAX 202/647–3000 for interactive hot line; ☎ 301/946–4400 for computer bulletin board); enclose a self-addressed, stamped, business-size envelope.

➤ PAMPHLETS: **Consumer Information Center** (⊠ Consumer Information Catalogue, Pueblo, CO 81009, ☎ 719/948–3334 or 888/878–3256) for a free catalog that includes travel titles.

## VISITOR INFORMATION

➤ ISRAEL GOVERNMENT TOURIST OFFICE: In the U.S.: ⊠ 800 2nd Ave., 16th floor, New York, NY 10017, ☎ 212/499–5650, FAX 212/499–5645; ⊠ 5 S. Wabash Ave., Chicago, IL 60603, ☎ 312/782–4306, FAX 312/782–1243; ⊠ 5151 Belt Line Rd., Suite 1280, Dallas, TX 75240, ☎ 214/991–9097 or 800/472–6364, FAX 214/392–3251; ⊠ 6380 Wilshire Blvd., Suite 1700, Los Angeles, CA 90048, ☎ 213/658–7462, ext. 03, FAX 213/658–6543. In Canada: ⊠ 180 Bloor St. W, Toronto, Ontario M5S 2V6, ☎ 416/964–3784, FAX 416/964–2420. In the U.K.: ⊠ 18 Great Marlborough St., London W1V 1AF, ☎ 0171/434–3651. The Israel Ministry of Tourism also staffs a toll-free information line at 888/774–7723. For on-line information, try the IGTO Web site at www.infotour.co.il.

## WHEN TO GO

There is no bad time to visit Israel. There are no rainy days at all from May through September, but some travelers prefer to risking rain and come in the cooler, less- expensive season of November through March. In the winter months, snow falls occasionally in the northern and central hills. In April, May, September, and October, the weather is generally sunny but not uncomfortably hot. March and April have the added attraction of a lush countryside splashed with vivid wildflowers.

During school holidays, particularly in July and August, Israelis themselves take vacations; accommodations and attractions get very crowded, and

THE GOLD GUIDE / SMART TRAVEL TIPS

surcharges are often added to hotel rates. Hotel prices also jump during the Passover and Sukkoth holiday periods (early April and late September–early October, respectively), and services and commerce are sharply curtailed; many Israelis simply go away for Passover. Reservations for this busy week should be booked at least four months in advance, and plane reservations six months to a year in advance. Some hotels require full board for the week of Passover.

### CLIMATE

Temperatures along the Mediterranean coast are similar to those of Tel Aviv; hill cities and towns have climates more like that of Jerusalem. Temperatures at the Dead Sea and in Eilat can get very high and stay high through the night; in the Negev Desert, on the other hand, the higher altitudes cause nighttime temperatures to drop sharply. The following are average daily maximum and minimum temperatures for Tel Aviv, Jerusalem, and Eilat.

➤ FORECASTS: **Weather Channel Connection** (☎ 900/932–8437), 95¢ per minute from a Touch-Tone phone.

## Climate in Israel

### EILAT

| | | | | | | | | |
|------|------|-----|------|------|-----|-------|------|-----|
| Jan. | 70F | 21C | May | 95F | 35C | Sept. | 97F | 36C |
|      | 49 | 9 |      | 70 | 76 |       |       | 24 |
| Feb. | 74F | 23C | June | 100F | 38C | Oct. | 92F | 33C |
|      | 52 | 11 |      | 76 | 24 |       | 68 | 20 |
| Mar. | 79F | 26C | July | 102F | 39C | Nov. | 81F | 27C |
|      | 58 | 14 |      | 77 | 25 |       | 61 | 16 |
| Apr. | 86F | 30C | Aug. | 102F | 39C | Dec. | 72F | 22C |
|      | 65 | 18 |      | 77 | 25 |       | 52 | 11 |

### JERUSALEM

| | | | | | | | | |
|------|------|-----|------|------|-----|-------|------|-----|
| Jan. | 52F | 11C | May | 77F | 25C | Sept. | 81F | 27C |
|      | 45 | 7 |      | 59 | 15 |       | 65 | 18 |
| Feb. | 58F | 14C | June | 81F | 27C | Oct. | 77F | 25C |
|      | 45 | 7 |      | 65 | 18 |       | 61 | 16 |
| Mar. | 61F | 16C | July | 83F | 28C | Nov. | 67F | 19C |
|      | 49 | 9 |      | 67 | 19 |       | 54 | 12 |
| Apr. | 68F | 20C | Aug. | 83F | 28C | Dec. | 56F | 13C |
|      | 54 | 12 |      | 67 | 19 |       | 47 | 8 |

### TEL AVIV

| | | | | | | | | |
|------|------|-----|------|------|-----|-------|------|-----|
| Jan. | 63F | 17C | May | 70F | 21C | Sept. | 85F | 29C |
|      | 49 | 9 |      | 61 | 16 |       | 70 | 21 |
| Feb. | 65F | 18C | June | 81F | 27C | Oct. | 81F | 27C |
|      | 50 | 10 |      | 68 | 20 |       | 65 | 18 |
| Mar. | 68F | 20C | July | 85F | 29C | Nov. | 74F | 23C |
|      | 52 | 11 |      | 72 | 22 |       | 58 | 14 |
| Apr. | 74F | 23C | Aug. | 85F | 29C | Dec. | 67F | 19C |
|      | 58 | 14 |      | 72 | 22 |       | 52 | 11 |

# 1 Destination: Israel

# SMALL COUNTRY, BIG HISTORY

**I**SRAEL IS A LAND of pastel landscapes and primary-color people; a land where the beauty of nature is subtle but the natives often are not. The sometimes rambunctious Israeli affability may envelop you as soon as you board your flight to Tel Aviv, especially if you're flying El Al, Israel's national carrier. Cries of recognition and the chatter of passengers exchanging stories about their trips and their duty-free loot recall first days back at school after summer vacations. Some passengers greet El Al touchdowns on Holy Land soil with spontaneous applause, but these are the sentimental tourists; the red-blooded Israelis are already on their feet collecting their bags, despite pleas from the cabin staff.

Israelis' feistiness can come across as assertive, intrusive, even aggressive; their fighter-pilot style of driving may be the best example. On the other hand, many claim that this attitude is what helped Israel tame its land and successfully defend it. The related lack of inhibition leads to fast and genuinely warm human contacts that come as a refreshing surprise to many visitors from more reserved cultures.

Hospitality has been a deeply ingrained tradition in this part of the world since the days of Abraham's tent. If an Israeli even casually invites you home for coffee or a meal, he or she probably expects that you'll accept the invitation. Do. There is no better way to dive into the culture, and you'll probably pick up instant expertise on local politics, ethnic differences, food, the cost of buying a house, and what your host earns. Be prepared for similar questions about *your* life; there are fewer conversational taboos in Israel than in most English-speaking countries. An oft-quoted example is that of the Israeli company rep sent abroad, who was advised to avoid discussing politics, religion, and sex in social situations. "What *else* is there to talk about?" asked the astonished Israeli.

The key to understanding Israel is to understand that it was created as the modern reincarnation of an ancient Jewish state. Israel was the "Promised Land" of Abraham and Moses, the Israelite kingdom of David and Solomon, and the home of Jesus of Nazareth and the Jewish Talmudic sages. Although the Jewish presence in the country has been unbroken for more than 3,000 years, several massive exiles—first by the Babylonians in 586 BC and then by the Romans in AD 70—created a diaspora, a dispersion of the Jewish people throughout the world.

The Jewish attachment to the ancient homeland weaves through the entire fabric of Jewish history and religious tradition. For the last 2,000 years, wherever they have lived, Jews have turned their faces toward Jerusalem daily in prayer. The Jewish liturgy is saturated with prayers for the restoration of "Zion and Jerusalem." Over the centuries, many Jews trickled back to Eretz Yisrael (the Land of Israel) while others looked forward to fulfilling their dream of return in some future—many felt imminent—messianic age. An 18th-century story tells of a certain Rabbi Yitzhak of Berdichev in Poland who sent out invitations to his daughter's wedding: "It will take place next Tuesday in the Holy City of Jerusalem. If, God forbid, the Messiah has not arrived by then, it will take place in the village square."

Not all were prepared to wait for divine intervention. In the late 19th century, Zionism was founded as a political movement to give structure and impetus to the idea of bringing the Jewish people home to Israel. Some early Zionist leaders, like founding father Theodore Herzl, believed that the urgent priority was simply a Jewish haven safe from persecution, wherever that haven might be. Argentina was suggested, and Great Britain offered Uganda. In light of their historical and emotional links to the land of Israel, most Jews rejected such suggestions as bizarre. British statesman (later Earl) Arthur James Balfour was perplexed by this attitude and asked Zionist leader Chaim Weizmann to explain it. "Mr. Balfour," Dr. Weizmann responded, "if I were to offer you Paris instead of London, would you accept it?" "Of course not," Balfour replied, "London is our capital." "Precisely," said

Weizmann, "and Jerusalem was *our* capital when London was still a marsh!"

The establishment of the state of Israel did not, of course, meet with universal rejoicing. To the Arab world, it was anathema, an alien implant in a Muslim Middle East. To many ultra-Orthodox Jews, it was an arrogant preempting of God's divine plan; and to make matters worse, the new state was blatantly secular, despite its concessions to religious interests. This internal battle over the character of the Jewish state and the implacable hostility of Israel's neighbors—which has resulted in half a century of almost constant conflict—have been the two main issues engaging the country since its birth.

About 81% of Israel's 6 million citizens are Jewish. Some can proudly trace their family roots back many generations on local soil; others are first-, second-, or third-generation *olim* (immigrants) from more than 100 countries. The first modern pioneers arrived from Russia in 1882, purchased land, and set about developing it with romantic zeal. A decade or two later, inspired by the socialist ideas then current in Eastern Europe, a much larger wave founded the first *kibbutzim*—collective villages or communes. In time, these fiercely idealistic farmers became something of a moral elite, having little financial power but providing a greatly disproportionate percentage of the country's political leadership, military officer cadre, and intelligentsia. "We are workers," they liked to say, "but not working-class!" The kibbutz movement still makes its voice heard and its economic presence felt, but it is not the dominant force it once was. A more ambitious younger generation has increasingly eschewed the communal lifestyle in favor of the lures of the big city.

Although most who immigrated before Israel's independence in 1948 were Ashkenazi Jews (those of Central or Eastern European descent), the biggest waves of immigration in the first decade of statehood were of Sephardic Jews, who came from the Arab lands of North Africa and the Middle East. Israel's Jewish population—600,000 at the time of its independence—doubled within 3½ years and tripled within 10. For a long time, the visible differences between the haves and have-nots seemed to break down along the lines of the more established and better-educated Ashkenazim and the poorer, un-skilled Sephardim. Resentment may still simmer in some disadvantaged neighborhoods, and some stereotypes may survive, but generally both the distinction and the prejudices have subsided.

THE STATE OF ISRAEL was founded just three years after the end of World War II, in which the Nazis annihilated fully a third of the world's Jewish population. The new state's first order of business was to provide a haven for the scattered remnants of Europe's shattered Jewish communities, so the 1949 Law of Return recognized the right of any Jew to Israeli citizenship. Immigration and immigrant absorption became national priorities, warranting a full government ministry. Absorption centers were eventually established to give new immigrants an orientation and teach them Hebrew in the renowned immersion method known as the *ulpan*.

Although the system has been generally very successful, its resources and creativity have been sorely taxed in recent years. Between 1989 and 1997, Israel absorbed some three-quarters of a million new immigrants from the former Soviet Union, increasing the population by more than 10%. The initial housing crisis has been resolved, but unemployment and underemployment linger, and only a minority of the often well-trained immigrant professionals are able to work in their own fields. The 14,400 Ethiopian Jews airlifted to Israel in just one day in May 1991 posed a radically different challenge: how to help this group bridge a centuries-wide cultural and technological gap and adjust to a modern society.

The vast majority of Israel's 1 million non-Jewish minority are Muslim Arabs, followed by about 70,000 Christian Arabs, 90,000 Druze, and a similar number of Bedouin (nominally Muslim Arabs, but a community apart). All are citizens, equal under the law, who vote for and may serve in the Knesset, the Israeli parliament. (Not included are the almost 2 million *Palestinian* Arabs of the partly autonomous West Bank and the autonomous Gaza Strip, who are not Israeli citizens.)

The Muslims in Israel are mainstream Sunnis, regarded as both politically and religiously moderate by the standards of the region. Recent years have seen some radicalization of the community's youth, however, and with it a tendency to identify politically with the Palestinian liberation movement or religiously with the Islamic fundamentalism currently sweeping the Middle East.

Of the Christian Arabs, most belong to the Greek Catholic, Greek Orthodox, or Roman Catholic church; a handful of Eastern denominations and a few Protestant groups account for the rest. The Western Christian community is minuscule, consisting mainly of clergy and temporary sojourners, such as diplomats and foreign professionals on assignment.

The Druze, though Arabic-speaking, follow a separate and secret religion that broke from Islam about 1,000 years ago. Larger kindred communities exist in long-hostile Syria and Lebanon, but Israeli Druze have solidly identified with Israel, and the community's young men are routinely drafted into the Israeli army. The Arab community itself is not liable for military service, in order to avoid the possibility of battlefield confrontations with kinsmen from neighboring countries.

There is no firm separation of religion and state in Israel. Matters of personal status—marriage, divorce, adoption, burial, inheritance—are the preserve of the religious authorities of the community concerned. For this reason there is no civil marriage; if one partner does not convert to the faith of the other, the couple must marry abroad. Within the Jewish community, such functions fall under the supervision of the Orthodox chief rabbinate, much to the chagrin of members of the tiny but growing Conservative and Reform movements (many of whom are American expatriates) and of the large number of nonobservant Jews.

The confrontation between secular Israelis and the hard-line ultra-Orthodox has escalated over the years, as the religious community tries to impose on what it considers an apostate citizenry its vision of how a Jewish state should behave. Hot issues include the Orthodox definition of what a Jew is (either born of a Jewish mother or converted by strict Orthodox procedures) for the purpose of Israeli citizenship, and public observance of the Sabbath and of dietary laws. For many nonreligious Israelis, already irked by what they consider religious coercion, the fact that many ultra-Orthodox Jewish men have been able to avoid military service on the grounds of continuing religious studies just rubs salt in the wound.

ISRAEL PRIDES ITSELF on being the only true democracy in the Middle East, and it sometimes seems bent on politically tearing itself apart in the democratic process. This is how the system works (or doesn't): once every four years, prior to national elections, every party publishes a list of its candidates for the 120-member Knesset. There are no constituencies or voting districts; each party that breaks the minimum threshold of 1.5% of the *national* vote gets in, winning the same percentage of seats as its *proportion* of nationwide votes (hence "proportional representation").

The good news is that the system is intensely democratic. A relatively small grouping of like-minded voters *countrywide* (currently about 40,000) can elect an M.K. (Member of the Knesset) to represent its views. The largest party able to gain a parliamentary majority through a coalition with other parties becomes the government. The bad news is that the system creates a proliferation of small parties, whose collective support the government needs in order to rule. Since no party has ever won enough seats to rule alone, Israeli governments have always been based on compromise, with small parties exerting a degree of political influence quite out of proportion to their actual size. Attempts to change the system have been doomed to failure, because the small parties, which stand to lose if the system is changed, are precisely those on whose support the *current* government depends.

Traditionally, the leader of the victorious large party became prime minister, but as of the general elections of May 1996, the prime minister is now elected directly on a separate ballot. The move was designed to reduce the influence of the small parties by giving the PM a popular mandate, but the innovation may have complicated the system rather than improved it. In the 1996 elections many voters split their vote, supporting one of the two big-party candidates as PM but casting their *party* vote in favor of the small party that most closely represented their views. The parliamentary strength of the big parties, Labor and Likud, declined dramatically as a result, with a proportionate rise in the power of the small parties.

THE COUNTRY IS SMALL—just 460 km (under 300 mi) long, from Metulla, on the northern border with Lebanon, to Eilat, on the Red Sea; 110 km (69 mi) wide at its widest, across the Negev Desert; and as little as 50 km (31 mi) wide at its narrowest, across the Galilee. In area Israel is exactly the size of Wales, or just larger than Massachusetts. The American writer Mark Twain was astonished by the smallness of the Holy Land when he visited in 1867. He had envisioned, he wrote, "a country as large as the United States. . . . I suppose it was because I could not conceive of a small country having so large a history."

Mark Twain's astonishment is instructive: in Israel the past is more present than almost anywhere else on earth. There is something about the place that seeps into one's soul. For the Jewish visitor, it's a feeling of coming home, of returning to one's roots. For the Christian, it's the awe of retracing Jesus's footsteps in the Scripture's actual landscape, of seeing the Bible take on entirely new meaning.

Indeed, the country's biblical past has made names like Jerusalem, the Galilee, and the Jordan River household words for almost half the human race. Many a pilgrim has reached Israel expecting a Jerusalem preserved as an uncommercialized shrine, a Galilee of donkey traffic and tiny fishing boats, and a Jordan River "deep and wide." The reality hits as you find the ancient names shouted from store billboards and highway signs. You discover that Jerusalem is a modern metropolis of 600,000 people; Galilee is the name of a professional basketball team; and Jericho, Joshua's first target 33 centuries ago, is now a Palestinian autonomous zone. To top it all off, the Jordan River is for the most part a little stream.

The past is far from forgotten, however. Archaeology is almost a national sport here (though less for today's video-game generation than for its parents), and any unusual find in one of the ongoing excavations is sure to make the prime-time news.

There are prehistoric settlement sites more than a million years old; the world's oldest walled town, at Jericho; echoes of the biblical patriarchs; and evidence of the kings of Israel. You can stand on the Temple Mount steps that Jesus almost certainly climbed, or marvel at an ancient wooden boat by the Sea of Galilee. The word *ancient* has a particular currency here.

Despite its small size, Israel offers an astonishing diversity of climate and terrain. Drive east from Tel Aviv via Jerusalem to the Dead Sea, and in 1½ hours you pass from classic Mediterranean white beaches and orange groves through olive-draped hills and up rugged pine-wooded mountains, only to plunge almost 4,000 ft down the other side, through wild, barren desert, to the subtropical oasis of Jericho and the Dead Sea, the lowest point on the planet.

Half of Israel is desert, but don't picture endless sand dunes. Awesome canyons slice through the Judean Desert to the Dead Sea, a few with sweet waterfalls and brilliant shocks of greenery. The Negev highlands, south of Beersheva, are punctuated by three huge craters caused by eons of water erosion, the only such formations in the world. The resort city of Eilat sits on the coral-reef Red Sea against a backdrop of jagged granite peaks and desert moonscapes. And in the spring, after the meager winter rains, the deserts burst into startling bloom, the hard landscapes softened by a fuzz of grass and multicolored wildflowers. A desert excursion here—by foot, jeep, or camel—is not quickly forgotten.

The northern and western parts of the country are a complete antidote to the desert. True, it's also hot in the summer and somewhat parched in the rainless season from May through October, but it's a land of good winter rains, some springs and streams, miles of Mediterranean beaches, extensive irrigated fields and orchards, mountainsides of evergreen forests, lush nature reserves, and the freshwater "Sea" of Galilee.

Despite its heritage and location—think of it as Eastern Mediterranean rather than Middle Eastern—Israel is as European as it is Levantine. Scientifically, the country is at the forefront of agriculture, electronics, computer technology, lasers, medicine, and biotechnology. Seven universities, some world-renowned, set exceptional standards. Although Israel's health system is groaning under the weight of financial deficits, and hospital conditions sometimes reflect this, the country's high medical standards do not seem to have been compromised. Doctors on call for your hotel will speak English and likely be on par with physicians back home.

Violent crime is extremely low in Israel. Politically motivated violence is infrequent and, despite occasional random outbreaks, has typically occurred in areas at the center of Israel's conflict with the Palestinians (like the West Bank) that are not recommended tourist destinations anyway. You *will* see automatic weapons on the street, obviously in the hands of uniformed security personnel, but also sometimes over the shoulder of a young off-duty soldier in civvies. The Israeli Defense Force is a people's army: almost everybody serves, and a national serviceman or servicewoman, once issued a weapon, is *wedded* to it for the duration. The criminal misuse of army-issue firearms is very, very rare.

There are many large towns in Israel, but only three major cities. Jerusalem, the capital and spiritual center, lies 60 km (38 mi) inland, at an elevation of 2,500 ft, and is a limestone blend of the ancient and the modern. Tel Aviv, on the Mediterranean coast, is unlovely but lively—the country's commercial and entertainment center, the city that never sleeps. Two out of every five Israelis live within its metropolitan area. Haifa, 100 km (63 mi) north of Tel Aviv, sprawls up the slopes of Mt. Carmel, offering sweeping views and serving as one of the country's two main ports and industrial areas.

Urban life, at least in the metropolis, has changed dramatically over the years. Greater affluence and a sharp sense of international fashion and style have produced a consumerism not unlike that of North America or Western Europe. You can see it in the delis and supermarkets, the boutiques and home-furnishing stores. The growing popularity of dining out as an evening activity has created a clientele with sophisticated expectations, which are reflected in the large number of great restaurants and local fine wines. A good climate and fine beaches have spawned a burgeoning leisure industry as well. Add all of this to Israel's physical attractions,

historical fascination, and profound religious impact, and you have one of the most intriguing destinations in the world.

—Mike Rogoff

# WHAT'S WHERE

## Around Jerusalem

This is less a unified region than an eclectic variety of sights that you can visit in day trips from Jerusalem. The most spectacular are the Judean Desert, east of Jerusalem, a land of baked rock cliffs and lush oases; the briny Dead Sea, in which you cannot help but float; and the broodingly unassailable ancient palace-fortress of Masada. West of Jerusalem, toward the Mediterranean coast, are evergreen forests, an exquisite stalactite cave and mazes of man-made ones, and the dueling ground of David and Goliath. Essential for the Christian traveler is Bethlehem, just south of Jerusalem, where Jesus was born.

## Eilat and the Negev

Most travelers to Israel fly into or whiz down to the sun-and-fun city of Eilat, on the Red Sea. Eilat's beaches, tropical reefs (for snorkeling and diving), nightspots, and restaurants make it the quintessential winter escape. But if you have the time to take it slow, and if your soul expands in the quiet vastness of desert landscapes, explore the Negev proper. Here you'll find stunning desert craters and canyons, the footprints of dead civilizations, and the brilliant achievements of new ones trying to "make the desert bloom." Get off the beaten path.

## Jerusalem

For some, Jerusalem is a place where the past and the future merge, sometimes joyously, sometimes perplexingly. For others, romantic illusions splinter on the concrete of a modern city. The city is both history and today's headlines, both spiritual and decidedly temporal. It is holy to Jews, Christians, and Muslims—to each in a different way—and the age-browned limestone walls and prayer-encrusted shrines of its Old City document centuries of often competing devotions. Modern Jerusalem, the capital of Israel, has all the bustle and press of a city of half a million souls, but its airy vistas, stone architecture, museums, and markets make it an absorbing place to visit.

## Lower Galilee

Travel with a Bible in hand. Gideon and Deborah both fought here; King Saul died here; Solomon built; Elijah ranted. Jesus grew up in the hill country of Nazareth and spent most of his ministry around the lovely Sea of Galilee. This region is best known for its antiquities and churches, but its beautiful scenery, outdoor activities, and good food are worth discovering. The Lower Galilee is a year-round destination, but it's best in March and April, when wildflowers blanket the hillsides and touch the fields with brilliance.

## Northern Coast and Western Galilee

This region is custom-made for the pampered explorer. Wending your way up the Mediterranean coast, you're never too far from a good hotel, a good beach, and a good restaurant. The city of Haifa, Israel's third largest, is the local center of gravity, and it alone is worth a chunk of time, along with the rugged Mt. Carmel, over which it sprawls. Classic stops are the Roman city of Caesarea and the Crusader town of Akko, both in the process of re-excavation and restoration. In Western Galilee, the wild natural beauty of forested hillsides and ravines mixes dreamily with archaeological traces of the past.

## Tel Aviv

It's brash and unsightly, but it has the sea—and it's where the action is. A cosmopolitan center of commerce, entertainment, and fashion, Tel Aviv likes to bill itself as "the city that never stops." Between fine sandy beaches; a pleasure-boat marina; restaurants, pubs, and clubs; and culture on tap any day of the week, Tel Avivians see little reason to go elsewhere. Aesthetic high points are Old Jaffa, a landscaped blend of greenery and revived stone buildings; some early 20th-century neighborhoods now being renovated and gentrified; the European International Style of the 1930s and '40s, which still survives in the streets of Tel Aviv; and the clean lines of tall modern buildings, which brand Tel Aviv as a city on the move.

## Upper Galilee and the Golan

Here you'll find what is arguably the finest scenery in Israel. Hike to a waterfall, boat on the Jordan, watch birds, explore a medieval castle, dine on trout, taste wine on the Golan Heights, hit Israel's only ski slope, wrap yourself in Jewish mysticism in the mountain city of Zfat (Safed), and make use of high vantage points to better understand "the situation" between Israel and its northern neighbors. This is a region where you can recharge your batteries and be as active or as indolent as you choose.

## Beyond Israel

Travelers to Israel can easily sample two neighboring countries while they're in the area. The Sinai, in Egypt, attracts both adventurous outdoor travelers who want to trek or dive among its awesome beauty, and pilgrims seeking biblical sights, such as St. Catherine's Monastery and Mt. Sinai. From Eilat, you can travel in luxury buses or join a jeep safari. Israelis and visitors alike are flocking to nearby Jordan to see Petra, the remains of an ancient Nabatean city carved into sandstone; Petra's gigantic rose-red buildings are treasures even in an area studded with impressive antiquities.

# PLEASURES AND PASTIMES

## Antiquities

For some, ancient sites are a chore; for others, such sites bring to momentary life the clash of ancient arms, the roar of long-dead crowds, and the boom of silent orators. In Israel this is even more true. Not everyone comes here with Bible in hand, but a vast majority of Israel's visitors have at least a childhood familiarity with the names that mark the country's history. Jerusalem, Beersheva, Bethlehem, the Jordan River, and Armageddon are as much concepts as map references. To walk in the footsteps of Abraham, King David, and Jesus of Nazareth is to relive significant chunks of the history of Western civilization. And where stone remains of the past can be connected—whether scientifically or by tradition—to the very well-springs of religious faith or cultural identity, the experience is often exultant.

## Beaches

Beach-lovers have their choice of an appealing variety of shorelines. The long Mediterranean coast has many excellent public beaches. Eilat, on the Red Sea, has its sandy North Shore for sun worshipers, and the pebbly beaches near the coral reefs for snorkelers. Beaches around the freshwater Sea of Galilee tend to be rocky. At the Dead Sea, don't miss the unique experience of floating in the intense brine; facilities are good, and the better beaches are sandy.

## Culture

Classical music is Israel's strong suit, with several excellent orchestras—most notably the Israel Philharmonic—and smaller ensembles performing a variety of programs. Many Russian immigrants have made their mark here, and young native virtuosos seem to be maintaining the tradition of Israeli superstars such as Itzhak Perlman, Pinchas Zuckerman, Daniel Barenboim, Shlomo Mintz, and Gil Shaham, all of whom periodically reappear on Israeli stages. The revival of opera in Tel Aviv—new location, new company—recalls the days more than 30 years ago when a young tenor named Placido Domingo got his start here.

Jazz and blues are popular, and their excellent summer festivals have gained international recognition, though the lineups consist largely of foreign artists. The local pop scene tends to be of the softer type, but superstars from abroad help heat it up. Middle Eastern sounds remain very popular, and fusions that incorporate Western musical elements have won adherents. Folk music is also alive and well, both the native Israeli and the "Anglo" variety.

There is very little English-language theater, but quite a few Hebrew productions provide simultaneous translation. Dance—particularly modern—can be very good; look especially for the renowned Bat Sheva company.

## Dining

Israel's culinary scene has undergone a revolution in the last decade or so. Traditionally, Israeli food was a grab bag of Middle Eastern specialties: a *meze* (appetizer) of well-flavored salads with warm pita bread, some fresh grilled fish, or a skewer of shish kebabs. But soaring tourism and a new, more affluent generation of Israelis have created a demand for a more cosmopolitan range of specialty restaurants. Add to that the country's rainbow of cultural influences and year-round availability of first-rate local produce, and the

burgeoning food scene seems a natural development. Fine steaks and tasty pies, the cuisines of France and Italy, of China and India, and even (perish the comparison!) international fast-food chains—it's all here, though obviously more so in the cities (with Tel Aviv in the lead) than in the country.

## Museums

Throughout Israel, museums help bring the past alive. Local museums tell the story of a particular site or display archaeological artifacts found there; regional museums do much the same thing but often add the area's natural history. At national museums, the art of museology is more finely honed; these include such historical or ethnographical museums as the Diaspora and Eretz Israel museums, both in Tel Aviv; and, in Jerusalem, Yad Vashem, the Holocaust museum and memorial, and the Tower of David Museum of the city's history. Jerusalem's marvelously eclectic and world-renowned Israel Museum is a repository of many of the nation's finest art and archaeological treasures.

## Outdoor Activities

Israel has become known to adventure travelers as a real destination for everything from desert treks to scuba diving. Many Israelis are avid hikers, and the country has several thousand miles of officially marked hiking trails as well as national parks and nature reserves. In the process of development is a long route called the Israel Trail, running the length of the country from the village of Metulla, on the northern border with Lebanon, to Eilat, on the Red Sea. Cliff rappelling has developed a following, particularly on the precipices of the Judean and Negev deserts. Scuba diving and snorkeling are popular among the world-renowned coral reefs off Eilat, but also off the Mediterranean beaches at Ashkelon, Tel Aviv, Caesarea, Haifa, Akko, and Nahariya.

While you're here, you can take advantage of pools and gyms, tennis and squash courts, sailboats and Windsurfers, scuba equipment and Para-Sails, horses, and canoes; trek the Negev by jeep or camel; and, in early spring, water-ski on the Sea of Galilee and snow-ski on Mt. Hermon on the same day.

# NEW AND NOTEWORTHY

## Jerusalem

Jerusalem's new **park,** which will stretch from the Garden of Gethsemane (at the foot of the Mount of Olives) down the Kidron Valley to the ancient City of David, and west up the Hinnom Valley, is being developed at a leisurely pace. The most visible results so far are the **observation point** near the Old City's southeastern corner, with a panorama of the Kidron Valley; and a pedestrian path above the heavy traffic along the Old City's eastern wall. Eventually (say the planners), the park will provide explanations of newly renovated archaeological sites en route, as well as refreshment stands and rest rooms.

Another high-visibility project is the *re*excavation and restoration of the **Ophel Archaeological Garden** (better known as the Western and Southern Wall Excavations), just inside the Old City's Dung Gate. This process has brought to light vast underground sewage tunnels and enormously evocative sections of one of Jerusalem's main streets from 2,000 years ago. Currently being prepared for public access, the site will offer frozen-in-time evidence of the Romans' destruction of the city in AD 70.

With Israel's 50th birthday behind it, the Holy City is bracing for the year 2000—the Christian bimillennium—and the expected rush of pilgrims. Poised to help relieve the lodging shortage are the new deluxe **Jerusalem Hilton** and **Dan Pearl** hotels, both part of the still-unfinished Mamilla complex, outside the Jaffa Gate. Two large but less expensive hotels are under construction along Road 1, near the American Colony Hotel.

## Around Jerusalem

At press time, the long-awaited second **cable-car system** at **Masada,** the great ancient citadel near the Dead Sea, was nearing completion. The cars will whisk 80 visitors at a time to its upper station, on the summit (the current system ends 90 steps below the top), but the powers that be are still debating whether the entrance from there to the site itself will be through a tunnel or a bridge. By almost tripling the present cable-car capacity, the new system will provide a long-term solution to peak-season delays. Also planned is a sophisticated **visitor center,** with visual and audiovisual aids.

## Tel Aviv

Driving in Tel Aviv is becoming increasingly difficult because of the sheer number of cars on the road and the according lack of parking. But if you can wait 20 years, you may be able to ride an **electric rail** that links Tel Aviv with the surrounding suburbs; this quiet, nonpolluting system will replace the buses now in use. Meanwhile, **intercity roads** are being improved; the Ayalon Highway (Route 1), for example, is being widened to ease congestion on Tel Aviv's access roads.

One of the biggest problems for visitors to Tel Aviv is a shortage of reasonably priced accommodations. With any luck, this will change in the next several years: several thousand new hotel rooms are slated to open by the year 2000, and many of these, say city officials, will be much more affordable than the average room today.

Four marked **walking tours** were introduced in 1995; they are called the Orange (Tapuz) Routes. Although they can also be done as driving tours, walking is preferred. The routes cover numerous points of historic and cultural interest in the city. Maps are available from the Tel Aviv Tourist Information Office in the Central Bus Station.

The city's **architectural history** gets its due in City Hall's aim to make Tel Aviv "the world's largest open-air International Style museum": 1,000 buildings designed in the International Style and dating from the 1930s and '40s are slated for restoration. Although you can study these buildings' characteristic straight lines and simple forms right now, their whitewash is blackened, and their dominant visual elements are plastic shutters and ugly air conditioners. Progress is slow, because money for the massive project is hard to come by, but the city's change in attitude toward preservation and restoration is a step in the right direction.

## Northern Coast and Western Galilee

**Haifa** is a hillside city with pale-gold beaches below and show-stopping views from the crest above. Good museums, old neighborhoods, religious landmarks, and several excellent restaurants make it a destination in itself. What Haifa has always lacked is a choice of top **hotels.** Though the hilltop Dan hotels are wonderfully located, two new hotels have other virtues: the secluded Carmel Forest Spa Resort, 30 km (19 mi) southeast of Haifa, offers the sybaritic pleasures of spa facilities, and the Carmel Beach Towers and Suites is right on the beach.

In **Caesarea,** archaeologists have recently identified the **prison cell of Paul** the Apostle.

## Lower Galilee

**Nazareth** seems finally to be coming of age as a tourist destination. Inspired by expectations of an upsurge in pilgrimage at the bimillennium of the Christian era (the year 2000), the city of Nazareth and the Israel Ministry of Tourism are investing huge sums in **infrastructure and face-lifting.** Visible results are flower beds, resurfacing of roads, and the renovation of the old market off Casa Nova Street. Transforming the market into a colorful tourist attraction, like the *souk* in Jerusalem's Old City, may be difficult, of course; such phenomena need to develop organically to feel authentic. Parking areas and public rest rooms are in the works; and the city's hotels—old, new, and still-to-be—should provide a total of 2,000 rooms by the year 2000.

Nazareth has always celebrated **Christmas** with parades, fireworks, and choral singing; but the Ministry of Tourism has given these events even greater support since Bethlehem came under Palestinian autonomous control in December 1995. Nazareth's international Christmas choir assembly seems set to rival Bethlehem's longer-established event.

The ancient city of **Zippori,** west of Nazareth, has become famous (and a national park) mostly because of its fine **mosaic floors** from the Roman period. In addition to the famous "Mona Lisa" floor, the restored "Nile" mosaic has been reopened; and the poorly preserved but intriguing synagogue floor will soon be on view as well.

## Upper Galilee

The range of accommodations in this region is constantly expanding, with a recent emphasis on the great outdoors. Among the new arrivals are **vegetarian inns** that offer health-and-beauty packages and **sports-oriented packages** centered

on activities such as horseback riding and kayaking.

## Eilat, the Negev, and Petra

Peace is upon Israel, at least from some directions, making **Eilat** a convenient departure point for trips to neighboring Jordan, just as it has long been a base for diving and sightseeing trips to the Egyptian **Sinai.** The main attraction is the ancient, pink-hued stone city of **Petra,** once the capital of the Nabatean kingdom, which controlled a lucrative perfume-and-spice route some 2,000 years ago. Another Nabatean city, **Avdat,** was one of the stops on the road that linked the Indo-Chinese markets to the Mediterranean world, running from Transjordan through Israel's Negev Desert and on to the coastal city of Gaza.

It's a pleasure to report that the managers of Eilat's newer **hotels** have taken into consideration the tastes of travelers who can live without loud music and nightly entertainment in the lobby. These hotels have been built with two lobbies; in the local lexicon, the one without entertainment is the "quiet lobby."

Hotels in **Eilat** and **Ein Bokek** get larger and plusher by the minute. There's not a hotel in the Dead Sea's Ein Bokek that doesn't boast a fine spa. Those built in the last two years are the final word in indulgent luxury, and the older ones have hastened to update their spa facilities. The newest lodging at the lowest place on earth is the sparkling white Caesar, with 300 rooms.

---

# FODOR'S CHOICE

## Quintessentially Israeli

★ **The Western (Wailing) Wall on Monday and Thursday mornings, Jerusalem.** Both local families and Jewish families from abroad welcome their 13-year-old bar mitzvah boys into the adult Jewish community.

★ **The Machaneh Yehuda market on Thursday and Friday, Jerusalem.** In the pre-Shabbat shopping frenzy, vendors hawk their wares, and a great variety of Jerusalem "types" rub shoulders among stalls piled with excellent produce and baked goods.

★ **Nahalat Binyamin street market and Sheinkin Street, Friday afternoon, Tel Aviv.** Install yourself in a café and enjoy music and local color.

★ **The Arab *souk* (outdoor market), Akko.** Middle Eastern flavors and aromas create a feast for the senses.

★ **Saturday lunch in Caesarea.** Gaze at the Mediterranean as you take a meal in the Crusader city.

★ **A visit to a nature reserve, Upper Galilee.** Take in the wildflowers at the Tel Dan or Hermon River (Banias) nature reserve.

★ **Sunset on the Gulf of Eilat.** Sip a drink on the Promenade and watch the distant Red Sea go crimson.

## Biblical Highlights and Holy Places

★ **Western (Wailing) Wall, Jerusalem.** The most important Jewish shrine in the world, this stone wall was part of the retaining wall of the ancient Temple Mount.

★ **Calvary, Jerusalem.** Different theories claim either the Church of the Holy Sepulcher or the Garden Tomb to be the site of Jesus' crucifixion.

★ **Dome of the Rock and El-Aqsa Mosque, Jerusalem.** Muslim tradition identifies these buildings with Muhammad's ascent to heaven to receive the teachings of Islam.

★ **Warren's Shaft and Hezekiah's Tunnel, Jerusalem.** These underground passages—the first an access shaft, the second an underground aqueduct—once saved the precious water supply of the ancient City of David.

★ **Via Dolorosa, Jerusalem.** The 14 Stations of the Cross on the Way of Sorrow mark the path Jesus is believed to have walked to his Crucifixion.

★ **Church of the Nativity, Bethlehem.** Israel's oldest church encompasses the cave in which Jesus is believed to have been born.

★ **Carmelite Monastery, Muhraka.** Near this site, Elijah defeated the priests of Ba'al in the struggle against paganism.

★ **Baha'i Shrine, Haifa.** Topped by a golden dome, the mausoleum of Mirza Husayn Ali, a central figure in the Baha'i faith, sits amid the shrine's magnificent gardens.

★ **Mt. Tabor, Lower Galilee.** Both the biblical victory of the prophetess-judge Deborah and the Church of the Transfiguration lend this site religious significance.

★ **Church of the Annunciation, Nazareth.** Roman Catholics believe it is here that the angel Gabriel announced the upcoming birth of Jesus to the Virgin Mary.

★ **Mount of Beatitudes, Lower Galilee.** The site of the Sermon on the Mount has a tranquil garden and a fine view of the Sea of Galilee.

★ **Tel Dan Nature Reserve, Upper Galilee.** Joshua led the Israelites through this area to victory against the Canaanites.

★ **Tel Beer Sheva, the Negev.** Some consider this well atop the hill of biblical Beersheva to be Abraham's Well.

## Archaeological Gems

★ **The archaeology wing of the Israel Museum, Jerusalem.** Artifacts from the past brilliantly illumine the area's long and colorful history.

★ **Herodian Quarter/Wohl Archaeological Museum, Jerusalem.** Learn ancient interior design from the remains of mansions from the Second Temple period.

★ **Herod's Palace/Fortress of Masada.** This monument to King Herod's taste for opulence is also the site of the Jews' last stand against the Romans.

★ **Tel Maresha and Bet Guvrin, west of Jerusalem.** Wander through the man-made caves that served as storerooms, cisterns, and quarries during the Hellenistic period.

★ **Crusader City, Akko.** A stroll through this area—both above and below ground—gives a sense of Akko's past glory.

★ **Herodian port and Crusader city, Caesarea.** Look down to see Byzantine mosaic floors—some with inscriptions, and several in a glorious bathhouse—along the seashore.

★ **Zippori, Lower Galilee.** Recently excavated mosaic floors and elaborate water systems recall Jewish life in the Roman period.

★ **Bet She'an, Lower Galilee.** The impressive remains of the great Roman-Byzantine city of Scythopolis are a showpiece of Israeli archaeology.

★ **Avdat, the Negev.** The ancient ruins of this hilltop city were left by the Nabateans, Romans, and Byzantines.

## Dining

⭐ **Michael Andrew, Jerusalem.** Stone arches enshrine a gourmet Belgian fish restaurant, where the chef's work is pure artistry. *$$$–$$$$*

⭐ **Le Tsriff, Jerusalem.** Locals flock to this backstreet gem for meat, seafood, and vegetable pies in perfect crusts. *$$$*

⭐ **Mul-Yam, Tel Aviv.** Dine on imported oysters and seafood in an attractive setting at the old port. *$$$$*

⭐ **Shipudei Hatikva, Tel Aviv.** This simply decorated, family-style eatery serves wonderful grilled meats. *$*

⭐ **The Pine Club Restaurant, Mt. Carmel.** Local ingredients help create a memorable experience in French dining. *$$$$*

⭐ **Uri Buri, Akko.** is a fish restaurant long famed for Uri's creative ways with seafood and fish, newly relocated from Nahariya to a spot near the lighthouse in old Akko. *$$$$*

⭐ **Picciotto, Zichron Ya'akov.** The menu is re-created daily, making use of seasonal produce and such fowl as quail, and you can sample wines from nearby wineries. *$$$$*

⭐ **Pagoda and The House, Tiberias.** Both specialize in excellent Chinese and Thai food (no pork or shellfish). *$$–$$$*

⭐ **Auberge Shulamit, Rosh Pina.** Home-smoked meats and sophisticated fish dishes draw crowds to this charming inn. *$$$$*

⭐ **Salsa, Eilat** is a rousing experience. The multicolored interior is stunning—all curves, angles, and soaring spaces over a huge bar—and the California-Mexican-Cajun–style meat, pasta, fish, and seafood dishes are sophisticated. A guitarist strums Mexican melodies. *$$$*

## Lodging

⭐ **American Colony, Jerusalem.** Guest rooms are modest, but this 19th-century limestone oasis draws travelers for its ambience and service. *$$$$*

⭐ **Lev Yerushalayim, Jerusalem.** Comfortable and spacious suite accommodations with kitchenettes provide convenience in the city center. *$$$*

⭐ **Ramat Rachel, Jerusalem.** Great views and superb facilities give this rustic kibbutz hotel a resort feel, yet it's only 15 minutes from downtown. *$$$*

⭐ **Dan Tel Aviv.** A welcoming atmosphere and personal touches set the tone at this landmark establishment. *$$$$*

⭐ **Sheraton Tel Aviv Hotel and Towers.** A well-designed lobby, comfortable rooms, and plenty of activities make the Sheraton a haven. *$$$$*

⭐ **The Carmel Forest Resort and Spa, near Haifa.** Pine trees are the setting, health and serenity the themes; indulge in sybaritic delights. *$$$$*

⭐ **Gai Beach, Tiberias.** Waterfront ambience and a quiet, edge-of-town location give the Gai Beach an edge over its downtown peers. *$$$$*

⭐ **Church of Scotland Centre, Tiberias.** Stone buildings with porches and high-ceilinged rooms; a serene wild garden; and a private beach are the draws here. *$$*

⭐ **Rimon Inn, Zfat.** Stone walls and a mountain setting add to the rustic mood of this well-equipped inn. *$$$$*

⭐ **Dan Eilat, Eilat.** This strikingly modern luxury hotel—the city's newest—has an incredible array of facilities. *$$$$*

# GREAT ITINERARIES

## Highlights of the Holy Land

History wraps its mantle around the present in Jerusalem. Abraham brought Isaac to Mt. Moriah; King David made the city his capital; and David's son, King Solomon, built the First Temple here. Conqueror after conqueror battled for Jerusalem, but the city transcends its martial past. You'll be struck both by its beauty and by its spiritual quality.

Jerusalem is a busy city—even frenetic on Friday, when people hurry through the streets to prepare for the Sabbath—but it has never quite shaken off its charming provincialism. Tel Aviv, in contrast, is a new city, founded on sand dunes by early 20th-century pioneers. It's modern, fast-paced, and fun-loving, Israel's headquarters of commerce, entertainment, and fashion. This is where the money is.

Tiberias is a small city on the shore of the Sea of Galilee. While its own attractions are limited, its splendid location makes it a perfect base for exploring the Galilee and Golan.

By booking hotel rooms in these three cities, you can see most of Israel in a short time and keep packing and unpacking to a minimum.

## Duration

8 days

## The Main Route

➤ 3 NIGHTS: OLD AND NEW JERUSALEM: Wear good walking shoes for Old City tours. Begin with a visit to the Tower of David Museum (just inside Jaffa Gate, in the Old City), which recounts the history of Jerusalem. Spend an evening at a folklore show. Have dinner at an ethnic restaurant—local specialties are *kubeh* soup (a rich vegetable soup with semolina-wrapped meatballs), Jerusalem mixed grill, and hummus. Have coffee or onion soup on Ben Yehuda Street and enjoy the atmosphere of a street fair. For the fourth day, book a full-day tour to the Dead Sea and Masada with a tour company or private guide. Return to Jerusalem for dinner.

➤ 2 NIGHTS: TEL AVIV: Frequent buses make the trip between Jerusalem and Tel Aviv in less than an hour. Military vehicles from the War of Independence have been left on the roadside as memorials to the days when the city was under siege. Farther along, the bus passes through the Ayalon Valley, named in the Bible as the site where the sun stood still in the heavens for Joshua.

In Tel Aviv, window-shop on Dizengoff Street and visit the Diaspora Museum. Shop at the outdoor Carmel Market. Have dinner at a beachside restaurant or eat authentic falafel. Catch local performers at a Jaffa nightclub, or hear the Israel Philharmonic Orchestra in the Mann Auditorium.

➤ 2 NIGHTS: TIBERIAS: Hovering around the Sea of Galilee on the first day, see the Mount of Beatitudes, the synagogue at Capernaum, the Hammat Gader hot springs in the remains of the Roman baths, Israel's oldest kibbutz, and Tabgha, said to be where Jesus multiplied the loaves and the fishes. Swim or go boating on the lake. Have dinner on the wharf; the local specialty is St. Peter's fish (*amnoon* in Hebrew). On the second day, take a day trip to the Upper Galilee and the Golan Heights to see sights like the old Syrian bunkers, the Banias Waterfall, ancient Gamla, the town of Katzrin, the Mt. Hermon ski resort, and Nimrod's Castle. Return to Tiberias via Zfat, a city of mystics and artists, and take a nighttime cruise on the Sea of Galilee.

On the eighth and last day of the complete tour, return to the airport via Rosh Hanikra and Haifa. In Haifa, take a cable car to the top of Mt. Carmel to enjoy the view.

## Getting Around

Pick up a rental car at Ben-Gurion Airport and drive to Jerusalem. From Jerusalem to Tel Aviv, leave Jerusalem from the same main westbound exit, near the Central Bus Station, and follow signs for Route 1, past the Ben-Gurion Airport, into Tel Aviv. Leave Tel Aviv by the Haifa Road (Route 2), drive north along the coast, and turn east onto Route 65 (look for power-station chimneys on your left) toward Afula to reach Tiberias.

You can also cover this itinerary by bus. Buses leave the airport about every half hour for Jerusalem; buses from North Tel Aviv (Arlozorov Street; Bus 480) and from the new Central Bus Station (Bus 405) leave every 10–15 minutes. There are also frequent buses to Tiberias from Tel Aviv's Central Bus Station.

## Information

Chapters 2, 3, 4, 6, and 7.

# Action Tour

The weather is so good in Israel that outdoor enthusiasts can always find plenty to do. The only limits are your energy and, sometimes, the heat. Drink a lot of fluids and watch out for the sun. Israelis are great hikers; you can add day hikes to any of the suggested activities below, and trails are well marked.

## Duration

11 days

## The Main Route

➤ 3 NIGHTS: JERUSALEM: Park outside Jaffa Gate and walk along the walls of the Old City. Join a walking tour through the archaeological tunnels under the Western Wall. Eat in an ethnic restaurant and attend a folklore show. On the second day, visit key West Jerusalem sites, including Yad Vashem, the Knesset, the Chagall windows at Hadassah Hospital, and the Israel Museum. Return to the Old City for a moonlight tour.

On the third day, take a vigorous walking tour through the Judean Hills. Visit a kibbutz, the Sorek Stalactite Cave, and the manmade caverns of Maresha/Bet Guvrin.

➤ 2 NIGHTS: DEAD SEA AREA: Visit Masada (by way of the steep Snake Path, if you're fit) and hike in the Ein Gedi Nature Reserve. Stay overnight at a kibbutz guest house on the shore of the Dead Sea; a hotel at Ein Bokek; or the SPNI field school at Ein Gedi. The next day, go cliff rappelling at Metzukei Dragot, near Kibbutz Shalem. Soothe your skin in the local mud baths. Take a nighttime jeep tour of the whole area.

➤ 2 NIGHTS: EILAT: Take a one-day camel tour into the breathtaking hills around Eilat. Swim with the dolphins and snorkel at a superb coral beach. Take a self-driven jeep tour or go for a desert hike in the magnificent Red Canyon and in Ein Netafim.

➤ 1 NIGHT: TEL AVIV: Rest up in Tel Aviv with a stroll on the boardwalk. Rent a sailboat at the marina.

➤ 2 NIGHTS: TIBERIAS: Hike or ride horseback in the Golan Heights, or depending on the weather, ski on Mt. Hermon or take an inner-tube or kayak ride down the Jordan River. Try parasailing on the Sea of Galilee.

### Getting Around

To cover this itinerary, pick up a rental car at Ben-Gurion Airport and follow signs east to Jerusalem. You can park at one of the lots adjacent to the Old City. Alternately, take a bus from the airport; they leave about every half hour or, from Tel Aviv to Jerusalem, every 10–15 minutes.

### Information

Chapters 2, 3, 4, 6, and 8.

## Archaeology Tour

Israel is an archaeology buff's dream, with an immense variety of fascinating sites in a small geographical area. Visitors may want to consider joining a dig for part of their trip. Most prehistoric sites are in the Lower Galilee and along the northern coast; Jerusalem is a treasure trove of sites from all periods of ancient history. Following the archaeologists' trails will take you around most of the country.

### Duration

8–10 days

### The Main Route

➤ 4 NIGHTS: JERUSALEM WITH DAY TRIPS: Plan on at least two days in the Old City and two days in museums. Some essential archaeological sites in Jerusalem are the City of David (including Warren's Shaft and Hezekiah's Tunnel), the Ophel Archaeological Garden, the Pools of Bethesda, the Jewish Quarter (including the Herodian Mansions and Burnt House, the Broad Wall, and the Cardo), and the Western Wall tunnel. Visit the Tower of David Museum, the Israel Museum (where the Dead Sea Scrolls are on display, as well as countless other ancient artifacts), the Bible Lands Museum, and the Rockefeller Museum. Have dinner at the Cardo Culinaria (✉ Jewish Quarter, Old City, ☎ 02/626–4155), a restaurant modeled after a Roman *triclinium*, a dining establishment of 2,000 years ago.

Make a day trip to the Qumran caves, where the Dead Sea Scrolls were found; the Chalcolithic temple at Ein Gedi (a considerable climb); and the great desert fortress at Masada (where the sound-and-light program makes a perfect evening). Also visit the Bet Guvrin caves, southwest of Jerusalem.

➤ 2 NIGHTS: TIBERIAS: Travel along the Jordan Valley to Bet She'an, then on to the Crusader castle Belvoir and Hammat Gader, with its excavated Roman baths, hot springs, and pools. Leave time to bathe in the hot pools and visit the alligator farm. Travel to the Golan town of Katzrin to see its small but fascinating museum. Don't miss the gates and "high place" of Tel Dan, the water system of Hazor, the ancient synagogues of Capernaum and either Hammat Tiberias or Bet Alfa, the mosaics of Zippori, and the prehistoric museum at Ma'ayan Baruch.

➤ 1 NIGHT: NAHARIYA: See the mosaics in the church at Givat Katznelson, the Crusader city in Akko, and the ancient city of Megiddo, one of the inspirations for James Michener's *The Source*. Stay either in the resort town of Nahariya or in a coastal kibbutz guest house.

The next day, visit a cluster of sites in the Western Galilee and along the northern coast: Bet She'arim, with its Jewish catacombs dating from the 2nd–4th centuries AD; the healing center and baths at Shuni, near Zichron Ya'akov; and the Roman city and port of Caesarea.

➤ 2 NIGHTS: BEERSHEVA AND EILAT: If you have two extra days, head south to the Negev to see the biblical city at Tel Beer Sheva (Beersheva) and the ancient copper works of Timna Valley, north of Eilat.

### Getting Around

Except in Jerusalem, it's best to rent a car to reach most of the archaeological sites. Buses will get you to many places, but you'll have to plan carefully to ensure return transportation.

### Information

Chapters 2, 3, 5, 6, and 8.

# NATIONAL AND RELIGIOUS HOLIDAYS

Time is figured in different ways in Israel. The Western Gregorian calendar—the solar year from January to December—is the basis of day-to-day life and commerce, but the school year, for example, which runs from September through June, follows the *Hebrew* lunar calendar (dated to when Creation is believed to have occurred). Thus fall 1999–fall 2000 is the Hebrew year 5760, reckoned from Rosh Hashanah, the Jewish New Year, which usually falls in September. Since the lunar year is 11 days shorter than the solar year, Jewish holidays are out of sync with the Gregorian calendar and fall on different dates (though within the same season) from one year to the next. Jewish religious festivals are observed as national public holidays, when businesses and some museums are closed (on Yom Kippur, the Day of Atonement, *all* sites are closed).

The Muslim calendar is also lunar, but without the compensatory leap-year mechanism of its Hebrew counterpart. Muslim holidays thus drift through the seasons and can fall at any time of the year.

Even the Christian calendar is not uniform: Christmas in Bethlehem is celebrated on different days by the Roman Catholic ("Latin") community, the Greek Orthodox Church, and the Armenian Orthodox Church.

## Jewish Holidays

Here is a calendar of holidays as they're observed in Israel. Remember that Jewish holidays begin at sundown the previous evening and end at nightfall; the dates listed for Jewish holidays in 1999 and 2000 are for the day itself, not for the beginning of the holiday on the previous evening. The phrase "Not religious" in the text indicates that the holiday might be part of the religious tradition, but few or no public restrictions apply. On holy days, most of the Sabbath restrictions apply.

➤ SHABBAT (SABBATH): The Day of Rest in Israel is Saturday, the Jewish Sabbath, which begins at sundown Friday and ends at nightfall Saturday. By Friday afternoon, you can feel the country winding down, as most Jewish-owned businesses close until Saturday night or Sunday morning. Religious neighborhoods grow frantic as families do last-minute cooking and cleaning before the Sabbath begins. Devout Jews do not cook, travel, answer the telephone, or use money or writing materials during the Shabbat, hence the Sabbath ban on photography at Jewish holy sites like the Western Wall. In Jerusalem, where religious influence is strong, the downtown area dies on Friday evening, and some religious neighborhoods are even closed to traffic. In more secular and urbane Tel Aviv, Haifa, and Eilat, much of the populace spills onto the streets and into the nightspots.

Kosher restaurants close on the Sabbath, except for the main hotel restaurants, where some menu restrictions apply. In the Holy City itself, your dining choices are considerably reduced. Outside Jerusalem, however, you'll scarcely be affected; in fact, many restaurants do their best business of the week on the Sabbath because nonreligious Israelis take to the roads.

In Arab areas, such as East Jerusalem and Nazareth, Muslims take time off for the week's most important devotions at midday Friday, but the traveler will notice this much less than on Sunday, when most Christian shopkeepers in those towns close their doors. Saturday is market day, and these towns buzz with activity.

There is no public intercity transportation on the Sabbath, although the private *sherut* taxis drive between the main cities. Urban buses operate only in Nazareth and, on a reduced schedule, in Haifa. Shabbat is also the busiest day for nature reserves and national parks—indeed, anywhere the city folk can get away for a day. Keep this in mind if you fancy a long drive; the highways toward the main cities can be choked with returning weekend traffic on Saturday afternoon.

Sunday, then, is the first day of the regular work week (in Israel, says the old quip, the Monday-morning blues begin on Sunday). The country is moving rapidly toward a five-day work week, but, unlike Western countries, the weekend will include Friday—already a half day and holy to the country's Muslim minority—and Saturday, the Jewish Sabbath. The public sector and most corporations already work Sunday through Thursday only, and the schools may soon follow suit.

➤ TU B'SHEVAT: Feb. 1, 1999, and Jan. 22, 2000. Not religious. Israelis eat fruit and plant trees on the New Year of Trees, when the white- and pink-blossomed almond trees are in bloom.

➤ PURIM: Mar. 2, 1999, and Mar. 21, 2000 (one day later in Jerusalem). Not religious. Children dress up in costumes on the days leading up to Purim. In synagogues and on public television, devout Jews read the Scroll of Esther, the story of the valiant Jewish queen who prevented the massacre of her people in ancient Persia. Many towns hold street festivals.

➤ PESACH (PASSOVER): Apr. 1–7, 1999, and Apr. 20–26, 2000. First and last days religious; dietary restrictions in force throughout. Passover is preceded by vigorous spring cleaning to remove all traces of leavened bread and related products from the household. During the seven-day holiday itself, no bread is sold in Jewish stores, and the crackerlike matzo replaces bread in most hotels and restaurants. On the first evening of the holiday, Jewish families gather to retell the ancient story of their people's exodus from Egyptian bondage and to eat a festive and highly symbolic meal called the seder (Hebrew for "order"). Hotels have communal seders, and the Ministry of Tourism can sometimes arrange for tourists to join Israeli families for Passover in their homes.

➤ YOM HASHO'AH (HOLOCAUST MEMORIAL DAY): Apr. 13, 1999, and May 2, 2000. Not religious. Special services take place at Jerusalem's Yad Vashem Holocaust Memorial and elsewhere in the country. Entertainment venues are closed, and at 11 AM all stand silent as a siren sounds in memory of the 6 million Jews who were annihilated by the Nazis in World War II.

➤ YOM HAZIKARON (MEMORIAL DAY): Apr. 20, 1999, and May 9, 2000. Not religious. This is a day of mourning for Israel's war dead. Commemorative ceremonies are held around the country, entertainment sites are closed, and at 11 AM a siren sounds in memory of the fallen.

➤ YOM HA'ATZMA'UT (INDEPENDENCE DAY): Apr. 21, 1999, and May 10, 2000. Not religious. Israel achieved independence in May 1948; the exact date of Yom Ha'atzma'ut follows the Hebrew calendar. Although there are gala events, fireworks displays, and military parades all over the country, most Israelis go picnicking or swimming. Stores and a few tourist sights are closed, but public transportation runs.

➤ LAG BA'OMER: May 4, 1999, and May 23, 2000. Not religious. The 33rd day between Passover and Shavuot marks both the end of the anniversaries of a string of historic tragedies, and the commemoration of the death of the great 2nd-century AD rabbi Shimon Bar

Yochai. Kids build bonfires, and the devout visit the rabbi's grave in Meron, near Zfat.

➤ SHAVUOT (FEAST OF WEEKS): May 21, 1999, and June 9, 2000. This holiday, seven weeks after Passover, marks the harvest of the first fruits and, according to tradition, the day on which Moses received the Torah ("the law") on Mt. Sinai. Many observant Jews stay up all night studying the Torah. It is customary to eat meatless meals with an emphasis on dairy products.

➤ TISHA B'AV (THE NINTH OF AV): July 23, 1999, and Aug. 10, 2000. Not religious. Among the calamities believed to have occurred on this day was the destruction of both the First and Second Temples. Observant Jews fast and recite the biblical Book of Lamentations. Entertainment venues and many restaurants are closed.

➤ ROSH HASHANAH (JEWISH NEW YEAR): Sept. 11–12, 1999, and Sept. 30–Oct. 1, 2000. Yom Kippur and this two-day holiday are collectively known as the High Holy Days. Rosh Hashanah traditionally begins a 10-day period of introspection and repentance. Observant Jews attend relatively long synagogue services and eat festive meals, including apples and honey to symbolize the hoped-for sweetness of the new year. Nonobservant Jews often use this holiday to picnic and go to the beach.

➤ YOM KIPPUR (DAY OF ATONEMENT): Sept. 20, 1999, and Oct. 9, 2000. Yom Kippur is the most solemn day of the Jewish year. Observant Jews fast, wear white clothing, and avoid leather footwear. There are no radio and television broadcasts. All sites, entertainment venues, and most restaurants are closed. Much of the country comes to a halt, and in towns like Jerusalem the roads are almost completely empty aside from emergency vehicles. It is considered a privilege to be invited to someone's house to "break fast" as the holiday ends, at nightfall.

➤ SUKKOTH (FEAST OF TABERNACLES): Sept. 25–Oct. 2, 1999, and Oct. 14–21, 2000. First and last days religious. Jews build open-roof "huts" or shelters called sukkot (singular sukkah) on porches and in backyards to remember the makeshift lodgings of the biblical Israelites as they wandered in the desert. The more observant will eat as many of their meals as possible in their sukkah, and even sleep there for the duration of the holiday.

Right before Sukkoth, colorful street markets sell special decorations and the four kinds of "species" used in the Sukkoth ceremonies—the etrog (citron, like a yellow lime) and the elements that make up the *lulav* (a palm frond and sprigs of willow and myrtle). The first day is observed like the Sabbath, except that food can be cooked. The intervening days are half holidays, and shopkeepers often take vacations. Many Israelis, and some tourists, join in the hugely colorful annual hike to Jerusalem through the surrounding hills. Many Evangelical Christians come to Israel to celebrate this festival as well, obeying the passage in the prophecy of Zechariah 14.

➤ SIMHAT TORAH: The last day of Sukkoth (☞ *above*), this holiday marks the end—and the immediate recommencement—of the annual cycle of the reading of the Torah, the Five Books of Moses. The evening and morning synagogue services are characterized by joyful singing and dancing as people carry the Torah scrolls.

➤ HANUKKAH: Dec. 4–11, 1999, and Dec. 22–29, 2000. Not religious. A Jewish rebellion in the 2nd century BC renewed Jewish control of Jerusalem. In the recleansed and rededicated Temple, the tradition tells, a vessel was found with enough oil to burn for a day. It miraculously burned for eight days, hence the eight-day holiday marked by the lighting of an increasing number of candles (on a candelabrum called a *hanukkiah*) from night to night. Customary foods are potato pancakes (latkes or *levivot*) and a local version of the jelly doughnut called *sufganiah*. Schools take a winter break. Shops, businesses, and services all remain open.

## Christian Holidays

For up-to-date holiday information, contact the Israel Government Tourist Office (IGTO) in your country or region, or the Christian Information Center in Jerusalem (☎ 02/628–7647).

➤ EASTER: Apr. 4, 1999, and Apr. 23, 2000. This major festival celebrates the resurrection of Jesus. The nature and timing of its ceremonies and services are colorfully different in each Christian tradition represented in the Holy Land—Roman Catholic, Protestant, Greek Orthodox, Armenian Orthodox, Ethiopian, and so on; check the dates for different groups.

➤ CHRISTMAS: Except in towns with a large indigenous Christian population, like Nazareth and Bethlehem, Christmas is not a high-visibility holiday in Israel. The Christmas of the Catholic and Protestant traditions is, of course, celebrated on December 25; but the Greek Orthodox calendar observes it on January 7, and the Armenian Orthodox wait until January 18. Shuttle buses from Jerusalem run to Bethlehem's Manger Square on Christmas Eve (December 24) for the annual international choir assembly and the Roman Catholic midnight mass. For more information, contact the Palestinian Authority in Bethlehem (☎ 02/674–1581 or 02/674–1582) or the Christian Information Center (☞ *above*) in Jerusalem.

## Muslim Holidays

Muslims observe Friday as their holy day, but it's accompanied by none of the restrictions and far less of the solemnity than those of the Jewish Shabbat and the Christian Sabbath (in their strictest forms). The noontime prayer on Friday is the most important of the week and is typically preceded by a sermon, often broadcast from the loudspeakers of the mosques.

The dates of Muslim holidays vary widely each year because of the lunar calendar.

➤ RAMADAN: Beginning Dec. 8, 1999, and Nov. 30, 2000. This month-long fast commemorates the month in which the Koran was first revealed to Muhammad. Devout Muslims must abstain from food, drink, tobacco, and sex during daylight hours; the conclusion of the period is then marked by the three-day festival of Id el-Fitr (begins Jan. 1, 1999, and Dec. 12, 2000). The dates are affected by the sighting of the new moon and can change slightly at the very last moment. The Muslim holy sites on Jerusalem's Temple Mount offer only short morning visiting hours during this time and are closed to tourists during Id el-Fitr.

# FESTIVALS AND SEASONAL EVENTS

New festivals appear on Israel's national calendar every year. Some, like the Israel Festival and the Red Sea Jazz Festival, are international in scope, with reliable dates. Some are permanent seasonal features, timed to coincide with the Jewish holidays in spring and fall. Still others are more local "occasionals," where scheduling is probable but not definite. Most dates were not available at press time; check with the Israel Government Tourist Office or the nearest Israeli consulate (☞ Visitor Information *in* The Gold Guide) for details. You can buy tickets for major events in advance at ticket agencies in the major cities.

## WINTER

➤ DEC.: A gala pre-Christmas performance of **Choirs from Around the World** takes place in Jerusalem. Choirs from around the world perform at the **International Christmas Choir Assembly** in Manger Square, Bethlehem, on Christmas Eve. International choirs also sing at Nazareth's **Christmas Parade** and songfest on December 26 and often give free performances as they tour the country.

➤ LATE DEC.–EARLY JAN.: The **Liturgical Festival of Choral Music,** sponsored by the Jerusalem Symphony Orchestra, runs from the end of December

through the beginning of January. Also in Jerusalem is the **Classical Music Winter Festival.**

➤ JAN.: The **International Marathon** is run in Tiberias in early January. Eilat hosts renowned classical musicians at the **Red Sea International Music Festival** toward the end of the month.

## SPRING

➤ MAR.: The **Spring Migration Bird-watchers' Festival** is held in Eilat around the end of the third week. Mid-March brings the **Tel Aviv half-marathon.** The **Mt. Tabor Run,** in the Lower Galilee, is scheduled for the third week of the month. The **Artur Rubinstein Piano Master Competition** generates great interest among music lovers.

Many communities organize joyous street festivities to mark **Purim.**

➤ APR.: During **Passover,** when many Israelis go on vacation, the country hums with activities and events. Inquire at the local tourist office and watch newspapers for details. The **Ein Gev Festival,** on the Sea of Galilee, features Israeli music of various kinds. **Days of Music and Blossoms,** in the Misgav region of the Western Galilee, is eclectic. The **International Festival of Sacred Music** comes to Nazareth. **Sounds of Spring,** a potpourri of musical events, in Zichron

Ya'akov, is worth checking out. The **Haifa Festival of Children's Theater** appeals to families. The **National Parks Authority** in Tel Aviv (☎ 03/576–6834) can update you on the various performances and activities (many of them great for kids) scheduled for this period in parks throughout the country. **Stone in the Galilee** is a sculpture symposium in the Upper Galilee town of Ma'alot.

➤ LATE APR.–EARLY JUNE: The **International Book Fair** comes to Jerusalem, usually in May, alternating with the **International Judaica Fair** (books in 1999, Judaica in 2000). Jerusalem's **Independence Day Gala Concert** marks Israel's birthday, along with celebrations elsewhere in the country.

Israel's premier festival, the international **Israel Festival** of all the performing arts, takes place in Jerusalem (May 25–June 12, 1999; May 25–June 15, 2000). Get tickets to major events well in advance. The village of Abu Ghosh, west of Jerusalem, hosts a **Vocal Music Festival** during Shavuot. Eat yourself silly at the **International Ethnic Food Fair,** in Jaffa's port.

The popular **Food Trail,** in the Western Galilee, begins in late May and continues through early summer. Participating restaurants work up special menus, and guests work off the tasty food on guided nature walks between meals, accompanied by eclectic live music.

## SUMMER

➤ LATE JUNE–EARLY JULY: The **International Folklore Festival,** much of which takes place in small villages, draws performers and artists from Israel and abroad. The **Israeli Folk-Dance Festival,** in Karmiel in early July, hosts ethnic-dance groups from around the world as well as community dancing. The **Jacob's Ladder Folk Festival** (mostly Anglo-American) takes place at Ha'on, on the Sea of Galilee, the first weekend in July. The late-June **Cherry Festival** at Kibbutz Kiryat Anavim, west of Jerusalem, features musical events in natural surroundings, and a cafeteria devoted to cherry-based delicacies.

Jerusalem celebrates the **U.S. and Canadian Independence Days** the first week in July. Film buffs should watch for the **International Student Film Festival** in Tel Aviv in early June. Jerusalem's prestigious **International Film Festival** is held in early July.

➤ LATE JULY–AUG.: The **Voice of Music in the Upper Galilee,** on Kibbutz Kfar Blum, may be the high point of the year for chamber-music lovers.

The **Klezmer Festival,** in Zfat (Safed), showcases Jewish soul music. The Upper Galilee's **Jewish Music Festival** features a variety of music. The **Arts and Crafts Fair** outside Jerusalem's Jaffa Gate has a huge display of hand-made items and nightly entertainment. Jerusalem hosts the **Zimriya,** the triennial World Assembly of Choirs, next up in August, 2000.

Eilat's fine **Red Sea Jazz Festival** has become an important date on the international jazz calendar. Israeli pop stars are in the limelight at the Negev's **Arad Festival. Nights of Love,** in Tzemach, at the southern end of the Sea of Galilee, brings in national pop stars. The **Jaffa Nights** festival offers music, theater, and general entertainment in the Old Jaffa square. The one-day **Wine and Vintage Festival,** in Binyamina, features wine-tasting and vocal and dance performances. The **Sea of Galilee Crossing** is a 4-km (2½-mi) swim from Kibbutz Ha'on to Tzemach.

## AUTUMN

➤ OCT.: The weeklong holiday **Sukkoth** brings almost as busy a calendar of events as Passover, in the spring.

The **Israel Fringe Theater Festival,** in Akko, features original Israeli plays, street theater, children's shows, and musicals. Rishon Lezion, south of Tel Aviv, and Zichron Ya'akov, on Mt. Carmel, both have festivals of **Wine and Song. Music in Tabgha,** on the Sea of Galilee, sponsors vocal and chamber music in the Church of the Loaves and Fishes. Haifa holds its **International Film Festival** in the fall. Yehiam, in the Western Galilee, is the site of the **Renaissance Festival.**

As in late spring, Abu Ghosh, west of Jerusalem, hosts the **Vocal Music Festival** during the week of Sukkoth. The **Christian Celebration of the Feast of Tabernacles** takes place in Jerusalem.

➤ NOV.: Tel Aviv hosts the **International Guitar Festival.**

**Days of the Olive Branch** features crafts, food, and folklore in celebration of the olive harvest. It's held in villages throughout the central and Western Galilee over a series of weekends from late October through November.

# 2 Jerusalem

*Revered by three of the world's great religions—Judaism, Christianity, and Islam—Jerusalem has drawn pilgrims and plenipotentiaries to its splendid mountain isolation for thousands of years. Yet the city's domes, spires, and ancient walls share the skyline with modern office towers, and its archaeological treasures vie for attention with rich museums, quirky shops, and fine restaurants.*

**T**HE WORD "UNIQUE" IS EASY to throw around, but Jerusalem has a real claim on it. Continuously occupied for more than 5,000 years now, this mountainous walled city is sacred to more than one-third of the world's population.

By Mike Rogoff

For Jews, Jerusalem has always been the focal point of devotion and spiritual yearnings and the psychic center of their nationhood. "The world is like a human eye," wrote a Jewish sage in the 1st century AD: "the white is the ocean that girds the earth, the iris is the earth upon which we dwell, the pupil is Jerusalem, and the image therein is the Temple of the Lord."

For 2,000 years Christians have also venerated Jerusalem as the place where their faith was shaped—the site of the death, burial, and resurrection of Jesus of Nazareth. A famous Renaissance map shows the continents of Asia, Africa, and Europe as the leaves of a clover meeting in the holy city, a reality at once spiritual, historical, and (almost) geographically accurate.

Islamic tradition identifies Jerusalem as the *masjad el aksa,* the "farthermost place" from which Muhammad ascended to Heaven for his portentous meeting with God, making it Muslims' third-holiest city, after Mecca and Medina. A Muslim tradition claims that the great rock of Jerusalem's Mt. Moriah, site of the onetime Jewish Second Temple and present Dome of the Rock, is made of stones from the Garden of Eden, and that on the Day of Judgment, "the holy Kaaba stone of Mecca will come to Jerusalem to be joined with it."

The first known mention of Jerusalem is in Egyptian "hate texts" of the 20th century BC, although recent archaeological evidence gives the city a founding date at least 1,000 years earlier. Many scholars identify Jerusalem with the Salem of Abraham's time (18th century BC). Joshua defeated the Amorite king of Jerusalem in the mid-13th century BC, but the Israelites were unable to retain possession of the city. It was only King David, in 1000 BC, who took it again, made it his capital, and thus propelled it onto the center stage of history. His son Solomon built the Temple of the Lord, now known as the First Temple, giving the city a preeminence it enjoyed until its destruction by the Babylonians in 586 BC.

Returning exiles at the end of the 6th century BC rebuilt the Temple—which would become known as the Second Temple—and began the slow process of revival. By the 2nd century BC, Jerusalem was again a vibrant Jewish capital, albeit one with a good dose of Hellenistic cultural influence. Herod the Great (who reigned 37 BC–4 BC) renovated the Second Temple on a magnificent scale and expanded the city into a cosmopolis of world renown. This was the Jerusalem Jesus knew, a city of monumental architecture, teeming—especially during the Jewish pilgrim festivals—with tens of thousands of visitors from elsewhere in the country and from abroad. It was here that the Romans crucified Jesus (circa AD 29) and here, too, that the Great Jewish Revolt against the Roman overlords erupted, ending in AD 70 with the total destruction (once again) of the city and the Temple.

The Roman emperor Hadrian redesigned Jerusalem as the pagan polis of Aelia Capitolina (AD 135), an urban plan that became the basis for the Old City of today. The Byzantines made it a Christian center, with a massive wave of church-building (4th–6th centuries AD), until the Arab conquest of AD 638 brought the holy city under Muslim sway. Except during the golden age of the Ummayad dynasty, in the late 7th and early 8th centuries, Jerusalem was no more than a provincial town under the Muslim regimes of the early Middle Ages, until the Crusaders stormed it in 1099 and made it the capital of their Latin Kingdom. With the reconquest of Jerusalem by the Muslims, the city again lapsed into a languid provincialism for 700 years under the Mamluk and Ottoman empires. The British conquest in 1917 thrust the city back into the world limelight, as rising rival nationalisms vied to possess it.

Jerusalem was divided by the 1948 war, with Jordan annexing the smaller, predominantly Arab eastern sector (including the Old City); the much larger Jewish western sector became the capital of the State of Israel. The Six-Day War of 1967 reunited the city under Israeli rule, but the concept of an Arab "East" Jerusalem and a Jewish "West" Jerusalem still remains, even though new Jewish neighborhoods in the northeastern and southeastern sections have rendered the distinction somewhat oversimplified.

The focal point of any visit to Jerusalem is the walled Old City, a square kilometer of exotic sights, sounds, and smells, its air as thick with chants as with charcoal smoke, the *souk* (market) redolent with the tang of tamarind and alive with the tinkle of trinkets. Its 40,000 inhabitants—Jewish, Christian, and Muslim—jostle in the cobblestone lanes with an air of ownership, at best merely tolerating the "intruders" from other quarters. Devout Jews in black and white scurry from their neighborhoods north and west of the Old City, through the Damascus Gate and the Muslim Quarter, toward the Western (or Wailing) Wall, a holy relic of the Second Temple enclosure. Arab women with baskets of fresh produce on their heads flow across the Western Wall plaza to the Dung Gate and the village of Silwan beyond it. It is not unusual to stand at the Western Wall, surrounded by the burble of devotions, and hear the piercing call to prayer of the Muslim *muezzin* above you, with the more distant bells of the Christian Quarter providing a counterpoint.

Step outside the Old City and you'll see a vibrant modern city of half a million—not as cosmopolitan as Tel Aviv, to be sure, but with a variety of good restaurants, concert halls, markets, and high-quality stores, as well as quaint neighborhoods that embody an earlier simplicity. In a city that prides itself on its sense of historical continuity, a municipal by-law makes it mandatory to face even high-rise commercial buildings with the golden "Jerusalem stone," the local limestone that has served Jerusalem's builders from time immemorial. The result is an unusual sense of historical significance, even in the most modern quarters.

No matter how oblivious they are to the burden of the city's past or the various grand designs for its future, contemporary Jerusalemites are not untouched by the subtle spirit that infuses the place. Even the irreverent Mark Twain, who visited Jerusalem in 1867, was moved to write, "The thoughts Jerusalem suggests are full of poetry, sublimity, and, more than all, dignity." He may have gotten a bit carried away, but to see these limestone buildings glow golden in the sunset is to understand the mystical hold Jerusalem has had on so many minds and hearts for so many thousands of years.

# Pleasures and Pastimes

## Antiquities
If you thrill to the thought of standing where the ancients once stood, you'll be in your element in this city of memories. From Old Testament walls and water systems to Second Temple streets and stones, the past calls to the attentive soul like a siren to a sailor. Scale models and outstanding local museums, such as the Israel Museum and the Bible

Lands Museum, help give depth and perspective to the intense experience of exploring Jerusalem's past.

### Arts and Crafts

Handicrafts in Israel are worth seeking out, with jewelry and Judaica exceptional standouts in design and workmanship. Jerusalem offers good selections of these, as well as fine works in other specialties: paper-cutting, ceramics, weaving, and harp-making.

### Dining

Although dining out is less an institution in Jerusalem than in the more cosmopolitan Tel Aviv, you still can eat very well in the holy city, and its timeworn stone and unique ambience create some magical corners in which to do so. Jerusalem favors Middle Eastern cuisine and vegetarian meals, either Italian-style or of the lighter, quiche-and-salad variety. Less popular are seafood and Far Eastern cuisines, though there are some outstanding exceptions. There's a reason for this trend: the high percentage of religious Jews who live in or visit Jerusalem (in contrast, again, with epicurean Tel Aviv) has resulted in a considerable number of kosher restaurants. Drop your preconceptions: "kosher" does not mean Grandma's traditional Eastern European delicacies (though you'll find these, too). It implies a set of culinary restrictions, rather than a specific cuisine: no pork or shrimp, for example; no mixing of meat and milk products; no cooking on the Sabbath. These requirements account for the popularity of meatless restaurants and those cuisines, like Middle Eastern, that don't use dairy products anyway. But the quality of meals need not suffer; some of Jerusalem's finest dining rooms are kosher (and, incidentally, closed for Friday dinner and Saturday lunch in observance of the Jewish Sabbath). Having said that, several *non*kosher restaurants—not all of them pricey—help to keep the flag of haute cuisine flying.

### Holy Places

Central to two faiths and holy to a third, Jerusalem is an almost bewildering collage of religious traditions and the shrines that have sanctified them. Pilgrims of one faith still tend to make time to view the shrines of the others. Sites such as the Western Wall, Calvary, Gethsemane, and the Haram esh-Sharif bring the thrill of recognition to ancient history. The devout cannot fail to be moved by the holy city, and its special, if sometimes dissonant, moods and modes of devotion tend to fascinate the nonbeliever as well.

### Scenic Views

Jerusalem is a city of hills—hard going for cyclists, but marvelous for the photographer and the romantic. Quite different views of the Old City unfold from Mt. Scopus and the Mount of Olives (you're facing west, so it's best to go in the morning) and the Haas Promenade, to the south. Mt. Scopus also looks east, to the Judean Desert and the Dead Sea; Mt. Herzl looks west; and Nebi Samwil, in the northwest, gives a commanding view in all directions.

# EXPLORING JERUSALEM

Jerusalem is built on a series of hills, part of the Judea-Samaria range, and straddles the "watershed," the mountain divide that runs north–south through much of the country. The city's eastern edge is marked by the high ridge of Mt. Scopus–Mount of Olives, beyond which the arid Judean Desert tumbles down to the Dead Sea. To the west are the Judean Hills, or the Mountains of Judah, many capped by modern farming villages and draped in the new pine forests that have transformed and softened their rugged landscape. North and south of the city—

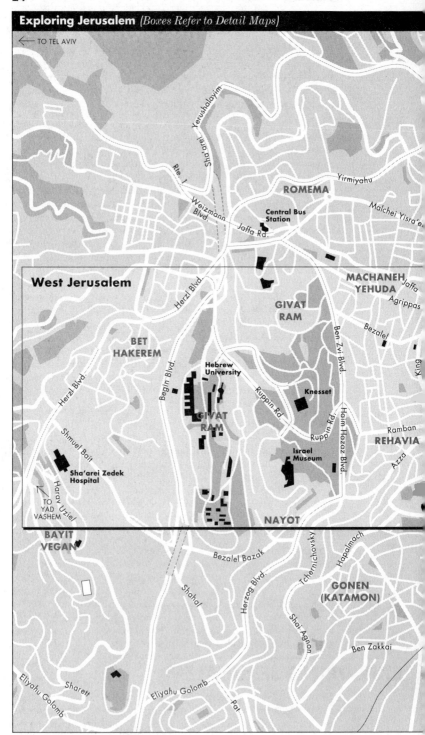

**Exploring Jerusalem** *(Boxes Refer to Detail Maps)*

TO TEL AVIV

ROMEMA

Yirmiyahu

Malchei Yisra'el

Central Bus Station

Jaffa Rd.

Yerushalayim

Sha'arei

Rte. 1

Weizmann Blvd.

MACHANEH YEHUDA

Jaffa

Agrippas

West Jerusalem

Herzl Blvd.

GIVAT RAM

Bezalel

King

BET HAKEREM

Begin Blvd.

Hebrew University

Ben Zvi Blvd.

Knesset

Ruppin Rd.

Herzl Blvd.

GIVAT RAM

Ruppin Rd.

Haim Hazaz Blvd.

Ramban

Shmuel Bait

REHAVIA

Azza

Sha'arei Zedek Hospital

Israel Museum

Harav Uziel

TO YAD VASHEM

NAYOT

BAYIT VEGAN

Bezalel Bazak

GONEN (KATAMON)

Shahal

Herzog Blvd.

Tchernichovsky

Hapalmach

Shai Agnon

Ben Zakkai

Eliyahu Golomb

Sharett

Eliyahu Golomb

Pat

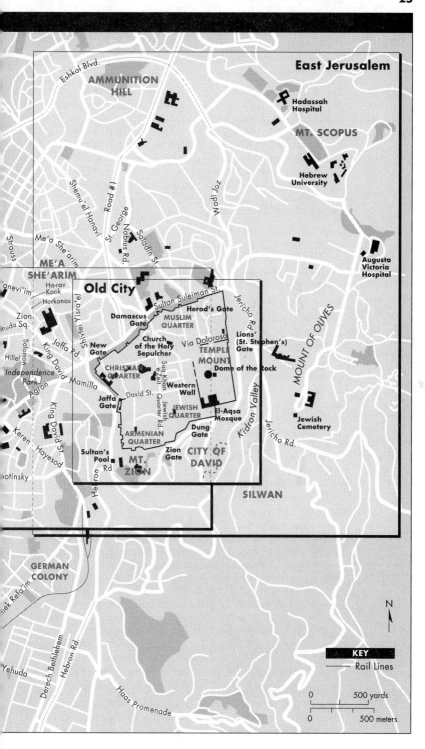

**East Jerusalem**

AMMUNITION HILL

Eshkol Blvd.

Hadassah Hospital

MT. SCOPUS

Hebrew University

Wadi Joz

Shemu'el Hanavi

St. George

Nablus Rd.

Saladin St.

Road #1

Strauss

Me'a She'arim

Augusta Victoria Hospital

ME'A SHE'ARIM

**Old City**

Ha-rav Kook

anevi'im

Horkonas

Zion nuda Sq.

Jaffa Rd.

Hillel

Salomon

Independence Park

Agron

Mamilla

King David Rd.

Shivtei Yisra'el

Damascus Gate

Sultan Suleiman St.

MUSLIM QUARTER

Herod's Gate

Jericho Rd.

MOUNT OF OLIVES

New Gate

Church of the Holy Sepulcher

Via Dolorosa

Lions' (St. Stephen's) Gate

CHRISTIAN QUARTER

Suq Khan ez-Zeit

Jewish Quarter Rd.

TEMPLE MOUNT

Dome of the Rock

Western Wall

Jericho Rd.

Jaffa Gate

David St.

JEWISH QUARTER

El-Aqsa Mosque

Kidron Valley

Keren

King David St.

ARMENIAN QUARTER

Dung Gate

Jewish Cemetery

Hayesod

Sultan's Pool Rd.

MT. ZION

Zion Gate

CITY OF DAVID

otinsky

Hebron

SILWAN

GERMAN COLONY

nek Refa'im

N

Yehuda

Derech Bethlehem

Hebron Rd.

Haas Promenade

**KEY**
— Rail Lines

0        500 yards

0        500 meters

Samaria and Judea, respectively—is the so-called West Bank, since 1967 a contested area administered mostly by Israel, apart from those cities and areas now under autonomous Palestinian control. The West Bank is part of the same highlands, geographically and historically, as Jerusalem itself.

The city has two centers of gravity: the downtown area, West Jerusalem (the "New City"), with its central triangle of Jaffa Road, King George Street, and Ben Yehuda Street; and the Old City, farther east. Most of the restaurants and many of the hotels we recommend are in or near the downtown area. Almost all the rest are farther west, where the modern Jewish neighborhoods share the hills with the city's best museums. The walled, squarish Old City is divided into four major residential quarters—Jewish, Christian, Muslim, and Armenian—and entered through seven gates, of which the Jaffa and Dung gates are the most frequently used by tourists.

Since 1987 the nationalist unrest in the Arab community (one-quarter of the city's population) has made East Jerusalem a less welcoming place than it once was. Exercise some caution in the Arab neighborhoods north of the Damascus Gate and in the Old City's Muslim Quarter, lest you run afoul of an occasional local incident.

When all is said and done, however, Jerusalem is a safe city, as Israeli cities are in general. Jerusalem is a great city to see on foot, and most of its outlying sights are reasonably accessible by public transportation. In many parts of Jerusalem, a rental car is sometimes more a bother than a boon; you can spend the same money more productively on cabs.

Of the key areas described, our Old City walking tour takes you from the Western (Wailing) Wall to the Church of the Holy Sepulcher and plunges you in at the deep end, with a heady whirl of ancient ruins and the all-important shrines of the three religions that call this city holy. The Jewish Quarter walk explores that attractively restored quadrant of the Old City, with its intriguing potpourri of archaeological sites unearthed in the 1970s. The Tower of David and Mt. Zion tour begins and ends with a museum, as it skirts (or climbs) the Old City walls en route to David's Tomb and the site of Jesus' Last Supper. The City of David tour concentrates on Old Testament Jerusalem, exploring a geographically tiny area below and outside the Dung Gate. Mainly Christian landmarks are explored under the title Mount of Olives and East Jerusalem, with highlights including the Mount of Olives itself and its spectacular view; the Garden of Gethsemane; and the Garden Tomb. Also included are the Rockefeller Museum, Damascus Gate, and the option of a walk along the Old City ramparts. Swing across town to West Jerusalem to visit Yad Vashem, Israel's most prominent Holocaust memorial and museum complex; Marc Chagall's famous stained-glass windows at the Hadassah Hospital; the village of Ein Kerem; and a large-scale model of Second Temple–period Jerusalem. Take time off to walk the Center City and visit the magnificent Israel Museum, where the Dead Sea Scrolls (and much else) are on display. Nearby are the Knesset (Israel's parliament) and the newer Bible Lands Museum.

## Great Itineraries

Most travelers spend only a few days in Jerusalem, but if you have more time or your interest ranges beyond the classic sights, a combination of the following suggestions can easily fill your days.

IF YOU HAVE 1 DAY: A GENERAL ORIENTATION

Catch the morning view from the top of the Mount of Olives or the view anytime from the Haas Promenade. Enter the Old City through the Dung Gate to visit the Western Wall, El-Aqsa Mosque, and Dome of the Rock. Return via the Western Wall plaza and ascend to the Jewish Quarter to explore its fascinating archaeological treasures. Visit the Church of the Holy Sepulcher en route to the Jaffa Gate. Take a cab or bus over to West Jerusalem (the New City) to visit the Israel Museum (Dead Sea Scrolls, archaeology, Judaica, and art) or Yad Vashem (a museum and memorial to the Holocaust).

### IF YOU HAVE 1 DAY: A CHRISTIAN ORIENTATION

Begin with the view from the Mount of Olives, and then walk or drive down to the Garden of Gethsemane, with its ancient olive trees. Enter the Old City through the Dung Gate to visit the Western Wall (the holiest Jewish site) and the Muslim shrines, the El-Aqsa Mosque, and Dome of the Rock, on the Temple Mount just above it. Join the Via Dolorosa near the serene courtyard of St. Anne's Church and the Pools of Bethesda (site of the healing of the lame man) and follow the Stations of the Cross to the Church of the Holy Sepulcher. If you're Catholic, you may want to join the Franciscans' Friday-afternoon walk of the stations. If you're Protestant—particularly, Evangelical—be certain to include the Garden Tomb (check times) in addition to or instead of the Holy Sepulcher. After this, you have four options. Option one: visit the Room of the Last Supper on Mt. Zion after lunch, and go on to the Church of the Nativity, in Bethlehem (a 15-minute drive; ☞ Bethlehem and the Etzion Bloc *in* Chapter 3). Option two: have lunch in and explore the archaeological finds of the Jewish Quarter, ending at the Room of the Last Supper. Option three: have lunch near the Jaffa Gate, and visit the Tower of David Museum on the history of Jerusalem, also ending the day (time permitting) at the Room of the Last Supper. Option four: have lunch on the way to the Room of the Last Supper, and then go to the Israel Museum to see the Dead Sea Scrolls. Check the sites' opening hours when planning your day.

### IF YOU HAVE 2-3 DAYS: A GENERAL ORIENTATION

Begin with the view from the Mount of Olives; then explore the City of David. Cab around to the Jaffa Gate to visit the Tower of David Museum, which covers the action-packed history of Jerusalem (try to catch the 11 AM tour). Eat lunch inside Jaffa Gate and follow the Ramparts Walk to Mt. Zion. Explore the Jewish Quarter, ending the day there or at the Western Wall. On the second day, plunge back into the Old City through the Dung Gate and visit the Western Wall and the Muslim shrines on the Temple Mount. Stroll through the *souk* (Arab bazaar) to the Church of the Holy Sepulcher and end at the Jaffa Gate. Have lunch in the Israel Museum (note hours). If you're a museum person, this will fill your afternoon; if not, see the Dead Sea Scrolls, and then head over to downtown Ben Yehuda Street for coffee and serious people-watching. Begin the third day at Yad Vashem, the Holocaust museum and memorial. Visit the stained-glass Chagall windows at Hadassah Hospital. Have a leisurely lunch in picturesque Ein Kerem; then take in the Church of the Visitation. Take the rest of the afternoon off for a well-earned break at your hotel pool or in the shops.

### IF YOU HAVE 2-3 DAYS: A CHRISTIAN ORIENTATION

On the first day, see the Western Wall, El-Aqsa Mosque, and Dome of the Rock, the Pools of Bethesda and St. Anne's Church, the Ecce Homo Convent (site of the fortress where Jesus was tried), the Via Dolorosa, and the Church of the Holy Sepulcher. In the afternoon, visit Bethlehem (☞ Bethlehem and the Etzion Bloc *in* Chapter 3). On the second day, start with the view from the Mount of Olives (Catholics should add the Pater Noster Convent on the Mount of Olives—with the Lord's Prayer in more than 70 languages on ceramic tiles—and Dominus Flevit, halfway down the slope), and then walk or drive down to the Garden of Gethsemane. Visit the Room of the Last Supper on Mt.

Zion (Catholics should add the Dormition Abbey, where, tradition says, Mary fell into eternal sleep) and enter the Jewish Quarter through Zion Gate. If biblical archaeology speaks to you, consider a walking tour with Archaeological Seminars (☞ Contacts and Resources *in* Jerusalem A to Z, *below*). In the afternoon, visit the Israel Museum or Yad Vashem. Spend the third day on the west side of town (the New City), picking up whichever of the two museums you didn't manage the day before. Visit the biblically inspired Chagall windows at Hadassah Hospital; and the Holyland Hotel's scale model of Jerusalem in the days of Jesus, built to a fiftieth of the city's actual size then. Protestants should use this day to visit the Garden Tomb, in East Jerusalem. Catholics will want to visit the Church of St. John the Baptist and the Church of the Visitation, in Ein Kerem, on the western edge of town.

*Numbers in the text correspond to numbers in the margin and on the Exploring the Old City, Exploring East Jerusalem, and Exploring West Jerusalem and Center City maps.*

## Old City: The Classic Sights

Drink in the very essence of Jerusalem as you explore the city's primary religious sites and touch the different cultures that share it. All of these holy places demand modest dress: no shorts and no sleeveless shirts.

### A Good Walk

You can begin at the Dung Gate (literally, "Refuse Gate" in Hebrew), named apparently because of the ancient practice of dumping garbage over the adjacent city walls. Just inside the gate is the **Ophel Archaeological Garden** ①, often known as the Western and Southern Wall Excavations. The most impressive and evocative remains here are those of King Herod the Great's grand structures, ones that Jesus knew well.

It's a few steps to the entrance of the **Western (Wailing) Wall** ② plaza. (Expect a routine check of your bags by security personnel at the plaza's entrance.) This is the most important Jewish shrine today, not because the structure itself is historically sacred but because it's close to the onetime Jewish Temple and is the last remnant of the enclosure of that temple.

Between the Western Wall and the Ophel Archaeological Garden, a ramp ascends to the vast plaza covering the summit of the biblical Mt. Moriah, called the **Temple Mount** by Jews and Christians, Haram esh-Sharif (the Noble Enclosure) by Muslims. The ancient Jewish Temple once stood here, both the "First" of King Solomon, and the "Second." Today the Temple Mount is administered by the Waqf, the Muslim religious council. Tall cypress trees create shady retreats from the glare of the whitish limestone pavements. Immediately in front of you as you enter the area is the large, black-domed **El-Aqsa Mosque** ③, the third-holiest mosque in the Muslim world. Two hundred yards to the left is the brilliantly golden **Dome of the Rock** ④, with its wondrously decorated interior.

As you exit the Temple Mount at its northeastern corner, through the al-Asbat Gate, the Lions' (also known as St. Stephen's) Gate is on your right. Stay within the city walls and turn left. Twenty yards on, an unobtrusive dark wooden door on your right opens onto the tranquil courtyard-garden of the **Pools of Bethesda and St. Anne's Church** ⑤. The Pools of Bethesda are the authentic site of the healing described in the New Testament (John 5), and the Romanesque St. Anne's Church has amazing acoustics, which visiting groups often sample by singing hymns.

NEED A
BREAK?
About 100 yards up the road after you turn right outside St. Anne's Church, a little **café** serves freshly squeezed orange juice, Turkish coffee, and mint tea. It's on the corner of a lane on your left. There are public toilets across the street.

About 300 yards up the road, look for a ramp on your left leading to the turquoise-color door of a school. On Friday afternoon at 3, the brown-robed Franciscans begin their procession of the **Via Dolorosa** ⑥ (Way of the Cross) in the school courtyard. Chapels along the way are open at that time. (In summer, the procession starts at 4; contact the Christian Information Center for specifics; ☞ Visitor Information *in* Jerusalem A to Z, *below*.)

Just beyond the start of the Via Dolorosa, an arch crosses the street. Before the arch, on the street corner on the right, is the entrance to the **Ecce Homo Convent of the Sisters of Zion** ⑦, with a basement of ancient pavements and cisterns. Just beyond the arch, steps on your right bring you into a small vestibule, separated from the convent's chapel by a glass panel; from here there's a view back onto a second span of the same arch.

The Via Dolorosa runs down into El-Wad Road, one of the Old City's most important thoroughfares. To the right, the street climbs toward the Damascus Gate; to the left, it passes through the heart of the Muslim Quarter and reaches the Western Wall. It's a sensory experience to sit at a café here sipping cardamom-flavored Turkish coffee and watch the passing parade. Buxom Arab matrons in bright embroidered dresses rub shoulders with black-hatted Hasidic Jews in beards and side curls; and local Muslim kids in the universal uniform of T-shirt, jeans, and sneakers dodge around groups of pious Christian pilgrims almost oblivious to the tumult.

As you turn left onto El-Wad Road, Station III of the **Stations of the Cross** is immediately on your left. A few steps beyond it, also on the left, is Station IV, and on the next corner, Station V. The Via Dolorosa turns right and begins its ascent toward Calvary. Halfway up the street, a brown wooden door on your left marks Station VI. At the top of the stepped street is a brown metal door: Station VII. The little chapel contains one of the columns of the Byzantine Cardo, the main street of 6th-century Jerusalem, which ran from the Damascus Gate (off to your right) to today's Jewish Quarter, some 300 yards to your left. Step to the left, and then walk 30 yards up the street facing you—you are now at Station VIII, marked by nothing more than an inscribed stone. Return to the main street (Suq Khan e-Zeit) and turn right (left as you reach Station VII from VI). The street is almost impossibly crowded on Saturday, when Arab Jerusalem does its shopping—beware of pickpockets in these quarters. One hundred yards from Station VII, a ramp parallel to the street ascends to your right; take the ramp and the small lane above it to its end. A column in the Wall represents Station IX.

Step through the open door on your left into the courtyard of the **Ethiopian Monastery** ⑧, also known as Deir es-Sultan, an esoteric enclave of this poor but colorful sect. From the monastery's upper chapel, descend through a lower one and out a small wooden door to the court of the **Church of the Holy Sepulcher** ⑨ (☞ Site map, *below*). (If you continue along Suq Khan e-Zeit without going up to the Ethiopian Monastery, a right turn brings you more quickly to the Holy Sepulcher.) Most Christians venerate this site as that of the death, burial, and resurrection of Jesus; you'll find Stations X, XI, XII, XIII, and XIV here. (Many Protestants believe these events occurred at Skull Hill and the Garden Tomb, north of the Damascus Gate; ☞ Mount of Olives

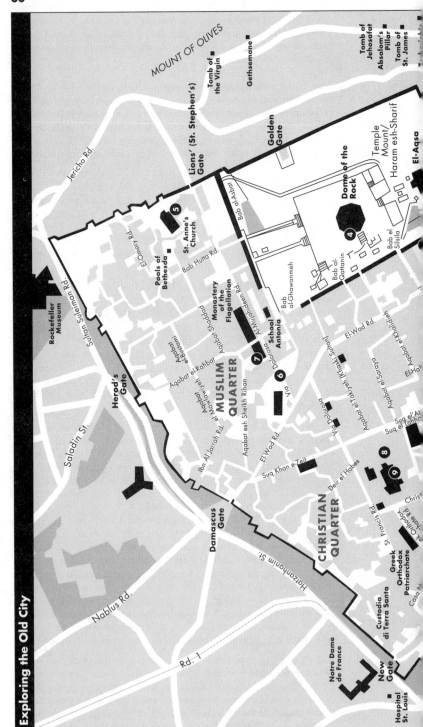

MOUNT OF OLIVES

Tomb of the Virgin

Gethsemane

Tomb of Jehosafat

Absalom's Pillar

Tomb of St. James

Lions' (St. Stephen's) Gate

Golden Gate

Jericho Rd.

El-Omariy Rd.

Pools of Bethesda

St. Anne's Church ⑤

Bab Hutta Rd.

Bab al-Asbat

Temple Mount/ Haram esh-Sharif

El-Aqsa

Dome of the Rock ④

Bab el Silsila

Bab al-Qattanin

Bab al-Ghawanmeh

Rockefeller Museum

Sultan Suleiman Rd.

Monastery of the Flagellation

School Antonia ⑦

Aqabat Shaddad

Aqabat el-Bustami

Al-Mujahideen Rd.

Herod's Gate

Saladin St.

Aqabat el-Rahbat

Ibn Al Jarrah Rd.

Aqabat el Mawlawiyeh

Aqabat esh Sheikh Rihan

**MUSLIM QUARTER**

Via Dolorosa ⑥

El-Wad Rd.

El-Wad Rd.

Aqabat el-Takiyeh (Khaski Sultan)

Aqabat el-Saraya

Aqabat el-Khalidieh

El-Hai

Suq el-At

Suq el-Tahhc

Suq Khan e-Zeit

Damascus Gate

Deir el Habes

⑧

⑨

**CHRISTIAN QUARTER**

St. Francis Rd.

Greek Orthodox Patriarchate

Greek Orthodox Patriarchate Rd.

Chris

Casa N

Haizenbanim St.

Nablus Rd.

Custodia di Terra Santa

Notre Dame de France

Rd. 1

New Gate

Hospital St. Louis

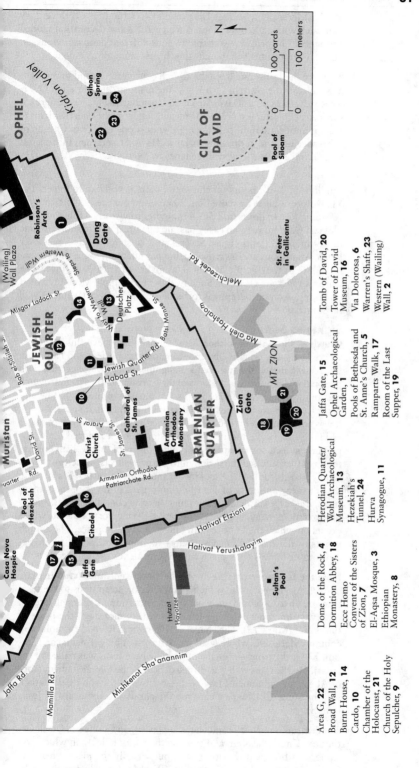

31

100 yards
100 meters

Area G, **22**
Broad Wall, **12**
Burnt House, **14**
Cardo, **10**
Chamber of the
Holocaust, **21**
Church of the Holy
Sepulcher, **9**

Dome of the Rock, **4**
Dormition Abbey, **18**
Ecce Homo
Convent of the Sisters
of Zion, **7**
El-Aqsa Mosque, **3**
Ethiopian
Monastery, **8**

Herodian Quarter/
Wohl Archaeological
Museum, **13**
Hezekiah's
Tunnel, **24**
Hurva
Synagogue, **11**

Jaffa Gate, **15**
Ophel Archaeological
Garden, **1**
Pools of Bethesda and
St. Anne's Church, **5**
Ramparts Walk, **17**
Room of the Last
Supper, **19**

Tomb of David, **20**
Tower of David
Museum, **16**
Via Dolorosa, **6**
Warren's Shaft, **23**
Western (Wailing)
Wall, **2**

and East Jerusalem, *below.*) The present vast structure is 12th-century Crusader, with a plethora of interior structures and decorations added since then. The property is shared by four different denominations, an unusual arrangement that lends the church much of its color.

To get to the Jaffa Gate from the church courtyard, ascend to the right as you leave the church, turn left at the main street (Christian Quarter Road), go as far as David Street, and turn right again. You can reach the Jewish Quarter (☞ *below*) by turning left from the courtyard, making an immediate right past the high white-stone Lutheran Church of the Redeemer and continuing as far as David Street, then turning left and taking any of the next three lanes to the right.

TIMING

You'll need 3–3½ hours for this walk, more if you like to linger. The Via Dolorosa takes no more than 20 minutes, but the full pilgrim procession takes an hour. Add 30–45 minutes to visit the Ophel Archaeological Garden; you can easily pass up this site if you're short on time or on interest in antiquities. Several sites close for a few hours over lunch. Afternoons are less crowded, but pay attention to the short opening hours of the Temple Mount (Haram esh-Sharif). Note that some Christian sites are closed on Sunday, the entire Temple Mount is closed on Friday, and photography is forbidden at the Western (Wailing) Wall on Saturday.

## Sights to See

★ ➒ **Church of the Holy Sepulcher.** Most Christians believe this is the site where Jesus was crucified by the Romans, was buried, and rose from the dead. Belief in the transcendent significance of those events, both personal and universal, is the basis of the Christian faith. The first church was built here circa AD 326 by Helena, mother of the Byzantine emperor Constantine the Great, and destroyed by Persian invaders in 614. It was rebuilt almost immediately, destroyed again by the Egyptian caliph El-Hakim in 1009, and once more restored, on a reduced scale, apparently as a cluster of shrines not under one roof. In the 12th century the Crusaders unified the shrines into the present vast structure (which is only two-thirds the length of its Byzantine predecessor). Many claim that the very antiquity of the tradition argues in favor of its authenticity; the early Christian community, fiercely committed to the point of martyrdom, would likely have preserved the memory of the site where events on which their entire faith hinged had taken place. The church is outside the city walls of Jesus' day—an important point, for no executions or burials took place within Jerusalem's sacred precincts.

Note the fine stone carving above the Gothic entrance (☞ Site plan, *above*). As you enter the church's dim interior, steep steps to the right take you up to **Golgotha** (the word comes from Aramaic, through Greek), otherwise known as Calvary (through Latin), meaning "the place of the skull" (Mark 15). The chapel on the right is Roman Catholic and contains **Station X** (where Jesus was stripped of his garments) and **Station XI** (at the front—note the mosaic—where Jesus was nailed to the cross). On the right wall is a mosaic depicting the Old Testament story of Abraham's binding of Isaac—the sacrifice of the son by the father, seen by some Christians as a symbolic parallel to the death of Jesus himself.

The central chapel—all candlelight, oil lamps, and icons—is Greek Orthodox. Under the altar, and capping the rocky hillock on which you stand, is a bronze disc with a hole, purportedly the place where the cross actually stood and thus **Station XII**, where Jesus died on the cross. (You can reach through the hole to touch the rock.) The Franciscans

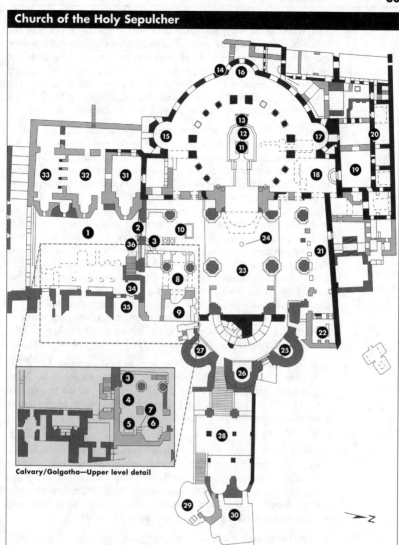

**Church of the Holy Sepulcher**

Calvary/Golgotha—Upper level detail

1. Entrance courtyard, 1
2. Twelfth-century facade and entrance to church, 2
3. Calvary/Golgotha steps, 3
4. Station X, 4
5. Station XI, 5
6. Station XII, 6
7. Station XIII, 7
8. Chapel of Adam, 8
9. Rock of Golgotha, 9
10. Stone of Unction, 10
11. Chapel of the Angel, 11
12. Tomb of Christ (Station XIV), 12
13. Coptic Chapel, 13
14. Tomb of Joseph of Aramathea, 14
15. Southern apse, 4th-century church, 15
16. Western apse, 4th-century church, 16
17. Northern apse, 4th-century church, 17
18. Altar of Mary Magdalene, 18
19. Chapel of the Apparition, 19
20. Franciscan Convent, 20
21. Arches of the Virgin, 21
22. Prison of Christ, 22
23. Crusader church, 23
24. "Center of the World," 24
25. Chapel of St. Longinus, 25
26. Chapel of the Division of the Raiment, 26
27. Chapel of the Mocking, 27
28. Chapel of St. Helena, 28
29. Chapel of the Holy Cross, 29
30. Byzantine wall etching of ship, 30
31. Chapel of 40 Martyrs, 31
32. Chapel of St. John, 32
33. Chapel of St. James, 33
34. Chapel of the Franks, 34
35. Chapel of St. Michael and exit from Ethiopian Monastery, 35
36. Tomb of Philip d'Aubigny, 36

33

indicate the spot between XI and XII, at the icon of Mary, as **Station XIII**, where Jesus' body was taken down. At ground level opposite the entrance is a rectangular, pink stone slab called the **Stone of Unction**, where it is said that the body of Jesus was cleansed and prepared for burial. Greek pilgrims can often be seen rubbing crosses and clothing on the stone in order to take home a trace of the site's sanctity. The tomb itself (**Station XIV**) is in the cavernous, dimly lit rotunda to the left of the entrance, encased in a small, pink marble edifice.

Some 50 ft above the tomb is the great dome that is the landmark of the Christian Quarter. Though repaired in the early 1980s as part of critical structural renovations to the church, the dome remained unfinished for another decade, a symbol (and a victim) of the denominational rivalry that has beset Holy Land sites, and the Holy Sepulcher in particular, for centuries. An agreement in 1995 between the Greeks, "Latins" (Roman Catholics), and Armenians on the great dome's interior decoration was hailed as an almost miraculous breakthrough in ecumenical relations, and the dome was dedicated in December 1996 in an unprecedented interdenominational service. (Both the artist and the philanthropist who resolved the stalemate were American Catholics.) The Status Quo Agreements—a list of possessions and privileges that was frozen in the 19th century—apply to this church; so, for example, in late afternoon, each of the church's four "shareholders" in turn—Greek Orthodox, Latins, Armenians, and Copts (Egyptians)—exercises its right to a procession from Calvary to the tomb, with fully frocked chanting clergy and censers streaming pungent smoke.

Enter the tomb between the sentinels of giant brass candleholders. The only hint of what it must have been like 2,000 years ago is the ledge in the inner chamber (now covered with marble) on which Jesus' body would have been laid. This detail resembles hundreds of Jewish tombs from the Second Temple period (the time of Jesus), both in Jerusalem and elsewhere.

The Holy Fire ceremony takes place here on the Greek Orthodox Easter. The church is typically packed with candle-carrying pilgrims tense with excitement; the patriarch enters the tomb, a flash of fire appears through its portholes, a messenger emerges with a flaming torch, congregants light their candles from those of their neighbors, and within moments the whole church seems to be ablaze.

Among the church's many chapels, the most interesting is the **Chapel of St. Helena**. From the corridor at the eastern end of the church, steps lead down to a crypt adorned with a fine Armenian mosaic floor and an ancient wall etching, probably Byzantine, of a ship. Tradition has it that Helena, mother of Constantine the Great, found the True Cross of Christ here circa AD 326. ⊠ *Between Suq Khan e-Zeit and Christian Quarter Rd.,* ☎ *02/627–3314.* 🎟 *Free.* ☉ *Apr.–Sept., daily 5 AM–8 PM; Oct.–Mar., daily 5 AM–7 PM.*

★ ❹ **Dome of the Rock.** This splendid octagonal building is the original one completed in AD 691 over the great rock—the summit of Mt. Moriah—from which the prophet Muhammad is said to have risen to heaven, where he received from God the teachings of the faith. Considering the original builders were immediate heirs of Byzantine artistic traditions, it's hardly surprising that the shrine's layout resembles those of its contemporaries, like the Byzantine Church of San Vitale in Ravenna, Italy. The exterior glazed ceramic tiles, in shades of blue, were applied during renovations in the 1950s and '60s, but the marvelous gold dome was restored more recently, with 176 pounds of 24-carat gold electroplated on copper.

The shrine's interior is wondrous. Granite columns support arches, some bearing the original green-and-gold mosaics set in arabesque motifs—in observance of Islamic religious tradition, no human or animal forms appear in the artwork. The mosaics were restored in 1027, preserving much of the original work. Some of the Arabic inscriptions in the mosaics are quotations from the Koran; others are dedications. One of the latter originally lauded Abd el-Malik, caliph of the Damascus-based Ummayad dynasty, who built the shrine; some 140 years later, the caliph of a rival dynasty removed el-Malik's name and replaced it with his own, but he neglected to change the date! Notice the outstanding marble slabs that adorn the walls. Without the benefit of power tools, medieval stonemasons were able to expose the natural grain of the marble, creating impressive symmetries.

The huge **rock** around which the shrine is built is considered by more than one faith to be the center of the world. In addition, Jewish tradition identifies it as the place where Abraham bound and almost sacrificed his son Isaac (Genesis 22). With King David's conquest of Jerusalem in 1000 BC, however, the rock became part of (relatively) indisputable history. Against the warning of his counselors—who said it was arrogant to count the people of Israel, as they were like "the sands of the sea and the stars of the sky"—the triumphant king undertook a national census, thus inviting divine retribution in the form of a plague (II Samuel 24). At the last minute, God stayed the hand of the Angel of Death, who was about to smite Jerusalem. It was on the rock—"the threshing floor of Araunah [or Ornan] the Jebusite"—that David saw the angel and here that he erected an altar and burned a repentance offering to the Lord. In the absence of other convincing candidates, modern scholars identify the rock with that threshing floor.

One generation later, David's son Solomon built his temple here. Did the rock become the innermost chamber, the Holy of Holies, of the Temple (meaning the sanctuary would have stood where the Dome of the Rock stands today)? Or did it become the altar in the Court of the Israelites (with the sanctuary a bit to the west)? Judaism grapples with the question to this day.

At the southwestern corner of the rock, a 10-ft-high ornamented canister is said to contain several hairs of the prophet Muhammad's beard. The reliquary is opened for faithful Muslims one day a year, during the holy month of Ramadan. A small opening in the marble facade below it allows you to put your hand in and feel the indentation in the rock; the faithful believe it was created by the prophet's foot as he ascended to heaven. A few steps to the right bring you to a staircase leading down to a small grotto, perhaps once a cistern or a grain store in the pre-Davidic days. Legend calls it the Well of Souls, the entrance to the netherworld and the place where the dead pray. An Islamic tradition relates that as Muhammad rose to heaven, the rock tried to follow him and had already left a void (the cave) when the archangel Gabriel intervened to hold it down. *For times and entrance fees, see* Temple Mount, *below.*

**❼ Ecce Homo Convent of the Sisters of Zion.** The arch that crosses the Via Dolorosa outside the convent and continues into the present-day Ecce Homo Church was once thought to have been the gate of Herod's Antonia Fortress and thus the spot where the Roman governor Pontius Pilate presented Jesus to the crowd with the words *"Ecce homo!"* ("Behold, the man!"). Recent scholarship, however, has established that the structure was a triumphal arch built by the Roman emperor Hadrian in the 2nd century AD.

The basement of the convent has two points of interest. The first is an impressive arched reservoir with a barrel-vault roof, apparently built by Hadrian in the moat of Herod's older Antonia Fortress. The second is the famous *lithostratos,* or stone pavement, etched with games played by bored Roman legionnaires. One such diversion—the notorious Game of the King—called for the execution of a mock king, a sequence tantalizingly reminiscent of the New Testament description of the treatment of Jesus by the Roman soldiers. Contrary to tradition, however, the pavement of large, foot-worn brown flagstones is not from Jesus' day but was laid down a century later. ⊠ *Via Dolorosa,* ☎ 02/ 627–7292. ⊡ *NIS 5 ($1.50).* ♥ *Apr.–Sept., Mon.–Sat. 8:30–12:30 and 2–5; Oct.–Mar., Mon–Sat. 8:30–12:30 and 2–4:30.*

❸ **El-Aqsa Mosque.** The name of the mosque—"the Farthermost Place"— comes from the Koranic story of Muhammad ascending to heaven from the nearby rock (☞ Temple Mount, *below*) to meet with God. At the far (southern) end of this cavernous building, under the landmark copper dome, is the *mihrab,* the niche indicating the direction of prayer toward Mecca. This wall is believed to be the only remnant of the original building created by the Ummayad dynasty in the early 8th century AD. Since then the mosque has been destroyed, usually by earthquake, and rebuilt several times. The rows of square stone columns on the right (west) as you enter date from the 14th century; the round marble ones in the center and on the left are the products of renovations in the 1920s and '30s. Persian rugs are interspersed with modern runners, on which individual prayer mats have been patterned. The mosque's finest feature is the wonderfully complex set of stained-glass windows beneath the dome.

In the 12th century, the Templars, one of the Crusader monastic orders, made its headquarters here, taking its name from the ancient site itself; but this spot has been the setting for more-recent dramas, too. In 1951, King Abdullah of Jordan (the late King Hussein's grandfather) was assassinated in the mosque; and in 1969, a demented arsonist set fire to a priceless wooden *minbar,* or pulpit, in an attempt to destroy the building. West of the mosque is the **Islamic Museum,** displaying some fine stone-relief work and carved wood from El-Aqsa's earlier incarnations. *For times and entrance fees, see* Temple Mount, *below.*

❽ **Ethiopian Monastery.** Standing in the monastery's courtyard beneath the medieval bulge of the Church of the Holy Sepulcher, you are surrounded by those churches of Christendom that revere this site. An Egyptian Coptic monastery lies close by, next to the Ninth Station of the Cross; and around you the skyline is broken by a Russian Orthodox gable, a Lutheran bell tower, and the crosses of Greek Orthodox, Armenian, and Roman Catholic churches.

The robed Ethiopian monks, tall and slender, gentle and shy, live in tiny cells in the rooftop monastery. Their small, dark church is adorned with modern paintings, one of which depicts the visit of the Queen of Sheba to King Solomon. Ethiopian tradition holds that more passed between the two than is related in the Bible (I Kings 10) and that their supposed union produced an heir to the Ethiopian royal house. The script in the paintings is Gehz, the ecclesiastical language of the Ethiopian church. ⊠ *Roof of the Church of the Holy Sepulcher, access from Suq Khan e-Zeit.* ⊡ *Free.* ♥ *Daily during daylight.*

❶ **Ophel Archaeological Garden.** Often known as the Western and Southern Wall Excavations, this extensive 1970s dig, under the direction of archaeologist Benjamin Mazar, unearthed very little of Old Testament Jerusalem but a great deal from the Herodian, Byzantine, and Arab periods. Have a look at the artist's reconstruction of the area on display at the entrance (you can buy your own copy from the attendant) and walk down to the corner of the massive wall facing you. King Solomon's First Temple on Mt. Moriah was destroyed by the Babylonians in 586 BC. Fifty years later, Jews returning from the Babylonian Exile began building the Second Temple on the same site (where the Dome of the Rock now stands). In the 1st century BC, when King Herod the Great rebuilt the Second Temple, he expanded the enclosure around it by constructing a massive retaining wall on the slopes of Mt. Moriah and filling the inside with thousands of tons of rubble, thus producing the huge plaza still known today as the Temple Mount. The great stones near the corner—their well-cut borders characteristic of the Herodian period—are not held together with mortar; their sheer weight gives the structure its stability.

Now exposed and accessible to the left of the corner is the pavement of a street from the Second Temple period. Two thousand years ago, the retaining wall would have been more than 50% higher above the street than it is today, and its foundations, plumbed by British army engineer Charles Warren in 1867, extend as deep below you as the present height of the wall rises above you. Left of the corner and far above your head is the protrusion known as **Robinson's Arch** (named for the 19th-century American explorer Edward Robinson), which is the beginning of a bridge to the Temple Mount, once reached by a staircase from the commercial area where you now stand.

On the wall a few yards north of the arch is an upbeat piece of biblical graffiti in Hebrew, written possibly in the 4th century AD by a Jewish pilgrim and filled with messianic dreams: "You shall see, and your heart shall rejoice, and your bones shall flourish like the grass" (Isaiah 66).

Return to the fork in the path and turn left. Fifty yards on, a small, modern spiral staircase on your left descends below present ground level to an intriguing, partially reconstructed labyrinth of Byzantine dwellings, mosaics and all; from here you reemerge outside the present city walls. Alternately, go straight, passing through the city wall by a small arched gate. The wide staircase to your left, a good part of it original, once brought hordes of pilgrims through the now-blocked gates of the southern wall of the Temple Mount and into the sacred temple precincts. A prominent archaeologist, interviewed on live American TV on these steps, committed himself to this statement: "Ladies and gentlemen, this is the one place in the city I can guarantee you Jesus walked!" The rock-hewn *mikva'ot* (plural of *mikveh*), Jewish ritual baths, at the bottom of the steps, are a visual reminder of the purification rites once demanded of Jews before they entered the Temple Mount. ✉ *Dung Gate*, ☎ *02/ 625–4403.* 🎟 *NIS 10 ($3); combined ticket including Ramparts Walk, Damascus Gate, and Hezekiah's Tunnel NIS 25 ($7).* ⊘ *Sun.–Thurs. 9–4, Fri. and holiday eves 9–2.*

**⑤ Pools of Bethesda and St. Anne's Church.** The transition is sudden and complete from the raucous cobbled streets and persistent vendors to the drooping pepper trees, flower patches, and birdsong of this serene Catholic cloister. The Romanesque Crusader **St. Anne's Church,** built in 1140, was restored in the 19th century, and with its austere and unadorned stone interior, it is one of the finest examples of medieval architecture in the country. According to local tradition, Anne, the mother of the Virgin Mary, was born in the grotto over which the church is built. It's worth waiting for one of the frequent pilgrim groups, who invariably test the church's extraordinarily reverberant acoustics by singing some hymns.

On the facade of the church, above the main door, is an unexpected five-line inscription in Arabic. After Saladin's defeat of the Crusaders in 1187, the church was turned into a *madrasa,* a Muslim house of study, and despite the Christian restoration, the inscription—a dedication to Saladin—has survived.

In the same compound, and just a few steps from the church, are the excavated **Pools of Bethesda,** a large, double public reservoir in use during the 1st century BC and 1st century AD. The New Testament (John 5) speaks of Jesus' miraculously curing a lame man by "a pool, which is called in the Hebrew tongue Bethesda [the Place of Mercy]." The actual bathing pools were the small ones, east of the reservoir, but it was over the big pools that both the Byzantines and the Crusaders built churches, now ruined, to commemorate the miracle. ✉ *Al-Mujahideen Rd.,* ☎ *02/628–3285.* 🎫 *NIS 5.50 ($1.60).* ☉ *Apr.–Sept., Mon.–Sat. 8–noon and 2–6; Oct.–Mar., Mon.–Sat. 8–noon and 2–5.*

**Temple Mount.** Covering some 35 acres, the Temple Mount is regarded by some scholars as one of the greatest religious enclosures of the entire ancient world. King Herod the Great (1st century BC) had an immense stone wall built around the hill to retain the rubble used to level off the crest and create the massive plaza. At its center stood Herod's rebuilt Second Temple, a splendid edifice that gained international fame as one of the architectural wonders of its day. (This was the Temple Jesus knew.) The Romans reduced it to ashes in the summer of AD 70. The Temple Mount today is a Muslim preserve (modest dress is essential), administered by the Waqf, the Supreme Muslim Religious Council.

When the Arab caliph Omar Ibn-Khatib seized Jerusalem from the Byzantines in AD 638, he found the Temple Mount covered with rubbish and had to clear the site to expose the great rock at its summit. It is said that Omar asked his aide Ka'ab al'Akhbar, a Jew who had converted to Islam, where he should build his mosque. Ka'ab recommended a spot north of the rock, hoping, the tale suggests, that the Muslims, praying south toward Mecca, would thus include the old temple site in their obeisance. "You dog, Ka'ab," bellowed the caliph. "In your heart you are still a Jew!" Omar's mosque, which he built south of the rock, has not survived, but the splendid gold-domed shrine, completed in AD 691, still stands.

Jerusalem is not mentioned in the Koran, but Muhammad's Night Ride is. Awakened one night by the archangel Gabriel, Muhammad was taken on the fabulous winged horse el-Burak to the *masjad el-aqsa,* the "farthermost place"—hence, the **El-Aqsa Mosque** (☞ *above*). From there he rose to heaven, came face-to-face with God, received the teachings of Islam, and returned home—all in the same night. The tradition evolved that the masjad el-aqsa was none other than Jerusalem, and the great rock the spot from which the prophet ascended.

The triumphant Arabs of the generation after Muhammad clearly venerated Jerusalem as the city of biblical kings and prophets. Many modern scholars also believe, however, that the feeling of being Johnnies-come-lately in the holy city of rival faiths did not sit well with the new masters of Jerusalem. The masjad el-aqsa tradition and the magnificent Dome of the Rock were designed to proclaim the ascendancy of the "true faith" and the new Arab empire over the rival Byzantine Christians.

The splendid **Dome of the Rock** (☞ *above*) dominates the center of the plaza and, in fact, the entire old cityscape, despite its relatively low elevation.

To the west of the Dome of the Rock is a large *sabil*, a public drinking fountain (now defunct), with an elaborate ornamented stone dome built by the Egypt-based Mamluk rulers in the 14th or 15th century. A large number of the nearby buildings lining the western edge of the Temple Mount date from this period, distinguished by their impressive jigsaws of fitted red, white, and black stone.

Overlooking the plaza from its northwestern corner is a long building, today an elementary school, built on the artificial scarp that once protected Herod's Antonia Fortress. The Christian tradition, probably accurate, identifies the site as the *praetorium* where Jesus was tried.

In the eastern outer wall, facing the Mount of Olives, is the ornate, domed inner **Golden Gate**, or Gate of Mercy, now blocked. The present masonry is restored Byzantine, though the gate—the Eastern Gate of Christian tradition through which Jesus is believed to have entered the area on Palm Sunday—existed in the Second Temple period. In the Jewish tradition, the long-awaited Messiah will one day enter the city through the same gate. ☎ *02/628–3292 or 02/628–3313.* 🎟 *Combined ticket for El-Aqsa Mosque, Dome of the Rock, and Islamic Museum NIS 22 ($7.40). Buy tickets to the right of El-Aqsa. Guards will require you to leave shoes, bags, and cameras outside (at your own risk, though theft is rare here); a small purse is usually allowed, but be sure your outfit has pockets just in case.* ☉ *Sat.–Thurs. 8–11:30 and 12:30–3. Seasonal changes are made without notice to accommodate changing prayer times; approximate summer hrs are 8–12:30 and 1:30–3. Last entry to area 30 min before closing.*

**❻ Via Dolorosa.** The Way of Suffering—or Way of the Cross, as it's more commonly called in English—is the route Jesus walked when he carried his cross from the place of his condemnation by Pontius Pilate to the site of his crucifixion and burial. The present tradition is essentially 12th-century Crusader, but it draws on older Byzantine beliefs. Some of the incidents represented by the 14 Stations of the Cross are scriptural; some (III, IV, VI, VII, and IX) are not. Many of the stations on the route, which winds through the Muslim and Christian quarters, are marked by tiny chapels open only during the Franciscan ceremonies. The last five stations are inside the Church of the Holy Sepulcher. (For walking directions and information, *see* A Good Walk *and* Church of the Holy Sepulcher, *above*.)

**Station I.** Jesus is tried and condemned by Pontius Pilate.

**Station II.** Jesus is scourged and given the cross. This station is at the Monastery of the Flagellation, whose shaded cloister and cool greenery offer some relief from the noisy street. The Roman pavement within the two chapels dates from the century after Christ. It's open April to September, Monday–Saturday 8–noon and 2–6; October to March, Monday–Saturday 8–noon and 1–5.

**Station III.** Jesus falls for the first time. (The chapel was built after World War II by soldiers of the Free Polish Forces.)

**Station IV.** Mary embraces Jesus.

**Station V.** Simon of Cyrene picks up the cross.

**Station VI.** A woman wipes the face of Jesus, whose image remains on the cloth. (Her name has come down to us as Veronica, apparently derived from the words *vera* and *icone*, meaning true image.)

**Station VII.** Jesus falls for the second time. (The little chapel contains one of the columns of the Byzantine Cardo, the main street of 6th-century Jerusalem.)

**Station VIII.** Jesus addresses the women in the crowd.

**Station IX.** Jesus falls for the third time.

**Station X.** Jesus is stripped of his garments.

**Station XI.** Jesus is nailed to the cross.

**Station XII.** Jesus dies on the cross.

**Station XIII.** Jesus is taken down from the cross.

**Station XIV.** Jesus is buried.

★ ❷ **Western (Wailing) Wall.** The Wall (*Kotel* in Hebrew), the most important *existing* Jewish shrine, was not itself part of the ancient Second Temple but of King Herod's retaining wall surrounding the Temple Mount (☞ *above*). After the Roman destruction of Jerusalem in AD 70, and especially after the dedication of its pagan successor in 135, the city was off-limits to Jews for generations. Although the general location of the Temple was known (it was in the vicinity of today's Dome of the Rock; ☞ *above*), its precise location was lost. Even when they eventually gained access, Jews avoided ascending the Temple Mount for fear of unwittingly trespassing on the most sacred—and thus forbidden—areas of their ancient sanctuary. With time, the closest remnant of the period took on the aura of the temple itself. The Western Wall is thus really a holy place "by proxy," and in a sense, it is *through* the stones rather than *to* them that devout Jews pray. It is the tears of generations of such worshipers, grieving for the lost temple, to which its Gentile name—the Wailing Wall—refers.

The Western Wall functions under the aegis of the rabbinic authorities, with all the trappings of an Orthodox synagogue: a dress code (modest dress; men are required to cover their heads), segregation of men and women in prayer (men on the left), and prohibition of smoking and photography on the Sabbath and religious holidays. The cracks between the massive stones are stuffed with slips of paper bearing petitions, and the swaying and praying of the devout leave no doubt of the powerful hold this place still has on the minds and hearts of many Jews.

On Monday and Thursday mornings, the place bubbles with often colorful bar-mitzvah ceremonies, when Jewish families celebrate the coming of age of their 13-year-old sons. The fervor is still greater on Friday evenings just after sunset, when the young men of a nearby yeshiva (Jewish seminary) come dancing and singing down to the wall to welcome in the "Sabbath bride." But many people find that it's only when the crowds have gone (the wall is floodlit at night and always open), and you share the warm, prayer-drenched stones with just a handful of bearded stalwarts, that the true spirituality of the Western Wall is palpable.

A long **tunnel** beyond the men's side (north of the plaza) was excavated in recent years, exposing ancient arches and chambers and several courses of the Western Wall along nearly its entire length. Among the masonry were two stones estimated to weigh an incredible 400 and 540 tons, respectively. The tunnel is open only to organized tour groups; you can join a prescheduled local tour. The tour takes about 80 minutes and ends at the beginning of the Via Dolorosa, in the Muslim Quarter. (Call **Western Wall Heritage,** ☎ 02/627–1333, or **Archaeological Seminars,** ☎ 02/627–3515, for details.)

If you're going directly to the Western Wall, you can take Bus 1, which will deposit you inside the Dung Gate. You can also reach the wall by descending from the Jewish Quarter or from the Street of the Chain, in the Arab souk. ☉ *Daily 24 hrs.*

# Jewish Quarter

When the Crusaders reached Jerusalem in 1099, the Jewish community was concentrated in the northeastern quadrant of the city, which is now the Muslim Quarter of the Old City. The Crusaders' destruction of that quarter and its population was so complete that when the Spanish rabbi Nachmanides (known as the Ramban, an acronym of his name) reached the city in 1267, he found "only two Jews, brothers, dyers by trade." The men established themselves in the city's southern quadrant—perhaps on Mt. Zion—eventually occupying the medieval building in today's Jewish Quarter that still bears the Ramban's name. The Ramban Synagogue is on Jewish Quarter Road, adjacent to and south of the Hurva. The community slowly revived, then mushroomed with the influx of Sephardic Jews expelled from Spain in 1492, and again with the flow of Ashkenazi Jews from Central and Eastern Europe in the early 18th century. By 1865 more than half the population of Jerusalem was Jewish, most living in the Jewish Quarter in very difficult conditions, some in the Muslim Quarter, and a handful in the new neighborhoods developing beyond the city walls.

During Israel's War of Independence in 1948, the Jewish Quarter was severely damaged, forced to capitulate to Transjordan's (now Jordan's) Arab Legion, evacuated, plundered, and abandoned for a generation. With the reunification of Jerusalem after the Six-Day War of 1967, the restoration of the quarter began in earnest. With so many buildings little more than rubble, Israeli archaeologists were given a unique opportunity to explore the area systematically, and a decade of frenetic excavation (in order to keep ahead of construction schedules) yielded a harvest of archaeologically important sites. The simultaneous reconstruction of the quarter emphasized the restoration of the old, as well as the design of new, buildings that would preserve the neighborhood's original architectural flavor. The result is an eye-pleasing harmony of limestone masonry, arched windows and buttresses, cobblestone alleyways, open archaeological sites, and splashes of greenery, making the Jewish Quarter the Old City's most attractive.

## A Good Walk

This walk's starting point, the parking lot of the Jewish Quarter, can be reached from a number of directions. You can follow Armenian Orthodox Patriarchate Road from the Jaffa Gate (700 yards) or enter through the Zion Gate and continue right (200 yards). With your back to the bus stop, cross the lot and enter Jewish Quarter Road (there will be a small supermarket on your right). One hundred yards down the road on your left and some 20 ft below you are the excavated and partly restored remains of the **Cardo** ⑩, the colonnaded main street of 6th-century AD Byzantine Jerusalem.

Some 50 yards farther and on the right is the entrance to the ruined **Hurva Synagogue** ⑪, the great landmark of the Jewish Quarter until it was blown up in 1948. Visual aids help reconstruct its past splendor. The second lane to the right beyond the Hurva Synagogue brings you to the **Broad Wall** ⑫, 23 ft thick and 27 centuries old.

Facing the Broad Wall with your back to the Cardo, bear right for 50 yards to Hurva Square, the center of the Jewish Quarter. Here you can duck into a shady spot, take the weight off your feet, and have some refreshments. On the eastern side of the square, take a few steps down the lane that begins some 20 yards to the right of Tony's Deli, where you'll find the **Herodian Quarter/Wohl Archaeological Museum** ⑬, containing the impressive remains of Second Temple–era mansions.

Once outside the Herodian Quarter, you can go down a wide staircase to the Western Wall and the Dung Gate (☞ Old City: The Classic Sights, *above*). To return to Hurva Square, go up the staircase. Just beyond the top of the steps, on your right, is the 2,000-year-old **Burnt House** ⑭, once a basement industrial workshop, destroyed by fire in the great conflagration of AD 70.

TIMING

Allow two hours for this walk, though the many good stores and restaurants may tempt you to spend more time. The Herodian Quarter, Burnt House, and all commercial establishments close early Friday afternoon and remain closed on Saturday.

## Sights to See

⑫ **Broad Wall.** The discovery in the 1970s of the rather modest-looking 23-ft-thick foundations of an Old Testament city wall was hailed as one of the most important archaeological finds in the Jewish Quarter. The wall was built in 701 BC by Hezekiah, King of Judah and a contemporary of the prophet Isaiah, to protect the city against an Assyrian invasion (II Chronicles 32). The unearthing of the Broad Wall—a biblical name—resolved a century-long scholarly debate about the extent of Old Testament Jerusalem: a large on-site map shows that the ancient city was far larger than was once thought. Seemingly attached to the wall are the scanty foundations of a dwelling, once in an unfortified outer neighborhood, possibly inhabited by refugees from the devastated northern Kingdom of Israel (721 BC): "And you [Hezekiah] counted the houses of Jerusalem, and you broke down the houses to fortify the Wall" (Isaiah 22). In an ancient version of eminent domain, Hezekiah's city planners expropriated private houses for the more urgently needed city wall.

⑭ **Burnt House.** During the Second Temple period, this was the basement industrial workshop of the priestly Bar Katros family, a fact gleaned from inscribed stone weights discovered on this spot in the 1970s. The evidence of the city's fiery destruction by the Romans is stronger here than anywhere else, with charred cooking pots and debris giving a vivid sense of the devastation 19 centuries ago. The archaeologists were riveted by the discovery of the skeletal hand and arm of a woman clutching a scorched staircase in a futile attempt to escape the flames. An audiovisual presentation illuminates the period, putting the artifacts in clear context. ⊠ *Tiferet Israel St.,* ☎ *no phone.* ☑ *Combined ticket with Herodian Quarter NIS 12 ($3.50); Burnt House only NIS 6 ($2).* ☉ *Sun.–Thurs. 9–5, Fri. and holiday eves 9–1.*

⑩ **Cardo.** In AD 135, the Roman emperor Hadrian built his town of Aelia Capitolina on the ruins of Jerusalem, an urban plan essentially preserved in the Old City of today. Hadrian's *cardo maximus* (the generic name for the city's main street) began at the strategic Damascus Gate, in the north, where sections of it have been unearthed. It did not originally run so far south into today's Jewish Quarter, but with the Christianization of the Roman Empire in the 4th century, access to Mt. Zion and its important Christian sites became a priority, and the main street was eventually extended. The original width—today you see only half—was 73 ft, about the width of an eight-lane highway. Some 20 ft below modern ground level, you can walk on the flagstones and among the columns of Byzantine Jerusalem in its heyday.

★ ⑬ **Herodian Quarter/Wohl Archaeological Museum.** Excavations in the 1970s exposed this area's most visually arresting site: the remains of mansions from the luxurious Upper City of the Second Temple period. Preserved in the basement of the seminary built later over the ruins, the geometrically patterned mosaic floors, colorful frescoes, and costly glassware, stone objects, and ceramics provide a peek into domestic life at the top in the days of Herod and Jesus. In the first hall, several small stone cisterns have been identified as private *mikva'ot,* Jewish ritual baths; holograms depict their use. A small ascending staircase ends abruptly, a reminder that nothing above ground level survived the Roman devastation of AD 70.

The quality, and even rarity, of some of the goods displayed in the second hall would have been the pride of any aristocratic household in those days: decorated ceramic plates, a ribbed green glass bowl, an imported mottled-alabaster vase. Large stone water jars are just like those described in the New Testament story of the wedding at Cana (John 2; ☞ Nazareth and the Galilee Hills *in* Chapter 6). Rare stone tables resemble the dining-room furniture depicted in Roman stone reliefs found in Europe.

Ancient steps bring you down to the last of the three distinct levels, a mansion with an estimated original area of more than 6,000 square ft. None of the upper stories have survived, of course, but the frescoes (half replaced by the later, more fashionable stucco) and the quality of the artifacts found here indicate a standard of living so exceptional that some scholars have suggested this might have been the long-sought palace of the high priest. At the southern end of the fine reception hall is a badly scorched mosaic floor with a charred ceiling beam lying on it. The Upper City held out against the Roman army for a month after the destruction of the Second Temple, but in September of AD 70, "on the eighth day of [the Hebrew month of] Elul," wrote the Jewish historian Josephus in his contemporary account of Jerusalem's last hours, "the sun rose over a city in flames." Precisely 19 centuries later, the victims' compatriots uncovered evidence of destruction so vivid, wrote archaeologist Nahman Avigad, "that we could almost smell the burning and feel the heat of the flames." ✉ *Hakara'im Rd.,* ☎ *02/628– 3448.* 🎟 *Combined ticket with Burnt House NIS 12 ($3.50); Herodian Quarter only NIS 10 ($3).* ☾ *Sun.–Thurs. 9–5, Fri. 9–1.*

⓫ **Hurva Synagogue.** Ruined walls, alcoves that once housed sacred texts, and a modern arch retracing the old are all that remain of what was once the Jewish Quarter's most prominent building. In 1700, a large group of devout Eastern European (Ashkenazi) Jews arrived in the holy city, led by the venerable Rabbi Yehuda Hehassid (Judah the Pious). The old man died days after their arrival, throwing his followers into despair and leaving them with a problem: with the death of the rabbi, the promised funds from the Old Country never materialized, and the funds for the construction of a synagogue had to be borrowed from the Jews' Muslim neighbors. By 1720 the loan was still outstanding, and the creditors burned down the synagogue, exiling Ashkenazi Jews from the city for more than 100 years. In 1862, a new and splendid synagogue was completed on the ruins—*hurva,* in Hebrew—of the old. It became the preeminent synagogue of the neighborhood, its high dome a Jewish Quarter landmark until the surrender of the quarter in the War of Independence, in 1948, and the destruction of the synagogue by local Arabs.

# Tower of David and Mt. Zion

"From Jaffa Gate to Zion Gate" could be the title of the walk we suggest here. It takes in a fine museum of the history of Jerusalem, a section of the Ramparts Walk, and a clutch of sights, both Christian and Jewish, on Mt. Zion.

## A Good Walk

Begin at the **Jaffa Gate** ⑮, served by Buses 19, 20, 30, 38, and 99. If you have your own car, look for parking in the Mamilla area opposite the walls. Walk to the bottom of the road that leads to Jaffa Gate and pause to look at the **Old City walls.** Above your head is the photogenic Tower of David—actually a Turkish tower and minaret—which has become one of Jerusalem's landmarks.

The road that enters the Jaffa Gate is a mere 100 years old; the gate to your left, which you would enter if you came from the downtown area via Jaffa Road, dates from the 16th century. The road immediately bends to the right. Directly ahead is David Street, one of the main streets of the *souk*, the Arab bazaar (not to be confused with King David Street, in West Jerusalem). Follow the vehicular road (Armenian Orthodox Patriarchate Road). On your left, 30 yards after the bend, is the entrance to the Anglican Christ Church, a neo-Gothic structure built in the 1840s and the oldest Protestant church in the Middle East. On your right is the platform from which British general Edmund Allenby officially reviewed his victorious troops on December 11, 1917, after the Turkish army had abandoned the city.

Go up the ramp, cross the moat, and enter the **Tower of David Museum** ⑯, a museum of the history of Jerusalem, and one of the city's highlights. From the entrance hall, a winding outside staircase on your right brings you to the roof. Turn left at once to reach the auditorium, where a film is shown, and a second staircase to the top of the great tower. The view is marvelous in all directions but especially looking east across the Old City to the Temple Mount and Mount of Olives. Return to the roof and follow the red signs marked EXHIBIT.

The exit from the museum puts you outside the Jaffa Gate, from which there are two ways to walk to Zion Gate. You can follow the road down to the left, then take an ascending path that hugs the Old City wall; the views across the Hinnom Valley to the Yemin Moshe neighborhood and the New City are splendid. At the southwestern corner of the Old City, turn left and continue 150 yards along the city wall to Zion Gate. Alternately, you can reach the same point by way of the **Ramparts Walk** ⑰, on top of the city walls. As you leave the museum, do not rejoin the road; instead, walk south across the terrace, which only seems like a blind alley. A left at the end brings you to the ticket office for the ramparts. Follow the route—watch the steep steps—and descend at Zion Gate.

Turn right a few steps past Zion Gate and follow the path away from the Old City wall. Bear right at the first fork and turn right at the second. You're now outside the **Dormition Abbey** ⑱, whose black conical dome and tall clock tower are prominent landmarks of Mt. Zion. The church preserves the tradition that Mary, mother of Jesus, did not die but fell into "eternal sleep" (hence *dormition*).

Return to the corner on the main path (the second fork) and turn right. Twenty yards on, step through a doorway to your left and climb one flight of steps to the **Room of the Last Supper** ⑲. Also known as "the Upper Room," this site has been enshrined by tradition as the place where Jesus instituted the Eucharist ("This is my body . . . this is my blood") and where his disciples gathered on Pentecost.

The exit leads to a small courtyard. A second, tranquil courtyard (to the left as you go down the stairs), surrounded by flowerpots and a colonnaded corridor, was once the cloister of a medieval monastery. The arched windows of the Room of the Last Supper are above you, and immediately beneath the cloister, in an inner chamber, is the traditional **Tomb of David** ⑳, draped in velvet and silver. As you emerge from the tomb, turn left and leave the cloister from the side opposite where you entered. Across the road is the **Chamber of the Holocaust** ㉑, a small but powerful exhibit dedicated to the Jews killed by the Nazis. To return to Zion Gate, turn right as you leave the memorial.

TIMING
Allow 1½–2 hours for the Tower of David Museum and a similar amount of time for the rest of the route.

## Sights to See

㉑ **Chamber of the Holocaust.** Not to be confused with Yad Vashem, a few miles to the west, this small museum dedicated to the memory of the 6 million European Jews annihilated by the Nazis in the Second World War contains artifacts salvaged from the death camps, including items that the Nazis forced Jews to make out of sacred Torah scrolls (the Five Books of Moses). With grim humor, one Jewish tailor fashioned the inscribed parchment into a vest, choosing sections that contained the worst of the biblical curses. Ceremonial plaques commemorate some of the 5,000 Jewish communities wiped out by the Nazis. ⊠ *Mt. Zion,* ☎ *02/671–5105.* ⌦ *NIS 10 ($2.90).* ☉ *Summer Sun.–Thurs. 8–6, Fri. 8–3; winter Sun.–Thurs. 8–5, Fri. 8–3.*

⑱ **Dormition Abbey.** Built of limestone, with a black dome, ornamented turrets at each "corner," and a tall clock tower, this large German Benedictine church stands on a site given by the Turkish sultan to Kaiser Wilhelm II during the kaiser's 1898 visit to Jerusalem; it was dedicated in 1910. The echoing interior is ringed by six small recessed chapels. At the eastern end is a large Byzantine-style apse with a wall mosaic of Jesus and Mary. The mosaic floor is decorated with expanding circles of names of the Trinity, the evangelists, the disciples, the Old Testament prophets, and the signs of the zodiac. In the basement is a cenotaph with the carved-stone figure of Mary in repose, embracing the tradition of her "dormition," which holds that she did not die but fell into eternal sleep. Among the little chapels on the lower level is one donated by the Ivory Coast, whose wooden figures and motifs are inlaid with ivory. The premises include a bookstore and a pleasant coffee shop. ⊠ *Mt. Zion,* ☎ *02/671–9927.* ⌦ *Free.* ☉ *Mon.–Sat. 8–noon and 12:30–6, Sun. 9:30–noon and 12:30–6.*

⑮ **Jaffa Gate.** The gate got its name from its westerly orientation, toward the once-important Mediterranean harbor of Jaffa, now part of Tel Aviv. In Arabic, the gate is called Bab el-Halil, the Gate of the Beloved (referring to Abraham, the "Beloved of God" in Muslim tradition), because from here another road strikes south toward Hebron—*El-Halil* in Arabic—where Abraham is buried. The vehicle entrance was created by the Ottoman Turks in 1898 to accommodate the carriage of the visiting German emperor, Kaiser Wilhelm II. In December 1917, during the First World War, the victorious British general Allenby had a different approach: he and his staff dismounted from their horses in order to enter the holy city with appropriate humility. The older bent gate is attributed by the Arabic inscription outside it to the Ottoman Turkish sultan Suleiman the Magnificent (1536).

On your left as you enter, a Tourist Information Office offers maps and information; next to the office is a tiny recessed terrace fronted by a grille. Between the two tall cypress trees in the recess are two Muslim tombs, said to be those of the architects of Suleiman's city walls. One story says that the angry Suleiman had them executed for rebuilding the city walls without encompassing Mt. Zion and the venerated Tomb of David. Another version has it that they met their fate for being too good at their jobs: Suleiman wanted to make sure they never built anything grander for anyone else.

Opposite the Tourist Information Office is a huge stone tower built of well-cut stones reminiscent of those in the Western Wall. Once called Phatza'el, after King David's brother, it is the last survivor of the three towers built by King Herod the Great in the 1st century BC. It has become known as the Tower of David, but it has as little to do with that biblical king as the photogenic 16th-century Turkish tower, *also* known as the Tower of David, visible from outside Jaffa Gate. Apart from this tower, there are scant remains of Herod's fortress, but in later centuries Crusaders and Muslims continued to fortify this vulnerable spot in the city's defenses, creating the Citadel (as it is still known locally today).

**Old City walls.** Built between 1536 and 1542 by the Ottoman sultan Suleiman the Magnificent, the walls incorporate clearly visible chunks of the so-called First Wall, some 21 centuries old. In some places, the older stones, distinguished by the chiseled border characteristic of the Hasmonean period, project out of the line of the Turkish wall, tracing the foundations of ancient defense towers.

**⑰ Ramparts Walk.** From atop the Old City walls, you'll get to play voyeur as you catch glimpses into the gardens and courtyards of the Armenian Quarter, which occupies the southwestern quadrant of the Old City. As you walk along the narrow stone catwalks and peer through the crenellated shooting niches, you'll also gain some empathy for the medieval soldiers who defended the city under great duress. There are a large number of fairly high steps on this route; the railings are secure, but small children should not walk alone.

The northern section of the Ramparts Walk is accessible at two points—the Jaffa Gate and the Damascus Gate—and you can exit at either of these as well as at the New Gate. There is no connection at the Jaffa Gate between the two sections of the walk. ☎ 02/625–4403. ⌨ *NIS 10 ($3); combined ticket with Ophel Archaeological Garden, Damascus Gate, and Hezekiah's Tunnel NIS 25 ($7).* ☉ *Sat.–Thurs. 9–4, Fri. and holiday eves 9–2.*

**⑲ Room of the Last Supper.** According to tradition, it was on this location—*inside* the city walls of 2,000 years ago—that Jesus celebrated the Passover seder meal with his disciples. The bread and wine consecrated at the Last Supper became the elements of the Christian Eucharist. Alternately known as the Cenacle or the Coenaculum—the "Upper Room" referred to in the Gospels (Mark 14)—the present room is a large, bare medieval chamber with flagstones and Gothic arches, apparently built in the 14th century. A second tradition identifies the same room with the "one place" of Acts 2, where Jesus' disciples gathered on Pentecost, seven weeks after his death: "They were all filled with the Holy Spirit and began to speak in other tongues. . . ."

Incongruously, the chamber has the trappings of a mosque as well: stained-glass Arabic inscriptions in the Gothic windows (with modern glass); one window blocked by an ornate mihrab (a chamber indicating the direction of Mecca); two Arabic plaques in the wall; and a Levantine dome. The Muslims were not interested in the site's Christian tradition but in the supposed Tomb of David (☞ *below*) on the level below. ⊠ *Mt. Zion.* ⌨ *Free.* ☉ *Sat.–Thurs. 8–5, Fri. 8–1.*

**⑳ Tomb of David.** The Bible refers to Jerusalem, King David's capital in the 10th century BC, as the "City of David." Medieval Jewish pilgrims erroneously placed it on this, the current southwestern hill; and apparently because the City of David was also called the "Stronghold of Zion" (II Samuel 5), the hill was named Mt. Zion. Since the Bible also relates that David was buried in the City of David, the tomb of the great king was sought—and supposedly found—here. The real City of David has been excavated to the east of Mt. Zion, but at least nine centuries of tears and prayers have sanctified this place.

Enter the antechamber behind the blue-painted barred windows (modest dress is required, and men must cover their heads) and pass on to the tomb itself. The cenotaph, a massive stone tomb marker, is draped with a velvet cloth—changed periodically—typically embroidered with stars of David and inscriptions in Hebrew: "David, King of Israel, lives forever" (meaning that David's dynasty, from which the Messiah is to come, is eternal) and "If I forget thee, O Jerusalem, may my right hand lose its cunning" (Psalm 137).

On top of the cenotaph are several ornaments used to crown Torah scrolls and two beautifully engraved silver canisters, used by Sephardic Jews as containers for the Torah. Behind the cenotaph is an age-blackened stone alcove, thought by scholars to be the oldest remnant of a synagogue in Jerusalem (from about the 5th century AD). In the antechamber opposite the tomb is a mihrab surrounded by green ceramic tiles, which once oriented the Muslim faithful toward Mecca in honor of Nebi Daoud—the prophet David—whom Islam has retroactively beatified. ✉ *Mt. Zion,* ☎ *02/671–9767.* 🎟 *Free.* ☉ *Sun.–Thurs. 8–5, Fri. 8–2.*

★ ⑯ **Tower of David Museum.** Entered through a gated tower and over a moat, the museum is housed in a series of medieval halls in what is known locally as the citadel (*Hametzuda* in Hebrew). Confusingly enough, although the name "Tower of David" has traditionally been applied to the 17th-century Turkish minaret at the citadel's southern edge, other traditions attach it to the massive Herodian tower at the opposite end. Neither claimant has the slightest connection to the biblical King David. The museum tells the city's 5,000-year-old history, not with original artifacts but through a variety of interesting visual and audiovisual aids, including models, maps, holograms, and videos. You can rent an audio guide at the entrance. Be sure to inquire about the next screening of the animated introductory film, which has English subtitles.

The site's old stones and arches lend an appropriately antique atmosphere to the entire exhibit, whose galleries are organized by historical period around the citadel's central courtyard. Landscaped archaeological remains in the courtyard form an eye-catching but incomprehensible jumble, except for the massive Herodian tower and the Hasmonean First Wall (2nd–1st centuries BC) to which it is attached. A walk on the citadel's ramparts, with sometimes unexpected panoramas from odd angles, is also worthwhile, though certainly a lesser priority. Ask about the occasional temporary exhibits. On summer evenings, a sound-and-light show in the citadel creates a magical atmosphere in an area out of sight of the modern city. (Dress warmly, even in midsummer.) A year-round evening experience is "Mystery in the Citadel," a lively, interactive Sherlock Holmes–type game in which you and others try to solve an actual historical murder. ✉ *Jaffa Gate,* ☎ *02/626–5333 or 02/626–5310 for recorded info.* 🎟 *Museum or sound-and-light show NIS 25 ($7); combined ticket to museum and sound-and-light show NIS 42 ($12); electronic audio guide NIS 10 ($3); mystery NIS 28 ($8); combined ticket to mystery and sound-and-light show NIS 38 ($9).* ☉ *Museum Apr.–Oct., Sun.–Thurs. 9–5, Fri.–Sat. 9–2; Nov.–Mar., Sun.–Thurs. 10–4, Fri.–Sat. 10–2. Free guided tour in English Sun.–Fri. at 11; sound-and-light show in English Apr.–Oct., Mon. and Wed. at 9:30 PM, Sat. at 9 PM; mystery in English: Apr.–Oct., Sat. 10 PM; Nov.–Mar., Sat. 9 PM (call ahead to verify).*

# City of David

The City of David is mentioned in the Bible (II Samuel 5) as a synonym for Jerusalem, once King David had conquered it (1000 BC) from the Jebusites and established it as his capital. In the mid-10th century BC, David's son Solomon expanded the city northward and built the Temple of God on Mt. Moriah, where the Dome of the Rock now stands. In time, Jerusalem spread farther west and north, but in recent years the name "City of David" has been revived to indicate the city's ancient core.

## A Good Walk

Begin at the Dung Gate. (If you're driving, you can park your car outside the gate.) Walk east on Ophel Road, so that the Old City wall is on your left, followed by the Ophel Archaeological Garden (☞ Old City: The Classic Sights, *above*). Where the Ophel Road swings left, cross the road—*carefully.* The **Kidron Valley** yawns beneath you, and from the lookout terrace you can see ancient funerary monuments below and to your left.

Return to the bend in Ophel Road. This was the northern limit of the City of David and the only side not protected by a valley. The city has been conquered at least 35 times in its 5,000-year history, almost always from the north. Continue south along the paved path that skirts the steep Kidron slope to the excavation site known as **Area G** ㉒, one of the areas dug up between 1978 and 1985 to great public interest, and the one with the most interesting finds. When you're ready to go, leave the site by the gate on the opposite side of the excavations.

From here on, the route is not recommended for visitors who have difficulty with steps. Go down the stairs and follow a small sign on the right to **Warren's Shaft** ㉓, an extraordinary access shaft to the Gihon Spring. It is still widely accepted that King David's commandos penetrated the city through this shaft in 1000 BC, although recent scholars have argued otherwise. The room at the top of the shaft has several visual aids to help explain the site.

The main stairway continues down to the Kidron Valley. Under a modern building on the right, a short flight of steps descends to the spring itself. This was the original water supply of ancient Jerusalem, and probably the reason the city was first built on this small hill. In 701 BC, in the face of an Assyrian invasion, King Hezekiah built a remarkable water tunnel, a third of a mile long, to bring the spring water to an innercity reservoir; it's now commonly known as **Hezekiah's Tunnel** ㉔. Walking the tunnel is a memorable experience, but you must bring flashlights or candles and be prepared to walk through thigh-deep water.

The tunnel emerges at a small pool, the "pool of Siloam" in the New Testament story of the healing of the blind man (John 9). Climb the steep road back to the Dung Gate. Bus 1 runs from here to Jaffa Gate and skirts the city center.

TIMING

Allow two hours for the walk, three if you walk Hezekiah's Tunnel. The tunnel involves 30–40 minutes' walking in knee- to thigh-deep water. The sights are closed on Friday afternoon, Saturday, and Jewish religious holidays.

## Sights to See

㉒ **Area G.** Archaeologists, notably Kathleen Kenyon in the 1960s, have sporadically dug up bits of the City of David for more than a century. The most thorough expedition, however, was led by the late Israeli archaeologist Yigal Shiloh from 1978 to 1985. In this sector, he confirmed that the city wall dated from the 2nd century BC (marked 1, 2, and 3 on the site) but redated the so-called stepped structure (marked 4) to the 10th century BC, the time of Israelite kings David and Solomon. It once supported a palace or fortification; in the 7th century BC, a house (now partially restored on a platform) was built against it.

The most intriguing artifacts the dig yielded were 51 bullae, clay seals used for documents, just as hot wax might be used today. All had personal names impressed on them in ancient Hebrew script. All of the seals were found in one chamber, suggesting that it was used as an archive; and the name on one of the seals—Gemariah ben Shafan, the royal secretary in the days of Jeremiah—reinforces this idea. The clay seals were seared into ceramic permanence, apparently from the fire of the Babylonian destruction of Jerusalem in 586 BC. ⊠ *Off Ophel Rd.,* ☎ *02/ 628–8141.* ▨ *NIS 5 ($1.50), including Warren's Shaft.* ☉ *Sun.– Thurs. 9–4, Fri. 9–1.*

| NEED A BREAK? | Immediately opposite the exit from Area G is a vine-shaded **terrace** with a view of the Kidron Valley. The enterprising owner sells soft drinks, fresh orange juice, and Turkish coffee, which you can sip leisurely at one of the stone tables. The toilet facilities are poor, but they're the only ones in this area. |
| --- | --- |

❷❹ **Hezekiah's Tunnel.** In 721 BC, the Assyrian Empire destroyed the northern Kingdom of Israel, exiled most of its population into historical oblivion—rendering them the so-called Ten Lost Tribes—and subjugated Israel's sister kingdom, Judah, in the south. Twenty years later, Judah revolted against its overlords, triggering a devastating, punitive military invasion. Preparing for an imminent assault by the Assyrians on his capital city of Jerusalem, the Judean king Hezekiah rushed to protect his precious water supply. The Bible describes the siege in three parallel accounts. Hezekiah gave instructions to "stop the water of the springs that were outside the city . . . saying, 'Why should the kings of Assyria come and find much water?' " Racing against time, Hezekiah's men dug a water tunnel a third of a mile long through solid rock, one team starting from the Gihon Spring and another from the new inner-city reservoir (called Shilo'ach in Hebrew, Siloam in English). Miraculously, considering the serpentine course of the tunnel, the two teams met in the middle. The chisel marks, the ancient plaster, and the zigzags near the halfway point (each team sought each other by sound) bear witness to the project. Again the Bible: and Hezekiah "closed the upper outlet of the waters of Gihon and directed them down to the west side of the city of David" (II Chronicles 32).

Most exciting was an inscription in ancient Hebrew, found in the 19th century near the exit of the tunnel (and now in a Turkish museum): "This is the story of the boring through. . . ," it began, echoing the biblical account; "the tunnelers hewed the rock, each man toward his fellow, pickax against pickax. And the water flowed from the spring toward the reservoir for 1,200 cubits [577 yards]."

Note the following: there is no lighting in the tunnel, so you must come with a flashlight or a good supply of candles and matches. Because the flow of the spring is unpredictable, the water level varies but can sometimes reach a depth of 3 ft in places; and the water is very cool, even in summer. This is no place for small children or claustrophobes, and although there are guards here, women visiting alone may attract unwanted attention from local youths. ☎ *02/625–4403.* ▨ *NIS 8 ($2.50); combined ticket with Ophel Archaeological Garden, Ramparts Walk, and Damascus Gate NIS 25 ($7).* ☉ *Sun.–Thurs. 9–4, Fri. and holiday eves 9–2; last entry to tunnel 45 min before closing.*

**Kidron Valley.** This valley separates the Old City from the high ridge of the Mount of Olives. Jewish tradition predicts that the Messiah will make his appearance here. The cliff face below the houses on the opposite side of the valley is marked with symmetrical holes, which are mouths of tombs from both the First Temple (Old Testament) and Second Temple (Hellenistic-Roman) periods. From the new lookout terrace near the bend in Ophel Road, you can look down and to your left at the impressive group of 2,200-year-old funerary monuments. The huge, square stone structure with the conical roof is known as **Absalom's Pillar**; the one crowned by a pyramidal roof, a solid block of stone cut out of the mountain, is called **Zachariah's Tomb**—but neither has anything to do with the Old Testament personalities for whom they're named. Wealthy Jerusalemites of the Second Temple period had themselves entombed at the foot of the Mount of Olives to await the Messiah and the resurrection that would follow his coming.

㉓ **Warren's Shaft.** Charles Warren was an inspired British army engineer who explored Jerusalem in 1867. In the City of David he discovered this spacious access shaft, which burrowed vertically under the city wall to a point 40 ft above the Gihon Spring, in the valley; water was hauled up through it in ancient times, perhaps by "the lame and the blind" of II Samuel 5. Conventional wisdom until Yigal Shiloh's dig (1978–85) said the shaft was pre-Davidic, the actual shaft—called the *tzinnor* (gutter or water shaft) in that same biblical passage—through which David's warriors penetrated the city in 1000 BC. Shiloh disagreed and dated the shaft to the 9th century BC, based on its similarity to water systems of that later period found elsewhere in Israel. Yet no one quite knows what the word *tzinnor* meant in Old Testament times (the word appears only twice in the Bible), so there *is* room for interpretation. Until the traditional explanation has been discredited, it is too good a story to surrender.

As you descend into the bowels of the earth, note the ancient chisel marks on the walls. It is now accepted that a good part of the shaft was a natural fissure reamed out by workmen in antiquity. The bottom of the last vertical section is now a dry chamber, walled off from the spring in the Israelite (Old Testament) period. ⊠ *Off Ophel Rd.,* ☎ *02/628–8141.* ▣ *NIS 5 ($1.50), including Area G.* ☉ *Sun.–Thurs. 9–5, Fri. 9–1.*

## Mount of Olives and East Jerusalem

The sights in this area are for the most part distinctly Christian. Some are well off the beaten path, but the walk, though long, is feasible; you can also cover this route by car or public transportation. A few words of caution: pickpockets continue to be a problem on the Mount of Olives lookout and on the road down to Gethsemane. The walk takes you through East Jerusalem's Arab neighborhoods, areas that Israelis have avoided in recent years because of political tensions. At press time the situation was fairly relaxed, but you're still advised to stick to the main streets and spend your evenings in some other part of town. If you're driving, choose your parking lot carefully, as Palestinian nationalist zeal has been known to spill over into old-fashioned vandalism: the Seven Arches Hotel on the Mount of Olives, the Rockefeller Museum compound, and the American Colony Hotel are recommended.

### A Good Drive and Walk

Begin on the **Mount of Olives** ㉕, at the panoramic lookout outside the Seven Arches Hotel. This is the classic picture-postcard view of the Old City, looking west across the Kidron Valley. Below you is a huge and ancient Jewish cemetery; around you are Christian spires and domes.

## Exploring East Jerusalem

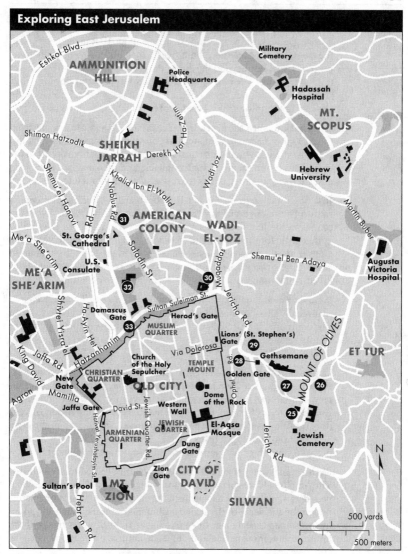

Leave your car near the Seven Arches Hotel and walk some 150 yards back along the approach road to the hotel. In a bay on your right, through a stone gateway, is a round stone structure about 10 ft in diameter called the **Dome of the Ascension,** built over a rock alleged to bear the footprint of Jesus. Just beyond the dome, the road turns sharply right. Enter the **Pater Noster Convent** ㉖ through a light-gray metal door on your right. Here, it is said, Jesus taught his disciples what is known as the Lord's Prayer, now recalled here in dozens of languages on ceramic tiles.

Walk back toward the hotel. If you're on foot, begin the descent from the Mount of Olives via the steps to your right before the parking lot. If you have a car, you can drive on an asphalt road that breaks off to the right just beyond the steps, switches back, and then begins a *very* steep descent. Note that despite its narrowness, this is *not* a one-way street!

Just down the steps on the left is a courtyard with a burial complex said to be the **Tombs of the Prophets** Haggai and Malachi. Below the tombs, in the Jewish cemetery, is the common grave of 48 Jews killed in the battle for the Jewish Quarter in 1948. Hastily buried within the quarter itself, their remains were disinterred in 1967 and reburied here. Among those buried with military honors were 10-year-old boys killed while running messages between defensive positions.

**Dominus Flevit** ㉗, halfway down the mountain, is a small, modern church that recalls Jesus' sorrowful prediction of the destruction of Jerusalem. The courtyard is a nice place to enjoy the view in peace between waves of tour groups. (Equally worthy of mention are the rest rooms, rare on this route!)

Continue down the hill. The gold onion domes and sculpted white turrets of the Russian **Church of Mary Magdalene,** straight out of a fantasy, can be seen in tantalizing glimpses over a high wall to the right. At the bottom of the road on the left—marked by a platoon of vendors outside—is the **Garden of Gethsemane** ㉘, mentioned in the New Testament as the site of Jesus' arrest. The ancient olive trees and impressive Church of All Nations are the prominent features here.

Gethsemane abuts Jericho Road at the foot of the Mount of Olives. The road bends sharply at this point, and to the right a staircase takes you deep into the subterranean Church of the Assumption, better known by the name of the shrine within it—the **Tomb of the Virgin** ㉙, the presumed burial place of Mary. To the right of the entrance is the Franciscan-administered **Grotto of Gethsemane.**

As you continue toward the Old City, the first left takes you to the City of David, Dung Gate, and Mt. Zion. For this tour, however, continue right. Turn left at the traffic light onto Sultan Suleiman Street. Immediately on your right is a steep driveway leading up to the **Rockefeller Museum of Archaeology** ㉚, with its landmark octagonal tower. Don't park on the street; you can park on the museum grounds. You may want to bring a lunch to enjoy in the shade of the lovely garden.

Continue along Sultan Suleiman Street and turn right at the post office into Saladin Street. Where Saladin Street meets Nablus Road (about 1½ km, or 1 mi, from the Rockefeller Museum), on the right, are the **Tombs of the Kings** ㉛. If you're driving, turn right at the intersection and again into the second street on the right (a dead-end road) to the American Colony Hotel (☞ Lodging, *below*), where you'll find safe parking. If you intend to complete the tour, leave your car here and see the other sights on foot. The immensely impressive tombs, once thought to be of Old Testament vintage, date to the 1st century AD and are the finest such catacombs in Israel. You will need a flashlight or several candles.

Continue down Nablus Road, heading back toward the Old City. Almost immediately on your left is the neo-Gothic Anglican St. George's Cathedral, built at the beginning of the 20th century as a copy of New College at Oxford University. Its tower is a landmark in Jerusalem's skyline. Some 500 yards farther, beyond the U.S. Consulate and opposite the bus station, a well-marked narrow lane to the left—Conrad Schick Street—leads to the **Garden Tomb** ㉜.

Back on Nablus Road, turn left and continue for 200 yards. You are now at the Old City walls opposite **Damascus Gate** ㉝. The archaeological remains of the Roman period found beneath the gate are worth your time and the small fee.

You now have several options: return by foot to the American Colony Hotel; take a cab from Damascus Gate to your next destination; walk up Hativat Hatzanhanim Street (outside the Old City, with its walls on your left) toward Jaffa Gate and the New City; walk the Ramparts (☞ Tower of David and Mt. Zion, *above*) to Jaffa Gate; or plunge into the Old City to reach the Via Dolorosa and the Western Wall (left fork inside Damascus Gate) or the Church of the Holy Sepulcher and the Jewish Quarter (right fork).

### TIMING
You can easily spend a day on this walk, with a stop for a picnic lunch on the grounds of the Rockefeller Museum. If archaeology is not your thing, you can start early and see most of the sights in time for a leisurely lunch at the American Colony, with just a bit of sightseeing left for the afternoon. The Mount of Olives is best in early morning, when you can see the Old City with the sun at your back, or at sunset on days with some clouds, when the golden glow can compensate for the glare. Several of the Christian sights are closed on Sunday.

## Sights to See
**Church of Mary Magdalene.** Dedicated in 1888, this church is Russian Orthodox and part of the Garden of Gethsemane tradition. It has very limited hours, but its icon-studded interior is well worth a look if you happen to be here at the right time. ⊠ *Mt. of Olives,* ☎ 02/628–4371. ⊠ *Free.* ⊙ *Tues. and Thurs. 10–11:30.*

㉝ **Damascus Gate.** The name of the gate gives away its location: it faces north toward Damascus, Syria. Its Hebrew name—Sha'ar Shechem, for the Nablus Gate—delivers the same message. With its tapered carved-stone crenellations and ornamented embrasures, the gate is the most beautiful of the seven still open in the present 16th-century Old City wall. It is also the busiest, the main link between the Old City and the Arab neighborhoods of East Jerusalem.

To the left and below the approach bridge is a surviving arched entrance of the pagan **Roman town** built by Emperor Hadrian in AD 135 on the ruins of its Jewish predecessor. Hadrian's plan to build the town touched off the Jewish Bar Kochba Revolt in AD 132. Excavations just inside the arch (reached by walking to the right of Damascus Gate, then left under the bridge) have brought to light an almost entirely intact Roman tower that connects with the Ramparts Walk (a separate ticket; ☞ Tower of David and Mt. Zion, *above*) and is part of an open plaza from the 2nd-century town. A tall column topped by the emperor's statue once dominated the plaza. With the Christianization of the Roman Empire in the 4th century, the statue was removed; but the column remained, exactly as depicted in the famous 6th-century mosaic floor map of Jerusalem found in Madaba, Jordan. The column, the point of reference for road distances throughout the country, has not survived, but the Arabic name for the gate—*Bab el-Amud,* the Gate of the Column—

preserves its memory. ✉ *Damascus Gate,* ☎ *02/625–4403.* ☜ *Roman plaza NIS 5 ($1.50); combined ticket with Ramparts Walk, Ophel Archaeological Garden, and Hezekiah's Tunnel NIS 25 ($7).* ⊙ *Sat.–Thurs. 9–4, Fri. 9–2.*

**Dome of the Ascension.** This building dates from the Crusader period and was once open to the sky. Credulous medieval pilgrims were shown an indentation in the natural rock, said to be the footprint of Jesus as he ascended to heaven, and the identification became part of local lore. The dome is actually Islamic in style, and, curiously, the current caretakers are Muslim. ✉ *Mt. of Olives.* ☜ *Small fee, about NIS 3 ($1).* ⊙ *No set hrs; ring bell to enter.*

**㉗ Dominus Flevit.** Designed by Antonio Barluzzi and built between 1953 and 1955, the tear-shape church (whose name means "the Lord wept") provides a potentially tranquil haven with a superb view of the Old City. (Crowds of pilgrims often keep the calm at bay.) The outstanding feature of the church's simple interior is the picture window facing west, with an iron cross on the altar silhouetted against the Old City and the Dome of the Rock. Although many small archaeological items have been found here, the tradition holding this as the site where Jesus wept over Jerusalem as he prophesied its destruction—"and they shall not leave in thee one stone upon another" (Luke 19)—is apparently no older than the Crusader period. ✉ *Mt. of Olives,* ☎ *02/627–4931.* ☜ *Free.* ⊙ *Daily 8–11:45 and 2:30–5.*

**㉘ Garden of Gethsemane.** The New Testament does not specifically refer to Gethsemane as a garden but as the "place" where Jesus came with his disciples after the Last Supper, where he prayed and sweated blood (Matthew 26), and where, in the end, he was betrayed and arrested. The name Gethsemane derives from the Aramaic *gat shamna* or the Hebrew *gat shemanim,* both meaning "oil press." The olive tree, which gives this hill its name (Mount of Olives), grew in greater profusion in antiquity than today, its fruit providing precious lamp oil. The "Garden of the Oil Press" still boasts eight enormous, gnarled trees—still productive—that may, according to some botanists, be as old as Christianity itself.

Within the garden is the **Church of All Nations,** designed by the architect Antonio Barluzzi and dedicated in 1924. Within each of its interior domes are mosaic symbols of the countries that contributed to its building (the seal of the United States is in the first dome as you enter the church; Canada is two up in the same line; and the English dome is the first, nearest the door, in the middle line). The windows are glazed with translucent alabaster in somber browns and purples, creating a mystical atmosphere in the dim interior. At the altar is the so-called Rock of the Agony, where Jesus is said to have endured his Passion. The large wall mosaics depict the events associated with the site. Small windows in the floor show sections of the Byzantine mosaics that inspired those in the contemporary church. ✉ *Jericho Rd.,* ☎ *02/628–3264.* ☜ *Free.* ⊙ *Oct.–Mar., daily 8–noon and 2:30–5; Apr.–Sept., daily 8–noon and 2:30–6.*

**★ ㉜ Garden Tomb.** The theory identifying this site with Calvary and Jesus' burial place goes back to 1883, when the British general Charles Gordon (of later Khartoum fame) spent several months in Jerusalem. From his window just inside the Old City walls, Gordon was struck by the skull-like features of a cliff face north of the Damascus Gate. He was convinced that this, rather than the traditional Calvary, in the Church of the Holy Sepulcher (☞ Old City: The Classic Sights, *above*), was "the place of the skull" (Mark 15) where Jesus was crucified. His conviction was infectious, and after his death a fund-raising campaign in

England resulted in the purchase of the adjacent site in 1894. An ancient rock-cut tomb uncovered there some years earlier took on new importance for its proximity to Skull Hill (already becoming known as Gordon's Calvary). Subsequent excavations exposed cisterns and a wine press, features typical of an ancient garden.

The newly formed Garden Tomb Association was jubilant, as all the elements of the Gospel account of Jesus' death and burial were here. Jesus was buried in the fresh tomb of the wealthy Joseph of Arimathea (Matthew 27), and contemporary archaeologists lent their authority to the identification of the tomb as an upper-class burial place of the Second Temple period. Recent research has strongly challenged that conclusion, however. The tomb might be from the Old Testament period, making it too old to have been Jesus', since his was one "in which no man had yet been laid." It should be noted that the gentle guardians of the Garden Tomb do not insist on the identification of the site as that of Calvary and the tomb of Christ but suggest that (as their brochure puts it) "the features of the Garden . . . provide an atmosphere which brings into focus the relevance of the Death and Resurrection of the Lord Jesus Christ." Indeed, the beautifully tended garden of trees, flower beds, and seats for private meditation makes this an island of tranquillity in the hurly-burly of East Jerusalem. For many Protestant visitors, especially those of Evangelical orientation, this site represents the climax of their pilgrimage to Jerusalem. ⊠ *Conrad Schick St.,* ☎ *02/627–2745.* ▨ *Free.* ◷ *Mon.–Sat. 8:30–noon and 2–5:30; Sun. service only (nondenominational Protestant in English) at 9.*

**Grotto of Gethsemane.** The rock ceiling in this hewn chapel seems to press down on you. Franciscans identify the *Garden* of Gethsemane with Christ's Passion and this spot with his arrest. ⊠ *Jericho Rd.,* ☎ *02/628–3264.* ▨ *Free.* ◷ *Daily 8:30–noon and 2:30–5.*

★ ㉕ **Mount of Olives.** The Mount of Olives has been bathed in sanctity—both past and future—since time immemorial. Separating you from the Old City is the Kidron Valley, which continues south for a way before breaking east and beginning its steep descent to the Dead Sea. On the slope beneath you, and spreading off to your left, is the vast **Jewish cemetery,** the oldest cemetery still in use anywhere in the world. Jews have been buried on the Mount of Olives for more than 2,000 years to await the coming of the Messiah and the resurrection to follow. It is said that elsewhere you die and disintegrate; in Jerusalem you die and mingle. The raised structures over the graves are merely tomb markers, not crypts; burial is still below ground.

In the Old City wall facing you, and just to the right of the Dome of the Rock, is the blocked-up, double-arched Gate of Mercy, or Golden Gate. Jewish tradition holds that the Messiah will enter Jerusalem this way; Christian tradition says he already has. To the south of the Dome of the Rock is the black-domed El-Aqsa Mosque, behind which are the stone arches of the Jewish Quarter. Some distance behind the Dome of the Rock is the large, gray dome of the Church of the Holy Sepulcher. To the left of the Old City, the cone-roofed Dormition Abbey and its adjacent tower mark the top of Mt. Zion, today outside the walls but within the city of the Second Temple period.

㉖ **Pater Noster Convent.** The focal point of this Carmelite convent is a grotto, traditionally identified as the place where Jesus taught his disciples the so-called Lord's Prayer: "Our Father [*Pater Noster*], Who art in Heaven . . ." (Mark 11; Luke 11). The site was purchased by the Princesse de la Tour d'Auvergne of France in 1868 and the convent built on the site of earlier Byzantine and Crusader structures. The ambitious Basilica of the Sacred Heart, begun here in the 1920s and designed to follow the lines of Constantine's 4th-century Basilica of Eleona, was never completed; its aisles, open to the sky, are now incongruously lined with pine trees, and its altar is more reminiscent of an Aztec high place than a Catholic church. The princess, entombed in a beautiful marble sarcophagus, lies in state in the cloister, oblivious to the abandonment of the master plan. Ceramic plaques lining the cloister walls quote the Lord's Prayer in more than 70 different languages. ⊠ *Mt. of Olives,* ☎ *02/589–4904.* ⊠ *Free.* ☉ *Mon.–Sat. 8:30– noon and 3–5.*

**30  Rockefeller Museum of Archaeology.** Built in the 1930s during the British Mandate, the stone halls of this museum still have an old-world atmosphere. The chronological presentation of its fine archaeological collection recalls the British Museum. If you have only a passing interest in archaeology, the Israel Museum's finely presented collection will probably suffice (☞ Center City, *below*); the Rockefeller is for the enthusiast.

The finds are all from Israel, dating from prehistoric times to around AD 1700. Among the most important exhibits are cultic masks from Neolithic Jericho, ivories from Canaanite (Bronze Age) Megiddo, the famous Israelite "Lachish Letters" (6th century BC), Herodian inscriptions, and decorative reliefs from Hisham's Palace, in Jericho, and from the Church of the Holy Sepulcher. ⊠ *Sultan Suleiman St.,* ☎ *02/ 628–2251.* ⊠ *NIS 22 ($6.30); inquire about combined ticket with Israel Museum.* ☉ *Sun.–Thurs. 10–5, Fri.–Sat. 10–2.*

**29  Tomb of the Virgin.** The Gothic facade of the underground Church of the Assumption, which contains this shrine, clearly dates it to the Crusader era (12th century), but the tradition that this is where the Virgin Mary was interred and then "assumed" into heaven apparently goes back to the Byzantine period. In an otherwise gloomy church—hung with age-darkened icons and brass lamps—the marble sarcophagus, thought to date from the 12th century, remains illuminated. The Status Quo Agreement in force in the Church of the Holy Sepulcher and Bethlehem's Church of the Nativity pertains here, too: the Greek Orthodox, Armenian Orthodox, and even Muslims control different parts of the property. The Roman Catholic Franciscans were expelled in 1757, a loss of privilege bitterly recalled to this day. ⊠ *Jericho Rd.* ⊠ *Free.* ☉ *Daily 6–11:45 and 2:30–5.*

**31  Tombs of the Kings.** These catacombs were explored in the 19th century by the Frenchman Félicien de Saulcy, who accepted the local tradition identifying them with the biblical kings of Judah. Royal tombs they were, but they weren't quite that old. In the 1st century AD, Queen Helene of Adiabene, a country on the border of Persia, converted to Judaism and came to live and die in the holy city. Although she built her palaces in the onetime City of David in the south of the city, she and her descendants were buried here.

Wide, rock-hewn steps descend to rain-catchment pools and into a spacious courtyard, all excavated out of solid rock. The entrance to the tombs is across a porch that once boasted two massive stone columns and still has its Hellenistic-style frieze, above. The "rolling stone" that once sealed the mouth of the catacombs is still in situ, a graphic example of those described in the New Testament.

The "weeping chamber" immediately inside the low doorway has rock benches for mourners and tiny triangular niches for oil lamps. Other chambers branching off this one contain the many alcoves and ledges where the dead were laid, wrapped in shrouds. ⊠ *Saladin St.,* ☎ *no phone.* ⊠ *Small fee for attendant.* ☉ *Daily 8:30–5, but hrs are unreliable and site is sometimes closed during these hrs. Bring flashlight or candles.*

NEED A
BREAK?
The **American Colony Hotel** (⊠ Nablus Rd., ☎ 02/628–5171) is a 19th-century limestone building with cane furniture, Armenian ceramic tiles, and a delightful courtyard. The food is generally very good, and a light lunch or afternoon tea in the cool lobby lounge, at the poolside restaurant, or on the patio can make for a well-earned break.

**Tombs of the Prophets.** The tradition that holds these to be the burial places of the prophets Haggai and Malachi is spurious, but the site is interesting in its own right: it's a burial cave from the Byzantine period, about 1,500 years ago. From the round entrance hall, three passages radiate out to meet the two semicircular inner corridors containing the cave's 26 burial niches. ⊠ *Mt. of Olives.* ⊡ *Gratuity for resident attendant.* ☉ *No fixed hrs; usually open.*

## West Jerusalem

Understandably, travelers tend to focus on the historical and religious sights on the eastern side of town; but exploring West Jerusalem gives more insight into the contemporary life in Israel's largest city. These attractions are most easily accessible by car or by a combination of buses, short cab rides, and a little patience.

### A Good Drive

Begin at **Yad Vashem** ㉞, the national Holocaust memorial and museum, 700 yards west of Mt. Herzl. Only Bus 99 stops at the site, but Mt. Herzl, a 10-minute walk away, is served by many lines (Buses 18 and 27 run from the city center). The experience of the Holocaust is so deeply seared into the Jewish national psyche that understanding it goes a long way toward understanding the Israelis themselves.

A good plan for seeing this complex site is the following: walk up the slope to the right of the bookstore near the entrance to the small but riveting Children's Memorial. Continue past the tall aluminum memorial to the Jewish resistance to visit the heavy basalt-and-concrete Hall of Remembrance. Step down through the carob trees of the Avenue of the Righteous and turn right onto Warsaw Ghetto Square. Here is the entrance to the Historical Museum. The Art Museum is in the same building, accessible from the end of the Historical Museum or by a separate rear entrance. Scattered around the grounds are many impressive sculptures. From the parking lot a road descends (about 1 km, or ⅔ mi) to the Valley of the Communities. If you're on foot, a path to the left of Warsaw Ghetto Square (opposite the museum entrance) will lead you down to the valley by a shorter route.

Return toward Herzl Boulevard, but turn left into the large parking lot that abuts it (*before* you reach the traffic lights). This is the entrance to **Mt. Herzl (National Memorial Park)** ㉟, named for Theodor Herzl, the founder of the modern Zionist movement, whose grave is at its summit. The path to the left of the Herzl Museum entrance eventually turns right across a huge plaza (used for state ceremonies) to the unadorned, black stone grave marker. To the left (west) of the grave site, a path leads down to a section containing the graves of national leaders, among them assassinated prime minister Yitzhak Rabin.

Continue west for a few yards, descending to the **Mt. Herzl Military Cemetery** ㊱. The paths through the cemetery bear around to the right, double back to the cemetery entrance, and reach Herzl Boulevard 300 yards below the first entrance where you entered Mt. Herzl. An alternative is to enter the military cemetery directly, without going through the park.

One hundred yards down Herzl Boulevard from the entrance to Mt. Herzl, turn right at the next traffic light, into Harav Uziel Street. After

# Exploring West Jerusalem and Center City

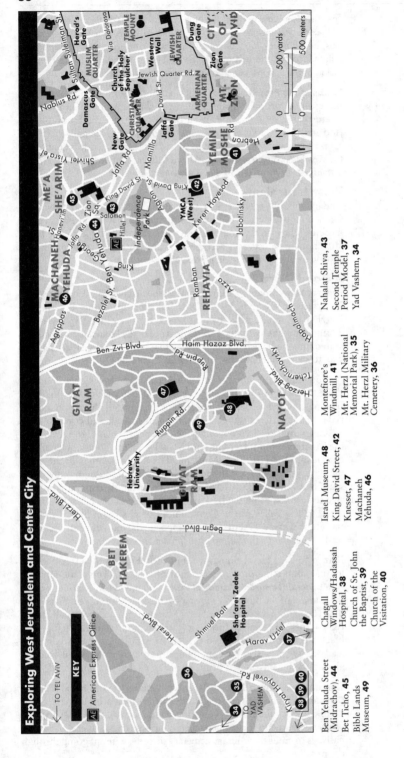

**KEY**

→ TO TEL AVIV

AE American Express Office

Ben Yehuda Street (Midrachov), **44**
Bet Ticho, **45**
Bible Lands Museum, **49**

Chagall Windows/Hadassah Hospital, **38**
Church of St. John the Baptist, **39**
Church of the Visitation, **40**

Israel Museum, **48**
King David Street, **42**
Knesset, **47**
Machaneh Yehuda, **46**

Montefiore's Windmill, **41**
Mt. Herzl (National Memorial Park), **35**
Mt. Herzl Military Cemetery, **36**

Nahalat Shiva, **43**
Second Temple Period Model, **37**
Yad Vashem, **34**

2 km (1 mi)—keep bearing left—the road passes the Holyland Hotel, and 150 yards farther is the **Second Temple Period Model** ㊲, a huge open-air scale model of Jerusalem as it existed 2,000 years ago. Park and take the short path on the left.

If you're driving, return to the intersection with Herzl Boulevard and turn left. Stay on the winding main road, the name of which changes several times: Kiryat Hayovel Road, Hantke Street, and Henrietta Szold Road. The road swings sharply right to Hadassah Hospital. There is a relatively remote parking lot on the hospital grounds and a free shuttle bus to the main buildings. What draws visitors here are the world-famous, stained-glass **Chagall windows** ㊳ of the hospital's synagogue. The theme is biblical: Jacob's deathbed blessings on his sons. The effect is magical.

As you leave from the hospital's main entrance, turn right and descend to where the road joins Route 386. Turn right again, reentering Jerusalem through the village of **Ein Kerem.** Dominating the center of the village (on the left as you approach from the west, from the bottom of the village) is the **Church of St. John the Baptist** ㊴, its orange tile roof a distinctive local landmark. Opposite the church, a short street takes you to the small Spring of the Virgin. Turn right and climb a steep, stepped street, past a Russian Orthodox monastery, to the impressive Franciscan **Church of the Visitation** ㊵, said to have been the home of John the Baptist's parents, Zechariah and Elizabeth.

Return to the main road of the village and turn right onto the steep road that emerges at Mt. Herzl.

TIMING

This tour takes a full day, even with the convenience of your own car. Allow two to three hours to do Yad Vashem justice, though you can see its highlights in less time. It's best to visit the Second Temple Period Model *after* you've become familiar with the Old City of today; 45 minutes is the most you need here. Note that Yad Vashem, Mt. Herzl, and the Chagall windows close very early on Friday and are not open on Saturday or on Jewish religious holidays.

## Sights to See

㊳ **Chagall windows/Hadassah Hospital.** Hadassah is one of the two largest general hospitals in the Middle East and is the teaching hospital for Hebrew University's medical and dental schools. When the Hadassah organization approached the Russian-born Jewish artist Marc Chagall in 1959 about designing stained-glass windows for the synagogue at the new hospital, he was delighted and contributed his work for free. Taking his inspiration from Jacob's deathbed blessings on his sons (Genesis 49) and, to a lesser extent, from Moses' valediction to the tribes of Israel (Deuteronomy 33), Chagall created 12 vibrant windows in primary colors, with an ark full of characteristically Chagallian beasts and a scattering of Jewish and esoteric symbols. The innovative techniques of the Reims glassmakers give the wafer-thin windows an astounding illusion of depth in many places. To see them, take the tour of the synagogue, which includes a film about the hospital. Buses 19 and 27 serve the hospital. ⊠ *Hadassah Hospital, Henrietta Szold Rd., Ein Kerem,* ☎ *02/641–6333.* ≦ *NIS 9 ($2.60).* ☉ *Guided tours of synagogue Sun.–Thurs. at 8:30, 9:30, 10:30, 11:30, 12:30, and 2:30; Fri. and holiday eves 9:30, 10:30, 11:30.*

㊴ **Church of St. John the Baptist.** The orange tile roof of this large, late-17th-century Franciscan church is a visual icon in Ein Kerem (☞ *below*). Though not mentioned by name in the New Testament, the village has long been identified as the birthplace of John the Baptist, a tradition that apparently goes back to the Byzantine period (5th century AD). The church's old paintings and glazed tiles alone make it worth a visit, and you can also see the grotto where John the Baptist is said to have been born. ⊠ *Ein Kerem Rd., Ein Kerem,* ☎ *02/641–3639.* ⊡ *Free.* ☉ *Apr.–Sept., weekdays 8–noon and 2:30–6, Sun. 9–noon and 2:30–5; Oct.–Mar., weekdays 8–noon and 2:30–5, Sun. 9–noon and 2:30–5.*

**④** **Church of the Visitation.** Built over what is thought to have been the home of John the Baptist's parents, Zechariah and Elizabeth, this church is high up the hillside in Ein Kerem (☞ *below*), with a wonderful view of the valley and the surrounding wooded hills. When Mary, pregnant with Jesus, came to visit her pregnant cousin, the aging Elizabeth, "the babe leaped in [Elizabeth's] womb" with joy at recognizing the unborn Jesus, and Mary pronounced the paean to God known as the Magnificat ("My soul doth magnify the Lord . . . ."—Luke 1). One wall of the courtyard here is thus covered with ceramic tiles quoting the Magnificat in 41 languages. The upper church is adorned with large wall paintings depicting the various mantles with which Mary has been endowed—Mother of God, Refuge of Sinners, Dispenser of All Grace, Help of Christians—and the Immaculate Conception. Other frescoes depict Hebrew women of the Bible also known for their "hymns and canticles," as the Franciscan guide puts it. ⊠ *Ein Kerem,* ☎ *02/641–7291.* ⊡ *Free.* ☉ *Apr.–Sept., Sun.–Fri. 8–11:45 and 2:30–6; Oct.–Mar., daily 8–11:45 and 2:30–5.*

**Ein Kerem.** Now part of Jerusalem, this village boasts a mix of its original working-class population along with artists and professionals. Most live in renovated old stone buildings that have become upscale showpieces. Among the landmarks here are the ☞ **Church of St. John the Baptist** and the ☞ **Church of the Visitation.** Ein Kerem is served by Bus 17.

**㉟** **Mt. Herzl (National Memorial Park).** The simple grave marker of Theodor Herzl, founder of modern Zionism, lies at the top of Mt. Herzl, inscribed in Hebrew with the name Herzl. The site is beautifully landscaped, with cedars of Lebanon lording it over the native pine and cypress. The **Herzl Museum,** to the left of the entrance, preserves Herzl's Viennese study intact.

In 1894 the Budapest-born Herzl was the Paris correspondent for a Vienna newspaper when the Dreyfus treason trial hit the headlines. The anti-Semitic outbursts that Herzl encountered in cosmopolitan Paris shocked him—Dreyfus, a Jewish officer in the French army, had actually been framed and was later exonerated—and thereafter Herzl devoted himself to the problem of Jewish vulnerability in "foreign" host countries and the need, in his eyes, of creating a Jewish state where Jews could control their own destiny. The result of his activities was the first World Zionist Congress, held in Basel, Switzerland, in 1897. That year Herzl wrote in his diary: "If not in five years, then in 50, [a Jewish state] will become reality." The United Nations approved the idea just 50 years later, in November 1947. Herzl died in 1904, and his remains were brought to Israel in 1949.

To the left (west) of the grave site, a gravel path leads down to a section containing the **graves of national leaders,** among them assassinated prime minister Yitzhak Rabin; his predecessors of the 1960s and '70s, Levi Eshkol and Golda Meir; and Zalman Shazar, Israel's third president. ⊠ *Herzl Blvd.,* ☎ *02/651–1108.* ⊡ *Free.* ☉ *Park and museum Apr.–Sept., Sun.–Thurs. 9–6:30, Fri. and holiday eves 9–1; Oct.–Mar., Sun.–Thurs. 9–4, Fri. 9–1.*

**❸❻ Mt. Herzl Military Cemetery.** The tranquillity and well-kept greenery of Israel's largest military cemetery almost belie its purpose. Different sections are reserved for the veterans of the various wars the nation has fought. The large number of headstones, all identical, is a sobering reminder of the price Israel has paid for national independence and security. Officers and privates are buried alongside one another, expressing an Israeli belief that lost lives are mourned equally, regardless of rank. ⊠ *Herzl Blvd.,* ☎ *02/643–7257.* 🎫 *Free.* ☉ *Daily.*

**❸❼ Second Temple Period Model.** Seven years in the building, this huge open-air model—the size of a tennis court—represents ancient Jerusalem at its largest, in the mid-1st century AD. The scale is 1:50, roughly ¼ inch to the foot. Although built around a concrete core, the miniature structures are faced with the same Jerusalem stone as the originals. The model's designer, the late Professor Michael Avi-Yonah, was guided by ancient literary descriptions of Jerusalem and modern archaeological finds. Public works, such as the city's fortifications and King Herod's great reconstructed marble temple (the Second Temple), are thought to be substantially accurate, although private buildings are more generic, reflecting the known architectural style of the period. The model is constantly evolving; whenever new evidence contradicts old assumptions, elements of the model are changed. Pick up an explanatory booklet in the bookstore, or eavesdrop on one of the many guided tours. Buses 21 and 21A arrive here from the city center and the Central Bus Station. ⊠ *Grounds of Holyland Hotel,* ☎ *02/643–7777.* 🎫 *NIS 15 ($4.30).* ☉ *Daily 8 AM–10 PM.*

**★ ❸❹ Yad Vashem.** It's no accident that Yad Vashem—the world's primary national Holocaust memorial and museum—is a mandatory stop on the itineraries of most official guests of the State of Israel. Created in 1953 by an act of the Knesset, it holds the largest Holocaust archive in the world, with more than 50 million documents, and attempts—through its museum, research, and publication departments and its youth-education programs—not merely to document the Holocaust but to convey the challenge of understanding it, especially to younger generations. The name Yad Vashem—"an everlasting memorial"—comes from the biblical book of Isaiah.

Perhaps the most riveting component of Yad Vashem is the **Children's Memorial.** Of the 6 million Jews murdered by the Nazis in World War II, fully a quarter were children, a fact that emphasizes the single-mindedness of the "Final Solution." In trying to do the seemingly impossible—to convey the enormity of the crime without numbing the visitor's emotions or losing sight of the victims' individuality—architect Moshe Safdie found an ingenious solution. Five candles and some 500 mirrors create an infinity of living flames in the dark interior (there are no steps, and guide rails throughout), while recorded narrators intone the names, ages, and countries of origin of known victims. The effect is electrifying.

The **Avenue of the Righteous,** which encircles the site, contains some 5,500 trees bearing plaques with the names of Gentiles in Europe who risked and sometimes lost their lives trying to save Jews from the Nazis. Raoul Wallenberg, King Christian X of Denmark, Corrie ten Boom, and Oskar Schindler are among the more famous honorees. The **Hall of Remembrance** is a heavy basalt-and-concrete building that houses an eternal flame, with the names of the death camps inscribed on the floor.

The **Historical Museum,** entered from Warsaw Ghetto Square, is the centerpiece of Yad Vashem. Through artifacts, photographs, videos, recordings, and explanations in English, it documents the period from

Hitler's rise to power in 1933 through the following 12 nightmarish years to the postwar turmoil that precipitated the birth of Israel. In the same building is the **Art Museum**, a simultaneously beautiful and heart-wrenching display of art and sculpture by Jewish artists—known and unknown, adults and children—who either perished in the Holocaust (while their work survived) or who survived the period and expressed their experiences in their art.

The **Valley of the Communities** was a project of individual Holocaust survivors and survivors' organizations. Walls of enormous rough-hewn limestone boulders create a series of canyons, each representing a region of Nazi Europe, laid out geographically. The names of 5,000 destroyed Jewish communities are inscribed in the stone, with the largest letters highlighting those that were particularly important in prewar Europe.

There is an information booth next to the bookstore at the entrance. Photography is permitted in the Historical Museum, but not in the Children's Memorial or the Art Museum. There is a cafeteria next to the parking lot. ⊠ *Near Herzl Blvd.,* ☎ *02/675–1611.* ▨ *Free.* ☉ *Sun.– Thurs. 9–4:45, Fri. and holiday eves 9–1:45.*

## Center City

West Jerusalem's downtown and near-downtown areas are a mix of old neighborhoods and new limestone edifices, of monuments and markets, of landscapes and peoplescapes. Add the readily accessible (by walk or a quick bus or cab ride) Givat Ram district—with the Israel Museum, the Bible Lands Museum, and the Knesset—and you have an absorbing day's sightseeing.

### A Good Walk and Drive

Begin in the **Yemin Moshe** neighborhood at the famous **Montefiore's Windmill** ④, named for the Anglo-Jewish benefactor who built it in the mid-19th century. The restored carriage in which Moses Montefiore once traveled the country was on display here until it was torched by vandals some years ago; the one you see now is an exact replica. Walk to the edge of the patio adjacent to the windmill—immediately below you is the long roof of **Mishkenot She'ananim,** the first settlement outside the walls of Jerusalem, built by Montefiore in 1860. Today it's a prestigious guest house for visiting artists, writers, and musicians.

Separating you from Mt. Zion and the Old City is the deep **Hinnom Valley,** mentioned in the Bible (Joshua 15) as the border between the Israelite tribes of Judah (to the south) and Benjamin (to the north) and as the site of renewed pagan sacrifices in the 7th century BC. As you face the valley, look to the right. On a hill just a few hundred yards away is the Scottish Church of St. Andrew. Below and to the left of the church, on the bend in the valley known as Ketef Hinnom (the Hinnom Shoulder), an excavation in the late 1970s uncovered a series of tombs. Cut out of the rocky scarp and still visible today, the tombs in turn yielded a treasure trove of archaeological finds.

To your left is the prestigious neighborhood of Yemin Moshe, one of Jerusalem's most affluent. The top of Yemin Moshe is separated from **King David Street** ④ by a small park. Follow the street a short distance to the landmark King David Hotel, a handsome, rectangular limestone building with a back terrace overlooking some well-kept gardens and the Old City walls. Across the street is the imposing YMCA; take the elevator to the top of its tower for stunning panoramas.

Turn left onto Abraham Lincoln Street, immediately after the YMCA. From the small intersection a hundred yards beyond it, a narrow pedestrian lane (George Eliot Street) continues in the same direction, emerging at Agron Street, next to the U.S. Consulate-General. Cross Agron and enter **Independence Park** (not recommended at night) by way of the road 100 yards to your right.

The park's crossroad emerges at Hillel Street, to the north. Immediately across the road is Yoel Moshe Salomon Street, and to the right and parallel is Yosef Rivlin Street, named after two of the seven founders of **Nahalat Shiva** ㊸, the second neighborhood built outside the city walls, established in 1869. At the other end of Salomon Street is Zion Square, where Jaffa Road, Jerusalem's main thoroughfare, is met by **Ben Yehuda Street** ㊹. If you've had enough for one day, take a stroll up Ben Yehuda (on your left) and poke around the shops and cafés of its bustling pedestrian mall.

If you still have strength, time, and patience, cross Jaffa Road at Zion Square and turn left. The first street on the right is Harav Kook, named after Rabbi (*Harav,* in Hebrew) Kook, chief rabbi of Palestine in the British Mandate period. Two hundred yards up the road on the left, a path (clearly signposted in orange) takes you to **Bet Ticho** ㊺, a magnificent limestone house that now houses a small art exhibit and a fine restaurant.

Return to Jaffa Road and turn right. Cross the intersection of King George and Strauss streets (a rare example of a *six*-way pedestrian crossing) and keep going. Six hundred yards farther up Jaffa Road, on your left just beyond the high-rise Clal Center, is the entrance to the **Machaneh Yehuda** ㊻ produce market. At the opposite end of Machaneh Yehuda is Agrippas Street. Across the street and through an arch is a small, somewhat neglected park in the turn-of-the-century neighborhood of Ohel Moshe, where you can sit under a tree and munch on the goodies you've just bought. A left turn on Agrippas Street, on the other hand, brings you down to King George Street and the city center. Bus 9—make sure you take it in the right direction (outside the Hamashbir department store)—will get you in 10 minutes to Givat Ram, site of the Knesset, the Israel Museum and the Bible Lands Museum.

To drive to Givat Ram, take the wide, divided Ruppin Road west from the tall, white condominium complex known as the Wolfson Buildings (on the edge of the Rehavia neighborhood, opposite Sacher Park). Five hundred yards from Sacher Park, at the first traffic light, turn right. The modern, flattop building on the rise to your right is the **Knesset** ㊼, Israel's parliament. The next turn to the right brings you to the security barrier. You may be able to gain entry and let the guards guide you to the parking lot; otherwise, simply park on the street before reaching the barrier. City Bus 9 drops you right at the main gate. Note: you'll have to produce your passport for identification and will be asked to check your camera before entering the building.

The world-class **Israel Museum** ㊽ was built in 1965 as a series of glass and white-stone pavilions clinging to a 22-acre hilltop across Ruppin Road from the Knesset; Buses 9, 17, and 24 stop here. A shuttle bus for passengers with disabilities runs on request from the main gate to the main entrance 200 yards away. The museum's eclectic collection includes the famous Dead Sea Scrolls and extensive art exhibits.

The **Bible Lands Museum** ㊾, across the Israel Museum parking lot, is highly recommended for the archaeology buff and the student of ancient cultures.

## TIMING

This route can easily be separated into the walk (2–2½ hours, not counting breaks) and the Givat Ram cluster of the Knesset and the two museums. Except for the first part of the route (up to the YMCA), the walk is pointless on Saturday, when the downtown area is dead. Friday is great, but shops close early in the afternoon for the Sabbath. You can *view* the Knesset from the outside any time, but there are tours only Sunday and Thursday morning. Allow at least 1½ hours for the tour, more in summer, when the lines are longer. The museums are closed Friday afternoon and have shorter hours on Saturday; visiting during their weekly evening hours is a time-efficient option. The eclectic Israel Museum demands from two to six hours; the Bible Lands Museum is pure archaeology—conceptually challenging, and best done with a local guide.

## Sights to See

**44** **Ben Yehuda Street.** Ben Yehuda has become the nerve center of downtown Jerusalem. Part of the downtown triangle formed with King George Street and Jaffa Road, the street is named after Eliezer Ben Yehuda, who in the late 19th century almost single-handedly revived Hebrew as a modern spoken language. The decision some years ago to close Ben Yehuda to vehicular traffic was opposed by some local merchants, who feared that changing patterns of pedestrian traffic would adversely affect their business. This was true for a few, but most prospered. The mall is called the Midrachov in Hebrew, a combination of *midracha* (sidewalk) and *rechov* (street). Cafés have tables out on the cobblestones, vendors display cheap, arty items like funky jewelry and prints, and buskers are everywhere, playing tunes old and new, good and indifferent. It's a great place to sip coffee and watch the passing crowd.

**45** **Bet Ticho.** This fine, large stone house was built by Dr. A. A. Ticho, a renowned early 20th-century ophthalmologist. Ticho married his cousin, Anna, a trained nurse, who had emigrated from Eastern Europe to join him in his pioneering struggle against the endemic scourge of trachoma. Her artistic talent gradually earned her a reputation as a brilliant chronicler—in charcoal, pen, and brush—of the landscape of Jerusalem's hills. Set among pine trees, off the busy streets of downtown, Bet Ticho houses a permanent exhibit of Anna Ticho's works and a very good restaurant serving light fare (☞ Dining, *below*). ⊠ *Ticho La.,* ☎ *02/624–5068.* ☜ *Free.* ☉ *Sun.–Thurs. 10–5, Fri. 10–2.*

**49** **Bible Lands Museum.** Most archaeological museums group artifacts according to their place of origin (Egyptian, Babylonian, and so on), but the curators here have abandoned this method in favor of a chronological display. This allows a comparison of objects of neighboring cultures of the same period, the better to explore cross-cultural interactions and influences. The museum was the brainchild of Canadian collector Elie Borowski, whose personal collection of ancient artifacts forms its core.

The exhibits cover a period of more than 6,000 years—from the prehistoric Neolithic period to that of the Byzantine Empire—and sweep geographically from Afghanistan to Nubia (present-day Sudan). Rare clay vessels, fertility idols, cylinder seals, ivories, and sarcophagi line the soaring, naturally lit galleries. Look especially for the ancient Egyptian wooden coffin, in a stunning state of preservation. ⊠ *Givat Ram,* ☎ *02/561–1066.* ☜ *NIS 23 ($6.60).* ☉ *Sun.–Tues. and Thurs. 9:30–5:30, Wed. 9:30–9:30 (Nov.–Mar. 1:30–9:30), Fri. and holiday eves 9:30–2, Sat. 11–3. Guided tours in English Sun.–Tues. and Thurs.–Fri. at 10:15, Wed. at 5:30, Sat. at 11:15.*

**Hinnom Valley.** The Hinnom Valley achieved notoriety in the 7th century BC during the long reign of Menasseh (697–640 BC), son of King

Hezekiah. Menasseh was an idolater who "burned his sons as an offering [to the god Moloch] in the valley of the son of Hinnom" (II Chronicles 33). The very name of the valley in Hebrew—Gei Ben Hinnom, contracted to Gehennom or Gehenna—has become a synonym for hell in both Hebrew and Yiddish.

At the bend in the valley, below the fortresslike Scottish Church of St. Andrew, Israeli archaeologist Gabriel Barkai discovered in the late 1970s a series of Old Testament–period tombs cut out of the rocky scarp. An unplundered pit came to light that contained "grave goods" like clay vessels and jewelry. The most spectacular finds were two tiny rolled strips of silver designed to be worn around the neck as talismans. When experts finally unrolled the fragile pieces, they discovered the biblical priestly benediction inscribed in the ancient Hebrew script: "The Lord bless you and keep you; the Lord cause his face to shine upon you and be gracious unto you; the Lord give you peace." This text dates to the 7th century BC, four centuries earlier than the Dead Sea Scrolls, and is the oldest biblical passage ever found.

**Independence Park.** This is a lovely spot for lounging around, throwing Frisbees, or eating a picnic lunch in warm weather. It also holds a Muslim cemetery with several well-preserved tombs dating from the 13th century. A huge reservoir just below the graves, known as the Mamilla Pool, is probably medieval, though it may have even earlier origins.

★ ㊽ **Israel Museum.** Some of these exhibits are among the best of their kind in the world, especially the ones devoted to archaeology and Judaica. The most distinctive edifice in the museum complex is the white, dome-like Shrine of the Book, which houses the famous **Dead Sea Scrolls,** arguably the most important archaeological find ever made in the region. The first of the 2,000-year-old scrolls was discovered by a Bedouin boy in 1947 in a Judean desert, not far from the Dead Sea. The adventures of these priceless artifacts before they finally came to rest here is the stuff of which Indiana Jones movies are made (☞ Dead Sea Region *in* Chapter 3). The shape of the pavilion in which they're housed was inspired by the lids of the clay jars in which the first scrolls were found.

The scrolls were written in the Second Temple period by a fundamentalist Jewish sect generally identified as the Essenes. All of the archaeological, laboratory, and textual evidence dates the earliest of the scrolls to the late 3rd or early 2nd century BC; none could have been written later than AD 68, the year in which their home community, Qumran, was destroyed by the Romans. Written on parchment, and still in an extraordinary state of preservation because of the exceptional dryness of the Dead Sea region, the scrolls contain the oldest Hebrew manuscripts of the Old Testament ever found, authenticating the almost identical Hebrew texts still in use today. Sectarian literature includes "The Rule of the Community" (also known as "The Manual of Discipline"), a constitution of this ascetic group, and "The War of the Sons of Light Against the Sons of Darkness," a blow-by-blow account of a final cataclysmic conflict that would, they believed, presage the messianic age.

Also in the Shrine of the Book, in the basement of the main hall, are artifacts from a slightly later period, that of the Bar Kochba Revolt of AD 132–135. With the collapse of the revolt, Jews fled the Roman legionnaires to remote caves in sheer desert canyons, taking with them their most prized possessions, including woolen blankets, prayer shawls, and a glass bowl of stunning perfection, regarded by scholars as one of the finest examples of ancient glassware ever found.

Next to the shrine is the open-air **Billy Rose Sculpture Garden,** donated by the American impresario and designed by the landscape architect Isamu Noguchi as a series of semicircular terraces divided by stone walls. Crunch over the gravel amid works by Daumier, Rodin, Maillol, Moore, Lipchitz, Nadelman, and Picasso, among many others, all seen against a Judean Hills cityscape. It's a dreamy setting for a picnic.

In the main building, the **Judaica** section, part of the Jewish Heritage collection, has perhaps the world's greatest collection of Jewish ceremonial art and artifacts. Among the highlights are medieval illuminated Haggadot (Passover texts) and Ketubot (wedding contracts), a huge collection of Sabbath spice boxes and Hanukkah menorahs; the interior of a 17th-century Venetian synagogue brought here virtually intact; and a reconstructed 19th-century German sukkah, a temporary booth associated with the holiday of Sukkoth (mentioned in Tabernacles), decorated inside with stylized scenes of Jerusalem. Recently installed is the almost complete 16th-century Kadavumbagam Synagogue, which served the ancient but now defunct Jewish community of Cochin, in India.

Ethnographic exhibits—including dazzling formal costumes and jewelry as well as everyday objects from Jewish communities throughout the Middle East, North Africa, and Eastern Europe—separate the Judaica from the fine-art section. A modest but high-quality collection of European art includes paintings by Van Dyck, Monet, van Gogh, and Renoir. Period rooms reflecting 18th- and 19th-century European design are an unexpected presence. The adjacent **Cummings 20th-Century Art Building** is dedicated to modern and contemporary art, from Cézanne, Picasso, and Chagall to Dubuffet, Rothko, and Lipchitz.

The **archaeology wing,** in the main building, boasts a lucid exhibit of objects found in Israel (and some from elsewhere in the Near East). Visitors are often surprised by Israel's *pre*history. Israel lies on the only land bridge between Africa and Asia, and the museum's wealth of important prehistoric objects from across the country attests to significant movement and settlement across it in the misty past. For many, of course, the focal point of this display is the biblical (Old Testament) period. Pots from the time of Abraham, a Solomonic gateway, and inscriptions from Isaiah's day are just a few of the artifacts that help shed light and immediacy on the history of this ancient land. A side hall holds a superb collection of glass, from rainbow-patinated Roman pieces to sleek Art Deco objects.

☾ There's also a **youth wing,** where delightful hands-on exhibits and workshops encourage children to appreciate art—and a changing variety of other subjects—and try their hand at creation in a do-it-yourself craft workshop. Parents with restless kids will also be grateful for the outdoor play areas. ⊠ *Givat Ram,* ☏ *02/670–8811.* ⊠ *NIS 28 ($8).* ☾ *Sun.–Mon. and Wed.–Thurs. 10–5, Tues. 4–10, Fri. 10–2, Sat. 10–4. Call for details on the many free tours in English.*

㊷ **King David Street.** The famous **King David Hotel** (⊠ 23 King David St.; ☞ Lodging, *below*) was built in 1931 as the country's premier hotel and is one of the most luxurious in the Middle East. Its guest book lists most of the heads of state and other international personalities who have passed through Jerusalem. The artist who decorated the interior columns and ceilings aimed to capture the spirit of the ancient Near East; you might call the result a Mesopotamian motif.

In the 1940s the hotel acquired a degree of notoriety as the British military headquarters in Jerusalem in the twilight of the British Mandate. Great Britain had governed Palestine since seizing it from Ottoman

Turkey in 1918, and the 1939 British "White Paper" severely restricted Jewish immigration to Palestine (European Jews were already being persecuted by the Nazis) and banned Jewish land purchases here. Despite the ensuing outcry, the Palestinian Jewish community (the *Yishuv*) put its opposition to the British on hold when World War II broke out, and joined ranks with Allied forces. When the war ended and the hoped-for British support for the Jewish state (as envisioned by the League of Nations back in 1922) failed to materialize, the Jewish underground became active again. The radical Irgun blew up the south wing of the King David Hotel as a military target in July 1946, with considerable loss of life. The Irgun's claim that its advance warning to evacuate the building was ignored by the British is still a matter of controversy. The wing was rebuilt, with two extra floors, in the 1950s.

The Jerusalem **YMCA** (✉ 26 King David St.; ☞ Lodging, *below*) was dedicated in 1933. Its almost palatial white-limestone facade and high, domed bell tower often surprise visitors who associate that international organization with modest buildings and sports facilities. The Y has those, too, of course, as well as an auditorium with excellent acoustics, built with a Levantine-inspired dome and decorative motifs. The tower, served by a small elevator, is 150 ft high, giving superb views in all directions; you can ride up to the view Monday through Friday between 8 and 5, Saturday between 8 and 1, for NIS 5 ($1.50).

NEED A BREAK? | The **King David Hotel coffee shop** (✉ 23 King David St.) is not cheap, but it serves the best cheese blintzes around. In good weather, the ambience on the garden patio, with its view of the Old City walls, is unbeatable. For a simple cold beer and snack, take a seat on the **YMCA patio** (✉ 26 King David St.), across the street from the King David.

**47** **Knesset.** Both the name Knesset and the number of seats (120) in Israel's one-chamber parliament were taken from Haknesset Hagedolah, the Great Assembly of the Second Temple period. You may see the building only on a 40-minute guided tour (conducted only on Sunday and Thursday), which includes the Knesset session hall and the reception hall, with its three enormous, brilliantly colored tapestries designed by Marc Chagall on the subjects of the Creation, the Exodus, and Jerusalem. On other days, you can attend open sessions of the Knesset (in Hebrew, of course); call ahead for the schedule. You'll need your passport.

"Take two Israelis," runs the old quip, "and you've got three political parties!" The saying is not without truth in a nation where everyone has a strong opinion and will usually not hesitate to express it. The Knesset reflects this rambunctious spirit, sometimes to the point of paralyzing the parliamentary process and driving the public to despair. Israel's electoral system, based on proportional representation, is a legacy of the dangerous but heady days of Israel's War of Independence, in 1948–49. To avoid an acrimonious and divisive election while the fledgling state was still fighting to stay alive, the founding fathers developed a one-body parliamentary system that gave representation to rival ideological factions in proportion to their comparative strength in the country's *pre*-State institutions.

Instead of the winner-takes-all approach of the constituency system, the Israeli system grants any party that wins 1.5% of the *national* vote its first seat in the Knesset. As a result, even fringe parties can have their voices heard. The disadvantage of this system is that it spawns a plethora of political parties, making it virtually impossible for one party to get the majority needed to govern. Israeli governments have thus always consisted of a coalition of parties, often a government of compromise. The smaller parties—whose support is critical for the government to keep its ruling majority—have thus been able to extract major political and material concessions for their own party interests, which are often at odds with those of the nation at large. Extensive discussion, public campaigns, demonstrations, and even proposed legislation to change the system have produced one important result: as of the 1996 general elections, the prime minister is no longer simply the leader of a victorious large party but is elected directly by the voters. This system could produce a deadlock, where the successful candidate for prime minister fails to win a parliamentary majority for his party; already it has produced the unexpected result of strengthening the smaller parties at the expense of the big ones. ⊠ *Givat Ram,* ☎ *02/675–3333.* ⚏ *Free.* ☾ *Guided tours Sun. and Thurs. 8:30–2.*

Across the road from the Knesset main gate is a 15-ft-high bronze menorah, a seven-branch candelabra based on the one that once graced the First and Second Temples in Jerusalem and now the official symbol of the State of Israel. Designed by artist Bruno Elkin and a gift of the British Parliament to the Knesset in 1956, the menorah is decorated with bas-relief depictions of events and personages in Jewish history, from biblical times through the modern day. Behind the menorah (enter below the security barrier) is the Wohl Rose Garden, filled with hundreds of varieties of roses and plenty of lawns for children to romp on.

❹❻ **Machaneh Yehuda.** This block-long alley is filled with the brilliant colors of the city's best-quality fruit and vegetables, pickles and cheeses, fresh fish and poultry, and confection stalls and falafel stands. It's riotously busy, especially on Thursday and Friday, when Jewish Jerusalem shops for the Sabbath. ☾ *Sun.–Tues., about 8 AM–sunset (later on Wed. and Thurs.), Fri. and holiday eves 8 AM–2 hrs before sunset.*

**Mishkenot Sha'ananim.** This building was the first modern neighborhood outside the walls of Jerusalem. Built by Moses Montefiore in 1860, with funds donated by the New Orleans philanthropist Judah Touro, it offered small apartments rent-free to destitute Jews who were prepared to abandon the wretched conditions of the Jewish Quarter and begin a new life. People did not rush to the new project at first, for however dismal life was within the city walls, at least the city gates were shut at night to keep bandits and beasts at bay. In time, however, the neighborhood of Yemin Moshe—named after Moses (Moshe in Hebrew) Montefiore—grew up around it. Today, this splendidly renovated property, with balconies that face the Old City walls, is run by the city-connected Jerusalem Foundation as a retreat for visiting writers, musicians, and artists. ⊠ *Yemin Moshe.*

❹❶ **Montefiore's Windmill.** Moses Montefiore was a prominent and wealthy Jew in the financial circles of 19th-century London—a rare phenomenon at the time. He devoted much of his long life to aiding fellow Jews in distress, wherever they might be. To this end he visited Palestine (as this district of the Ottoman Empire was then known) seven times. The windmill was built in 1857 to provide a source of income for Jews in the new planned neighborhood of Mishkenot She'ananim (☞ *above*), but its location in relation to the prevailing winds was less than strategic. In any event, the windmill was soon superseded by new-fangled steam-driven rivals. The narrow interior of the attractive, tapered limestone structure has a small photographic exhibit on Montefiore's life and works. ⊠ *Yemin Moshe,* ☎ *02/625–4321.* ⚏ *Free.* ☾ *Sun.–Thurs. 8–4, Fri. 8–1.*

❹❸ **Nahalat Shiva.** The name translates roughly as "the Estate of the Seven," for the seven Jewish families that formed an association and established this neighborhood—only the second outside the Old City walls—in 1869. Defying both physical and bureaucratic hostility, they persevered, and they ultimately determined the direction of the growth of the so-called New City. Salomon Street and its adjacent alleys and courtyards have been refashioned as a pedestrian mall and offer the keen photographer and the eager shopper many opportunities. There's a profusion of snack and lunch options.

**Yemin Moshe.** The core of this now-affluent neighborhood is its attractive turn-of-the-century stone buildings. Dangerously near the Jordanian sniper positions on the Old City walls across the valley, the area was largely run-down in the 1950s and '60s, home mainly to families who couldn't afford to move elsewhere. The reunification of Jerusalem after the Six-Day War, in 1967, changed all that. Developers bought up the area, renovated old buildings, and built new and spacious homes in a compatible style. Yemin Moshe is now a place to wander at random. Several artists' galleries are well signposted; the well-known French-style restaurant Mishkenot She'ananim (not part of the original complex) is on your right as you go down the stepped Yemin Moshe Street; and the Mishkenot She'ananim guest house has a pleasant patio café.

OFF THE
BEATEN PATH

**HAAS PROMENADE** – A great way to get your bearings in Jerusalem is to absorb the panorama from this attractive 1-km (⅔-mi) promenade along one of the city's highest ridges. Hidden behind a grove of trees to the east (your right as you pan the view) is a turreted limestone building, the residence of the British High Commissioner for Palestine in the 1930s and '40s. In Hebrew, the whole ridge is known as Armon Hanatziv (the Commissioner's Palace). When the War of Independence ended, in early 1949, the building became the headquarters of the U.N. Truce Supervision Organization (UNTSO), specially formed to monitor the cease-fire line that divided the city. Until the reunification of the city in the Six-Day War of 1967, the site was an enclave between Israeli West Jerusalem and Jordanian-controlled East Jerusalem. You can see quite a bit of West Jerusalem off to your left; it's the downtown area easily distinguished by its high-rises. The Old City, identified by the walls and golden Dome of the Rock, is directly in front of you. To its right is the ridge of Mt. Scopus–Mount of Olives, with its three towers (from left to right, Hebrew University, Augusta Victoria Hospital, Russian Church of the Ascension), separated from the Old City by the deep Kidron Valley. Between the Kidron Valley, to the east, and the Cheesemakers' Valley (now just an asphalt road), to the west, is a blade-shape strip of land that Jerusalem occupied for its first 2,000 years—the City of David. To get here, drive south along Hebron Road. Turn left at the second traffic light, about 1¼ km (¾ mi) beyond the Ariel Hotel, following signs to East Talpiot and the Haas Promenade. The parking lot is on the left.

# DINING

A brief glossary of culinary terms will help you appreciate the pleasures of eating out in Jerusalem. When used in reference to food, the word *Oriental* (the translation of the Hebrew *mizrachi*—"eastern") means Middle Eastern cuisine, *not* Far Eastern (such as Chinese, Japanese, or Thai). Dairy restaurants are simply those serving meals without meat; many such places serve fish as well. Hummus, a ubiquitous dish in this region, is a creamy paste made from chickpeas, moistened with olive oil and often tahini (a sauce based on ground sesame), and scooped up with pieces of flat pita bread. Have hummus at a place that specializes in Middle Eastern dishes; many "Western" establishments serve poor imitations. Also look for a Kurdish-Iraqi specialty called *koubeh,* seasoned ground meat formed into small torpedo shapes and deep-fried in a jacket of bulgur (cracked wheat).

Falafel, the region's fast food, consists of deep-fried chickpea balls served in pita pockets and topped with a variety of vegetables and sauces. It's filling, nutritious, and cheap, at about NIS 7 ($2) for a full portion. About twice that price is *shwarma,* grilled slices of meat (traditionally lamb but now more commonly turkey) also served in pita bread with vegetables and sauces. Both falafel and shwarma are sold at stands; try King George Street, the Ben Yehuda Street open-air mall, the area near the Machaneh Yehuda produce market, or the good cluster of fast-food places on Emek Refa'im Street at the corner of Rachel Imenu, in the German Colony. A specialty of the grills at Machaneh Yehuda, on Agrippas Street, is *me'oorav yerushalmi* (Jerusalem mixed grill), a deliciously seasoned meal of grilled chicken hearts and other organ meats in pita. It's a popular stop after the movies.

Dress codes are pretty much nonexistent in Jerusalem's restaurants (as in the rest of Israel). People tend to dress very casually: jeans are perfectly appropriate in most restaurants, the only possible exceptions being dining rooms at deluxe hotels. Even then it's only a matter of degree; informal dress is acceptable, but a modicum of neatness is expected. Still, if you've taken the trouble to bring your dressy duds, you won't be out of place thus attired in Jerusalem's more exclusive eateries. Remember that kosher restaurants are closed for Friday dinner and Saturday lunch in observation of the Jewish Sabbath.

| CATEGORY | COST* |
| --- | --- |
| $$$$ | over $35 |
| $$$ | $22–$35 |
| $$ | $12–$22 |
| $ | under $12 |

*per person for a three-course meal, excluding drinks and 10% service charge*

## Chinese

**$$**  ✕ **Sini Ba-Moshava (Chinese Colony).** Better known to locals by its Hebrew name, this restaurant occupies an old stone house with a pleasant courtyard for outdoor dining in good weather. It's run by a Taiwanese couple: the wife runs the dining area with charm and panache, while the husband cooks with a sure and creative hand. The crispness of the food—the spring rolls are a good example—testifies to the fact that all dishes are made to order. The hot-and-sour and corn soups are excellent, and the oxtail soup—a local rarity—is fantastic. The long list of entrées includes the usual duck, chicken, beef, pork, shrimp and fish, but each dish has its own character, some strong, some more subtle. The slices of meat are thin and tender, the sweet-and-sour chicken (despite the lurid red sauce) is as good as you'll find anywhere, and the unusual beef in chili-garlic sauce is worth trying. The desserts may not be for the purist, but the Western palate will enjoy *balagan* (chaos), a platter of sweet delights. ⊠ *48 Emek Refa'im St.,* ☎ *02/567–1788. AE, DC, MC, V.*

## French

**$$$$**  ✕ **Arcadia.** You're unlikely to stumble on this place, but it's worth hunting for, housed in an old stone-arched building (with a courtyard for outdoor dining) in a narrow alley between Agrippas Street and Jaffa Road. The menu is imaginative—there's a rich parade of daily specials—and the service, excellent. Two tiny complimentary appetizers set the tone. From the regular appetizer menu, try the calf's brain with sun-dried tomatoes and garlic, or any of the shrimp dishes. For the main course there are several fine beef and lamb dishes, and fish eaters will love the fillet combinations, one in a bouillabaisse sauce, others in aromatic herbal sauces of the day. Save space for dessert: the chocolate praline is exceptional, and the seasonal fruit pies and passion fruit ice cream particularly good. ⊠ *Off 10 Agrippas St.,* ☎ *02/624–9138. Reservations essential. AE, DC, MC, V. Closed Sun.*

**$$$$** ✕ **Mishkenot Sha'ananim.** With a picture window overlooking the illuminated Old City walls, this veteran restaurant is a landmark in its own right. It has one of the region's best wine cellars, extensive if expensive. Melt-in-the-mouth rolls start you off well, but you can pass on the mixed hors d'oeuvres. Excellent main courses include duck à l'orange, veal marsala, veal sweetbreads in a mushroom-and-pastis sauce, and several steak options. An intriguing (and successful) combination is the sea-bass steak cooked in a sweet, fruit-based "exotic" sauce. Desserts are good, not exceptional. ⊠ *Yemin Moshe St., below the Windmill,* ☎ *02/625–4424. AE, DC, MC, V.*

## Grills

**$$$** ✕ **Stanley's.** Stanley combines a native South African's respect for good meat (aged steaks, slow cooking) with some French kitchen techniques and sauces to produce an aesthetic and satisfying dining experience. The arches and niches of the old stone building break the room into intimate sections, and the wooden roof deck is wonderful in nice weather. Excellent appetizers include a foie-gras terrine, a skewer of Portobello mushrooms, chicken wings in an orange sauce, and delicious South African *boerewors* (beef sausage). The best meats are the sirloin steaks and the lamb spare ribs, but you can't go wrong with any of the other carnivorous choices, and there are fish and salad options if you eschew the meat. The "Struggling Artist Lunch Menu" is a real find, with a good steak meal for NIS 35 ($10). A good bar attracts those looking for a drink and a light bite. ⊠ *3 Horkanos St.,* ☎ *02/625–9459. AE, DC, MC, V.*

**$$–$$$** ✕ **El Gaucho.** It's all about red meat at this Argentine grill in the Nahalat Shiva neighborhood. To a stone building with interior arches and a flagstone floor, El Gaucho adds rustic wooden tables, lattice screens, and artifacts from the Argentinian pampas. Munch a delicious beef empanada while you wait for your steak. Best here are the steak entrecôte and the steak chorizo (no relation to the sausage of the same name, though it's also available) with a parsley-based *chimichurri* (herbs with olive oil and vinegar) sauce. The grilled udders and innards are very much an acquired taste. There is a separate children's menu and a few fish dishes for the steak avoider. ⊠ *22 Rivlin St.,* ☎ *02/624–2227. AE, DC, MC, V. Closed Fri. No lunch Sat.*

**$** ✕ **Burger Ranch.** This is a fast-food place, pure and simple, with the expected array of hamburgers, hot dogs, chicken sandwiches, and french fries (known in Israel as chips). The quality is good, but the prices are probably higher than the equivalents in your hometown. ⊠ *16 King George St.,* ☎ *02/623–3766;* ⊠ *43 Emek Refa'im St.,* ☎ *02/666–2318. AE, DC, MC, V. No dinner Fri., no lunch Sat.*

**$** ✕ **La Brasa.** This unassuming eatery on the Salomon Street mall, near Zion Square, specializes in grilled chicken but serves other inexpensive dishes as well, such as beef or chicken sandwiches on crispy rolls. You can fill up for under NIS 35 ($10), a feature that draws a young, budget-conscious crowd. In good weather, take to the street and chow at one of the outdoor tables. ⊠ *7 Salomon St.,* ☎ *02/623–1456. Reservations not accepted. AE, DC, MC, V. No dinner Fri., no lunch Sat.*

# Indian

**$$–$$$** ✕ **Kohinoor.** Graciousness and impeccable service are the hallmarks
**★** of this national tandoori chain, and the Jerusalem branch is no exception.
Low lighting and Indian ornaments and background music set a tone
of quiet yet informal elegance. The cuisine is northern Indian, subtler
and less fiery than the curries of the south. Best of the appetizers are
the chicken wings marinated in ginger, garlic, and spices, then deep-
fried. The breads, served with piquant chutneys and sauces, are great—
just don't fill up on them. Try the *rani nan,* stuffed with shredded chicken,
or the tandoori-baked *kulcha,* stuffed with a nondairy "cheese." For
the main course, try the wonderfully flavored lamb dishes—the *bhuna
gosht* or the *rogan gosht*—or the succulent marinated chicken chunks
baked to redness in a tandoor (clay oven). Vegetarians are far from neglected; the vegetable curries, *sabzi* pilaf, and spinach pureed with a
cottage-cheese substitute will have meat eaters reaching across the
table. End the meal with one (or all) of the fragrant *kulfi*-type ice creams.
The lunch buffet is an excellent value. ✉ *Crowne Plaza Hotel, Givat
Ram,* ☎ *02/658–8867. Reservations essential for dinner Thurs. AE,
DC, MC, V. No dinner Fri., no lunch Sat.*

# Italian

**$$$** ✕ **Spaghettim.** This nonkosher restaurant in an old stone building is
tucked into a side street off one of the city's downtown arteries. The
decor is spare but attractive; the dining rooms are tastefully painted
in pastel neutrals. In summer, the courtyard is filled with tables for al-
fresco meals. Spaghettim is popular with the fashionable young set, but
you can still take the family without breaking the bank. Sauces are
grouped in three categories: tomato-, oil-, and cream-based. The *Bolo-
gnese* sauce is ordinary, but the *arrabbiata* (fiery tomato sauce flavored
with chili peppers) is good; the smoked salmon (with optional as-
paragus), delicious; and the fresh mushrooms (with optional bacon),
sublime. Some of the oil-based sauces are quite spicy. The pasta por-
tions are generous; two youngsters can easily share one. Friendly and
efficient service adds a final welcoming touch, as does the no-smoking
section if you'd prefer it. ✉ *8 Rabbi Akiva St.,* ☎ *02/623–5547 or
02/623–5548. AE, DC, MC, V.*

**$$–$$$** **Pepperoni's.** They do things differently here: the price of a meal in-
cludes a rich selection of tasty antipasti, home-baked rolls, and smoked
sausage as well as an entrée from the chalkboard menu. House spe-
cialties include veal escalope with Parmesan cheese on a bed of pasta;
linguini with olive oil, smoked goose breast, herbs, and cherry toma-
toes; and trout prepared any of several ways. By popular demand, the
menu departs from Italian cuisine to include good steak and pork
chops. We recommend the *panna cotta* or hot chocolate cake for
dessert. The marvelous, age-worn flagstone floor, arched windows, and
ingenious ceiling—cheesecloth stretched taut between wooden beams
and illuminated from behind—create a warm ambience. ✉ *4 Rabbi
Akiva St.,* ☎ *02/625–7829. AE, DC, MC, V.*

**$$** ✕ **Mamma Mia.** A nicely renovated stone building with a shady courtyard houses a restaurant that virtually pioneered the concept of vege-
tarian Italian food in Jerusalem. For an appetizer, try focaccia with
*insalata alla siciliana* (salad of tomato and grated mild feta cheese with
a basil dressing), or the antipasti for two. The cannelloni entrées—especially with salmon—are superb, as is the lasagna; or you can choose
from a wide selection of pizza. All of the pasta is homemade. A refreshing
summer offering is spaghetti primavera, with an uncooked sauce of tomatoes, olive oil, and garlic. ✉ *38 King George St., behind parking lot,*
☎ *02/624–8080. AE, DC, MC, V. No dinner Fri., no lunch Sat.*

**$$** ✕ **Sergio's Friends (Hachaverim Shel Sergio).** The name refers not to Sergio's longtime buddies but to you, his instant friends. This family-run trattoria resembles a village restaurant in Tuscany, Sergio's birth-place. The decor is simple, but the food (no meat, no shellfish) is delicious, and the service lives up to the promise implied in the restaurant's name. The menu changes constantly, depending on the best produce available that day at the market nearby. Good starters include focaccia with rosemary and garlic, and mixed antipasti. The spinach cannelloni is delicious, and there is good pizza for the young 'uns. The kitchen prides itself on its fish dishes: if it's available, try the sea bream (known locally as *denise*), cooked in white wine and capers. Desserts of choice are the tiramisu and the especially good panna cotta. There's no sign outside; go strictly by the address. ⊠ *34 Agrippas St.,* ☎ *02/ 625–5665. Closed Fri. No lunch Sat. No credit cards.*

## Mediterranean

**$$$** ✕ **Le Tsriff.** This very Jerusalemite restaurant, on a downtown back-
★ street, occupies an old house with a great stone patio. Since 1978, it has cultivated a faithful local clientele, from students to celebrities, and earned a reputation for savory pies encased in terrific crusts: chicken with nuts and raisins; veal and prunes; vegetables such as mushrooms and broccoli; and the popular "Mediterranean" pie of eggplant, zucchini, mozzarella cheese, and pesto. The soups, salads, and pies are still good (try the Moroccan *harira* soup), but owner-chef Michal has stirred the menu even further by introducing flavors from her native southern France. For starters, try the hot breaded goat cheese on a bed of leafy salad, or the salmon carpaccio. Specialty entrées include succulent grilled salmon and scallops, tender sirloin with a lovely French-style wine sauce, excellent lamb cutlets, shrimp in a spicy "Spanish" sauce, and roasted sea bream denise in a delectable citrus-ginger sauce. The house dessert is a hot sweet pie, but the pear tart Tatin is excellent, too, and the crème brûlée with ginger is as good as it gets. ⊠ *5 Horkonos St.,* ☎ *02/625–5488 or 02/624–2478. AE, DC, MC, V.*

## Mexican

**$$–$$$** ✕ **Amigos.** Mexican restaurants are rare in Israel, but this one—on the Nahalat Shiva pedestrian mall—would stand proud even in North America. There are sidewalk tables in good weather, and in the evenings the waiters serve to the beat of recorded Latin American music. Sip an arctic-cold margarita (lemon, strawberry, mango, or melon) while you discuss the menu with one of the owners ("If you don't like the food, you don't pay!"). Along with the expected burritos and chili con carne (as well as several vegetarian options) are fajitas, the house specialty: a sizzling combination of grilled slices of beef, chicken, and vegetables served with warm tortillas, refried beans, and guacamole. There's an $8 (NIS 28) lunch menu, and an even cheaper takeout option. At press time, the restaurant was about to open a second-floor "Latin Bar" with counter service. ⊠ *19 Salomon St.,* ☎ *02/623–4177. AE, DC, MC, V. No dinner Fri., no lunch Sat.*

## Middle Eastern

**$$–$$$** ✕ **Eucalyptus.** The traditional cooking of yesteryear's Israel is the pas-
★ sion of owner Moshe Basson, who has rambled across the country quizzing old-timers and searching for wild greens that few people use anymore. The result is an intriguing experience for adventurous palates (and there's good, more typical Middle Eastern fare for their less curious companions). For a tasty appetizer, try the unusual, salty mixture of *sabanach* (wild spinach) with *postulaka* or *hobeiza* greens

(depending on the season); fried koubeh; and either the almond or the Jerusalem-artichoke soup. Stuffed leaves (grape, cyclamen, and many others) come in both meat and vegetarian versions. Especially recommended among the meat dishes are the casserole of chicken, vegetables, and rice, and the figs stuffed with meat and nuts. A "banquet" choice allows you to sample just about everything, a great way of spending the evening if you come with good company, a hearty appetite, and a bigger budget. Arched windows and vaulted ceilings, earth-tone decor, and early 20th-century artifacts, both rural and urban, give the meals an apt period setting. The tree-shaded tables on the adjacent square are a treat in good weather. ⊠ *4 Safra Sq. (next to City Hall complex; opposite 19 Jaffa Rd.),* ☎ *02/624–4331. AE, DC, MC, V. No dinner Fri., no lunch Sat.*

**$$** ✕ **Ima.** It's pronounced "*ee*-mah," means "mom," and is named for Miriam, the owner's Kurdish mother, who still does all the cooking. This restaurant, at the bottom of the Nahla'ot neighborhood, opposite Sacher Park, serves traditional, plentiful, very good Middle Eastern food. First courses include a modest *meze* of some half-dozen salads, such as hummus and *baba ghanoush* (eggplant dip), as well as the excellent koubeh and stuffed vine leaves. Try the tangy koubeh soup, full of dumplings—it's almost a meal in itself. The entrée, which could be *shishlik* (shish kebab) or a Jerusalem mixed grill, is accompanied by *majadra* (rice and lentils). ⊠ *189 Agrippas St.,* ☎ *02/624–6860. AE, DC, MC, V. Closed Sat. No dinner Fri.*

**$–$$** ✕ **Armenian Tavern.** Once a cistern, one floor below street level, this medieval arched restaurant is decorated with fine Armenian wall tiles, a fountain, wooden furniture, and old-style chandeliers. Good starter choices are the excellent koubeh and the *lachmajun,* a so-called Armenian pizza, made with meat and served like a crepe. The best homemade salad is the tahini; some others are blander than their standard Arab equivalents. The most distinctive entrée is the *khaghoghi* (pronounced cha-ror-i) *derev,* vine leaves wrapped around well-flavored ground beef. Both the baklava and the coffee (don't call it *Turkish* coffee here!) are first-class. ⊠ *79 Armenian Patriarchate Rd., Old City, inside Jaffa Gate,* ☎ *02/627–3854. AE, DC, MC, V. Closed Mon.*

**$–$$** ✕ **Mifgash Ha'esh.** Here's a good example of the wisdom of eating where the locals eat. When the restaurant opened a few years ago in the Romema industrial zone behind the Central Bus Station, it gained an almost instant reputation for good food and good value and began attracting Jerusalemites from farther afield—and even the occasional tourist. People flock here for the skewers of grilled meat and particularly the house specialty, succulent grilled pieces of marinated chicken. Appetizers include unusually good hummus, koubeh, and a finely chopped green salad. ⊠ *23 Yirmiyahu St., Romema,* ☎ *02/538–8888 or 02/528–8889. Reservations not accepted. AE, DC, MC, V. No dinner Fri., no lunch Sat.*

## Moroccan

**$$$$** ✕ **Darna.** In an era of (near) peace, Darna's Moroccan-born owner has indulged his nostalgia for his native land, and brought an architect from back home to re-create the "real" Morocco here. The results are delightful: a vaulted peach-painted tunnel deposits you in a corner of Morocco, an asymmetrical arrangement of different-size rooms with stone arches and decorative motifs of wood, copper, pottery, brass, and fabrics. The set menu is a good value, but ordering à la carte gives you more flexibility if you're not up to the generous portions. There's a great selection of salads, with a quite different range of tastes than those in the local Arabic *mezes.* Another excellent starter is *pastilla,* thin phyllo pastry stuffed with almonds, cinnamon, and Cornish hen; there are both vegetarian and fish versions. The couscous is competent, and the various *tagines,* or Moroccan stews, are very good. End the meal with refreshing, green mint tea (served with fine ceremony), and, if you have room, the candied fruits or the exquisite *toubkal* delight, a sweet pastilla done in cinnamon and (nondairy) almond milk. ⊠ *3 Horkonos St.,* ☎ *02/624–5406. AE, DC, MC, V. Closed Fri. No lunch Sat.*

## Seafood

**$$$$**   ✕ **Aqua.** Softly lit and tastefully decorated (creams predominate), this tranquil corner of the new Jerusalem Hilton was created by renowned French chef Jacques Le Divellec, and his local understudy, Eric Attias, does very well. Aqua's hallmark is superb service: the staff is professional, friendly, and intelligent. Follow the complimentary hot and cold starters with the tantalizingly unusual Fisherman's Soup or the delicious sautéed mushrooms. Among the entrées (no shellfish; the restaurant is kosher), a standout is the sea bream baked with sesame seeds and served with a smoked-salmon risotto. Chocolate lovers will enjoy the "Degrade" for dessert, but do ask about the seasonal sabayon with lightly cooked, unsweetened mixed berries. The prices, while high, are quite reasonable for a restaurant of this caliber. ⊠ *Jerusalem Hilton Hotel, 7 King David St.,* ☎ *02/621–1111. Reservations essential. AE, DC, MC, V. Closed Fri.–Sat. No lunch.*

**$$$–$$$$**   ✕ **Michael Andrew.** Housed in a stone building overlooking the Old
★   City (ask for a window table), this fine restaurant defines itself as Belgian. Chef-owner Michael, half-Belgian himself, spent several years working in highly rated Brussels restaurants and now blends his imported skills with local produce. The results are impressive. All fish are served filleted, complemented by delectable, imaginative, and well-balanced sauces, lighter and more subtle than you'd expect from their French counterparts (no two dishes use the same sauce). The menu changes completely every two months, and half the offerings at any given time are specials of the day. Try the fish soup, typically a consommé in summer, a piquant tomato-based chowder in winter. Those avoiding fish can choose from a few vegetable-based entrées. The superb crème brûlée, when available, is the dessert of choice. For an intimate dinner for two in good weather, ask for the balcony table off the kitchen, where the ethereal views of the illuminated Old City walls create an unmatched ambience (just dress warmly). The staff is charming, and the business lunch is a good deal. ⊠ *12 Emil Botta St. (in Zionist Confederation House, in the park),* ☎ *02/624–0090. AE, DC, MC, V. In summer, no dinner Fri., closed Sat. In winter, closed Fri., no lunch Sat.*

## Vegetarian

**$$–$$$**   ✕ **Little Jerusalem ("Bet Ticho").** This is one of downtown Jerusalem's loveliest, most tranquil nooks. Now a national monument, the imposing stone building was built in the 1920s as the home and office of the famous ophthalmologist A. A. Ticho and his even more famous wife, artist Anna Ticho, whose evocative drawings of Jerusalem adorn the place. The lobby and patio have been turned into a fine restaurant for light meals. House specialties include sublime salmon blintzes, onion soup served *inside* a crusty loaf of bread, fish in fresh ginger sauce, and a variety of pasta and sautéed veggie dishes. Portions are very generous: share rather than over-order. Desserts are sinfully wonderful, from the apple strudel and various cakes to the ice cream cake topped with hot fudge. On Tuesday night there's a wine-and-cheese buffet, accompanied by a jazz combo (reserve in advance); on Friday at 11 AM, there's live chamber music. Angle for a table on the patio in nice weather. ⊠

# Jerusalem Dining and Lodging

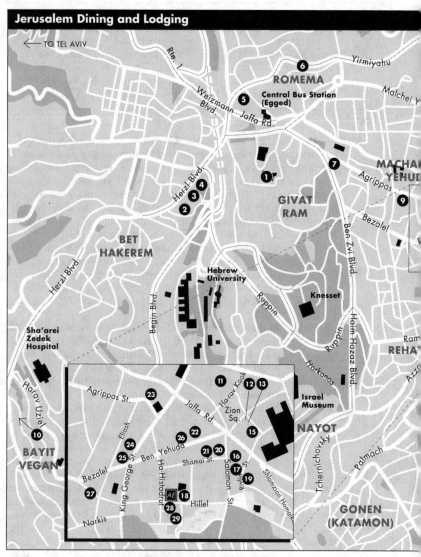

← TO TEL AVIV

**Dining**

Amigos, **17**
Aqua, **34**
Arcadia, **8**
Armenian Tavern, **50**
Burger Ranch, **25, 47**
Darna, **13**
El Gaucho, **19**
Eucalyptus, **14**
Ima, **7**
Kohinoor, **1**
La Brasa, **16**
Le Tsriff, **12**

Little Jerusalem **11**
Mamma Mia, **31**
Michael Andrew, **36**
Mifgash Ha'esh, **6**
Mishkenot
Sha'ananim, **48**
Pepperoni's, **28**
Sergio's Friends, **9**
Sini Ba-Moshava, **46**
Spaghettim, **29**
Stanley's, **15**
Te'enim, **45**
Village Green, **26, 27**

**Lodging**

American Colony, **52**
Ariel, **44**
Bet Shmuel, **33**
Christ Church, **51**
Crowne Plaza, **1**
Eyal, **21**
Four Points
Jerusalem, **3**
Hyatt Regency, **53**
Jerusalem Hilton, **34**
Jerusalem Inn, **14**
Jerusalem Tower, **18**
Kikar Zion, **20**

King David, **35**
King Solomon, **39**
Laromme, **41**
Lev Yerushalayim, **24**
Louise Waterman-
Wise, **10**
Mercure–Jerusalem
Gate, **5**
Mount Zion, **43**
Palatin, **23**
Park Plaza, **4**
Prima Kings, **32**
Radisson Moriah
Plaza, **38**

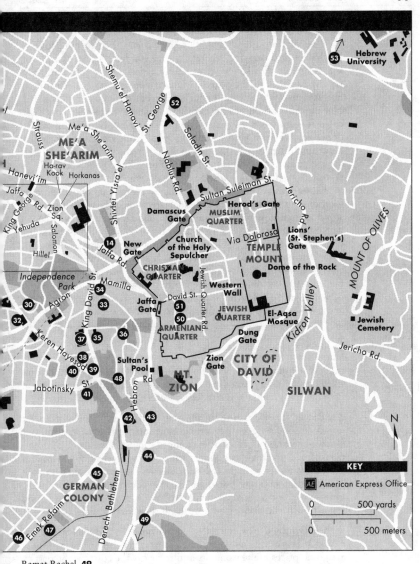

*7 Harav Kook St., ☎ 02/624–4186. Reservations not accepted for outdoor tables. AE, DC, MC, V. No dinner Fri., no lunch Sat.*

**$$**   ✕ **Te'enim.** The name means "figs," and if you're a vegetable lover— let alone a card-carrying vegetarian—the Garden of Eden association is inescapable. The soups are excellent, especially the refreshing soy-flavored miso and the sorrel (when available). Try the Portobello mushrooms with polenta, or the simple but delicious arugula salad. Hot quiches and pies change constantly, and every weekday is dedicated to a different culinary tradition—Japanese, Italian, Indian, Indonesian, Mexican, and Middle Eastern. Regulars choose their day accordingly. Apart from the delicately flavored coffee parfait, desserts are the restaurant's weak spot. ⊠ *21 Emek Refa'im St., ☎ 02/563–0048. No credit cards. Closed Sat. No dinner Fri.*

**$–$$**   ✕ **Village Green.** This purely vegetarian restaurant has two downtown locations, both self-service. On Bezalel Street you can retreat into a quiet stone courtyard, while on bustling Ben Yehuda Street you can people-watch as you eat. There is a good variety of soups, quiches, pies, and wonderfully fresh vegetable salads, with a choice of great dressings. Several menu items have three prices—these indicate the item by itself, with a small salad, and with a large salad. Every meal comes with home-made bread. The dessert pies are worth trying. ⊠ *1 Bezalel St., ☎ 02/625–1464; ⊠ 10 Ben Yehuda St., ☎ 02/625–2007. Reservations not accepted. AE, DC, MC, V. Closed Sat. No dinner Fri.*

## Cafés

Sitting down for coffee and cake in one of Jerusalem's fine cafés is something of a tradition. The selection of sweets includes the gooey, cream-filled pastries many Israelis favor; more sophisticated cheesecakes and pies; and yeast cakes and strudels, a Central European inheritance.

The downtown **Midrachov,** the open-air mall of Ben Yehuda Street and its side lanes, has several venerable hangouts from an earlier era, but a new generation of cafés offers a more sophisticated menu and better coffee. Two neighborhood arteries—Azza Street, in **Rehavia,** and Emek Refa'im Street, in the **German Colony**—are well stocked with popular watering holes, a few of which serve decent light meals as well. On summer evenings in particular, these places teem with the young set; arrive in mid-evening to beat the après-show crowd.

In the downtown area, the self-service **Aroma** (⊠ 18 Hillel St., ☎ 02/625–5365) is brash and young and almost never closes. The croissants are good, prices are reasonable, and some say the coffee is the best in town. Just up the road is the newly fashionable **Hillel** (⊠ 8 Hillel St., ☎ 02/624–7775), with a spacious interior, a breakfast menu, and good prices. Opposite, and in a wide alley, is **Second Cup** (⊠ 4 Shammai St., but just off Hillel St., ☎ 02/623–4533), with good brownies and muffins, a remarkable selection of coffees, and some upholstered armchairs in the no-smoking section.

**Conus** (⊠ 18 King George St., ☎ 02/625–5317), next to the Hamashbir department store, is the outlet for a local maker of excellent Italian-style ice cream and gelato. **Dalia Renaud's Bistro** (⊠ In the lane off 10 Agrippas St., ☎ 02/625–7647) has a lot of atmosphere—arches and flagstones, genteel personal attention—and superb but very pricey cakes (and light meals).

A sign of the times is **Netcafe** (⊠ 9 Helene Hamalka St., ☎ 02/624–6327), where you can surf the Net and check your e-mail over a good cup of coffee.

**Paradiso,** at a new location opposite the King Solomon Hotel (✉ 36 Keren Hayesod St., ☎ 02/563–4805), does light meals, coffee, and exceptional cakes.

**Jan's** (✉ 20 Marcus St., ☎ 02/561–2054), under the plaza of the Sherover (Jerusalem) Theater, is a one-of-a-kind café. You sit or lounge on soft pillows and rugs, with low lights and Asian ornaments adding to the mysterious atmosphere. The menu isn't extensive—the ambience is all—but what's served is very good (and not cheap). It's better for romantic assignations than clubby conversation.

# LODGING

Some travelers insist on a hotel in a central location; others prefer to retreat to a haven at the end of the day, with ambience more important than accessibility. Jerusalem has more of the first kind of hotel than the second; even hotels once considered remote are now no more than 10 minutes by cab or hotel minibus from the city center. In truth, with only a few exceptions, most hotels are modern, with little claim to old-world charm.

Many Jerusalem hotels can be grouped by the following locations: on or near the downtown triangle formed by King George Street, Jaffa Road, and Ben Yehuda Street (Sheraton Jerusalem Plaza, Lev Yerushalayim, Jerusalem Tower, Kikar Zion, Eyal, Zion); near the city center (and most convenient to Jaffa Gate and the Old City), near the intersection of King David and Keren Hayesod streets (King David, Laromme, King Solomon, Radisson Moriah Plaza, Mt. Zion, Windmill, Ariel, YMCA [West], Scottish Hospice); in West Jerusalem between the Central Bus Station and Givat Ram, on major city bus routes (Holiday Inn Crowne Plaza, Renaissance Jerusalem, Caesar, Jerusalem Gate, Park Plaza, Four Points Jerusalem). A few defy the above categories (Hyatt Regency, Ramat Rachel, Waterman-Wise). An interesting alternative is a kibbutz guest house in the forested hill country, a 20-minute drive from the city center (Neve Ilan, Ma'aleh Hahamisha, Kiryat Anavim, and Shoresh); it's best to have a car to reach these (☞ West of Jerusalem *in* Chapter 3).

Hotels in Arab East Jerusalem, which are generally in the less-expensive categories, were seriously affected by Palestinian street violence in the late 1980s and early '90s. The ensuing shrinkage of hotel occupancy there has, unfortunately, led to a widespread decline in standards as well. We still recommend, however, the American Colony Hotel.

Rates quoted by hotels are the maximum regular-season rates, but remember that it's quite common to get a room at a price below the published rate, especially off- season. The high season typically includes 10 days to a month around the Jewish holiday of Passover (March–April), a similar period over the Jewish holidays in September and October (High Holy Days and Sukkoth), part of the summer, and, for some hotels, the Christmas season. Because there is considerable variation in what different hotels consider high season, and because the dates of Jewish holidays shift annually in accordance with the Jewish calendar, the difference in room rates can be significant; it's worth confirming the rate before making a firm reservation.

All hotels are heated, and all in the $$$$ and $$$ categories (as well as some of those more moderately priced) have air-conditioning and telephones in the rooms.

| CATEGORY | COST* |
| --- | --- |
| **$$$$** | over $200 |
| **$$$** | $100–$200 |
| **$$** | $60–$100 |
| **$** | under $60 |

*All prices are for two people in a standard double room, including breakfast and 15% service charge.*

**$$$$**   **American Colony Hotel.** This onetime pasha's palace, a cool lime-
★   stone oasis with a flower-bedecked inner courtyard, has been a hotel
for more than a century. It's a 10-minute walk from the Damascus Gate,
in East Jerusalem, but worlds away from the hubbub of the Old City.
A favorite haunt of American and British expats, international journalists, and diplomats, the hotel (now affiliated with Relais & Châteaux)
is noted for its ambience and good service. The recently refurbished
guest rooms are comfortable but not sumptuous, with unexceptional
furniture, the occasional Turkish or Syrian artifact, and Oriental area
rugs covering stone floors. The better rooms are spacious and more
individualized, usually topped with vaulting or an antique painted-wood
ceiling. Some have hot tubs. In the public areas, decorative touches such
as turquoise-and-blue tilework, Damascene wood inlay, and plenty of
potted palms lend a Mediterranean air. The restaurant Arabesque is
known for its excellent (nonkosher) Continental dishes, though at
press time it was on the way to increasing and highlighting the Middle Eastern side of its menu. ⊠ *Nablus Rd., Box 19215, 97200,* ☎
*02/627–9777,* ℻ *02/627–9779. 7 suites, 77 rooms with bath. 3
restaurants, bar, pool. AE, DC, MC, V.*

**$$$$**   **Crowne Plaza.** A quintessential business and convention hotel, the
Crowne Plaza is a tower block that dominates the city's western skyline, giving almost all of the rooms—and particularly those on the top
five floors—sweeping views of some part of Jerusalem. Rooms are not
especially large, but their decoration, in tasteful pastels and light earth
tones, makes them feel light and airy. The lobby-level dairy restaurant–
cum–bar–cum–coffee shop, serves superb cakes and pastries, and the
Kohinoor Indian restaurant and the new Oasis fish restaurant are real
treats. The small, informal health club is privately owned, but guests
of the hotel enjoy a special rate. ⊠ *Givat Ram (West Jerusalem),
91130,* ☎ *02/658–8888,* ℻ *02/651–4555. 397 rooms with bath.
4 restaurants, bar, pool, sauna, hot tub, miniature golf, tennis court,
health club, playground, business services. AE, DC, MC, V.*

**$$$$**   **Hyatt Regency.** Cascading down Mt. Scopus, the Hyatt Regency has
the most dramatic setting of any hotel in Jerusalem, and the boldest
design (it's built around seven courtyards). The lobby is a stylish combination of stone, leather seating, and greenery. Guest rooms, about
one-third of which have views of the Old City, are spacious and decorated with stone-top tables, Castel prints, and light colors. Thorough-
going renovations (through 1999) are not expected to inconvenience
guests. The pool area, with an adjacent playground, is a cool enclave
of palms and plants. The sophisticated, independently owned Jerusalem
Spa offers cosmetic and therapeutic treatments in addition to the standard facilities, and hotel guests receive a discounted day rate. Valentino's,
the in-house Italian restaurant, is recommended. ⊠ *32 Lehi St., 97856,*
☎ *02/533–1234,* ℻ *02/581–5947. 503 rooms with bath. 4 restaurants, bar, 1 indoor pool (fee) and 1 outdoor pool, beauty salon, sauna,
steam room, hot tub, 2 tennis courts, health club, nightclub, business
services. AE, DC, MC, V.*

**$$$$**   **Jerusalem Hilton.** This hotel makes a powerful first impression with
its stonework and arches, and the fine aesthetics are carried over into
the spacious guest rooms. Furnishings are in soft tones of beige and
cream; wall hangings include stone mosaics in an ancient style; and bath-

rooms are well appointed. The lobby, however, is cold and uninviting, a monument to the architect rather than a welcoming vestibule. The in-house fish restaurant, Aqua (☞ Dining, *above*), is an excellent excuse to dine in. ⊠ *7 King David St., 94101,* ☎ *02/621–1111,* FAX *02/621–1000. 381 rooms with bath. 3 restaurants, bar, pool, sauna, exercise room, business center. AE, DC, MC, V.*

$$$$ 🏨 **King David Hotel.** The grande dame of Israeli luxury hotels opened ★ in 1931 and has successfully defended its title ever since. The lobby, whose ceilings, columns, and walls are covered with "ancient" geometric decoration, is comfortable but bustling, very much a part of the nearby reception area. For more privacy, try the bar. Renovations have transformed the already spacious and elegant rooms into symphonies of tasteful cream and brown, with old-fashioned writing tables a gracious addition. The pricier rooms have views of the Old City. The large pool, in a beautifully landscaped garden behind the hotel, may tempt you away from your touring in hot weather. The in-house French-style grill restaurant, La Régence, is highly regarded locally. ⊠ *23 King David St., 94101,* ☎ *02/620–8888,* FAX *02/624–6847. 249 rooms with bath. 3 restaurants, bar, 2 pools, tennis court, exercise room, shops, business services. AE, DC, MC, V.*

$$$$ 🏨 **Laromme.** A low-rise building of Jerusalem stone (limestone) wrapped around a central courtyard and atrium, the Laromme is more appealing for its architecture and friendly, energetic staff than for its decor. The furnishings in the public areas are rather ordinary, though they're helped by a profusion of plants. Recent refurbishing has improved the guest rooms, some of which have balconies and fine views. The newly enlarged pool is chlorine-free, kept clean by a newfangled substitute. Despite its unexceptional aesthetics, there's something about the hotel— perhaps the lively atmosphere and amiable staff—that has made the Laromme one of the most popular in its category. Its location next to the playgrounds of Liberty Bell Garden is a plus for families. ⊠ *3 Jabotinsky St., 92145,* ☎ *02/675–6666,* FAX *02/675–6777. 294 rooms with bath. 3 restaurants, bar, pool, beauty salon, sauna, hot tub. AE, DC, MC, V.*

$$$$ 🏨 **Radisson Moriah Plaza.** The Moriah has long been outclassed by its luxury peers, but planned major renovations through 1999 are expected to upgrade both the guest rooms and the public areas radically. The small size of the rooms, however, remains a drawback. Advantages are the excellent location, convenient to downtown and the Old City; the pleasant atmosphere; and the ministrations of the hotel's efficient staff. ⊠ *39 Keren Hayesod St., 94188,* ☎ *02/569–5695,* FAX *02/623–2411. 292 rooms with bath. 3 restaurants, bar, pool, health club, beauty salon. AE, DC, MC, V.*

$$$$ 🏨 **Renaissance Jerusalem.** Polished stone walls and copper fixtures in the reception and lounge areas add class to this large, modern hotel, whose rates are modest for this price category. The recently renovated rooms are quite spacious, though the bathrooms are small. The high points are the large outdoor pool and the equally large heated indoor pool and health club, all free to registered guests. The hotel is on the west side of town, adjacent to Hebrew University's Givat Ram campus. A complimentary shuttle bus transports you downtown, to Jaffa Gate, and to the Western Wall. ⊠ *Ruppin Bridge, at Herzl Blvd., 91033,* ☎ *02/659–9999,* FAX *02/651–1824. 650 rooms with bath. 3 restaurants, 2 bars, 1 indoor and 1 outdoor pool, beauty salon, saunas, hot tub, tennis court, health club. AE, DC, MC, V.*

$$$$ 🏨 **Sheraton Jerusalem Plaza.** Not far from the lively shopping area on Ben Yehuda Street, the 22-story Sheraton looks like a big business hotel anywhere, complete with look-alike guest rooms (big beds, big closets), but it actually has more to recommend it. The balcony views

of the Old City are spectacular, and those of the New City are almost as impressive. The nonmeat Italian restaurant, Primavera, has won kudos locally, and the expensive French restaurant, Cow on the Roof, is considered the hotel's calling card. At press time, the hotel was about to embark on a major renovation. ⊠ *47 King George St., Box 7686, 91076,* ☎ *02/629–8666,* ℻ *02/623–1667. 300 rooms with bath. 4 restaurants, bar, pool, beauty salon, massage, sauna. AE, DC, MC, V.*

**$$$** 🏨 **Ariel.** The Ariel was originally conceived as an apartment hotel, so an early change in plans left it with a good number of spacious guest rooms, some large enough to accommodate families. About a third of the rooms have excellent views of Mt. Zion. Extensive bathroom renovations and some new bedroom furniture have raised the comfort level. The public areas—lobby, bar, and dining room—have been completely redone as well, with copious plants balancing the new marble. The railway station is nearby. ⊠ *31 Hebron Rd., 93546,* ☎ *02/568–9999,* ℻ *02/673–4066. 128 rooms with bath. Restaurant, bar. AE, DC, MC, V.*

**$$$** 🏨 **Eyal.** A central downtown location makes this well-kept hotel a good choice at the very bottom of this price range. Rooms are not too cramped, and although the decor is unexceptional (think faux-wood paneling), the presence of TVs and refrigerators—unusual in this category—adds up to good value. Ask for an "outer" room, facing the street. ⊠ *21 Shammai St., 94631,* ☎ *02/623–4161,* ℻ *02/623–4167. 71 rooms with bath. Restaurant, bar. AE, DC, MC, V.*

**$$$** 🏨 **Four Points Jerusalem.** Although there's nothing particularly remarkable in the look of this hotel on Jerusalem's west side, its recreational facilities make it a standout in its price category. The health club—complete with indoor pool, exercise room, sauna, and whirlpool bath—and the grassy pool area provide delightful, relaxing environments at the end of an intense day of sightseeing. ⊠ *4 Vilnai St., 91036,* ☎ *02/655–8888,* ℻ *02/651–2266. 200 rooms with bath. Restaurant, bar, 1 indoor and 2 outdoor pools, hot tub, sauna, exercise room, health club. AE, DC, MC, V.*

**$$$** 🏨 **Jerusalem Tower.** This hotel is in a choice location: bang in the center of downtown. The café-bar is an inviting asymmetrical room with quiet corners. Guest rooms are small but tastefully decorated, with upholstered headboards and stone tabletops. Ask for a room above the sixth floor to guarantee a view. ⊠ *23 Hillel St., Box 2656, 94581,* ☎ *02/620–9209,* ℻ *02/625–2167. 120 rooms with bath. Restaurant, bar, café. AE, DC, MC, V.*

**$$$** 🏨 **Kikar Zion.** Although this seven-story building dominates downtown Zion Square (Kikar Zion in Hebrew), the entrance is a very modest doorway off Shammai Street a half block away, where the elevator takes you up to the huge lobby. High above street level, the guest rooms are quiet and spacious, with light-gray felt wall coverings lending warmth and intimacy. The rooms wrap around the building, affording good views of the city; insist on a high floor facing either the Old City or Independence Park. Guests pay a nominal fee to use the privately owned health club. ⊠ *25 Shammai St., 94631,* ☎ *02/624–4644,* ℻ *02/624–4136. 120 rooms with bath. 2 restaurants, bar, health club. AE, DC, MC, V.*

**$$$** 🏨 **King Solomon.** The centerpiece of the lobby is a huge, spherical sculpture of Jerusalem by Frank Meisler. Alcoves in the adjacent coffee shop allow a degree of privacy. A split-level atrium reveals shops one floor down and restaurants below that. The standard guest rooms are not spacious, but the more deluxe ones are quite large. The rooms are attractive, with brown and tan predominating, enhanced by sepia prints above the beds. The well-equipped bathrooms are more spacious than most. Rates are at the upper end of the price range, but the deluxe aesthetic makes them a good value. ⊠ *32 King David St., 94101,* ☎ *02/*

569–5555, ⨳ 02/624–1774. *142 rooms with bath, 6 suites. 2 restaurants, bar, pool, beauty salon. AE, DC, MC, V.*

**$$$** ⊞ **Lev Yerushalayim.** One of the best bargains in its price category, this all-suite hotel is in the heart of the city center. You leave the heat and noise behind as you enter the stone-walled, plant-filled lobby. Suites are decorated in soothing pinks and grays. Prices are per suite for two guests; additional guests using the sofa beds pay an extra $50 per night for an adult and $25 per night for a child under 12. Deluxe suites are defined by an additional room with sofa beds—for a family, easily worth the small extra charge—not by a higher grade of furnishings. Breakfast is included, but you can make other meals in your kitchenette. The use of the on-site Samson's Gym (gym, whirlpool bath, sauna, solarium) is free to hotel guests. ⊠ *18 King George St., 91079,* ☎ *02/530–0333,* ⨳ *02/623–2432. 57 suites, 27 deluxe suites, 2 royal suites, 6 penthouses. 2 restaurants, hot tub, sauna, exercise room, health club, coin laundry. AE, DC, MC, V.*

**$$$** ⊞ **Mercure–Jerusalem Gate.** The Jerusalem Gate caters to business travelers and tour groups. It's adjacent to the old Central Bus Station and on many convenient bus routes, though not a short walk to anywhere in particular. The guest rooms are reasonably spacious, and their pastel colors make them look more so. Ask for a room that faces north, so you'll have a view across the hills and beyond the city. The attractive bar on the mezzanine overlooking the lobby has a copper ceiling. The rooftop sundeck is a welcome haven. ⊠ *43 Yirmiyahu St., 94467,* ☎ *02/500–2225,* ⨳ *02/500–2121. 298 rooms with bath. Restaurant, bar, business services. AE, DC, MC, V.*

**$$$** ⊞ **Mount Zion.** The core of the Mount Zion is a renovated 19th-century building that once served as a British eye hospital. To this a new, similar wing was added in the 1970s. Columns, arched doorways, and windows in Jerusalem stone all frame ethereal views of Mt. Zion and create attractive nooks filled with wall hangings, Armenian tiles, and plants. New ownership and management seem to be realizing the hotel's phenomenal potential and thus changing its once mediocre reputation. The rooms in the new wing were recently renovated, but the rooms in the old wing are still superior; they have character and better views. An octagonal swimming pool and children's pool overlook the Hinnom Valley. The gym (with its own picture window) is free to guests; the charming new "water spa" (hot pool, sauna, and both indoor and outdoor whirlpool baths) asks a nominal fee. ⊠ *17 Hebron Rd., 93546,* ☎ *02/568–9555,* ⨳ *02/673–1425. 135 rooms with bath, 5 with shower. 2 restaurants, bar, pool, wading pool, health club. AE, DC, MC, V.*

**$$$** ⊞ **Park Plaza.** This West Jerusalem hotel—the old Sonesta—has a good local reputation. Its rooms are small and its facilities limited, but recent renovations have made a difference and added a touch of class to both guest rooms and public areas. ⊠ *2 Vilnai St., Box 3835, 95435,* ☎ *02/658–2222,* ⨳ *02/658–2211. 217 rooms with bath. Restaurant, bar. AE, DC, MC, V.*

**$$$** ⊞ **Prima Kings.** The Kings—the name by which it's still known—is on a noisy intersection less than 10 minutes' walk from the city center. It's been transformed by ongoing renovations, so be sure to ask for one of the new rooms. Cane furniture and deep sofas create comfortable, if not particularly intimate, public areas. Most of the guest rooms are fairly spacious, an effect that's enhanced by light colors. ⊠ *60 King George St. (entrance on Ramban St.), 94262,* ☎ *02/620–1201,* ⨳ *02/620–1211. 187 rooms with bath. 2 restaurants, bar. AE, DC, MC, V.*

**$$$** ⊞ **Ramat Rachel.** As a rustic kibbutz hotel less than 15 minutes' drive
★   from downtown, at the southern end of the Bus 7 route, Ramat Rachel enjoys the best of both worlds. Most rooms have stunning views of

Bethlehem and the Judean Desert. The older rooms have all been brought up to the standard of those in the new wing, which opened in 1998. The pleasant if unexceptional decor is offset by the brilliant colors of Calman Shemi quilted "soft art" originals above each headboard. With its fine pool and other sports and health facilities, all free to guests, Ramat Rachel feels like an isolated resort. ⊠ *Kibbutz Ramat Rachel, Jerusalem 90900,* ☎ *02/670–2555,* FAX *02/673–3155. 164 rooms with bath. Restaurant, bar, pool, beauty salon, saunas, hot tub, 3 tennis courts, basketball, exercise room, playground. AE, DC, MC, V.*

$$$ 🏨 **Windmill.** This hotel is comfortable but fairly nondescript, with unobtrusive decor other than an abundance of plants in the public areas. Its rates are high for what it offers, but the location—on a side street opposite the Radisson Moriah Plaza, near the city center and on good bus routes—counts for something. ⊠ *3 Mendele St., off Keren Hayesod, 92147,* ☎ *02/566–3111,* FAX *02/561–0964. 133 rooms with bath. Restaurant, bar. AE, DC, MC, V.*

$$$ 🏨 **YMCA (West)–3 Arches.** Built in 1933, this limestone building with its famous domed bell tower is a Jerusalem landmark. Stone arches, exotic murals, wooden cupboards, and Armenian tiles give it charm and character. The guest rooms are not large, but renovations have made them attractive and comfortable, and added air-conditioning. These and an excellent location make the Y an attractive deal at the upper end of this price category. On the premises are excellent sports facilities, an auditorium for concerts and folkloric performances, and the privately run Le Tsriff restaurant (☞ Dining, *above*). ⊠ *26 King David St., Box 294, 91002,* ☎ *02/659–2692,* FAX *02/623–5192. 52 rooms with bath, 4 with shower. Restaurant, café, pool, sauna, 4 tennis courts, basketball, exercise room, indoor track, squash. AE, DC, MC, V.*

$$ 🏨 **Bet Shmuel.** This relatively new stone building, with cool inner
★ courtyards and fabulous views of the Old City from the roof and almost half the rooms, was built not just as a guest house but as a cultural and educational center of the World Union for Progressive Judaism. Its spacious rooms, which can sleep six, are bright and pleasant, with blond-wood furniture, if a little spare. The location is excellent: only 5 minutes' walk to the Old City, 10 to the center of town. There's just one drawback: in good weather the central courtyard is used for Friday-night concerts and occasional receptions, rendering the guests in many rooms involuntary participants. ⊠ *13 King David St. (entrance on Shammai St.), 94101,* ☎ *02/620–3456,* FAX *02/620–3467. 41 rooms with shower. Restaurant, coffee shop. AE, DC, MC, V.*

$$ 🏨 **Christ Church.** This is the guest house of the adjacent Anglican church, the oldest Protestant church (1849) in the Middle East. Rooms in the two old stone buildings (once a pilgrim hospice) are comfortably furnished, if not exactly luxurious; the eight new rooms are air-conditioned. The location, in the Old City just inside Jaffa Gate, is excellent for sightseeing, though many people are more at ease in modern West Jerusalem. Children 12 and under pay only a small supplement. ⊠ *Jaffa Gate, Old City, Box 14037, 91140,* ☎ *02/627–7727 or 627–7729,* FAX *02/628–2999. 32 rooms with bath. Dining room, coffee shop. MC, V.*

$$ 🏨 **Jerusalem Inn.** All of these rooms have little balconies overlooking shady side streets near Zion Square, downtown. Inside, they have wooden furniture and private (though tiny) shower and toilet facilities, and TVs. Half the rooms have air-conditioning. Renovations are planned to add rooms and create a far more stylish entrance area. Note that there is no elevator, and breakfast is not included. ⊠ *7 Horkonos St., Box 2729, 94230,* ☎ *02/625–2757,* FAX *02/625–1297. 18 rooms with shower. Restaurant, coffee shop. AE, DC, MC, V (Cash or personal checks preferred; 5% surcharge for credit cards).*

**$$** 🏨 **Palatin.** The rooms are small at this personable family-run hotel, just off the intersection of King George Street and Jaffa Road, but the updated furnishings include pine furniture, moldings and other details, brighter colors, and TVs. Complimentary coffee and tea are available 24 hours a day. ⊠ *4 Agrippas St., 94301,* ☎ *02/623–1141,* ℻ *02/ 625–9323. 28 rooms with bath. AE, DC, MC, V.*

**$$** 🏨 **Scottish Hospice.** Part of the St. Andrew's Church complex, the Presbyterian-operated hospice—a guest house, not a medical facility!—is as much a retreat as a place to stay overnight. Opened in 1930, the building has the pleasing stone arches, alcoves, and atriums that characterize the local architecture of that period. The rooms are small, somewhat sparsely furnished, and not air-conditioned (though they have overhead fans), but most compensate with views of the garden, and some have views of Mt. Zion. Meals are available upon request. ⊠ *Off corner of King David and Emek Refa'im Sts., opposite rail station, Box 8619, 91086,* ☎ *02/673–2401,* ℻ *02/673–1711. 17 rooms with shower. AE, DC, MC, V.*

**$$** 🏨 **Zion.** The Parisian-style Zion is right in the center of town, its little balconies overlooking a pedestrian-only side street off the Ben Yehuda mall. The down side is a lot of street noise till late hours. The building is 140 years old, so stone walls, alcoves, traditional furniture, and brass ornaments in some of the public areas only add to the old-world ambience. The simply but pleasantly furnished rooms have TVs and fans but no air-conditioning. Note well: the rooms are two and three flights up, and there is no elevator. Prices are at the lower end of this category. ⊠ *10 Dorot Rishonim St., 94646,* ☎ *02/625–9511,* ℻ *02/625–7585. 26 rooms with bath. Bar. AE, MC, V.*

**$–$$** 🏨 **Louise Waterman-Wise.** Once a youth hostel, now upgraded to a guest house (in keeping with the Youth Hostel Association's successful attempt to march with the times), this large facility offers simply but neatly furnished rooms. They vary in size, sleeping anywhere from one to six, but all have en-suite baths. The setting, opposite Mt. Herzl in the Bayit Vegan area of West Jerusalem, has sweeping views of the Judean Hills yet is only a 10-minute cab ride (there's a taxi stand next door) or a 15-minute bus ride from downtown. Guests have access to a garden and other common rooms and to occasional evening activities, such as folk dancing and movies. Meals are substantial and very cheap. The rate jumps on weekends. ⊠ *8 Hapisgah St., Bayit Vegan, Box 16350, 91162,* ☎ *02/642–3366,* ℻ *02/642–3362. 80 rooms. No credit cards.*

# NIGHTLIFE AND THE ARTS

## Nightlife

Jerusalem's nightlife is a great deal more limited than Tel Aviv's—almost provincial—but some lively spots do keep late hours.

### Bars and Lounges

All of the major hotels have bars, but the quiet, comfortable, low-lit room at the **King David Hotel** (⊠ 23 King David St., ☎ 02/620–8888) is a bit more intimate than most.

### Dance Clubs

Primarily the preserve of the 17- to 21-year-old crowd (Israel's drinking age is 18), Jerusalem dance clubs come alive on Thursday, Friday, and Saturday nights. Admission runs NIS 30–NIS 35 ($8.60–$10). Don't even *think* about going before midnight.

The veteran downtown **Underground** (⊠ 1 Yoel Salomon St., off Zion Sq., ☎ 02/625–1918) looks like something out of Dante's *Inferno*, with rough black walls, murals, and sculptures of prisoners. The bar, up at street level, is only marginally saner. You can also have a drink at the upper level, where the dance floor is free. The **Orient Express** night-club (⊠ 32 Lehi St., ☎ 02/581–1334), at the entrance to the Hyatt Regency Hotel on Mt. Scopus, is decorated to recapture the bygone era of that famous train, but the sound system is marvelously state-of-the-art. Tuesday night is reserved for '60s and '70s nostalgia and draws a more mature crowd; Wednesday attracts the students from the Hebrew University campus next door; and on Thursday and Saturday anything goes.

The **Talpiot Industrial Zone,** 4 km (2½ mi) out of the city center, may seem an unlikely place to find a clutch of discos, but it makes sense in a city where the Jewish Sabbath is sacrosanct to so many. Nothing much happens before midnight, but by then parking is tight and the snack bars are crowded. Most places are geared to the college-age set, a few to a slightly older crowd. Individual clubs appear and disappear with such bewildering rapidity that specific listings have little long-term significance; ask your hotel staff for recommendations.

### Folk-Music Clubs

Jerusalem has a modest folk scene, with performances by local artists and occasional visits by international performers. Watch for listings, usually under Entertainment in the *Jerusalem Post* and elsewhere, or call folk singer Jill Rogoff (☎ 02/679–0410) for connections with the local folk community.

### Jazz Clubs

The **Pargod Theater** (⊠ 94 Bezalel St., ☎ 02/623–1765) hosts a regular jam session on Friday afternoon and often features evening jazz programs, especially in July and August.

### Pubs

A half-dozen totally nondescript pubs populate a courtyard off **31 Jaffa Road,** where a drink is just a drink and the ambience is secondary. There's another cluster in and around the **Russian Compound,** but the pubs themselves have little atmosphere.

## The Arts

For schedules of performances and other cultural events, consult the Friday weekend section of the *Jerusalem Post* and its insert *In Jerusalem,* the free local booklets *Your Jerusalem* and *This Week in Jerusalem,* and the monthly *Hello Israel,* all in English. Particularly useful is the Ministry of Tourism's monthly bulletin, *Events in Jerusalem,* available at TIOs and most better hotels.

The main ticket agencies for performances in Jerusalem are **Ben-Naim** (⊠ 38 Jaffa Rd., ☎ 02/623–1273), **Bimot** (⊠ 8 Shammai St., ☎ 02/624–0896), and **Kla'im** (⊠ 12 Shammai St., ☎ 02/625–6869).

Student discounts are sometimes available; present your card at the ticket office.

Top Israeli and international orchestras, choirs, singers, theater companies, dance troupes, and street entertainers participate in the **Israel Festival,** usually held in May or early June. All of the performing arts are represented, and offerings range from the classical to the avant-garde.

### Dance

The **Israel National Ballet** and the modern **Bat-Dor** have a varied performance record; the better-known **Batsheva** modern-dance troupe is the one to look out for.

## Film

The usual Hollywood fare is available at the comfortable modern cinemas clustered in the center of town, in the Jerusalem Mall, and farther out in the Talpiot Industrial Zone. They're closed Friday night. Movies are subtitled in Hebrew and, when appropriate, English. The **Jerusalem Cinemateque** (⊠ Hebron Rd., ☎ 02/672–4131) specializes in old, rare, and art films, but its wide-ranging programs often include current offerings. Its monthly series focuses on specific directors, actors, or subjects, and its annual **Jerusalem Film Festival,** held in July, is a must for film buffs. The theater is open Friday night.

## Music

Classical music abounds in Jerusalem, with Israeli orchestras and chamber ensembles performing year-round and a trickle of international artists passing through. The **International Convention Center,** or ICC (☎ 02/655–8558), still known locally by its old name Binyanei Ha'ooma, is opposite the Central Bus Station and is the local venue for occasional concerts by the world-renowned **Israel Philharmonic Orchestra.** For tickets, contact the orchestra's offices in Tel Aviv (⊠ Hechal Hatarbut, 1 Huberman St., ☎ 03/525–1502). The **Jerusalem Center for the Performing Arts** (20 Marcus St., ☎ 02/561–7167), still best known as the Jerusalem Theater, houses the Jerusalem Sherover Theater, the Henry Crown Auditorium, and the more intimate Rebecca Crown Theater. All in all, this is Jerusalem's most active and interesting venue.

**Bet Ticho,** or Ticho House (⊠ Off Harav Kook St. near Zion Sq., ☎ 02/624–5068), holds intimate recitals on Friday mornings in a charming setting. The atmosphere is rustic at the **Targ Music Center,** in Ein Kerem (⊠ Hama'ayan St., ☎ 02/641–4250), 7 km (4½ mi) from the city center, where noontime chamber-music performances are common on Friday and Saturday. The popular (and free) **Etnacha** series of concerts, produced by Israel Radio's classics station, takes place Monday at 5 PM, October through June, at the Henry Crown Auditorium (⊠ 20 Marcus St., ☎ 02/561–7167). Always check listings before you make plans.

Hearing music in one of Jerusalem's many churches can be a moving experience. The most common venues are the **Church of the Redeemer** (⊠ Muristan, in the Old City's Christian Quarter, ☎ 02/627–6111) and **Dormition Abbey** (⊠ Mt. Zion, ☎ 02/671–9927).

A rousing concert of Israeli folklore—mostly singing and folk dancing—is presented at the **YMCA (West)** (⊠ 26 King David St.; call Zion at ☎ 050/233210 or 052/233210), usually on Monday, Thursday, and Saturday evenings. Call ahead to confirm. Reservations are advised; but as the 500-seat hall is generally inundated by tour groups and seats are unmarked, it's recommended that you arrive early. The cost is $15.

The **Bible Lands Museum** (⊠ Givat Ram, next to Israel Museum, ☎ 02/561–1066) hosts Saturday-evening concerts, preceded by cheese and wine in the foyer. The delightfully eclectic programs range from chamber music to jazz and gospel to folk music and country-and-western. An added attraction: the museum's galleries are open to concertgoers for half an hour before and after the concert.

To rub shoulders with the locals, look into the Friday-night Oneg Shabbat series at **Bet Shemuel** (⊠ Eliyahu Shama'a St., off King David St., ☎ 02/620–3456), which typically hosts some of the top performers on the Israeli pop scene. The evening will be in Hebrew, of course, but the music and the atmosphere may speak to you in an international language of good feelings.

### Theater

Most plays are performed in Hebrew, but there is the odd offering in English. Some performances have simultaneous translation. Your best bet for plays in English is the **Khan Theater** (⊠ 2 David Remez Sq., near the railway station, ☎ 02/671–8281), but check newspaper listings for other venues as well.

# OUTDOOR ACTIVITIES AND SPORTS

For a change of pace from sightseeing, keep in shape or pursue a favorite sport.

## Bicycling

The informal **Jerusalem Bicycling Club** (☎ 02/561–9416; ask for Benny) leads rides on Saturday morning at 7 starting from the International Convention Center, Binyanei Ha'ooma (opposite the Central Bus Station). The club is a good source for information on bike rentals and can recommend routes within the city.

## Bowling

The **Jerusalem Bowling Center** (⊠ Achim Yisrael Mall "Kenyon Talpiot," 18 Yad Harutzim St., Talpiot Industrial Zone, ☎ 02/673–2195) has 10 lanes, a small cafeteria, and billiard tables. The center is open daily 10 AM–2 AM (Saturday from 11 AM). From Sunday through Thursday, the cost per game (including shoe rental) is NIS 17 ($4.90) 10 AM–6 PM and NIS 22 ($6.30) 6 PM–2 AM; from Friday evening through Saturday night the cost is NIS 25 ($7.20).

## Health Clubs

The best health clubs in Jerusalem are in hotels; some are privately run concessions. All welcome health-seekers who are not hotel guests. The most comprehensive facilities are at the **Crowne Plaza** (⊠ Givat Ram, ☎ 02/653–5821), **Four Points Jerusalem** (⊠ 4 Wolfson St., ☎ 02/655–8888), **Hyatt Regency** (⊠ 32 Lehi St., Mt. Scopus, ☎ 02/532–2906), and **Renaissance Jerusalem** (⊠ 6 Wolfson St., ☎ 02/659–9999).

The following have good facilities but no pools:

**Kikar Zion** (⊠ 25 Shammai St., Zion Sq., ☎ 02/624–4644) and **Lev Yerushalayim** (Samson's Gym; ⊠ 18 King George St., ☎ 02/530–0333).

## Horseback Riding

A number of stables offer lessons and trail riding, including those suitable for children, as well as longer (and more interesting) trails.

**King David's Riding Stables** (⊠ Neve Ilan, north of Rte. 1, ☎ 02/534–0535), in the wooded Judean Hills, 16 km (10 mi) west of Jerusalem, charges NIS 90 ($25.70) for a trail ride (45 minutes–1 hour). Longer guided trails in the area are offered at a lower hourly rate. **Meir Mizrachi Stables** (⊠ Kfar Adumim, north of Rte. 1, ☎ 02/535–5419 [stables] or 02/535–4769 [home]), in the Judean Desert, 17 km (11 mi) east of Jerusalem, charges NIS 50 ($14.30) for an hour. The **Riding Club** (⊠ Kiryat Moshe, behind Angel's Bakery, ☎ 02/651–3585; do not call between 1 and 3 PM), run by Yehuda Alafi, breeds Arabians. The charge is NIS 70 ($20) for an hour.

# Squash

The **YMCA (West)** (⊠ 26 King David St., ☎ 02/569–2692) has three squash courts for hourly rental. They're available for NIS 35 ($10) an hour 7:15 AM–8:45 PM, Monday–Saturday.

# Swimming

The enthusiast can swim year-round at these pools (those at hotels welcome nonguests). Indoor: **Bet Hano'ar Ha'ivri** (or YMWHA; ⊠ 105 Herzog Blvd., ☎ 02/678–9441), **Djanogly** (⊠ Bet Avraham Community Center, Ramot Allon, ☎ 02/586–8055), and **Renaissance Jerusalem Hotel** (⊠ 6 Wolfson St., ☎ 02/659–9999). Outdoor (covered and heated in winter): **Laromme Hotel** (⊠ 3 Jabotinsky St., ☎ 02/675–6666).

Other recommended outdoor pools (except in winter) include the public **Jerusalem Pool** (⊠ 43 Emek Refa'im St., ☎ 02/563–2092), which gets very crowded in July and August; and the beautifully landscaped facilities at the following hotels:

**Crowne Plaza** (⊠ Givat Ram, ☎ 02/658–8888); **Hyatt Regency** (⊠ 32 Lehi St., Mt. Scopus, ☎ 02/533–1234); **King David Hotel** (⊠ 23 King David St., ☎ 02/620–8888); and **Renaissance Jerusalem** (6 Wolfson St., ☎ 02/659–9999). A little less expensive are the facilities at the **Four Points Jerusalem** (⊠ 4 Wolfson St., ☎ 02/655–8888) and **Mt. Zion Hotel** (⊠ 17 Hebron Rd., ☎ 02/568–9555), also in attractive locations.

# Tennis

Tennis has really taken off in Israel in the last 10 years. Advance reservations are always required.

**Hebrew University at Mt. Scopus** (☎ 02/581–7579 or 02/588–2796) has 10 lighted courts and rental equipment. Courts go for NIS 24 ($6.90) an hour in daylight and NIS 28 ($8) an hour in evenings and are open Sunday–Thursday 8 AM–10 PM, Friday 7–6, and Saturday 7–5. The **Israel Tennis Center** (⊠ 5 Almaliach St., Katamon Tet, ☎ 02/679–1866 or 02/679–2726) has 18 lighted courts, available for NIS 17 ($4.90) per hour Sunday–Thursday 7 AM–4 PM, NIS 25 ($7.20) per hour Sunday–Thursday 7 PM–10 PM, Friday 7–6, and Saturday 7–2. You'll need your own equipment. The **YMCA (West)** (⊠ 26 King David St., ☎ 02/569–2692) has four courts that rent for NIS 25 ($7.20) per hour; they're open Monday–Saturday 8 AM–sunset. Several major **hotels** have their own courts, but they often restrict usage to guests or club members. Ask your concierge to make inquiries if you want to play at a particular hotel.

# SHOPPING

Jerusalem has good shopping, for everything from jewelry and art to crafts and souvenirs. The several distinct shopping areas make it easy to plan expeditions. Prices are generally fixed in the city center and the Jewish Quarter of the Old City, though you can sometimes negotiate for significant discounts on expensive art and jewelry. Shopping in the Old City's colorful Arab bazaar, or *souk* (pronounced "shook" in Israel—rhymes with "book"), is fascinating but can be a trap for the unwary. Never buy gold, silver, or gem-studded jewelry here.

Weekday store hours are generally 8:30 or 9–1 and 4–7, but many stores now stay open throughout the day. Some close on Tuesday afternoon, a traditional but not mandatory half-day. Jewish-owned stores (that is, all of West Jerusalem—the "New City"—and the Old City's

Jewish Quarter) close on Friday afternoon at 1 or 2, depending on the kind of store and the season (food and souvenir stores tend to stay open later), and reopen on Sunday morning. Some stores geared to the tourist trade, particularly in the center of town (bounded by Jaffa Road, King George Street, and Ben Yehuda Street), are open on Saturday night after the Jewish Sabbath ends, especially in summer. Arab-owned stores in the Old City and East Jerusalem are busiest on Saturday and quietest on Sunday, when many (but not all) Christian storekeepers close for the day.

## Shopping Streets and Malls

**Arts and Crafts Lane** (known in Hebrew as Hutzot Hayotzer), opposite and downhill from the Jaffa Gate, has goldsmiths and silversmiths specializing in Judaica, generally done in an ultramodern, minimalist style. The work is exquisite and is priced accordingly. You can also find excellent jewelry, weaving, fine art, and musical instruments.

The **Cardo,** in the Old City's Jewish Quarter, began life as the main thoroughfare of Byzantine Jerusalem, was a street during the Crusader era, and has now been converted into an attractive shopping area. Beyond discovering souvenirs and Judaica, you'll find good-quality jewelry, art, and objets d'art here.

**King David Street** is lined with a sizable number of prestigious stores, with the emphases on art, Judaica, antiquities, and interesting jewelry.

The pedestrian-only **Midrachov** is simply downtown Ben Yehuda Street, the heartbeat of west Jerusalem (the New City). The selection of clothing, shoes, jewelry, souvenirs, T-shirts, and street food is prodigious here. You'll be serenaded by street musicians at every turn. It's a real scene, best appreciated from one of the many outdoor cafés. Summer evenings are lively, as the mall fills with peddlers of cheap jewelry and crafts, and young shoppers admiring them.

**Salomon Street,** in the old neighborhood of Nahalat Shiva, just off Zion Square, has also been developed as a pedestrian mall. Here and in adjacent alleys and courtyards, eateries abound, but you'll also find some attractive crafts galleries and arty jewelry and clothing shops.

**Hatachana** (the Mill) is a small arcade on Ramban Street, near the intersection with King George Street. Built around an old windmill, the complex houses expensive boutiques and an excellent beauty salon.

The new **Jerusalem Mall,** known locally as Kenyon Malcha, is—at 500,000 square ft not counting parking—the largest in the Middle East. It includes a department store, a supermarket, eight cinemas, and almost 200 shops and eateries (Pizza Hut and Burger King among them). The interior is an attractive mix of arched skylights and wrought-iron banisters in a quasi–art deco style. The mall is clearly signposted from the new Begin Boulevard, via Eliyahu Golomb Street, and from the Pat Junction–Gilo Road.

## Street Markets

Jerusalem's first and foremost market, of course, is the **souk** in the Old City. Spreading through a warren of intersecting streets, the souk is primarily for the Old City's Arab residents. Awash with color, it's redolent with the clashing scents of exotic spices. Village women's baskets of produce vie for attention with hanging shanks of lamb, fresh fish on ice, and fresh-baked delicacies, and food stalls are interspersed with those selling fabrics and shoes. The baubles and trinkets of the tourist trade often seem secondary, except along the well-trodden paths of the Via Dolorosa, David Street, and Christian Quarter Road.

The atmosphere in the Arab Quarter has relaxed a great deal since the tense years of the late 1980s. On the other hand, haggling with merchants—a time-honored tradition—is not the good-natured experience it once was. Unless you know what you want, know how much it's *really* worth, and enjoy the sometimes aggressive give-and-take of bargaining, you're better off just enjoying the local color (stick to the main streets, and watch your wallet or purse) and doing your shopping in the more modern and familiar New City.

Off Jaffa Road, near the Clal Center office buildings, is the **Machaneh Yehuda** produce market, a block-long alleyway that becomes a blur of brilliant primary colors as the city's best-quality fruit and vegetables, pickles and cheeses, fresh fish and poultry, confections, and falafel await inspection. The busiest days are Thursday and Friday, when Jews shop for the Sabbath; the market is closed on Saturday along with the rest of Jewish West Jerusalem.

On Thursday and Friday, **Hamartef** (the Cellar) arcade, beneath City Tower (✉ Corner of King George and Ben Yehuda Sts.), hosts jewelers and vendors of bric-a-brac and secondhand books. It's fun just to browse here, but sometimes the wares are really worth buying.

## Specialty Stores

### Art Galleries
Several galleries representing a range of Israeli artists are close to the city's premier hotels, on **King David Street.**

For large wall decorations (with prices to match), check out the appliqué-like "soft art" of **Calman Shemi** (✉ 22 King David St., ☎ 02/624–9557), whose marvelous effects must be seen to be appreciated. **Frank Meisler** (✉ 21 King David St., ☎ 02/624–2759) has an original and whimsical sense of humor; his caricaturish silver-plated pewter sculptures cover subjects from Noah's ark and Jerusalem cityscapes to Freud and animal figures that seem to be sharing Meisler's secret joke.

### Clothing
Clothing tends to be expensive in Israel, and in Jerusalem you have to search for really fashionable clothes. One homegrown women's clothing store with definite style is **A.B.C.** (✉ 33 King George St., ☎ 02/623–4934). The very pricey **Lagotte Studio,** in the Hatachana arcade (✉ 8 Ramban St., ☎ 02/566–5059), stocks well-designed imported women's wear, with the adjacent **Lagotte Plus** (☎ 02/561–2113) specializing in large sizes. In the same building, **Oui Set** (☎ 02/563–8365) stocks more casual but still elegant merchandise of a similar standard.

SWIMWEAR

Israeli swimsuits and beach accessories have revolutionized the market overseas with their dazzling designs and colors. Gottex swimwear is available at the downtown department store **Hamashbir** (✉ 28 King George St.). **Names** (✉ 23 Ben Yehuda St., ☎ 02/625–8430) sells Gideon Oberson suits.

### Crafts
For ceramics, glass, jewelry, wooden objects, and embroidery, try the **Jerusalem House of Quality** (✉ 12 Hebron Rd., ☎ 02/671–7430), which presents the work of some excellent Israeli craftspeople. Their studios are on the second floor, so you can often see them at work.

For Armenian hand-painted pottery—predominantly blue and brown, with geometric or stylized natural motifs—one of the best artisans is

Stefan Karakashian of **Jerusalem Pottery,** at the VI Station of the Cross, on the Via Dolorosa in the Old City. Karakashian's work is of a particularly high standard and includes plates, plaques, and bowls. Drop in at **Cadim** (⊠ 4 Salomon St., ☎ 02/623–4869), in Nahalat Shiva, for a selection of interesting contemporary Israeli ceramics. **Shemonah Beyachad** (⊠ 11 Salomon St., ☎ 02/624–7250) displays the work of several artists. At **7 Artists** (⊠ 6 Salomon St., ☎ 02/623–4210), pottery shares the showcases with embroidered and woven fabrics. Feast your eyes at the **Guild of Ceramicists** (⊠ 27 Salomon St., ☎ 02/624–4065), where artistic designs are applied to pottery both functional and decorative. **Danny Azoulay**'s store (⊠ 5 Salomon St., ☎ 02/623–3918) has fine porcelain items; many are traditional Jewish ritual objects—some of which are expensive—but you can also find less pricey items, such as napkin rings and bottle stoppers, all beautifully hand-painted in rich blues, reds and golds.

Opaque, smoky Israeli **glass** is available in both decorative and practical items in many tourist shops. The miniature vases, sometimes decorated with silver, are particularly attractive.

**Kakadu** (⊠ 1 Rivlin St., ☎ 02/625–6412) manufactures and sells exciting modern "art and design in wood," colorful items that range from desktop paraphernalia to full-size mirrors. **Klein** (⊠ 3 Ziv St., off Bar Ilan St., ☎ 02/538–9992 and 02/538–8784), in northern Jerusalem, has some of the highest-quality olive-wood objects in the country. This is actually the factory, so the showroom stocks everything they make, from bowls and yo-yos to attractive trays of Armenian pottery tiles framed in olive wood; picture frames; boxes; and desktop paraphernalia.

Paper-cutting was a well-established Jewish art form until about 100 years ago. **Yehudit Shadur** (⊠ 12 Hovevei Zion St., ☎ 02/566–3217), who has been primarily responsible for the Israeli revival of this tradition craft, makes pieces in styles that range from simple contrasts to richly colored and varied textures; call for an appointment. Working with traditional motifs, **Archie Granot** has evolved his own complex, multilayered style of paper-cut Judaica (⊠ 22 Yosef Rivlin St., ☎ 02/624–3956); call ahead.

Colorful, folk-style Druze weavings in the form of cloths, pillow covers, and wall hangings are sold at **Ben Shalom** (⊠ 19 Ben Yehuda St., ☎ 02/625–2948), which has a wide variety of beautiful items at reasonable prices. **G.R.A.S.** (⊠ 20 King George St., adjacent to Hamashbir department store, ☎ 02/625–6599) sells its own special line of pillow covers and curtains in its distinctive, Israeli-made fabrics in exotic patterns. The pillow covers are an especially good value and make great, easy-to-pack gifts. Two good general gift shops are **Pupi** (⊠ 2 Hillel St., ☎ 02/624–2236) and **Poenta** (⊠ 21 Salomon St., ☎ 02/624–0383), both of which carry an attractive selection of *hamsas,* the region's mystical hand-shaped talisman, in forms ranging from delicate charms to large wall-art.

## Harps

The **House of Harrari,** in Nahalat Shiva (⊠ Ma'alot Nahalat Shiva 7, ☎ 02/625–5191), sells a selection of beautiful harps, ranging from decorative door harps to 22- and 34-string folk instruments. You can choose from a variety of ornamentation, and the little door harps can be decorated with an appropriate inscription. The gallery will ship your purchase home.

## Jewelry

Jewelry in Israel is of a high international standard.

**Meshulash** (⊠ Arye Leib Hurwitz Alley, off Salomon St., ☎ 02/624–1762) makes and sells exquisite ultramodern pieces, characterized by their clean, almost minimalist lines. The very affordable **G.R.A.S.** (☞ Crafts, *above*) creates modern adaptations of traditional Yemenite silver jewelry. **Pick** (⊠ 11 Ben Hillel St., ☎ 02/623–2859) specializes in modern silver jewelry—the earrings are especially good—at reasonable prices. **Idit** (⊠ 21 King George St., ☎ 02/622–1911) has fine merchandise in a more formal style. One particularly outstanding craftsman is **Danny Alsberg** (☎ 02/628–9275), in the Arts and Crafts Lane (Hutzot Hayotzer), outside the Jaffa Gate. Not to be missed is **Sarah Einstein** (⊠ 7 Ma'alot Nachalat Shiva, off Salomon St., ☎ 02/622–1151), with a collection of one-of-a-kind necklaces and earrings made from antique silver, amber, and other materials.

The ubiquitous **H. Stern** (⊠ Just inside Jaffa Gate and at many major hotels) has high-quality, conventional pieces. Two large diamond manufacturers, **National Diamond Center (NDC)** (⊠ 143 Bethlehem Rd., ☎ 02/733770) and **Adipaz** (⊠ 20 Pierre Koenig St., ☎ 02/678–3887), each have a factory and showroom for jewelry and loose-cut gems. You can take a guided tour of the facilities upon request.

### Perfumes

**Judith Muller** sells her scents in pretty, smoky-glass flacons shaped to look like ancient bottles. The bottles are available in the usual measures, but you can also find gift sets of two, four, six, and eight miniature bottles.

### T-Shirts

Tourist shops all stock the same range of machine-stamped shirts, but most stores will also decorate shirts from a selection of designs. There are several on Ben Yehuda Street: Army/Navy Surplus (also on Ben Hillel St., adjacent to Ben Yehuda), Sweet, and Happening. Mr. T. and Lord Kitsch, on Zion Square, also stock a good selection.

# JERUSALEM A TO Z

## Arriving and Departing

### By Bus

The **Egged** National Bus Cooperative (☎ 03/694–8888) serves Jerusalem's **Central Bus Station** (⊠ 224 Jaffa Rd.) with comfortable, air-conditioned buses from all major cities in Israel. Egged buses in and out of Jerusalem stop running about a half hour before sunset on Friday and religious holiday eves and resume after dark on Saturday or religious holidays. The **East Jerusalem Bus Station** (⊠ Sultan Suleiman St., opposite Damascus Gate) is the terminus for private Arab-run lines serving West Bank towns such as Bethlehem.

### By Car

**Route 1** is the chief route to Jerusalem from both the west (Tel Aviv, Ben Gurion Airport, Mediterranean Coast) and the east (Galilee via Jordan Valley, Dead Sea area, Eilat). From Tel Aviv, Route 1 becomes Jaffa Road, which runs into the city center. The road from Tel Aviv is a divided highway that presents no problems except at morning rush hour (7:30–9), when traffic backs up at the entrance to the city.

### By Plane

INTERNATIONAL FLIGHTS

Most visitors entering Israel fly into **Ben Gurion International Airport** (☎ 03/971–0000 for information), 16 km (10 mi) east of Tel Aviv and 50 km (31 mi) west of Jerusalem.

**Egged** Buses 423, 945, and 947 run from the airport to Jerusalem's Central Bus Station on a reasonably frequent schedule (you'll seldom wait more than 30 minutes), except in the evenings, and cost NIS 18.50 ($5.30). There is no bus service from Friday afternoon to Saturday night, or on religious holidays. For bus schedules, call ☎ 03/694–8888.

The **drive** from the airport, on Route 1 east, takes about 35 minutes. A "special" taxi (as opposed to a shared one, a *sherut*) should cost (at press time) NIS 130 ($37), NIS 145 ($42) after 9 PM and on Saturday and holidays.

Seven-seat **sherut** taxis (limo-vans; ☞ *below*) depart when they fill up and drop passengers off at whatever Jerusalem address they request for NIS 34 ($9.70). To get *to* Ben-Gurion Airport from Jerusalem the same way, call **Nesher** (☎ 02/625–3233 or 02/623–1231) to book a place, preferably a day in advance. They'll pick you up at any address in Jerusalem.

DOMESTIC FLIGHTS

**Atarot Airport** (☎ 02/583–3440), 8 km (5 mi) north of Jerusalem off Ramallah Road, has domestic flights only—specifically, daily flights to and from Eilat and Haifa on Arkia, Israel's domestic carrier. **Arkia** runs a shuttle service between the airport and its downtown office, at the Clal Building (⊠ 97 Jaffa Rd., ☎ 02/625–5888 or 177/022–4888 toll-free); the service is geared to Arkia's flight schedule and costs NIS 10 ($2.90).

## By Sherut

Seven-seat sheruts (stretch cabs or minivans) ply the same routes as the Egged buses to and from Tel Aviv, Haifa, and Beersheva and charge about the same fares (25% more on Saturday and holidays, when the buses don't run). In Jerusalem, **Ha'ooma/Habira** (⊠ 1 Harav Kook St., near Zion Sq., and at the old Ram Hotel, behind Central Bus Station, ☎ 02/538–9999) goes to Tel Aviv. **Aviv/Kesher** (⊠ 12 Shammai St., ☎ 02/625–4034 or 02/625–7366) goes to Haifa. **Yael Daroma** (⊠ 12 Shammai St., ☎ 02/625–6985) serves Beersheva and Eilat. Sheruts from Tel Aviv to Jerusalem congregate at Tel Aviv's New Central Bus Station. Sheruts to Jerusalem from Haifa leave from the Hadar district.

## By Train

One rides the train between Tel Aviv and Jerusalem for the scenery and novelty of the experience (it's great for kids), not for the convenience. There is only one train a day in each direction: from Jerusalem, Sunday–Thursday at 2:50 PM and Friday at 11:55 AM; and from Tel Aviv, Sunday–Thursday at 10 AM and Friday at 8:45 AM. There is no service on Saturday or on religious holidays. The schedule is subject to change, so call ahead before setting out for the station. The train takes twice as long as the bus—about 1¾ hours—and costs NIS 18 ($5.20). The rail station (David Remez St., ☎ 02/673–3764) is on several city bus routes (Nos. 4, 7, 8, 21, and 48), and you can normally hail a passing cab out front. The route ends at Tel Aviv Central on Arlozorov Street, well served by taxis and numerous bus routes.

# Getting Around

## By Bus

The **Egged** National Bus Cooperative (☎ 02/530–4704 for local information; note that they're very difficult to reach) enjoys a monopoly on bus lines within Jerusalem. Routes within the city are extensive. Service begins at 5:30 AM and ends around midnight, depending on the route. Service stops half an hour before sunset on Friday (or on the eve of a religious holiday) until half an hour after sundown on Saturday. The fare on all routes is NIS 4.20 ($1.20), and you need to use Israeli money, but you don't need exact change. There are no transfers. Buses do not automatically stop at every bus stop; you need to signal the driver. Bus maps are sometimes available at the Central Bus Station, on Jaffa Road in West Jerusalem. If you need bus advice, your best bet is to inquire at your hotel or ask the locals.

The two small, Arab-run bus stations in **East Jerusalem** primarily serve routes to towns in the West Bank (☞ Around Jerusalem A to Z *in* Chapter 3).

Egged's **Bus 99** runs a loop that sets out from the small terminal on Ha'emek Street (near Jaffa Gate) and takes about 1½ hours to complete. The 36 stops include the downtown area (the New City), the Jerusalem Theater, the Jerusalem Mall, the Holyland Hotel (with its scale model of ancient Jerusalem), Mt. Herzl, Yad Vashem, the Israel Museum, the Knesset, the Central Bus Station, Mt. Scopus, and a circuit of the Old City walls (with stops at Damascus Gate, the Rockefeller Museum, Gethsemane, the Western Wall and Mt. Zion). Almost all of the hotel districts are serviced by this bus. The route stops at sites that are otherwise difficult to reach except by taxi. Buses leave the Jaffa Gate station Sunday–Thursday at 10, noon, 2, and 4, and on Friday and holiday eves at 10 and noon only. There is no service on Saturday or religious holidays. The cost is NIS 22.50 ($6.50) for a one-day ticket or NIS 24 ($8) for a two-day ticket, with unlimited transfers on this route.

## By Car

Navigating a rental car through unfamiliar territory and looking for legal parking make driving in Israel's big cities a dubious pleasure. A combination of walking and taking cabs or a guide-driven tourist limo-van is often more time-effective—and even more cost-effective. In Jerusalem the only sights that might be easier to reach by car are West Jerusalem and the panoramic overlooks, which are a bit out of the way.

Note that curbs painted with alternate bands of blue and white indicate legal parking, but only with the use of inexpensive parking cards, available for purchase at post offices and at many refreshment stands or curb vendors in or near the downtown area.

Gas stations are easy to find, and some never close, but gasoline is expensive in Israel—about NIS 14 ($4) a gallon. Drive defensively: many local drivers take hair-raising risks on the road.

## By Taxi

Taxis can be flagged on the street, ordered by phone, or picked up at a taxi stand or at major hotels. There are usually taxis waiting outside the Israel Museum and Yad Vashem. The law requires taxi drivers to turn on their meters, so you can insist on it, but if you want the cab badly you might need to compromise. Negotiating the fare puts you at a disadvantage unless you're familiar with the distance involved. A 10- to 15-minute ride (day rates until 9 PM) should cost between NIS 15 and NIS 25 (between $5 and $7). The fare is 25% higher after 9 PM and on Saturday and holidays. Any serious problem with the cabbie can be reported to the Ministry of Tourism: be sure to note the number on the illuminated yellow sign on the roof of the cab.

# Contacts and Resources

## Car Rental

**Avis** (✉ 22 King David St., ☎ 02/624–9001). **Budget** (✉ 8 King David St., ☎ 02/624–8991 or 02/624–8992). **Eldan** (✉ 24 King David

St., ☎ 02/625–2151). **Europcar (National)** (⊠ 8 King David St., ☎ 02/624–8464). **Hertz** (⊠ 18 King David St., ☎ 02/623–1351; ⊠ Hyatt Regency Hotel, 32 Lehi St., ☎ 02/581–5069). **Reliable** (⊠ 14 King David St., ☎ 02/624–8993).

## Consulates
**United States Consulate-General**: ⊠ 18 Agron St., West Jerusalem; 27 Nablus Rd., East Jerusalem (for consular services); ☎ 02/625–3288 for both. **British Consulate-General**: ⊠ Tower House, next to St. Andrew's Church, Remez St., West Jerusalem, ☎ 02/671–7724; ⊠ for consular services, Sheikh Jarrah, East Jerusalem, ☎ 02/582–8281. This consulate also serves citizens of New Zealand.

## Doctors and Dentists
The privately run, 24-hour **Terem Emergency Care Center** (⊠ 7 Hamag St., Romema, ☎ 02/652–1748) offers first aid and other medical attention. **Yad Sarah** (⊠ 43 Hanevi'im St., ☎ 02/644–4444) is a voluntary organization that lends medical equipment and accessories such as wheelchairs, crutches, and canes. There is no charge, but a contribution is expected. It's open Sunday–Thursday 9–7 and Friday 9–noon.

A private **dental clinic** offers an emergency service (⊠ 1 Mendele St., at 24 Keren Hayesod St., opposite Radisson Moriah Plaza, ☎ 02/563–2303) Sunday–Thursday 8–8, Friday 8 until just before sundown, and Saturday evening. Call first: when the office is closed, the call is automatically transferred to an on-call dentist.

## Emergencies
**Ambulance** (☎ 101 or 02/652–3133). The ambulance company, Magen David Adom, is the Israeli version of the Red Cross. **Police** (☎ 100 or 02/539–1111). **Fire** (☎ 102).

### HOSPITAL EMERGENCY ROOMS
Emergency rooms in major hospitals are on duty 24 hours a day in rotation; the schedule is published in the daily press. In an emergency, call Magen David Adom (☎ 101) to find out which hospital is on duty that day for your specific need (orthopedic or gastric, for example). Be sure to take your passport with you. There will be a fee. The major hospitals in Jerusalem are **Bikur Holim** (⊠ Strauss St., ☎ 02/670–1111); **Hadassah** (⊠ Ein Kerem, ☎ 02/677–7111, 02/677–7215 emergency room, 02/677–7204 children's emergency room); **Hadassah** (⊠ Mt. Scopus, ☎ 02/584–4111); **Sha'arei Tzedek** (⊠ Bayit Vegan, ☎ 02/655–5111; 02/655–5508 emergency room).

## Guided Tours
### ORIENTATION
Two tour operators offer half- and full-day tours of Old and New Jerusalem, with different itineraries on different days of the week:

**Egged Tours** (⊠ 8 Shlomzion Hamalka St., ☎ 02/622–2929) and **United Tours** (⊠ King David Hotel Annex, 23 King David St., ☎ 02/625–2187, 02/625–2188).

A tour costs about $24–$32 for a half day and $46–$56 for a full day, depending on itinerary. The price includes pickup and drop-off at your hotel. You can reserve directly or through your hotel concierge.

### PERSONAL GUIDES
At press time the daily rate for a private guide with an air-conditioned car or limousine was $280–$360, depending on the size of the vehicle. Many guides will offer their services without a car for about $140–$170. The customary rate for a half day is 60% of the full-day rate. For listings of private guides, contact **Eshcolot Tours** (⊠ 36 Keren

Hayesod St., ☎ 02/563–5555) or Fodor's writer and guide Mike Rogoff (☎ FAX 02/679–0410).

The **Society for the Protection of Nature in Israel** (✉ 13 Helene Hamalka St., ☎ 02/625–2357), or SPNI, emphasizes nature, often trekking off the beaten path. Tours in English cater to tourists, but sometimes the experience matters more than the explanations, so you might want to consider the richer menu of tours in Hebrew. Itineraries change throughout the year; call for details.

**Archaeological Seminars** (☎ 02/627–3515) specializes in visiting sites of archaeological importance. Tours are preceded by a slide lecture, and the guides are generally excellent. Two two- to three-hour itineraries ($16) are offered Sunday through Wednesday several times a week, and options are expanded in summer. No reservations are required. All tours depart from 34 Habad Street, in the Jewish Quarter of the Old City.

**Zion Walking Tours** (✉ Inside Jaffa Gate, opposite police station, ☎ 02/628–7866) has eight different itineraries, each running twice a week. Tours last about three hours and cost $10–$20.

## Late-Night Pharmacies

The daily press publishes the addresses of pharmacies on duty at night, on Saturday, and on holidays. This information is also available from Magen David Adom (☎ 02/652–3133).

**SuperPharm** (✉ 5 Burla St., Nayot, ☎ 02/678–4139) is open Sunday–Thursday 8:30 AM–midnight, Friday 8:30 AM–3 PM, and Saturday 9 PM–midnight. Its downtown location (✉ 3 Hahistadrut St., ☎ 02/624–6249) closes at 11 PM.

## Taxis

Twenty-four-hour service:

**Hapalmach** (☎ 02/679–2333 or 02/679–3333); **Hapisgah** (☎ 02/642–1111 or 02/642–2222 except on the Sabbath); **Rehavia** (☎ 02/625–4444 or 02/622–2444).

## Travel Agencies

**American Express** (✉ 40 Jaffa Rd., ☎ 02/623–1710 or 02/623–1908). **ISSTA** (✉ 31 Hanevi'im St., ☎ 02/625–7257), for students and academics. **Vaintours** (✉ 33 King George St., ☎ 02/625–2984). **Zion-tours** (✉ 19 Hillel St., ☎ 02/625–4326 or 02/625–4327).

## Visitor Information

Jerusalem's **Tourist Information Offices** (✉ Jaffa Gate, Old City, ☎ 02/628–0457 or 02/628–0382; ✉ 2 Luntz St., ☎ 02/625–8908) are open Sunday–Thursday 8:30–5 and Friday 8:30–1 (8:30–2 at Jaffa Gate).

The **Christian Information Center** (✉ Jaffa Gate, Old City, ☎ 02/627–2692) is open Monday–Saturday 8:30–1, except Christmas, New Year's Day, and Good Friday.

# 3 Around Jerusalem

*Including Bethlehem, Masada, and the Dead Sea*

*West of Jerusalem, rugged pine-forested hills fold down to a green region of soft landscapes, biblical echoes, and chalk caves. To the east, in stark contrast, you plunge at once through the Judean Desert to Masada and the Dead Sea, the lowest spot on earth, with bleak, dramatic vistas punctuated by brilliant green oases. And just south of the holy city is Bethlehem, birthplace of Jesus. Travelers based in Tel Aviv can easily reach these areas by adding an hour's transport in each direction.*

**J**ERUSALEM'S LOCATION IN THE HEART of Israel's central mountain range makes it an excellent base for day tours in the area. Furthermore, many people find visiting Jerusalem so intense that they need excursions like these for a change of pace and scenery.

By Mike Rogoff

By far the most interesting and dramatic sights are those in the Judean Desert–Dead Sea region. This is a rocky desert of extraordinary barrenness, throwing into brilliant relief the waterfalls and greenery of Ein Gedi, the springs and reed thickets of Ain Fashkha, and the sprawling oasis of the town of Jericho.

The road skirting the Dead Sea (Route 90) is hemmed in by awesome, fractured brown cliffs that soar in many places to heights of more than 1,600 ft. Slicing through these immense desert crags are Ein Gedi's two canyons, Nahal David and Nahal Arugot, both refreshing surprises of rivulets, pools, waterfalls, and subtropical vegetation. Wildlife abounds here, particularly the ibex (wild goat) and the hyrax (coney), though you can't rely on seeing them.

The Dead Sea itself—actually a lake—is a unique phenomenon: it is the saltiest body of water in the world, at the lowest point on earth. You can feel the tension seep away as you float in the balmy brine or as you smooth mineral-rich black mud all over your body. Bathing options range from free public beaches with minimal facilities to well-equipped spas; the best are in the Ein Bokek hotel district, at the southern end of the Dead Sea (☞ Chapter 8).

Masada, the great mountaintop palace-fortress built 2,000 years ago by King Herod, overlooks the Dead Sea. Its palaces, mosaics and frescoes, ingenious water system, and baths are a tribute to Herod's grand style; the remote location and almost unassailable position are evidence of his paranoia. Add the human drama of Masada's defense and fall during the Jewish revolt against Rome a century later, and it's easy to understand why this is one of the most visited sites in Israel.

Bethlehem, a stone's throw from Jerusalem, is a major place of pilgrimage for Christians. The cavernous and colonnaded Church of the Nativity, the oldest church in the country, is built over the grotto where Jesus is believed to have been born. Today's town is a West Bank Arab community of some 35,000 souls, one-third Christian, two-thirds Muslim, straddling the ancient high road through the rocky, olive-groved Judean Hills.

Still on the trail of the Bible, you'll find echoes of Joshua (though not his walls) at the palm-studded oasis of Jericho, to the east; and persuasive topographical detail of the dueling ground of David and Goliath in the Elah Valley, to the west.

The planted pine and cypress forests west of Jerusalem have an abundance of delightful views and picnic spots, and a few nature reserves. Don't miss the Sorek Cave, an almost fantastical cavern of stalagmites and stalactites; or the extraordinary network of ancient man-made chalk caves—the huge "bell caves" of Bet Guvrin and the adjacent underground complexes of Maresha.

## Pleasures and Pastimes

### Bird-Watching
Israel's varied climate and its position on major migratory routes make it a fascinating place for bird-watchers. Especially interesting in this region are the raptors in the skies of the Judean Desert.

### Dead Sea Beaches, Spas, and Mineral Pools

You cannot actually swim in the briny Dead Sea; you simply float in it. The incredible density of its water—about 10 times that of the ocean—makes it impossible to sink here. The Dead Sea area is recognized as one of the world's primary health retreats for sufferers of psoriasis and various rheumatic and arthritic ailments. But the hale, too, will enjoy the benefits of the incredible mineral concentration in the Dead Sea water and mud, the natural warm mineral springs, and the oxygen-rich atmosphere at the lowest point on earth. There are several places to swim along the Dead Sea and the Ein Gedi Spa. (For the sophisticated spas and therapeutic facilities of the Ein Bokek–Neve Zohar area, *see* Chapter 8.)

Doctors recommend confining your time in the water to 15 minutes or less because of the enervating effect of the salt; and if you have a heart condition or high blood pressure, you should not bathe here at all. Avoid the discomfort of getting the brine in your eyes and mouth, although you can rinse off at the outdoor showers and faucets found at recognized beaches. It's imperative to drink a lot of water, especially in the hot season (April to October). Many beaches are rocky (and hot in summer), so it's a good idea to wear protective rubber sandals, shoes, or sneakers. Don't leave your possessions unguarded on the beach.

### Dining

Beyond some passable lunch cafeterias, there are no restaurants in this area to tempt you out in the evening. Most tours bring you back by nightfall to Jerusalem or Tel Aviv, where your options are plenty (☞ Dining *in* Chapters 2 and 4).

### Hiking and Rappelling

The Judean Desert has some excellent hiking trails. Ein Gedi's two nature reserves, Nahal David and Nahal Arugot, are the best for beginners. Serious hikers can seek out more challenging walks in spectacular canyons but should only pursue these with expert local guidance. The combination of heat and dryness can be dangerous, so bring a hat and copious amounts of water when hiking in this region. Some of the awesome limestone cliffs near the Dead Sea are favorites with local rappelling clubs.

### Lodging

The lodgings of the Dead Sea region are heavily used by visitors, both local and international, who come to "take the waters." Many enjoy the quiet ambience between cliffs and coastline. Others just make this a convenient base from which to strike out over the Judean Desert. Facilities range from youth hostels to the luxury hotels of the nearby Ein Bokek area (☞ Chapter 8).

People typically explore the area west of Jerusalem as a day trip from Jerusalem or Tel Aviv. The only decent lodgings here are some fine guest houses 15–20 minutes outside the capital. Bethlehem, now governed by the Palestinian Authority, has a few unprepossessing hotels; Jerusalem, only 10 minutes away, is a far more convenient and congenial base. For price-category definitions, *see* Lodging *in* Chapter 2.

## Exploring Around Jerusalem

This area offers day-trip options in three different directions. The Dead Sea has the richest fare and takes the most time, but you can see some of its sights en route to the Galilee via the Jordan Valley. The other two areas—west of Jerusalem, and Bethlehem and the West Bank— are closer to Jerusalem and can be combined with Jerusalem sights or, in a pinch, with each other.

## Great Itineraries

To explore the **Dead Sea region,** you journey east through the arid Judean Desert to Qumran, where the Dead Sea Scrolls were found; the salty Dead Sea, the lowest point on earth; the canyons and waterfalls of Ein Gedi; and the ancient palace-fortress of Masada. An interesting side trip (political climate permitting) includes the oasis town of Jericho, the oldest city known.

With an early start, you can see most of these sights in one day. A good combination is Masada (with its dramatic history and interesting archaeological remains), the Dead Sea (total relaxation), and one of the nature reserves at Ein Gedi (a refreshing antidote to the heat and brine of the Dead Sea). From April to October, later closing times allow a visit to Qumran as well. You can see Jericho (again, if accessible) as a day tour from Jerusalem, on the way to an overnight trip along the Dead Sea, or en route to the Jordan Valley and Galilee.

The area **west of Jerusalem** encompasses part of the Judean Hills and, farther southwest, the lowland area known as the Shefelah. Highlights include the exquisite Sorek stalactite cave; the Elah Valley, where David and Goliath clashed; and the intriguing man-made caves of Bet Guvrin and Maresha. It's a full but comfortable day trip.

**Bethlehem,** with its famous Church of the Nativity, is no more than a 10-minute drive south of Jerusalem. You can see the church and be back in the city within two hours. There is the option (recommended only with a licensed guide) of continuing deeper into the West Bank as far as the Etzion Bloc, now accessible by a new road that leaves Jerusalem from the Gilo neighborhood, bypassing several unfriendly Arab villages on the way. From the Etzion Bloc, Route 367 descends west to the Elah Valley (☞ West of Jerusalem, *below*), if you want to link two areas on your trip.

## When to Tour Around Jerusalem

The Dead Sea region is pleasant in the cool season (October–April) but often very hot the rest of the year. Getting a very early start and beginning the day with Masada can help beat the heat and the crowds. *Ending* the day with Masada often achieves the same result. Bethlehem is best first thing in the morning or late in the afternoon if you want to avoid the crowds, especially the seasonal cruise-boat traffic; but do note the hours for the Grotto of the Nativity. The area west of Jerusalem is good anytime, although the Sorek Cave has limited hours and no guided tour on Friday.

*Numbers in the margin correspond to points of interest on the Around Jerusalem map.*

# DEAD SEA REGION

From the ridges of Jerusalem's Mt. Scopus and Mount of Olives, the view to the east is of barren hills that cascade almost 4,000 ft down to the Dead Sea. Clouds off the Mediterranean warm and disperse as they cross the high ridge and descend toward the chasm of the Dead Sea, creating what is called a "rain shadow." Within a map distance of about 24 km (15 mi), the average annual rainfall drops from 22 inches in Jerusalem to 2 inches at the Dead Sea. This "shadow" region is the Judean Desert, and its proximity to Jerusalem has always made it part of that city's consciousness. Refugees fled to it; hermits sought its solitude; and in ancient times, before the Jewish Day of Atonement, the scapegoat symbolically bearing the sins of the people was driven into oblivion among its stark precipices.

## Around Jerusalem

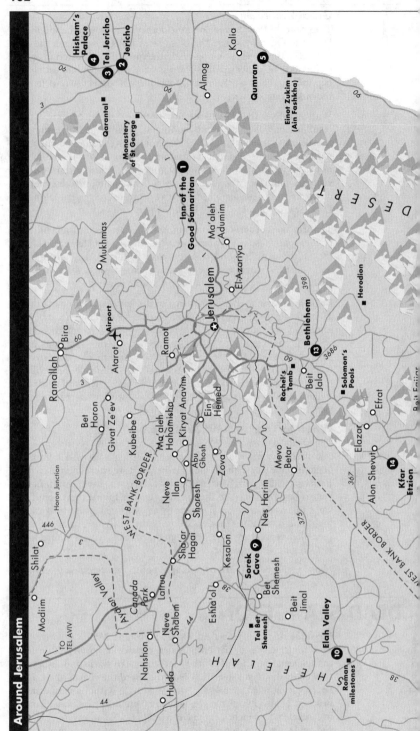

Hisham's Palace **4**
Tel Jericho **3**
Jericho **2**
Kalia
90
Almog
Qarantal ■
Monastery of St George ■
Qumran **5**
Einot Zukim (Ain Fashkha) ■
90
3
Inn of the Good Samaritan **1**
Mukhmas
Ma'aleh Adumim
El-Azariya
D E S E R T
Jerusalem
Airport
Bira
Ramallah
60
Atarot
Ramot
398
Bethlehem **13**
Herodion ■
Ramot
3
Bet Horon
Givat Ze'ev
Kubeibe
Ma'aleh Hahamisha
Kiryat Anavim
Ein Hemed
Rachel's Tomb ■
Beit Jala
60
3686
Solomon's Pools ■
Efrat
Horon Junction
WEST BANK BORDER
Neve Ilan
Abu Ghosh
Shoresh
Zova
Mevo Betar
Elazar
Alon Shevut
Beit Fajjar
446
Shilat
Sha'ar Hagai
Nes Harim
367
Kfar Etzion **14**
WEST BANK BORDER
Modiin
Ayalon Valley
Canada Park
Latrun
Kesalon
Sorek Cave **9**
375
TO TEL AVIV
Nahshon
Neve Shalom
Eshta'ol
38
Bet Shemesh
Beit Jimal
Elah Valley **10**
Roman milestones ■
38
Hulda
3
Tel Bet Shemesh ■
S H E F E L A H
44
44

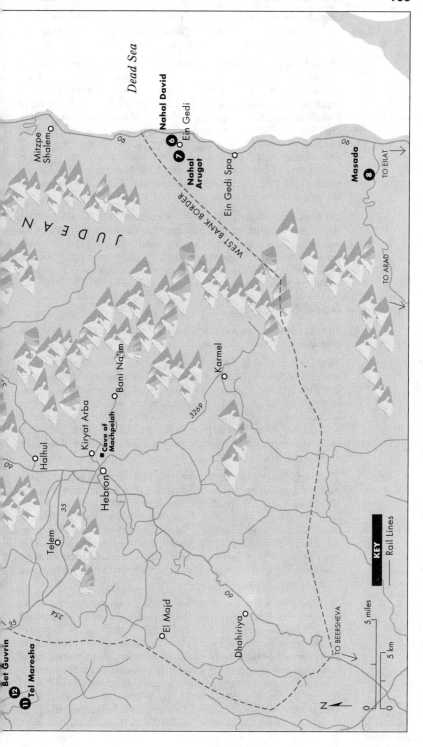

*Dead Sea*

Mitzpe Shalem

**Nahal David**

**6** Ein Gedi

**7** **Nahal Arugot**

Ein Gedi Spa

**Masada**

**8**

TO EILAT

J U D E A N

Bani Na'im

Kiryat Arba

■ Cave of Machpelah

Karmel

3269

Halhul

Hebron

Telem

El Majid

Dhahiriya

Bet Guvrin

**12**

**11** Tel Maresha

WEST BANK BORDER

TO ARAD

TO BEERSHEVA

**KEY**

Rail Lines

5 miles

5 km

N

60
35
3
354

Important words of caution: it is vital to wear a hat and drink plenty of water here in hot weather. Approach the desert with respect—do not attempt unfamiliar trails without expert guidance.

Route 1 leaves Jerusalem just north of the French Hill neighborhood, runs east, swings back below the eastern slopes of Mt. Scopus and the Mount of Olives (look for their distinctive towers on your right), and begins its steep descent to the Dead Sea. Some 8 km (5 mi) on, ahead and above you, is the edge of the town of Ma'aleh Adumim, built in the 1970s and '80s as a bedroom community of Jerusalem. This and the handful of small Jewish villages in the Judean Desert are some of the so-called West Bank settlements that so often make the news. Because of their isolation, however, they have been spared the constant friction with Palestinian Arab neighbors typical of such settlements in the mountain region.

On both sides of the road you'll see encampments of tent-dwelling Bedouins (Arab nomads) still clinging to their ancestors' way of life and eking out a livelihood by herding sheep and goats. Yet they have made concessions to modernity: water tanks and tractors, synthetic fabrics flapping on clotheslines, and even the occasional TV antenna sprouting from a tent bear witness to a culture in flux.

## Inn of the Good Samaritan

**❶** *20 km (13 mi) east of Jerusalem on Rte. 1, 500 yards east of the junction with Rte. 458.*

The lone one-story building, its courtyard surrounded by a low stone wall, was a Turkish police fort a century ago, the halfway point on what was then a two-day journey between Jerusalem and Jericho. Known in the Hebrew Bible as Ma'aleh Adumim (the Red Ascent) because of its distinctive patch of red limestone, this spot was once the border marker between the biblical Israelite tribes of Benjamin, to the north, and Judah, to the south (Joshua 15). (Don't confuse it with the town of the same name closer to Jerusalem.)

The popular name of the site, the Inn of the Good Samaritan, is not necessarily spurious. The New Testament (Luke 10) relates the parable of a man ambushed on the Jericho road and helped only by a Samaritan (a member of a people hostile to the Jews), who lodged him at the nearby inn. Because Jesus' parables used images familiar to his listeners, it's entirely possible that he had a specific inn in mind and that the inn was at this perennially strategic spot. The original Jericho road, now tarred but not much used, is off to the left of the highway as you continue east.

No remains of a 1st-century inn have been found, but other ages have left their mark. If you're energetic, turn your back on the commercialized "Inn," carefully cross the road, and climb the dirt track to the top of the hill opposite. Amid the scanty ruins of the small 12th-century Crusader fort of **Maldoim**—from which you can see the outskirts of Jerusalem and Jericho—the Gospel passage comes alive. The medieval Burchard of Mt. Sion wrote that the Red Ascent (called the "Blood Ascent" by Arabs) got its name "from the frequent blood shed there. Of a truth it is horrible to behold and exceedingly dangerous! . . ."

## Jericho

★ **❷** *45 km (28 mi) northeast of Jerusalem.*

The oasis town of Jericho, immortalized as the place where "the walls came tumblin' down" at the sound of Joshua's trumpets, is the oldest city in the world, and at 850 ft below sea level, it's (currently) the lowest as well. It may be worth a trip through Jericho just to be able to say "I was there," but the town does have enough to hold you a little longer. The wide, tree-lined main artery is more country lane than city street. The riot of greenery—date palms, orange groves, banana plantations, bougainvillea, and papaya trees—takes the edge off the neglect and dilapidation that are everywhere apparent. The Arab population of about 20,000 is mostly Muslim, with a tiny Christian minority.

Jericho has been under autonomous Palestinian control since May 1994, and although the atmosphere at press time was generally relaxed, the situation is not always predictable, and you should check it before you plan your tour. There have been times when tourists in private cars were discouraged from visiting the town.

Entering the town from the south, take the left fork at the traffic island. A few hundred yards farther, the road swings sharply to the left. To the right of the bend and one block away is a huge, fenced-off sycamore tree, which tradition (and the postcard vendor across the way) identifies as the very one Zacchaeus climbed to watch Jesus pass by (Luke 19).

**3** **Tel Jericho** is the mound of accumulated earth that entombs the famous ancient city. Archaeologists have extensively excavated it, looking for its most famous ruins: Joshua's walls. Jericho was the first Canaanite objective of the Israelite army in the mid-13th century BC. The Israelites marched around the city once a day for six days, says the Bible. On the seventh day, they marched around seven times, and on the seventh time they blew their ram's horns and shouted, "and the wall fell down flat, so that the people went up into the city, every man straight before him, and they took the city" (Joshua 6:20).

Those walls have not been found, but remains of the world's oldest walled city have. An excavation pit at the top of the *tel* (hill) reveals a massive, round stone tower 30 ft in diameter, preserved to a height of 25 ft and attached to an 8-ft-thick wall. The structures predate the invention of pottery, and carbon-14 tests have placed human skulls and bones found here in the Neolithic period (Late Stone Age), between 6500 and 7800 BC. Little is known about who these early urbanites were, or why they needed such stout fortifications thousands of years before they became common in the rest of the region, but a wealth of artifacts, most displayed in the Israel and Rockefeller museums in Jerusalem (☞ Exploring Jerusalem *in* Chapter 2), helps us imagine their domestic life and customs. One such custom was decapitating the bodies of deceased relatives and burying the head beneath the floor of the house, apparently to keep the ancestor's spirit—and thus his strength and wisdom—within the home.

From the sun shelter at the top of the tel, there is a fine sweeping view of Jericho, the biblical "City of Palms." The generous spring that was always the secret of its fecundity is across the road, capped today by a pump house. It is known as **Ain es-Sultan,** the Sultan's Spring, or Elisha's Spring, in recognition of the Old Testament prophet's miracle of sweetening the water with a bowl of salt (I Kings 2). In the distance to the east are the high mountains of the biblical kingdoms of Ammon and Moab, in Jordan, among them the peak of Mt. Nebo, from which Moses viewed the Promised Land.

To the south, among the banana trees some 3 km (2 mi) away, is a small but distinctive mound of earth. This is **Tel Abu Alaik,** where archaeologists' spades have uncovered the remains of the royal palace of the Jewish Hasmonean dynasty (2nd–1st centuries BC), described by the

Jewish historian Josephus Flavius (AD 37–circa 100). A synagogue of the period, believed to be the oldest ever found, was unearthed in the complex in 1998. In the last decades of the 1st century BC, Mark Antony gave the valuable oasis of Jericho to his beloved Cleopatra; the humiliated King Herod, Antony's local vassal, was then forced to lease the property back from the Egyptian queen. Herod expanded and improved the palace, turning it into his winter retreat. He died here in 4 BC.

To the west is the **Mount of Temptation,** identified by tradition as the "exceedingly high mountain" from which Satan tempted Jesus with dominion over "all the kingdoms of the world" (Matthew 4). The peak is surrounded by a modern wall. Halfway down the mountain and a bit to the left is a remarkable Greek Orthodox monastery, built right into the cliff face on Byzantine remains (note also the many caves, which once housed hermits). Both mountain and monastery (the Monastery of Temptation) are known locally as Qarantal, a corruption of *quarantena*—a period of 40 days (the source of the English word *quarantine*)—the period of Jesus' temptation. ✉ *Turn left at sharp bend in the road; enter from the west,* ☎ *02/992–1909.* ☒ *NIS 10 ($2.90).* ☉ *Apr.–Sept. daily 8–6, Oct.–Mar. daily 8–5; subject to change.*

NEED A BREAK?    The **Temptation Restaurant,** next to the Tel Jericho parking lot, has excellent *bourma,* a honey-rolled pastry filled with whole pistachio nuts. The lunches offer good value, with tasty *mezes* (Middle Eastern salads) and meats. The nearby fruit stands tend to overcharge, but try the pomelo (related to the grapefruit), in season from December to March.

❹ A spacious site in pastoral surroundings, the remains of **Hisham's Palace** have some interesting stonework and a spectacular mosaic floor. Hisham was a scion of the Ummayad dynasty, which built the Dome of the Rock and El-Aqsa Mosque, in Jerusalem. Like Herod eight centuries earlier, he was attracted by the balmy winter climate of the Jericho oasis and decided to build what is known as Hisham's Palace (Hirbet el-Mafjar, in Arabic). While still under construction, the structure was badly damaged by the great earthquake of AD 749 and never completed, but the high quality of the mosaics and stone and plaster reliefs that survive are evidence of its splendor.

To get here from Tel Jericho, go north for 2 km (1 mi) and turn right. After that, the left turn toward the site itself is another kilometer (½ mi) down the road but is marked only by a low stone pillar on the right. You enter the ruins through a small gatehouse, which leads into a wide plaza dominated by a large, star-shape stone window that once graced an upper-floor chamber. The basement bathhouse and one of the palace's two mosques (open to the sky) are an interesting juxtaposition of both the worldly and the spiritual character of the Arab empire of the time. North of the plaza is a series of columns—some artless reconstructions in concrete—that supported the roof of a large bath and recreation area. Several sections of the fine geometric mosaics have been left exposed; others are covered by sand.

The most impressive part of the complex is the reception room, off the plaza. Its intricate **mosaic floor,** depicting a lion hunting a stag, is one of the most beautiful in the country, the tiny colored tesserae producing a realism astonishing for this medium. You can still see fragments of ornate stucco reliefs on some of the walls, but the best examples found here are now in Jerusalem's Rockefeller Museum (☞ Exploring Jerusalem *in* Chapter 2). The balustrade of an ornamental pool reflects the artistic influences of both East and West. ✉ *Jericho,* ☎ *02/992–2522.* ☒ *NIS 10 ($2.90).* ☉ *Apr.–Sept. daily 8–6, Oct.–Mar. daily 8–5; subject to change.*

*En Route*   Route 90 south brings you back toward the **Dead Sea.** A milestone by the side of the road just before the gas station (at the Kalia Junction) announces that you have now reached the bottom of the world, and a Bedouin is often here with his camel to help you immortalize the moment. The Dead Sea has shrunk in recent years, so the shore at this point is almost a kilometer (½ mi) away. You'll see heaps of white potash, the primary product of the Dead Sea, off to the left, though today all extraction of potash, bromine, and magnesium takes place at the huge plant at Sodom, at the southern end of the lake.

## Qumran

**⑤** *6 km (4 mi) south of the Kalia Junction on Rte. 90, 20 km (13 mi) south of Jericho, 50 km (31 mi) east of Jerusalem.*

The ancient remains of Qumran are not especially impressive to the layperson, but caves in the cliffs west of the small site yielded the most significant archaeological find ever made in Israel: the **Dead Sea Scrolls,** found under extraordinary circumstances. In 1947, a young Bedouin goatherd stumbled on a cave containing a cache of the now-famous scrolls, hidden in earthen jars. Because the scrolls were written on parchment—treated animal hide—one of the nomads sought out a Bethlehem shoemaker to turn them into sandals! The shoemaker alerted a local antiquities dealer, who brought them to the attention of Professor Eliezer Sukenik of the Hebrew University of Jerusalem. Five other major scrolls and several thousand fragments came to light in subsequent years, some from pirate digs conducted by the Bedouin themselves in other caves in the area, others from methodical excavations by Israeli, French, and British archaeologists.

The scrolls were written by an ultradevout Jewish sect generally identified as the Essenes, who had set up a monastic community at Qumran in the late 2nd century BC. During the Great Revolt against Rome (AD 66–73), they apparently spirited away their precious scrolls to the caves visible in the cliffs and canyons behind the town. Their fears were well founded—Qumran was destroyed in AD 68, never to rise again—giving scholars a terminus date, or last possible date, for the age of the scrolls.

The Dead Sea Scrolls include books of the Old Testament and sectarian literature of the Qumran community. Among the biblical scrolls is one containing the full 66 chapters of the Book of Isaiah, which, except for minor variations, is almost identical to the text used in Jewish communities to this day, putting to rest any doubts about the authenticity of the modern version. Sectarian texts include the constitution of the community, known as the "Rule of the Community" (or as the "Manual of Discipline"); a description of a battle that ends the world ("War of the Sons of Light Against the Sons of Darkness"); and the "Thanksgiving Scroll," containing hymns reminiscent of biblical psalms.

Apart from the bonanza the scrolls represented for Bible scholars and students of ancient Hebrew, they gave researchers rare insights into this previously shadowy Jewish sect. Christian scholars in particular have long been intrigued by the suggestion that John the Baptist, whose lifestyle seems to have paralleled that of the Essenes, may have been a member of the Qumran community. Several of the scrolls are on display in the Israel Museum in Jerusalem (☞ Exploring Jerusalem *in* Chapter 2).

Qumran sits on a narrow plateau between the craggy limestone cliffs to the west and the narrow shores of the Dead Sea to the east. The site was excavated in the 1950s. Climb the tower for a good view, and note the unusual number of water channels and cisterns that gathered run-off winter floodwater from the cliffs to the west. Just below the tower (in front of you as you look toward the Dead Sea) is a long room identified as the **scriptorium.** A plaster writing table and bronze and ceramic inkwells found here confirm that this was where the scrolls were written. A good air-conditioned cafeteria and gift store now serve the site. ✉ *Rte. 90,* ☎ *02/994–2235.* 🎟 *NIS 13 ($3.70).* ◷ *Apr.–Sept., Sat.–Thurs. 8–5, Fri. 8–4; Oct.–Mar., Sat.–Thurs. 8–4, Fri. 8–3.*

### Beaches and Pools

**Attraktzia** offers a Dead Sea beach, freshwater pools with water slides, two go-cart tracks (separate fee), and full facilities. ✉ *3 km (2 mi) north of Qumran off Rte. 90,* ☎ *02/994–2393.* 🎟 *NIS 59 ($16.90); after 2 PM NIS 40 ($11.50).* ◷ *Apr.–Oct., daily 9–5.*

**Siesta Beach** has good access to the Dead Sea, free black mud, showers, and changing rooms. You can buy disposable or regular towels (with soap and shampoo). ✉ *3 km (2 mi) north of Qumran off Rte. 90,* ☎ *02/994–2781.* 🎟 *NIS 12 ($3.50).* ◷ *Apr.–Oct., daily 8:30–6:30; Nov.–Mar., daily 8:30–5:30.*

### Hiking, Rappelling, and Desert Safaris

**Metzukei Dragot,** the Center for Desert Tourism (✉ M.P. Jericho Valley, ☎ 02/994–4222, 🖷 02/994–4333), is on a cliff top overlooking the Dead Sea. The turnoff from Route 90 is 17 km (10½ mi) south of Qumran, 16 km (10 mi) north of Ein Gedi; the Center is about 5 km (3 mi) off the main road. Run by Kibbutz Mitzpe Shalem, it specializes in desert safaris in go-anywhere vehicles, and in rappelling (even for novices) on the impressive cliff faces nearby.

### Shopping

**Kibbutz Mitzpe Shalem** (✉ 20 km, or 12½ mi, south of Qumran on Rte. 90, ☎ 02/994–5117) manufactures the excellent—but not inexpensive—Ahava line of skin and hair-care products based on (but not smelling like!) the Dead Sea minerals. The factory outlet here is open Sunday–Thursday 8–6, Friday and holiday eves 8–4, and Saturday 8:30–5:30, but the products are sold elsewhere (at Masada and the Ein Gedi Spa, for example) and at pharmacies in major cities.

## Einot Zukim (Ain Fashkha)

*3 km (2 mi) south of Qumran on Rte. 90.*

A Dead Sea beach, fresh (though brackish) springs, a variety of trees and reeds rare in the arid Judean Desert, and picnic and changing facilities make the nature reserve Einot Zukim (Ain Fashkha, in Arabic; the name means "Cliff Springs") a popular spot. It's especially crowded on Friday and Saturday. The most beautiful part of the reserve, with bubbling brooks and thickets of giant reeds, is closed to the general public to preserve its fragile ecosystem, but the Nature Reserves Authority occasionally conducts tours of this section; call for information. ☎ *02/994–2355.* 🎟 *NIS 25 ($7.20).* ◷ *Mar.–Oct., daily 8:30–5.*

*En Route*  Four kilometers (2½ mi) south of Qumran, Route 90 enters a wider area, the delta of the dry **Kidron stream.** One of the very few canyons in the area with a gentle enough slope to be used as a caravan route in ancient times, the Kidron comes down from the heart of Jerusalem itself. Look for the remains of a 21-centuries-old Hasmonean fort on your left, built to protect royal caravans carrying valuable tropical produce from Ein Gedi to the Mediterranean world.

# Ein Gedi

★ *33 km (21 mi) south of Qumran, 20 km (12½ mi) north of Masada, 83 km (52 mi) east and south of Jerusalem.*

The wondrous oasis of Ein Gedi—two nature reserves and a verdant kibbutz-type village—bursts upon you with a splash of vivid green against the burnt browns and beiges of the desert rock.

**❻ Nahal David** (David's Stream), where David hid from the wrath of King Saul (I Samuel 24) 3,000 years ago, is a delightful nature reserve, with cliffs soaring to more than 1,600 ft above the streams, waterfalls, and tropical reeds. These features plus the wildlife would make this a delightful spot anywhere, but in the midst of a harsh desert, it's nothing short of spectacular. As you reach Ein Gedi from the north, the first turnoff to the right takes you to the parking lot at the entrance to Nahal David.

It's a bit of a climb up the clearly marked trail, which takes you past several pools and small waterfalls to the beautiful top waterfall, but it's not too daunting. Allow at least 1¼ hours to include a refreshing dip under one of the lower waterfalls. Floods in the winter of 1997– 98 wrought changes in the landscape, carrying away some of the reed thickets but happily deepening the bathing holes. Look out for ibex (wild goat), especially in the afternoon, and for the small, furry hyrax, often seen on tree branches. Leopards were rediscovered in this area some years ago but face extinction again because of breeding problems; they're seldom seen nowadays, and never in the reserve.

If you're a hiker, don't miss the trail that breaks off to the right some 50 yards down the return path from the top waterfall. It passes the remains of Byzantine irrigation systems and offers breathtaking views of the Dead Sea. The trail doubles back on itself toward the source of Nahal David. Near the top, a short side path climbs to the remains of a 4th-millennium BC (Chalcolithic) temple. The main path leads on to a streambed, again turns east, and reaches Dudim (Lovers') Cave, formed by boulders and filled with the crystal-clear spring water. You are directly above the waterfall of Nahal David (don't throw stones— there are people below). Since this trail involves a considerable climb (and hikers invariably take time to bathe in the "cave"), access to the trail is permitted only up to 2½ hours before closing time. ✉ *Ein Gedi,* ☎ *07/658–4285.* 🎫 *NIS 15 ($4.30); includes Nahal Arugot on same day only (☞ below).* ☉ *Sat.–Thurs. 8–4, Fri. 8–3; closes 1 hr later during daylight saving time (late spring and summer); last admission 1 hr before closing.*

**❼ Nahal Arugot,** like Nahal David to its north, is a splendid nature reserve. Aside from its natural beauty—though perhaps because of it— Ein Gedi has attracted settlement for thousands of years. Near the mouth of the canyon is a small mound known as **Tel Goren,** where excavations in the 1960s exposed five noncontinuous strata of settlements from the 7th century BC (Israelite period) to the 6th century AD (Byzantine period). An intriguing Hebrew and Aramaic inscription removed from a 6th-century AD mosaic synagogue floor nearby invokes the wrath of heaven on troublemakers of different stripes, including "whoever reveals the secret of the town to the Gentiles." The "secret" is believed to refer to the revived cultivation of the balsam tree, which produced the prized perfume for which the town was once famous.

Although not quite as green as Nahal David, the deep canyon of Nahal Arugot is, if anything, more spectacular. Enormous boulders and slabs of stone on the opposite cliff face seem poised in mid-cataclysm, and the whole effect is powerfully primordial. The hour-long hike to the **Hidden Waterfall** (quite a lot of steps, but not especially steep) takes you by delightful spots where a stream bubbles over rock shelves and shallow pools offer relief from the heat. The Hidden Waterfall is reached by a short marked trail down to the left. Do not continue on the trail beyond the waterfall without prior arrangement with the Nature Reserves Authority. From the waterfall, if you're adventurous and have appropriate footwear, you can return through the greenery of the streambed, leaping the boulders and wading the pools. ⊠ *Ein Gedi,* ☎ *07/658–4285.* ⊡ *NIS 15 ($4.30); includes Nahal David on same day only (☞ above).* ☉ *Sat.–Thurs. 8–4, Fri. 8–3; closes 1 hr later during daylight saving time (late spring and summer); last admission 2 hrs before closing.*

### Beaches and Pools

**Ein Gedi Spa** offers decent facilities (indoor showers, changing rooms with lockers, disposable towels for a fee), access to the Dead Sea, a freshwater pool, free Dead Sea mud, and marvelously relaxing, warm indoor sulfur pools. There's a restaurant downstairs from the changing rooms and snack bar. ⊠ *3 km (2 mi) south of Ein Gedi gas station,* ☎ *07/659–4813.* ⊡ *NIS 45 ($12.90), NIS 49 ($14) on Sat. and holidays, including locker and restaurant discount; NIS 35 ($10), including light lunch, if accompanied by licensed guide.* ☉ *Months of daylight saving time (late spring and summer), daily 7–6; rest of year, daily 7–5.*

A somewhat rocky **public beach,** 200 hundred yards south of Nahal David behind the gas station, has free access to the Dead Sea, freshwater showers (absolutely essential) by the water's edge, and basic changing facilities for NIS 5 ($1.50). Some words of advice: avoid getting the saltwater in your eyes and mouth, and do not leave valuables unguarded.

### Lodging

**$$$**   🏨 **Kibbutz Ein Gedi.** This motel-style guest house on the kibbutz grounds is set between 1,600-ft-high cliffs and the Dead Sea and surrounded by subtropical landscaping. There is no maid service. Prices per double range, according to season, from NIS 579 to NIS 680 ($174 to $204) and include breakfast, another full meal, and unlimited entry to the nearby spa, to which there's a free shuttle throughout the day. ⊠ *Rte. 90, M.P. Dead Sea 86980,* ☎ *07/659–4222,* 𝖥𝖠𝖷 *07/658–4328. 120 rooms with shower. Kitchenette, pool, 2 tennis courts. AE, DC, MC, V.*

**$**   🏨 **Bet Sarah** is a newly renovated youth hostel belonging to the official YHA network. It has 350 beds in either dormitory or (far better) guest-house configurations, all with facilities *en suite.* ⊠ *Rte. 90, M.P. Dead Sea 86980,* ☎ *07/658–4165,* 𝖥𝖠𝖷 *07/658–4445. Cafeteria. AE, DC, MC, V.*

### Outdoor Activities and Sports

The newcomer to Ein Gedi will have no problem hiking the area alone, on well-marked trails through magnificent scenery. For advice on more serious trails and information on organized hikes, contact the **Society for the Protection of Nature in Israel (SPNI)** (⊠ 13 Helene Hamalka St., Jerusalem, ☎ 02/624–4605; ⊠ 3 Hashefela St., Tel Aviv, ☎ 03/638–8677; or the Society's field school in Ein Gedi, ☎ 07/658–4288).

## Masada

★ ❽   *19 km (12 mi) south of Ein Gedi on Rte. 90, 103 km (64 mi) east and south of Jerusalem, 20 km (12½ mi) north of Ein Bokek.*

The great, isolated flattop rock of Masada commands its surroundings, its Herodian remains a witness to the chimera of ancient power and glory. Hated by his subjects and threatened by Cleopatra of Egypt, Herod the Great—King of the Jews by the grace of Rome—built a fortress here in the 1st century BC to which he could escape if necessary. Terrified by the thought of being an uncomfortable refugee, Herod had the mountaintop complex built in the finest palatial style; nowhere in the land are both his paranoia and sense of grandeur more evident. Long before you reach it, Masada is visible to the west of the highway.

Masada's very name has become a symbol and a rallying cry, having entered history as the site of the dramatic last stand of Jewish rebels against the legions of Rome. With Herod's death in 4 BC and the exile of his oldest son, Archelaus, 10 years later, the central districts of Judea and Samaria (south and north of Jerusalem, respectively) came under direct Roman control. Decades of oppression and misrule precipitated the Great Revolt of the Jews against Rome in AD 66, spearheaded by an ultranationalist group called the Zealots. Masada fell to the rebels early on, but with the Roman reconquest of the country and the fall of Jerusalem in AD 70, the fortress became the last refuge for almost a thousand men, women, and children. The new governor, Silva, came down with a full legion of troops and thousands of slaves to crush the last vestige of resistance. The long Roman siege wall at the foot of the mountain and the eight square Roman camps in strategic locations on all sides attest to the thoroughness of the siege.

The 1st-century Jewish historian Josephus Flavius sets the final scene. Despite the Jews' vigorous defense, the Romans succeeded in constructing a massive earth assault ramp from the high western plateau to the very summit of the mountain. Seeing that the battle was lost, the rebel leader, Elazar Ben Yair, assembled his warriors and exhorted them to "at once choose death with honor, and do the kindest thing we can for ourselves, our wives and children" rather than face the brutal consequences of capture. The decision was not an easy one, relates Josephus, but once taken, it impelled each man to "carry out his terrible resolve" without delay. Having dispatched their own families, the men then drew lots to select 10 executioners for the rest; and the 10 similarly chose the last man, who would kill them all and afterward take his own life.

Josephus, who went over to the Romans in the course of the revolt, has long been suspect in the eyes of modern historians, and his melodramatic account was taken with more than a grain of salt. His description of Masada has been borne out by archaeologists, however, and the human skeletal remains and inscribed potsherds (the lots, perhaps?) seem to give weight to his story as well.

Most visitors ride up to Masada on the large **cable car** (three minutes), with a scheduled run every half hour starting at 8 AM, and intermediate runs depending on demand. The intrepid climb the **Snake Path** (45 minutes of steep walking), some even going before dawn to watch the sunrise. Others take the easier, western Roman Ramp path, accessible only from Arad (☞ Exploring Eilat and the Negev *in* Chapter 8). The desert climate makes it imperative to drink lots of water and wear a hat. Running water (but no other refreshments) is available on Masada itself, so save your bottles for refilling. Allow at least 1½ to two hours to explore the site. Maps, brochures, and a very useful electronic guide are available at the top entrance.

The 90 steps from the cable car to the top of Masada pass a large plastered cistern, one of a dozen (many are much larger) that gave Herod's fortress an incredible 11 million gallons "on tap." The secret was the winter floodwaters in streambeds west of the mountain, diverted to cisterns in the slope and then hauled to the top by hand.

The entire mountaintop—an area of more than 20 acres—is surrounded by a 4,250-ft-long **casemate,** a double wall that included living quarters and guardrooms. Most of the important buildings are concentrated in the site's high northern area. A street passes between storerooms, where quantities of broken jars, seeds of grain, and dried fruit pits were found, bearing out Josephus's story that the Jews burned their possessions but spared their food supply in order to show the Romans that they did not die of want.

At the highest and most northerly point of Masada stands the **Northern Palace,** an extraordinary structure that seems to hang off the mountain. The wonderful view from its upper terrace takes in the Roman camps and "runner's path" (used for communication between the camps), as well as Ein Gedi, 16 km (10 mi) to the north, from which Silva had to get his water. The effect is awesome: baked brown precipices and bleached valleys shimmering in the midday glare, or awash in the gentler light of the early morning or late afternoon. Designed to serve as an inner citadel in time of crisis, the palace is protected by an outer plastered wall.

Facing you as you return from the upper terrace is the **bathhouse,** a state-of-the-art facility in Herod's time, with its *apodyterium* (changing room), *frigidarium, tepidarium,* and *caldarium* (cold, lukewarm, and hot rooms, respectively). Frescoes and floor tiles are evidence of the Herodian opulence; intrusive benches and a pool represent alterations by the later occupants. The caldarium was once a closed room, heated, sauna-style, from below, and through wall pipes by hot air pumped in from an outside furnace. West of the bathhouse, steps descend to the middle and lower terraces—interesting (note Herod's hidden spiral staircase as well as the columns and frescoes on the lower terrace), but a long climb back up.

The **mikveh** is one of two Jewish ritual baths found on Masada and built during the revolt. Their discovery in the 1960s created a sensation in Israel's ultra-Orthodox circles, especially after a rabbinic inspection team confirmed that the mikvehs had been built in precise obedience to Jewish law—thus demonstrating both the longevity and tenacity of the religious tradition.

Continue down to the western casemate and the **synagogue** of Masada, one of only four ever found from this period. The building's orientation toward Jerusalem suggested its function, but the stone benches (synagogue means "place of assembly") and man-made pit for damaged scrolls (a *geniza*) confirmed it. It was likely here, in the community's spiritual center, that Elazar's men made their fateful decision.

At a break in the walls of the western edge, a modern winch marks the place where the Roman legionnaires broke into Masada. The original wedge-shape **ramp** (the upper part has since collapsed) is below. Here, too, is the Western Gate, from which a modern trail takes you down this side of the mountain (access via Arad only).

The small **Byzantine chapel,** complete with mosaic floor and wall designs, comes as something of a surprise on Masada. The monastic movement of the 5th century swirled and eddied into the most remote corners of the Byzantine Empire and found solitude here, too. South of the chapel is the **Western Palace,** the largest structure on Masada and originally its residential and administrative center. Its most interesting features are two colorful Herodian mosaics, the larger with especially meticulous geometric and fruit motifs.

The message of the Jews' last stand on Masada was not lost on Palestinian Jews fighting for independence in the 1930s and '40s, or on the modern Israel they created. "Masada shall not fall again!" became not just a rallying cry but a state of mind. It reflected Jews' determination (made more poignant by the Nazi Holocaust) to become masters of their own destiny in their own land.

If you have time and energy, explore the sparser, southern part of Masada, with its huge water cistern and spectacular view from the southern citadel. Test the echoes here as you face the great canyon to the south.

A fine summer-night diversion is the **sound-and-light show** at Masada's western base, accessible from Arad.

✉ *Off Rte. 90,* ☎ *07/658–4207 or 07/658–4208.* 🎫 *Site NIS 17 ($5). Cable car,* 🚠 *one-way NIS 18 ($5.20), round-trip NIS 30 ($8.60).* ☉ *Apr.–Sept., Sat.–Thurs. 8–5 (last car down at 5), Fri. and holiday eves 8–4 (last car down at 3), eve of Yom Kippur until noon. Oct.–Mar., Sat.–Thurs. 8–4 (last car down at 4), Fri. and holiday eves 8–3 (last car down at 2). Sound-and-light show (access only from Arad;* ☞ *Exploring Eilat and the Negev in Chapter 8)* 🎫 *NIS 30 ($8.60).* ☉ *Mar.– Oct., Tues. and Thurs. 9 PM. Translation headsets (from Hebrew)* 🎫 *NIS 12.50 ($3.60). Shuttle bus, by prior reservation: Yoel Tours,* ☎ *07/658–4432 or 053/913149.* 🎫 *NIS 50 ($14.30) from Arad, NIS 60 ($17.20) from Ein Bokek (Dead Sea); call ahead to verify show times.*

### Beaches and Pools
The **Ein Bokek** hotel district, about 15 minutes' drive south of Masada, has a free public beach with showers (between Kapulsky's and Hordos restaurants); there are better facilities, such as changing rooms, at the adjacent **Hammei Zohar** (☎ 07/658–4161). Nonguests can pay to use the beaches and freshwater pools at the **Lot** (☎ 07/658–4321 or 07/658–4324) and **Tsell Harim** (☎ 07/658–4121 or 07/658–4122) hotels. Also available to nonguests are the beaches, pools, and full spa facilities at the more expensive **Caesar Premier** (☎ 07/668–9666), **Crowne Plaza** (☎ 07/659–1919), **Hod** (☎ 07/658–4644), **Hyatt Regency** (☎ 07/659–1234), **Nirvana** (☎ 07/658–4626), and **Radisson Moriah Plaza** (☎ 07/659–1591) hotels. For more information on Ein Bokek, *see* Chapter 8.

### Lodging
One inexpensive option at the foot of Masada itself is the **Taylor Hostel,** part of the YHA network, with a few dormitories and 20 "family rooms," all with baths *en suite* (✉ Rte. 90, M.P. Dead Sea 86935, ☎ 07/658–4349, ℻ 07/658–4650). About 15 km (9 mi) south of Masada are the excellent hotels of **Ein Bokek** (☞ Beersheva to Ein Bokek *in* Chapter 8).

# WEST OF JERUSALEM

The rugged and reforested Judean Hills drop you—with a stop at an exquisite stalactite cave—onto the gentler landscapes of the Shefelah lowland. This is not a region of towns but of rural landscapes, biblical ghosts, and ancient fingerprints. To get here from Mt. Herzl, in West Jerusalem, take the steep descent to Ein Kerem and out the other side. One kilometer (⅔ mi) beyond the neighborhood is the Kerem Junction. Continue straight (left fork) on Route 386. On the hills to your left is the Hadassah Hospital complex (☞ West Jerusalem *in* Chapter 2), one of the largest in the Middle East. Most of these hillsides have the terraced effect of the natural strata of sedimentary limestone; many were laboriously widened by farmers over the centuries by enclosing them with drystone walls. One of the landscape's dominant features is the result of reforestation undertaken by the Jewish National Fund to restore something of the area's ancient scenery. The mostly pine and cypress groves have begun restoring the topsoil lost through centuries of erosion, providing recreation areas and a new lease on life for animals such as the gazelle, which is now seen near Jerusalem itself.

The road crosses the Jerusalem–Tel Aviv railway line, where the Refaim Valley merges with Nahal Sorek, and at once begins climbing, offering fine views of the deep gorge below. Most of the villages in these hills are *moshavim,* cooperative farming settlements of a kind pioneered in the 1920s by veteran settlers who found the communal life of the kibbutz too stifling. In a moshav, the family unit is completely autonomous but is contractually bound to other members in areas such as cooperative purchasing and marketing, social and educational services, and mutual assistance in time of need.

The socialism of the kibbutz was another turnoff for Jewish refugees from Arab lands in the 1950s. Most went to the towns, of course, but for those who settled the land, the moshav lifestyle, in which the patriarchal family structure of the old country could be preserved, was an ideal solution. There are more than 450 moshavim in Israel today, accounting for about 3% of the population. Moshavim in this area typically raise poultry and dairy cattle or sheep and cultivate fruit orchards in the lowland valleys.

## Sorek Cave

★ ❾ *25 km (17 mi) southwest of Jerusalem on Rtes. 386 and 3866, 16 km (10 mi) east of Bet Shemesh on Rte. 3855.*

The Avshalom Reserve contains the justly renowned Sorek Cave, a stalactite cave that is small in comparison to similar caverns elsewhere but is said to include every type of formation known. It was discovered in 1967, when a routine blast in the nearby quarry tore away the rock face, revealing a subterranean wonderland that no human had ever seen.

In developing the site, the Nature Reserves Authority faced the problem of how to allow public access to the cave yet minimize impact on its unique environment. The authority's sensitive solutions have generally won kudos. Colored lights have been eschewed in favor of white ones, which highlight the stones' natural whites and honey browns. The cave's forms have names like "macaroni," "curtains," and "sombreros," the products of tour guides vying with each other to find imaginative familiarity in the shapes of the formations. In a series of "interfaith" images, some guides find rocky evocations of Moses, the Madonna and Child, Buddha, and the Ayatollah Khomeini. Photography is allowed only on Friday morning, when there are no guided tours. Despite the almost 100% humidity, the temperature and the atmosphere in the cave are very comfortable year-round.

A stepped path winds down to the cave entrance—visitors with medical problems should bear in mind the climb back to the parking lot. Local guides take groups into the cave every 15 minutes for a 30-minute tour (English tours on request). A video in an acclimatization room (English version available) explains how the cave was formed. ✉ *Avshalom Reserve. Rte. 3866,* ☎ *02/991–1117.* 🎟 *NIS 15 ($4.30).* ☉ *Sat.–Thurs. 8:30–3:45, Fri. and holiday eves 8:30–12:45.*

## Lodging

There are four very good kibbutz guest houses in wooded enclaves of the Judean Hills, 15–20 minutes' drive west of Jerusalem and about 10 km (6 mi) north of the Sorek Cave. All have commanding hilltop views, quiet surroundings, rural ambience, comfortable if not luxurious accommodations, and good swimming pools. Bed-and-breakfast for two runs NIS 300–NIS 500 ($90–$150), depending on the season.

**Kiryat Anavim.** Besides the better-appointed rooms in the main building, there are garden rooms, more spartan but also more private, with quiet little arbors nearby. ⊠ *8 km (5 mi) west of Jerusalem, north of Rte. 1, M.P. Judean Hills 90833,* ☎ *02/534–8999,* FAX *02/534–8848. 50 rooms with bath. AE, DC, MC, V.*

**Ma'aleh Hahamisha.** In this largest, and thus least intimate, of this area's guest houses, new additions have provided a health club, including an indoor heated pool, gym, saunas, and whirlpool baths. Some rooms lead to a garden patio. ⊠ *12 km (7 mi) west of Jerusalem, north of Rte. 1, M.P. Judean Hills 90835,* ☎ *02/533–1331,* FAX *02/534–2144. 231 rooms, most with bath. AE, DC, MC, V.*

★ **Neve Ilan.** A cut above its neighbors, this hotel has larger and better-furnished rooms. You can also reserve superior-grade rooms, and minisuites with their own whirlpool baths. The pool is covered year-round and heated in winter, and there is now a well-equipped exercise room. ⊠ *15 km (10 mi) west of Jerusalem, north of Rte. 1, M.P. Judean Hills 90850,* ☎ *02/533–9339,* FAX *02/533–9335. 160 rooms with bath. AE, DC, MC, V.*

**Shoresh.** An ambitious building program aims to convert this guest house to the largest and best-appointed in the area. Options include bed-and-breakfasts arrangements, modest hotel rooms, and suites. The new pool is covered and heated year-round. ⊠ *15 km (8½ mi) west of Jerusalem, south of Rte. 1, 88 M.P. Judean Hills 90860,* ☎ *02/533–8338,* FAX *02/534–0262. 94 rooms with bath, 120 2-bedroom apartments. AE, DC, MC, V.*

## Swimming

Several villages and kibbutzim have beautiful pools in wooded parts of the Judean Hills, to the north of the Sorek Cave (☞ Lodging, *above*).

**Kiryat Anavim.** ☎ *02/534–8999.* 🎫 *Sun.–Fri. NIS 30 ($8.60), Sat. and holidays NIS 35 ($10).* ☉ *May–Sept., Sun.–Thurs. 10–7, Fri. and holiday eves 10–6:30, Sat. 9:30–7.*

**Ma'aleh Hahamisha.** ☎ *02/533–1331.* 🎫 *Sun.–Fri. NIS 35 ($10), Sat. and holidays NIS 45 ($13).* ☉ *Mid-May–Aug., daily 9–6.*

**Neve Ilan.** ☎ *02/533–9339.* 🎫 *Sun.–Fri. NIS 40 ($11.50), Sat. and holidays NIS 55 ($15.70).* ☉ *Mon.–Thurs. 5:30 AM–9 PM, Fri.–Sat. 8–6, Sun. 8 AM–9 PM.*

# Tel Bet Shemesh

*12 km (7½ mi) west of Sorek Cave on Rtes. 3855 and 38, 35 km (22 mi) west of Jerusalem.*

The modern town of Bet Shemesh takes its name from its ancient predecessor, now entombed by the *tel,* or archaeological mound, on a rise on Route 38, 2 km (1 mi) south of the town's main entrance. This is Samson country. Samson, one of the judges of Old Testament Israel, is better known for his physical prowess and lust for Philistine women than for his shining spiritual qualities, but it was here, "between Zorah and Eshta'ol," that "the Spirit of the Lord began to stir him" (Judges 13). Today, Eshta'ol is a moshav a few minutes' drive north, and Tzora (Zorah) is the kibbutz immediately to the west.

There is a clearing to pull off the road next to the tel. From the top of the tel there is a fine view of the fields of Nahal Sorek, where Samson dallied with Delilah (Judges 16). The city of Bet Shemesh controlled access through the valley to the mountains of Judah, to the east. According to the Bible, when the Philistines captured the Israelite Ark of the Covenant in battle (11th century BC), they found that their prize brought divine retribution with it, destroying their idol Dagon and afflicting them with tumors and their cities with rats (I Samuel 5). In consternation and awe, the Philistines rid themselves of the jinxed ark by sending it back to the Israelites at Bet Shemesh.

## Elah Valley

⓾  *10 km (6 mi) south of Bet Shemesh, 42 km (26 mi) west of Jerusalem.*

The Elah Valley is one of those delightful places—not uncommon in Israel—where you can relate the scenery to a specific biblical text and confirm the maxim that once you've visited Israel, you'll never read the Bible the same way again.

Just beyond the junction of Route 38 with Route 383, and up to your right above the pine-wooded slopes, is a distinctively bald flattop hill, **Tel Azekah,** the site of an ancient Israelite city. The hills are crisscrossed by dirt roads, especially delightful in spring when the wildflowers are out.

You are now in the Elah Valley. A small bridge spans a usually dry streambed; just after crossing, park carefully on the shoulder. If you have a Bible with you, open it to I Samuel 17 and read about the dramatic duel between David and the giant Philistine champion Goliath. The battle probably took place within a half mile or so of where you're standing. Skeptical? Review the following passage:

*Now the Philistines gathered their armies for battle; and they were gathered at Socoh, which belongs to Judah [identified by a mound 800 yards east of the junction ahead of you], and encamped between Socoh and Azekah [your location]... And Saul and the men of Israel were gathered, and encamped in the valley of Elah, and drew up in line of battle against the Philistines. And the Philistines stood on the mountain on the one side, and Israel stood on the mountain on the other side, with a valley between them.*

Try this: as you look east up the valley (across the road), you'll see the mountains of Judah in the distance and the road from Bethlehem—now, as then—by which David reached the battlefield. The white northern ridge, a spur of the mountains of Judah, may have been the emplacement of the Israelite army; the southern ridge (where the gas station is today)—including Tel Socoh, where, as the Bible says, the Philistines gathered—ascends from the Philistine territory to the west. And the stream you crossed is the only one in the valley: "And David... chose five smooth stones from the brook...; his sling was in his hand, and he drew near to the Philistine." The rest, as they say, is history.

*En Route*   About 1½ km (1 mi) south of the Elah Junction (Routes 38 and 383), a terrace on the right is planted with a few slim cypress trees. The five broken pillars here are **Roman milestones** that were found nearby. The second from the left bears a lengthy (though damaged) Latin inscription dedicated to the glory of the emperors Septimus Severus and

Caracalla and to the latter's brother (later murdered by him), Septimus Geta. Dating from around AD 210, the milestones marked the road from Ashkelon through the Elah Valley to Bethlehem and Jerusalem, which by that time was called Aelia Capitolina. The Latin was for the benefit of the Roman legionnaires; but Greek was the language of the region, and the last three lines say, "COL[onia] AEL[ia] CAP[itolina], MIL[le], K[24]," meaning 24 Roman miles to Aelia Capitolina, specifically to the city's northern (Damascus) gate.

About 2 km (1 mi) farther, a road to the right climbs to the forest watchtower of Mitzpeh Massua. A small restaurant (closed on Saturday) serves light meals and draft beer, and there are picnic facilities nearby. The fabulous view is free.

## Tel Maresha and Bet Guvrin

*21 km (13 mi) south of Bet Shemesh, 52 km (33 mi) southwest of Jerusalem.*

The Bet Guvrin-Maresha national park is a wonderland, both under the ground and above it.

★ ⑪ The flattop mound of ancient Maresha, known today as **Tel Maresha,** was already the site of an important city in the Israelite period (early 1st millennium BC); but it was during the Hellenistic period (4th–2nd centuries BC) that the endless complexes of chalk caves that riddle the site—and make it so delightful—were excavated. Maresha was finally destroyed by the Parthians in 40 BC, and its place was subsequently taken by the new nearby Roman city of Bet Guvrin.

Even before you enter the park, the antiquities greet you: sprawled around the kibbutz of Bet Guvrin, on the junction of Routes 30 and 35, are bits and pieces of the 2nd- to 3rd-century AD "free city" of Bet Guvrin, renamed (around the year 200) Eleuthropolis, "the city of free men." A particularly great find was the amphitheater, an arena for blood sports, one of only a handful discovered in Israel. The main part of the Roman city was on the southeast side of the road, where a few old buildings, at least one of them Roman, peek tantalizingly out of a rubble-strewn hill that still awaits archaeologists' attention. (The scanty ruins of a 12th-century church are virtually the only evidence of the Crusader town of Bethgibelin.)

The layout of the park's roads encourages but does not compel you to begin with its older sites. Nothing remains of earlier excavations that unearthed the Hellenistic city on the tel's top, but more recent digs have exposed the masonry of ancient fortifications from the Old Testament period at the corner of the mound. The view from the tel is worth the short climb.

What you have really come for, however, is a vast series of underground chambers carved out of the soft chalk by the Hellenistic citizens more than 2,000 years ago. One impressive complex (to the right before you reach the tel) is the so-called **Columbarium,** dug underground in the shape of a double cross (of no religious significance; this is older than Christianity) some 30 ft deep. The walls are lined with symmetrical niches. The Latin word *columba* means dove or pigeon, and a leading theory is that these birds were raised here to eat and to provide fertilizer from the droppings but especially to use in ritual sacrifices. Other scholars question the pigeon theory because chemical analysis of the surrounding chalk has failed to support it; they suggest instead that the niches contained urns of cremated human remains. The term *columbarium* has nevertheless entered the archaeological lexicon to describe this style of niche-filled walls, whatever their purpose.

The most interesting and extensive of the mazes is just off the road on the opposite side of the tel. Here, under their houses, the ancient Mareshans dug their own personal water cisterns and storerooms. The excitement of exploration makes this sight a must for kids (with close parental supervision, though the safety features are good), but the many steps make it impractical for the infirm. The last chamber of the maze route displays a restored ancient olive press in situ where an estimated 9 tons of that precious commodity were processed each year.

Warning: other fascinating but undeveloped complexes of caves near the tel have dangerous pits and are off-limits to visitors. Keep to the marked sites only. The leaflet you're given with your ticket has a good diagram of the site.

On a ridge to the north of Tel Maresha, look for a large **apse** standing in splendid isolation on the ridge to the north. Known as Santahanna in Arabic, it has been identified by scholars as a remnant of the Crusader Church of St. Anne.

★ ⑫ The great "bell caves" of **Bet Guvrin** date from the Late Roman, Byzantine and even Early Arab periods (2nd century–7th century AD), when the locals created an ecologically sound quarry to extract lime for cement. These caves are very different from the functional underground chambers of Maresha. At the top of each "bell" is a hole through the 4-ft-thick hard stone crust; the moment they reached the soft chalk below, the diggers began reaming out their quarry in the structurally secure bell shape, each bell eventually cutting into the adjacent one. The effect of the soaring domed ceilings and the interplay of shadow with shafts of sunlight is awesome.

The open areas outside the bell caves were once such caves themselves, but their roofs have since collapsed. They have a wild look, now that fig and carob trees, cacti, and small bushes struggle for dominance. (Photographers: the caves are not dark, yet the light is dim in places.) Claustrophobes need have no fear here: the cavernous bell caves reach up 50 ft in places and are open to the outdoors.

Although not built to be inhabited, the caves may have been used as refuges by early Christians. In the North Cave (currently closed for restoration), a much later cross high on the wall, at the same level as an Arabic inscription, suggests a degree of coexistence even *after* the Arab conquest of the area in AD 636. Some scenes in the rock-musical movie *Jesus Christ Superstar* were filmed here. *Rte. 35,* ☎ *07/681-1020.* 🎟 *NIS 17 ($5).* 🕑 *Apr.–Sept., Sat.–Thurs. 8–5, Fri. and holiday eves 8–4; Oct.–Mar., Sat.–Thurs. 8–4, Fri. and holiday eves 8–3.*

An attractive alternative route back to Jerusalem is east from the Elah Valley on Route 375, past Israel's main satellite communications receiver, and up through fine, wooded hill country to Tzur Hadassah (look out for the rock-hewn Roman road on the right). Route 386 runs north to Jerusalem. The right turn (continuation of Route 375) takes you to Bethlehem and on to Jerusalem, but this road goes through some inhospitable West Bank villages and is not recommended at this time. Avoid Route 35 from Bet Guvrin to Hebron as well.

# BETHLEHEM AND THE ETZION BLOC

**Warning:** The sites covered in this section are in the West Bank. Because of sporadic Arab unrest in the area, most travelers confine themselves to Bethlehem. You are strongly urged to explore other sites in the region only in the company of a licensed guide and to remain on the main arterial roads in any case.

The West Bank is that part of the onetime British Mandate of Palestine, west of the Jordan River, that was occupied by the Kingdom of Transjordan in its war with Israel in 1948 and unilaterally annexed shortly afterward. That country then changed its name to the Hashemite Kingdom of Jordan to reflect its new territorial reality. The territory was lost to Israel in the Six-Day War of 1967 and, with the exception of recently autonomous areas (mostly urban), has remained under Israeli military administration ever since. In Israel itself, the region is usually referred to by its ancient biblical names: *Yehuda*, or Judea, for the area south of Jerusalem, and *Shomron*, or Samaria, for the much larger area north of it. The term *Green Line* denotes the pre-1967 border between the West Bank and Israel proper.

The West Bank is a kidney-shape area, a bit larger than the U.S. state of Delaware and almost half the size of Northern Ireland. The Arab population of almost 1 million is more than 90% Muslim, with the Christian minority living mostly in the Greater Bethlehem area (in Judea) and in Ramallah (in Samaria).

Palestinian nationalism in the West Bank and the Gaza Strip flared into street violence in the late 1980s (a wave known as the *intifada*); however, in the last few years, the series of negotiated agreements between Israel and the Palestinians, along with related political developments, have had a significant effect on the general atmosphere in the Territories, as they are sometimes called. On the one hand, the Autonomy Agreement, signed in Cairo in 1994, gave Palestinian Arabs control of their own internal affairs in the Gaza Strip, Jericho, and, more recently, seven other West Bank cities. On the other hand, Muslim fundamentalists who reject the entire peace process with Israel (like the Hamas and Islamic Jihad movements) have stepped up their attacks on Israeli citizens. In response, Israel has severely restricted the access of Palestinian Arab workers from these areas to Israel proper—a security measure that may be necessary to contain the violence but that has caused economic hardship among the Palestinians. At press time, Israel was poised to implement a second redeployment in the West Bank, releasing further territory to Palestinian autonomous control; but an impasse on the extent of this phrase of redeployment—and, by implication, on what would remain to be negotiated in the "final-status" talks—has encouraged more rhetoric than dialogue.

The nonviolent majority of Palestinians is caught between a rock and a hard place. Despite the frustration of military occupation, the West Bank's economic development, educational standards, and medical services have improved dramatically since 1967; but these developments do not impress a new generation for whom political independence is the top priority. The prognosis is not entirely bleak, however: since the beginning of the current peace process in Madrid in 1991, the street activists and clandestine terrorist cells have had to share local glory with a legitimate, recognized leadership representing its people's cause.

The Jewish population in Judea and Samaria numbers about 160,000, dispersed in a handful of small towns and more than 100 villages. Although some of the towns are really suburbs of Jerusalem and Tel Aviv, other settlements were set up by fiercely nationalist Israelis—the majority of them religious Jews—who see the region as an integral and inalienable part of their ancient homeland and who consider the almost miraculous "homecoming" of 1967 as nothing less than a first rumble of the messianic age. With its mountain heights dominating Israel's main population centers and the area thrusting to within 14 km (9 mi) of the Mediterranean Sea, the West Bank has a strategic value that has convinced many moderate Israelis that it would be folly to relinquish it to potentially hostile Arab control. A person's attitude toward the questions of continuing settlement in the West Bank and the ultimate status of the region is an important touchstone of political affiliation in Israel, and the country is completely divided on these issues.

This section takes in Bethlehem, less than 8 km (5 mi) south of Jerusalem, and continues southwest to the Jewish settlements of the Etzion Bloc. The Hebron Road leaves Jerusalem heading south to become Route 60.

## Bethlehem

⓭ *8 km (5 mi) south of Jerusalem on Rte. 60. You may experience delays at the Israeli army checkpoint when returning to Jerusalem.*

Christian visitors are often surprised by how close Bethlehem is to Jerusalem (10 minutes' drive), as if the temporal separation of the two in the New Testament should somehow be reflected in distance. As you leave Jerusalem, a good view of the modern city opens up on your right. Kibbutz Ramat Rahel, on the hill to your left, was an important Israeli position in the War of Independence of 1948 and then a border outpost in the years that followed, when the Green Line ran through the valley immediately below it. The next ridge is capped by the Greek Orthodox monastery of Mar Elias (St. Elijah)—once a Jordanian stronghold—and immediately beyond is your first view of Bethlehem.

Way off on the eastern horizon is a prominent flattop hill. This is Herodion, one of Herod's great palace-fortresses, later used by the Zealots in the Great Revolt against Rome (AD 66–73) and by Bar Kochba's fighters in the 2nd century AD. On the ridge to the right as you pass Jerusalem's Gilo neighborhood is Tantur, an ecumenical institute set up in the afterglow of the Second Vatican Council (1962) as a sabbatical retreat for Christian clergy of all denominations.

**Rachel's Tomb,** at the entrance to Bethlehem, is the only Israeli enclave in a Palestinian area, its once-landmark white dome now invisible behind a new security wall. This is an important Jewish holy site: the biblical patriarchal couples (Abraham and Sarah, Isaac and Rebecca, Jacob and Leah) are all buried in the Cave of Machpelah, in Hebron, to the south—all but Rachel, Jacob's second and favorite wife. The Bible relates that Rachel died in childbirth on the outskirts of Bethlehem, "and Jacob set up a pillar upon her grave" (Genesis 35).

The present building is probably medieval, with 19th-century additions made by the renowned British Jewish philanthropist Sir Moses Montefiore. The large, velvet-draped, blocklike cenotaph inside is certainly not the original pillar set up by Jacob, and the thread of authenticity is lost in the distant past, but centuries of prayers have hallowed the spot for observant Jews. The tomb's interior is decorated with Hebrew biblical quotations referring to Rachel. People come to pray here for good health and fecundity (Rachel was long barren), and the keening of a particularly afflicted soul is not an unknown sound. Another tradition is to wind a red thread seven times around the tomb marker, take it off, and give snippets of it as talismans to cure all ills.

Rachel is respected by Islam as well. Next to the tomb is a Muslim cemetery, reflecting the Middle Eastern tradition that it is a special privilege to be buried near a great personage. ✉ *Rte. 60.* 🖾 *Free.* ☯ *Sun.–Thurs. 8–5, Fri. 8–1.*

Even from a distance, **Bethlehem** is easily identified by the minarets and church steeples that struggle for control of its skyline. Immediately beyond Rachel's tomb, the road forks; the right fork goes toward the Etzion Bloc and Hebron, the left into Manger Street and onto Manger Square. Note that Bethlehem is now an autonomous Palestinian enclave, with all security and tourism matters in the hands of the Palestinian Authority.

The wide Manger Street winds into town past large gift shops and the high stone walls of various religious institutions. To the east are occasional panoramas of what geographers call "marginal land"—still more or less arable, but very close to the desert. Fields that now belong to the adjacent town of Beit Sahour are traditionally identified with the biblical story of Ruth the Moabite, daughter-in-law of Naomi, who "gleaned in the field" of Boaz, Naomi's kinsman. Boaz eventually "took Ruth and she became his wife" (Ruth 4); and it was in Bethlehem that their great-grandson, King David, was born.

The same fields are identified by Christian tradition as those where shepherds "keeping watch over their flock by night" received word of the birth of Jesus in Bethlehem. Several denominations maintain sites in the valley venerated as the authentic "Shepherds' Fields."

★ Manger Square is Bethlehem's central plaza and the entrance to its primary sight, the **Church of the Nativity,** built over the grotto thought to be the birthplace of Jesus. The square has a tourist-information office, a few restaurants, and some shops. At press time the atmosphere in Bethlehem was fairly relaxed, and the area of the Nativity well monitored by the Palestinian Tourist Police, but the town's political vicissitudes and occasional incidents in recent years make it inadvisable to wander away from Manger Square into the *souk* (market) and narrow alleys.

The unprepossessing stone exterior of the Church of the Nativity is crowned by the crosses of the denominations sharing it. Above the central gable is the Greek Orthodox cross; to the left, the square Jerusalem cross of the Franciscans (Roman Catholic); and to the right, the Armenian Orthodox cross. The now blocked but still impressive square entranceway dates from the time of the Byzantine emperor Justinian (6th century AD). Twelfth-century Crusader repairs created the arched entrance (also now blocked) within the Byzantine one. The current low entrance (watch your head) was designed in the 16th century to protect the worshipers from attack by their then-hostile Muslim neighbors.

The church interior is vast and gloomy. On the left side of the central nave, a wooden trapdoor reveals a remnant of a mosaic floor from the original church, built in the 4th century by Helena, mother of Constantine the Great, the Roman emperor who first embraced Christianity. Emperor Justinian's rebuilding two centuries later enlarged the church, creating its present-day structure and plan. The high columns, which run the length of the nave in two paired lines, are also from the 6th century, making this the oldest standing church in Israel.

When the country was invaded by the Persians in AD 614, they destroyed every Christian church and monastery across the land except the Nativity. The story holds that when the Persians reached Bethlehem and discovered the splendid Byzantine church, they noticed particularly the wall mosaics and frescoes depicting the Nativity, including the tale of the Three Wise Men of the East. For the local artist, "east" meant Persia, and he had thus dressed his wise men in Persian garb. The Persians understood nothing of the picture's significance, but they "recognized" themselves in it, and spared the church.

The church was pillaged by the early Muslims in the 7th century (much of the marble used at the Temple Mount in Jerusalem came from here), but the patches of 12th-century mosaics high on the walls and the faded burned-wax figures of saints on the Corinthian pillars hint at its revived medieval splendor. The ceiling beams are medieval English oak and are said to have been covered by lead, which the Turks later melted down for bullets in their wars with the Venetians, in the late 11th and early 12th centuries.

The elaborately ornamented front of the church serves as the parish church of Bethlehem's Greek Orthodox community. The right transept is theirs, too, but the left transept belongs to the Armenian Orthodox. All three "shareholders" in the church have vied for centuries for control of the holiest Christian sites in the Holy Land. A 19th-century status-quo agreement that froze their respective rights and privileges in Jerusalem's Church of the Holy Sepulcher and the Tomb of the Virgin pertains here, too: ownership, the timing of ceremonies, the number of oil lamps, and so on are all clearly defined. The agreement has not, however, prevented fisticuffs between rival monks in recent years over the privilege of cleaning this or that part of the birthplace of Jesus.

Below the altar is the **Grotto of the Nativity.** Once a cave—precisely the kind of place that might have been used as a barn—the grotto has been reamed, plastered, and decorated beyond recognition. Immediately on your right as you enter is a small altar, and on the floor below it is the focal point of the entire site: a 14-point **bronze star** with the Latin inscription HIC DE VIRGINE MARIA JESUS CHRISTUS NATUS EST (Here of the Virgin Mary, Jesus Christ was born). The original star was placed here in 1717 by the Roman Catholic Church, which lost control of the altar 40 years later to the more influential Greek Orthodox Church. In 1847 the star mysteriously disappeared, and pressure from the Turkish sultan compelled the Greeks to allow the present Latin replacement to be installed in 1853. The Franciscan guardians do have possession, however, of the little alcove a few steps down on your left as you enter the Grotto (behind the candles). This is said to be the manger where the infant Jesus was laid. There is clear evidence of the fire that gutted the grotto in the 19th century; the asbestos wall hangings were a French gift to prevent a recurrence. ⊠ *Manger Sq.,* ☎ *02/674–1020.* ▤ *Free.* ☉ *Daily 6–6 (access to grotto restricted until about 9:30 AM daily for Armenian mass).*

The **Church of St. Catherine,** adjacent to the Church of the Nativity and accessible by a passage from its Armenian chapel, is Bethlehem's Roman Catholic parish church. Completed in 1882, the church incorporates remnants of its 12th-century Crusader predecessor and has fine acoustics but is otherwise unexceptional. It is from this church that the midnight Christmas mass is broadcast around the world. Steps descend from within the church to a series of dim grottoes, clearly once used as living quarters. Chapels here are variously dedicated to Joseph; to the Innocents killed by Herod; and to St. Jerome, bishop of Bethlehem in the late 4th century, who is said to have written here the Vulgate, the Latin translation of the Bible. At the end of a narrow passage, a small wooden door (kept locked) connects the complex with the Grotto of the Nativity.

The cloister outside the church, with its restored Crusader minicolumns, flower beds, and young lemon trees, is probably one of the most tranquil spots in Bethlehem. ⊠ *Manger Sq.,* ☎ *02/674–2425.* ☉ *Daily 5–noon and 2–6.*

**Manger Square** is brilliant with lights and bursting with life on Christmas Eve (December 24; the Greek Orthodox celebrate Christmas Day on January 7, the Armenian Orthodox on January 19). Traditionally, choirs from around the world perform carols and sacred music in the square between 8:30 PM and 11:30 PM, and at midnight the Roman Catholic mass from the Franciscan Church of St. Catherine is simultaneously relayed on closed-circuit television onto a large outside screen and, via satellite, to all parts of the globe.

There have been changes, however. The celebration of Christmas 1995 came just days after Bethlehem had become an autonomous Palestinian zone and thus was far more a political rally than a religious event. The traditional framework of the Christmas Eve celebrations will most likely be preserved in seasons to come, but the logistics and other arrangements for tourists need to be clarified close to the date. For information, contact the **Office of Tourism of the Palestinian Authority** in Bethlehem (☎ 02/674–1581 or 02/674–1582). Regarding the mass, contact the Christian Information Center at Jerusalem's Jaffa Gate (☎ 02/627–2692). General advice: you'll probably need to leave your car in Jerusalem and take public transportation to Bethlehem; there is no seating in Manger Square; very warm clothing is essential; you should have your passport with you; you may not bring in alcohol; and it's not ideal to carry large bags (because of security checks). The Israel Ministry of Tourism extends its patronage to parallel Christmas celebrations in Nazareth.

## Shopping

Bethlehem craftspeople make carved olive-wood and mother-of-pearl objects, mostly of a religious nature, but the many stores along the tourist route in town sell jewelry and a range of baubles and notions as well. For quality and reliability, most of the half-dozen or so large establishments on Manger Street, where the tour buses stop, are worth investigating, but some of the merchants near the Church of the Nativity, on Manger Square, have good-quality items as well.

# Etzion Bloc

*24 km (15 mi) south of Jerusalem on the new bypass road, which begins near the Jerusalem Mall. From Bethlehem, return to Jerusalem and take the bypass (rather than continuing south on Rte. 60).*

Midway between Jerusalem and Hebron, the Etzion Bloc—*Gush Etzion* in Hebrew—is today made up of two small Jewish towns (Efrat and Alon Shevut) and a handful of rural communities. In the 1940s there were four kibbutzim here, built because of their strategic proximity to the important Jerusalem–Hebron highway. During Israel's War of Independence, their ability to disrupt troop movements of the Jordanian (then Transjordanian) Arab Legion led to the Legion's attack, conquest, and destruction of the Bloc in May 1948. Jewish settlers, some of them survivors of the 1948 disaster, returned here after the Six-Day War of 1967, when the area came under Israeli control. Since the Bloc had been an area of Jewish settlement long before Israel became a state, it remains sacrosanct even among Israelis who would otherwise support a large-scale Israeli withdrawal from the West Bank.

The small, restored fortresslike building at the entrance to the Etzion Bloc, facing the Jerusalem–Hebron road (Route 60), was a turn-of-the-century Russian Orthodox monastery and the Bloc's forward position in the War of Independence. The road west passes Alon Shevut on the right.

**⑭ Kfar Etzion,** the oldest settlement in the Etzion Bloc, was founded as far back as 1921, but its poor land, lack of water, and harsh winters deterred many from settling here. By the early 1940s, however, the situation had stabilized with the addition of three more villages: Revadim, Ein Tzurim, and Massu'ot Yitzhak. When the Arab Legion overran the

Bloc, the survivors of these three kibbutzim were taken prisoner. Those of Kfar Etzion were not so lucky: almost all were gunned down after their surrender. Among the group that resettled the site in the late 1960s were those who had been evacuated as children before the battle. Make time for the story of Kfar Etzion, told in a dramatic audiovisual presentation in the auditorium, and at the small museum. To get to the settlement, ignore the first gate and continue along the periphery of the village to the second, southern gate. Park at the cafeteria–gift shop, and ask for directions to the museum and auditorium. ⊠ *Rte. 367, just west of Rte. 60,* ☎ *02/993–5160. Visits by prior arrangement only.* 🎫 *NIS 8 ($2.30).* ☉ *Sun.–Thurs. 9–3:30; Fri., spring–summer (daylight saving time) 9–12:30, autumn–winter 9–11:30.*

From the Etzion Bloc, Route 367 descends west to the Elah Valley (☞ West of Jerusalem, *above*).

### Shopping
**Kibbutz Kfar Etzion** (⊠ Off Rte. 367, near the junction with Rte. 60, ☎ 02/993–4040) runs a gift shop near its museum, specializing in, but not limited to, Judaica.

# AROUND JERUSALEM A TO Z

## Arriving and Departing

The points of departure for the three areas explored in this chapter are Jerusalem and Tel Aviv. For information about arriving and departing, *see* Jerusalem A to Z *and* Tel Aviv A to Z *in* Chapters 2 and 4, respectively.

## Getting Around

### By Bus
With few exceptions, the **Egged Bus Cooperative** enjoys a nationwide monopoly on intercity bus routes. Buses are modern, comfortable, air-conditioned, and reasonably priced. Service is solid on main routes but infrequent to outlying rural districts. For fares and schedules, call 02/530–4704 (Jerusalem) or the more accessible 03/694–8888 (Tel Aviv).

Jerusalem's **Central Bus Station** is in the city's northwestern corner, on Jaffa Road. Give yourself ample time to buy a ticket and get in line for the often crowded Dead Sea routes.

Since Jericho became autonomous under the Palestinian Authority, Egged no longer serves it. For the Dead Sea area (Qumran, Ein Gedi, Masada, and Ein Bokek), take Bus 421 or 486 (or 487 only as far as Ein Gedi) and the busy 444 to Eilat (which does not drive into Masada). Service is approximately hourly. Only one bus departs daily from Tel Aviv to the Dead Sea area—Bus 421, currently at 8:30 AM.

You can get to Rachel's Tomb on (the infrequent) Bus 163. Bus 160 (the Hebron route) stops at the Etzion Bloc Junction, while Bus 161 takes you into Kfar Etzion itself. All originate at the Central Bus Station, but you can also pick them up near downtown Jerusalem, on **Keren Hayesod Street** opposite the Radisson Moriah Hotel, and at the **Jerusalem Train Station.** From the **East Jerusalem Bus Station,** on Sultan Suleiman Street near the Damascus Gate, an Arab company operates Bus 22 to Manger Square, in the heart of Bethlehem. There is no direct bus service from Tel Aviv to Bethlehem.

The sights west of Jerusalem are difficult to reach by public transportation. The only bus going to Bet Guvrin (Bus 011) leaves at 8 AM from the town of Kiryat Gat. There are frequent buses to Kiryat Gat: Bus 446 from Jerusalem and Bus 369 from Tel Aviv.

## By Car

Driving is much better than relying on public transportation here, as many of the sights in this chapter are on secondary roads, where bus services are infrequent or in some cases nonexistent. Roads range in condition from fair to excellent, and most destinations are clearly marked. Drive defensively—many Israeli drivers are frustrated fighter pilots. Gas stations are plentiful, and some are open 24 hours a day. Still, it's wise to play it safe and keep your tank at least half-full at all times. Pay special attention to keeping the radiator topped in the hot Israeli summer.

Masada, the farthest of the Dead Sea sites in this chapter, is 100 km (62 mi) from Jerusalem, about 1½ hours' drive, on Routes 1 and 90; add one hour from Tel Aviv. Jericho, which is 40 km (25 mi) from Jerusalem, can be reached in 35 minutes via Routes 1 and 90 north. Since Jericho is now a Palestinian Autonomous Zone and occasionally off-limits to visitors, check the town's accessibility before you set out. As you head southwest from Jerusalem, it takes 40 minutes to get to the Sorek Cave via Route 386 (about 24 km, or 15 mi) and another 30 minutes' driving time (about 30 km, or 19 mi) to Bet Guvrin via Route 38. From Tel Aviv (east on Rte. 1, south on Route 38), you can reach Bet Shemesh in about 40 minutes. Bethlehem is a mere 8 km (5 mi) from downtown Jerusalem—a 15-minute drive—and the Etzion Bloc 16 km (10 mi) farther south on Route 60. A new bypass road from the Jerusalem Mall avoids Bethlehem en route to the Etzion Bloc. Driving your own car in other areas of the West Bank is definitely not recommended.

## By Guide-Driven Limousine/Minivan

This is by far the best way (if not the cheapest) to see the areas covered in this chapter. With a private licensed guide in a 4-, 7-, or 10-passenger, air-conditioned limousine/minivan, *you* determine the tour's character and pace (☞ Guided Tours *in* Contacts and Resources, *below*).

## By Sherut and Taxi

A *sherut* is a shared taxi (seating up to seven passengers) that runs along a set route. Usually it follows a major bus route and charges a comparable fare. From Jerusalem you can get an Arab sherut to West Bank towns such as Bethlehem and Jericho, which will give you some local flavor—and sometimes a hair-raising driving experience. An Arab taxi is likely to be delayed at military checkpoints, however. Depending on the destination, Egged buses (☞ By Bus, *above*) are a more comfortable and reliable alternative.

Using a regular **taxi** to tour is not cheap. Define your itinerary, get a quote from one of the main West Jerusalem taxi companies, and use that as a starting point for negotiating a better deal with an individual cabbie (outside your hotel, or the Arab cabbies at the Jaffa Gate). Hiring a taxi for seven hours to Ein Gedi, the Dead Sea, and Masada, for example, costs about NIS 620–NIS 700 ($180–$200). Hiring a qualified tour guide with an air-conditioned limo for the same trip is a far better value for the money.

## Contacts and Resources

### Bird-Watching

For more information on birds in this area, contact the **Society for the Protection of Nature in Israel** (SPNI), which has a bird-watching center and a center for raptors; the group is based in Tel Aviv (☎ 03/638–8677, FAX 03/688–3940).

## Car Rental

### JERUSALEM

**Avis** (✉ 22 King David St., ☎ 02/624–9001); **Budget** (✉ 8 King David St., ☎ 02/624–8991); **Eldan** (✉ 24 King David St., ☎ 02/625–2151); **Europcar** (National; ✉ 8 King David St., ☎ 02/624–8464); **Hertz** (✉ 18 King David St., ☎ 02/623–1351; ✉ Hyatt Hotel, ☎ 02/581–5069 [open on Saturday]); **Reliable** (✉ 14 King David St., ☎ 02/624–8993).

### TEL AVIV

**Avis** (✉ 113 Hayarkon St., ☎ 03/527–1752); **Budget** (✉ 99 Hayarkon St., ☎ 03/524–5233); **Eldan** (✉ 112 Hayarkon St., ☎ 03/527–1166); **Europcar** (National; ✉ 126 Hayarkon St., ☎ 03/524–8181); **Hertz** (✉ 144 Hayarkon St., ☎ 03/522–3332); **Reliable** (✉ 96 Hayarkon St., ☎ 03/524–9794).

## Emergencies

**Ambulance and medical emergencies—Magen David Adom** (☎ 101).

The major **hospitals** in Jerusalem are as follows: **Bikur Holim** (✉ Strauss St., ☎ 02/670–1111); **Hadassah** (✉ Ein Kerem, ☎ 02/677–7111, 02/677–7215 for emergency room, 02/677–7204 for children's emergency room); **Hadassah** (✉ Mt. Scopus, ☎ 02/584–4111); **Sha'arei Tzedek** (✉ Bayit Vegan, ☎ 02/655–5111 or 02/655–5508 for emergency room).

**Police** (☎ 100).

## Guided Tours

"Regular" bus tours, as they're known locally (as opposed to charter tours), pick you up at your hotel and bring you back there at the end of the tour. Guided bus tours departing from Tel Aviv offer the same itineraries as those leaving Jerusalem. There are discounts for children. The two main operators are **Egged Tlalim Tours** (✉ 8 Shlomzion Hamalka St., Jerusalem, ☎ 02/622–1999 or 622–2929; ✉ 59 Ben Yehuda St., Tel Aviv, ☎ 03/527–1212, 03/527–1213, 03/527–1214, or 03/527–1215); and **United Tours** (✉ King David Hotel Annex, Jerusalem, ☎ 02/625–2187 or 02/625–2188; ✉ 113 Hayarkon St., Tel Aviv, ☎ 03/693–3412 or 03/522–2008). Most hotels carry the tour companies' brochures and can book tours for you.

Both companies offer full-day tours of Masada, the Dead Sea, Ein Gedi, and sometimes Jericho. Tours cost between $60 and $70 per person (not including lunch) and depart daily. The Church of the Nativity, in Bethlehem, and sometimes Rachel's Tomb can be seen as part of half-day or full-day Jerusalem tours (daily departures, $24 to $46 per person).

Touring in a private **guide-driven limo/van** can be comfortable and convenient (☞ Getting Around, *above*), and for four or more people, it's cost-effective as well. Current recommended rates (always quoted in U.S. dollars) are $281, $318, and $360 per day for 4-, 7-, and 10-passenger vehicles respectively. Rates include all guiding and car expenses (up to 200 km, or 120 mi, per day, averaged out over the days of the tour). There is a charge for the guide's expenses for overnights away from the home base.

Some guides have organized into cooperatives, but all are essentially freelancers. In Jerusalem, try **Eshcolot Tours** (✉ 36 Keren Hayesod, ☎ 02/563–5555, FAX 02/563–2101); and in Tel Aviv, **Twelve Tribes** (✉ 29 Hamered St., ☎ 03/510–1911, FAX 03/510–1943) or **Tar-Hemed** (✉ 59 Hayarkon St., ☎ 03/517–6101, FAX 03/510–0165).

You can get free travel advice from two of Fodor's in-field writers, themselves qualified guides: **Mike Rogoff** (✉ 67/35 Shahal St., 93721 Jerusalem, ☎ FAX 02/679–0410) and **Judy Goldman** (✉ Gan Rehavia A, Apt. 6, 92461 Jerusalem, ☎ 02/624–5827, FAX 02/623–3834). Hotel concierges can usually recommend guides as well.

SPECIAL-INTEREST TOURS

**Metzukei Dragot** (✉ Kibbutz Mitzpe Shalem, M.P. Jericho Valley, ☎ 02/994–4222, FAX 02/994–4333) provides one variety of desert adventure. It offers one-day "safaris" twice weekly (currently Tuesday and Saturday) from Jerusalem to the Judean Desert in a 31-seat off-road safari truck; the cost is $64, including a picnic lunch. If you can't live without air-conditioning or plush seats, don't consider it. But if you want unforgettable desert vistas that are really off the beaten track, this is for you.

The **Society for the Protection of Nature in Israel** (✉ 13 Helene Hamalka St., Jerusalem, ☎ 02/624–4605, FAX 02/625–4953; ✉ 3 Hashefela St., Tel Aviv, ☎ 03/638–8677, FAX 03/688–3940; U.S. office: ✉ 89 5th Ave., Suite 800, New York, NY, ☎ 212/645–8732 or 800/323–0035, FAX 212/645–8749), also known as SPNI, runs several off-the-beaten-track excursions, with an emphasis on nature and some hiking. Their English-speaking tours in this region include Masada, the Dead Sea, and the Ein Gedi Nature Reserve (including hiking); a trip into the Judean Desert in a go-anywhere vehicle (no hiking); a more energetic trip into Wadi Kelt, with its marvelous desert spring and St. George's Monastery; and a monthly moonlight hike into the same area, timed for a bright moon. An occasional tour to the area west of Jerusalem includes the Neot Kedumim Biblical Landscape Reserve, the Sorek Cave, and Bet Guvrin. Day tours range from $59 to $64; the two-day Masada–Ein Gedi combination costs $185 (including lodging and some meals); and longer, more complex packages are available.

## Visitor Information

There are **Tourist Information Offices** (TIOs) at the following locations (✉ Manger Sq., opposite the Police Station, 3rd floor, Bethlehem, ☎ 02/741581 or 02/741582, FAX 02/647–0604; ✉ Jaffa Gate, Jerusalem, ☎ 02/628–0382 or 02/628–0457; 2 Luntz St., Jerusalem, ☎ 02/625–8908; ✉ Shop No. 6018, 6th floor, New Central Bus Station, Tel Aviv, ☎ 03/639–5660).

# 4 Tel Aviv

*Although it is not the official capital of Israel—a right reserved for age-old Jerusalem—Tel Aviv is the country's pulse, the center for Israel's economy, business, culture, and cuisine. Brash and unlovely at first glance, this teeming, cosmopolitan city on the Mediterranean has fine sandy beaches, excellent restaurants and nightlife, and a serious performing-arts scene. It's hard to believe that less than a century ago, these streets were nothing but sand dunes.*

**P**ROUD RESIDENTS CALL IT the city that never stops, and if you don't believe them, just come around at 4 AM, when you may find yourself waiting in line for a table at a café or stuck in a traffic jam on Hayarkon Street. True, there are no buses at that hour, but that doesn't stop the young and the restless of surrounding towns from finding their way to the country's throbbing heart.

By Lisa Perlman

Next to the magical holy city of Jerusalem, Tel Aviv seems more like the city of sin. Your first reaction to it may be negative—to the newcomer it appears muggy, congested, ill-planned, and scarred with boxy, concrete buildings. But what it lacks in grandeur, Tel Aviv makes up for in vitality. One-third of Israel's population—a number approaching 2 million—lives in this 138-square-km (55-square-mi) metropolis. Half a million cars enter and leave the city every day. Residents of other towns swell the population further on weekends, when they make Tel Aviv their playground. The city is Israel's center of commerce and culture, and it bustles with restaurants, art galleries, museums, and beaches.

Having risen from empty sand dunes less than a century ago, Tel Aviv could never hope for the ancient beauty of Israel's capital. Still, the city's southern border, the port of Jaffa, is as old as they come: Jonah set sail from here for what turned out to be his journey to the belly of a whale. The cedars of Lebanon that were used to build Solomon's Temple arrived in Jaffa before being transported to Jerusalem. According to archaeologists, Jaffa was founded in the Middle Canaanite period, around 1600 BC. For the next thousand years it was dominated by one ancient people after another: Egyptians, Philistines, Israelites, Phoenicians, and Greeks. After being taken by Crusaders twice, in the 11th and 12th centuries, Jaffa was recaptured by the Muslims and remained largely under Arab control until the 20th century. During much of this time it was abandoned; it did not regain its importance as a port until the 19th century.

In the second half of the 19th century, Jewish pioneers began immigrating here from other parts of the world, and their numbers strained the capacity of the small port. By the late 1880s, Jaffa was overcrowded, rife with disease, and stricken with poverty. A group of Jewish families moved to the empty sands north of Jaffa to found Neve Tzedek, the first specifically Jewish neighborhood. This was followed by Ahuzat Bayit (literally, "housing estate"), an area to the north of Neve Tzedek that became the precursor of Tel Aviv. The city was named Tel Aviv in 1909; Arab riots in Jaffa in the 1920s then drove more Jews to Ahuzat Bayit, spurring further growth. These Jews were joined by immigrants from Europe, mostly Poland, and a decade later by an influx of German Jews fleeing the Nazis. These new, urban arrivals—unlike the pioneers from earlier immigrant waves—brought with them an appreciation for the arts and a passion for the sidewalk cafés that began to sprout like mushrooms in this city. It was they who made the strongest social and cultural impact on Tel Aviv.

The fact that Tel Aviv began as separate neighborhoods helps to explain its eclectic (some would say discordant) appearance, its Mediterranean-style buildings jostling each other in the shadow of towering skyscrapers. In the 1930s and '40s, the city became known as the "white city," because it was the only one in the world dominated by the International Style of Le Corbusier and Mies van der Rohe—an aesthetic of functional forms, flat roofs, and whitewashed exteriors. By the 1950s, however, shoddy imitations of this style led to its decline, and many of its buildings fell into disrepair. Happily, recent efforts by preservationists are helping to reclaim these architectural treasures.

The Tel Aviv of today is already vastly different from the Tel Aviv of 50 years ago. Although northern Tel Aviv has traditionally been the city's flashy, affluent half, it's the oft-neglected south that gets attention now. Here, gentrification projects in many neighborhoods are changing the area's face; each week the scaffolding rises on another building, and new restaurants and shops appear. Tel Aviv has come a long way in its short life; look around and try to imagine the scene just 90 years ago, when this teeming metropolis was nothing but sand.

# Pleasures and Pastimes

### Beaches

Tel Aviv's western border, an idyllic stretch of Mediterranean sand, has miles of beaches and a beachfront promenade. Sunsets here are spectacular. Still, the Med can be moody; the lapping of gentle waves offers respite and relaxation for most of the year, but it's not always as uplifting as you might expect. Because the Med is a closed sea, its water turns warm and decidedly unrefreshing in the dead of summer. If the jellyfish are out in force—as they are in July and August—you may find that an air-conditioned café with a view of the sea is a more civilized place to be.

### Cultural Activities

As Israel's undisputed cultural capital, Tel Aviv puts on a pretty good show, even at the street level. There's a stimulating range of museums; dance and music of all kinds are popular; opera is budding; and theater (almost all in Hebrew) is prolific. As for pop culture—well, it's all around you.

### Dining

Tel Aviv's culinary scene has improved radically in the last few years, so that the city's cosmopolitan character is now happily represented in its food. That's not to say that you can't still enjoy the Middle Eastern fast foods for which this part of the world is famous—falafel and shwarma (spit-grilled meat) stands still occupy countless street corners. But beyond these are restaurants serving everything from American burgers to Chinese dim sum. In contrast to Jerusalem, Tel Aviv makes you really search to find a kosher restaurant outside the hotels (where all restaurants are required to be kosher).

Tel Aviv is also very much a café society. Everyone from idle shoppers to hard-driving businesspeople frequents the scores of coffee shops in this city. Don't miss an opportunity to join them at least once; the murmur of varied languages and the range of exotic coffees at these cafés will convince you as nothing else will that you are in a world-class cosmopolitan city.

Many of Tel Aviv's restaurants are concentrated in an area known as Little Tel Aviv, at the northern end of Ben Yehuda and Hayarkon streets (around the old Tel Aviv port). In addition, there are numerous establishments along the seafront south of Little Tel Aviv—all the way to Jaffa, at the city's southern end—as well as east of there, in the inner city. In Herzliya Pituach, a suburb north of Tel Aviv, most restaurants are housed in one complex in the industrial area, about a 10-minute walk from the Herzliya hotels.

### Lodging

Nothing stands between Tel Aviv's luxury hotels and the Mediterranean Sea except the golden beach and the Tayelet (promenade), outfitted with chairs and gazebos. Even the small hotels are only a short walk from the water. Tel Aviv's hotel row is on Hayarkon Street, which becomes Herbert Samuel Esplanade as you proceed south between Little Tel Aviv (the old port area) and Jaffa. This means that no matter where you stay, you're never far from the main thoroughfares of Ben Yehuda and Dizengoff streets, with their shops and outdoor cafés, or the city's major concert hall, museums, art galleries, and open-air Carmel Market.

Note that in the winter (mid-November to March), Tel Aviv hotels close their outdoor pools, and the lifeguards at the public beaches take a break as well. And aside from the Hilton, most hotels don't have room for tennis courts. Hotel health clubs are open to anyone over age 18.

## Water Sports

Tel Aviv has no shortage of water-sports opportunities, even some that may come as a surprise. In addition to enjoying the more obvious swimming, sailing, and windsurfing, you can rent pleasure boats on the Hayarkon River, and also water-ski—not in the sea, but on a cable in a man-made lake.

# EXPLORING TEL AVIV

Tel Aviv's western border is the Mediterranean. The beachfront Tayelet runs from north Tel Aviv to Jaffa, some 3 km (2 mi) to the south, and provides a great walk, especially at sunset. The north–south thoroughfares of Hayarkon, Ben Yehuda (which becomes Allenby), Dizengoff, and Ibn Gvirol streets run more or less parallel to the shore. The hotels are almost all concentrated on the seafront, along Hayarkon Street, which is also bursting with cafés, restaurants, and pubs. Allenby Street, one of the oldest in the city, crosses Hayarkon and Ben Yehuda streets and becomes the latter at its southern terminus. The change in affluence is as immediate as the change in street name, with a different socioeconomic situation reflected in the shabbier buildings and more budget-oriented shops along Allenby. You might say that the "border" between south and north is Carmel Market, a real junction of East-meets-West and old-meets-new. In the north, the business center dwindles north of Arlosoroff Street, which runs east–west near Kikar Hamedina (Hamedina Square). The residential area continues north and takes in the Yarkon River, once the city's northern boundary and now a popular recreational spot. South of downtown is Jaffa, once a separate city but now part of the municipality of Tel Aviv. An ancient port, Jaffa contains an impressively restored section known as Old Jaffa.

Technically, there are boundaries between Tel Aviv and the numerous towns and cities that surround it, but the urban sprawl is so great that residents of these surrounding municipalities will often tell you they live in Tel Aviv.

*Numbers in the text correspond to numbers in the margin and on the Exploring Tel Aviv map.*

## Great Itineraries

Spending three or four days in Tel Aviv is ideal. You'll have time to explore a variety of neighborhoods and museums and still have time left over to cool off on the beach. A shorter stay will require a lot of action, though you'll still be able to catch the highlights.

IF YOU HAVE 2 DAYS

Begin in Old Jaffa, wandering around the restored section and delving into the small galleries and shops. Enjoy a meal of fresh fish on the waterfront at the port, and walk along the coastal Tayelet (promenade) back to central Tel Aviv. In the afternoon, head for the Sheinkin Street area (Israel's wanna-be Greenwich Village) to get a feel for the contemporary Israeli lifestyle. This area is a meeting point between the city's trendiest trendy and a local ultra-Orthodox (Hasidic) Jewish community. In a way, it's hard to tell the difference: both groups wear black. Nearby Rothschild Boulevard has good examples of the city's various architectural styles and periods, from Middle East–influenced to Bauhaus to latter-day steel and glass.

On the second day, take in a museum on a subject that interests you: the Tel Aviv Museum of Art; the Eretz Israel Museum, with its excellent archaeological exhibits; or Beth Hatefutsoth (Diaspora Museum), which depicts Jewish life around the world throughout the ages. You may want to squeeze in some shopping after that, then spend a few hours doing what Tel Avivians do best—*beten-gav* (tummy-back), in Hebrew—cooling off on the beach.

IF YOU HAVE 4 DAYS

If your first day is a Tuesday or a Friday, head straight for the Nahalat Binyamin street fair and the Carmel produce market. From there, it's a hop, skip, and a jump to Sheinkin Street for a coffee break. Spend the afternoon at the Tel Aviv marina, either on the port or on the Mediterranean (rent a small boat with or without a captain). The next day, walk through Old Jaffa and Neve Tzedek, where you'll get an excellent idea of Tel Aviv's origins. Rest up in the late afternoon and go out for a late dinner on Ha'arba'a Street, which is lined with bars and eateries. Begin the third day on the beach, and then hit a museum (☞ If You Have 2 Days, *above*). Spend the evening in Jaffa; the atmosphere is very different at night. Leave the last day for wandering around the city center—browsing and shopping. Stroll the Tayelet again before you leave.

## From the Market to the Theater

It's only 2 km (1¼ mi) from the *shuk*, or marketplace, to the national theater, yet this walk traverses a good part of the city's nine-decade history, its ethnic mix, and its various social strata.

### A Good Walk

Begin at **Bialik Street** ① (off Allenby Street), one of the city's quaintest corners, with well-preserved architecture characteristic of Tel Aviv's early years. The change from bustling, polluted Allenby to Bialik is striking: quiet descends upon you in an instant. Walk to the end of the street and you'll find a mosaic and a fountain (which rarely flows). Strolling from the fountain back toward Allenby Street, stop in at No. 22, **Bet Bialik** ②, the home of the "father of Hebrew poetry." Three doors down, at No. 14, is **Bet Rubin** ③, an art gallery that houses painter Reuven Rubin's works as well as changing exhibits.

Return to Allenby Street, cross at the traffic light, and head south (left). In less than a minute you'll be at the entrance to the **Carmel Market** ④; soak up the lively atmosphere and perhaps purchase some dry goods or samples of Israel's fresh produce. On Tuesday and Friday, Tel Aviv's artisans (and would-be artisans) create a street fair along **Nahalat Binyamin** ⑤, east of the market.

Nahalat Binyamin forms a V with the marketplace at Allenby Street, at **Kikar Magen David** ⑥. Cross Allenby at this intersection by taking the underpass (otherwise you risk life and limb), and you'll end up on the corner of Sheinkin and Allenby streets. Cross narrow Sheinkin Street to King George Street and make your way downhill. Halfway down King George Street, on the right, the alley called **Simtat Plonit** ⑦ is identifiable by the two obelisk-style plaster structures at its entrance; pop in here to see some of the city's older architecture.

**Gan Meir** ⑧, a park that's a bit farther along on the other side of King George, is a nice place to rest your feet. Walk north from the park and turn right onto Ben Zion Boulevard. It's a few minutes' walk up a slight incline to the culturally rich **Kikar Habimah** ⑨, a square containing the **Habimah National Theater**; the **Helena Rubinstein Pavilion,** an annex of the Tel Aviv Museum (TAM); and the **Mann Auditorium.** A 1-km (½-mi) detour northeast to Shaul Hamelech Boulevard would bring you to another cultural highlight, the **Tel Aviv Museum of Art.**

Ben Zion Boulevard swings right (south) at Kikar Habimah to become **Rothschild Boulevard.** It's a 15-minute walk south to the **Independence Hall Museum** ⑩; you'll see it on your left after you cross Allenby. Israel's statehood was announced here in 1948. Nearby, in the middle of the boulevard, stands the stark, square **Founders' Monument and Fountain** ⑪.

TIMING

This walk can take the better part of the day, if you include time spent at the Nahalat Binyamin street fair and stops for coffee and a light meal along the way. Allow about three hours for a straight stroll.

## Sights to See

★ ❷ **Bet Bialik.** Bialik House is the charmingly restored home and library of Chaim Nachman Bialik (1873–1934), the national poet who is considered the father of Hebrew poetry. Bialik was already a respected poet and publisher by the time he moved to Tel Aviv from Russia in 1924; in the remaining 10 years of his life, his house became the intellectual center of Tel Aviv, and Bialik himself became the city's inspiration. His two-story, cream-color house, with its pointed arches and turrets, is a harmonious blend of Mediterranean and European styles. Built in 1927, it was almost palatial by the harsh standards of the time: mosaic-tile floors; Islamic-style arches and pillars; a small tower for meditating; sturdy, dark wood; and European-style furniture, including shelves for some 3,000 books. All labels are in Hebrew (an explanatory pamphlet is available in English), but the house is still a highly recommended stop. ⊠ *22 Bialik St.,* ☎ *03/525–4530.* ⊡ *Free.* ☉ *Sun.–Thurs. 9–5, Sat. 10–2.*

❸ **Bet Rubin.** Recognized as one of Israel's major painters, Reuven Rubin (1893–1974) bequeathed his house to Tel Aviv along with 45 of his works, which make up the permanent collection here. Unlike the still-furnished Bet Bialik (☞ *above*), this house functions solely as an art gallery, with changing exhibits by Israeli artists in addition to the great Rubin's work. Upstairs, there is a small but well-stocked art library where you can pore over press clippings and browse through art books. Note that on most days, the museum has limited hours. ⊠ *14 Bialik St.,* ☎ *03/525–4230.* ⊡ *NIS 12 ($3.40).* ☉ *Sun.–Mon. and Wed.–Thurs. 10–2, Tues. 10–1 and 4–8; Sept.–June, also Sat. 11–2.*

❶ **Bialik Street.** This area has been more successful than many other Tel Aviv neighborhoods in maintaining its charming older buildings. Bialik has long been a popular address with many of the city's artists and literati, so it's not surprising that some of the houses have been converted into small museums. One end of the street has a fountain and a **mosaic,** designed by painter-cum-writer Nahum Gutmann, which depicts the history of the city from the ancient days of Jaffa to the rise of Tel Aviv. Gutmann, a renowned children's author as well as a painter, was among the elite group of Tel Aviv's first artists and one of the first pupils at the city's first school, in Neve Tzedek. His writer father, Simcha Ben Zion, had a special place in the city's beginnings, too, and a boulevard, Ben Zion, is named for him.

## Exploring Tel Aviv

**KEY**

AE American Express Office

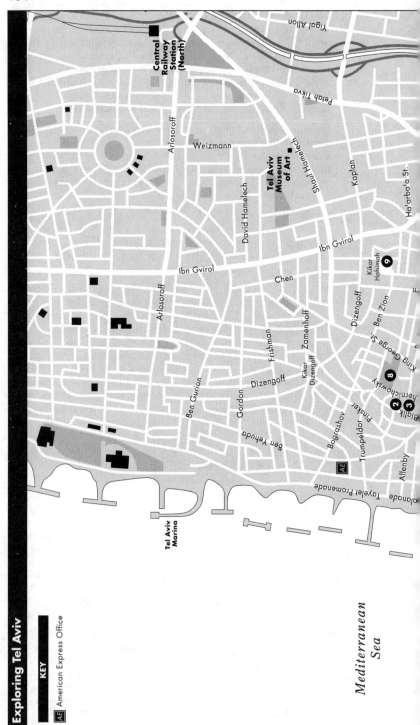

Central Railway Station (North)

Arlosoroff

Weizmann

Tel Aviv Museum of Art

Shaul Hamelech

Kaplan

Ha'arba'a St.

David Hamelech

Ibn Gvirol

Ibn Gvirol

Kikar Hohimah ⑥

Chen

Dizengoff

Ben Zion

Arlosoroff

Frishman

Zamenhoff

Chernichowsky

King George St.

⑧

Kikar Dizengoff

② Bialik ③

Ben Gurion

Dizengoff

Pinsker

Gordon

Bograshov

Trumpeldor

Allenby

Ben Yehuda

olande

Tayelet Promenade

AE

Tel Aviv Marina

*Mediterranean Sea*

Yigal Allon

Petah Tikva

**135**

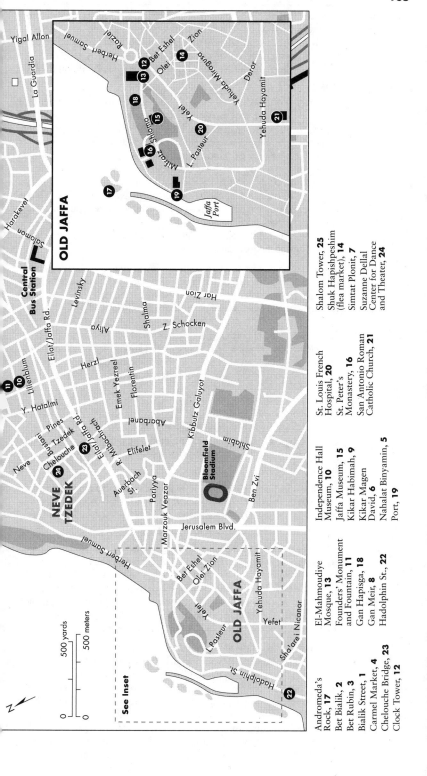

OLD JAFFA

Andromeda's Rock, **17**
Bet Bialik, **2**
Bet Rubin, **3**
Bialik Street, **1**
Carmel Market, **4**
Chelouche Bridge, **23**
Clock Tower, **12**

El-Mahmoudiye Mosque, **13**
Founders' Monument and Fountain, **11**
Gan Hapisga, **18**
Gan Meir, **8**
Hadolphin St., **22**

Independence Hall Museum, **10**
Jaffa Museum, **15**
Kikar Habimah, **9**
Kikar Magen David, **6**
Nahalat Binyamin, **5**
Port, **19**

St. Louis French Hospital, **20**
St. Peter's Monastery, **16**
San Antonio Roman Catholic Church, **21**

Shalom Tower, **25**
Shuk Hapishpeshim (flea market), **14**
Simtat Plonit, **7**
Suzanne Dellal Center for Dance and Theater, **24**

★ ❹ **Carmel Market.** Consisting of one long street and numerous short streets branching off it in both directions, the Carmel market (commonly referred to as the *shuk*) is invariably crowded on weekdays from about 9 through the afternoon, especially on Friday, as people rush to finish the shopping before the Sabbath and the weekend. Take a deep breath before you dive in.

The first section is devoted mainly to dry goods and assorted items. If you're looking for, say, a pair of slippers or a can opener, you'll find it here. A little farther down is the fruit and vegetable section, where everyone yells. Here, Israel's famous oranges, avocados, and mangoes are as fresh as they get, and if you think the vendor is insulting you for not taking a large enough quantity, he probably is—but it's all part of the show. With prices fixed, the days of market-style bargaining are over, but all the atmosphere and vigor of the past are retained. These days, in addition to coming across veteran Tel Avivians, you'll find Russian immigrants and foreign workers looking for bargains, even if they don't yet understand the Hebrew of the merchants who squawk the praises of their produce.

If you feel like trying something new, stop at one of the stalls that sell dried fruit and ask for *ledder* (a variation on the English *leather*). It's a Moroccan version of the dried apricot, beaten to a pulp and rolled out into a superthin, square sheet that resembles . . . leather.

NEED A BREAK?
The Carmel Market borders the **Yemenite Quarter,** which hides a score of delicious and cheap little eateries (closed Friday night and Saturday) offering shwarma and barbecued skewered meats, all kosher. Dig into any that catch your fancy, and wash them down with a cold beer.

⓫ **Founders' Monument and Fountain.** Dedicated in 1949, the Founders' Monument names those who founded Tel Aviv. This large slab of stone also encapsulates the city's past in three bas-relief panels representing the earliest pioneer days of planting and building as well as modern structures and houses. ⊠ *Rothschild Blvd. on the island at Nahlat Binyamin St.*

❽ **Gan Meir.** In this park you can rest on one of the benches and take in a free performance by city birds. It's something of a green haven in muggy Tel Aviv, and although also favored by local derelicts, it is perfectly safe.

You are now close to the Dizengoff Center, Israel's first shopping mall (☞ Shopping, *below*). Before the center opened in the early 1980s, this area was known as the **Nordiya Quarter,** a neighborhood set up in the 1920s by Jewish refugees seeking a home in the wake of Arab attacks in Jaffa. If you proceed north from Meir Park, you'll reach Bograshov Street, named for the man who founded the Nordiya Quarter and served as one of the headmasters of Tel Aviv's first school.

**Habimah National Theater.** The origins of Israel's national theater are rooted in the Russian Revolution, when a group of young Jewish actors and artists in Russia established a theater company that performed in Hebrew—this at a time when Hebrew was barely considered a living language. Subsequent tours through Europe and the United States in the 1920s won wide acclaim. In the late 1920s and '30s, many of the group's members moved to Israel and helped to establish the theater here. The cornerstone was laid in 1935; the current large, rounded glass-front building dates from 1970. ⊠ *Kikar Habimah.*

<table>
<tr><td>NEED A<br>BREAK?</td><td>Stop in for a coffee and a strudel topped with whipped cream at **Cafe Habimah** (⊠ 2 Tarsat St., ☎ 03/620–4113), near the wide, round window in the Habimah National Theater complex. If you do attend a play at the Habimah, you might even see some of the actors here afterward. In any case, this café is something of a theater in itself, with many of the Who's Who of Tel Aviv vying for the spotlight.</td></tr>
</table>

**Helena Rubinstein Pavilion.** This annex of the Tel Aviv Museum of Art (☞ *below*) houses changing contemporary-art exhibitions. The gallery is next to the Habimah National Theater (☞ *above*), on Tarsat Street. (Tarsat is the Hebrew-calendar acronym of 1948, the year in which Israel became independent.) ⊠ *6 Tarsat St.,* ☎ *03/528–7196.* ☑ *Combination ticket with Tel Aviv Museum of Art NIS 27 ($7.70).* ☉ *Sun.– Mon. and Wed.–Thurs. 10–6, Tues. 10–10, Fri.–Sat. 10–2.*

**⑩ Independence Hall Museum.** This impressive structure, with its wide ground-floor entrance and narrow horizontal windows, was originally the home of longtime mayor Meir Dizengoff; he donated it to the city in 1930 for use as the first Tel Aviv Museum. More significantly, the settlement's leaders assembled here in May 14, 1948, to announce to the world the establishment of the State of Israel. Today the museum's **Hall of Declaration** stands as it did on that dramatic day, with the original microphones on the huge table where the dignitaries sat. Behind the table is a portrait of the Zionist leader Herzl. ⊠ *16 Rothschild Blvd.,* ☎ *03/517–3942.* ☑ *NIS 12 ($3.40).* ☉ *Sun.– Thurs. 9–2.*

**⑨ Kikar Habimah.** Habimah Square is a center of culture in Tel Aviv— home of the **Habimah National Theater** (☞ *above*), the **Mann Auditorium** (☞ *below*), and the **Helena Rubinstein Pavilion** (☞ *above*), an annex of the Tel Aviv Museum. Nestled between the theater and the museum is a charming little junglelike garden, **Gan Ya'akov,** whose centerpiece is a sycamore that's been here almost longer than the city itself. Legend has it that camels were brought here to relax in the shade of the sycamore and drink from the nearby well.

**⑥ Kikar Magen David.** This meeting point of six streets is named for the six-point Magen David, or Star of David. The intersection gives you an all-too-close look at the Israelis' hair-raising driving style; if you need to cross the street here, use the underpass.

<table>
<tr><td>OFF THE<br>BEATEN PATH</td><td>**SHEINKIN STREET** – This street off Kikar Magen David recalls New York's Greenwich Village, with its artists and would-be artists, trendoids and wanna-bes, and endless cafés. Shopping here is fun, too, if you're not looking for anything in particular. Half the street is closed to vehicular traffic on Friday afternoons, allowing for street performances in good weather (though it's hard to see much through the crowds).</td></tr>
</table>

**Mann Auditorium.** One of the several cultural centers on Kikar Habimah (☞ *above*), Mann Auditorium is Israel's premier concert hall and the home of the Israel Philharmonic Orchestra, led by maestro Zubin Mehta. The low-slung gray building, among the most distinguished and sophisticated cultural buildings in the country, has excellent acoustics and a seating capacity of 3,000. It also hosts pop and rock concerts (☞ Nightlife and the Arts, *below*).

**★ ⑤ Nahalat Binyamin.** The selection at this street market, open Tuesday and Friday, is broad—ranging from tacky plastic trinkets to sophisticated crafts such as hand-carved wooden boxes and attractive glassware—but the real drawing card is the handmade silver jewelry. Nahalat Binyamin is further enlivened with a relatively new (for Israel) profusion of street performers and buskers. For a finishing touch of local color, cafés serving cakes and light meals line the street. Throughout the summer, the street is packed on market days, and you have to slalom through other pleasure-seekers and bargain-hunters to see anything. It's more enjoyable in spring and autumn, when you actually have room to wander among stalls and appreciate the wares.

When Tel Aviv first began to spread out from Jaffa, Nahalat Binyamin served as the eastern border of the city's premier neighborhood, **Ahuzat Bayit.** In those days, this area was so far removed from the center of things that only the poorest Jews ended up here. In recent years, much of Nahalat Binyamin has been gentrified, although the contrast between the "befores" and "afters" is all too clear. Look up while strolling here, for some of the architectural detail is particularly interesting. At **No. 8,** for example, built in the early 1920s, a number of Jewish symbols were incorporated into the original eclectic design. Note especially the way the bricks at the top form steps: this kind of deliberate incompleteness is a common motif to remind viewers of the destruction of the Temple in Jerusalem.

**Rothschild Boulevard.** Half a century ago, this was the most exclusive street in the city, and its real estate still commands astronomical prices. Many of the 1940s buildings have been allowed to deteriorate; others have been restored. Still others are examples of the International Style, a look that's charming on this tree-lined street but poorly imitated elsewhere in the city.

**❼**   **Simtat Plonit.** It's worth a wander down this alley to see old Tel Aviv decorative (now derelict) architecture at its best. Note the stucco lion in front of **No. 7,** which used to boast glowing eyes fitted with light-bulbs. The tract of land that incorporates Simtat Plonit was bought in the 1920s by an outspoken builder from Detroit named Meir Getzel Shapira. (He established what is still known as the Shapira Quarter, just south of the Central Bus Station and now one of the city's seedier neighborhoods.) After buying the land, Shapira insisted that this pint-size street be named after him, and the story goes that he fought furiously with Tel Aviv's first mayor, Meir Dizengoff, to get his way. (Dizengoff had already planned to name another street Shapira, after a different Shapira.) The mayor emerged victorious and named the alley Plonit, meaning "What's-His-Name."

**Tel Aviv Museum of Art.** The TAM houses a fine collection of Israeli and international art, including works by Israeli artist Reuven Rubin and a Roy Lichtenstein mural commissioned for the museum in 1989. There's also an impressive French Impressionist collection and an extensive collection of sculptures by Aleksandr Archipenko. ⊠ *27 Shaul Hamelech Blvd.,* ☎ *03/696–1297.* ◻ *NIS 27 ($7.70); includes entry to Helena Rubinstein Pavilion (☞ above).* ◷ *Sun.–Mon. and Wed.– Thurs. 10–6, Tues. 10–10, Fri.–Sat. 10–2.*

# Jaffa

The origin of Jaffa's name is unclear: some say it derives from the Hebrew *yafeh* (beautiful); others claim the town was named after its founder, Japhet, son of Noah. Nor is it known exactly when Jaffa was established. What is certain is its status as one of the oldest ports in the world—perhaps the oldest. Excavations have turned up artifacts as many as 4,000 years old. The Bible mentions Jaffa in connection with a number of significant events: the cedars used in the construction of the Temple passed through Jaffa on their way to Jerusalem; the prophet Jonah set off from Jaffa before being swallowed by the whale;

and St. Peter raised Tabitha from the dead here. In the ancient world, Jaffa was an important stop on the Via Maris, the trade route that extended from Egypt to Mesopotamia.

Jaffa's history has been one of fits and starts. The city has been razed and rebuilt scores of times as various powers fought to control it. Napoléon was but one of a succession of invaders who brought the city walls down; these walls were rebuilt for the last time in the early 19th century by the Turks and torn down yet again as recently as 1888.

By that time, Jaffa was a thriving cosmopolitan center, host to international businesspeople, bankers, and diplomats. Christian and Jewish pilgrims on their way to Jerusalem were a familiar sight. Jewish immigrants lived peacefully with Arabs here until the riots of 1921, when discord sent most of Jaffa's Jews fleeing to the sandy north that would become Tel Aviv. Now part of the municipality of Tel Aviv, Jaffa has a Jewish majority (most hailing from North Africa and from other Middle Eastern countries) and is also home to many Arab Christians and Muslims.

The restored section, Old Jaffa, is only a small part of this fascinating port; it caters primarily to tourists and fishermen. Beyond the restored section, a visit to Jaffa can take in the city's shabbier side, where trading, bargaining, and arguing are as much a part of life as ever.

## A Good Walk

To get to Jaffa, you can take Bus 8, 10, 25, 46, or 90 from downtown Tel Aviv. If you're driving, you can park for free during the day on weekdays and Sunday; there's a charge on weekday evenings and Saturday.

A good starting point is the northwestern corner of Jaffa's main square—known familiarly as the "clock square"—in front of the **police station** on Yefet Street. On the empty patch of land across the road, you can see the remains of what used to be Jaffa's northern wall. This patch was the *saraya* (administrative center) of the Turkish government in the early 20th century and was one of the corners of what was later called Government Square (its official, though rarely used, name is Jewish Agency Square). The square was eventually destroyed by a Jewish underground group seeking to root out Arab terrorist gangs.

Head south on Yefet for about 100 ft, passing the **clock tower** ⑫, on an island in the middle of the street—a popular meeting place for anyone with any kind of rendezvous in Jaffa. On the southwestern corner of the square is the beautifully preserved **El-Mahmoudiye Mosque** ⑬.

Turn onto Beit Eshel Street, opposite the mosque, and wander through what was a bustling business district some 300 years ago: the old Jerusalem Road, with handy access to the harbor. No. 11, which you'll recognize by the numerous arches forming its facade, was the local *khan*, the rough equivalent of a motel, built in the early 18th century by an Armenian family named Manouli. The ground floor was used as stables, with rooms upstairs for travelers. Today the building houses a furniture store. Any of the small streets leading south from Beit Eshel Street will take you into the **shuk hapishpeshim** ⑭, a flea market where you can find anything from silver earrings and Indian-style clothes to a kilo of shrimp. The ambience seems a world away from modern Tel Aviv.

Return to Yefet Street, south of the clock tower. Cross the street and enter the passage between Nos. 10 and 12: this used to be the local fish market. The aroma lingers—there are still a few excellent fish stores and restaurants in the vicinity—but these days you'll find more shoe stores than seafood here.

You are now very close to the ancient port. Walk south (you'll be going uphill) on Mifratz Shlomo Street until you come to a square on the left. Note the fountain here: when it was built by Turkish governor Mohammed Abu Najat Aja in the early 19th century, the fountain boasted six pillars and an arched roof, providing shade as well as water. The archway just beyond formed the entrance to the *hamam*, or old Turkish baths. Today archaeologists are digging beneath the floor of what is now an events hall here in search of ancient artifacts. Their finds—most of which were parts of Jaffa's ancient fortifications dating from the town's beginnings around 2000–1500 BC—have been preserved beneath the building's center stage as well as in the **Jaffa Museum** ⑮, also on Mifratz Shlomo Street.

Before you continue up the hill to the main square of Old Jaffa, cast your gaze north to see the dramatic contrast between the ancient and the modern, linked by the soft waves of the Mediterranean. As you make your way toward **Kikar Kedumim,** Old Jaffa's central plaza, you'll see the beautiful ocher-and-russet **St. Peter's Monastery** ⑯, on the right.

Before leaving the square, go through the restaurant Yamit (it's on an outdoor terrace, with a narrow walkway beside the tables), on the western side, for the best view of an unassuming piece of rock that rises from the sea here and is known as **Andromeda's Rock** ⑰. Now climb the hill from Kikar Kedumim, passing wide, shady yucca and fig trees, and cross the wooden bridge to a park called **Gan Hapisga** ⑱—literally "Summit Garden."

Return to Kikar Kedumim and follow one of the stepped alleyways leading down to the **port** ⑲, which makes for pleasant exploring. If you have the energy to continue walking, some very interesting sights and sounds remain. You can either follow the coast north for about five minutes to return to the clock tower or take the official port exit, walk a few steps up the hill, and turn left onto Louis Pasteur Street. About 300 ft ahead, you'll notice a bronze sculpture of a roly-poly little whale by sculptor and jewelry maker Ilana Goor, a resident of Old Jaffa. (Goor recently opened her house, 4 Mazal Dagim St., as a museum.) The whale keeps watch over a small parking area, beyond which stands a remnant of the city's ancient wall.

Continue on Louis Pasteur Street and return to **Yefet Street,** a few strides ahead, which links Jaffa sights both old and new. Most face you at the T-junction of Pasteur and Yefet streets, including the **St. Louis French Hospital** ⑳. A little farther south, on the left at No. 51, is the **San Antonio Roman Catholic Church** ㉑.

A few steps farther south, turn right into Sha'arei Nicanor Street and wander down to the charming little **Hadolphin Street** ㉒. The sightseeing walk ends here. To the south is the **Ajami Quarter** of Jaffa, one of many neighborhoods around the country benefiting from a rejuvenation program known as Project Renewal, financed by Jewish communities around the world.

TIMING

Allow about three hours for a daytime walk around Jaffa. Jaffa Port and restored Old Jaffa are good for a stroll at any time; consider coming at night for a romantic dinner.

## Sights to See

**Ajami.** Though still suffering from poverty, lack of infrastructure, and crime and drug problems, Ajami boasts some of the most gracious, luxurious houses in the country. Some ambassadors and other diplomats stay in this area. Tel Aviv has numerous projects in store for Ajami, and property prices are rising rapidly. Within a few years this part of Tel Aviv may be radically different—just as Old Jaffa, though still retaining the flavor of the past, is unrecognizable to anyone who saw it 30 years ago. ⊠ *South of Old Jaffa.*

**⑰ Andromeda's Rock.** To look at this rock from Kikar Kedumin (☞ *below*) is to see the stuff of myth and legend: Nireus, father of mermaids, was incensed that Andromeda, daughter of King Copeus of Ethiopia and his queen, Xaiopa, was more beautiful than the mermaids. He implored Poseidon, the god of the sea, to intervene. Poseidon obligingly set the sea astorm and sent a monster to eat whatever approached. In an attempt to restore calm, the people tied Andromeda to this rock. Only Perseus, riding the winged horse Pegasus, dared to save her. Soaring down from the sky, he beheaded the monster, rescued the lovely Andromeda, and promptly married her.

**⑫ Clock tower.** The tower is the focus of Jaffa's central square and stands at the center of town, with restored Old Jaffa to the west and the flea market to the east. The clock tower was completed in 1906, in time to mark the 30th anniversary of the reign of Sultan Abdul Hamid II; similar clock towers were built for the same occasion in Akko and in Jerusalem. The four clock faces stood still for many years until 1965, when the city renovated the tower and set them in motion again; the renovation also added stained-glass windows depicting events in Jaffa's history. ⊠ *Yefet St.*

NEED A BREAK?   There's always a line outside **Abulafia Bakery** (⊠ 7 Yefet St.), south of the clock tower. The Middle East's answer to pizza goes like hot cakes here—literally. For a simple snack with an exquisite flavor, order a pita topped with the indigenous herb *za'atar* (hyssop, a relative of mint). Other pitas are topped with egg or mushroom, or stuffed with salty cheese and baked until crisp.

**⑬ El-Mahmoudiye Mosque.** Built in 1809, the mosque was renovated for the first time in 1812 by Turkish governor Mohammed Abu Najat Aja. The governor rebuilt much of the city during his rule (1807–22), including the city walls that Napoléon's army had torn down in 1799.

The mosque managed to escape the fate of other sites in Jaffa that were destroyed during the War of Independence. In the late 19th century a separate entrance was built into the east wall to save the governor and other dignitaries the bother of having to push through the market-square crowds at the main entrance, on the south wall. With a minaret and two colorful domes, this is one of the local Muslim community's most important mosques and is not usually open to the general public.

The original mosque had a huge, splendid **drinking fountain** built into its southern wall, where travelers refreshed themselves after long journeys. In recent times, however, the Suleiman Fountain has lost its glory, and it sits sadly between two soft-drink stores that offer today's wanderers a less romantic means of quenching their thirst. ⊠ *Yefet St.*

**⑱ Gan Hapisga.** You might have to vie for space in the Summit Garden with a long line of newlyweds, who come here to be photographed in their wedding garb at sunset. Seven archaeological layers have been unearthed in a section of the park called Ramses II Garden. The oldest sections of wall (20 ft thick) have been identified as part of a 17th-century BC Hyksos city. Other remains include part of a 13th-century BC city gate inscribed with the name of Ramses II; a Canaanite city; a Jewish city from the time of Ezra and Nehemiah; Hasmonean ruins from the 2nd century BC; and traces of Roman occupation. At the summit, disturbing the ancient aura, is a kitschy stone sculpture—the Statue of Faith—from the 1970s, in the shape of a gateway.

**㉒ Hadolphin St.** This enclave is a hive of activity, with an art gallery, a French restaurant, a Greek Orthodox church dating from 1924, one of the best hummus joints in the city (open only in the morning), and a ceramics store run by local potter Eytan, all within a stone's throw of one another.

**⑮ Jaffa Museum.** This building has a lengthy history. It was first built during the Crusades; in the 18th century, the Turks added to what was left of the original building and used it as their Government House until 1897. In the first half of the 20th century it was a soap factory, and since 1961 the upper level has been operating as the Jaffa Museum, displaying many of the finds unearthed during archaeological digs here and in other parts of Tel Aviv. ☒ *10 Mifratz Shlomo St.,* ☎ *03/ 682–5375.* ☒ *NIS 10 ($2.85).* ☉ *Sun.–Mon. 9–2, Tues.–Wed. 9–7, Thurs. 9–2.*

**Kikar Kedumin.** This is Old Jaffa's central plaza. Old Jaffa used to be Tel Aviv's red-light district, plagued with crime of all kinds and raw sewage in the streets. Today, however, thanks to efforts begun by the Tel Aviv municipality in the late 1950s, the square is chockablock with excavation sites, restaurants, expensive gift and souvenir shops, and galleries. The artists who live here complain that there's too much noise on summer nights; some visitors say it's too touristy. But Old Jaffa is indisputably charming and should not be missed. The labyrinthine network of tiny alleys snakes in all directions from Kikar Kedumim down to the modern port. The focus of Kikar Kedumim is an archaeological site that exposes 3rd-century BC catacombs; the site has been converted into an underground visitor center with large, vivid, illustrated descriptions of Jaffa's history. Admission is free.

**Police station.** On the whole it's an uninteresting structure, but the station has an Ottoman-designed arch above its entrance. The design over the door is the seal of Turkish sultan Abdul Hamid II. During the British Mandate, the British used the building to intern both Arabs and members of the Zionist group Irgun. ☒ *Yefet St.*

**★ ⑲ Port.** A great many fishing boats are stuffed into this small marina, as well as a handful of houseboats. Along the waterfront are a plethora of restaurants, all expensive but most pretty good.

**⑳ St. Louis French Hospital.** This building was named for Louis IX, leader of the Seventh Crusade, who landed in Jaffa in 1251. Established by Roman Catholic nuns in the late 19th century, it was Jaffa's first modern hospital. Its neo-Renaissance style, popular in Europe at the time, includes high ceilings and tall arched windows. The building also had strategic importance, occupying the southwestern corner and highest point of Jaffa's encircling wall. It's now a community health center. ☒ *Yefet St.*

**⑯ St. Peter's Monastery.** Established by Franciscans in the 1890s, St. Peter's was built over the ruins of a citadel that dates from the Seventh Crusade, which was led by King Louis IX of France. It remained Jaffa's principal Roman Catholic church until the church of San Antonio was built in 1932. A monument to King Louis stands today at the entrance to the friary. Napoléon is rumored to have stayed here during his Jaffa campaign of 1799. To enter, ring the bell by pulling the string on the right side of the door; you will probably be greeted by one of the custodians, who speak Spanish and some English. ☎ *03/682–2871; call ahead if you want to visit.*

㉑  **San Antonio Roman Catholic Church.** Although it looks quite new, with its clean white-stone bricks, this church actually dates from 1932, when it was built to accommodate the growing needs of Jaffa's Roman Catholic Church. (St. Peter's, ☞ *above*, was in a heavily populated Muslim area and was unable to expand due to lack of land.) The church is named for St. Antonius of Padua, friend and disciple of St. Francis of Assisi. ✉ *51 Yefet St.*

★ ⑭  **Shuk hapishpeshim.** The flea market actually began as one of many small bazaars that surrounded the clock tower in the mid-19th century, and it's now the only survivor of that era. The market's main street is **Olei Zion,** but there are a number of smaller streets and arcades to explore at your leisure, so take your time. Today there's more junk than there are treasures, and bargaining is not as vigorous as it once was; but it's still important to play the game, so don't agree to the first price the seller demands.

**Yefet Street.** Think of Yefet as a sort of thread between eras: beneath it is the old market area, while all around you stand the Christian and Western schools and churches of the 19th and 20th centuries. Nos. 21, 23, and 25 deserve mention. The first is the **Tabitha School,** established by the Presbyterian Church of Scotland in 1863. Behind the school is a small cemetery where some fairly prominent figures are buried, including Dr. Thomas Hodgkin, the personal physician to Sir Moses Montefiore and the first to define Hodgkin's disease; he died in Jaffa in 1866. **No. 23** was a French Catholic school (it still carries the sign COLLÈGE DES FRÈRES) from 1882, but has long since been used by the French Embassy for administrative purposes. And next door, the neo-Tudor, fortresslike **Urim School,** with its round tower, was set up as a girls' school in 1882 by nuns of the same order that built the St. Louis French Hospital. It's now a local school.

# Neve Tzedek

In 1887 a small group of Jewish families concentrated their efforts to get out of crowded, poverty-stricken Jaffa and began creating an infrastructure on the sand to the north of the mainly Arab port town. Building at a rate of 10 houses a year, they laid the cornerstone for Neve Tzedek (Dwellings of Justice) in 1890. This was the forebear of Tel Aviv. The area is off the beaten path for most tourists, but as time and money are invested in its restoration, it attracts renewed interest. Today Neve Tzedek is the home of many of Tel Aviv's artists, rich and poor; it also has a splendid dance and arts complex (the Suzanne Dellal Center) and a growing number of small trendy galleries, gift stores, and restaurants. Though bordered on three sides by major thoroughfares (Eilat Road to the south, Herzl Street to the west, and Kaufman Street along the sea), this little quarter is very tranquil. Made up of only about a dozen tiny streets stuffed with one- and two-story dwellings in various stages of either depressing disrepair or enthusiastic renovation, Neve Tzedek is rich with tales of 100 years ago.

## A Good Walk

Begin your visit at **Chelouche Bridge** ㉓, on Chelouche Street just in from Eilat Road. Get used to the name: the Chelouches, one of the quarter's founding families, are remembered all over Neve Tzedek. The shell of Aaron Chelouche's house—the first in the quarter—still stands at what later became **32 Chelouche Street.**

Continue on Chelouche Street to Yehieli Street to see the main attraction of Neve Tzedek, the **Suzanne Dellal Center for Dance and Theater** ㉔. The two buildings from early in the century are now venues for a wide range of performances. Backtrack on Chelouche Street; the restored house at **No. 35,** at the corner of Rokach Street, was home to Nobel Prize–winning writer S. Y. Agnon from 1909 to 1912.

Turn right into Rokach Street. As you approach the intersection of Rokach and Neve Tzedek streets, consider what life was like before electricity or running water. On the northwestern corner, where the cream-color bomb shelters stand today, were Neve Tzedek's wells; here residents waited eagerly for their "water man," a Yemenite by the name of Yosef Minz, who pumped the water and even offered home delivery. Toward the end of the century people began digging their own wells; running water did not start to flow until after World War I.

At **36 Rokach Street** is the house of another of Neve Tzedek's founders, Shimon Rokach; family members still live here. A few steps on, you'll come to Pines Street. To the left and across the road, on the corner of Pines and Lilienblum streets, the pink-and-yellow shell of a building was the Eden Cinema, the first movie house in the country and a curious phenomenon altogether in 1914, set up as it was in the middle of the sand. The Eden became a cultural center, hosting the city's earliest opera and theater performances as well as films.

Continue up Lilienblum to Herzl Street and turn left. End your walk at the huge, ungainly **Shalom Tower** ㉕, where the view from the rooftop observatory takes in both the sprawling city and the Mediterranean.

TIMING

Allow around two hours for this walk, including time for coffee or a light meal. There are few sites to enter, but these are closed on Friday afternoon and Saturday, so it's better to visit on a weekday.

## Sights to See

㉓ **Chelouche Bridge.** The bridge was named for Aaron Chelouche, who began his career as a money-changer and quickly started buying up property north of Jaffa with his profits. It was built on top of the first railroad track in the country—linking Jaffa and Jerusalem, the railroad was laid in 1892 by Egyptian workers and operated by a French company. Aaron Chelouche was one of the agents for the French firm, and he added the bridge soon after the railway line was built, as a convenient means of getting from Jaffa to Neve Tzedek.

**32 Chelouche St.** Aaron Chelouche was prominent in Jaffa's Jewish community, but he was intent on setting up a Jewish town elsewhere. He thus built the first house here, in 1887. The shell of the huge house still stands, with hints of its grandeur in the arched terrace that spans the facade on the second floor. It held more than just the Chelouche clan (including Aaron's two daughters, three sons, and their families): by the time Aaron "persuaded" other Jews to come here to live—by selling them cheap plots—the house was doubling as a community center. There was even a synagogue out back. The dynasty would continue, and one of Aaron's grandsons—Moshe—even became mayor of Tel Aviv, albeit only for a day. Following the 1936 death of the city's first mayor, Meir Dizengoff, Moshe was elected to replace him; but he was quickly deposed by the city's rightist bloc, backed by the ruling British, who preferred another son of Neve Tzedek, Yisrael Rokach.

**35 Chelouche St.** Drawn to this quarter like so many other Israeli literati and artists, writer S. Y. Agnon lived here from 1909 to 1912. At the time, the young Agnon was working as a literary assistant to the more senior writer Simcha Ben Zion, the namesake of the boulevard leading from King George Street to Habimah Square; and his first story was published in literary journals produced by Ben Zion. Much of Agnon's writings reflects these very surroundings.

**36 Rokach St.** Shimon Rokach moved to the area from Jerusalem in 1884, and his son was born here three years later. This grandiose house changed the face of the street; it was designed by an Austrian architect whose touches included a bronze dome at the rear. Rokach became known as the Parisian Street because of its obvious grand-European influence.

Rokach the younger was already ensconced in politics by the time he was 28. After Mayor Dizengoff died in 1936, Rokach bumped out Moshe Chelouche as the preferred choice to succeed him. He served as mayor until 1952. In 1953, he became Israel's interior minister. The house is still occupied by the family; Shimon's sculptor granddaughter renovated it and now opens it up to the public on Saturday from 10 to 2.

㉕ **Shalom Tower.** Israel's first skyscraper stands on the site of the first high school ever to hold its classes entirely in Hebrew: the Herzliya Gymnasium (named, like the street, for the founder of the Zionist movement, Theodor Herzl). The building is your basic office block, but it has a rooftop observatory well worth a visit for its magnificent city and sea views. ⊠ *Herzl St.,* ☎ *03/517–0991.* 🎫 *NIS 15 ($4.30).* ☉ *Sun.–Thurs. 10–6:15, Fri. 10–1:30, Sat. 11–4.*

㉔ **Suzanne Dellal Center for Dance and Theater.** The two large whitewashed buildings that make up this attractive complex started as schools, one in 1892 and the other in 1908. Both were used for education until the 1970s, though they also served as headquarters for the political force Etzel and the underground military group Haganah, which marched on Arab Jaffa in the 1940s, when Arab residents terrorized Jewish neighborhoods. The complex was always something of a meeting place for theater folk, and it opened as a dance center after extensive renovations in 1990 (☞ Nightlife and the Arts, *below*). You can enter the attractive grounds, but the halls are open only for performances. ⊠ *6 Yehieli St.,* ☎ *03/510–5656.*

# Northern Tel Aviv

Among the sights north of the Yarkon River are two important museums. The Eretz Israel Museum is close to Tel Aviv University; Bet Hatefutsoth (Diaspora Museum) is farther north, on the university campus. The museums are about 8 km (5 mi) from the downtown hotels; Buses 24, 25, 27, 45, or 49 will take you to both. Allow at least two hours for each.

## Sights to See

★ **Beth Hatefutsoth (Diaspora Museum).** Presented here are 2,500 years of Jewish life in the Diaspora (the settling of Jews outside Israel), beginning with the destruction of the First Temple in Jerusalem and chronicling such major events as the exile to Babylon and the expulsion from Spain in 1492. Also covered is the world of Eastern Europe before the Holocaust. Photographs and text labels provide the narrative, and films and music enhance the experience. One highlight is a replica collection of miniature synagogues throughout the world, both those destroyed and those still functioning. ⊠ *Tel Aviv University Campus (Gate 2), Klausner St., Ramat Aviv,* ☎ *03/646–2020.* 🎫 *NIS 24 ($6.80).* ☉ *Sun.–Tues. and Thurs. 10–4, Wed. 10–6, Fri. 9–1.*

★ **Eretz Israel Museum.** This national museum comprises eight pavilions that present such facets of Israeli life as ethnography and folklore, ceramics and other handicrafts, and coinage; the displays span 3,000 years of history. In the center of the complex is the ancient site of Tel Kassile, where archaeological digs have so far uncovered 12 layers of settlements. ⊠ *2 Levanon (University) St.,* ☎ *03/641–5244.* 🎫 *Museum*

NIS 25 ($7), planetarium NIS 15 ($4.30). ☉ Sun.–Tues. and Thurs.
9–2, Wed. 9–7, Sat. 10–2.

# DINING

Most Tel Aviv restaurants are open throughout the day and well into
the night year-round, except Yom Kippur. Keep in mind that many serve
business lunches at reasonable prices, making them less-expensive options than the price categories suggest. (Eating well in Tel Aviv can be
very expensive.) Like many of their counterparts around the Mediterranean, Israelis dine late; chances are you'll have no trouble getting a
table at 7 PM, whereas at 10 you may face a long line. Casual attire is
always acceptable in Tel Aviv, even in the poshest restaurants.

Although the quality of Tel Aviv's cuisine has improved significantly,
be warned that the same cannot be said about service. Even in good
restaurants, staff members may make you feel as though they're doing
you a favor by waiting on you. It's customary to leave a 10%–15%
tip, but don't feel obliged to do so if you've received poor service. Occasionally, the service charge is added to the bill, so look for it; this is
uncommon enough that it generally goes unnoticed, and diners end up
paying twice for service.

| CATEGORY | COST* |
|----------|-------|
| **$$$$** | over $35 |
| **$$$** | $22–$35 |
| **$$** | $12–$22 |
| **$** | under $12 |

*per person for a three-course meal, excluding drinks and 10%–15% service
charge

## American

**$$$**  ✕ **Dixie.** This bar and grill is away from the main tourist areas and
serves mostly the surrounding offices and commercial centers. But
grab a taxi and go (any time—it's open 24 hours a day) if you're in
the mood for a breakfast of eggs Benedict, a hearty steak, or Cajun
food. The bar is well stocked. ⊠ 120 Yigal Allon St., ☎ 03/696–6123.
AE, DC, MC, V.

## Barbecue

**$**  ✕ **Shipudei Hatikva.** This family-style restaurant chain is one of many
★  grills along Ha'etzel Street, in the Hatikva Quarter. The Las Vegas–
style lights along the street contrast with the plain Formica tables and
fluorescent lighting inside, where you can pick from a range of sump-
tuous skewered meats grilled over hot coals. The specialty is barbe-
cued goose liver. ⊠ 37 Ha'etzel St., ☎ 03/687–8014. AE, DC, MC,
V. No dinner Fri., no lunch Sat.

## Cafés

**$$**  ✕ **Cafe Cazeh.** A true survivor on Tel Aviv's capricious restaurant
scene, Cafe Cazeh has good food, warm service, and a little courtyard-
garden in back with a very relaxing atmosphere. No meat is served,
but the vegetable pies and quiches are hearty and come with fresh salads. Desserts are the real specialty here—you may have trouble decid-
ing between lemon-meringue or pecan pie, apple cake, and brownies. ⊠
19 Sheinkin St., ☎ 03/629–3756. No credit cards. Closed Sat. No dinner Fri.

**$$**  ✕ **Cafe Tnuva.** Big, hearty salads and fresh juices can help perk you
up on a day of touring Tel Aviv on foot. End an already outstanding

meal with one of the many tasty cakes. ⊠ *34 Ben-Gurion Blvd.,* ☎ *03/527–2972. AE, DC, MC, V.*

$$  ✕ **Espresso Bar.** This is one of Tel Aviv's three Italian-style cafés, and it really does recall Rome. "*Rustico*" sandwiches and hearty cakes are the main attraction—beyond, of course, the potent coffee. ⊠ *46 King George St.,* ☎ *03/528–7307. No credit cards.*

$$  ✕ **Orna and Ella.** Consistently good for light meals and excellent for cakes and desserts, Orna and Ella is worth several trips. Have the sweet-potato latkes, but don't leave here without trying something from the dessert corner, such as a tart Tatin (apple tart) or pear pie. ⊠ *33 Sheinkin St.,* ☎ *03/620–4753. AE, DC, MC, V.*

$  ✕ **Internet Inbar.** If you must surf the Web or check your e-mail while you're here, you may as well do it with an espresso in hand. And why turn down blueberry pie with chocolate sauce? Just don't be surprised if your neighbors don't acknowledge you when you ask the time—the Net can give you that. ⊠ *87 King George St.,* ☎ *03/528–2228.*

## Chinese

$  ✕ **Fu-Xing.** It's noodles, noodles, and more noodles in this, the humblest of the Chinese restaurants owned and run by Yisrael Aharoni, who figures high on the city's culinary scene. They make for a pleasant light meal, especially if you're wandering near the Gan Ha'Ir shopping mall; you can watch shoppers go by as you eat. There's also a takeout counter and a Chinese grocery store, a relative rarity in Israel. ⊠ *71 Ibn Gvirol St., Gan Ha'Ir,* ☎ *03/527–9119. AE, DC, MC, V.*

## Contemporary

$$$$  ✕ **Tamuz.** Tucked away in a quiet corner of the city, this so-called "bistro-bar" offers an eclectic and varied menu that varies from season to season. Sauces are very much emphasized, most of them a tad sweet. Highlights include a beef fillet in light pickle; goose thigh cooked with port, onions, and dried fruit; salmon in orange sauce; and risotto with calamari in tomato butter. For dessert, try the sumptuous baked pears and marzipan coated with white chocolate. The decor is in warm tones, with Santa Fe–style terra-cotta stucco walls complementing old-style Mediterranean tile floors. ⊠ *6 Ahad Ha'am St.,* ☎ *03/516–7888. Reservations essential. AE, DC, MC, V.*

$$$  ✕ **Kachol.** Were it not for the crowd of trendy Tel Avivians here, you could forget you were still in the city. *Kachol* means "blue," and the restaurant has a suitably romantic and relaxing setting on the Tel Baruch beach, in north Tel Aviv: there's nothing like a Mediterranean sunset with your glass of wine. For starters, dip into the scrumptious salmon pâté with fresh bread, or *halumi* salad (fresh vegetables dotted with deep-fried goat's cheese); for dinner itself, lean toward the baked fish. ⊠ *Tel Baruch Beach,* ☎ *03/699–6574. AE, DC, MC, V.*

## Continental

$$$$  ✕ **King Solomon Grill.** Dim lights and partial curtains between tables create an intimate atmosphere here, despite the restaurant's large size. The eclectic menu ranges from Continental (pâté de foie gras, baked sweetbreads) to Middle Eastern (hummus and tahini) to North American (New York–style pastrami on rye). And everything is kosher. ⊠ *Hilton Hotel, Independence Park,* ☎ *03/520–2222. Reservations essential. AE, DC, MC, V. No lunch.*

$$  ✕ **Alexander's.** Dress trendy if you want to fit in here: the crowd at Alexander's is Tel Aviv yuppie, in keeping with the atmosphere along this street. The international menu changes frequently, and runs the

gamut from roast-beef sandwiches to lasagna. Light meals and toasted sandwiches are well garnished with fresh vegetables; the Persian kebabs are among the more creative options. You may have to wait for a table if you haven't made reservations, but service is generally quite good. ✉ *81 Yehuda Hamaccabi St., ☎ 03/546–3591. AE, DC, MC, V.*

## Eastern European

$ ✕ **Bebale.** With its old-style Jewish food amid photographs and mementos from the past, Bebale now serves young, hip Israelis newly appreciative of their Eastern European roots. Specialties include gefilte fish, chopped liver, meatballs in tomato sauce, and cold cherry soup. ✉ *177 Ben Yehuda St., ☎ 03/546–7486. AE, DC, MC, V. No dinner Fri.*

## French

$$$$ ✕ **Kapot Tmarim.** Over the years, a small number of restaurants have been credited with turning Israel's culinary tide, and Kapot Tmarim is one of them. The pleasant ambience and friendly staff enhance a compelling French menu with contemporary influences, from hot goose liver with onions and dates right down to the restaurant's own ice cream. ✉ *60 Ahad Ha'Am St., ☎ 03/566–3166. Reservations essential. AE, DC, MC, V. Closed Sat.*

$$$$ ✕ **Keren.** Ranked among the finest restaurants in Israel, Keren is housed in the only fully restored building in Jaffa's run-down American Colony. The bar downstairs proves a restful spot after the inevitable daytime traffic jam on Eilat Street. You'll forget the state of the neighboring buildings when you enter the upstairs dining room, with its smooth wood floors and welcoming armchairs. Foie gras features prominently on the menu, in various forms; but the range is wide. ✉ *12 Eilat St. (at Auerbach St.), Jaffa, ☎ 03/681–6565. Reservations essential. AE, DC, MC, V. No lunch Sun.*

## Italian

$$$$ ✕ **PastaLina.** One of the most innovative restaurants in Tel Aviv, PastaLina is worth the trek to this less-well-known corner of Jaffa, near the American Colony. Antipasti cover a large table by the entrance, and you're served generous samples thereof upon sitting down. The fixed-price menu, which changes daily, includes antipasti and a pasta, meat, or fish dish. Glass bricks in the front wall allow natural light to highlight the russet walls and wood furniture. ✉ *16 Elifelet St., Jaffa, ☎ 03/683–6401. Reservations essential. AE, DC, MC, V. No dinner Fri.*

$$$$ ✕ **Prego.** An easygoing atmosphere—you dine in a glassed-in terrace on the boulevard—encourages lingering over your fine Italian meal. Most of the restaurant occupies a terrace overlooking Rothschild Boulevard, in one of Tel Aviv's older quarters. For something delicate and tasty, go for the spinach-and-ricotta ravioli with tomato sauce, accompanied by a glass of cold white wine from the Golan. ✉ *9 Rothschild Blvd., ☎ 03/510–7319. AE, DC, MC, V.*

## Mediterranean

$$$$ ✕ **Twelve Tribes.** Regulars call this the best hotel restaurant in Tel Aviv
★ (and, of course, it's kosher). They don't come here for the '70s decor, though, as it's out of sync with the "Mediterranean fusion" cuisine—a contemporary notion reflecting the Sea's many nationalities. Favorite dishes include hot goose liver in sultana sauce and a sliced rack of lamb with red-wine sauce. ✉ *Sheraton Hotel, 115 Hayarkon St.,*

☎ 03/521–1111. *Reservations essential. AE, DC, MC, V. Closed Fri.–Sat. No lunch.*

**$$$** ✗ **Suzanna.** This century-old building once housed the first coffee shop in Tel Aviv, and Suzanna's owners retained the early Israeli furnishings, such as decorative ceramic floor tiles, when they renovated several years ago. A pleasant café and eatery by day, the restaurant bustles by night, when it's especially nice to sit on the leafy terrace. The menu is odd, but very successful, drawing on both traditional and contemporary cuisines. Do you feel like Iraqi *kube* (meat-filled semolina dumplings) and pumpkin soup, or Moroccan silk soup with chick peas, veal, and coriander? If you're still in a Middle Eastern mood, will it be lamb in yogurt, grilled chicken salad with pine nuts and shallots, or couscous-stuffed chicken with a sweet date-and-plum sauce? The choices don't end there: for dessert, there's home-style sorbet, ice cream, and cakes: pear-and-apple tart, chocolate cake with cream and biscuits, and chocolate fudge cake. ✉ *9 Shabazi St., Neve Tzedek,* ☎ *03/517–7580. AE, DC, MC, V.*

## Mexican

**$$$$** ✗ **Chimichanga.** Located in a light-industrial area, this New Mexican restaurant joins the ranks of Tel Aviv eateries that stay alive and hopping long after everything—and everyone—else has gone to sleep. It's large, but friendly. Start with a margarita; then tuck into a meal of chicken in tequila and lime, all sautéed in "Indian butter" and served with grilled vegetables. ✉ *6 Kriminitzky St.,* ☎ *03/561–3232. Reservations essential. AE, DC, MC, V. No lunch Fri.*

**$$** ✗ **Cactus.** South-of-the-border–inspired graphics in bold yellows, reds, blues, and greens compliment the terra-cotta tones of this small, happy Tex-Mex restaurant. The menu is largely traditional, with nachos and salsa, burritos, chili con carne, and fajitas. The margaritas are not quite the real thing, but they do the trick. ✉ *66 Hayarkon St.,* ☎ *03/510–5969. MC, V.*

## Indian

**$$$** ✗ **Tandoori.** This veteran restaurant—the oldest of the Tandoori chain,
★ which introduced Israelis to fine Indian cuisine—has maintained the high quality of its food and service over the years, which in Tel Aviv is noteworthy in itself. The curries come in three strengths, but tandoori chicken is the specialty: it comes to the table sizzling hot, and finger bowls of rose water mean you can dig in with abandon. ✉ *2 Zamenhoff St. (Kikar Dizengoff),* ☎ *03/629–6185. AE, DC, MC, V.*

## Pizza

**$** ✗ **Big Mama.** The thin-crust pizza here is excellent, and the owners
★ take pride in using only the freshest ingredients. Toppings range from the traditional basil to more unusual ideas, such as zucchini or prosciutto and egg. It's ideal for a quick, light meal. ✉ *22 Rabbi Akiva St.,* ☎ *03/510–7805. No credit cards. Closed Sun. No lunch.*

## Seafood

**$$$$** ✗ **Mul-Yam.** This is Israel's first true-to-life oyster and seafood bar. Every-
★ thing is flown in fresh from abroad—including Nova Scotia lobsters—so the prices are not low. Still, it's a true pleasure: the dishes are tasty and well presented, and the great location, in the old port by the Mediterranean, adds to the flavor. ✉ *Tel Aviv Port,* ☎ *03/546–9920. Reservations essential. AE, DC, MC, V. No dinner Sat.*

## Tel Aviv Dining and Lodging

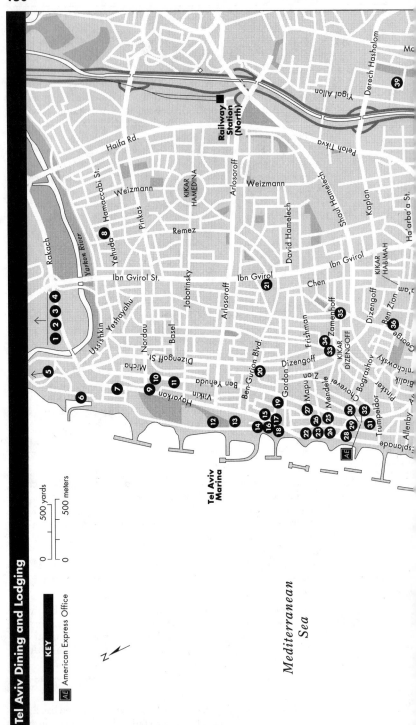

**KEY**

**AE** American Express Office

0 ——— 500 yards
0 ——— 500 meters

Railway Station (North)

Haifa Rd.

Weizmann

Hamaccabi St.

Pinkas

Yehuda

Remez

KIKAR HAMEDINA

Arlosoroff

Weizmann

David Hamelech

Shaul Hamelech

Kaplan

Ha'arba'a St.

Yigal Allon

Derech Hashalom

Peah Tikva

Rakach

Yarkon River

Ussishkin

Yeshayahu

Ibn Gvirol St.

Jabotinsky

Arlosoroff

Ibn Gvirol

Chen

Ibn Gvirol

KIKAR HABIMAH

Nordau

Basel

Dizengoff St.

Micha

Ben Yehuda

Viktin

Hayarkon

Ben-Gurion Blvd.

Frishman

Dizengoff

Gordon

Mapu

Zion

Mendele

Trovelet

Bograshov

Zamenhoff

KIKAR DIZENGOFF

Dizengoff

Pinsker

Bialik

Trumpeldor

Trichowsky

Ben Zion

George

Allenby

Esplanade

Mediterranean Sea

Tel Aviv Marina

N

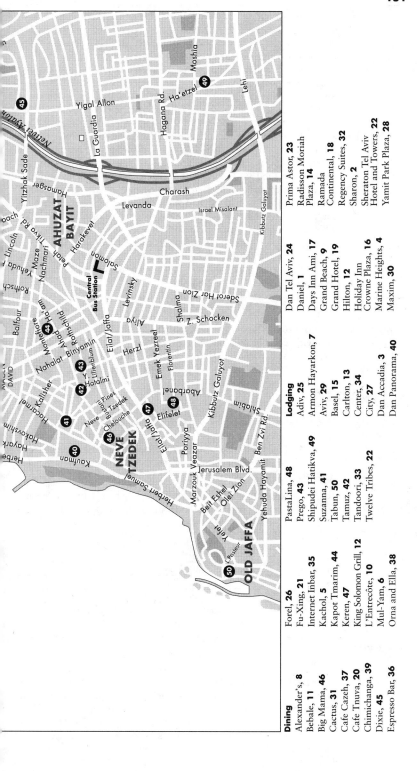

**Dining**
Alexander's, **8**
Bebale, **11**
Big Mama, **46**
Cactus, **31**
Cafe Cazeh, **37**
Cafe Tnuva, **20**
Chimichanga, **39**
Dixie, **45**
Espresso Bar, **36**

Forel, **26**
Fu-Xing, **21**
Internet Inbar, **35**
Kachol, **5**
Kapot Tmarim, **44**
Keren, **47**
King Solomon Grill, **12**
L'Entrecôte, **10**
Mul-Yam, **6**
Orna and Ella, **38**

PastaLina, **48**
Prego, **43**
Shipudei Hatikva, **49**
Suzanna, **41**
Tabun, **50**
Tamuz, **42**
Tandoori, **33**
Twelve Tribes, **22**

**Lodging**
Adiv, **25**
Armon Hayarkon, **7**
Aviv, **29**
Basel, **15**
Carlton, **13**
Center, **34**
City, **27**
Dan Acadia, **3**
Dan Panorama, **40**

Dan Tel Aviv, **24**
Daniel, **1**
Days Inn Ami, **17**
Grand Beach, **9**
Grand Hotel, **19**
Hilton, **12**
Holiday Inn
Crowne Plaza, **16**
Marine Heights, **4**
Maxim, **30**

Prima Astor, **23**
Radisson Moriah
Plaza, **14**
Ramada
Continental, **18**
Regency Suites, **32**
Sharon, **2**
Sheraton Tel Aviv
Hotel and Towers, **22**
Yamit Park Plaza, **28**

$$$$   ✕ **Tabun.** Your best bet here is the catch of the day—fresh fish or seafood—lightly herbed and baked in olive oil in the *tabun* (stone) oven, which imparts a rich and faintly barbecued flavor. If you can't wait for the main course—ideally, baked sea bass or bream with herbs—the carpaccio of salmon and grouper is delectable, and the bouillabaisse is excellent. Whitewashed walls, crisp, white linen tablecloths, and turquoise trimmings lend sophistication to the Mediterranean ambience. ✉ *Main Gate, Jaffa Port (turn left at pier),* ☎ *03/681–1176. Reservations essential. AE, DC, MC, V.*

$$$   ✕ **Forel.** Pleasant, unassuming, and always friendly, Forel (which means "trout" in German) has a consistently appealing menu of—you guessed it—trout, in all forms and flavors: blue trout, stuffed trout, smoked trout, and more. Specialties include a thick fish soup with seafood and vegetables; a seafood platter with shrimp, calamari, crab, and mussels; trout on a charcoal grill; and *daurade (denise)* fillet with charcoal-roasted peppers. An antipasti table near the entrance gets the taste buds whirring. Despite its name, Forel is particularly known for its apple strudel, and takes additional pride in its chocolate-orange parfait. The decor is subtle, with neat, clean lines in soft beige and pink. The clientele is largely older, with a sizable business contingent. ✉ *10 Frishman St.,* ☎ *03/522–3167. AE, DC, MC, V.*

## Steak

$$   ✕ **L'Entrecôte.** The mood is distinctly Parisian in this intimate restaurant with wood beams and a cozy upper-level garret. As the name implies, steaks are the focus. There are only a few tables, so the noise level is low. ✉ *195 Ben Yehuda St.,* ☎ *03/546–6726. AE, DC, MC, V.*

# LODGING

Hotel reservations are essential during all Jewish holidays and are advised throughout the year. Keep in mind that most hotels (except as noted) include breakfast in the price: fresh vegetables, salads, and fruit; cereals and pastries; and eggs and cheeses are usually among the options.

Tel Aviv is known for a dearth of middle-price hotels, but the few hotels listed in the $$ and $ categories are generally clean and comfortable, with friendly employees who create a warm atmosphere.

| CATEGORY | COST* |
| --- | --- |
| $$$$ | over $120 |
| $$$ | $80–$120 |
| $$ | $60–$80 |
| $ | under $60 |

*All prices are for a standard double room, including breakfast and excluding 15% service charge.*

## Tel Aviv

$$$$   🏨 **Carlton.** The warm European ambience is evident as soon as you enter the lobby, with its muted colors, pale wood paneling, and soft music. The Carlton caters to a mix of tourists and businesspeople with efficient yet personal service. Most rooms have sea views, as does the swimming pool, which is on the roof. ✉ *10 Eliezer Peri St., 61064,* ☎ *03/520–1818,* ℻ *03/527–1043. 278 rooms with bath. 2 restaurants, bar, 2 coffee shops, pool, beauty salon, chapel, parking (fee). AE, DC, MC, V.*

$$$$   🏨 **Dan Panorama.** The location—south of the main stretch of hotels, near Jaffa—is not ideally convenient to Tel Aviv, but rates are lower than

at comparable luxury hotels. Rooms in this high-rise are compact and attractive, with decorative wall hangings adding spots of color. Each room has a tiny balcony overlooking the sea, either south toward Jaffa or north facing the hub of the city. Poolside barbecues in the summer are a plus. ⊠ *10 Y. Kaufman St., 68012,* ☎ *03/519–0190,* FAX *03/517–1777. 504 rooms with bath. Restaurant, bar, coffee shop, pool, massage, sauna, exercise room, health club, nightclub, parking (fee). AE, DC, MC, V.*

$$$$ ⊡ **Dan Tel Aviv.** Despite its reputation for exclusivity, this landmark
★ hotel has a warm, congenial atmosphere. Patterned coverlets decorate olive-green furniture in the rooms; the bathrooms have hair dryers, phones, and radios. Rooms are larger in the luxurious King David wing and have panoramic sea views as well as double-glazed windows to muffle city noise; however, none of these have balconies. Guests have access to both the beach below and free golf at the Dan Accadia Hotel (☞ *below*), about 25 km (15½ mi) north of Tel Aviv. Tel Avivians themselves come to La Regence, the hotel's restaurant, for elegant dining. ⊠ *99 Hayarkon St., 63903,* ☎ *03/520–2525,* FAX *03/524–9755. 238 rooms with bath, 50 suites. 3 restaurants, bar, café, minibars, pool, sauna, steam room, health club, parking (fee). AE, DC, MC, V.*

$$$$ ⊡ **Grand Beach.** All of these rooms are decorated in turquoise, gray, and yellow, and have unusually good reading lamps. There is a rooftop pool, and the beach is a five-minute walk away. The main dining room has a view of city streets, and light food is served in the large lobby lounge. ⊠ *250 Hayarkon St., 63113,* ☎ *03/543–3333,* FAX *03/546– 6589. 212 rooms. Bar, lobby lounge, pool, chapel. AE, DC, MC, V.*

$$$$ ⊡ **Hilton.** Tel Aviv's most expensive hotel—and the one that caters most directly to business travelers—the Hilton fairly bristles with the energy of negotiations and deal-making. It offers a full range of executive services, including Japanese-language services and two business lounges. The Hilton's large seawater pool is the best in town, and the hotel has its own beach (so you don't need to get dressed to get undressed again). In addition to enjoying classic French cuisine in the first-class King Solomon Grill, you can grab a pastrami-on-rye in the Deli Room or, in summer, a poolside barbecue lunch. Note that the room rate does not include breakfast. ⊠ *Hayarkon St., Independence Park, 63405,* ☎ *03/520–2222,* FAX *03/527–2711. 582 rooms with bath. 2 restaurants, 2 bars, deli, saltwater pool, tennis court, health club, beach, parking (fee). AE, DC, MC, V.*

$$$$ ⊡ **Holiday Inn Crowne Plaza.** The light and attractive Holiday Inn Crowne Plaza is decorated in soothing pastels in both the guest rooms and the public spaces. Executive floors are available. The main restaurant, Bellissima, serves meat at lunchtime and becomes an Italian dairy restaurant at night. In addition, there is the Pacific China Grill, which serves Western food cooked with an Eastern influence, and the English-style Pub Inn, a nice spot for a seaside beer. ⊠ *145 Hayarkon St., 63453,* ☎ *03/520–1111,* FAX *03/520–1122. 266 rooms with bath. 2 restaurants, pub, snack bar, sushi bar, in-room safes, no-smoking rooms, beauty salon, massage, sauna, health club, parking (fee). AE, DC, MC, V.*

$$$$ ⊡ **Radisson Moriah Plaza.** In this 17-floor hotel, all rooms (except singles) have sea views from their balconies. Public areas are freshly decorated in earth tones; the lobby has photos of old Tel Aviv. Rooms have Mediterranean color schemes and good reading lights. The outdoor pool (with daily children's activities in summer) overlooks the beach, to which you have direct access. The restaurant presents a wide range of Israel dishes, including *taboon* (clay oven) baked fish. ⊠ *155 Hayarkon St., 63453,* ☎ *03/521–6666,* FAX *03/527–1065. 372 rooms with bath. Restaurant, bar, patisserie, in-room safes, minibars, room service, saltwater pool, children's programs in summer, parking (fee). AE, DC, MC, V.*

$$$$ ⊞ **Ramada Continental.** The Ramada's rooms are decorated in a variety of soft hues, and all have double-glazed windows and balconies with sea views. Some even have queen-size beds, unusual in Israel. Bathrooms include hair dryers and scales. The lobby, with windows overlooking the sea, has a bar with a pianist, and the main dining room opens onto a patio, where barbecues are held. An outdoor terrace coffee shop, also overlooking the water, serves light meals. ⊠ *121 Hayarkon St., 61032,* ☎ *03/521–5555,* FAX *03/521–5588. 330 rooms with bath, 10 suites. Restaurant, 2 bars, coffee shop, 2 pools, sauna, exercise room, parking (fee). AE, DC, MC, V.*

$$$$ ⊞ **Regency Suites.** This Best Western hotel is made up entirely of fully equipped, modern one-bedroom suites, each of which also has a small living area. It's a tad cheaper than the big hotels, and you have the added advantage of being able to cook for yourself and entertain a few friends. The decor is tasteful and the atmosphere is homey, especially in the tiny coffee shop, where breakfast is served (for an extra charge). ⊠ *80 Hayarkon St., 63432,* ☎ *03/517–3939,* FAX *03/516–3276. 20 suites. Coffee shop, kitchenettes. AE, DC, MC, V.*

$$$$ ⊞ **Sheraton Tel Aviv Hotel and Towers.** Combining a personal touch
★ with the efficiency and experience of the international Sheraton chain, this is one of the most attractive lodging options in Tel Aviv. An excellent lobby design allows for private areas within the public space, and there's a lounge bar, often with live entertainment. Most of the rooms are decorated in soft hues and color-coordinated fabrics, and all have double-glazed windows. The well-run executive Sheraton Towers floors have their own check-in, and there is a 24-hour business center. The Twelve Tribes restaurant (☞ Dining, *above*) is widely considered the best hotel restaurant in Tel Aviv. ⊠ *115 Hayarkon St., 61032,* ☎ *03/521–1111,* FAX *03/523–3322. 346 rooms with bath. 2 restaurants, bar, minibars, 2 pools, health club, nightclub, business services, parking (fee). AE, DC, MC, V.*

$$$$ ⊞ **Yamit Park Plaza.** Roughly half the accommodations in this beachfront hotel are in suites with fully equipped kitchenettes, unusual for Tel Aviv. One building contains the one- and two-bedroom suites, which include living areas as well as kitchenettes; the standard rooms in the adjacent building are less expensive. ⊠ *79 Hayarkon St., 63903,* ☎ *03/519–7111,* FAX *03/517–4689. 42 rooms with bath, 43 suites. 2 restaurants, bar, pool, nightclub, parking (fee). AE, DC, MC, V.*

$$$ ⊞ **Armon Hayarkon.** Though hardly the Hayarkon Palace (its English translation), this small, family-run hotel is pleasant enough to attract a high percentage of repeat customers. It's in Little Tel Aviv, at the northern end of Hayarkon Street, near a number of good restaurants and a minute's walk from the beach. The small rooms are decorated in basic brown, and some have balconies facing the sea. The lobby (also small) has coffee-making facilities and a soda machine. ⊠ *268 Hayarkon St., 63504,* ☎ *03/605–5271,* FAX *03/605–8485. 24 rooms with bath. Parking (fee). AE, DC, MC, V.*

$$$ ⊞ **Basel.** It's not on the beach side of Hayarkon Street, but this seven-story hotel lives up to its reputation as a good deal. All but five rooms on each floor have sea views; their decor includes well-designed wooden furniture and patchwork-style fabrics. Expect personalized service—a legacy of the original Swiss owners? The lobby, with a corner bar, overlooks the small swimming pool. ⊠ *156 Hayarkon St., 63451,* ☎ *03/520–7711,* FAX *03/527–0005. 120 rooms with bath. Bar, coffee shop, room service, pool, parking (fee). AE, DC, MC, V.*

$$$ ⊞ **City.** On a quiet street near the beach, this six-story hotel is at the
★ bottom of its price range. The light, airy lobby has a small sitting area on one side, a cozy dining room on the other. The basic but pleasant outdoor café, which faces the neighbor's hedge across the street, con-

sists of a dozen plastic chairs and tables under a sidewalk canopy. The rooms have blond-wood furniture and TVs. The City is known for its fine food, including an acclaimed Israeli breakfast and a Friday night Shabbat (Sabbath) dinner with gefilte fish. ⊠ *9 Mapu St., 63577,* ☎ *03/524–6253,* ℻ *03/524–6250. 96 rooms with bath. Restaurant, café, room service, free parking. AE, DC, MC, V.*

$$$   🏨 **Grand Hotel.** The bar and the lobby share one relatively small space here, so you can have a drink as you check in. The pleasant guest rooms are decorated with warm colors and wood trim. You have easy access to both the city center and the beach. ⊠ *87 Ben Yehuda St.,* ☎ *03/527–8282,* ℻ *03/527–8304. 60 rooms with bath. Dining room, lobby lounge, free parking. AE, DC, MC, V.*

$$$   🏨 **Prima Astor.** Built on a rise on the corner of Frishman and Hayarkon streets, the Astor has an excellent view of the sea. The rooms in this 30-year-old hotel are not large, but those facing the sea have enclosed balconies with picture windows. The small, homey lobby has prints of Israeli scenes and a coffee bar. The restaurant, Shangri-La, serves authentic Thai cuisine and has a beautiful canopied terrace that faces seaward. ⊠ *105 Hayarkon St., 63903,* ☎ *03/520–6666,* ℻ *03/523–7247. 70 rooms with bath. Restaurant, bar, business services, free parking. AE, DC, MC, V.*

$$   🏨 **Center.** This is one of the new breed of tourist-class hotels in Tel Aviv—simple rooms, warm but basic service, and far more reasonable prices than the luxury properties on the beach, which is just a 15-minute walk from here. The Center is well situated in town on Dizengoff Square, next to the Tandoori Indian restaurant (☞ Dining, *above*). Rooms are small and tasteful, though there is no Mediterranean view. ⊠ *2 Zamenhoff St.,* ☎ *03/629–6181,* ℻ *03/629–6751. 56 rooms with bath. AE, DC, MC, V.*

$$   🏨 **Days Inn Ami.** This small hotel is half a block from the sea, heading down a side street off Hayarkon Street, with a pleasant sidewalk café out front. Most of the guest rooms are relatively small, but each has a small desk and chair. Four rooms on each floor have balconies with views of rooftops and other cityscapes. ⊠ *152 Hayarkon St., 63455,* ☎ *03/524–9141,* ℻ *03/523–1151. 60 rooms with bath. Café, room service. AE, DC, MC, V.*

$$   🏨 **Maxim.** Moderately priced amid pricier accommodations, Maxim is a good value. The rooms are basic, but most have sea views. Europeans like to stay here, and there is indeed a kind of Continental atmosphere about the place, due in part to the many languages heard in the lobby. The lobby café is a popular place to relax. ⊠ *86 Hayarkon St.,* ☎ *03/517–3721,* ℻ *03/517–3726. 60 rooms with bath. Bar, café. AE, DC, MC, V.*

$   🏨 **Adiv.** This amiable hotel is on a side street off Hayarkon Street. Rooms have pleasing modern furnishings and pastel-print bedspreads and curtains, if no sea views. The staff is polite. ⊠ *5 Mendele St., 63907,* ☎ *03/522–9141,* ℻ *03/522–9144. 68 rooms with bath. Bar, café, room service. AE, DC, MC, V.*

$   🏨 **Aviv.** More a hostel than a hotel, this three-story 1950s building was renovated when the trendy Picasso restaurant opened on its ground floor. You enter through the restaurant, and register at a desk behind the kitchen. There's no elevator, and the decor is spare; don't expect telephones or TVs. The rooms in back are said to be quiet, but their location on Hayarkon Street and over the restaurant (which is open until 5 AM) is not ideal for those who seek serenity. A real plus here is the breakfast (omelet, salad, juice, and bread) at Picasso, which is included in the room rate. ⊠ *88 Hayarkon St., 63432,* ☎ *03/510–2784,* ℻ *03/522–3060. 20 rooms with bath. DC, MC, V.*

## Herzliya Pituach

Herzliya Pituach, or Herzliya-on-the-Sea, is a resort area 12 km (7½ mi) up the coast from Tel Aviv. It has a number of beachfront hotels, a wide range of eating options (some on the beach, but most a short distance inland, in the industrial area), public squares with outdoor cafés and shops, and a new marina. Affluent suburbanites live here, as do diplomats and foreign journalists; there's a cosmopolitan, holiday air to the place. An express tourist bus (Bus 90) plies the route between the Herzliya hotels, the center of Tel Aviv, and ancient Jaffa.

**$$$$** 🏨 **Dan Accadia.** This well-known seaside hostelry (part of the Dan Hotel chain) opened in 1956 and is still going strong. Its two buildings are surrounded by plant-filled lawns, which in turn surround a pool overlooking the sea. Sixty rooms face the pool, with direct access to the beach; others face the marina. The rooms are not huge, but they have balconies with sea views; interior decor includes quilted bedspreads and matching blue-and-pink drapes. Organized activities help keep children and teenagers amused on Friday and Saturday. Guests have access to the golf course at the Dan Caesarea, farther north. The dining room has a glass wall looking out to sea, and a second, poolside restaurant is open for lunch. The Wednesday-night poolside barbecue, complete with a band and dancing, has been a local fixture for years. ⊠ *Herzliya-on-the-Sea 46851,* ☎ *09/959–7070,* ⅋ *09/959–7091. 185 rooms with bath. 2 restaurants, bar, coffee shop, pool, beauty salon, massage, sauna, tennis courts, exercise room, children's programs, free parking. AE, DC, MC, V.*

**$$$$** 🏨 **Daniel.** Almost anywhere you stand (or recline) in the Daniel, you can see the Mediterranean: from the rooms, restaurant, and lobby. One of the bonuses here is the state-of-the-art spa, whose facilities include an indoor pool and single and double treatment rooms. All rooms look onto the Mediterranean; the deluxe rooms have balconies. The decor is a tasteful mixture of sea-blue and mustard hues. ⊠ *60 Ramot Yam, Herzliya-on-the-Sea 46769,* ☎ *09/952–8282,* ⅋ *09/954–4675. 200 rooms with bath. 4 restaurants, bar, sushi bar, room service, 1 indoor and 1 outdoor pool, spa, 2 tennis courts, business services, parking (fee). AE, DC, MC, V.*

**$$$$** 🏨 **Marine Heights.** The Marine Heights is made up of one- and two-bedroom suites, each fully equipped with a pleasant kitchenette and dining corner as well as a terrace overlooking the sea. ⊠ *93 Ramot Yam, Herzliya-on-the-Sea 46851,* ☎ *09/950–8787,* ⅋ *09/958–0320. 19 suites with bath. Restaurant, room service, pool. AE, DC, MC, V.*

**$$$$** 🏨 **Sharon.** The Sharon first opened its doors in 1948. Today the rooms have light-color furniture, pink-and-gray color schemes, and bright reading lamps; most overlook the sea. The garden rooms are near the seawater pool. The Sharon's health club (popular with Tel Avivians) has a heated indoor pool, a workout room, dry and wet saunas, massage, and Dead Sea mineral baths. ⊠ *5 Ramot Yam, Herzliya-on-the-Sea 46748,* ☎ *09/957–5777,* ⅋ *09/956–8741. 150 rooms with bath. Restaurant, bar, room service, pool, saltwater pool, beauty salon, tennis court, health club, free parking. AE, DC, MC, V.*

# NIGHTLIFE AND THE ARTS

## Nightlife

"The city that never stops" stays up later than many of the world's capitals. Peak hours on Hayarkon Street on a Friday or Saturday night continue until about 3 AM, when things finally begin to wind down.

Partygoers are not daunted by the fact that nightspots come and go about as quickly as the tides.

Bars and nightspots in Tel Aviv usually open in the daytime, long before the night owls descend; typically, they offer either full dinners, beer and fries, or, at the very least, the coffee and cake they've been serving throughout the afternoon.

## Bars, Pubs, and Nightclubs

**Bar Mitzvah** (⊠ 16 Ha'arba'a St., ☎ 03/561–1869), one of numerous fun corners on this street, makes an admirable play on words. Have some light smoked snacks with your beer.

**Bar Yehuda** (⊠ 90 Ben Yehuda St., ☎ 03/527–3394) is popular with the over-25 crowd. Live jazz on Friday afternoons helps launch the weekend.

**Camelot** (⊠ 16 Shalom Aleichem St., ☎ 03/528–5222) has been described as "neo-yuppie" by the local newspaper. Quiet jazz is the main item on the menu, with some blues thrown in; the bar is upstairs, the music downstairs.

**Fresco** (⊠ 11 Rambam St., ☎ 03/516–3764) can make for an interesting travel experience; it specializes in Middle Eastern music and Israeli sing-alongs.

**Hakossit** (⊠ 6 Kikar Rabin, ☎ 03/522–3244) appears to be nothing more than a simple pub, but some of Israel's most successful jazz musicians began their careers on a wooden barstool here.

**Hamisba'a** (⊠ 344 Dizengoff St., ☎ 03/604–2360) is usually packed, and people really do dance on the tables here.

**Hard Rock Cafe** (⊠ Dizengoff Center, ☎ 03/525–1136), the Israeli version of the international pub-café, serves up music with your hamburger.

**Hashoftim** (⊠ 39 Ibn Gvirol St., at the corner of Hashoftim St., ☎ 03/695–1153), one of Israel's first pubs, has stood the test of time. Longtime regulars still hang out here, and newcomers will enjoy the atmosphere.

**Lemon** (⊠ 17 Hanagarim St., ☎ 03/681–3313) is a small place with a nice bar, showcasing a variety of music and often attracting an over-30 crowd (unlike many Tel Aviv nightspots). It sometimes organizes parties.

**Logus** (⊠ 8 Hashomer St., corner of Nahalat Binyamin, ☎ 03/516–1176) has live music inside, for which there's a cover charge, but it's usually loud enough to hear from the mall outside, where food and drinks are also served.

**Lola** (⊠ 54 Allenby St., ☎ 03/516–7803) features alternative and electronic music, and a crowd to match.

**Paco** (⊠ 87 Yehuda Halevy St., ☎ 03/560–7345) is all bar; but you can get Spanish-style ham and sausages with your drinks.

**Rose** (⊠ 147 Yehuda Halevy St., ☎ 03/685–0340) is one of the chicest bars in town. There's good music, too.

**Soweto** (⊠ 6 Frishman St., ☎ 03/524–0825) is still going strong; reggae and R & B are the order of the day.

**Swing** (⊠ 52 Nahalat Binyamin St., ☎ 03/510–0865) is known for its large, round bar, downstairs. Music is generally light.

**Yuazar** (⊠ 2 Yuazar Ish Habira, near clock tower, Jaffa, ☎ 03/683–9115), a posh wine bar, is owned and operated by one of Israel's best-known gourmets.

### Gay Bars

In Tel Aviv, a park serves the purpose of a gay bar: it's perfectly acceptable for gays to meet in Independence Park, next to the Hilton Hotel. Elsewhere, gay bars open and close even faster than other bars and restaurants, though a few seem to be standing the test of time.

**Cafe Nordau** (⌧ 145 Ben Yehuda St., ☎ 03/524–0134) is one of the oldest establishments around, with especially good cakes.

**Litvinsky** (⌧ 22 Ahad Ha'am, ☎ 03/510–7722) is popular for loud rock and techno, complete with dance space.

## The Arts

Tel Aviv is Israel's cultural capital, and it fulfills this role with relish. Like New York, the city is full of people who devote their lives to the arts without necessarily getting paid for it. It's entirely likely that your waitress, taxi driver, or salesperson is also a struggling actor, painter, or musician.

You can purchase tickets to events at the box office or through one of Tel Aviv's three major ticket agencies:

**Hadran** (⌧ 90 Ibn Gvirol St., ☎ 03/527–9955), **Castel** (⌧ 153 Ibn Gvirol St., ☎ 03/604–4725), and **Le'an** (⌧ 101 Dizengoff St., ☎ 03/524–7373).

All accept major credit cards. You must pick up your tickets in person. Although there is never a shortage of events in Tel Aviv, some of the arts—opera in particular—are still developing. The Friday editions of the English-language *Jerusalem Post* and *Ha'aretz* contain extensive entertainment listings for the entire country.

### Dance

Most of Israel's dance groups perform in the **Suzanne Dellal Center for Dance and Theater** (⌧ 6 Yehieli St., Neve Tzedek, ☎ 03/510–5656), and Neve Tzedek itself is home to artists and a growing number of trendy galleries and gift shops. A visit here is a cultural experience, as the complex itself is an example of new Israeli architectural styles used to restore some of the oldest buildings in Tel Aviv. (For more about Neve Tzedek, ☞ Exploring Tel Aviv, *above*).

### Music

The **Mann Auditorium** (⌧ 1 Huberman St., ☎ 03/528–9163), Israel's largest concert hall, is home to the Israel Philharmonic Orchestra and hosts rock, pop, and jazz concerts.

The **Enav Cultural Center** (⌧ Gan Ha'Ir [roof level], 71 Ibn Gvirol St., ☎ 03/528–9163) is a more intimate venue, also with eclectic fare.

Large outdoor concerts are held in the open air in **Hayarkon Park** (☎ 03/642–2828); within the park is a smaller venue called the Wohl Amphitheater.

### Opera

The **Tel Aviv Performing Arts Center** (⌧ 28 Leonardo da Vinci St., ☎ 03/692–7700) is home to the budding New Israeli Opera.

### Theater

Performances are almost always in Hebrew.

Most of the plays at **Bet Liessin** (⌧ 34 Weizmann St., ☎ 03/695–6222) are by Israeli playwrights. The **Cameri Theater** (⌧ 101 Dizengoff St., ☎ 03/524–5211) sometimes offers simultaneous (taped) English translations. **Habimah** (⌧ Habimah Sq., ☎ 03/526–6666) is the national theater; plays here are all in Hebrew, but some have simultaneous translation. **Hasimta Theater** (✉ 8 Mazal Dagim St., ☎ 03/681–2126), in Old Jaffa, features avant-garde and fringe performances.

# OUTDOOR ACTIVITIES AND SPORTS

## Beaches

Beaches in the heart of the city are free. Hatzuk, on the northern edge of Tel Aviv, charges an entrance fee, as do the beaches in Herzliya (except Sidney Ali).

Beaches are generally named after something nearby—a street or a hotel, for example. Thus, you have Hilton Beach in front of the hotel of that name, Gordon Beach at the end of Gordon Street, and likewise Bograshov Beach. Sometimes, however, this gets a bit confusing: Sheraton Beach is at the site of the first Sheraton Hotel in Tel Aviv, about 1 km (½ mi) north of today's Sheraton; and Jerusalem Beach, at the bottom of Allenby Road, is named after the city, not after something in Tel Aviv.

When choosing a beach, look for one with timber lifeguard huts, where first aid is available. Lifeguards are on duty from roughly May to October, from 7 AM until between 4 PM and 7 PM, depending on the month (check with your hotel's concierge). Be forewarned: Tel Aviv's lifeguards are fond of yelling commands over the loudspeakers if they think swimmers are misbehaving. All beaches have public amenities, including bathrooms and changing rooms, and many have kiosks and the omnipresent ice cream man, who paces up and down the sand proffering his treats throughout the summer. These days, he even hangs on to the wrappers when he hands over the goods—his contribution to the fight against litter.

## Participant Sports

### Boating
**Yehoshua Gardens (Hayarkon Park)** (☎ 03/642–0541), in the northern part of the city, rents out pedal boats and rowboats (NIS 50, or $14.20, per hour) and motorboats (NIS 70, or $20, per half hour). You can also opt for pleasure boats, which take up to 120 people for 15-minute rides (NIS 9, or $2.60, per person); bicycles; or tandems that take up to six people.

### Health Clubs
Most of the city's luxury hotels have health clubs, normally free for guests.

The **Hilton** (✉ Hayarkon St., ☎ 03/520–2291) has the largest gym and is open to nonguests; the fee for each visit is $17.50. The club is open Sunday–Thursday 6:30 AM–11 AM and 1 PM–9 PM (Friday 1–5 PM).

The **Gordon Health Club** (✉ 165 Hayarkon St., at the end of Gordon St., ☎ 03/527–1555), a Tel Aviv institution since the 1950s, includes an Olympic-size saltwater pool, a gym, and a sauna. Entrance to the health club alone costs NIS 60 ($17.20), and pool use is an additional NIS 36 ($10). You must present a passport. It's open daily from 6:30 AM–10 PM, except on Saturday in July and August, when hours slim down to 8 AM–2 PM.

### Sailing
The **Sea Center** (✉ Tel Aviv Marina, ☎ 03/522–4079, with another branch at the Hilton) rents out sailboats and windsurfing equipment by the hour. Windsurfers cost NIS 65 ($18.40) per hour; small boats, NIS 95 ($27) per hour; and catamarans, NIS 150 ($42.80) per hour. The unskilled can hire a boat with an instructor.

### Swimming

The **Gordon Health Club** (☎ 03/527–1555) has an Olympic-size salt-water pool, a real Tel Aviv landmark (☞ Health Clubs, *above*). The pool is open daily 5 AM–7 PM; admission is NIS 36 ($10), NIS 42 ($12) on Saturday.

### Waterskiing

**Park Darom** (☎ 03/739–1168), in southern Tel Aviv, runs waterskiing without boats: cables attached to a revolving crane pull you around an artificial lake, a system that holds no appeal for some but is particularly good for beginners. Costs around NIS 50 ($14.20) for half an hour.

## Spectator Sports

**Yad Eliahu Stadium** (☎ 03/537–6376) is the place to go for basketball games. **Bloomfield Stadium** (⌖ 1 Hatehiya St., Jaffa, ☎ 03/682–1276) and the **Israel Football Stadium** (⌖ Abba Hillel Rd., ☎ 03/579–9966), in nearby Ramat Gan, host soccer matches.

# SHOPPING

Tel Aviv's shopping scene has made rapid advances in recent years, as prosperous Israelis have begun demanding higher-quality goods.

## Shopping Districts and Malls

**Kikar Hamedina,** in northern Tel Aviv, is arguably the most expensive real estate in the country; this is where the wealthy shop. Hit the shops on this circular street for, say, a Sonia Rykiel or Chanel suit, perhaps a Kenzo creation, or a pound of Godiva chocolates. The middle of the square is an unkempt plaza that, alas, is the perfect foil to the luxury surrounding it but does nothing to bring prices down.

The northern end of **Dizengoff Street** has a number of boutiques, including those of such popular Israeli designers as Yuval Kaspin (check out his wedding dresses), Tovale (very avant-garde), and Hagara (for all body types).

**Dizengoff Center** (⌖ Dizengoff and King George Sts.), Israel's first shopping mall, bursts with stores selling everything from air conditioners to camping equipment, with many a fashion boutique and gift shop in between. Stay away from it during school holidays if you'd rather avoid crowds of teenyboppers.

**Opera Tower** (⌖ 1 Allenby St.), near the sea, has a small but eclectic range of stores. It's particularly good for jewelry.

**Allenby Street,** a less affluent strip in the southern part of the city, offers some real bargains on clothes, jewelry (especially gold), and Judaica (religious and decorative objects).

Malls have mushroomed here in recent years. They include **Gan Ha'Ir** (⌖ 71 Ibn Gvirol St.), **Azrieli Center** (⌖ Hashalom Rd., above the railway station), **Ramat Aviv Mall** (⌖ 40 Einstein St.), and **Canion Ayalon** (⌖ Ramat Gan).

## Department Stores

**Hamashbir** (⌖ Dizengoff Center, Dizengoff and King George Sts., ☎ 03/528–5136) carries, for the most part, a rather banal selection of goods, often at prices a little higher than those in smaller stores. On the second floor, however, its Designer Avenue features women's clothing by local designers, who also have boutiques at the northern end of Dizengoff Street or in the surrounding area—sample the range here, and then ask for the address if you'd like to see more of a particular designer's line. Hamashbir is also the Israeli outlet for the British St. Michael's label (of Marks & Spencer).

The French **Galleries Lafayette** now has a branch in the Azrieli Center, but unlike its "parent" in Paris, it stocks only clothes and cosmetics.

## Street Markets

At the **Nahalat Binyamin** street fair, held Tuesday and Friday, local crafts ranging from handmade puppets and pincushions to olive-wood sculptures and silver jewelry attract throngs of shoppers and browsers (☞ Exploring Tel Aviv, *above*). The **shuk hapishpeshim,** in Jaffa, is mostly full of junk these days, but you can still find a bargain, even if it's not an authentic antique. The flea market has a wide selection of reasonably priced Middle Eastern–style jewelry that uses chains of small silver coins and imitation stones.

## Specialty Stores

### Jewelry, Judaica, and Ethnic Crafts

You can find good prices on gold in the many hole-in-the-wall jewelry stores on **Allenby Street.** For silver, hit the **Nahalat Binyamin** street fair on Tuesday or Friday (☞ Street Markets, *above*). Shop for sophisticated gems and jewels at **H. Stern,** with branches in the Dan, Sheraton, and Hilton hotels.

### Leather

Stick with traditional browns or blacks or branch out to reds, purples, and mustards.

**Beged-Or** (✉ Dizengoff Center, Gate 3, ☎ 03/525–4294) has sophisticated fashions. **Ofnat Or** (✉ 134 Dizengoff St., ☎ 03/523–9021) can deck you out in the latest styles.

### Swimwear

Although swimsuits and accessories sometimes cost less in the United States than in their country of origin, it's worth checking out the sales here.

Tel Aviv–based **Gideon Oberson** (✉ 36 Gordon St., ☎ 03/524–3822) is well known. **Gottex** (✉ 148 Dizengoff St., ☎ 03/524–5383) is internationally known for its designer swimwear.

# TEL AVIV A TO Z

## Arriving and Departing

### By Bus

Bus travel in Israel is generally very convenient. The main interurban bus company, **Egged** (☎ 03/694–8888), operates primarily from Tel Aviv's **Central Bus Station** (✉ Levinsky St.) but also from the **Central Railway Station** (✉ Arlosoroff St.). The Central Bus Station may look like a big, confusing marketplace, but the bus service is actually very efficient. (Buses leave for Jerusalem every 15 minutes throughout most of the day.) You can purchase your ticket at the booth on each platform (signs at each platform indicate destinations) or, if your booth is closed, from the driver on the bus. Only the Eilat line requires advance reservations—particularly necessary in peak season.

### By Plane

Israel's international airport is **Ben-Gurion** (☏ 03/971–0111), 16 km (10 mi) southeast of Tel Aviv. All international flights to Israel land here, except for charters to Eilat. The airport is modern and efficient and is served by most major American and European carriers, with frequent and convenient connections to major cities around the world.

From **Sde Dov Airport** (☏ 1800/444888), 4 km (2½ mi) north of the city center, the domestic airline Arkia flies to Eilat (some 10 flights per day), Jerusalem (3 flights), Haifa (3 flights), and the Upper Galilee (2 flights or more).

##### BETWEEN BEN-GURION AND CITY CENTER

**United Bus 222** (☏ 03/971–1711) runs between the airport and the city roughly every hour from 4 AM to midnight on weekdays, and on Saturday at 45-minute intervals from noon to midnight. From the airport it stops at the Central Railway Station (✉ Arlosoroff St.), the youth hostel (✉ Weizmann St.), and numerous points along the promenade, Tel Aviv's main hotel strip. The fare is NIS 15 ($4.30) from downtown Tel Aviv and NIS 11.50 ($3.30) from Arlosoroff.

**Bus 475,** a local, runs to the Central Bus Station (Platform 613) from 5:10 AM to 11 PM. The fare is NIS 9 ($2.60). Like all state-run buses, it does not run on the Sabbath (Friday afternoon to Saturday evening) or on holidays.

**Tal Limousine Service** (✉ Ben-Gurion Airport, ☏ 03/972–1701, FAX 03/972–1705) can supply a limousine (that is, a van) and driver for the trip into Tel Aviv for NIS 116 ($28). It's slightly cheaper to go from Tel Aviv to the airport, because the driver has to pay taxes only to exit the airport.

There is a fixed tariff for **taxis** from the airport into town (and vice versa); it's printed in a booklet that the driver carries. Verify the price before you get in, and don't let the driver switch the meter on: the rate is NIS 68 ($19.20), going up to NIS 78 ($22) after 9 PM and on the Sabbath. The price includes one piece of baggage per person; for each additional piece there is a baggage charge of NIS 2.50 (70¢). The airport has a supervised taxi stand.

##### BETWEEN SDE DOV AND CITY CENTER

City **Bus 26** runs between Sde Dov and the Central Bus Station every 10–15 minutes, following Ibn Gvirol Street. The fare is NIS 4.20 ($1.20). There is no service on the Sabbath or on holidays. Taxi is the most convenient way to get from Sde Dov to the center of town; the fare is determined by the meter (unlike from Ben-Gurion, where it's a fixed rate) but should be about NIS 25 ($7) (excluding baggage charge).

### By Sherut

*Sherut* taxis are a fleet of stretch Mercedes-Benzes at the Central Bus Station that run the same routes as the buses, at comparable one-way prices (unlike buses, sheruts do not offer round-trip tickets). The "schedule" of arrivals and departures is determined by how long it takes to fill all seven seats of each car. You'll find sheruts at various points (depending on destination) in front of the bus platforms; you can usually hear someone yelling the destination before you even approach. (If you don't, try yelling yourself—someone is sure to point you in the right direction.) Sheruts do run on Saturday.

### By Train

Train travel is not as common as bus travel in Israel, yet this is one of the most scenic and relaxing ways to travel between Tel Aviv and cities and towns to the north, such as Netanya, Hadera, Haifa, and Nahariya. The northbound train leaves the **Central Railway Station** (⊠ Arlosoroff St., ☎ 03/577–4000). The information office is open Sunday–Thursday 6 AM–9 PM and Friday 6–2, roughly every hour on weekdays from 6 AM to 8 PM; there are fewer trains on Friday and holiday eves and no service on Saturday or holidays. There is also a line to and from Beersheva. Timetables are available in English at all rail stations. Note that the Tel Aviv–Jerusalem line is undergoing renovations and is currently out of service.

## Getting Around

### By Bus

The city bus system is well developed, with lines run primarily by the Dan bus cooperative, as well as by Egged. The fare is a fixed NIS 3.70 ($1.20) within the city center, and you buy your tickets on the bus. If you think you might use the buses between 21 and 25 times during your stay, you can buy a *kartisia*, which offers 25 journeys for the price of 20. Remember, however, that Dan's kartisia is only good for Dan lines and Egged's for Egged (but you'll be able to use the Egged ticket in other cities).

Two of the major lines, Bus 4 (Ben Yehuda and Allenby streets) and Bus 5 (Dizengoff Street and Rothschild Boulevard), are also serviced by privately run red minibuses. You can flag these down and ask to get off at any point along their routes; the fare is the same as on regular buses. Minibuses also run on Saturday, when regular buses do not.

### By Car

Driving in Tel Aviv is not recommended, especially if you get nervous on the road. Aside from the aggressive tactics of other drivers, Tel Aviv's layout seems more the creation of an absent-minded philosopher than a city planner. Moreover, some street names may not be marked in English—or, indeed, at all—which makes getting to your destination nothing short of a headache. Parking is yet another problem, and the last thing you want is to deal with the Israeli bureaucracy if your illegally parked car has been booted (clamped) or towed.

Tel Aviv is more fun on foot, anyway. Most attractions and sights are in the heart of the city within walking distance of one another; and when you get tired, a bus or taxi is never far away.

### By Taxi

Taxis here can be any car model or color; they're identified by lighted signs on top. Cabs are plentiful, even in bad weather; drivers will honk their horns to catch your attention, even if you're not trying to catch theirs. If you're traveling within the metropolitan area, make sure the driver turns the meter on when you get into the car. Rates are NIS 6.50 ($1.80) for the first 18 seconds and 40 agorot (10¢) in increments thereafter. For interurban trips, there is a fixed tariff; if you think you're being quoted a price that's too high, ask to see the tariff in the booklet each driver carries. Expect night rates to be about 25% higher than day rates. Tipping taxi drivers is not customary in Israel.

## Contacts and Resources

### Car Rental

Rental agencies include **Budget** (⊠ Dan Hotel, 99 Hayarkon St., ☎ 03/523–1551), **Hertz** (⊠ Sheraton Hotel, 115 Hayarkon St., ☎ 03/527–1881), and **Eldan** (⊠ 112 Hayarkon St., ☎ 03/527–1166), Israel's largest rental company.

## Dentists

**Ichilov Hospital** (✉ Weizmann St., ☎ 03/697–3696 or 03/697–3676) has dental service Sunday, Monday, and Wednesday 8–7, Tuesday and Thursday 8–1. The **dental clinic** inside the Dizengoff Center (✉ Gate 3, 50 Dizengoff St., ☎ 03/629–6716 or 050/502050) is open daily from 8 AM to 10 PM.

## Embassies

**U.S. Embassy** (✉ 71 Hayarkon St., ☎ 03/519–7575). **U.K. Embassy** (✉ 1 Ben Yehuda St., ☎ 03/510–0166). **Canadian Embassy** (✉ 9 Hashlosha St., ☎ 03/636–3300). **Australian Embassy** (✉ Europe House, 37 Shaul Hamelech St., ☎ 03/695–0451).

## Emergencies

**Ambulance** (☎ 101). **Fire** (☎ 102). **Police** (☎ 100).

**Magen David Adom** (✉ 2 Alkalai St., ☎ 03/546–0111) provides 24-hour emergency first aid.

**Emergency calls** are free at public phones; no tokens or telecards are necessary.

### HOSPITAL

The casualty ward of **Ichilov Hospital** (✉ Weizmann St., ☎ 03/697–4444) has 24-hour emergency service. Bring your passport.

### POLICE

The main **police stations** are at 14 Harakevet Street, near the Central Bus Station (☎ 03/564–4444), and 221 Dizengoff Street (☎ 03/545–4444). Harakevet Street also has a lost-and-found.

## English-Language Bookstores

**Steimatzky** (✉ 107 Allenby St., ☎ 03/566–4277; ✉ 109 Dizengoff St., ☎ 03/522–1513) is a large chain.

## Guided Tours

### BOAT TOURS

**Kef** (✉ Jaffa Port, ☎ 03/682–9070) and **Sababa 5** (✉ Jaffa Port, ☎ 03/681–6739) run hourly boat tours (weekends and summer evenings) from the Jaffa Port to the Tel Aviv Marina and back. Fare is around NIS 15 ($4.30).

### ORIENTATION TOURS

**Egged Tlalim** (✉ 59 Ben Yehuda St., ☎ 03/527–1212) and **United** (✉ 113 Hayarkon St., ☎ 03/522–2008) bus companies offer half-day tours of Tel Aviv for $26 per person. The tour takes in Old Jaffa and the flea market, the Mann Auditorium, Yitzhak Rabin Square, the Oppenheimer Diamond Museum, and the Eretz Israel Museum.

**Egged Tlalim** (☎ 03/527–1212) also runs the 101 Citybus (the Tel Aviv–Jaffa Circle Line). NIS 20 ($5.70) buys you a one-day pass that allows you to jump on and off the bus at any of the sights along the route. The complete tour is designed to last around two hours.

### PERSONAL GUIDES

**Twelve Tribes** (✉ 29 Hamered St., ☎ 03/510–1911, FAX 03/510–1943) and **Tar-Hemed Tours** (✉ 59 Hayarkon St., ☎ 03/517–6101, FAX 03/510–0165) provide personal guides, usually with a car, who will take you anywhere in the city and even around the country.

### SPECIAL-INTEREST TOURS

**Late Night Tel Aviv** (✉ 9 Hess St., ☎ FAX 03/525–6484) organizes nightlife tours, in which choice restaurants and bars are mixed into the sightseeing. You can join one of the regular jaunts or tailor one to your own interests.

WALKING TOURS

The Tel Aviv–Jaffa municipality has laid out four self-guided tours of the city called the **Tapuz (Orange) Routes**; these take in both historic and current cultural sites. Maps are available from the Tel Aviv Tourist Information Office in the Central Bus Station (☞ Visitor Information, *below*). Free, city-sponsored walking tours of **Old Jaffa** begin at the clock tower on Wednesday at 9 AM; no prior registration is required.

## Late-Night Pharmacies

Pharmacies take turns keeping late hours, and the duty roster changes daily. Check the *Jerusalem Post* or *Ha'aretz* for those currently on call.

## Travel Agencies

Ben Yehuda Street, in central Tel Aviv, is full of travel agencies large and small. Among the biggest are:

**Diesenhaus** (✉ 21 Ben Yehuda St., ☎ 03/517–2140) and **Ophir Tours** (✉ 32 Ben Yehuda St., ☎ 03/526–9777).

## Visitor Information

The **tourist bureau** at Ben-Gurion Airport is open 24 hours. You'll find the latest local information at the **Tel Aviv Tourist Information Office** (✉ Store No. 6108, Central Bus Station, Levinsky St., 6th floor, ☎ 03/639–5660, FAX 03/639–5659), open Sunday–Thursday 9–5, Friday 9–1. They can also provide a list, albeit not comprehensive, of *zimmerim* (bed-and-breakfast-type accommodations).

# 5 Northern Coast and Western Galilee

*Including Haifa, Caesarea, and Akko*

*North of Tel Aviv and up to the border with Lebanon lies the only part of Israel where you can drive for long stretches with unimpeded views of the Mediterranean. Coastal cities speak from the past: Caesarea, a 2,000-year old port, was built by King Herod, and the vast underground ruins of the ancient walled city of Akko hark back to Crusader victories. Mt. Carmel meets the sea in the city of Haifa, where steep streets climb to sharp, white hotel towers at the crest of Mt. Carmel, a backdrop for the sparkling golden dome of the Baha'i Shrine. "The Carmel" is the name of the area at the top of the city.*

By Karen
Wolman

Updated by
Judy Stacey
Goldman

**S**TRETCHED TAUT ON A NARROW COASTAL STRIP between Tel Aviv and the chalky cliffs of the Lebanese border, this region offers more than just balmy Mediterranean beaches. Sand and sea meet archaeology here—historical sights line the shore along with the gently undulating dunes, fields, and citrus groves of the Sharon Plain, a fertile swath encompassing Netanya, Hadera, and Caesarea that was converted from a wasteland of malarial swamp early in the 20th century by Jewish pioneers. Today, Caesarea is a delightful resort full of whitewashed villas and romantically crumbling Roman and Crusader ruins. The arches of an ancient aqueduct disappear into the sand, and Israeli children splash in the cove in summertime, heedless of the feats of King Herod's engineers.

It was in the softly contoured foothills and valleys at the base of Mt. Carmel that the philanthropic Baron Edmond de Rothschild came to the Jews' succor in helping Israel create a wine industry, still one of its most successful enterprises. The Carmel range rises dramatically to its pine-covered heights over the coast of Haifa, a friendly, hardworking, thoroughly modern port city. Haifa was the site of some heartrending and historic scenes in the decade prior to Israel's independence: scores of ragtag ships filled with Jewish refugees fleeing Nazi persecution were turned away by the British just off the shore of Haifa, within view of relatives and residents. North of Haifa is the Western Galilee, which runs along a fertile plain up to the Lebanese border. Just across the sweeping arc of Haifa Bay lies Akko, a jewel of a Crusader city that combines Romanesque ruins, Muslim domes and minarets, and swaying palms. To the north are the resort town of Nahariya, popular with Israelis; Montfort, arguably Israel's most magnificent Crusader castle; more Crusader ruins at Kibbutz Hanita; and, straddling the Lebanese border, the caves at Rosh Hanikra, scooped out of rock by the relentless tides.

As the scenery changes, so does the ethnic mix of the residents and their ancestors: Druze, Carmelite monks, Ottomans, Baha'is, Christian and Muslim Arabs, and Jews. Paleontologists continue to study on-site the artifacts of the most ancient natives of all, the prehistoric people of the caves of Nahal Me'arot, on Mt. Carmel. In Haifa and perhaps at absorption centers at kibbutzim, you'll meet the region's latest arrivals, Jews from Ethiopia and the former Soviet Union. The Baha'is, whose universalist religion embraces the teaching of many others, dominate Haifa's mountainside setting with their gleaming golden temple and handsome gardens. Robed Carmelite monks preside quietly over their monasteries in Haifa and in Mukhraka, on Mt. Carmel, next door to the Druze villages. Although the north-coast Druze consider themselves an integral part of Israeli society, they maintain a unique cultural and religious enclave on Mt. Carmel, with the secret rites and rituals of their faith and the distinctive handlebar moustaches and white head scarves favored by the older men. Arabs and Jews live side-by-side in Akko, whose dilapidated, cramped, and dusty old quarter belies its pristine, picture-postcard reputation. Yet Akko's subterranean knights' halls, Ottoman skyline, and outdoor *shuk* (market), awhirl with fascinating colors and sounds, can still enchant. Throughout the region, you'll encounter the ghosts of the Crusaders at castles and fortifications built to maintain the warriors' tenuous hold over Palestine; after two centuries of rule, they were chased out in 1291 with the fall of Akko to Egypt's powerful Mamluk dynasty.

Running the length of the region up to Haifa are two main highways: Route 2, a multilane highway that gets you from Tel Aviv to Haifa in just over an hour, and the inland Route 4, otherwise known as the Old Haifa Road. Route 4 continues all the way to the border. Most sights are a short drive from one of these two roads. In the spring, you'll pass fields ablaze with the color of wild anemones, tulips, and buttercups; cyclamen and narcissus grow a bit higher up. And you don't have to be an ornithologist to appreciate the astonishing variety of birds here, sometimes perched casually on telephone wires. Flocks of storks, pelicans, herons, cormorants, and ducks pass through every spring and fall on their migratory routes between Europe and Africa.

## Pleasures and Pastimes

### Archaeology

It is said that wherever you put down a shovel in Israel, you'll find ancient ruins. Even onetime visitors to Caesarea have been known to find old coins after a rainfall, when the surface earth is washed away. Archaeologists continue to uncover history, while restorers lovingly assemble shards and patch up ancient buildings. Caesarea and Akko are two of Israel's star archaeological sites, where even repeat visitors are amazed to find new and stunning discoveries each time. Such museums as the underwater museum at Nachsholim-Dor and the Hecht Museum at Haifa University display finds in unusually engaging style. And Herod's fabulous port, which subsided beneath the Ceasarea waters 2,000 years ago, beckons scuba divers to an underwater tour.

### Arts

On many a balmy summer night in towns up and down the coast, you're bound to find an outdoor concert, play, or dance performance. In summer, the performances held under the stars on the reconstructed stage of Caesarea's Roman theater are particularly memorable; in other seasons, catch chamber music in Ein Hod and Zichron Ya'akov. For printed listings, check the Friday issue of the *Jerusalem Post* or pick up a copy of the monthly brochure "Events in Haifa and the Northern Region," available at hotels and tourist offices.

### Beaches

Between Tel Aviv and the Lebanese border are miles and miles of beautiful sandy beaches, most of them public and attended by lifeguards from early May to mid-October. Many Israeli beaches are left untended off-season and get pretty grubby as a result, but they're generally cleaned up and well maintained once warm weather returns. Beware of swimming in the absence of a lifeguard, as the currents and undertows can be dangerous.

### Dining

You won't have to look hard in this region for a restaurant with either an excellent view of the Mediterranean or good fresh fish. The fish you'll most often find on your menu—served grilled or baked, with a variety of sauces—are *locus* (grouper), *mulit* (red mullet), *churi* (red snapper), and *farida* (sea bream). Also fresh, but hailing from commercial fishponds and the Sea of Galilee, are *buri* (gray mullet) and the ubiquitous *tilapia* (St. Peter's fish), as well as the hybrid *iltit* (salmon-trout).

The coastal restaurants are generally not as refined as those in Tel Aviv, with some notable exceptions in Haifa and Mt. Carmel. Haifa—not unlike Tel Aviv—is livened by the growing number of funky cafés sprouting up in both commercial and residential neighborhoods. In the Druze village of Daliyat el Carmel you can sample the locally famous falafel and other authentic Mediterranean fare. Netanya has the region's highest concentration of kosher restaurants. Otherwise, fare runs the gamut from pita and hummus to sophisticated French cuisine.

Even at the most expensive restaurants in this region, dress is informal (but tasteful). Ties are never required.

| CATEGORY | COST* |
| --- | --- |
| $$$$ | over $35 |
| $$$ | $22–$35 |
| $$ | $12–$22 |
| $ | under $12 |

*per person for a three-course meal, excluding drinks, service, and sales tax*

## Hiking and Walking

Magnificent parks and nature reserves grace the coastal area, both along the Mediterranean shore and in the hilly areas to the east. The largest of these is the flourishing Carmel Park, which comprises 20,000 hilly acres and covers the top of Mt. Carmel. Several parks and reserves have visitor centers, where staff can explain maps and trails, and all have parking lots, rest rooms, and picnic areas. Though parks and reserves are generally not signposted from the road in English, you can spot the entrances by looking for distinctive dark wooden boards with white or yellow letters.

## Lodging

Options range from campgrounds to luxury hotels, though you won't find the selection and quality of deluxe accommodations comparable to those in, say, Tel Aviv or Eilat. In some places, such as Akko, the pickings are slim indeed; but because this region is so compact, you can cover many sights along the coast from a single base.

The chart below lists peak-season prices, which normally kick in for July and August; Passover, Rosh Hashanah, and Yom Kippur; and Hanukkah (☞ National and Religious Holidays *in* Chapter 1). There are variations, however, so be sure to inquire at each hotel. In addition, many hotels are considerably less expensive—sometimes off 40%—during low season, from November through February.

Camping facilities, including some bungalows and cabins, dot the coastline north of Netanya. Note that the wooded slopes of Carmel National Park, however inviting, do not have facilities. Contact the tourist office in Tel Aviv or Haifa (☞ Visitor Information *in* Northern Coast and Western Galilee A to Z, *below, and in* Tel Aviv A to Z *in* Chapter 4) for complete lists of campgrounds and maps as well as a brochure on "Isra-chalets" and bungalows.

| CATEGORY | COST* |
| --- | --- |
| $$$$ | over $120 |
| $$$ | $80–$120 |
| $$ | $55–$80 |
| $ | under $55 |

*All prices are for a standard double room, including breakfast and excluding service charge.*

## Wine

Wine lovers, take note: this is one of the country's prime wine-growing areas (its classification is "Shomron"). Though wine has been produced in Israel for thousands of years, and the Rothschilds updated viniculture around Zichron Ya'akov some 120 years ago, truly high-quality wines have appeared on the market only in the last decade or so. The Zichron Ya'akov Carmel Winery's best (and most expensive) wines are those in the Rothschild series, whose best vintage, in turn, is the 1985 cabernet sauvignon. Also distinctive are the wines of the less exclusive Selected series, especially the chardonnay. Israelis enjoy the semidry Emerald Riesling, fruity and aromatic.

# Exploring the Northern Coast and Western Galilee

Starting from Tel Aviv, Route 2 (the Coastal Road) hugs the coast, introducing travelers to the northern coast via Netanya, Caesarea, and Haifa, with archaeological sites Nachsholim-Dor and Atlit in-between. Zigzagging along to the east, parallel to Route 2 (at the most about 10 km, or 6 mi, away) is Route 4, also known as the Old Road. Just off Route 4 is the Rothschild wine country—the scenic back-door route to Haifa—which meanders through the foothills and up the spine of Mt. Carmel, taking in Zichron Ya'akov, Shuni, the Carmel Park, the Carmelite monastery at Mukhraka, and two Druze villages near Haifa. (A branch of Route 4, going north and then inland, winds through the huge Carmel National Park and later connects with Route 672, leading to the Druze villages.) Haifa is Israel's third-largest city and is a good base for two other sights to the south, Ein Hod and the Carmel Caves. The Western Galilee is the area north of Haifa, including Akko, Nahariya, and Rosh Hanikra, with several sights along the way and inland. All sights in this region are within easy driving distance of Caesarea and Haifa, the former a quiet overnight spot and the latter a thriving city.

## Great Itineraries

Remember to allow time for swimming, hiking, or golfing if you're so inclined. Here the Mediterranean coast is lined with beaches, the land is packed with scenic trails, and Caesarea has Israel's only golf course. Less-conventional sporting options include paragliding and underwater diving to shipwrecks.

*Numbers in the text correspond to number in the margin and on the Northern Coast and Western Galilee map.*

### IF YOU HAVE 2 DAYS

For a quick tour of the highlights, start with King Herod's port city, **Caesarea** ②, bursting with Roman, Byzantine, and Crusader ruins. Then travel through Rothschild wine country, in the rolling Carmel Hills, and **Benyamina** ⑳, one of the area's first settlements. Set aside several hours to half a day for the pioneer village of **Zichron Ya'akov** ㉒ and the picturesque Druze villages of **Daliyat el Carmel** ㉕ and **Isfiya** ㉖. Stay overnight in modern 🏨 **Haifa** ⑤–⑲, atop Mt. Carmel. The next day, get an early start so you can see the Baha'i Shrine and gardens on your way down the hill and out of Haifa. Head north to the walled Crusader city of **Akko** ㉙–㊲, and after a late lunch, head up to the Lebanese border and watch the waves crash through the caves at **Rosh Hanikra** ㊶.

### IF YOU HAVE 3 DAYS

Start with a visit to the **Carmel Wine Cellars** (reserve a tour in advance) and **Zichron Ya'akov** ㉒; then head through the hilly wine country to see the Carmelite Monastery at **Mukhraka** ㉔. Stop at **Daliyat el Carmel** ㉕ en route to 🏨 **Haifa** ⑤–⑲. Bright and early the next morning, visit the Baha'i Shrine and Gardens; then head north to **Akko** ㉙–㊲ and zip up the coast to **Rosh Hanikra** ㊶. Return to Haifa for the night. On the third day, explore **Caesarea** ② and the artists' village of **Ein Hod** ㉗.

### IF YOU HAVE 5 DAYS

On a hot summer's day, stop at **Netanya** ① for a swim beneath the cliffs. Then drive through Rothschild wine country to the restored Roman theater and Ottoman fortress at **Shuni** ㉑, and continue on to the **Carmel Wine Cellars** and the pioneer town of **Zichron Ya'akov** ㉒. Travel through the foothills of Mt. Carmel to the Carmelite Monastery at **Mukhraka** ㉔ and the Druze villages of **Daliyat el Carmel** ㉕ and **Isfiya** ㉖. Spend the night in 🏨 **Haifa** ⑤–⑲, and devote the next day to exploring the city. On day three, leave Haifa early for the walled Crusader city of **Akko** ㉙–㊲, the Holocaust memorial museum at **Lochamei Hageta'ot** ㊴, and the seaside town of **Nahariya** ㊵. Now that you're almost at the Lebanese border, a short drive north brings you to the incredible sea caves at **Rosh Hanikra** ㊶. If you have energy left, walk up to the medieval castle of **Montfort,** perched high on a wooded mountain. (If not, you can see it long-distance from Goren Park.) You can spend the night in Haifa, but you may want to move on to tomorrow's stomping ground, **Caesarea** ②. After exploring the myriad ruins, head south to **Nachsholim-Dor** ③ to see the intriguing Underwater Museum. From here you'll zigzag between Route 2 and Route 4 to see the reconstructed British detention camp at **Atlit** ④, the artists' village of **Ein Hod** ㉗, and the prehistoric **Carmel Caves.** Nearby is the entrance to the **Nahal Me'arot Nature Reserve** ㉘, where you might want to set aside a few hours for a hike on the wooded slopes of Mt. Carmel.

### When to Tour the Northern Coast and Western Galilee

The summer sun is strong and hot here, but there's no humidity, and soft sea and mountain breezes cool things down. Spring (April–May) and fall (October–November) are balmy and crisp. Winter (late December, January, February, and into March) brings cold weather (sun interspersed with rain), while the sea makes the wind chilly. If you have warm clothes, you can wander with impunity.

As in the rest of Israel, hotels and other lodgings tend to fill up on weekends, so it's best to make reservations well ahead of time. On Saturdays and national holidays, Israelis themselves hit the road, so it's best to avoid north-to-south travel out of Tel Aviv or Jerusalem altogether, and prepare for crowds at beaches and sights. If you're taking a two-day trip, try to make it Thursday and Friday (Shabbat calm reigns on the highway Friday night) or Saturday and Sunday.

Summer brings theater and dance to Caesarea's Roman theater and a blues festival to Haifa, usually in July.

# THE NORTHERN COAST

## Netanya

❶ *30 km (18 mi) north of Tel Aviv, off Route 2; take second exit (Central Netanya).*

Netanya is a seaside resort, the geographic capital of the Sharon Plain, and a center for diamond-polishing. Once a sleepy town of farmers and orange groves, Netanya, named after Jewish philanthropist Nathan Strauss, steadily burgeoned to its present population of 160,000 from a few settlers in 1929.

Though citrus farming is still evident on Netanya's rural outskirts, there are few traces of small-town charm and few sights to see in the rambling clusters of apartment buildings, some built on the coast itself. Travelers come here for the sandy public beaches just below the cliffs—ideal for swimming, sunbathing, windsurfing, and paragliding—and the pleasant cafés.

Lively **Ha'atzmaut Square,** near the beach, is the heart of the city, surrounded by open-air cafés and restaurants that are crowded late into the night. The square has just been repaved, and new benches sit among the flower beds and palm trees. Saturday nights are enlivened by folk dancing here, and the amphitheater hosts free concerts in summer and an arts-and-crafts fair on Friday morning and several other

**Northern Coast and Western Galilee**

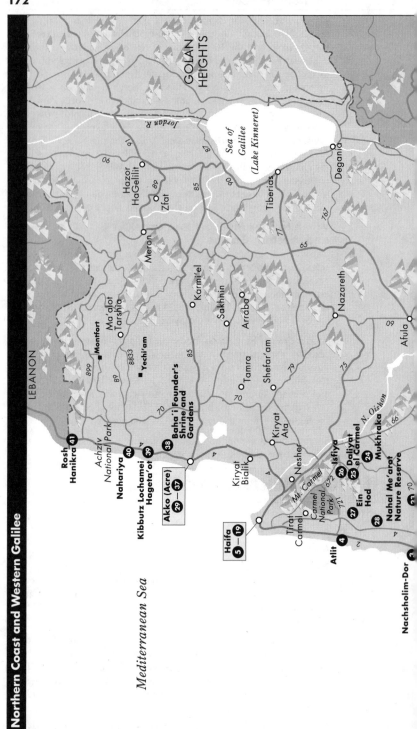

GOLAN HEIGHTS

LEBANON

*Mediterranean Sea*

Sea of Galilee
(Lake Kinneret)

*Jordan R.*

91

90

87

89

85

90

767

77

65

09

79

75

72

66

70

70

85

70

89

899

8833

Rosh Hanikra 41

Achziv National Park

Nahariya 40

Kibbutz Lochamei Hageta'ot 39

Akko (Acre) 29 — 37

Montfort

Ma'alot Tarshia

Yechi'am

Baha'i Founder's Shrine and Gardens 38

Meron

Zfat

Hazor HaGelilit

Karmi'el

Sakhnin

Arraba

Tamra

Shefar'am

Kiryat Ata

Nazareth

Afula

Tiberias

Degania

Kiryat Bialik

Nesher

N. Oishon

Mt. Carmel

Carmel National Park

Tirat Carmel

Haifa 5 — 19

Atlit 4

Isfiya 26

Daliyat el Carmel 25

Mukhraka 24

Ein Hod 27

Nahal Me'arot Nature Reserve 28

Nachsholim-Dor 3

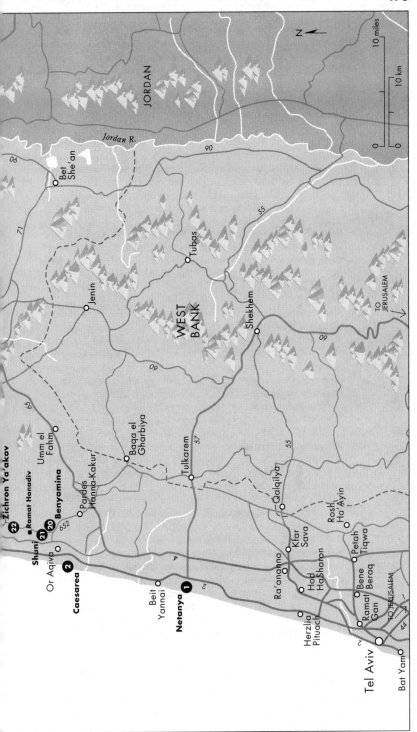

late afternoons each week. Netanya attracts droves of French travelers, and in the summer their lilting tones float above the café au lait and croissants (now popular all over Israel) served in the outdoor cafés. To get to your hotel or the beach, drive down the town's main artery, Herzl Street, which ends at the **pedestrian mall** and Ha'atzmaut Square; access to the beaches is south and north of the mall.

Israel's large diamond industry (its leading export is polished diamonds) was launched with the arrival of Jewish diamond-cutters from Belgium and Holland during World War II, many of whom settled in Netanya. You can take a free tour of one of the larger **diamond factories** and showrooms, where raw stones of various hues and quality are cut, polished, and set into jewelry; tours end in the showroom, where prices are generally good, though not better than those in New York City's wholesale diamond district. *See* Shopping, *below,* for phone numbers of those factories that will pick you up at your hotel.

OFF THE BEATEN PATH

**Fields of Flowers –** In February and March, detour a few kilometers south of the city to see fields carpeted with a rare, exotic variety of deep-indigo **wild iris** indigenous to this area. Marked paths lead the way, and there's a parking lot on Ben-Gurion Boulevard.

## Dining

$$$$ ✕ **El Gaucho.** Tucked into the Carmel Hotel, El Gaucho is one of Israel's few high-quality (and kosher) steak houses. Decorated in a rustic style, the restaurant is nonetheless dominated by a dramatic view of the sea, with a picturesque garden below. Professional grill man Ernesto, from Uruguay, cooks South American–style meat specialties over embers on a giant grill that forms part of the restaurant. Juicy steaks, grilled chicken, and fish are highlights and are served by very professional waiters. Ask for the extensive wine list. ⊠ *Carlton Hotel, Jabotinsky St.,* ☎ *09/884–1263 or 09/884–1264. Reservations essential. AE, D, MC, V. Closed holidays. No dinner Fri., no lunch Sat.*

$$$ ✕ **Lucullus.** Tunisian owner Bernard Gabay has run this reliable French restaurant on the southern edge of town for more than 20 years. (There's also a kosher version, at 5 Ha'atzmaut Square.) Although the menu is French, the ambience is Israeli. Candles and fresh flowers add a touch of class, and there's a pianist in the bar several times a week. Gabay recommends his coquilles St. Jacques or chateaubriand, and for dessert the chocolate mousse or profiteroles. ⊠ *2 Jabotinsky St.,* ☎ *09/861–9502. Reservations essential.*

$$ ✕ **Apropo.** This restaurant—something of a glorified coffee shop—is in King George Park and serves breakfast, lunch, and dinner overlooking the scalloped coastline below a jutting cliff. There's something for everyone (and the portions are generous) on the eclectic menu: fresh fish, Italian pastas, soups and salads, a variety of omelets, and even some Thai specialties. All dishes are glatt kosher, meaning that meal preparation undergoes extra-strict supervision by the *kashrut* authorities. There's a pianist every evening after 8. ⊠ *Gan Hamelech park, at end of Ha'atzmaut Sq.,* ☎ *09/862–4482 or 09/862–4483. Reservations essential for dinner Sat. and Apr.–Sept. AE, DC, MC, V. Closed Fri.–Sat.*

$$ ✕ **Casa Mia.** Replete with pizza oven, this centrally located, family-run restaurant is not unlike a traditional Italian trattoria, if a bit short on charm. The chef takes pride in being well versed in both language and cuisine: he makes a mean *fegato alla veneziana* (liver with bacon and onion in a red-wine sauce) as well as calamari *fritti,* lasagna, and minestrone. When in doubt, you can stick with pizza. ⊠ *10 Herzl St.,* ☎ *09/834–7228. Reservations essential for dinner Fri.–Sat. AE, DC, MC, V.*

**$$** ✕ **Yotvata.** Here's the *original* Yotvata, opened 11 years ago and named for the Negev kibbutz whose dairy products are famous nationwide. Farm-fresh products are what you get: extra-large salads, fish dishes, cheeses, sandwiches, and blintzes help stuff the menu, which lists a whopping 200 items. The desserts are huge; even the most voracious sweet-lovers will be able to share their portions. The fresh juice drinks (a mixture of several fruits is tasty) and drinks made with yogurt, milk, or cream are generous and refreshing. ✉ *3 Ha'atzmaut Sq.,* ☎ *09/862–9151. Reservations essential on weekends. AE, D, MC, V.*

**$** ✕ **Pundak Hayam.** The three friendly brothers who own this unprepossessing place have run it for 30 years. It's a favorite among locals, a no-frills Middle Eastern diner with counter seating and wooden tables. You'll find fresh fish, shish kebabs, and roast goose as well as the usual salads. ✉ *1 Harav Kuk St.,* ☎ *09/861–5780 or 09/834–1222. Reservations not accepted. AE, D, MC, V. Closed Sat. No dinner Fri. or holidays.*

## Lodging

**$$$$** ▥ **Blue Bay.** It's removed from the bustle of the city center (3 km, or 2 mi, away), but you're only a short ride away via the hotel's hourly shuttle or a public bus. Blue Bay offers direct access to the beach below, and all rooms in the main wing, and the back, have sea views. Five of the seven floors, including the lobby, were renovated in 1997. The hotel opens its own dance club on Friday night. ✉ *37 Hamelachim St., 42228,* ☎ *09/860–3603,* ℻ *09/833–7475. 196 rooms with bath. Restaurant, bar, coffee shop, pool, beauty salon, hot tub, sauna, health club, 2 tennis courts. AE, DC, MC, V.*

**$$$$** ▥ **Carmel.** New and sparkling, and built on a cliff overlooking the Mediterranean, the Carmel makes the most of its beautiful views—the lobby has floor-to-ceiling windows; glass elevators serve the 20 stories; and the decor in the guest rooms reflects the blues and greens of the sea outside. Most of the rooms have sea views, each has its own air conditioner, and most have kitchenettes (with dishes, pots, and utensils furnished upon request). The swimming pool, which includes a whirlpool, is covered and heated in winter. It's fun to sit on the lawn and watch the paragliders, who use the the grass as their springboard into the blue. ✉ *Jabotinsky St., south of Ha'atzmaut Sq.,* ☎ *09/860–1111,* ℻ *09/860–1171. 200 rooms with bath. Restaurant, lobby lounge, pub, pool, wading pool, 2 saunas, health club, children's programs. AE, DC, MC, V.*

**$$$$** ▥ **La Promenade.** This six-year-old apartment hotel, with its snappy, modern design, is just south of the main square, near the city center and the beach. Each unit, accommodating up to five people, has a bedroom and living room, furnished with marble tiles and sleek furniture, plus a kitchenette, all topped off with a balcony and a stunning sea view. The indoor pool includes a whirlpool. Guests eat breakfast at the Jeremy Hotel, across the street. ✉ *6 Gad Machness St., 42279,* ☎ *09/862–6450,* ℻ *09/862–6450. 15 apartments with bath. Restaurant, indoor pool, pub. AE, DC, MC, V.*

**$$** ▥ **Seasons.** Just outside the city center, with stair access to the beach
★ below, Seasons is well maintained and provides consistently good service. The hotel was built 28 years ago, but most of the rooms and all of the public areas have been redecorated in the last few years. The bedrooms are quite spacious, with private terraces and sea views; the newer ones, decorated in pleasing pastels, are especially comfortable, and their baths are luxurious. ✉ *Nice Blvd., 42269,* ☎ *09/860–1555,* ℻ *09/862–3022. 85 rooms with bath. Restaurant, coffee shop, pool, hot tub, massage, sauna, tennis court, exercise room. AE, DC, MC, V.*

## Outdoor Activities and Sports

Much of the sophisticated equipment at the **Wingate Institute,** Israel's national Center for Sports and Physical Education, 8 km (5 mi) south of Netanya (☎ 09/863–9521, 𝔽𝔸𝕏 09/865–3070), is now available to the public, albeit generally only in the afternoon. Facilities include a 25-meter pool with a retractable roof; squash courts; tennis courts; and a fitness center. You can even get a full medical checkup in the sports-medicine division.

### BEACHES

Standard facilities, including lifeguards, first-aid station, showers, toilets, and changing rooms, are available free at all of Netanya's beaches, which cover 12 km (7 mi) of soft, sandy coastline. Most beaches also rent beach chairs and umbrellas. The main beach, **Sironit,** is open year-round; the parking lot is on the beach, just off Jabotinsky Street south of the main square, and costs NIS 10.50 ($3) per car. The beach has volleyball nets and two snack bars. South of town is the Orthodox beach **Kiryat Sanz,** where men and women have different bathing days and hours. There's another beach near the **Seasons Hotel,** with a restaurant and refreshment stand as well as standard facilities. **Herzl** is right in front of Ha'atzmaut Square and has a water slide, restaurant, and refreshment stand. **Argamon** has a refreshment stand but no chair or umbrella rentals. At press time Netanya's southernmost beach, **Poleg,** was closed because of pollution problems. (Pollution levels are monitored regularly by the Health Department; the other beaches have received clean bills of health.)

There's a lovely **private beach** (☎ 09/866–6230) 5 km (3 mi) north of Netanya, next to Moshav Bet Yannai. Amenities include grills, picnic tables, a lifeguard in season, toilets, cold showers, and chair and umbrella rentals. There is no entrance fee, but parking costs NIS 25 ($7) per car Sunday–Friday and NIS 35 ($10) Saturday and holidays. Because this beach is only 2,400 ft long and cannot comfortably accommodate crowds, it's wise to come on a weekday.

The beach at **Mikhmoret,** 7½ km (4½ mi) north of Netanya, is very popular. The huge dirt parking lot, which charges NIS 20 ($5.70) per car, is 1 km (½ mi) after the turnoff from Route 2. There are three lifeguard stations, a restaurant, a café, and chair and umbrella rentals.

### GOLF

The Center for Golf Instruction and Practice at the **Wingate Institute** (☎ 09/863–9546 after 10 AM, 𝔽𝔸𝕏 09/865–3070; ☞ *above*) has a driving range, putting and pitching greens. It's open both days and evenings year-round.

### HORSEBACK RIDING

The **Ranch** (☎ 09/866–3525) is in northern Netanya, 2 km (1 mi) up the road from the Blue Bay Hotel. It's wise to reserve for Saturday or for moonlight rides on the beach; you can also take a pastoral ride though orange groves. The stables are open daily 9–6; the cost is NIS 70 ($20) per hour.

### PARAGLIDING

If you're between 6 and 60 and want to fly without an engine or a cockpit but with an instructor beside you, call **Dvir Paragliding** (☎ 09/899–0277 or 052/546077) for a thrilling experience.

## Shopping

Netanya is known for quality diamonds. Shoppers will be dazzled by the profusion of earrings, necklaces, bracelets, and loose stones with international diamond certificates. Two reliable merchants are **Inbar Jewelry** (⊠ 1 Ussishkin St., ☎ 09/882–2233) and the **National Dia-**

mond Center (✉ 90 Herzl St., ☎ 09/862–0436). Prices are competitive. The tourist office may be able to recommend other firms currently known for fairness and authenticity.

<table>
<tr>
<td>NEED A<br>BREAK?</td>
<td>Always doing a brisk roadside business, the **Kfar Vitkin Pancake House** (✉ 7 km, or 4 mi, north of Netanya on Rte. 2, ☎ 09/866–6112) is the local equivalent of a truck stop. The down-home menu includes pancakes and eggs as well as Middle Eastern mainstays like hummus and pita bread. It's open daily 6 AM–1 AM.</td>
</tr>
</table>

## Caesarea

❷ *16 km (10 mi) north of Netanya, 49 km (29½ mi) south of Haifa*

By turns ancient Roman port city, Byzantine capital, and Crusader stronghold, Caesarea marks the northern tip of the Sharon Plain. Chock-full of Roman, Byzantine, and Crusader ruins, it's a delightful place to spend half a day sightseeing followed by a leisurely lunch or a swim at the beach. (Swim only if a lifeguard is on duty.) Stretched out over 3 km (2 mi) are a Roman theater, a Crusader city, and newly discovered Roman-Byzantine remains that include a bathhouse complex, a Herodian amphitheater, parts of Herod's port, and, in the sand dunes themselves, an ancient aqueduct.

Herod the Great gave Caesarea its name, dedicating the magnificent Roman city he built to his patron Augustus Caesar: He called the port itself Sebastos, the Greek translation of Augustus. It was the Roman emperor who had crowned Herod—born to an Idumean family that had converted to Judaism—King of the Jews around 30 BC. Construction began in 22 BC at the site of an ancient Phoenician and Greek port called Strato's Tower. Herod spared nothing in his elaborate designs for the port—a major engineering feat at the time—and the city itself, which included palaces, temples, a theater, a marketplace, a hippodrome, and water and sewage systems. When Caesarea was completed, 12 years later, it was outshone only by Jerusalem. Its population under Herod grew to around 100,000, larger than that of Jerusalem, and the city covered some 164 acres.

In AD 6, a decade after Herod died, Caesarea became the seat of the Roman procurators. Herod's kingdom had originally been divided among his surviving sons, with his eldest, Archelaus, getting Judea and Samaria; but the Romans were unhappy with Archelaus's rule and banished him to Gaul. With Jerusalem predominantly Jewish, the Romans preferred the Hellenistic Caesarea, with its Jewish minority, as the seat of their administration.

Religious harmony did not prevail here. The mixed population of Jews and Gentiles (mainly Greeks and Sytians) repeatedly clashed, with hostilities exploding in the Jewish revolt of AD 66. The first Jewish rebellion was squelched by Vespasian, who was proclaimed emperor here by his legions in AD 69. A year later, his son and co-ruler, Titus, captured and razed Jerusalem and celebrated his brutal suppression of the Jewish revolt. Henceforth Caesarea was a Roman colony and the local Roman capital of Palestine for nearly 600 years. It was here that Peter converted the Roman centurion Cornelius to Christianity—a milestone in the spread of the new faith—and where Paul preached and was imprisoned for two years. In the 2nd century, Rabbi Akiva, the spiritual mentor of the Bar Kochba Revolt, was tortured to death here.

Caesarea is distinguished by well-marked signs in English. The **Roman theater,** along with the port area, is under the aegis of the National

Parks Authority. One ticket admits you to both the theater and the Crusader city, so save your stub. At the entrance you can pick up a free brochure with a basic map and layout of the sites. (Be sure to lock your car and keep valuables out of sight.)

Entry to the theater is through one of the vomitoria (arched tunnels that led the public into Roman theaters). Herod's theaters—here and elsewhere in Israel—were the first of their kind in the ancient Near East. Although smaller than the better-preserved Roman theater at Bet She'an (☞ Chapter 6), Caesarea's has become famous in its own right. The theater today seats 3,600 and is a spectacular venue for summer concerts and dance performances (☞ Arts, *below*). The backdrop of the sea steals any show, especially when set ablaze by the setting sun.

What you see today is predominantly a reconstruction. Only a few of the seats of the *cavea* (where the audience sat) near the orchestra are original, in addition to some of the stairs and the decorative wall at the front of the stage. Just inside the main gate is proof that one of the Roman rulers who spent time here was Pontius Pilate, governor of Judea when Jesus was crucified; it's the only archaeological evidence of the governor's presence in Palestine. The fragmented Latin inscription on a mounted plaque (a replica of the original, which is in the Israel Museum in Jerusalem) is believed to say that "Pontius Pilate, the prefect of Judaea, built and dedicated the Tiberieum [probably a temple or shrine dedicated to the Emperor Tiberius] to the Divine Augustus." ☎ 06/ 636–1358. 🎟 *Theater and Crusader city NIS 17 ($4.85).* ☉ *Daily 8–4, Fri. and holiday eves 8–3.*

In the large area of **ongoing excavations** along the shore, you'll see the streets of a Roman-Byzantine administrative area built over vaults that served as storehouses. Worth a special look are the beautiful and imaginative mosaic floors in the bathhouse complex. The huge, horseshoe-shape "entertainment area," its sloping sides filled with rows of stone seats, was an amphitheater built by Herod (most likely the one mentioned by first-century historian Flavius Josephus in both *The Jewish War* and *The Antiquities of the Jews*), where some 10,000 spectators watched horse races, chariot races, and various sporting events some 2,000 years ago.

★ The walls that surround the **Crusader city** were built by King Louis IX of France. They enclose both the remains of the Herodian port and the Crusader city itself, which was actually only one-third the size of Herod's original city. The bulk of what you see today—the moat, escarpment, citadel, and walls, which once contained 16 towers—dates from 1251, when the French king actually spent a year pitching in with his own two hands to help restore the existing fortifications. The Crusaders first besieged and conquered Caesarea in 1101 after it had been ruled for nearly five centuries by Arabs, who had allowed the port to silt up. As a reward for furnishing the fleet that was instrumental in the victory, the Genoese were awarded a green glass vessel found in Caesarea by the Crusaders and believed to be the Holy Grail.

You enter the Crusader city over a dry moat. However impressive, the 42-ft-deep moat was of little use in repelling an attack under Sultan Baybars in the late 13th century. The invading Mamluks then destroyed the city to prevent its resettlement by the Christians. Still, the fortifications and the gatehouse (at the entrance) are fine examples of medieval architecture. Note the sloping glacis against the outer wall, the shooting niches, and the groined vaults of the gatehouse.

Arrows and signs direct you on a designated walking tour. Especially after heavy rains, keep a vigilant eye out for old bronze coins, some smaller than a dime. As you walk under a series of four arches, spanning a ruined Crusader street, you can see just to your right the remains of a Frankish house. At the southeast corner of the fortress is a postern gate, designed for counterattack against an enemy. You're on the high area, above the remains of the harbor—walk toward the sea and the observation point to find the remains of the unfinished Crusader cathedral. To the west are the remains of the unfinished **Crusader cathedral,** built on the site of a Byzantine church; the three graceful curves of its apses stand out. Both churches stood on the ruins of the temple Herod dedicated to Augustus on this promontory dominating the port. The collapse of the underlying vaulted chambers halted construction of the cathedral.

At the railing in front of the church ruins, there's a lookout over the ancient port, now under water, as well as a view up the coast to Zichron Ya'akov and Haifa. On a clear day, you can see the shadowy outlines of the submerged harbor constructions from the top terrace of the tower, now the Citadel restaurant. The diving center in Caesarea's port offers underwater tours with marked maps of the port area (☞ Outdoor Activities and Sports, *below*).

Even today, **Herod's port** can be regarded as an awesome achievement. Flavius Josephus described the wonders of the port in glowing terms, comparing it to Athens's port of Piraeus. Once archaeologists explored the underwater ruins, beginning in the 1960s and continuing sporadically into the 1990s, it became clear that what had been long dismissed by many historians as hyperbole was exactly as Josephus described it.

The construction of the port was an unprecedented challenge—there was no artificial harbor of this size anywhere in the world. There were no islands or bays to provide natural protection, and the work itself was hindered by bad weather. During preliminary underwater digs in 1978, archaeologists were stunned to discover concrete blocks near the breakwater offshore, indicating the highly sophisticated use of hydraulic concrete (which hardens underwater). Historians knew that the Romans had developed such techniques, but before the discoveries at Caesarea, they never knew hydraulic concrete to have been used on such a massive scale. The main ingredient in the concrete, volcanic ash, was probably imported from Mt. Vesuvius, in Italy, as were the wooden forms. Teams of professional divers actually did much of the trickiest work, laying the foundations hundreds of yards offshore. To inhibit the natural process of silting, engineers designed sluice channels to cut through the breakwaters and flush out the harbor. Herod's engineers also devised underwater structures to break the impact of waves.

Once finished, two massive breakwaters—one stretching west and then north from the Citadel restaurant some 1,800 ft and the other 600 ft long, both now submerged—sheltered an area of about 3½ acres from the waves and tides. Two towers, each mounted by three colossal statues, marked the entrance to the port; and although neither the towers nor the statues have been found, a tiny medal bearing their image was discovered in the first underwater excavations here, in 1960. The finished harbor also contained the dominating temple to Augustus and cavernous storage facilities along the shore. The port was devastated by an earthquake in AD 130. The Crusaders only reutilized a small section of the harbor when they conquered Caesarea in 1101. ☎ 06/636–1358. ◻ *Theater and Crusader city NIS 17 ($4.85).* ⊙ *Daily 8–4, Fri. and holiday eves 8–3.*

NEED A
BREAK?

Relax in the shadow of the vaulted remains of Herod's inner harbor, on the raftered **patio** in the middle of the Crusader city (near the rest rooms). The kiosk sells hot and cold drinks, snacks, and ice cream, and souvenir shops and restaurants hug the water's edge.

East of the main entrance to the site (across the road), a small, sunken, fenced-in area encloses Caesarea's **Byzantine street.** It was during the Byzantine period and in late Roman times that Caesarea thrived as a center of Christian scholarship and as an episcopal see; in the 7th century, Caesarea had a famous library of some 30,000 volumes that originated with the collection of the Christian philosopher Origen (185–254), who lived in Caesarea for two decades. Eusebius, who was an ecclesiastical advisor to Emperor Constantine and is known as the Church's first historian, became Caesarea's first bishop in the 4th century. Once lined with workshops and stores, the street is paved with marble slabs. The inscription you see dates the area to the late 6th or early 7th century. Towering over the street are two monumental marble statues that face each other, both probably carted here from nearby Roman temples. The provenance of the milky white one is unknown; the purple porphyry figure might have been commissioned by the Emperor Hadrian when he visited Caesarea. In Byzantine times, the city's area grew an estimated eight times the size of the fortified Crusader city. The Byzantine street is just across the street from the entrance to the Crusader city.

The **Caesarea Museum** houses many of the artifacts found by kibbutz members as they plowed their fields in the 1940s. The museum has arguably the best collection of late-Roman sculpture in Israel; impressive holdings of rare Roman and Byzantine gemstones; and a large variety of coins minted in Caesarea over the ages, as well as oil lamps, urns excavated from the sea floor, and fragments of jewelry. ✉ *On grounds of Kibbutz Sdot Yam, about 600 ft south of entrance to theater,* ☎ *06/ 636–4367.* ✆ *NIS 9 ($2.60).* ☉ *Sat.–Thurs. 10–4, Fri. 8–2.*

A wonderful finale to your trip to Caesarea (especially at sunset) is the ★ **Roman aqueduct** on the beach. The chain of arches tumbling north toward the horizon, where they disappear beneath the sand, is a captivating sight and forms a unique backdrop for a swim at the pretty beach (☞ Beaches, *below*). During Roman times, the demand for a steady water supply was considerable, but the source was a spring about 13 km (8 mi) away in the foothills of Mt. Carmel. Workers had to cut a channel approximately 6½ km (4 mi) long through solid rock before the water was piped into the aqueduct, whose arches spanned that entire length. In the 2nd century, Hadrian doubled its capacity by adding a new channel. Today you can walk along the sea side of the aqueduct and see marble plaques dedicated to the support troops of various legions who toiled here. On your way back to the road, you might want to drive around the villa area and admire some of Israel's tonier homes, some brand-new and many covered with swaths of brilliant bougainvillea. ✉ *Villa area: north of Crusader city.*

## Dining and Lodging

$$$  ✕ **Charley's.** It's a delight to eat on one of Charley's several patios on a clear day. Located under the stone watchtower in the Crusader city's port, right above the sandy cove beach, Charley's is especially known for its way with fresh seafood, grilled or baked. Depending on the catch of the day—supplied by fishermen from a neighboring Arab village— you might choose from red snapper, mullet, or grouper, or simpler and cheaper alternatives such as a Middle Eastern salad or just coffee and crème caramel or cheesecake. ✉ *Crusader city,* ☎ *06/636–3050.*

*Reservations essential in high season (roughly Apr.–Oct.). AE, D, MC, V.*

$$$ 🏨 **Dan Caesarea.** Quiet comfort is combined here with accessibility
★ to a range of sports facilities and Caesarea's many archaeological sites. The four-story hotel is unobtrusively set in attractively landscaped grounds. All the rooms have balconies, overlooking either the sea or the open countryside. Especially recommended are the newly renovated deluxe doubles, with marble bathrooms and modern decor in cheerful hues. Adjacent to the hotel's 15-acre gardens lies Israel's only (18-hole) golf course, which offers Dan guests a discount. ⊠ *North of Crusader city (opposite entrance to villa area), Caesarea 30600,* ☎ *06/ 626–9111,* 🆉 *06/626–9122. 114 rooms with bath. Restaurant, bar, café, pool, sauna, 18-hole golf course, 2 tennis courts. AE, DC, MC.*

$$$ ✕ **Harbor Citadel.** By Israeli standards, this place is an institution: it's been open for 28 years. You'll spot it under the Israeli flag at the far end of the port, at the top of a spiral stone staircase; the elevation gives a spectacular view of the coast. The versatile menu features seafood and salads, as well as schnitzel and chicken livers. In warmer weather, you can sit outdoors on the patio, shaded by a yellow awning, and gaze at the ruins of the ancient port. It's wise to make reservations on Friday, Saturday, and in summer. ⊠ *Crusader City,* ☎ *06/636–1988 or 06/636–1989. AE, DC, MC, V.*

For a longer vacation, you can rent a villa, one of the modern whitewashed houses near the beach. Contact **Chana Kristal Real Estate** (⊠ 23 Hamigdal St., Cluster 8, Caesarea 36060, ☎ 06/636–3896 or 06/ 636–2691, 🆉 06/636–0212) or **Real Estate Caesarea** (⊠ 32 Hadar St., Cluster 5, Caesarea 43660, ☎ 06/636–0969).

## Outdoor Activities and Sports

### BEACHES

Bathers have three choices here. In the Old City, in a sandy cove in Herod's ancient harbor, is the small **Caesarea Beach Club** (☎ 06/636–1441), where the admission charge of NIS 20 ($5.70) includes chairs, umbrellas, and the use of hot showers. The beach has a diving platform, and you can also rent kayaks. The Gal-Mor Diving Center is right next door. At the **Roman aqueduct,** just north of the Crusader city in the residential area, is a considerably more spacious beach with the dramatic backdrop of Roman arches disappearing into the sand. The amenities, however, are few: toilets, and a lifeguard in season. There is no entrance fee, but parking runs about NIS 5 ($1.40) per car. The beach and swimming area have been cleared of rocks and debris, but swimming outside the designated, guarded area is prohibited (never swim at all unless the guard is on duty). The largest and most popular beach in the area is **Hof Shonit** (☎ 06/636–2927), just south of Caesarea—from Route 2, turn left instead of right toward the Old City. The parking lot here accommodates a hefty 400 vehicles and charges NIS 12 ($3.40). There are lifeguards in season, a refreshment stand, and a restaurant, as well as toilets and cold showers.

### GOLF

Both Israeli and foreign golfers flock to the **Caesarea Golf Club** (☎ 06/ 636–1172), for an obvious reason: it's the only 18-hole course in Israel. Adjacent to the Dan Caesarea hotel, the club is open from sunrise to sunset, and the course is built on sandy soil so that you can even play after heavy rainfall. Reservations are advisable. The greens fee is NIS 297.50 ($85) Tuesday–Friday, NIS 350 ($100) weekends; the weekly rate is NIS 960 ($274). Golf-club rentals run NIS 87.50 ($25), electric-caddy rentals NIS 115.50 ($33).

The **Gal-Mor Diving Center,** in the Crusader city (☎ 06/636–1787), gives instruction in scuba diving. A unique diving tour explores Herod's largely submerged port, with a detailed map showing four different routes through the underwater ruins.

## Nightlife and the Arts

Caesarea's **Roman theater** hosts evening performances of the highest caliber, by both local and international artists and troupes. The season runs from May to mid-October. For advance information on programs, contact the **National Parks Authority** starting in April (✉ 35 Jabotinsky St., Ramat Gan, ☎ 03/576–6888). You can buy tickets in advance at the **Le'an ticket agency** in Tel Aviv (✉ 101 Dizengoff St., ☎ 03/524–7373); the box office in Caesarea is open on performance days.

## Shopping

The **Glass Center** (☎ 06/636–1890), open daily except Saturday, is a small store on the southern side of the port selling handblown colored glass. The pale-hued vases and vessels, lightly veined and streaked, are reminiscent of ancient glass. The factory warehouse, open Sunday–Friday 9–5, is next to a Paz gas station on the road leading to the highway toward Tel Aviv.

# Nachsholim-Dor

❸  *20 km (12 mi) north of Caesarea. Travel east at Zichron Ya'akov turnoff until the Fureidis Junction (marked "to Haifa"), turn south, and travel 1 km (½ mi) to sign for Nachsholim-Dor. Turn west and drive 3 km (2 mi).*

Founded 3,500 years ago, biblical Dor was once the maritime capital of the Carmel coast. Its small bay made it the best harbor between Jaffa and Akko and thus a target for many imperial ambitions, from the ancient Egyptians and the "Sea Peoples" through King Solomon and on down. It was renowned in antiquity for its precious purple dye, called Tyrian purple; reserved for royalty, this hue was extracted from a mollusk that was abundant along the coast. During the Arab period, the town was renamed Tantura, which is also the name of the town's popular beach today.

★  Well worth a visit is the **Nachsholim-Dor Museum** (or Mizgaga Museum), which is also the Center for Nautical and Regional Archaeology. It's housed in the partly restored former glass factory opened by Baron Rothschild in 1893 to serve the wineries of nearby Zichron Ya'akov. (Run by Meir Dizengoff, the first mayor of Tel Aviv, the glass enterprise failed after only two years because the poor quality of the sand used made the bottles black.) The museum is a rich trove of finds from both local nautical digs and excavations at nearby Tel Dor. The sequence of peoples who settled, conquered, or passed through Dor—from the Phoenicians to Napoléon—can be traced through these artifacts. Of particular interest is the bronze cannon that Napoléon's vanquished troops dumped into the sea during their retreat from Akko to Egypt in May 1799. Treacherous currents and winds have long made this shoreline a graveyard for ships and thus a source for many of the finds you see here. In 1982, a storm revealed a shipwreck about 300 ft offshore, an archaeologist's treasure chest: the ship contained 2,200 pounds of coins, bronze figurines, silver plates, and bracelets dating from the Byzantine and Mamluk periods. An interesting film in English illuminates the seminal work of Kurt Raveh, a Dutch-born member of the kibbutz who spearheaded many of the underwater digs. ✉ *Kibbutz Nachsholim,* ☎ *06/639–0950.* ⊡ *NIS 10 ($2.85).* ☉ *Sun.–Thurs. 8:30–2, Fri. 8:30–1, Sat. and holidays 10:30–3.*

**Tel Dor,** an ongoing archaeological excavation, is a five-minute walk away from the museum. During the Arab period, it was renamed Tantura, also a name the popular beach goes by today. The site is not formally open to visitors, but if you call the Nachsholim-Dor Museum (☞ *above*), someone will take you around and explain what's been uncovered. Among the finds are remains of a Crusader fortress, a temple to Zeus, and the industrial area for production of the purple dye.

### Dining and Lodging

$$  🏠 **Nachsholim Guest House.** Next to the museum, on a lovely, white, sandy beach called Tantura, this unadorned but well-maintained abode is ideal for a family beach holiday and as a base for sightseeing. Set among lawns, it consists of a series of one-story buildings, each with several units. These are furnished in the quintessentially austere style of the kibbutz, and many have kitchenettes. The dining room serves three meals a day. ⌂ *M.P. Hof Carmel, 30815,* ☎ *06/639–9533,* 𝖥𝖠𝖷 *06/639–7614. 80 rooms with bath (40 sleep 6). Restaurant, coffee shop. AE, DC, MC, V.*

### Beach

**Dor Beach,** also known as Tantura Beach (☎ 06/839–0922), is one of the most popular in Israel thanks to the fine sand lining its 1½ km (1 mi) of coastline. The parking facilities fit 2,000 cars and charge NIS 10 ($2.85) per person. Amenities are ample: lifeguards in season, a snack bar and restaurant, a first-aid station, a trampoline (fee), and chair and umbrella rentals, as well as changing rooms and showers.

## Atlit

❹ *9 km (6 mi) north of Nachsholim-Dor, 15 km (9 mi) south of Haifa.*

Atlit is a peninsula with the jagged remains of an important Crusader castle. Of more recent vintage, to the west (about 1,500 ft from the highway), is the **Atlit detention camp,** used by the British in the decade prior to Israeli independence. The reconstructed barracks, fences, and watchtowers stand as reminders of how Jewish immigration was practically outlawed under the British Mandate after the publication of the infamous White Paper in 1939. More than a third of the 120,000 illegal immigrants to Palestine passed through the camp from 1934 to 1948. The 45-minute tour includes the living quarters, complete with laundry hanging from the rafters. The authenticity of the exhibit is striking: it was re-created from accounts of actual detainees and their contemporaries. Call ahead to make sure the site is open. ⌂ *Rte. 2,* ☎ *04/984–1980.* ⊡ *NIS 10 ($2.85).* ☉ *Sun.–Thurs. 9–4, Fri. 9–12:30, Sat. 9–4.*

To see the **Crusader castle,** continue straight 1 km (½ mi) along the road toward the beach, passing the left turnoff to the new town of Atlit (or take Bus 122 from Haifa), and then cross the railroad tracks. Since 1948 the castle itself has been off-limits, property of the Israeli Navy, but you can take a good look at it from the windswept beach just north of the walls. Built by the Crusader order known as the Templars in 1217, this fortified castle with a natural port was known as Château des Pelerins, or the Pilgrims' Castle. After the fall of the Crusader capital at Akko in 1291, the Château became the last surviving Crusader fortress in the Holy Land. It was never taken by siege, but in August of that year, the last Crusaders set sail, and after their departure the Mamluks dismantled the fortifications just in case the Crusaders had second thoughts.

The castle's strategic location made it a natural stronghold that only needed fortifications on one side, facing landward; several towers were erected here, two of which are still visible. There was once a moat along the eastern side that could be flooded with seawater. During the Seventh Crusade, Louis IX of France extended the fortifications (and his wife gave birth to a son here); in the 18th century, stones from the castle were used to fortify Akko. An 1837 earthquake wreaked heavy damage, leaving the castle in its present ruined state.

# HAIFA

Spilling down from the pine-covered heights of Mt. Carmel to the blue Mediterranean is Haifa, whose vertiginous setting has led to perhaps hyperbolic comparisons with San Francisco. Israel's largest port and third-largest city, Haifa was ruled for four centuries by the Ottomans and gradually grew up the mountainside into a cosmopolitan city whose port served the entire Middle East. In 1902, Theodor Herzl enthusiastically dubbed it "the city of the future." Haifa's now coming into its own as a place worth a visit. For a long time, the city has been left behind on the tourist trail because of the steep slopes one had to climb to get from one place to another. Thanks to the beneficence of the Baha'is, whose world center's gold dome is Haifa's landmark, change is in the air. The construction work you'll encounter on the city's slopes is the partly finished 1-km-long (½-mi-long) swathe of precisely manicured gardens that start at the German Colony near the sea and climb up to the crest of Carmel and the Bahai center at the top. The gardens will make it both easier and more pleasurable to see the sights.

Haifa was already becoming a center for science and technology by 1924, when the Technion Institute opened. The Turks' construction at the turn of the century of the Hijaz Railway—which stretched from Constantinople via Damascus to the Muslim holy cities of Mecca and Medina—proved a boon to Haifa, which had its own branch of the new line to Damascus. Under the British Mandate, a deep-water port was dug and opened to world traffic in 1933, and Haifa was linked to Iraq by an oil pipeline the following year. After Israel's independence, Haifa's links with neighboring Arab states were broken, but today cruise ships from abroad ply its waters, and the Technion is still the nation's citadel of scientific research.

First mentioned in the Talmud, the area around Haifa had two settlements in ancient times. To the east, in what is today a congested industrial zone in the port, lay Zalmona, and 5 km (3 mi) west around the cape was Shiqmona. The Crusaders conquered Haifa while it was an important Arab town and maintained it as a fortress along the coastal road to Akko for 200 years; like much of the Crusader kingdom, it was lost and repeatedly regained by the Christians. During this period, in 1154, the Order of Our Lady of Mount Carmel (the Carmelite order) was founded on the slopes of Mt. Carmel by a group of hermits following the principles of the prophet Elijah and the rules of poverty, vegetarianism, and solitude. After Akko and Haifa succumbed to the Mamluk Sultan Baybars in 1265, Haifa was destroyed and left derelict, just as it had been at the end of Byzantine rule. It was a sleepy fishing village for centuries thereafter.

The city reawakened under the rule of Bedouin sheikh Dahr el-Omar, who had rebelled against direct Ottoman rule in the mid-18th century and independently governed Akko and the Galilee. Dahr recognized that Haifa's location left it vulnerable to attack; in 1761 he ordered the city to be demolished and moved about 3 km (2 mi) to the south. The new town was fortified by walls and protected by a castle, and its port began to compete with that of Akko across the bay—for while its harbor was not as good as Akko's, Mt. Carmel offered a natural barrier against the strong southwesterly winds and thus a comfortable anchorage.

Napoléon, too, came to Haifa, though only briefly, and en route to ig-nominious defeat at Akko during his Eastern Campaign. Napoléon left his wounded at the Carmelite Monastery (☞ *below*) when he beat a retreat in 1799, but the French soldiers there were killed and the monks driven out by Ahmed el-Jazzar, the victorious pasha of Akko.

*Numbers in the margin correspond to points of interest on the Haifa map.*

Today, the metropolis is divided into three main levels that run paral-lel to the harbor, crisscrossed by parks and gardens. The downtown port encompasses the largely uninhabited Old City; the midtown area, called Hadar HaCarmel (Hadar for short), was one of the early Jew-ish neighborhoods and is now a bustling shopping area; and Central Carmel, or Mercaz HaCarmel, on top, comprises upscale residential developments and the posher hotels. The most striking landmark on the mountainside is the gleaming golden dome of the Baha'i Shrine. The Carmelit subway (☞ Getting Around *in* Northern Coast and Western Galilee A to Z, *below*) makes several stops on its way up from the port. It is Israel's only subway.

## A Good Walk

Start by taking a taxi, bus, or the Carmelit subway down to the **Car-melite Monastery** ⑬ and the **Stella Maris lighthouse,** on a promontory overlooking Haifa Bay. From here a 20-minute walk takes you down to **Elijah's Cave** ⑭, sacred to Jews, Christians, and Muslims; tradition says it was here that the prophet took refuge from King Ahab, in the 9th century BC.

Walk down the flight of stairs that leads from the cave to Allenby Road. Turn left and cross the road to the **Clandestine Immigration and Naval Museum** ⑮, which tells the story of the efforts to bring European Jew-ish refugees to Palestine around the time of World War II. Up the road is the **National Maritime Museum** ⑯, which brings 5,000 years of mar-itime history to life via model ships, coins with nautical motifs, and other artifacts, including underwater finds from nearby excavations and shipwrecks.

For great views of Haifa from above, stroll scenic **Yefe Nof Street** ⑤. At 89 Yefe Nof Street is the **Mané Katz Museum** ⑥, the lattice-windowed former home of the Ukrainian-born Expressionist painter Emmanuel Katz. Parallel to and west of Yefe Nof is Hanassi Avenue; No. 88 is the **Tikotin Museum of Japanese Art** ⑦. Back on Yefe Nof Street, walk west (accompanied by great bay vistas) to Shomron Street, turn right, and turn right again into **Sderot Hatziyonut** (Zionism Boulevard). This street was originally named after the United Nations, but following the 1975 passage of a U.N. resolution that equated Zionism with racism, the city government quickly changed it (the resolution was rescinded in 1992).

On your left is the entrance to a **sculpture garden** ⑧ that overlooks Haifa Bay. A bit farther along, you'll come upon the ornately carved gates of the **Baha'i Shrine and Gardens** ⑨, the dazzling gold dome of the Shrine of the Bab (Gate) and the mainstay of Haifa postcards. Keep heading down the hill to the intersection of Sderot Hatziyonut and Shab-betai Levy, where you're flanked by the **Haifa Museum** ⑩ and **Bet Hagefen** ⑪. Turning left, onto Sderot Hagefen, walk three blocks to Ben-Gurion Boulevard, whereupon you'll turn right into what's known

**186**

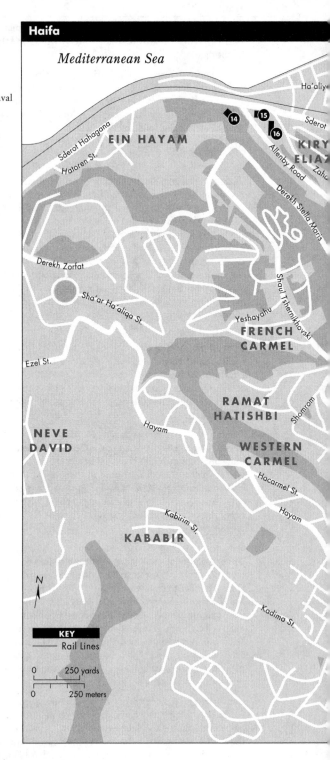

BAT GALIM

naron

ashnia

gana

*Mediterranean Sea*

Heyl Hayam St.

Tel Aviv St.

**KIRYAT
ELIAHU**

*Harbor*

Deror

de Rothchild

Sderot Hameginim

Yizhaq Sade St.

Haganim St.

Ben Gurion Blvd.

Allenby Rd.

Hagefen Blvd.

**12**

Jaffa

Sderot Ha'atzma'ut

Blvd.)

Khouri St.

**11** Wadi
Nisnas

(Zionism

**10**

Y. L. Perez St.

Hassan

Shabbetai Levy St.

Baerwald St. Shukri

Bialik

Yefe Nof

Sderot Hatziyonut

**8**
**9**

Gid'on St.

Hanassi Avenue

**5**

**6**

**7**

Eliyahu Golumb St.

Hatashmona'im St.

Arlosoroff St.

Balfour St.

Pevsner St.

Spinoza

**17**

Herzl St.

Nordau St.

Kibbutz Galuyot St.

**HADAR
HA'CARMEL**

Bilu

Hakishon

**19**

Sderot Wedgewood

Sderot Wingate

Sderot Kish

Hapoel St.

Geula St.

**CENTRAL
CARMEL**

**18**

Ha'asif St.

**TEL AMAL**

as the **German Colony** ⑫, a late-19th-century colony established by the German Templar religious reform movement, and the most important in the Holy Land. The street is no-nonsense straight, and the red-roofed houses solid enough to have withstood the years of neglect they've suffered since World War II, when the Germans were expelled. There are a few good restaurants along the way (☞ Dining, *below*).

Three additional sights are a bit farther afield. The closest, still downtown, is the **National Museum of Science and Technology** ⑰, with hands-on exhibits. Bus 30 takes you to Haifa University and the **Hecht Museum** ⑱, known for its archaeological collections. Bus 31 takes you to the **Technion** ⑲ scientific research center.

## Sights to See

⑨ **Baha'i Shrine and Gardens.** The most striking feature of the gardens is the Shrine of the Bab, whose gilded dome dominates as well as illuminates Haifa's skyline. Haifa is the world center for the Baha'i faith, which was founded in Iran in the 19th century and holds as its central belief the unity of mankind. Religious truth for Baha'is is not doctrinaire; rather, it consists of progressive revelations of a universal faith. Thus the Baha'is teach that great prophets have appeared throughout history to reveal divine truths, among them Moses, Zoroaster, Buddha, Jesus, Mohammed, and, most recently, the founder of the Baha'i faith, Mirza Husayn Ali, known as Baha'u'llah—the Glory of God. Baha'u'llah (1817–1892) was exiled from his native Persia by the Shah and then by the Ottomans to Akko, where he lived as a prisoner for almost 25 years. The Baha'is' holiest shrine is on the grounds of Baha'u'llah's home, where he lived after his release from prison and where he is now buried, just north of Akko (☞ *below*).

Here in Haifa, at the center of the shrine's magnificently manicured gardens, is the mausoleum built for the Bab (literally, the "Gate") the forerunner of this religion, who heralded the coming of a new faith to be revealed by Baha'u'llah. The Bab was martyred by the Persian authorities in 1850. The gardens and shrine were built by Baha'u'llah's son and successor, who had the Bab's remains reburied here in 1909. The building, made of Italian-cut stone and rising 128 ft, gracefully combines the canons of classical European architecture with elements of Eastern design and also houses the remains of Baha'u'llah's son. The dome glistens with some 12,000 gilded tiles imported from the Netherlands. Inside, the floor is covered with rich Oriental carpets, and a filigree veil divides visitors from the inner shrine.

The hush of the largely geometrically arranged gardens is now periodically disturbed by construction work, which will create new terraces extending down the slope all the way to the German Colony (☞ *below*) as well as up the mountain to Yefe Nof Street. The Shrine of the Bab, along with the Shrine of Baha'u'llah north of Akko, are sites of pilgrimage for the worldwide Baha'i community; visitors to the shrine are asked to dress modestly. ⊠ *65 Sderot Hatziyonut,* ☎ *04/ 835–8358.* ▣ *Free.* ☉ *Shrine daily 9–noon, gardens daily 9–5.*

⑪ **Bet Hagefen.** The Arab-Jewish Center is a striking but simple two-story stone building. Founded 33 years ago, it was the first and remains the only such institution in Israel. Bet Hagefen's location is not accidental: it stands at the meeting place between Wadi Nisnas (☞ *below*), with its large Arab population; the German Colony, with its mixed population; and Central Carmel, which is predominantly Jewish. Throughout troubled times, the center has promoted the principles of coexistence and understanding between Arabs and Jews through cultural projects and exhibitions.

You can wander into the visitor center and the small art gallery, with works by Arab and Jewish painters and sculptors. The center's involvement in the community goes far beyond art shows, however; activities include meetings between Arab and Jewish schoolchildren and performances by an Arab-Jewish dance group and an Arab theater company. Call ahead to see what's on the calendar. ⊠ *2 Hagefen*, ☎ *04/852–5252.* ⊠ *Free.* ☉ *Sun.–Thurs. 8–1 and 4–8, Fri. 8–1, Sat. 10–1.*

**⑬ Carmelite Monastery and Stella Maris lighthouse.** During the Crusader period, groups of hermits emulating the life of the prophet Elijah lived in caves on this steep mountain slope. In the early 13th century they united under the leadership of the Italian pilgrim (later saint) Berthold, who petitioned the patriarch of Jerusalem for a charter for the group. Thus was born the Carmelite order, which spread across Europe. The Carmelite monks were forced to leave their settlements on Mt. Carmel at the end of the 13th century, when Akko fell to the Mamluks, and did not return until nearly four centuries later. When they found Elijah's cave inhabited by Muslim dervishes, they set up a rudimentary monastery nearby. Dahr el-Omar drove them out again in 1767.

The church of the present monastery dates from 1836 and was built with the munificence of the French monarchy, hence the name of the surrounding neighborhood: French Carmel. The French connection is explained by a small pyramid, topped with an iron cross, that stands before the entrance of the basilica-style church. The monument commemorates those French who were slaughtered here by the Turks in 1799 after the retreating Napoléon left his ailing troops behind to be treated in what was then a military hospital at the monastery. Inside, the academic paintings in the dome depict Elijah in the chariot of fire in which he ascended to heaven, and other Old Testament prophets. The small cave a few steps down at the end of the nave is traditionally associated with Elijah and his pupil, Elisha. A small museum near the entrance contains some fossils and Byzantine artifacts discovered in the area. Across the street from the church, at the tip of the promontory, is the Stella Maris (Star of the Sea) lighthouse, built in the 19th century to guide the Turkish fleet to safe harbor and still in use. It is not open to the public. ⊠ *Carmelite Monastery, Stella Maris Rd.,* ☎ *04/833–7758.* ⊠ *Free.* ☉ *Daily 6:30–1 and 3–6.*

**⑮ Clandestine Immigration and Naval Museum.** The rather dull name of this museum belies the dramatic nature of its contents. The Clandestine Immigration and Naval Museum tells the story of the often heroic efforts to bring Jewish immigrants to Palestine from war-torn Europe in defiance of British policy. In addition to a clearly marked map showing the immigration routes, there are video presentations, photographs, and documents recording both deportations and successful missions. The exhibits are labeled in English.

Emigration to Palestine was well nigh impossible after the British imposed a naval blockade, bowing to pressure by Arabs opposed to Jewish immigration. In 1939, on the eve of World War II, the British issued the so-called White Paper, which effectively strangled Jewish immigration to Palestine and prohibited Jews from buying land there. Small boats sometimes managed to elude the vigilant British warships and unload their human cargoes at secret landing beaches; but for bigger ships the odds were daunting. Out of 63 clandestine ships that tried to run the blockade after the war's end, all but 5 were intercepted, and their passengers were deported to Cyprus.

The museum is full of moving stories of courage, tenacity, and disaster. A photomural of the celebrated ship the *Exodus* recalls the story of the 4,530 refugees aboard who were forcibly transferred back to Germany in 1947, but not before the British forces opened fire on the rebellious ship, convincing the passengers and crew to surrender. Another tragic episode befell the *Struma,* a leaky vessel that was forced to anchor in Istanbul for repairs in 1941. The Turks refused to assist the ship after warnings from the British; so, unable to continue but unwilling to return, the boat wallowed in Istanbul harbor for two months and finally sank a few miles offshore. Of the 767 on board, one person survived.

One of the blockade runners was an old American tank-landing craft renamed Af-al-pi-chen ("Nevertheless," in Hebrew), which serves as the museum's centerpiece. (It's accessible from the roof.) This ship left Italy in 1947 for Palestine and was intercepted by the British, at which point its 434 passengers, all survivors of the Holocaust, were sent to internment camps in Cyprus. ⊠ *204 Allenby Rd.,* ☎ *04/853–6249.* ☞ *NIS 6 ($1.70).* ☉ *Sun.–Thurs. 9–4, holiday eves 9–1.*

**⓮  Elijah's Cave.** This site is considered sacred by Jews, Christians, and Muslims; an early Byzantine tradition identified it as the cave in which Elijah found refuge from the wrath of Ahab, king of Israel from 871 to 853 BC. Graffiti from pilgrims of various faiths and different centuries are scrawled on the right wall, and written prayers are often stuffed into crevices. Some supplicants come to ask for fertility, others for better fortune or a cure for an illness. Modest dress is requested. The cave is a 20-minute walk down the fairly steep path across from the entrance to the Carmelite Monastery and church; you can also reach it by walking about 100 ft up from Allenby Road. ⊠ *230 Allenby Rd.,* ☎ *04/852–7430.* ☞ *Free.* ☉ *Sun.–Thurs. 8–5, Fri. and holiday eves 8–1.*

**⓬  German Colony.** Ben-Gurion Boulevard, ruler-straight, was the heart of a late-19th-century colony established by the German Templar religious reform movement. Note the robust two- and three-story stone houses, with red-tile roofs typical of the neighborhood; some houses still bear German names and inscriptions on the lintels above the doors. The disciplined Germans of yesteryear would no doubt be amazed to know that today their strictly arranged streets are the focus of renovation into what is being developed as an area of enjoyment for all, with sophisticated wine bars, restaurants, and shops. The new Baha'i gardens adjoin the area, making it easily accessible.

The Templars' colony in Haifa was the most important one in the Holy Land. The early settlers formed a self-sufficient community and enjoyed quite a comfortable standard of living; by 1883 they had built nearly 100 houses and filled them with as many families. They introduced several improvements in transportation to Haifa, including the horse-drawn wagon, unknown until their arrival. They started to make wagons locally and then built with their own funds a pilgrimage road from Haifa to Nazareth. The Germans' labors gave rise to modern workshops and warehouses, and it was under their influence that Haifa began to resemble a modern Western city, with well laid-out streets, gardens, and attractive homes.

Haifa's importance to Germany was highlighted in 1898, when Kaiser Wilhelm II sailed into the bay, his first stop on the first official visit to the Holy Land by a German emperor in more than 600 years. The ruling Turkish sultan ordered a new jetty built for the occasion. During World War II the Germans who lived in the colony were expelled, suspected of being Nazis.

The German Templars and the French Carmelite monks on the hill were on no better terms than their compatriots back home. A nationalistic

Flying to France on Friday? Get Francs from Chase on Thursday. Call Currency To Go at 935-9935 for overnight delivery.

r pounds for London. Or Deutschmarks for Düsseldorf. Or any of 75 foreign currencies. Call **Chase Currency To Go**[SM] **at 935-9935** in area codes 212, 718, 914, 516 and Rochester, N.Y.; all other area codes call 1-800-935-9935. We'll deliver directly to your door.\* Overnight. And there are no exchange fees. Let Chase make your trip an easier one.

## CHASE. The right relationship is everything.[SM]

# BONUS MILES MAKE GREAT SOUVENIRS.

MCI Calling Card
123 456 7891 2345
J.D. SMITH
WORLDPHONE

## Earn Miles With Your MCI Card.

Take the MCI Card along on this trip and start earning miles for the next one. You'll earn frequent flyer miles on all your calls and save with the low rates you've come to expect from MCI. Before you know it, you'll be on your way to some other international destination.

Sign up for MCI by calling 1-800-FLY-FREE

## Earn Frequent Flyer Miles.

American Airlines
AAdvantage®

Continental Airlines
OnePass®

Delta Air Lines
SkyMiles®

NORTHWEST AIRLINES
WORLDPERKS®

MILEAGE PLUS.
United Airlines

US AIRWAYS
DIVIDEND MILES

Is this a great time, or what? :-)

MCI

## Easy To Call Home.

1. To use your MCI Card, just dial the WorldPhone access number of the country you're calling from.
2. Dial or give the operator your MCI Card number.
3. Dial or give the number you're calling.

| | |
|---|---|
| # Bahrain | 800-002 |
| # Brunei | 800-011 |
| # China ✧ | 108-12 |
| For a Mandarin-speaking operator | 108-17 |
| # Cyprus ◆ | 080-90000 |
| # Egypt (CC) ◆ (Outside of Cairo, dial 02 first) | 355-5770 |
| # Federated States of Micronesia | 624 |
| # Fiji | 004-890-1002 |
| # Guam (CC) | 1-800-888-8000 |
| # Hong Kong (CC) | 800-96-1121 |
| # India (CC) ✧ | 000-127 |
| # Indonesia (CC) ◆ | 001-801-11 |
| Iran ÷ | (Special Phones Only) |
| # Israel (CC) | 1-800-940-2727 |
| # Japan (CC) ◆ | |
| To call using KDD ■ | 00539-121▶ |
| To call using IDC ■ | 0066-55-121 |
| To call using ITJ ■ | 0044-11-121 |
| # Jordan | 18-800-001 |
| # Korea (CC) | |
| To call using KT ■ | 009-14 |
| To call using DACOM ■ | 00309-12 |
| Phone Booths ÷ Red Button 03, then press ★ | |
| Military Bases | 550-2255 |
| # Kuwait | 800-MCI (800-624) |
| Lebanon ÷ Collect Access | 600-MCI (600-624) |
| # Macao | 0800-131 |
| # Malaysia (CC) ◆ | 1-800-80-0012 |
| # Philippines (CC) ◆ | |
| To call using PLDT ■ | 105-14 |
| Collect access via PLDT in Filipino ■ | 105-15 |
| Collect access via ICC in Filipino ■ | 1237-77 |
| # Qatar ★ | 0800-012-77 |
| # Saipan (CC) ÷ | 950-1022 |
| # Saudi Arabia (CC) ÷ | 1-800-11 |
| # Singapore | 8000-112-112 |
| # Sri Lanka (Outside of Colombo, dial 01 first) | 440-100 |
| # Syria | 0800 |
| # Taiwan (CC) ◆ | 0080-13-4567 |
| # Thailand ★ | 001-999-1-2001 |
| # United Arab Emirates ◆ | 800-111 |
| Vietnam ● | 1201-1022 |
| Yemen | 008-00-102 |

# Automation available from most locations. ✧ Available from most major cities. ◆ Public phones may require deposit of coin or phone card for dial tone. (CC) Country-to-country calling available to/from most international locations. ÷ Limited availability. ■ International communications carrier. ▶ Regulation does not permit intra-Japan calls. ★ Not available from public pay phones. ● Local service fee in U.S. currency required to complete call. Limit one bonus program per MCI account. Terms and conditions apply. All airline program rules and conditions apply. © 1998 MCI Telecommunications Corporation. All rights reserved. Is this a great time, or what? is a service mark of MCI.

battle arose in 1885, when the Germans bought some acreage on the mountain and the French monks refused to let them cross their land to get there. The case ended up in a Haifa court, and the monks were ordered to allow the Germans access.

🔟 **Haifa Museum** (Museum of Modern Art). Until recently, this was three "museums" in one building; now Ancient Art is housed at the Maritime Museum (☞ *below*), while Music and Ethnology has yet to find a home. One admission ticket is good for both Modern Art and Ancient Art, as well as the Tikotin Museum of Japanese Art, also under the auspices of the Haifa Museum.

The Museum of Modern Art displays work from all over the world, dating from the mid-18th century to the present. It's also a good place to learn about modern Israeli art: the many pieces include 20th-century graphics and contemporary paintings, sculpture, and photography. The print collection is of special note, and international photography shows are mounted several times a year. ⊠ *26 Shabbetai Levy St.,* ☎ *04/852–3255.* ☒ *NIS 20 ($5.70) includes all 3 museums.* ☉ *Sun.– Mon. and Wed.–Thurs. 10–4, Tues. 4–7, Fri. 10–1, Sat. 10–2.*

⓲ **Hecht Museum.** It's worth the trip to Haifa University for these fine archaeological holdings. At the summit of Mt. Carmel, in the main campus tower (designed by Brazilian architect Oscar Niemeyer), the collection spans the millennia from the Chalcolithic era to the Roman and Byzantine periods. The artifacts, all Jewish, range from religious altars and lamps to two coffins and figurines from the Early Bronze Age. Featured prominently are finds from the excavations of Jerusalem's Temple Mount. A separate wing displays a small collection of paintings, mostly impressionist and Jewish School of Paris. To get here, take Bus 37 from the Nof Hotel. ⊠ *Abu Hushi St.,* ☎ *04/824–0577.* ☒ *Free.* ☉ *Sun.–Thurs. 10–4, Fri. and holiday eves 10–1, Sat. 10–2.*

NEED A **Gan Ha'em** (Mothers' Park), opposite the Dan Panorama Hotel, has a
BREAK? small and happy collection of zoo animals and reptiles, along with a botanical garden, a picnic area, park benches, and a snack bar.

⑥ **Mané Katz Museum.** This is the house and studio where the Expressionist painter Emmanuel Katz (1894–1962) lived and worked for the last four years of his life. Katz spent the 1920s in Paris, where he exhibited with a group of Jewish artists from the École de Paris; as in the canvases of fellow members Marc Chagall and Chaim Soutine, a recurring theme in his work is the village life of Jews in Eastern Europe. A whitewashed building with ornamental grillwork on the windows, this intimate museum houses a collection of Katz's paintings, drawings, and sculptures, the Ukrainian-born artist's legacy to the city. The artist was an avid collector of rugs and 17th-century antiques from Spain and Germany, and these are also on display along with objects from his Judaica collection. ⊠ *89 Yefe Nof St.,* ☎ *04/838–3482.* ☒ *Free.* ☉ *Sun.–Thurs. 10–4, Tues. 2–6, Fri.–Sat. 10–1.*

⑯ **National Maritime Museum.** Here 5,000 years of maritime history is told (and made more interesting than it sounds) with model ships, archaeological finds, coins minted with nautical symbols, navigational instruments, and other artifacts. There are also a number of intriguing underwater finds from nearby excavations and shipwrecks. The ancient-art collection, formerly housed in the Haifa Museum, is one of the finest in the country; it comprises mostly Greek and Roman stone and marble sculpture, Egyptian textiles, Greek pottery, and encaustic grave portraits from Fayyum, in Lower Egypt. Particularly rare are the figures of fishermen from the Hellenistic period. Among numerous terra-cotta figurines from Syria and Egypt are several curious animal-shape vessels—once used as playthings, incense burners, or funerary gifts—from Haifa's nearby Shiqmona excavation. Also from Egypt are a group of finely carved alabaster vessels and funerary masks. ⊠ *198 Allenby Rd.,* ☎ *04/853–6622.* ☞ *NIS 20 ($5.70), including Museum of Modern Art and Tikotin Museum of Japanese Art.* ☉ *Sun.–Mon. and Wed.–Thurs. 10–4, Tues. 4–7, Fri. 10–1, Sat. 10–2.*

**⑰ National Museum of Science and Technology (Technoda).** Children and adults alike will be captivated by the hands-on chemistry and physics exhibits in this beautifully designed building, the original home of the Technion (☞ *below*). ⊠ *Balfour St.,* ☎ *04/862–8111.* ☞ *NIS 8 ($2.30).* ☉ *Mon. and Wed.–Thurs. 9–5, Tues. 9–7, Fri. 9–1, Sat. 10–3.*

**⑧ Sculpture garden.** From one of the benches on a winding path through the garden, you can contemplate the life-size bronzes of humans and animals by sculptor Ursula Malbin, who came to Israel as a refugee from Nazi Germany. ⊠ *Just west of Baha'i Shrine.*

**⑲ Technion.** Israel's foremost center for applied research, the 300-acre Technion City was relocated to this area in 1953. The original institute (known as the Technoda) was founded in 1912 and opened its doors in midtown 12 years later, due in part to the hardships of an intervening world war. Today, the Technion is highly fertile ground for Israel's scientific innovations: two-thirds of the nation's university research in such fields as science, technology, engineering, medicine, architecture, and town planning takes place here. Visitors can get an idea of the vast scope of these studies, plus the goals for the future, at the **Coler-California Center,** housed in a concrete-and-glass building. A 20-minute English-language film called "Vision" is an introduction to the multimedia touch screens and Internet stations available in the comfortable lounge. Laser-disc videos describe the various Technion departments. To get here, take Bus 31 from the Nof Hotel or the Dan Panorama Hotel. ⊠ *Kiryat Ha-Technion (Technion City), Neve Sha'anan,* ☎ *04/832–0664.* ☞ *Free.* ☉ *Sun.–Thurs. 8–3.*

**⑦ Tikotin Museum of Japanese Art.** Established in 1957 by Felix Tikotin, this graceful venue adheres to the Japanese tradition of displaying beautiful objects that are in harmony with the season, so exhibits change frequently. The Japanese atmosphere, created in part by sliding doors and partitions made of wood and paper, accompanies you through a display of scrolls, screens, pottery and porcelain, lacquer and metalwork, paintings from several schools, netsuke and inro, and fresh-flower arrangements. ⊠ *88 Hanassi St.,* ☎ *04838–3554.* ☞ *NIS 20 ($5.70), including Museum of Modern Art and Maritime Museum.* ☉ *Sun.–Mon. and Wed.–Thurs. 10–4, Tues. 4–7, Fri. 10–1, Sat. 10–2.*

OFF THE
BEATEN PATH

**WADI NISNAS –** This colorful quarter east of Bet Hagefen, around Khouri Street, is a slice of modern Arab life in Israel, yet still a place where men crouch on stools in front of stoops and women in traditional dress peer out from behind curtains or duck into doorways. The narrow streets are packed with shops selling housewares and groceries. St. John's pedestrian mall is a humming marketplace of stalls heaped with fruit and vegetables. Open on Saturday—when many other stores in Haifa are closed—the market draws Jewish customers from all over the city.

**⑤ Yefe Nof Street.** Also known as Panorama Road, this street skirts the backs of Haifa's biggest hotels and descends the mountain past the Baha'i Shrine. Included is the lushly planted, curving Louis Promenade, with shaded benches along the way, starting behind the Dan Carmel Hotel. On a clear day, from any of several lookouts, the naked eye can take in the port below; Akko, across the bay; and the cliffs of Rosh Hanikra, with Lebanon in the distance. It's a superlative view.

| | |
|---|---|
| NEED A BREAK? | In a city known for its falafel, we can still highly recommend a **falafel joint** just around the corner from the Wadi Nisnas market, on a small street parallel to St. John's. Turn left at the mall's end onto Khouri Street, and then take the first left. Some 300 ft up on your right is a tidy stand with fresh, steaming chickpea balls; warm pita bread; and all the toppings, as well as soft drinks to wash them all down. |

## Dining

**$$$$** ✕ **La Chaumière.** Occupying a two-story stone building in the German Colony, this restaurant offers authentic French charm in both its ambience and the virtuosity of its cuisine. Owner Michel Kaminski and his wife, who take turns in the kitchen, see to it that everything from the goose-liver pâté to the chocolate mousse and bread is fresh and homemade. Two fine choices are the fillet Chaumière with a cream sauce of tomatoes, cognac, and port, and sea scallops with Martini Blanco and cream sauce. ⊠ *40A Ben-Gurion Blvd.,* ☎ *04/853–8563 or 04/855–3154. Reservations essential. AE, DC, MC, V. No lunch Fri.*

**$$$$** ✕ **Restaurant 1873.** The name indicates when the German Colony was founded and suggests that you'll enjoy a bit of history with your meal. This charmingly renovated house has several small dining rooms, each with wooden floors and an intimate air. The French-Italian chefs create admirable dishes, such as a four-mushroom appetizer with Marsala sauce, seafood in lemon and thyme, fillet of veal with sweetbreads, and breast of moulard in blackberry sauce. A crepe filled with pastry cream in toffee sauce makes a grand finale. If you can't wait until dinner, try the business lunch. The wine bar upstairs provides a pleasant way to spend an evening. ⊠ *102 Jaffa St.,* ☎ *04/853–2211. Reservations essential. AE, D, MC, V. No lunch Fri.*

**$$$** ★ ✕ **Recital.** The atmosphere at this newly expanded restaurant (with a patio for summer dining) is decidedly artistic, with classical music playing softly in the background. The pastries and desserts are divine here, particularly the finger-licking hot apple pie served with ice cream or whipped cream, and the unbeatable cheesecakes. If you must dine properly *before* dessert, precede these delights with sliced steak in pepper sauce, or goose breast served on a hot plate with port and mint sauce. Lighter choices include quiche and a salad of fresh fruit and nuts. The sign outside is in Hebrew only; the address is opposite the Israel Discount Bank. ⊠ *131 Moriyya Blvd.,* ☎ *04/834–1269. AE, DC, MC, V.*

**$$$** ✕ **Shishkebab.** You'll see lots of locals slipping in for down-home kosher Middle Eastern food here in the German Colony. Formica tables and chairs indicate the no-nonsense approach to service and decor. Shishkebab is famous for its high-quality grilled meats, arrayed on skewers in a small glass counter by the entrance; other options include Middle Eastern salads and *kube* soup (ground-beef dumplings, often with pine nuts or raisins, rolled in cracked wheat and floated in a consommé). Aromatic coffee is served in tiny cups with cardamom. Don't balk at sharing a table; it's customary here. ⊠ *59 Ben-Gurion Ave.,* ☎ *04/852–7576. Reservations not accepted. No credit cards. Closed Fri.–Sat. and holiday eves.*

**$$$** ★ ✕ **Voilà.** Tucked downstairs off the Nordau pedestrian mall, this whitewashed hideaway is an exclusive haunt. The mood is cozy and offbeat, with tilted doorways, strange wooden trestle tables, a Bedouin woman's headdress hung with British soldiers' dog tags, flower pots, dolls, decorative *objets* from churches, and Oriental rugs. There are only eight tables inside, but there's also a garden enclosure that's heated in winter. Famous for its fondues (cheese, beef, or chocolate), the restaurant also prides itself on its beef fillet with port sauce and goose-liver pâté. A welcome accompaniment is another house specialty, the traditional Swiss potato dish called *rösti*. For dessert, don't miss the ice cream crepes draped with wild-blackberry or -raspberry sauce. Less expensive three-course business lunches are available noon–4 PM. ⊠ *21A Nordau St.,* ☎ *04/866–4529. Reservations essential. AE, DC, MC, V.*

**$$**  ✕ **La Trattoria.** This is not your typical Italian restaurant: along with pizza, pasta, and minestrone, the menu features the likes of couscous and chicken livers. It's this homey hodgepodge of Italian, French, and Tunisian atmosphere and cuisine that makes La Trattoria a hit with the locals. Jovial owner Edy Barby presides. ⊠ *119 Hanassi Blvd.,* ☎ *04/837–9029. AE, DC, MC, V.*

**$$**  ✕ **Palermo Pizza.** If you lean toward genuine, thin-crusted pizza,
★  you've come to the right place. Looking more like a fashionable salad bar than a pizzeria, this parlor in the Panorama Center shopping mall displays jars of spicy peppers and fresh flowers for a dash of color. The range of pizza toppings is prodigious—from tuna and salami to pineapple and peppers—and the crusts are crisp. The menu expands to fit plenty of other Italian specialties—like *caprese* salad (sliced mozzarella topped with tomatoes and basil leaves and drizzled with olive oil), gnocchi, and ravioli—as well as meat, fish, and salads. ⊠ *Panorama Center, Hanassi Ave.,* ☎ *04/838–9129. AE, MC, V.*

**$$**  ✕ **Taiwan.** One of Haifa's best Chinese restaurants, this family-owned place in the German Colony has been in business since the '70s. The chef is, fittingly enough, from Taiwan. House specialties are lemon chicken and meat and seafood with satay sauce. ⊠ *59 Ben-Gurion Blvd.,* ☎ *04/853–2082. Reservations essential Fri.–Sat. AE, DC, MC, V.*

## Lodging

**$$$$**  ⌸ **Carmel Beach Hotel and Suites.** Just opened in 1998, this hotel has a location unmatched by any other in Haifa: it's right on the beach. You can't miss the buildings that make it up—the two 14-story towers rise high on the sea side at the city's entrance, and three of the floors are connected mid-tower. Part of the hotel consists of individually owned suites; the rest comprises 86 one-room suites and 12 two-bedroom suites, each with a kitchenette (there are no shops or restaurants nearby). A business center and a health club are in the works. ⊠ *10 David Elazar St., Carmel Beach,* ☎ *04/850–8888,* FAX *04/850–0444. 85 rooms with bath. Restaurant, lobby lounge, room service, pool, wading pool, beach, tennis court. AE, D, MC, V.*

**$$$$**  ⌸ **Carmel Forest Spa Resort.** It's the ultimate escape: a top-of-the-line spa in a tastefully appointed hotel designed to pamper its guests in a calm and healthful setting (no cell phones or children under 16). Outside, you're surrounded by 15 acres of pine-covered hills; inside, there are 25 different treatment rooms dedicated to your well-being. Choose from a variety of massages, from aromatherapy to shiatsu; facials; body peels; seaweed wraps; and such treatments as hydrotherapy, mind-body harmony, reflexology, and body sculpture. (Reserve treatments in advance.) Green wicker chaises face the forest and the Mediterranean coast through the solarium windows. A sample day? Consult the nutritionist, strike out on a forest walk, and then sit down to a meal prepared with all-natural ingredients. Other comforting amenities include an authentic Turkish bath, a reading room, and a music room with stuffed armchairs in front of the lobby fireplace. Weight-loss and anti-stress packages are also available. ⊠ *Carmel Forest, Box 90000, Haifa 31900,* ☎ *04/832–3111,* FAX *04/832–3988. 126 rooms with bath. Restaurant, lobby lounge, pool, beauty salon, hot tub, sauna, spa, exercise room. AE, D, MC, V.*

**$$$$** ☷ **Dan Carmel.** The Dan is beautifully located on the heights of the Carmel. One of Haifa's first hotels, this thirtysomething institution still has a charm of its own, and the staff is devoted. The premises could use a renovator's touch, but the deluxe rooms on the upper floors are nicely furnished, with wooden bureaus and satin bedspreads. The other doubles are less luxurious, but they're cheerfully decorated in pastels. All guest rooms have balconies with stunning views over the city or the curving shore. The large garden around the pool, landscaped with potted geraniums and surrounded with fir trees, is always breezy and pleasant. ⊠ 85–87 Hanassi Ave., 31060, ☏ 04/830–6211, FAX 04/838–7504. 219 rooms with bath. Restaurant, café, pool, beauty salon, sauna, exercise room. AE, DC, MC, V.

**$$$$** ☷ **Dan Panorama.** Another member of the Dan hotel chain, this one
★ is glitzier than its sister down the road. The rooms, like the gleaming marble lobby, are spacious and sparkling; the blue-and-yellow color scheme, like the furnishings, is low-key. Some rooms look out onto the Baha'i Shrine and the bay. The hotel is connected to the Panorama Center shopping mall, filled with small restaurants and boutiques. ⊠ 107 Hanassi Ave., 31060, ☏ 04/835–2222, FAX 04/835–2235. 266 rooms with bath. Restaurant, 3 cafés, piano bar, 2 pools, sauna, exercise room, baby-sitting. AE, DC, MC, V.

**$$$** ☷ **Dvir.** Share the same great location as Haifa's priciest hotels without paying top shekel. In summer, guests at the Dvir even have free access to the pool at the nearby Dan Panorama. The hotel is built into the hillside, so there is a two-flight climb up to the reception area. About one-third of the simple, unpretentious rooms have sea or city views; all are spacious, clean, and recently painted. Ask for a front room (with a view), as some of the back rooms are on the small side. ⊠ 124 Yefe Nof St., 34454, ☏ 04/838–9131, FAX 04/838–1068. 35 rooms with bath. Guests have access to most facilities at Dan Panorama and Dan Carmel, ☞ above. AE, DC, MC, V.

**$$$** ☷ **Haifa Tower.** Housed in a brand-new, 17-floor office tower in downtown Haifa, this hotel is set in a busy shopping district near the Technion science center. Rooms are ample in size, and decor is subdued, tasteful, and spanking new. All rooms have either sea or city views. The breakfast area, which looks out over Haifa Bay, is bright and cheerful. ⊠ 63 Herzl St., 33212, ☏ 04/867–7111, FAX 04/862–1863. 100 rooms with bath (4 with shower only). Restaurant, bar. AE, MC, V.

**$$$** ☷ **Nof.** The rooms in this small, pleasant hotel are done up in turquoise, though renovations are in the works. What's unbeatable are the location and the view of the city spilling down to the sea from the top of Mt. Carmel. The guest rooms take full advantage, with large windows; the on-site Chinese restaurant and coffee shop also have superb views. The front desk and room service are quick and efficient. ⊠ 101 Hanassi Ave., 31063, ☏ 04/835–4311, FAX 04/838–8810. 93 rooms with bath. Restaurant, bar, room service, coffee shop, dance club. AE, DC, MC, V.

**$$** ☷ **Beth Shalom.** Across the street from Haifa's luxury hotels, in Cen-
★ tral Carmel, this guest house operated by an evangelical Christian organization gets high points for its prime location. The management runs a tight ship while preserving a family atmosphere, true to the reputation of Swiss-owned hotels worldwide. The rooms and lobby are spotless and well maintained, if the furnishings are a bit dated. Reservations are accepted only for stays of at least three nights. ⊠ 110 Hanassi Ave., Box 6208, Haifa 31061, ☏ 04/837–7481 or 04/838–3019, FAX 04/837–2443. 30 rooms with bath. Cafeteria. AE, DC.

## Nightlife and the Arts

For the latest information on performances, festivals, and other special events in and around Haifa, check Friday's *Jerusalem Post* or the monthly brochure "Events in Haifa and the Northern Region," available at hotels and tourist offices. In balmy weather, a stroll through the Baha'i Gardens or along the Louis Promenade is a relaxing way to end the day. For a more festive evening, try the wine bars and restaurants in the newly spruced-up German Colony. Nightspots in Haifa come and go, and some open only on certain evenings, so call first if possible.

### BARS

Three pubs of the moment are **Migdalor** (⊠ At Stella Maris, ☎ 04/833–6292), **Fever** (⊠ In Gan Ha'Em, opposite the Dan Panorama hotel, ☎ no phone), and **Shmura** (⊠ 38 Pica Rd., ☎ 04/834–7727).

### DANCE CLUBS

In the basement of the Dan Panorama hotel is the **Chaplin Club,** a disco catering to the thirtysomething crowd. There's no cover charge and no minimum on weekdays; on Friday the minimum per person is NIS 60 ($17.20) plus a 10% service charge. The club is open from 10:30 PM to 2 AM daily. On Friday, call for reservations (☎ 04/835–2206).

### FILM

In October, around the time of the holiday Sukkoth, Haifa hosts an **international film festival.** Contact the Haifa Cinemateque (☎ 04/838–3424) for schedules and venues.

### MUSIC

A **blues festival** takes place in July in Haifa's port; for information call 04/837–4010 or inquire at the tourist office (☎ 04/853–5606). The **Israel Philharmonic Orchestra** gives approximately 30 concerts at the Haifa Auditorium (⊠ 138 Hanassi Ave., ☎ 04/838–0013) from October through July. Ticket prices range from NIS 105 ($30) to NIS 280 ($80) and are generally sold only at Philharmonic box offices in Jerusalem, Tel Aviv, and Haifa (in Haifa, ⊠ 16 Herzl St., ☎ 04/866–4167). Concerts start at 8:30 PM or 9 PM, and the box office opens one hour before performances. The **Haifa Symphony Orchestra** also performs at the Haifa Auditorium about four times a week. It's best to buy tickets about 30 minutes before the performance, which generally begins around 8:30 PM; ticket prices range from NIS 40 ($11.40) to NIS 80 ($22.80). Contact the box office for more information (⊠ 50 Tezner St., ☎ 04/862–1973).

### WINE BARS

A welcome addition to Haifa's nightlife are two new wine bars, where you can settle down to a glass of wine, a loaf of bread, and other light victuals. The upper floor of the old stone building housing **Restaurant 1873** (⊠ 102 Yaffa St., ☎ 04/853–2211), in the lively German Colony, is open Thursday, Friday, and Saturday nights; reservations are a good idea. **Special Reserve** (⊠ 87 Hanassi St., beside the Dan Carmel hotel, ☎ 04/836–1187) is a well-organized store with a huge selection of wine. Owner and wine expert Andre hosts wine tastings and complements his wares with cheese and such novelties as six different kinds of local foie gras. He plans a second store in the German Colony.

## Outdoor Activities and Sports

### BEACHES

Haifa's coastline is one fine, sandy public beach after another. From south to north, **Bat Galim, Dado, Zamir, and Carmel** beaches (☎ 04/852–4231) cover 5 km (3 mi) of coast and have 13 lifeguard stations among them. There are no parking or entrance fees. The beaches have sports areas, changing rooms, showers, toilets, refreshment stands, 12 restaurants, and a promenade that connects them. At press time, additional Haifa beach developments were under way. (The new Carmel Beach Suites Hotel, at Bat Galim beach, had just been completed.)

BOWLING

It's hardly the national sport, but on the road from Haifa to Akko, about 5 km (3 mi) from the port, you'll find the 12-lane **Bowling Checkpoint** (⌧ 5 Maklef St., at Checkpost Junction, the eastern entrance to Haifa, ☎ 04/872–0529). It's open from 11 AM until after midnight, depending on the crowd; Friday and holiday-eve hours are 10–4. The daytime rate is NIS 17 ($4.85) per game. Shoe rentals are available.

ICE-SKATING

One of Israel's few ice-skating rinks (☎ ☎ 04/841–5388) is in the **Lev Hamifratz** shopping center, in northern Haifa on the road to Akko. The rink is open daily from 10 AM to 10 PM, but call ahead, as practice sessions sometimes tie up the rink in the afternoons. Admission, which includes skate rental, is NIS 35 ($10).

## Shopping

Haifa is studded with modern indoor shopping malls replete with boutiques, small restaurants, and movie theaters. The three main ones are the **Horev Center,** on Horev Street at Pica Street, in the Ahuza district; the **Panorama Center,** next to the Dan Panorama hotel, in Central Carmel; and **Migdal Haneve'im,** on Khouri Street, in the Hadar district.

Duck into **Sara's Gift Shop,** in the Dan Carmel hotel (☎ ☎ 04/830–6238), to pick up gifts for everyone, including yourself, at reasonable prices. It's crammed with jewelry made exclusively for these displays; the silver and Roman-glass pieces are particularly seductive. Other items include Judaica, souvenirs such as the *chamsa* (a hand for warding off the evil eye), and handmade textile hangings.

Oenophiles and cheese lovers will appreciate **Special Reserve** (⌧ 87 Hanassi St., next door to Dan Carmel hotel, ☎ 04/836–1187), a well-stocked wine and cheese shop run by wine expert Andre. You can taste at the counter. Call to see if there's a wine tasting (in English) while you're in town. One part of the shop is a wine bar, where excellent light food is served (☞ Wine Bars *in* Nightlife and the Arts, *above*).

# THE ROTHSCHILD WINE COUNTRY AND MT. CARMEL

This is the back-door route to Haifa, one that wanders through the foothills and up the spine of Mt. Carmel through Druze villages. Route 4 is smooth sailing, with the Carmel looming to the east beyond cultivated fields and huge banana plantations (though you may not see the bananas, as they're usually bagged in blue or gray plastic). The road leads through undulating countryside dotted with cypresses, palms, and vineyards.

## Benyamina

**㉑** *55 km (34 mi) north of Tel Aviv on Rte. 652.*

Coming from the south, you'll drive through Benyamina, the youngest settlement in the area. Founded in 1922, it was named after Baron Edmond de Rothschild (1845–1934), the head of the French branch of the famous family, who took a keen interest in the welfare of his fellow Jews in Palestine. (His Hebrew name was Benyamin.) With his prestige, vision, and financial contributions, Rothschild laid the foundations in the late 19th century for Zichron Ya'akov and Bat Shlomo, as well as other towns along the coastal plain and in the Upper Galilee.

The advice of the viniculture experts Rothschild hired in the 1880s paid off handsomely, at least in this region—after years of adversity and setbacks, the fruit of the vines flourished in the 1890s. Rothschild's paternalistic system was not without its pitfalls, however; some of his administrators ruled his colonies like petty despots, trying, for instance to impose use of the French language on the local settlers, who wished to speak Hebrew. Note that in Benyamina, as in many other Rothschild towns, the signs of early settlement are respectfully preserved: rows of lofty, willowy Washingtonian palms introduced to the area by the local hero and agronomist Aaron Aaronson, of neighboring Zichron Ya'akov; and groups of modest, one-story stucco homes capped with terra-cotta roofs, inspired by towns in Provence.

## Shuni

**㉑** *At railroad tracks in Benyamina, turn left onto Rte. 652; then drive 1 km (½ mi) north.*

This stone fortress was built by effendis in the 18th and 19th centuries, on the site of existing ruins, because of its sweeping command over the surrounding lands, some planted with grain (*shuni* is Arabic for granary). Now the landscaped **Jabotinsky Park,** this area was part of a parcel purchased by Rothschild in 1914, but its chief attractions today are Shuni (the Ottoman fortress) and the Roman theater. You can also dine in the fortress (☞ *below*). The spring at present-day Shuni was also the source of the spring water that was tapped for the aqueducts of ancient Caesarea. In the 1930s and '40s, the site was chosen for its remote location as a training ground for members of self-organized units inspired by Ze'ev Jabotinsky (1880–1940), the right-wing Zionist leader who was the spiritual head of the Jewish underground organization Irgun Zvai Leumi. Armed Irgun units later launched attacks from here.

Excavations of the well-preserved, 2nd-century **Roman theater** (which you enter through the fortress) have revealed the remains of bathing pools lined with 2nd-century Roman mosaics and a marble statue of the Greek god of medicine, Aesculapius, both now in storage at the Rockefeller Museum, in Jerusalem. These finds support the theory that this was once a sacred spa whose waters had healing powers—indeed, an early 4th-century pilgrim mentioned in his writings that women who bathed here always became pregnant, like it or not. The theater also contains an ancient olive press, carved lintels, and fragments of columns. On the right, before you enter the fortress, you can still see part of a mosaic floor. Call ahead to arrange a guided tour of the site. ⊠ *Rte. 652,* ☎ *06/638–9730.* 🎫 *NIS 4 ($1.15).* ☉ *Sun.–Thurs. 9–4, Fri. and holiday eves 9–12:30.*

OFF THE BEATEN PATH
**RAMAT HANADIV** – Literally "the Benefactor's Heights" (also known as the Rothschild Memorial Gardens)—is the splendid setting for the tombs of the baron and his wife, the Baroness Adelaide. Set in 1,112 acres of parkland, the stunning gardens that surround the family crypt lie 2 km (1 mi) up an unpaved road with memorable views back over the Sharon Plain. Over the wrought-iron gateway to the garden is the family coat of arms, a bronze shield supported by a gilded lion and unicorn, capped by a coronet. Inside, the well-tended gardens are filled with a mixture of indigenous and foreign flora. Cedars of Lebanon and cypresses punctuate lawns interspersed with rose and palm gardens. The western edge has a panoramic view of Caesarea and Hadera, to the south, and Dor and the fishponds of Kibbutz Ma'agan Michael, to the north; a stone map shows the regional settlements that the baron founded or spon-

sored. The Rothschilds' wish to be buried here was carried out only after the Jewish state was established; an Israeli warship brought their remains from France in 1954. Opposite the exit are a refreshment kiosk and picnic tables. A large billboard map next to the kiosk outlines the several hikes that start here, some with great views of the coast. *3½ km (2¼ mi) east of Shuni,* ☎ *06/639–7821.* ⌷ *Free.* ☉ *Sun.–Thurs. 8–4, Fri. 8–2, Sat. 8–4.*

### Dining

**$$$**  ✕ **Shuni Castle.** The setting alone—a few upper rooms in the stone
★    fortress with views of Israel's wine country—is memorable. Add to this the country charm of artfully arranged baskets of red peppers and dried sausage, laid out beside chubby loaves of homemade bread under hanging pots of trailing vines, and you've got a winner. The view is divine from the three tables on the patio, so you may want to reserve one in advance. In keeping with the informal style (chef Antoine likes to banter with regulars), there's no written menu, but you can expect to find some of the following: homemade goose liver pâté, leg of duck with honey and fruit, boeuf bourgignon with mushrooms, veal with white wine and artichokes, and braised entrecôte with peppers and tomatoes. Local red and white wines are served, or you can ask for the Riesling from Antoine's vineyard. ⌂ *In Jabotinsky Park, just off Rte. 652, 1 km (½ mi) north of Benyamina,* ☎ *06/638–0227. DC, V. Closed Sun.*

# Zichron Ya'akov

★ ㉒   *61 km (40 mi) north of Tel Aviv.*

The planted roundabout marks the entrance to Zichron Ya'akov, a town named by its original settlers in honor of Rothschild's father, James. Pick up a town map in the tourist office just opposite, next to the Founders' Monument and the central bus station. Most of the main sights are signposted in English. You can visit Zichron Ya'akov in an hour or so if you're on your way elsewhere; it also makes a nice day trip from Tel Aviv or Haifa, including a relaxing lunch at one of the town's new restaurants (make reservations if you're coming on Saturday).

Founded in 1882 by Romanian pioneers, this settlement nearly foundered until rescued by Edmond de Rothschild. A decade later, however, the town's winery took off, the same **Carmel Oriental Wine Cellars** that you'll find by veering to the right from the roundabout and driving down Jabotinsky Street. At the end of Jabotinsky, turn right on Hanadiv Street. Today the winery is Israel's second-largest, producing more than 80 different wines and spirits. The original storage vats and oak barrels are still on view, though wine is now stored mostly in stainless-steel vats and concrete tanks. A guided one-hour tour outlines the stages of local wine production, from the weighing-in of tractors laden with grapes to grape pressing and the aging of wine in caves. Fermentation is computerized, bottling lines automated. The tour includes a tasting of some five varieties and an audiovisual presentation that's pretty rudimentary; you may find yourself yawning before you even taste the wine. Tours leave at various times between 9 AM and 3 PM, and it's a good idea to reserve one in advance. The shop carries a superior selection of wine, and you get a 15% discount. The finest wines are the Rothschild vintages: cabernet sauvignon, sauvignon blanc, and fumé blanc. Locally made gin, vodka, and brandy are also available. A three-day autumn wine festival takes place here after the harvest, around the time of the holiday Sukkoth. ☎ *06/629–0280.* ⌷ *NIS 12 ($3.40).* ☉ *Sun.–Thurs. 9–3, Fri. 9–12:30.*

To visit the town itself, retrace your way up Jabotinsky Street to the town's entrance. The main street, **Hameyasdim,** starts at the stone arch with the red tile roof, just past the Founders' Monument. Residents have made every effort to maintain the original appearance of this short thoroughfare, so the cobblestone street is lined with small, red-roofed 19th-century homes. In those days, people needed courtyards behind their homes to house animals, carts, and farm equipment; several of these have been restored to look exactly as they did then. These days, however, upscale restaurants and an assortment of antiques shops, crafts shops, and offbeat boutiques occupy the courtyards and line the main street.

About halfway down the street is **Bet Aaronson** (Aaronson's House), whose late-19th-century architecture successfully combines Art Nouveau and Middle Eastern traditions. This museum was once the home of the accomplished agronomist Aaron Aaronson (1876–1919), who gained international fame for his discovery of an ancestor of modern wheat, a wild and hardy strain that grew in the surrounding mountains. The house remains as it looked after World War I, with family photographs and French and Turkish furniture. The museum also houses the library, diaries, and letters of Aaronson, who in his youth was sent by Rothschild to France to study agriculture.

Aaronson and his sisters became local heroes as leaders of the spy ring called the NILI (an acronym for a quotation from the Book of Samuel: "The Eternal One of Israel will not prove false")—a militant group dedicated to ousting the hated Turks from Palestine by collaborating with the British during World War I. They were spurred on by the harshness of such Turkish policies as the expulsion of Russian Jews from Palestine (the Russians were enemies of the Turks during World War I) and the confiscation of Jewish property.

Both sisters, Sarah and Rebecca, were in love with Aaron's assistant, Absalom Feinberg. A double agent was disrupting NILI's communications with the British, so Feinberg set off to cross the Sinai desert to make contact. He was killed in an ambush in the Gaza Strip. His remains were recovered some 50 years later from a grave marked simply by a palm tree, the tree having sprouted from some dates in Feinberg's pockets. (After the Six Day War, Feinberg's body was reburied in Jerusalem.) Sarah Aaronson was captured by the Turks and committed suicide in her brother's house after being tortured. Other NILI leaders were executed by the Turks upon discovery. Aaron returned to Zichron Ya'akov with the victorious British in 1918, but the following year his plane mysteriously vanished en route from London to the Paris Peace Conference. ⊠ *40 Hameyasdim St.,* ☎ *06/639–0120.* ▨ *NIS 7 ($2).* ☉ *Sun.–Thurs. 8:30–1, Tues. 3:30–5:30, Fri. 9–noon.*

A few doors up the street is **Binyamin Pool,** built in 1891 and originally the town's water tower. Zichron was the first village in Israel to have water piped to its houses; Meir Dizengoff, the first mayor of Tel Aviv, even came to town to see how it was done. The facade resembles that of an ancient synagogue. Farther on, at the corner of Hanadiv and Hameyasdim streets stands the actual town synagogue, **Ohel Ya'akov,** built by Rothschild in 1886 to satisfy the settlers' first request. Turn left onto Hanadiv Street, which will take you past a children's park to the **former town hall,** on the left. Commissioned by Rothschild, this is a fine example of late-19th-century Ottoman-style architecture, built of white stone with a central pediment capped by a tile roof. The building is being restored as a museum dedicated to the town's first pioneers.

NEED A
BREAK?

An inviting place to relax and watch the action in this rural town is **Tnuva b'Moshava,** at the main crossroads (✉ Hameyasdim and Hanadiv Sts.). This streetside vegetarian café offers in-season fresh-fruit drinks (try mango or peach), ice cream, high-rise cakes, and a wide choice of light meals.

**Bet Daniel** (Daniel's House) is a tranquil oasis for writers, musicians, and artists set in the woods on the western edge of town, with a wonderful view of the Carmel coast. Now a small cluster of one- and two-story buildings, it was built by Lillian Friedlander in 1938 as a retreat for musicians after the death of her son Daniel, a highly gifted pianist. A child prodigy, Daniel was sent to study at the Juilliard School in New York, where he committed suicide at the age of 18.

The complex hosts concerts, music classes, and workshops, in addition to being a guest house open to the public (☞ Dining and Lodging, *below*). Daniel's 1905 Steinway from New York still stands in the dining room, which is furnished with other family antiques and photographs. The guest roster bears such illustrious names as Isaac Stern, Leonard Bernstein, Aaron Copland, and Arturo Toscanini. A chamber-music festival is held twice a year in a small concert hall on the grounds (☞ Arts, *below*). To get here, turn right off Hanadiv Street onto Herzl Street, then left onto Habroshim Street.

## Dining and Lodging

$$$$ ✕ **Aroma.** Just up the hill from the winery, this restaurant presents a sophisticated menu in an old-fashioned setting, and the small, wood-paneled bar holds a large collection of drink. The decor is charming: peach-color walls are hung with paintings of the surrounding countryside; 18th-century implements used by the pioneers who settled Zichron; and a terra-cotta floor. The fare includes French-style meat dishes, fish, and seafood; try the marinated calamari heads to start, moving on to selections such as beef fillet, smoked trout, or shrimp with capers and lemon. For dessert, try marzipan parfait or homemade apple pie. ✉ *66 Hameassdim St.,* ☎ *06/639–0728. Reservations essential. Closed Sun. AE, DC, V.*

$$$$ ✕ **Pastoral.** The owner's grandfather headed one of Zichron Ya'akov's founding families. Here, in a little lane off the main street, the family has renovated several buildings, including a 100-year-old prison (now a wine cellar) and an even older tool shed (now Pastoral). The courtyard in front has a small pool and introduces you to the restaurant's theme: roses. They bloom in pots outside, in vases on the tables, and on all of the dishes, tableware, and napkins—it's luscious, and so is the food. Specialties include crab soup, goose liver with cherry-tomato conserve, fillet of steak or mullard (mallard) in honey and mustard. The homemade ice cream is a treat, and the family's own vineyard supplies the grapes for some of the local wines served here. ✉ *56 Hamayesdim St.,* ☎ *06/629–0489. Reservations essential. AE, D, MC, V. Closed Mon.*

$$$$ ✕ **Picciotto.** Not so long ago, Zichron was a sleepy village, and many of its old houses sat shuttered and closed. One of these, on the main street, retains its original wood shutters and warm clay color but has been restored inside. The ceiling is original, made of wood brought from the Carpathian mountains; settlers peer sternly out from photos on the pale-pink walls; and the dishes are ocher-colored pottery decorated with green palm trees. The young chef creates an eclectic menu depending on what's fresh in the market. Choices include quail breast baked with rosemary, calamari with ginger and lemon, or grilled drumfish in a sauce of shallots and butter. Dessert could be chocolate custard or tarte

Tatin with honey and lemon ice cream. ⊠ *41 Hameyasdim St.,* ☎ *06/629–0646. Reservations essential. AE, D, MC, V. Closed Sun.*

$$ ✕ **Hatemaniya shel Santo.** Settle down on this wooden porch, in a courtyard well off the main street, for a tasty and authentic Yemenite meal. There's no menu—the waiter brings you soft pita bread, black bread, and a large, fresh vegetable salad along with a rugged hummus dripped with olive oil. You can order stuffed vegetables or chicken, but make sure you also try the potato cakes and a plate of the small meat patties flavored with cilantro. It's all delicious, and nicely washed down by Yemenite coffee or cold water with lemon and mint. ⊠ *52 Hameysdim St.,* ☎ *06/639–8762. AE, DC, MC, V. Closed Sat.*

## Lodging

$$$$ 🏨 **Baron's Heights and Terraces.** Spread over the hillside on 14 terraced levels, this relatively new hotel was designed with clean, modern geometric lines. The rooms are furnished in pastels with terra-cotta tiles and carpeting, and each has a terrace (with a nice view), a separate living area, and a kitchenette. The specially designed mountain elevator reaches all levels. The pool, which adjoins the large coffee shop, overlooks the sea from the 15th floor. ⊠ *Box 332, Zichron Ya'akov 30900,* ☎ *06/630–0333,* 𝐅𝐀𝐗 *06/630–0325. 154 rooms with bath. Restaurant, bar, café, pool, hot tub, sauna, steam room, exercise room, children's programs. AE, DC, MC, V.*

$$$$ 🏨 **Radisson Moriah Gardens.** This large hotel occupies a mountainside 1 km (½ mi) from Zichron Ya'akov and has stunning views of the Mediterranean coast. Its newest wing, surrounded by trees and gardens, is very large and very contemporary. The public rooms are beautifully furnished with heavy, off-white wooden pieces plumped with seat covers and lots of white pillows dappled with blue, brown, or beige. Polished stone floors set off the modern look. Outdoors, on the terrace, a waterfall splashes down the hill to a pool below. The guest rooms (up 10 steps) are functional rather than fancy, but each has a smashing view. The hotel is designed for conventions, but the common areas are so large and spread-out that crowds are not likely to disturb those traveling independently. ⊠ *1 Etzion St. (at western entrance to Zichron Ya'akov), 30900,* ☎ *06/630–0011,* 𝐅𝐀𝐗 *06/639–7030. 112 rooms with bath. Lobby lounge, pool, massage.*

$$ 🏨 **Bet Daniel.** Set in a verdant park on Mt. Carmel, this guest house was founded in 1938 as a retreat for musicians. Its guests came to include artists and writers, and today it is open to the public. If you place a premium on quiet and charm, you'll love it. The living room boasts a 1905 Steinway and other antiques from England; old photographs hang on the walls; and the library is well stocked with books in German, Yiddish, French, and Hebrew. The rooms in the two 1930s-style stone buildings are newly redecorated. The Summer House has several apartments, each accommodating four guests. If you want to stay here during the biannual chamber-music festival (☞ Arts, *below*), reserve well in advance. Good home cooking is available under various meal-plan options including breakfast, half-board, and full board. ⊠ *Box 13, 30900,* ☎ *06/639–9001,* 𝐅𝐀𝐗 *06/639–7007. 14 rooms, most with bath. V.*

$$ 🏨 **Bet Maimon.** This family-run hotel on the western slopes of Zichron Ya'akov has a spectacular view of the coastal valley and the sea. The terrace restaurant serves both Middle Eastern and Eastern European cuisine. Inquire about the special health-vacation packages. Guests who are less than fit will feel the climb to the sundeck on the roof; the three-story building has no elevator. ⊠ *4 Zahal St., 30900,* ☎ *06/639–0212,* 𝐅𝐀𝐗 *06/639–6547. 22 rooms with bath. Restaurant, hot tub, sauna. DC, MC, V.*

## The Arts

The pastoral musicians' and artists' retreat, Bet Daniel (☎ 06/639–9001) is a perfect setting for the two **chamber-music festivals** held here during Sukkoth and Passover, which generally fall in October and April, respectively. The programs feature open rehearsals and discussions by musicians and teachers as well as alternating afternoon and evening concerts. Between concerts, you can walk around the lovely landscaped grounds, set in the woods with a fine view of Mt. Carmel. Try to reserve a room well in advance if you want to stay at Bet Daniel itself.

# Bat Shlomo

**㉓** *5 km (3 mi) northeast of Zichron Ya'akov on Rte. 4, then Rte. 70 (toward Yokneam).*

Bat Shlomo was established in 1889 and named after the Baron de Rothschild's mother, Betty, daughter of Solomon ("bat Shlomo" in Hebrew). Established for the children of Zichron Ya'akov's farmers, this tiny hamlet failed to grow, and the town remains virtually unchanged. The oldest part of the village has only one street; it's a charming stroll past small, square houses with red-tile roofs, the space between them leaving just enough room for the farmer's horse and wagon. The old synagogue is in the middle of the street. A few of the owners still cultivate the land and sell locally made cheese, olive oil, and honey, much like their forebears. The short walk ends with a dramatic view of vineyards below and, opposite, the lushly forested hill of a nature reserve established by the British in 1941.

# Mukhraka

**㉔** *18 km (11 mi) northeast of Bat Shlomo, on Rte. 70, then Rte. 672. Drive 3 km (2 mi) east on bumpy 672, then turn at sign for Mukhraka.*

Past open, uncultivated fields and a goatherd's rickety shack is the **Carmelite Monastery** at Mukhraka. The monastery stands on the spur of the Carmel range, at an altitude of 1,580 ft, on or near the site where the struggle between Elijah and the priests of Ba'al is believed to have taken place. *Mukhraka* is the Arabic word for a place of burning, referring to the fire that consumed the offering on Elijah's altar. The conflict developed because the people of Israel had been seduced by the pagan cults introduced by King Ahab's wife, Jezebel; Elijah demanded a contest with the priests of Ba'al in which each would erect an altar with a butchered ox as an offering and see which divinity sent down fire. Elijah drenched his altar with water, yet it burst into flames. On his orders, the priests were taken down to the Brook of Kishon and executed.

The stark stone monastery was built in 1883 over Byzantine ruins. Records show that the site was revered as early as the 6th century, when hermits dwelled here. The Carmelites, a Roman Catholic monastic order established in the 13th century, look to Elijah as their role model (Muslims revere Elijah as a prophet). (The courtyard contains a statue of a fearless Elijah brandishing a knife.) The monks who live here have no telephones and only a generator for power. Climb to the roof for an unforgettable panorama: to the east stretches the Jezreel Valley and the hills of Nazareth, Moreh, and Gilboa. On a clear day you can even see Jordan's Gilead Mountains beyond the Jordan River and Mt. Hermon. ☎ *No phone.* ✏ *NIS 1 (28¢).* ⊙ *Mon.–Sat. 8–1:30 and 2:30–5. Closed Sun. after noon mass.*

# Daliyat el Carmel

**㉕** *2 km (1⅓ mi) west of Mukhraka (at junction with Rte. 672).*

Daliyat el Carmel is Israel's largest Druze village. The Druze are a close-knit, Arabic-speaking people who practice a secret religion; they form one of the most intriguing entities in the mosaic of Israel's population (of which they number 2%). So exclusive is this sect that only around 6% of the community is initiated into its religious doctrine, one tenet of which is a belief in reincarnation. The Druze broke away from Islam about 1,000 years ago, believing in the divinity of their founder, al Hakim bi Amir Allah, the Caliph of the Egyptian Fatimid dynasty from AD 996 to 1021. The Druze who live in the two existing villages on Mt. Carmel (the other is Isfiya; ☞ *below*) serve in the Israeli Army, a sign of their loyalty to Israel. Though many of the younger generation wear jeans and T-shirts, some older men and women are easily recognizable in their traditional garb. Head coverings indicate the degree of religious belief, from high white turban (resembling a fez) to white kerchief covering the head and shoulders. Many men sport a bushy, walruslike moustache, a hallmark of the Druze, and some older ones wear flowing dark robes and black pantaloons. Although many women wear Western garments, they retain the diaphanous white headdress, often worn with an embroidered dress.

About 1 km (½ mi) inside town, take a right turn into the marketplace, a colorful jumble of shops lining the street. You can be assured of eating excellent falafel at any of the roadside stands or restaurants.

### Dining

**$$** ✕ **The House of Druze Heritage.** The Druze are famous for their hospitality. Here you get not only a warm welcome and a good, solid meal but a rare look at the Druze way of life. The traditional meal begins with an assortment of appetizers, such as hot-pepper salad, pickles, tahine (sesame paste), and hummus with big, flat Druze pita bread. The main course consists of skewers of grilled lamb, chicken, and steak; baklava and Turkish coffee provide the finishing touch. The museum in the back displays Druze clothing and an intriguing array of farm implements, household objects, handicrafts, and photos. ⌂ 4 Ahat St., ☎ 04/839–3242. AE, D, MC, V. Closed Fri.

### Shopping

Along a brief stretch of the main road that winds through Daliyat el Carmel are shops selling lightweight throw rugs, handwoven baskets, brightly colored pottery, brass dishes, characteristic woven wall hangings, and embroidered skull caps (for men). Bargaining is expected. Some shops close on Friday; the strip is crowded on Saturday.

# Isfiya

**㉖** *1 km (½ mi) north of Daliyat el Carmel on Rte. 672.*

Isfiya is very similar to neighboring Daliyat el Carmel, with flat-roofed homes built closely together into the hillside, many of them raised on pillars and cut with arched windows. Hospitality is second nature to the Druze; you may be able to visit a village home and watch as the woman of the house bakes crispy-thin pita bread in the courtyard, then eat it with yogurt cheese and spices while hearing about Druze life from an ornate sofa in the living room (☞ Guided Tours *in* Northern Coast and Western Galilee A to Z, *below*). As you leave the village, at the top of the hill, note the vista of the Jezreel Valley opening suddenly on your right. The final approach to Haifa also affords a magnificent view of the coast stretching up to Akko, across the bay.

### Dining

**$$$$** ✕ **The Pine Club Restaurant.** Nestled in the woods at the crest of the
★ mountain, the Pine Club is one of this region's finest restaurants.
You'll dine in a glass-enclosed pavilion, where the fireplace is always
well stoked in winter months. Fresh flowers and crisp white linens match
the French-inspired cuisine in elegance. Try the local venison with
sour cherry sauce, or the beef fillet stuffed with goose liver. A new dish:
ostrich with mint sauce. Dessert lovers will like the dark- and white-
chocolate mousse. It's all a 20-minute drive from Haifa's hotel area,
in the direction of the university. ⊠ *Road to Bet Oren (near Damon
Jail),* ☎ *04/832–3568. Reservations essential. AE, DC, MC. Closed
Sun. No lunch weekdays.*

**$$** ✕ **Nof Carmel.** Don't bother to look for an English sign; this Druze
★ restaurant is identifiable by the ubiquitous red Coca-Cola logo. Drive
to the northern edge of the village and it's on your left, encircled by a
picket fence. People come for the fine Middle Eastern fare, especially
the thick homemade hummus with pine nuts or *foule* (a baked broad-
bean concoction seasoned with oil, garlic, and lemon juice), and the
well-seasoned kebab. Those with a sweet tooth will want to sample
the *sahlab* (a warm, custardlike winter drink or pudding of crushed
orchid bulb with thickened milk and sugar, topped with raisins, almonds,
cinnamon, or ginger) or the scale-bending baklava. ⊠ *Rte. 672,* ☎ *04/
839–1718. Reservations not accepted. AE, MC, V.*

## Ein Hod

**㉗** *5 km (3 mi) west of Isfiya.*

To get to the artists' village of Ein Hod, head east straight past the coastal
highway to Route 4, where you turn right. The exit ramp, climbing
through olive trees and scrub, will be on your left. You can also get
there with Bus 921 or 202 from Haifa. Today, Ein Hod is home to around
135 families of sculptors, painters, and other artists. The setting is an
idyllic one, with rough-hewn stone houses built on the hillside with
sweeping views. As the Dadaist painter Marcel Janco (1895–1984) wrote
of the deserted Arab village slated for demolition after his first trip there,
in 1950: "The beauty of the place was staggering." Though the place
was ruled by scorpions and snakes and was without water or electricity,
Janco and a group of 20 artists set up a colony here two years later.

The town square is bordered by a restaurant and a large gallery where
works by present and past Ein Hod artists are exhibited (☞ Shopping,
*below*). Across the street is the **Janco-Dada Museum.** As one of the
founders of the Dada movement, the Romanian-born Janco already
had, of course, a well-established professional reputation when he im-
migrated to Israel in 1941. The museum, which opened in 1983, houses
a permanent collection of works in various media by the artist, reflecting
Janco's output in both Europe and Israel. A 20-minute slide show chron-
icles the life of the artist and the Dada movement. Also exhibited are
works by other Israeli modern artists. Don't miss the view from the
rooftop before leaving. ☎ *04/842350.* ☜ *NIS 6 ($1.70).* ☉ *Sun.–Thurs.
and Sat. 9:30–5, Fri. and holiday eves 9:30–4.*

Back in the square, walk up the stone staircase that skirts the restau-
rant to a ruined building with an old olive press. It leads to the town's
open-air theater where summer concerts are held (☞ Nightlife and the
Arts, *below*). Paths branch off to artists' studios and homes on a lovely
walk along the road that encircles the village.

### Dining

**$$** ✕ **Ein Hod Restaurant.** This rustic place is in the heart of the village.
Seating includes wooden tables beside arched windows and outdoor

settings on a stone patio. House specialties include stuffed vegetables, soups, Greek kebab with pine nuts, and steak with mustard or pepper sauce. You can accompany these with various salads, and top them off with fresh fruit or homemade cakes. ✉ *Main square,* ☎ *04/984–2016. Reservations not accepted. No credit cards.*

### Nightlife and the Arts

Ein Hod's **Gertrud Kraus House** (☎ 04/984–1058), just off the main square, features chamber music on some Saturday evenings at 6:30 between October and June. Admission is NIS 35 ($10), and coffee and cake are on the house.

### Shopping

The best place in this region for quality handicrafts is the **Gallery** (☎ 04/984–2548), on Ein Hod's main square. (You can also buy directly at various workshops.) Arrayed in the front room of the village's official gallery are silver, enamel, and gold jewelry; handblown glass; and ceramic jugs, mugs, and teapots. Three other rooms are devoted to paintings, watercolors, sculptures, and graphic works by resident artists, some of them internationally known. Tourists can ask for a small discount. The gallery is open Sunday–Thursday and Saturday 9:30–5, Friday and holidays 9:30–4. It's 3 km (2 mi) south of Ein Hod, east of Route 4.

The gallery **Silver Print** (☎ 04/984–1067), run by Vivienne and Roy Silver, a four-minute walk from the main square, is devoted to Israeli photography. A subspecialty is greeting cards, some of which are old photos of the Holy Land. The Silvers also sell a map (NIS 20, or $5.70) with a walking tour of Ein Hod, and stickers with photos of the 18 sites along the way. Call ahead for an appointment.

## Nahal Me'arot Nature Reserve

**28** *3 km (2 mi) south of Ein Hod, 1 km (½ mi) east of Rte. 4.*

The prehistoric **Carmel Caves** are located in the Nahal Me'arot Nature Reserve. The three excavated caves are up a steep flight of stairs, on a fossil reef that was covered by the sea 100 million years ago. The first discoveries of prehistoric remains were made when this area was being scoured for stones to build the Haifa port. In the late 1920s, the first archaeological expedition was headed by Dorothy Garrod of England, who received assistance from a British feminist group on condition that the dig be carried out exclusively by women. It was. In the Tannur cave, the first on the tour, the strata Garrod's team excavated are clearly marked, spanning about 150,000 years in the life of early man. The most exciting discovery made in the area was the existence of both Homo sapien and Neanderthal skeletons; evidence that both lived here has raised fascinating questions about the relationship between the two and whether they lived side by side. A display on the daily life of early man as hunter and food gatherer occupies the Gamal cave. The last cave you'll visit, called the Nahal, is the largest—it cuts deep into the mountain—and was actually the first discovered. A burial place with 84 skeletons was found outside the mouth of the cave, where you can see a hunched-up skeleton.

The bone artifacts and stone tools discovered in the Nahal cave suggest that people who settled here, about 12,000 years ago, were the forebears of early farmers with a modified social structure more developed than that of hunters and gatherers. There is also evidence that the Crusaders once used the cave to guard the coastal road. Inside, an audiovisual show sheds light on how early man lived here. There's a snack bar and parking lot at this site. ☎ *04/984–1750 or 04/984–*

1752. ⊟ NIS 15 ($4.30). ☉ *Sun.–Thurs., Sat., and holidays 8–4, Fri.
and holiday eves 8–1.*

### Outdoor Activities and Sports

At the entrance to the Carmel Caves is the stone office of the **Nature
Reserves Authority** (☎ 04/984–1750), where trained staff provide
maps and information about two well-marked nature walks that leave
from this point. The route of the "Botanical Path" takes two hours,
while the "Geological Path" takes 40 minutes; both include specially
built lookout points.

# THROUGH WESTERN GALILEE, FROM AKKO TO ROSH HANIKRA

## Akko

*22 km (13½ mi) north of Haifa.*

Akko—also known as Acre—is an enchanting mixture of mosques, markets, khans (Ottoman inns), and vaulted Crusader ruins (many of
which are underground) at the northern tip of Haifa Bay. You can approach it from Haifa on Route 4. A much slower but far prettier inland route takes you north on Route 70, a scenic drive that runs
roughly parallel to Route 4 about 7 km (4½ mi) to the east, through
rolling hills, avoiding the unattractive industrial pockets and drab
satellite towns of Haifa. Continue north past a small jog in the road
that you'll encounter 10 km (6 mi) ahead. Take Route 85 west some
14 km (9 mi) later to reach Akko's walled Old City, where you'll start
your visit. Plan on at least two hours here, half a day if you want to
see everything.

*Numbers in the margin correspond to points of interest on the Akko
Old City map.*

You approach the **Old City** on Weizman Street, proceeding through a
breach in the surrounding walls. Once inside, park at the Knights
parking lot, where you'll start a walking tour (the circular route brings
you back to your car). Double back a few steps to the entrance of the
Old City at the walls and climb the signposted blue-railing stairway
on your right for a stroll on the **ramparts.** Walking right, you can see
the stunted remains of the 12th-century walls built by the Crusaders,
under whose brief rule—just under two centuries—Akko flourished as
never before or since. The indelible signs of the Crusaders, who made
Akko the main port of their Christian empire, are much more evident
inside the Old City itself.

**29**

The wide wall you are walking on, which girds the northern part of
the town, was built by Ahmed el-Jazzar, the Pasha of Akko, who
added these fortifications following his victory over Napoléon's army
in 1799. With the help of the British fleet, which sunk the French heavy
artillery sent by sea, el-Jazzar turned Napoléon's attempted conquest
into a humiliating rout. Napoléon had dreamed of founding a new Eastern empire, thrusting northward from Akko to Turkey and then seizing India from Great Britain. His defeat at Akko hastened his retreat
to France, thus changing the course of history.

History clings to the stones of old Akko, with each twist and turn along
its warren of streets telling another tale. The city's history begins 4,000
years ago, when Akko was first mentioned in Egyptian writings that
refer to the mound, or tel, northeast of the walls you are standing on.
The Old Testament describes in Judges 1 that after the death of Joshua

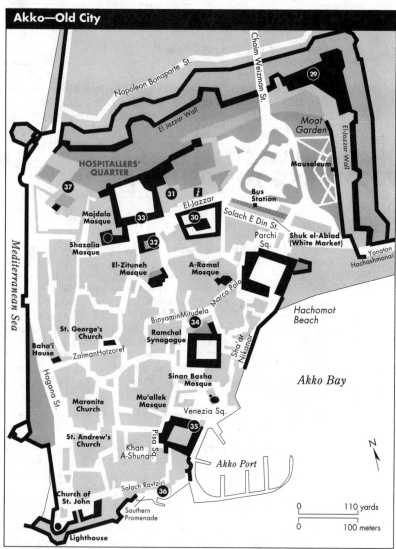

## Akko—Old City

Crusader Vaults
and Halls, **31**

El-Jazzar Mosque, **30**

Khan el-Umdan, **35**

Museum of the
Underground
Prisoners, **37**

Pisan Harbor, **36**

Ramparts, **29**

Refectory, **33**

Souk, **34**

Turkish Bath, **32**

the tribe of Asher was unable to drive the Canaanite inhabitants from Akko and so lived among them there. Akko was a prize worth fighting for throughout the course of history. It had a well-protected harbor, a well-watered and fertile hinterland, and a strategic position on the coastal road that links Egypt and Phoenicia (present-day Lebanon). In the 4th century BC, Akko eclipsed Tyre and Sidon as the principal port of the eastern Mediterranean. Alexander the Great's high regard for Akko is reflected in the fact that in the 3rd century BC he set up a mint in the city; it remained in operation for six centuries. For long periods Akko was a Phoenician city, but when the Hellenistic king Ptolemy II of Egypt gained control of the country in the 2nd century BC, he renamed it Ptolemais, the name it retained through the Roman and Byzantine periods.

Walk around to the guard towers and up an incline just opposite; there's a commanding view of the moat below and Haifa across the bay. Turn around and let your gaze settle on the exotic skyline of Old Akko, the sea-green dome of the great mosque its dominating feature. Walk down the ramp, crossing the **Moat Garden** at the base of the walls, and continue alongside the round arches on the backside of **Shuk el Abiad** (White Market). This market was built by Dahr el-Omar, the Bedouin sheikh who defied Turkish rule and set up his own fiefdom in the Galilee in the 18th century. In 1749 he moved his capital from Tiberias to Akko and rebuilt the walls of the city. Dahr el-Omar's rule here ended more than four centuries of desolation and isolation that had beset Akko after the Mamluks drove the Crusaders out in 1291. He rebuilt the port and also built access roads to the city. Continue along a pedestrian walkway, with a bank on your right.

★ ③ The **El-Jazzar Mosque** is considered one of the most magnificent in Israel. Ahmed el-Jazzar, who succeeded Dahr el-Omar simply by having him assassinated, ruled Akko from 1775 to 1804. During his reign he built this mosque along with other public structures. The Albanian adventurer's cruelty was so legendary that he earned the epithet "the Butcher." (He is buried next to his adopted son in a small white building to the right of the mosque.)

Just beyond the entrance, in the middle of the courtyard, is a pedestal mounted with a marble reproduction of a seal. Engraved with graceful calligraphy, it re-creates the seal of a 19th-century Ottoman sultan. Some of the marble and granite columns that adorn the mosque and courtyard were plundered from the ruins of Caesarea. On your left is the entrance to the underground **reservoir**; the ornate fountain with eight slender columns opposite the entrance to the mosque is used by the faithful for ritual washings of hands and feet. Bordering the courtyard are outbuildings once used as a religious school. Inside the mosque, enshrined in the gallery reserved for women, is a reliquary containing a hair believed to be from the beard of the prophet Muhammad; it is removed only once a year, on the 27th day of Ramadan.

The reservoir dates from the Crusader period and was actually a cathedral until converted into cisterns by Ahmed el-Jazzar. You can traverse the cavernous depths on a wooden walkway (children like this, but do keep an eye on them); the cisterns still fill up with rainwater. The mosque closes five times a day for prayers, so you might have a short wait. Dress modestly. ⊠ *Off El-Jazzar St., opposite entrance to Crusader Vaults and Halls.* 🕾 *NIS 2 (57¢).* ⊘ *Sat.–Thurs. 8–5, Fri. 8–11 and 1–5.*

| | |
|---|---|
| NEED A BREAK? | In the plaza outside the mosque are several outdoor restaurants where you can enjoy a falafel or simply a pita, fresh-squeezed orange juice, or coffee while sunning yourself and watching the world go by. |

**③①** Across from the mosque is the entrance to the **Crusader Vaults and Halls.** Your ticket also gets you into the **Turkish Bath** and **Refectory,** so hang on to it. You can pick up brochures and maps here and make inquiries at the helpful tourist office. There's a post office along one wall.

Here you begin a tour of the 12th-century subterranean city, which unfolds beneath the 18th- and 19th-century buildings you see today. Deep inside, following the arrows past fragments of marble capitals, you arrive in a series of barrel-vaulted rooms known as the **Knights' Halls,** one of which is sometimes used for chamber-music concerts. Six such halls have been discovered thus far. Above this part of the Crusader city stands the Ottoman **citadel,** which you can glimpse from the courtyard. Raised by Dahr el-Omar on the rubble-filled Crusader ruins, the citadel was the highest structure in Akko. It was later converted by the British into a prison (☞ Museum of the Underground Prisoners, *below*). Archaeologists are always busy delving into the mysteries of Akko here, but signs keep you on a safe path.

The Crusaders who conquered Akko in 1104 were led by King Baldwin I and assisted by the Genoese fleet. The port city, which the victorious French Hospitallers, the Knights of St. John, renamed for their patron saint—Jean d'Acre—was the Crusaders' principal link to their homeland. Commerce thrived, and the European maritime powers Genoa, Pisa, Venice, and Marseilles developed separate quarters here. After the disastrous defeat of the Crusader armies at the Horns of Hattin in 1187, Akko surrendered to the victorious Saladin without a fight, but England's Richard the Lionheart recaptured the Crusader stronghold four years later. In the 13th century, after the capture of Jerusalem by the Muslims, Akko became the effective capital of a shrunken Latin kingdom. In its Crusader heyday, Akko had about 40 churches and monasteries and a population of 50,000. Today its residents number 45,000, an ethnic mix of Jews and Arabs.

The seeds of the Crusaders' downfall in Akko were probably sown by the divisive factions within its walls. The Hospitallers and Templars, the so-called fighting monks, also had separate quarters (the Templars, also French, lived near the lighthouse by the western Crusader sea wall). By the mid-13th century, open fighting had broken out between the Venetians and Genoese. When the Mamluks attacked with a vengeance in 1291, the Crusaders' resistance quickly crumbled, and the city's devastation was complete. It subdued the city for centuries, and even today Akko retains a medieval cast. ✉ *Opposite El-Jazzar Mosque,* ☎ *04/991–1764.* 🎫 *Knights' Halls, Turkish baths, and Refectory NIS 15 ($4.30).* ☉ *Oct.–Mar., Sun.–Thurs. 8:30–5, Fri. 8:30–2, Sat. 8–3; Apr.–Sept., Sun.–Thurs. 8:30–7, Fri. 8:30–2, Sat. 8–5.*

**★ ③②** Akko's remarkable **Turkish Bath,** built for Pasha el-Jazzar in 1781, was in use until 1947, when it was damaged by the explosion at the British prison nearby. The bathhouse has been restored to a pristine condition and is slated to become a museum, with displays of copper objects, jewelry, coins, and other artifacts from both the city's collection and the latest archaeological digs. You'll notice colored glass bubbles protruding from the roof domes, sending a filtered green light to the steam rooms below; these skylights were actually made by the same Hebron workshop that made the originals a century ago. The dressing room is decorated with colorful handmade Turkish tiles and topped with a cupola; note the inlaid marble floors. For admission and hours, *see* Vaults and Crusader Halls, *above*.

**③③** The **Refectory** was once known as the Crypt of St. John—before excavation it was erroneously thought to have been an underground chamber. The dimensions of the colossal pillars that support the roof (note that they're girdled with metal bands for extra support) make this one of Israel's most monumental examples of Crusader architecture and one of the oldest Gothic structures in the world. In the right-hand corner opposite the entrance is a fleur-de-lis carved in stone—the crest of the French House of Bourbon—which has led some scholars to postulate that this was the chamber in which Louis VII convened the knights of the realm.

At the wooden stairs descending from the base of one of the columns, there's an opening to an extremely narrow **subterranean passageway.** Cut from stone, this was a secret tunnel that the Crusaders probably used to reach the harbor when besieged by Muslim forces. (Those who are claustrophobic can take an alternate route, which goes back to the entrance of the Turkish bath and continues straight.) You'll emerge to find yourself in the cavernous vaulted halls of the **Posta,** the fortress guardpost, with a 13th-century marble Crusader tombstone and map of the Crusader city at the exit. Go up the stairs to the left and turn right into the covered market, where artisans beat pieces of copper into bas-relief plates and bowls and sell other handcrafted items. Exit to the left.

Continue through a square with the whitewashed El-Zituneh Mosque on your right, and wend your way to the left through the angular streets

**34** to the local **souk** (market). Stalls with artfully arranged heaps of fresh produce alternate with specialty stores: a pastry shop with an astonishing variety of exotic Middle Eastern delicacies; a spice shop filled with the aromas of the East; a bakery with steaming-fresh pita. You'll often see fishermen sitting on doorsteps, intently repairing their lines and nets to the sounds of Arabic music blaring from the open windows above.

NEED A BREAK? | Here in the souk, duck into the **Oudah Brothers Cafe** (☎ 04/991–2013) and enjoy a coffee, hummus, or kebab in the courtyard of the 16th-century Khan el-Faranj, or Franks' Inn. Note the 18th-century Franciscan monastery and tower to your left.

Exiting the Khan el-Faranj from the south, you'll pass the Sinan Basha mosque on your left as you enter Venezia Square, in front of the port.

**35** On your right is the **Khan el-Umdan,** or Inn of the Pillars. Before you visit this Ottoman *khan*—the largest of the four in Akko—and the Pisan Quarter beyond, take a stroll around the port, with its small flotilla of fishing boats, yachts, and sailboats. Then walk through the khan's gate beneath a square clock tower, built at the turn of the century. The khan served vast numbers of merchants and travelers during Akko's golden age of commerce, in the 18th century. The 32 pink-and-gray granite pillars that give it its name are compliments of Ahmed el-Jazzar's raids on Roman Caesarea. There was once a market at the center of the colonnaded courtyard.

**36** You can walk along the sea walls at **Pisan Harbor.** Start at the café perched on high—a great lookout (where boys dive off the rocks into the sea in summer)—and head west in the direction of the 18th-century Church of St. John. You'll end up at the southwestern extremity of Akko, next to the lighthouse. The Templars once occupied this area. Head north along Hagana Street, which runs parallel to the crenellated western sea wall. After five minutes you'll reach the whitewashed, blue-trimmed Baha'i house (not open to the public), where the prophet of the Baha'i religion, Baha'u'llah, spent 12 years of his exile. His burial site is just north of Akko (☞ Baha'i Founder's Shrine and Gardens, *below*).

❸❼ The **Museum of the Underground Prisoners** is housed in several wings of the citadel built by Dahr el-Omar and then amended by Ahmed el-Jazzar in 1785. It became a British prison during the Mandate. On the way in, you pass the citadel's outside wall; the difference between the large Crusader building stones and the smaller Turkish ones above is easy to spot. Prison life is illustrated by the original cells and their meager contents, supplemented by photographs and documents that reconstruct the history of the Jewish resistance to British rule in the 1930s and '40s. During the Mandate, the citadel became a high-security prison whose inmates included top members of Jewish resistance organizations, including Ze'ev Jabotinsky. In 1947 a dramatic prison breakout by leaders of the Irgun captured headlines around the world and provided Leon Uris's novel *Exodus* with one of its most dramatic moments.

As you leave the museum, turn right after 60 ft and follow the massive walls around the northern part of town to the breach at Weizman Street and the parking lot where you entered the Old City. ⊠ *Haganah St. (a few min north of the Lighthouse)*, ☎ *04/991–8264.* ✉ *NIS 7 ($2).* ☉ *Sun.–Thurs. 9–3, Fri. 9–1.*

## Dining

$$$$ ✕ **Uri Buri.** If you're in Akko at mealtime, you're in luck: Uri's famous fish and seafood restaurant was relocated from Nahariya to Akko in the summer of 1998. It's now housed in an old stone Turkish building, with three arches, and one room is furnished in old Arab style, with sofas, copper dishes, and *nargillas* ("water pipes"). Everything on the menu is seasonal, i.e., very fresh, and the fish is steamed, baked, or grilled. Allow some time for a meal here, as it's not your everyday fish fry. Two house specialties are gravlax and Thai-style fish; chowder is another fixture. Look for the restaurant near the lighthouse, on one edge of the coast-side parking lot. ⊠ *93 Hagana St.,* ☎ *04/955–2212. Reservations essential. AE, D, MC, V. Closed Tues.*

$$ ✕ **Abu Christo.** This popular waterfront fish restaurant at the north-
★ ern edge of the Crusader port actually stands at one of the original 18th-century gates built by Pasha Ahmed el-Jazzar when he fortified the city after his victory over Napoléon. A family business opened in 1948 and passed from father to son, Abu Christo serves up the daily catch—often grouper, red snapper, or sea bass—prepared simply, either grilled or deep fried. Shellfish and a selection of grilled meats are also available. The covered patio on the water is idyllic in summer. ⊠ *Crusader Port,* ☎ *04/991–0065. Reservations essential July–Sept. AE, DC, MC, V.*

$$ ✕ **Galileo.** Here you can sit on a terrace alongside the Old City's ancient walls and dine on fresh fish, grilled meats, or Middle Eastern salads. You'll be right on the water in the Pisan Harbor, with nothing but a few ruins and an expanse of blue before you. The view, which often includes young boys diving off the rocks into crashing water below, compensates for the standard fare. ⊠ *Crusader Port,* ☎ *04/991–4610. Reservations essential Fri.–Sat. DC, MC, V.*

## Lodging

$$$ 🛏 **Beit Hava.** Eight kilometers (5 mi) north of Akko, not far from Nahariya (☞ *below*), Beit Hava is a country hotel at Moshav Shavei Zion, a communal settlement founded in 1938 by German Jews. The surrounding countryside invites strolls, as the beach and a 4th-century Byzantine church are a few minutes from your front door. The guest rooms are adequate, nothing fancy; the main attraction is peace and quiet, supplemented by a beautiful beach. If you're coming by public transportation, take Egged Bus 271 or the train from Akko or Haifa; both drop you off within a five-minute walk of the hotel. ⊠ *Box 82, Shavei Zion 25227,* ☎ *04/982–0391,* 𝔽𝔸𝕏 *04/982–0519. 90 rooms with bath. Dining room, pool, 2 tennis courts, baby-sitting. AE, MC, V.*

**$$$** 🏠 **Nes Ammim Guest House.** Founded in 1964, Nes Ammim is an ecumenical Christian settlement of about 90 people, where life and study center on the furthering of mutual respect and tolerance. Lodging options are two: double rooms, or family apartments with fully equipped kitchens. The furnishings are pleasant, and the setting, 10 km (6 mi) north of Akko, is picturesque and rural, providing pastoral views. Guests are invited to chat with members of the community, stroll the grounds, and visit the hothouse, blooming with roses. In the summer, classical music is performed near the large pool (drawing local music lovers as well as guests), often after a barbecue meal. To get here, drive north from Akko on Route 2. ✉ *D.N. Western Galilee, 25225,* ☎ *04/ 995–0000,* 🖷 *04/995–0098. 48 rooms with bath, 13 apartments. Grocery, lounge, pool. AE, D, MC, V.*

**$$$** 🏠 **Palm Beach.** The Palm Beach is on Route 4 just south of Akko— right on the beach, with a fine view of Haifa Bay and the rooftops of the Old City. Guests have access to the facilities of the adjoining country club, which include a pool and a whirlpool bath. Rooms are modest, but all face the sea. ✉ *Rte. 4,* ☎ *04/981–7777,* 🖷 *04/991–0434. 120 rooms with bath. Restaurant, dance club. AE, MC, V.*

## Outdoor Activities and Sports

BEACHES

Just south of the Old City on the Haifa–Akko road is a sandy stretch of municipal beach in Akko Bay, with parking, showers, toilets, and chair rentals. Admission is NIS 7 ($2).

SCUBA DIVING

In Akko's marina is the **Ramy Diving Center** (☎ 04/834–3006 or 052/ 667835). Ramy, a former navy diver, runs the diving school and offers guided dives. The three local dives explore the reef (NIS 140, or $40), the submerged city wall (NIS 105, or $30), and the wreck of an Italian submarine from World War II (NIS 210, or $60). Prices include equipment rental.

## Shopping

**I.E. Dany's Archaeological Galleries** (✉ 13/3 Salah Adin, ☎ 04/981– 3770), in the Old City, is a fascinating place to browse. (It's on your left before the plaza of the El-Jazzar Mosque.) The shop is lined with glass cases whose contents, some more than 4,000 years old, range from ancient coins to small statuary, delicate Roman glass, and urns and pottery. The pieces carry government-issued certificates, and those for sale are officially approved for export. Prices start around $50 and go into the thousands.

# Baha'i Founder's Shrine and Gardens

**㊳** *Rte. 4, 1 km (⅔ mi) north of gas station at northern edge of Akko.*

For the Baha'is, this is the holiest place on earth, the site of the tomb of the faith's prophet and founder, Baha'u'llah (☞ Sights to See *in* Haifa, *above*). First you'll pass the west gate of the gardens, open only to Baha'is. Take the first right (no sign) and continue to the unobtrusive turn, 500 yards up, to the north and main gate. Baha'u'llah lived in the redtile mansion here after he was released from jail in Akko and was buried in the small building next door, now the Shrine of Baha'u'llah. Visitors to the shrine are asked to dress modestly. The gardens and terrace are exquisitely landscaped. ☎ *04/981–2763.* 🎟 *Free.* ☉ *Gardens daily 9–4, tomb Fri.–Mon. 9–noon.*

*En Route*  To the west of the highway, as you travel north, stands a segment of the multitiered aqueduct built by Ahmed el-Jazzar in the late 18th century to carry the sweet waters of the Kabri springs to Akko.

# Lochamei Hageta'ot

**㊲** *2 km (1 mi) north of Akko, 6 km (4 mi) south of Nahariya.*

Kibbutz Lochamei Hageta'ot ("Ghetto Fighters") was founded in 1949 by survivors of the German, Polish, and Lithuanian Jewish ghettos and veterans of the ghetto uprisings against the Nazis. To commemorate their compatriots who perished in the Holocaust, and to perpetuate the memory thereof, the kibbutz members set up a **museum,** which you enter to the right of the main gate. Exhibits include a vast collection of photographs documenting the Warsaw Ghetto and the famous uprising, and halls devoted to different themes, among them Jewish communities before their destruction in the Holocaust; the death camps; and deportations at the hands of the Nazis. You can also see the actual booth in which Adolf Eichmann, architect of the "Final Solution," sat during his Jerusalem trial.

Opened in 1996, **Yad Layeled** (Children's Memorial) a white, cone-shaped building, is dedicated to the memory of the 1½ million children who perished in the Holocaust. It's designed for young visitors, who can begin to comprehend the events of the Holocaust through a series of tableaux and images accompanied by recorded voices, allowing them to identify with individual victims without seeing shocking details. There is a small restaurant on the premises. ☎ *04/995–8080.* ☒ *Free; donation appreciated.* ☉ *Sun.–Thurs. 9–4, Fri. 9–1, Sat. 10–5.*

# Nahariya

**㊵** *8 km (5 mi) north of Akko.*

Nahariya was the first Jewish settlement in the Western Galilee. It was founded in 1934 by German Jews who had fled the Nazis and come to eke out a living by farming. Eventually these pioneers turned from the soil to what they realized was their greatest natural resource—some of the country's best beaches—for a more lucrative livelihood. Thus a popular seaside resort was born. Nahariya's main thoroughfare, Haga'aton Boulevard, was built along the banks of a river, now dried up, lined with shady eucalyptus trees; the town's name comes from *nahar,* the Hebrew word for "river."

Although German was once the language of these streets, you're now just as likely to hear Russian or Amharic (spoken by Ethiopians), and blue-bereted U.N. soldiers from bases to the north are frequent visitors. In July and August, there's dancing in the amphitheater at the mouth of the river, and Israeli stars come out to perform on the beach and in the town square.

The **Byzantine church** has an elaborate, 17-color mosaic floor, discovered in 1964, that depicts peacocks, other birds, hunting scenes, and plants. It was part of what experts consider one of the largest and most beautiful Byzantine churches in the Western Galilee, where Christianity rapidly spread—as in the rest of Israel—from the 4th to the 7th centuries. Call the tourist office (☎ 04/987–9800) to arrange a visit, as the church is not always open. To get here, head east on Haga'aton to Route 4, making a left at the stoplight and then the first right into Yechi'am Street. From here take the third left and then an immediate right onto Bielefeld Street. The church is next to the Katzenelson school. ☒ *Bielefeld St.* ☒ *NIS 2 (70¢).*

### Dining

**$$$** ✕ **Golden River.** Locals consider a meal at this Chinese restaurant a special event. The Asian decor may be standard for Israel, but the authenticity of the cuisine is a pleasant surprise. The stir-fried shrimp with green peppers, onions, and mushrooms in a chili sauce is one of the more distinctive dishes, but the menu also has standbys, such as lemon chicken, batter-fried and covered with a sweet-and-sour lemon sauce; and sautéed chicken on a skewer, smothered in peanut sauce. ⌧ *43 Weizman St., ☎ 04/992–1088. Reservations essential Fri.–Sat. AE, D, MC, V.*

$$ ✕ **Penguin.** This casual, main-street institution opened its doors in 1940, well before the state of Israel was even created. Three generations of the same family work here, and the walls carry enlarged photographs of how the place looked when it was just a hut. Stop off for coffee and cake, or make a meal of fresh spinach blintzes with melted cheese; pasta; hamburger platters; or Chinese dishes. Management swears that the schnitzel gets accolades from Viennese visitors. All main dishes come with salad, rice, french fries, and vegetables. Finish off with a frozen yogurt from the adjacent stand, under the same venerable ownership. ⌧ *31 Haga'aton Blvd., ☎ 04/992–8855. V.*

## Lodging

$$$ ⊞ **Carlton.** The best traditional hotel in town, this centrally located, six-story hotel is blessed with a staff that will go the extra mile. The guest rooms are spacious, and many have sea views or a view of the mountain range rearing up to the northeast. Furnishings are not exceptional, but they're comfortable enough. The La Scala dance club attracts revelers from all over the north with live music in the summer. ⌧ *23 Haga'aton, ☎ 04/992–2211, ⸬ 04/982–3771. 196 rooms with bath. Restaurant, bar, pool, sauna, nightclub, baby-sitting. AE, MC, V.*

$$$ ⊞ **Club Med Arziv.** *Chic alors!* Overhauled in May 1998, this Club Med (Israel's only other is in Eilat) lays claim to one of the most beautiful locations in the country, a gentle rise with the sparkling sea stretching toward the horizon below. The grounds are crowded with flowering bushes and palm trees and include old, stone Turkish-style buildings. Club rules apply: the price includes everything from your straw hut (which sleeps two or three) to excellent food and wine, nightly entertainment, and all sports activities. Special prices are available midweek. The pool is especially lovely—you're looking at the sea as you dip and dive. In the Unusual Perks department, the in-house circus school gives trapeze and juggling lessons. The hotel is 6 km (4 mi) north of Nahariya, near the caves of Rosh Hanikra. ⌧ *Box 34, Achziv, Nahariya, ☎ 03/521–2525 for reservations, 04/982–1203 on site; ⸬ 03/527–1345 for reservations, 04/982–4414 on site. 276 huts. Restaurant, pool, aerobics, archery, basketball, exercise room, jogging, sailing, yoga, bicycles, dance club, children's programs. AE, MC, V.*

$$ ⊞ **Erna.** A bit off the beaten track, this family-owned hotel is nonetheless only a five-minute walk from Nahariya's main beach. The three-story building is unobtrusive from the outside but is spic-and-span and cheerful inside, and the service is solicitous. ⌧ *29 Jabotinsky St., ☎ 04/992–0170, ⸬ 04/992–8917. 26 rooms with bath. Restaurant, bar, baby-sitting. MC, V.*

## Nightlife and the Arts

Nahariya's flashiest disco is **La Scala** (☎ 04/992–2211), which draws the over-thirty crowd for standard dance tunes with a throbbing beat. It's in the passageway just west of the Carlton. The cover charge on Friday is NIS 50 ($14); doors open at 10 PM.

## Outdoor Activities and Sports

BEACHES

Nahariya's public bathing facilities, at **Galei Galil Beach,** just north of Haga'aton Boulevard, are ideal for families and not far from most hotels. Beyond the lovely beach, facilities include an Olympic-size pool, a wading pool and playground for children, and changing rooms and showers, plus a snack bar. In peak season, the beach offers exercise classes early in the morning. The entrance fee is NIS 12 ($3.40) for children.

Beautifully maintained because it's in the Achziv National Park just north of Nahariya, **Achziv Beach** is great for kids, with a protected man-made lagoon, lifeguards, and playground facilities. You can picnic on the grassy slopes or make use of the restaurant. Admission, which is NIS 12 ($3.40), includes the use of showers and toilets. **Betzet Beach,** a bit farther north, is part of a nature reserve and offers abundant vegetation, trees, and the ruins of an ancient olive press. There's a lifeguard on duty in season.

SCUBA DIVING

**Trek Yam Ltd.,** also known as Sea Treks (☎ 04/982–3671 or 04/982–5089), takes scuba divers to explore the Achziv Canyon and the caves at Rosh Hanikra, along the northern coast. The outfit also offers jeep tours and rappelling.

# Rosh Hanikra

**④** *7 km (4½ mi) north of Nahariya.*

The dramatic white cliffs on the coast signal both Israel's border with Lebanon and the sea **grottoes** of Rosh Hanikra. Even before you get in line for the two-minute cable-car ride down to the grottoes, take a moment to absorb the stunning view back down the coast. Still clearly visible is the route of the railway line, now mostly a dirt road, built by the British through the hillside in 1943 to extend the Cairo–Tel Aviv–Haifa line to Beirut. The caves beneath the cliff were sculpted by relentless waves pounding away at the white chalky rock. Footpaths inside the cliff itself lead from one carved-out cave to another, while the sound of waves echoes among the water-sprayed rocky walls. Huge bursts of seawater plunge into pools at your feet (behind protective rails). ☎ 04/985–7109. ☞ *NIS 30 ($8.60).* ☉ *Sun.–Thurs. and Sat. 8:30–4 (July–Aug., 8:30–11 PM); Fri. and holiday eves 8:30–4 (Apr.–June, 8:30–6). Call ahead for winter hrs.*

NEED A BREAK?

The cafeteria perched on top of the Rosh Hanikra cliff may not be a gourmet's dream, but you'd be hard pressed to find a more fabulous view. It's bright and breezy, with a wide range of snacks, drinks, and ice cream as well as hot meals. It's fun to take a photo outside at the sign on the cafeteria wall, which indicates the distance from there to Beirut.

OFF THE BEATEN PATH

**YEHIAM** – This kibbutz, set in a wooded area, has an unusual attraction, the ruins of the medieval **Castle Judin.** The memorial that you pass on the way commemorates the convoy that set out to bring fresh supplies and reinforcements to the besieged kibbutz in Israel's War of Independence, in 1948. Apparently built by the Templars in the late 12th century, Castle Judin was destroyed by the Mamluk sultan Baybars in the 13th century, but its ruins so impressed the 18th-century Bedouin sheikh Dahr el-Omar that he transformed it into a palatial citadel 500 years later. You can see the remains of a large reception hall and mosque, as well as a tower and bathhouse. There are picnic facilities on-site. The site is 12 km (8 mi) east of Nahariya: at Hanita Junction, turn south onto Route 70; then at Kabri Junction, head east 7 km (4½ mi) on Route 89. ☎ 04/985–6004. ☞ *NIS 8 ($2.30).* ☉ *Daily 8–4.*

# NORTHERN COAST AND WESTERN GALILEE A TO Z

## Arriving and Departing

### By Bus

The Egged bus cooperative (☞ Getting Around, *below*) serves the coastal area from Ben-Gurion Airport and from the Jerusalem and Tel Aviv central bus stations. Service to Netanya, Hadera, Zichron Ya'akov, and Haifa from both cities starts before 8 AM and usually ends around 8 PM. A bus leaves Tel Aviv for Haifa every 20 minutes between 5:20 AM and 11 PM. Travel to Caesarea requires a change at Hadera; service from Hadera to Caesarea runs only until 12:30 PM. You must change buses at Haifa to get to Akko and Nahariya. Keep in mind that Egged buses do not operate between late Friday afternoon and Saturday evening (sometimes Sunday morning). One exception is Haifa, where some buses do run on Saturday. For fares and information, call 03/694-8888 (Tel Aviv) or 02/530-4704 (Jerusalem).

### By Car

You can take either Route 2 or Route 4 north along the coast from Tel Aviv to Haifa, continuing on Route 4 all the way up to the Lebanese border. From Jerusalem follow Route 1 to Tel Aviv and then connect through the Ayalon Highway to Herzliya, where you can pick up Route 2.

### By Plane

Most travelers from abroad arrive at **Ben-Gurion International Airport,** at Lod on the outskirts of Tel Aviv. The airport is 105 km (65 mi) from Haifa, about a 90-minute drive. At the airport you can easily catch a bus, sherut taxi, or regular taxi to the north coast. **Haifa Airport** (☎ 04/847-6165), a small airport in the port area, is served by **Arkia Airlines** (☎ 02/585-3440 in Jerusalem, 03/690-2222 in Tel Aviv), which flies into the city from Jerusalem, Tel Aviv, Eilat, and the Dead Sea. Buses connect Haifa Airport with Haifa itself.

### By Ship

Many cruise ships that tour the Mediterranean stop at Haifa. You'll exit the docks area through either Gate 5 or the Passenger and Customs Terminal, depending on whether or not you're required to go through customs. Taxis are usually waiting at the exits. You can catch buses nearby for the central bus station, the Hadar district, and Mt. Carmel.

### By Train

A train line connects Tel Aviv with Netanya, Haifa, and Nahariya, with stops along the way. The trip from Tel Aviv to Haifa takes 90 minutes and costs NIS 19 ($5.15). There is also a fast (one hour) and comfortable direct train from Haifa to Tel Aviv; it runs hourly Sunday–Thursday 6 AM–10 PM (last train from Haifa 7 PM). It's advisable to buy tickets a day in advance, at the **Tel Aviv train station** (✉ Rakevet Zafon [Northern Train Station], 1 Arlozorov, ☎ 03/693-7515). Haifa has two train stations; the main one is **Haifa Bat Gallim,** located at the central bus station (☎ 04/856-4564). The **Netanya train station** is on Ha'Rakevet Road, just east of Route 2 (☎ 09/823470).

## Getting Around

### By Bus

The Egged network will get you just about anywhere in the region. Most buses depart hourly on weekdays. For nationwide information on routes and schedules, call 02/304555, 03/537–5555, or 04/549555, or contact the local bus stations directly: Haifa, 04/549131; Netanya, 09/337052.

## By Car

Driving is probably the most comfortable and convenient way to tour this region, and it allows you to explore some of the more scenic back roads. The distances are short: for example, 29 km (18 mi) from Tel Aviv to Netanya, 22 km (15 mi) from Haifa to Akko, 37 km (23 mi) from Haifa to Zichron Ya'akov.

Traffic gets particularly snarled along the coast at rush hour, especially entering and exiting major cities. The worst times are weekdays after 5 PM and Saturday evenings. Expect gridlock in Haifa's port area during morning and evening rush hours. Even in the best of conditions, Haifa traffic is sluggish, and because of the city's steep layout, streets zigzag up the slope and are difficult to negotiate. Remember to pay attention to Haifa's street signs indicating which streets close on Saturday.

## By Train

The North Coast and Western Galilee is, aside from Tel Aviv and Jerusalem, the one part of Israel with rail service. You can reach many of the region's main cities and towns by train, including Netanya, Hadera, Benyamina, Zichron Ya'akov, Haifa, Atlit, Akko, and Nahariya.

Haifa has Israel's only subway system: the six-station Carmelit subway runs from Hanassi Avenue in Central Carmel to Kikar Paris in the port area in six minutes. The fare is NIS 3.50 ($1), and the train operates Sunday–Thursday 6 AM–10 PM, Friday 6–3, and Saturday 7 PM–midnight.

# Contacts & Resources

## Car Rentals

**Haifa: Avis,** ✉ 7 Ben-Gurion St., ☎ 04/513050; **Budget,** ✉ 46 Histadrut St., ☎ 04/842–4004; **Eldan,** ✉ 95 Hanassi Ave., ☎ 04/837–5303; **Hertz,** ✉ 33 Histadrut St., ☎ 04/840–2127; **Reliable,** ✉ 33 Histadrut St., ☎ 04/842–2832. **Nahariya: Budget,** ✉ 62 Weizman St., ☎ 04/992–9252. **Netanya: Avis,** ✉ 1 Ussishkin St., ☎ 09/833–1619; **Budget,** ✉ 2 Gad Machness, ☎ 09/861–4711; **Eldan,** ✉ 2 Gad Machness, ☎ 09/861–6982; **Hertz,** ✉ 8 Ha'atzmaut Sq., ☎ 09/828890.

## Consulate

**Haifa:** Jonathan Freidland, **U.S. Consular Agent,** ✉ *Ben-Gurion Blvd., German Colony,* ☎ *04853–1446.* ⊙ *Sun.–Thurs. 9–1.*

## Emergencies

AMBULANCE

**Akko:** ☎ 101 (Magen David Adom) or 04/991–2333; **Haifa:** ☎ 101; **Nahariya:** ☎ 101 or 04/823332; **Netanya:** ☎ 101.

HOSPITALS

**Carmel,** ☎ 04/825–0211; **Haifa:** Rambam, ☎ 04/854–3111; **Nahariya:** Western Galilee Regional Hospital, ☎ 04/985–0766; **Netanya:** Laniado Hospital, ☎ 09/860–4666.

POLICE

**Akko:** ☎ 100; **Haifa:** ☎ 100; **Nahariya:** ☎ 100 or 04/992–0344; **Netanya:** ☎ 100.

## Guided Tours

GENERAL INTEREST

You can usually arrange to be picked up at your hotel for any of the following tours.

**Egged Tours** offers a one-day bus trip from Tel Aviv or Netanya that takes in Caesarea and Akko and goes north to Rosh Hanikra. The cost is NIS 227.50 ($65), and the tour departs Sunday, Wednesday, and Friday at 8 AM. You can reserve in Tel Aviv (☎ 03/527–1212) or Netanya (☎ 09/860–6206). For departures from Haifa call ☎ 04/854–9486.

For those in a hurry, Egged gives a half-day tour that follows the Western Coast to Nahariya, goes north to Rosh Hanikra, and visits Akko on the way back. It departs on Sunday, Wednesday, and Friday and costs NIS 96 ($32).

A **United Tours** excursion from either Tel Aviv or Netanya takes you to Caesarea, an observation point in Haifa, and Rosh Hanikra; the return trip stops at Akko to see the Crusader city, the Arab market, and the mosque. This one-day tour costs NIS 217 ($62) and leaves at 8 AM on Wednesday, Friday, and Sunday from the Tel Aviv train station. Contact United Tours in Tel Aviv (☎ 03/693–3412 or 03/522–2008).

The **National Diamond Center** offers a free half-day tour to Netanya from Tel Aviv, driving through the coastal Sharon Valley, visiting a kibbutz, and then visiting the center itself, where you'll see diamonds polished and set. Call 04/522–1081 to arrange for pickup in Tel Aviv or Herzliya. Departures are daily (except Saturday) between 9:15 and 10; the bus returns at about 2 PM.

From April through November, Israel's **Society for the Protection of Nature** (SPNI) sponsors two-day excursions along the Mediterranean coast and into the Carmel mountains. The tour, which costs NIS 385 ($110), leaves at 11:30 AM from Tel Aviv at the SPNI office (✉ 3 Ha'shfela St., ☎ 03/638–8673 or 03/638–8677); call for schedule of days. Participants can swim at Dor beach, explore the ancient tel (man-made mound of layers of civilization) nearby, bird-watch at Kibbutz Ma'agan Michael, hike Mt. Carmel, and visit the Carmel Caves. Accommodations are in a field-study center, which is a bit like a youth hostel; breakfast and dinner are included.

The **Haifa Tourist Board** (☎ 04/853–5606) conducts a free 2½-hour walking tour that departs on Saturday at 10 AM from the corner of Yefe Nof (Panorama Rd.) and Sha'ar Ha'levanon streets. The itinerary generally includes the Mane' Katz Museum and the Baha'i Shrine and ends at Haifa Museum, but it may change slightly; call ahead to confirm.

### BOAT TOURS

**Carmelit** (☎ 04/841–8765) offers boat tours of Haifa Bay from Magan Hadayag, beside the airport. The ride lasts one hour and costs NIS 16 ($4.50). Call ahead for departure times. From Akko's Crusader port, the *Princess of Akko* ferry makes a 40-minute jaunt around the bay (☎ 04/991–0606), setting out whenever the boat fills up, year-round. The cost is NIS 15 ($4). From Nahariya, **Trek Yam** (☎ 04/982–3671 or 04/982–5089) takes you on a 40-minute ride up the coast in a high-speed motorboat, the *Tornado,* for NIS 60 ($17.20).

### DRUZE HOSPITALITY

For an ethnic adventure in a Druze village in the Carmel, call **El Carmel** (☎ 04/839–0412 or 052/645100) and ask Amit to make the arrangements. You'll be invited into a private home, usually one with a courtyard where pita bread is baked over a traditional stove; and the head of the house will discuss the distinctive life of the Druze. The cost is $21.50 with lunch, $16 without.

### PERSONAL GUIDES

Caesarea resident and authorized tour guide **Illana Berger** (☎ 06/636–3936) provides an upbeat 2½-hour walking tour through Caesarea for $50. Haifa-based **Mitzpe Tours** (☎ 04/867–4341) offers guided tours in a private car or limousine, custom-tailored for individuals or small groups.

## Taxis

**Akko: Akko Zafon,** ☎ 04/981–6666. **Haifa: Carmel-Ahuza,** ☎ 04/838–2727; **Mercaz Mitzpe,** ☎ 04/866–2525. **Nahariya: Kefarim,** ☎ 04/992–3333; **Hasharon,** ☎ 09/833–3338.

## Travel Agencies

**Akko: Shefi Tours,** ✉ 37 Ha'Arba'a St., ☎ 04/991–2730. **Haifa: Histour,** ✉ 6 Derech Hayam, ☎ 04/836–2696. **Nahariya: Ler Tours,** ✉ 19 Ha'Ga'aton Blvd., ☎ 04/982–5636. **Netanya: Atlas Tours,** ✉ 29 Herzl St., ☎ 09834–5183.

## Visitor Information

The following towns have tourist offices:

➤ AKKO: The **Tourist Information Office** (✉ El Jazzar St., just inside Knights Hall, opposite mosque, ☎ 04/991–1764) is open Sunday–Thursday 9–5 (9–6 in winter), Friday 9–2.

➤ HAIFA: The **Haifa Tourist Board** (✉ 48 Ben-Gurion Blvd., German Colony, ☎ 04/853–5606) is open Sunday–Thursday 8–4; a second office, at the Central Bus Station (✉ Haganah Blvd., ☎ 04/851–2208), is open Sunday–Thursday 9:30–4:30, Friday 9:30–2.

➤ NAHARIYA: The **Tourist Information Office** (✉ 19 Ga'aton Blvd., ☎ 04/987–9800) is open Sunday–Thursday 9–1 and 4–7, Friday 9–1.

➤ NETANYA: The **Tourist Information Office** (✉ Next to amphitheater on Ha'atzmaut Sq., ☎ 09/882–7286) is open Sunday–Thursday 8:30–6 (8:30–4:30 in winter), Friday 9–noon.

➤ ZICHRON YA'AKOV: The **tourist office** (✉ Next to central bus station, Gidonim, ☎ 06/639–8811) is open Sunday–Thursday 9–1, Friday 9–noon.

# 6 Lower Galilee

*Including Nazareth, Tiberias, and the Sea of Galilee*

*Nowhere does the Bible resonate more powerfully than in this land of soft cultivated valleys, rocky hills, and the freshwater Sea of Galilee. The Jezreel Valley is the land of Deborah, Gideon, King Saul, and Elijah. Nazareth and the Sea of Galilee are rich with significance for the Christian pilgrim. Yet this is also a region of parks, one of Israel's most popular playgrounds.*

By Mike Rogoff

**T**O MOST ISRAELIS, THE GALILEE is synonymous with "the North," a land of mountains and fertile valleys, nature reserves and national parks. In short, they would claim, it's a great place to visit, but they wouldn't want to live there: it's provincial, rustic, and remote. Although much of the wild scenery associated with the North—rugged highlands, waterfalls, and panoramas that seem to go on forever—is in the Upper Galilee, the Lower Galilee has its own quiet beauty, varied landscape, and, more than anything else, rich history.

On a map, the Lower Galilee fits into a frame about 50 km (31 mi) square, divided into valleys, hill country, and the Sea of Galilee. To the south is the fertile Jezreel Valley, known in Hebrew simply as *Ha'emek*—the Valley—and sentimentally, if not scientifically, perceived by many Israelis as distinct from the rest of the Lower Galilee. To the east, the boundaries are easily defined by the Jordan Valley and the eastern shore of the Sea of Galilee (the *Kinneret* in Hebrew). To the north, the steep hillsides above the lake merge into the Upper Galilee, while Route 85 west follows the Bet Hakerem Valley, the natural division between the two regions. Toward the Mediterranean Sea, the hills flatten out as you reach the coastal plain; Route 70 follows the region's western edge. Farming forms the economic base: fruit orchards; fishponds; field crops such as wheat and cotton in the valleys; olive groves in the hills; livestock everywhere. The valley towns of Afula and Bet She'an are little more than small, nondescript rural centers, while the larger hill town of Nazareth, the region's automotive-service center, has more character—a noisy clash of pistons and politics. Tiberias, on the Sea of Galilee, depends on tourism for its livelihood, but its location is more impressive than the town itself.

Ancient history abounds here. In the Jezreel Valley, filled with Old Testament lore, you come face-to-face with the land of Deborah, Gideon, King Saul and Jonathan, King Solomon, the prophet Elijah, Ahab and Jezebel. After the Assyrian devastation of the northern kingdom of Israel in the 8th century BC, the region declined as the stream of history was diverted elsewhere; but in the late Roman and Byzantine periods (1st century BC–6th century AD), the vibrancy and wealth returned. The magnificent city of Scythopolis/Bet She'an, the opulent spa of Hammat Gader, the exquisite mosaics of Hammat Tiberias and Zippori, and the synagogues of Bet Alfa and Capernaum all illustrate this period.

For Christian pilgrims, of course, there is nothing more compelling than exploring the landscape where Jesus of Nazareth lived, walked, and forged his ministry. Although Nazareth and Cana play crucial roles in the Gospel stories, it is the Sea of Galilee and the many biblical sites near its shores that have the most powerful resonance. Here Jesus called his disciples, wrought miracles, cured the sick, and taught the multitudes.

But the Galilee is not all ancient history. Twentieth-century Jewish pioneers first tamed hostile ground here, draining malarial swamps and clearing boulders to transform the region into some of Israel's richest farmland. Here, too, they invented a new way of living together in perfect equality—the kibbutz. Travelers in the Galilee should take the opportunity to visit a kibbutz settlement and one of the handful of small museums exploring this uniquely Israeli social experiment.

The region's *kibbutzim* and a smaller number of *moshavim* (Jewish family-farm settlements) are concentrated in the Jezreel and Jordan valleys and around the Sea of Galilee. The rockier hill country is predominantly Arab (*Israeli* Arab; this is not disputed territory). Although

# In case you want to see the world.

At American Express, we're here to make your journey a smooth one. So we have over 1,700 travel service locations in over 120 countries ready to help. What else would you expect from the world's largest travel agency?

do more ®

http://www.americanexpress.com/travel

Travel

# In case you want to be welcomed there.

We're here to see that you're always welcomed at establishments everywhere. That's why millions of people carry the American Express® Card – for peace of mind, confidence, and security, around the world or just around the corner.

do more

Cards

# In case you're running low.

We're here to help with more than 118,000 Express Cash locations around the world. In order to enroll, just call American Express before you start your vacation.

do more

**Express Cash**

# And just in case.

We're here with American Express® Travelers Cheques and Cheques *for Two*.® They're the safest way to carry money on your vacation and the surest way to get a refund, practically anywhere, anytime.

Another way we help you...

do more

**Travelers Cheques**

Arabs and other Arabic-speaking minorities are only 19% of Israel's general population, they were long the majority in the Galilee. The demographics have shifted over time, however, so that half a dozen small Jewish towns and several dozen rural villages have brought the two communities to numeric parity; and the enmities of the 1940s have yielded to a pragmatic and often even amicable modus vivendi.

Whatever your agenda in the Lower Galilee, take time to savor the region's natural beauty. Follow a hiking trail above the Sea of Galilee or drive up to Belvoir, a mountaintop Crusader fortress; wade through fields of rare irises in the spring; bathe in warm mineral spas and spring-fed swimming pools; water-ski on the lake; canoe on the Jordan River; or slip down a water slide.

Culture and entertainment are not this region's strong suits. A number of annual festivals and other events are the highlights. Tiberias's pubs and restaurants probably come closest to providing lively nightlife; but there are worse ways to spend an evening than sitting by a moon-lit lake washing down a good St. Peter's fish, lamb *shishlik* (grilled skewered meat), or a Chinese meal with an excellent Israeli wine.

## Pleasures and Pastimes

### Biblical History
Biblical echoes are what make the Lower Galilee unique. The Jezreel Valley is saturated with Old Testament sites; and the hill country and, especially, the Sea of Galilee witnessed the beginnings of the ministry of Jesus and are second only to Jerusalem in its importance to the Christian story.

### Dining
Tiberias is the center of gravity for Lower Galilee tourism, so it's here that you'll find the better restaurants. St. Peter's fish (also known as tilapia) is a regional specialty. With only a few exceptions, the restaurants en route are cafeterias or forgettable local eateries, some very good, but all places to grab a meal rather than dine out. Restaurant attire, even at dinner, is strictly casual.

| CATEGORY | COST* |
|---|---|
| $$$$ | over $35 |
| $$$ | $22–$35 |
| $$ | $12–$22 |
| $ | under $12 |

*per person for a three-course meal, excluding drinks and 10% service charge*

### Festivals
Ein Gev, on the eastern shore of the Sea of Galilee, has an eclectic Israeli-music festival in the spring. The Misgav area, at the region's western edge, is even more eclectic: small and larger events alike take place during the week of Passover in a widespread series of venues, the better to encourage the Israeli public to mix their music with some sightseeing. Bet She'an has revived its ancient Roman theater for a short series of events in May, and in early July, Jacob's Ladder—the annual national folk festival—fills the air above Kibbutz Ha'on, on the Sea of Galilee with the traditional folk and country music of the British Isles and North America.

### Lodging
Tiberias, the region's tourist center, has a large number of hotels for every budget, from deluxe (though not top-drawer) to moderate—and even cheaper hostelries for those traveling on a shoestring. Within a radius of 20 to 30 minutes' drive from Tiberias are a number of ex-

cellent motel-type guest houses, some run by kibbutzim and some on the shore of the Sea of Galilee itself. A few of these also rent out cheaper huts or small mobile homes called caravans, with access to the same facilities as the better accommodations.

Nazareth has a few inexpensive hotels (not all recommended) that cater primarily to organized Christian pilgrim groups and attract few individual travelers. Tiberias, just 45 minutes away, has far more to offer after hours. Also in Nazareth, and to a lesser extent around Tiberias, are a number of hospices run by one or another Christian denomination or order (in the Holy Land, a hospice is a hotel for pilgrims, not a facility for the ill; some are good or interesting enough to attract general traffic as well).

Bed-and-breakfasts have sprung up in such profusion in recent years that it's hard to keep track of them. Many are in or adjacent to private homes in rural farming communities; others are within kibbutzim, where the collective has renovated older buildings, creating units with a kitchenette and a bath. These are usually good values for the money, especially for families.

The Sea of Galilee is a magnet for Israeli vacationers, especially during the two major Jewish-holiday seasons: Passover (March–April) and the High Holidays and Sukkoth (September–October). Because they're based on the Hebrew lunar calendar, the dates of these holidays shift from year to year; be sure to verify the dates before you decide when *not* to stay in the area. The weather is normally great during these periods, but everything is crowded, and rates soar. Some hotels charge high-season rates for part of the summer and during the week of Christmas. Some hotels raise weekend rates substantially.

Youth hostels are not what they used to be. Gone are the days of 10 people stuffed into a room with iron beds and communal showers. The Youth Hostel Association has seriously upgraded its facilities (including five in this region alone), with many hostels offering suite-type arrangements suitable for families. These are generally the cheapest deals around.

| CATEGORY | COST* |
|---|---|
| $$$$ | over $200 |
| $$$ | $120–$200 |
| $$ | $60–$120 |
| $ | under $60 |

*All prices are for a standard double room, including breakfast and 15% service charge.*

## Swimming and Water Sports

The Jezreel Valley has two fine pools (one actually a river) in national parks with delightful natural surroundings. The Sea of Galilee—really a freshwater lake—is a refreshing but rocky place for a swim. You can recline on pleasant commercial beaches with shaded lawns, facilities, cafeterias, and the occasional water park, or on free beaches with minimal facilities, particularly south of Tiberias. Serious swimmers may enjoy the internationally recognized Kinneret Swim, in September.

At several locations around the Sea of Galilee you can hire pedal boats, rowboats, kayaks, and motorboats, and arrange to water-ski. Very serious kayakers convene for an annual international competition in March. Water slides, some of which resemble extraterrestrial life-forms, are now available at some of the private beaches just south of Tiberias and some of the beaches on the northeastern shore, north of Ein Gev.

## Walking, Jogging, and Running

Two annual Tza'adot (Big Walks; *Tza'adah* is a Big Walk) take place in March or April, one along the shore of the Sea of Galilee (with distances from 3 km, or 2 mi, to 20 km, or 12½ mi), the other along the trails of Mt. Gilboa (11 km, or 7 mi). These mass scenic rambles attract folks from all over the country. A promenade suitable for jogging follows the lakeshore for about 5 km (3 mi) from Tiberias south. Dedicated runners might want to participate in the Sea of Galilee Marathon and Half-Marathon, which take place in December or January. A triathlon takes place at the beginning of May.

# Exploring the Lower Galilee

The Lower Galilee embraces three distinct subregions: the Jezreel and Jordan valleys, which traverse the southern part of the region from Mt. Carmel, in the west, to the Jordanian border, in the east; Nazareth and the rugged hill country north of the Jezreel Valley and west of the Sea of Galilee; and the Sea of Galilee itself.

The Jezreel Valley is most easily entered from the Mediterranean coast by Route 65 (the Wadi Ara Pass), which runs northeast from Caesarea. From Jerusalem, you're more likely to come up the Jordan Valley and begin exploring the area from the east. You'll find echoes of Old Testament stories throughout the area, but the most compelling attractions include fine natural sites as well as archaeological ones.

The hill country is permeated with the history of the New Testament, but it still defies a simple label. Olive groves dominate the landscape like scriptural illustrations. You can cover this whole area comfortably in a day if you time it right. If your itinerary includes the drive between Nazareth or Zippori and Akko, on the Mediterranean coast, and you aren't pressed for time or hampered by impending nightfall, consider a scenic return route from the Nazareth end of Route 79 west, 784 north (just west of the Hamovil Junction), and then west again from Karmiel on 85.

The third part of this chapter takes you clockwise along the shores of the entire Sea of Galilee starting at Tiberias, the main town. The shores are covered with sites hallowed by Christian tradition, but there are also important ancient synagogues at Capernaum and Hammat Tiberias, and Tiberias itself is one of Judaism's four holy cities. Those whose interests lie elsewhere will find plenty of ways to relax in, on, and around the water.

*Numbers in the text correspond to numbers in the margin and on the Lower Galilee map.*

## Great Itineraries

It's possible to get a feeling for this region in a few days, but you may want to expand your trip to include some highlights of the Upper Galilee and the Golan (☞ Chapter 7).

IF YOU HAVE 2 DAYS

Use Tiberias or the Sea of Galilee region as a base. Explore the archaeological excavations of **Megiddo** ① and/or **Bet She'an** ⑥ on the way into or out of the area. In hot weather, take a dip at Gan Hashelosha (Sachne). Visit the Church of the Annunciation in **Nazareth** ⑨ and the fine mosaics of **Zippori** ⑪, nearby. A Christian itinerary might also include **Mt. Tabor** ⑫ and **Yardenit** ㉑, on the Jordan River. For a more general approach, visit the ancient synagogue mosaics of **Bet Alfa** ⑤ or **Hammat Tiberias** ㉓, the Crusader fortress of **Belvoir** ⑦, and the **cemetery of Kibbutz Kinneret** ㉒. (The sequence will be determined by the

**Lower Galilee**

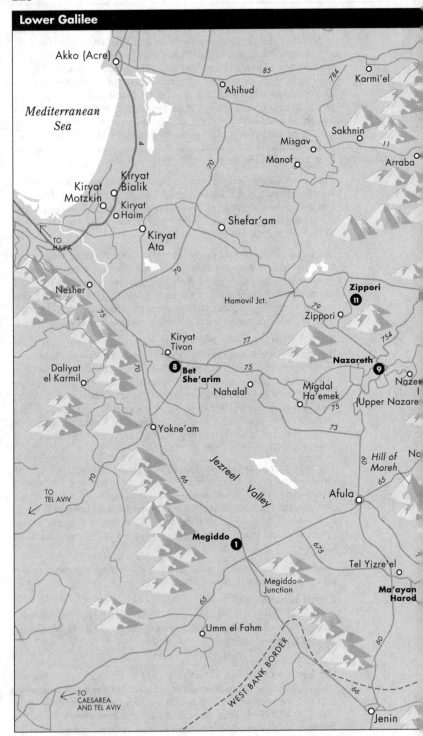

*Mediterranean Sea*

Akko (Acre)

Ahihud

Karmi'el

85

784

Misgav

Sakhnin

11

Manof

Arraba

Kiryat Bialik

Kiryat Motzkin

Kiryat Haim

Kiryat Ata

70

Shefar'am

Zippori **11**

Zippori

79

TO HAIFA

4

70

Hamovil Jct.

Nesher

75

754

Kiryat Tivon

77

Nazareth **9**

NazE

(Upper Nazare

Daliyat el Karmil

70

**8** Bet She'arim

75

Nahalal

Migdal Ha'emek

75

Yokne'am

73

TO TEL AVIV

70

66

*Jezreel Valley*

Hill of Moreh

Nc

65

Afula

**Megiddo 1**

675

Tel Yizre'el

Megiddo Junction

65

**Ma'ayan Harod**

60

Umm el Fahm

TO CAESAREA AND TEL AVIV

66

WEST BANK BORDER

Jenin

TO ZFAT (SAFED)

TO UPPER GALILEE

Maghar

85

8277

Jordan R.

Jordan R. Park

87

87

869

92

Almagar

**Mount of Beatitudes** 15

**Tabgha** 16

Capernaum

17

Eilabun

65

**Ginosar** 14

Migdal

Ramot

Arbel

Kursi 18

789

Lavi

7717

90

18

Turan

11

**Tiberias** 13

Sea of Galilee (Lake Kinneret)

Ein Gev

98

Golani Junction

65

867

**Hammat Tiberias** 23

GOLAN HEIGHTS

ana

Kafr Kamma

767

Cemetery of Kibbutz Kinneret 22

Ha'on

N. Yarmuk

**Mt. Tabor** 12

Yavne'el

**Yardenit** 21

20

Ma'agan

Shibli

7266

Kfar Tavor

Afikim

**Degania Alef**

98

**Hammat Gader** 19

Dovrat

90

Gesher

Ma'ad

717

**Belvoir** 7

JORDAN

Moledet

**Kibbutz Ein Harod (Me'uchad)** 4

Gidona

Waqqas

Hefziba

**Bet Alfa** 5

Gan Hashelosha/ Sachne

Marhaba

57

Ma'aleh Gilboa

6666

**Bet She'an** 6

**Mt. Gilboa** 2

669

TO JERUSALEM

Jordan R.

**KEY**

- - - - Ferry

N

0          5 miles

0          5 km

direction from which you enter the region: from Jerusalem via the Jordan Valley or from the Mediterranean coast.)

If you want to concentrate on Christian sights, spend the second day around the Sea of Galilee. Join a boat ride, admire the ancient boat at **Ginosar** ⑭, contemplate the multiplication of the loaves and fishes at **Tabgha** ⑯, eat St. Peter's fish near the water, explore the ruins of **Capernaum** ⑰, and end the day in the panoramic tranquillity of the **Mount of Beatitudes** ⑮. For a more general experience, ascend the Golan Heights via **Hammat Gader** ⑲ for a spectacular view, and in the Upper Galilee explore the nature reserves of Banias and Tel Dan (with a trout lunch along one of the rivers) or the synagogues and cobblestone lanes of Zfat (☞ Chapter 7).

IF YOU HAVE 3 OR MORE DAYS

Spend the first day in the Jezreel Valley, including **Megiddo** ①, visiting the scenic attractions of **Mt. Gilboa** ②–⑤, **Bet She'an** ⑥, and, time permitting, either the catacombs of **Bet She'arim** ⑧, in the west, the Crusader castle of **Belvoir** ⑦, in the east, or the church and fine views atop **Mt. Tabor** ⑫. Stay overnight in 🕾 **Tiberias** or one of the kibbutz guest houses in the Galilee. (The sequence of the following days will be determined to some extent by where you stay.)

The Christian explorer should spend the second day around the Sea of Galilee (☞ If You Have 2 Days, *above*). On the morning of the third day, drive up to Banias and Caesarea Philippi, in the Upper Galilee (☞ Chapter 7), and then head south via the Church of the Annunciation in **Nazareth** ⑨ and the mosaics of ancient **Zippori** ⑪. A more general approach might include a more leisurely outdoor exploration of the Golan Heights and Upper Galilee on the second day (eat some trout, go boating, or inner-tube the Jordan River in season; ☞ Chapter 7). On the third day, explore the old synagogues and artists' quarter of the mystical mountaintop city of Zfat, in the Upper Galilee, and **Nazareth** ⑨ and **Zippori** ⑪ on the way south.

## When to Tour the Lower Galilee

By far the best time to tour the Galilee (and Israel in general) is the spring—March, April, and early May—when the weather is usually excellent (though March is a bit less reliable) and the countryside is blanketed with wildflowers. At 700 ft below sea level, the Sea of Galilee region is very hot in summer. Avoid the week of Passover, when half the country is vacationing exactly where you are; weekends in general (Thursday night through Saturday night) are more crowded as well. Autumn—late September, October, early November—is fine, though the Jewish holidays bring crowds and high-season prices. Most panoramas are better in the afternoon, when the sunlight is gentler.

# JEZREEL AND JORDAN VALLEYS

"Highways of the world cross Galilee in all directions," wrote the eminent Victorian scholar George Adam Smith in 1898. The great international highway of antiquity, the Via Maris (Way of the Sea), swept up the Mediterranean coast from Egypt and broke inland along three separate mountain passes to emerge in the Jezreel Valley before continuing northeast to Damascus and Mesopotamia. The west–east through road that began at the Mediterranean coast just north of Mt. Carmel and led to the Jordan Valley (at Bet She'an) ran through the Jezreel Valley as well. And then, as now, roads connected the valley with the hill country of the Galilee, to the north, and Samaria, to the south. Its destiny as a kind of universal thoroughfare and its flat terrain made the Jezreel Valley a frequent and easy battleground, so much so that the Book of Revelation identified it—by the name Armageddon—as the stage for humanity's apocalyptic finale.

On a topographical map, the Jezreel Valley appears as an inverted equilateral triangle, each side about 40 km (25 mi) long, edged by low mountains. The narrow Harod Valley extends the Jezreel southeast to Bet She'an, in the Jordan Rift. Your first impression will be one of lush farmland as far as the eye can see, but as recently as 50 years ago, malarial swamps still blighted the area; some early pioneering settlements had cemeteries before their first buildings were completed. Today the valley is one of Israel's most fertile regions.

The sights in this section are covered from west to east (though they can easily be explored in the reverse order). Begin with the ancient city of Megiddo; continue via Tel Jezreel and a clutch of diverse attractions on or near Mt. Gilboa; go through the famous dig at Bet She'an; and end (if time permits!) at the glorious Crusader castle of Belvoir, overlooking the Jordan River. There are no fewer than six national parks here, making the Israel Nature Parks Protection Authority's monthly pass (☞ Nature Reserves and Parks *in* the Gold Guide) a worthwhile investment. Most people spend less than a day in these valleys, but a more leisurely pace will pay off.

With one notable exception, restaurants in this rustic area are confined to roadside cafeterias; lunch-only places next to archaeological sites and parks such as Megiddo and Sachne/Gan Hashelosha; and small restaurants and snack bars in the towns of Afula (especially) and Bet She'an.

# Megiddo

★ ❶ *2 km (1¼ mi) north of the Megiddo Junction, where Rtes. 65 and 66 meet; 12 km (7½ mi) west of Afula.*

Since the beginning of the 20th century, several archaeological expeditions have exposed no fewer than 25 strata of civilization—from the 4th millennium BC to the 4th century BC—in the historical urban layer cake (known to archaeologists as a *tel*) of Megiddo. The ancient city owed its great importance to its strategic position at the mouth of a pass, the main branch of the international highway between Egypt and Mesopotamia. Pharaohs and Assyrian satraps rushed their armies up and down these passes on their way to attack the other, and Megiddo's coveted location made it as much a target for foreign conquest as it was the center of power of its own small region.

A tiny museum at the site's entrance offers some good visual aids, including maps, a video, and a model of the tel itself. There is an unremarkable cafeteria.

The ramp up to the flattop mound brings you through the partially restored remains of a Late Canaanite (Late Bronze Age) **gate,** quite possibly the very one that unsuccessfully defended Megiddo against the Egyptian pharaoh Thutmose III in 1468 BC, as described in his victory stele. Above this is a larger and later gate, almost identical to those found at Hazor, in the north, and Gezer, to the south. Long identified with King Solomon (10th century BC)—the three cities were his regional military centers—the gate has been redated by some scholars to the time of Ahab, king of Israel a century later.

Evidence has indicated prehistoric habitation here as well, but among the earliest remains of the *city* of Megiddo are a round **altar** dating from the Early Bronze Age and the outlines of several Early Bronze Age **temples,** almost 5,000 years old, visible in the trench between the two fine lookout points.

The connection to King Ahab (9th century) is strong at Megiddo. Ruins of **stables,** also once thought to have been Solomon's, are now definitively dated to the reign of Ahab, who is known to have had a large chariot army. But nothing else at Megiddo is as impressive as the **water system.** Before its construction (again apparently by Ahab), residents had to leave the safety of the city walls to draw water from the subterranean spring. In a masterful stroke, the Israelite engineers dug a deep shaft and a horizontal tunnel through solid rock to reach the spring from within the city. With this access, the spring could be permanently blocked outside the defensive walls, securing the city's vital water supply. The spring, at the end of the tunnel, is no more than a trickle today, perhaps blocked by earthquakes of later centuries. As you descend 180 steps through the shaft, traverse the 65-yard-long tunnel under the ancient city wall, and climb up 83 steps at the other end, look for chisel marks and ancient steps hewed from the rock. A 10-minute walk takes you back to the parking lot.

The Jezreel Valley has so often heard the clash of arms that the very name of the site that commands it—Har Megiddo, Mt. Megiddo, or Armageddon (Revelation 16)—has become synonymous with the final cataclysmic battle of all time. In 1918, General Allenby swept up the pass by way of Megiddo to outflank the Ottoman Turks and seal the British victory; he was subsequently elevated to the peerage, taking as his title Viscount of Megiddo. ⊠ *National Park, Rte. 66,* ☎ *06/652–2105 or 06/652–6815.* ▨ *NIS 17 ($4.90).* ☉ *Apr.–Sept., Sat.–Thurs. 8–5, Fri. and holiday eves 8–4; Oct.–Mar., Sat.–Thurs. 8–4, Fri. and holiday eves 8–3; water tunnel closes 30 min before rest of site.*

### Shopping
A small **jewelry shop** at Megiddo (☎ 06/642–0314) specializes in handsome and reasonably priced silver and gold items, many made in nearby Kibbutz Megiddo. The jewelry that incorporates pieces of ancient Roman glass is particularly attractive.

*En Route*   From the Afula road (Route 65), Route 675 breaks southeast through a small farming region called the Ta'anach. On the left, 500 yards beyond the intersection with Route 60 and just after the entrance to Kibbutz Yizre'el, is the low-rise **Tel Yizre'el,** site of the Old Testament city of Jezreel. A short dirt road leads to a rise with a small thicket of trees. Here Ahab coveted Naboth's vineyard (I Kings 21), and his Phoenician wife, Jezebel, met the gruesome death predicted by the prophet Elijah (II Kings 9). From among the indecipherable ancient ruins recently unearthed by a Tel Aviv University expedition, you have a magnificent view of the valley below and a great place to sit and read those biblical passages.

Five hundred yards farther, on the right, the scenic Route 667 strikes up through the pine forests of Mt. Gilboa, eventually descending to Route 669 just east of Bet Alfa.

## Mt. Gilboa

★ ❷   *17 km (10½ mi) from Megiddo (on Rte. 675) to Rte. 667, descending via Rte. 6666 to Rte. 69, just east of Bet Alfa.*

Mt. Gilboa—actually a small, steep mountain range rather than a single peak—is geographically a spur of the far greater Samaria Range (the biblical Mt. Ephraim) to the southwest. Literally half the mountain is freshly reforested with evergreens, while the other half is left in its pristine rockiness; environmentalists prefer the latter, as it protects the profusion of wildflowers that splatter the slopes with color every March and April. From the gravel parking area off Route 667 on the summit of the ridge, easy and well-marked trails wind through the natural habitat of the rare black (actually purple) iris, which draws hordes of Israelis every spring to pay homage to Mother Nature. Years of tireless efforts by environmental groups, such as the Society for the Protection of Nature in Israel (SPNI), have paid off, to the extent that preschoolers will tell you imperiously that you are not allowed to pick the wildflowers! The views of the valley below and the hills of Galilee beyond are great year-round, but on a good winter or spring day they're amazing, reaching as far as the snowcapped Mt. Hermon, far to the north. Afternoon is the best time to come.

The view isn't the only attraction, however. Three thousand years ago, the Israelites were routed by the Philistines on Mt. Gilboa, and Saul, the mortally wounded Israelite king, took his own life on the battlefield. "On the morrow, when the Philistines came to strip the slain, they found Saul and his three sons fallen on Mt. Gilboa. And they cut off his head, and stripped off his armor, and sent messengers throughout the land of the Philistines to carry the good news to their idols and the people . . . and they fastened his body to the wall of Beth-shan"—thus the Bible (I Samuel 31) describes the aftermath of the debacle. The battle was presumably fought on the mountain's lower slopes, as the upper reaches are too craggy and steep; but from a vantage point on the crest, you can easily conjure up the din of a battle beneath you. Saul's death sowed panic in the ranks, and the Israelites "forsook their cities and fled; and the Philistines came and dwelt in them." In his lyrical eulogy, king-to-be David curses the battlefield—"Let there be no dew or rain upon you"—where "thy glory, O Israel" was slain (II Samuel 1).

❸ **Ma'ayan Harod** (the Spring of Harod), at the foot of Mt. Gilboa, is a small national park with an attractive spread of lawns, huge eucalyptus trees, and a big swimming pool fed by a spring. Today it's a bucolic picnic spot, but almost 3,200 years ago, Gideon, the reluctant hero of the biblical Book of Judges, organized his troops to fight the Midianite desert invaders: "And the camp of Midian was north of them, by the Hill of Moreh, in the valley" (Judges 7). At God's command—in order to emphasize the miraculous nature of the coming victory—Gideon dismissed more than two-thirds of the warriors, and by selecting only those who lapped up water from the spring "as a dog laps," further reduced the army to a tiny force of 300. Equipped with swords, ram's horns, and flaming torches concealed in clay jars, the army divided into three companies and surrounded the Midianite camp across the valley in the middle of the night. At a prearranged signal, the Israelite warriors shouted, blew the ram's horns, and smashed the jars. Waking to the commotion and the sudden appearance of flaming torches, the Midianites were panicked into flight, and the victory was won.

The spring has seen other armies in other ages. It was here in 1260 that the Mamluks stopped the invasion of the hitherto invincible Mongols. And in the 1930s, the woods above the spring hid clandestine Jewish self-defense squads training under British army officer Orde Wingate. Wingate died in the Burmese jungle in 1944, but his trainees, among them Moshe Dayan and Yigal Allon, became top military commanders of the fledgling State of Israel in 1948, when Wingate's principles of unconventional warfare served them well. ⊠ *National Park off Rte. 71, next to Gidona,* ☎ *06/653–2211.* ⊑ *NIS 22 ($6.30).* ☉ *Apr.– Sept., Sat.–Thurs. 8–5, Fri. and holiday eves 8–4; Oct.–Mar., Sat.– Thurs. 8–4, Fri. and holiday eves 8–3.*

❹ **Kibbutz Ein Harod (Me'uchad),** across the highway from Mt. Gilboa, has an **art museum** with a permanent collection that showcases Jewish artists past and present. Temporary exhibits are more general,

spanning cultures and genres. Don't confuse the place with its immediate neighbor to the west, Kibbutz Ein Harod (Ichud).

Also on the kibbutz is **Bet Sturman,** a museum of the region's natural
history (stuffed and preserved specimens) and human settlement. ✉
*Rte. 71 opposite gas station,* ☎ *06/653–1670 art museum; 06/653–
3284 Bet Sturman.* ✆ *Art museum NIS 12 ($3.50); Bet Sturman NIS
14 ($4).* ☽ *Bet Sturman Sun.–Thurs. 8–4, Sat. and holidays 10–2 (last
entry 1 hr before closing) Art museum Sun.–Thurs. 8–4:30, Fri. and
holiday eves 8–1:30, Sat. 10–4:30. A video in English is included. An
English-speaking guide can sometimes be arranged; call ahead.*

NEED A
BREAK?

The **Gan Hashelosha** National Park (✉ Off Rte. 669, ☎ 06/658–
6219), commonly known as Sachne, has won international recognition
for its natural beauty. The name, Gan Hashelosha—the Garden of the
Three—remembers three Jewish pioneers killed here by a land mine in
1938. The park is developed around a warm spring (28°C, or 82°F,
most of the year) and a deep stream (actually a small river deep enough
to dive into at spots, with artificial cascades in others). Admission is NIS
22 ($6.30). Facilities include changing rooms for bathers, a decent
snack bar at the west end, and a good cafeteria at the east end. In
good weather, the park is especially crowded on Friday and Saturday.
Don't leave your possessions unattended on the lawns.

❺ The ancient synagogue of **Bet Alfa** was accidentally discovered in 1928
by members of Kibbutz Hefziba who were digging an irrigation trench
(some say serendipity is the best archaeologist). Their tools hit a hard
surface, and careful excavation uncovered a lovely, multicolored **mosaic floor,** almost entirely preserved. The art is somewhat childlike, but
that, too, is part of its charm. An Aramaic inscription dates the building to the reign of Byzantine emperor Justinian, in the second quarter
of the 6th century AD; a Greek inscription credits the workmanship to
one Marianos and his son, Aninas. In keeping with Jewish tradition, the
synagogue faces Jerusalem, with an apse at the far end to hold the
holy ark. The building faithfully copies the architecture of the Byzantine basilicas of the day, with a nave and two side aisles; and the doors
lead to a small narthex and an erstwhile outdoor atrium. Stairs indicate a onetime upper story.

The large mosaic in the nave is divided into three panels. The top one
leaves no doubt that the building was a synagogue, as all the classic
Jewish symbols are here: the holy ark flanked by lions; the *menorah,*
a seven-branch candelabra; the ram's horn, called a *shofar;* the incense
shovel once used in the Temple; and the *lulav* and *etrog,* the palm frond
and citron used in the celebration of Sukkoth, the Feast of Tabernacles. The middle panel, however, is the most interesting: it's filled with
human figures depicting the seasons, the zodiac, and—even more in-
credibly for a Jewish house of worship—the Greek sun god, Helios.
Clearly these were more liberal times theologically; perhaps the prohibition on making graven images didn't apply to two-dimensional art
then. Most scholars agree that the mosaic's motifs do not suggest a di-
vergent Jewish sect or regional apostasy but a convenient artistic convention to symbolize the orderly cycles of the universe, since the
Creator himself could not be represented graphically. The last panel
tells the story of Abraham's near sacrifice of his son Isaac (Genesis 22),
again captioned in Hebrew. Take the time to watch the lighthearted
but informative film. ✉ *National Park on Kibbutz Hefziba, Rte. 669,*
☎ *06/653–2004.* ✆ *NIS 8 ($2.30).* ☽ *Apr.–Sept., Sat.–Thurs. 8–5,
Fri. and holiday eves 8–4; Oct.–Mar., Sat.–Thurs. 8–4, Fri. and holiday eves 8–3.*

## Dining and Lodging

**$$–$$$** ✕ **Herb Farm on Mt. Gilboa.** The sweeping view of the Jezreel Valley
★ from the wooden deck or the picture windows is reason enough to come
here, but this restaurant glories in the myriad tastes of fresh herbs (25
in use at any one time) and good produce. The homemade bread and
spreads and the "salad basket" of flavorful cold appetizers make delicious basic starters, but you can also branch out to smoked salmon
mousse and a chives crepe stuffed with chicken liver. Entrées include
the excellent tart, a pie of shallots, forest mushrooms, and goat cheese;
or ostrich breast stuffed with smoked goose liver and *kashkeval* cheese
and served with a pesto sauce. The less adventurous palate can choose
from a good selection of steak and other grilled meats and several fish
and pasta dishes. For dessert, agonize between tiramisu, hot apple cake,
and crème brûlée. ⊠ *Rte. 667,* ☎ *06/653–1093. Reservations essential for Sat. lunch. AE, DC, MC, V. Closed Sun.*

**$–$$** 🏠 **Hankin Youth Hostel.** "Youth" is a misnomer at this lodging in
Ma'ayan Harod National Park (next to the hamlet of Gidona, at the
foot of Mt. Gilboa); all are welcome. Mini-apartments sleep six; 20
"caravans" (cheaply built mobile homes) sleep four, with two more sleeping nine. All units are air-conditioned, but conditions are functional
and furnishings spartan. The surroundings—the pines and eucalypti
of Mt. Gilboa and the park—are a compensation. July and August rates
are slightly higher but include both breakfast and dinner. ⊠ *Ma'ayan
Harod National Park off Rte. 71, M.P. Gilboa 19120,* ☎ FAX *06/653–
1660. 146 beds (including 8 mini-apartments and 22 caravans, all with
private shower). Dining room. AE, DC, MC, V.*

## Outdoor Activities and Sports

### KITE FLYING

The **Janusz Korczak Kite-Flying Competition** is an annual event at
Ma'ayan Harod, drawing contestants from throughout Israel and
abroad. The less serious kite flier can buy a kite on the spot, or join a
kite-building workshop. The event is named after the great Polish-Jewish
educator, who visited the nearby kibbutz in the 1920s and subsequently perished in the Holocaust. The event takes place during the
week of Sukkoth, usually in October. For details, contact Hagilboa Community Centers (⊠ M.P. Gilboa 18120, ☎ 06/653–3242, FAX 06/653–
3362).

### WALKING

The annual **Gilboa Big Walk** (Tza'adat Hagilboa in Hebrew) takes place
in March and follows an 11-km (7-mi) route along Mt. Gilboa. Transportation to the starting point is provided from Ma'ayan Harod. The
views are delightful, and the weather, though still unstable in this season, can be superb. For details, contact Hagilboa Community Centers
(⊠ M.P. Gilboa 18120, ☎ 06/653–3242, FAX 06/653–3362).

# Bet She'an

★ ❻ *23 km (14 mi) east of Afula, 39 km (24 mi) south of Tiberias.*

"The hottest archaeological dig in Israel" is what many have dubbed
Bet She'an over the last decade or so. At the intersection of the Jordan
and Jezreel valleys and surrounded by farming settlements and fishponds, the town has one spectacular site and no other attractions. Once
in town, follow signs to the National Park or the Roman theater. The
theater was exposed more than 30 years ago, but the rest of the great
Roman-Byzantine city of Scythopolis, as the city was known in antiquity,
came to light only in the current excavations and partial restoration.

The high tel dominating the site to the north was the location of
**Canaanite/Israelite Bet She'an** three to four thousand years ago. There

is no visible evidence of the partial excavation undertaken by a University of Pennsylvania group in the 1920s, but a team of Israeli archaeologists is now working on this most ancient area. The climb to the top, though a bit strenuous, is short and worth every gasp. There is a fine panoramic view of the surrounding valleys and a superb bird's-eye view of the entire excavated area.

The impressive, semicircular **Roman theater** was built of contrasting black basalt and white limestone blocks around AD 200, when Scythopolis was at its height. Although the upper *cavea*, or tier, has not survived, the theater is the best preserved and largest in Israel, with an estimated original capacity of some 10,000 people. The large stage and part of the *scaena* (backdrop) behind it have been restored, and Bet She'an again hosts late-spring performances as in days of yore (☞ Nightlife and the Arts, *below*).

Until 1985, when the current excavations of the nearly 30-acre site began, the theater was ignored by most travelers in favor of the more famous one at Caesarea (☞ Chapter 5). Now, it's the jewel in the crown of one of Israel's most extensive and fascinating digs. The expedition has systematically exposed the downtown area of one of the region's greatest and most cosmopolitan cities during the Late Roman and Byzantine periods (2nd–6th centuries AD). Masterfully engineered colonnaded main streets, complete with storm drains and lined with shops, converge on a central plaza that once boasted a fine temple, a decorative fountain, and a public monument. An elaborate Byzantine bathhouse, covering 1¼ acres in area and built with *caldaria* (steam rooms) and mosaic-floored porticoes, once pampered the town's worthies. And the enormous haul of marble statuary and friezes says much about the opulence of Scythopolis in its heyday. One of the most interesting finds was a multicolored mosaic floor in a small room near the ancient *odeon* (a small auditorium for chamber music), showing Tyche (Fortuna), Greek goddess of good fortune, holding a cornucopia. Although a lack of funds has so far prevented extending the excavations to other parts of the town, restoration of what has already been unearthed continues.

On the main thoroughfare, Sha'ul Hamelech (King Saul) Street (a few hundred yards east of Bank Leumi), are the impressive remains of Scythopolis's **amphitheater,** where blood sports and gladiatorial combats were once the order of the day. ✉ *National Park off Sha'ul Hamelech St., at Bank Leumi,* ☎ *06/658–7189.* 🎟 *NIS 17 ($4.90).* ☉ *Apr.–Sept., Sat.–Thurs. 8–5, Fri. and holiday eves 8–4; Oct.–Mar., Sat.–Thurs. 8–4, Fri. and holiday eves 8–3.*

### Nightlife and the Arts

**Gesher Leshalom** (Bridge to Peace; ☎ 06/658–5349, 🖷 06/658–4761) is the name of the arts festival that enlivens Bet She'an each May. The emphasis is on large-scale mainstream productions featuring international artists—opera, modern dance, ballet, classical and choral ensembles. The main venue is the marvelous Roman theater, but secondary locations throughout the town spotlight local talents in street theater, folk dancing, children's programs, and so on.

## Belvoir

❼   *Rte. 717; turnoff 12 km (7½ mi) north of Bet She'an; continue 5 km (3 mi) to site. The road from Ein Harod via Moledet is passable but in very bad condition in places.*

The Crusaders chose their site well: Belvoir, they called it—"beautiful view"—and it was the most invincible fortress in the land. The Hebrew name Kochav Hayarden (the star of the Jordan) and the Arabic Kaukab el Hauwa (the star of the wind) merely underscore the splendid isolation. The breathtaking view of the Jordan River Valley and southern Sea of Galilee, some 1,800 ft below you, is worth the drive by itself (it's best in the afternoon).

The mighty castle was completed by the Hospitallers (the Knights of St. John) in 1173. In the summer of 1187 the Crusader armies were crushed by the Arabs under Saladin at the Horns of Hattin, west of Tiberias, bringing to an end the Latin Kingdom of Jerusalem. Their remnants struggled on to Tyre (in modern Lebanon), but Belvoir alone refused to yield; 18 months of siege brought the Muslims no further than undermining the outer eastern rampart. The Crusaders, for their part, even sallied out from time to time to battle the enemy, but their lone resistance had become pointless. They struck a deal with Saladin and surrendered the stronghold in exchange for free passage, flags flying, to Tyre.

Don't follow the arrows from the parking lot; instead, take the wide gravel path to the right of the fortress. This brings you right to the panoramic view, and the best spot from which to appreciate the strength of the stronghold, with its deep, dry moat, massive rock and cut-stone ramparts, and series of gates. Once inside the main courtyard, you are unexpectedly faced with a fortress within a fortress, a scaled-down replica of the outer defenses. It's little wonder the Muslims could not force its submission. Not much remains of the upper stories; in 1220, the Muslims systematically dismantled Belvoir, fearing another Crusade and the renewal of the fortress as a Frankish base. Once you've explored the modest buildings, exit over the western bridge (once a drawbridge) and spy on the postern gates (the protected and sometimes secret back doors of medieval castles). ✉ *National Park, Rte. 717, 5 km (3 mi) west of Rte. 90,* ☎ *06/658–1766.* ✑ *NIS 13 ($3.80).* ☯ *Apr.–Sept., Sat.–Thurs. 8–5, Fri. and holiday eves 8–4; Oct.–Mar., Sat.–Thurs. 8–4, Fri. and holiday eves 8–3.*

# NAZARETH AND THE GALILEE HILLS

Remove the modern roads and power lines, and the landscape of this region is an illustration of the Bible. Unplanned villages are splashed seemingly haphazardly on the hillsides, freeing the valleys for small-scale agriculture. Acres of olive groves, the source of the region's wealth in antiquity, are still harvested by whacking the trees. New Testament settings abound here: Nazareth, where Jesus grew up; Cana, with its miraculous wedding feast; Mt. Tabor, identified with the Transfiguration; and more. Jewish history resonates strongly, too: Tabor and Yodefat were fortifications in the Great Revolt against the Romans (1st century AD); Shefar'am, Bet She'arim, and Zippori were in turn the headquarters of the Sanhedrin, the Jewish high court, between the 2nd and 4th centuries AD; and latter-day Jewish pioneers, attracted to the region's wild scenery, put down roots where their ancestors farmed. Our suggested route reflects the area's diversity, moving from the catacombs of Bet She'arim to Nazareth, Cana, and Zippori and detouring to Mt. Tabor before descending to Tiberias and the Sea of Galilee.

## Bet She'arim

❽ *20 km (12½ mi) southeast of Haifa, 25 km (15½ mi) west of Nazareth.*

The chalk slopes are honeycombed with catacombs around the attractively landscaped site of ancient Bet She'arim. A Jewish town flourished here after (and to some extent because of) the eclipse of Jerusalem.

The little that was left of Jerusalem after Titus's legions sacked it and razed the Second Temple in AD 70 was plowed under by Hadrian in AD 135, following the Second Revolt (known as Bar Kochba) of the Jews against Rome. Hadrian built in its stead the pagan town of Aelia Capitolina, and the Jews were denied access to their holy city and the venerated burial ground of the Mount of Olives for generations. The center of Jewish life and religious authority retreated first to Yavne, in the southern coastal plain, and then for several centuries to the Lower Galilee.

By around AD 200 the unofficial Jewish capital had shifted to Bet She'arim, a city that owed its brief preeminence to the enormous stature of one man who chose to make it his home: Rabbi Yehuda Hanassi, the Patriarch—or, as he's sometimes called, the Prince. The title was conferred on the nominal leader of the Jewish community, who was responsible both for its inner workings and for its relations with its Roman masters. Alone among his contemporaries, Yehuda Hanassi brought to his dual office both a worldly understanding of the ways of diplomacy (he was a personal friend of one of the emperors, possibly Marcus Aurelius) and an awesome reputation as the foremost Jewish religious scholar and spiritual leader of his day.

The rabbi eventually moved east to Zippori (☞ *below*) because of its more salubrious climate, and there he gathered the great Jewish sages of his day and compiled the Mishnah, which remains the definitive interpretation of biblical precepts for religious Jews. Nonetheless, it was in his hometown of Bet She'arim that Yehuda Hanassi was finally laid to rest.

If Bet She'arim was a magnet for scholars and petitioners in Yehuda Hanassi's lifetime, it became a virtual shrine after his death. With Jerusalem still off-limits, Bet She'arim became the most prestigious burial site in the Jewish world. It was considered a privilege and good after-life insurance to be buried in the company of *rabenu hakadosh* (our holy teacher)—for when the Messiah came, surely the rabbi would be one of the first resurrected to accompany the Messiah to Jerusalem. Bet She'arim's prominence lasted until AD 352, when Gallus destroyed the town in suppression of yet another Jewish revolt.

Two major expeditions in the 1930s and '50s uncovered a huge series of 20 **catacombs.** The largest of these is open to the public, with 24 chambers containing more than 200 stone sarcophagi and *arcosolia* (arched burial niches). A wide range of both Jewish and Roman symbols are carved into the sarcophagi, and more than 250 funerary inscriptions in Greek, Hebrew, Aramaic, and Palmyrene throughout the site testify to the great distances some people traveled—from Yemen and Mesopotamia, for instance—to be buried here. Without exception, the sarcophagi were plundered over the centuries by grave robbers seeking the possessions with which the dead were interred.

The tiny but interesting **museum** next to the catacombs (closed for renovation at press time) includes a relic of Bet She'arim's industrial activity: a 9-ton slab of raw, unfinished glass, the largest such artifact from the ancient world. ⊠ *Follow the signs in Kiryat Tivon, off Rte. 75 or 722,* ☎ *04/983–1643.* ⊠ *NIS 13 ($3.80).* ⊙ *Apr.–Sept., Sat.– Thurs. 8–5, Fri. and holiday eves 8–4; Oct.–Mar., Sat.–Thurs. 8–4, Fri. and holiday eves 8–3.*

# Nazareth

★ ❾ *30 km (19 mi) east of Bet She'arim; about 56 km (35 mi) east of Haifa; 15 km (9½ mi) north of Afula.*

The Nazareth where Jesus grew up was an insignificant village nestling in a hollow in the Galilean hills. Today's city of 70,000 has burst out of the hollow with almost frenetic energy. It's a slightly bemusing and dissonant experience for the Christian pilgrim who seeks the spiritual Nazareth among the horn-blowing cars, vendors, and donkeys (at least *they* add some scriptural authenticity!) plying Paulus VI Street. The scene is hardly quieter even on Friday, the holy day of the Muslim half of the Arab population, but it calms down somewhat on Wednesday afternoon, when many businesses close for a midweek sabbatical; and on Sunday, the day of rest for the Christians who make up the other half of the town, it's positively placid. If you're out for local color (and traffic jams), come on Saturday, when Arab peasants come to town to sell produce and buy goods and Jewish families from the surrounding area come looking for bargains in the *souk* (market).

If you're coming from Bet She'arim, Route 77 breaks off to the north— to Zippori, the Golani Junction, and Tiberias. Route 75 skirts the north side of the picturesque Jezreel Valley as it climbs into the hills toward Nazareth; at the crest of the hill, it's joined by Route 60 from Afula. A turn to the left takes you down to Paulus VI, Nazareth's main drag.

The Franciscan **Church of the Annunciation,** the largest church in the Middle East, dominates the lower part of the town. Consecrated in 1969, it enshrines the Roman Catholic belief that the angel Gabriel visited Mary here to announce that she would be the mother of Jesus. (Casa Nova Street climbs steeply to the entrance of the church. Parking is hard to find here; try Paulus VI Street, in the direction of the Galilee Hotel.)

The artwork in and around the church is eclectic in the extreme, but the more interesting for it. The portico around the courtyard just inside the main gate is decorated with striking contemporary mosaics, most depicting the Madonna and Child, donated by Catholic communities around the world. Many carry the names of their countries of origin; for others you must rely on the script (such as Korean or Gaelic) or the artistic style (such as Thai) to tell you the provenance.

The main entrance of the church is marked by massive bronze doors, made in Germany, that relate in bronze relief the central events of Jesus' life. Here you can enter the dimly lighted **lower church,** with its brilliant, abstract stained-glass windows. The focal point of the entire church is the **grotto,** a small, sunken cave dwelling. The New Testament (Luke 1) relates, "The angel Gabriel was sent from God to a city of Galilee named Nazareth, to a virgin. . . and the virgin's name was Mary. And he came to her and said, 'Hail, O favored one, the Lord is with you! . . . And behold, you will conceive in your womb and bear a son, and you shall call his name Jesus.' " This event is known to Christians as the Annunciation, and Roman Catholic tradition identifies the grotto as the former home of Mary and the place where the angel appeared to her. A seating area before the cave is surrounded by a fence with a gate, opened only for groups of pilgrims holding prearranged masses. If you're on your own, you may be able to dart in and out as groups arrive and depart. Crusader-era walls still stand beneath the modern windows, and there are some restored Byzantine mosaics below the railings from which you view the grotto.

Just inside the entrance, a spiral staircase leads to the vast **upper church,** some 70 yards long and 30 yards wide, the parish church of Nazareth's Roman Catholic community. Note that the beautiful Italian ceramic reliefs on the huge concrete pillars representing the stations of the cross are captioned in the Arabic vernacular. The cupola, which soars 195 ft above the grotto of the lower church (seen down through a well), is formed by ribs representing the petals of an upside-down lily chalice rooted in heaven. The lily, a symbol of purity, represents Mary's unblemished nature, and the petals are repeatedly inscribed with the letter M. The huge, Italian-designed mosaic behind the altar shows Jesus and Peter at the center and an enthroned Mary behind them, flanked by figures of the hierarchical church (to your right) and the charismatic church (to your left). The modern concrete trusses over the nave evoke the wooden roofs of the early Christian basilicas.

On the walls of the upper church are the so-called banners, large panels of mosaics and ceramic reliefs contributed by Roman Catholic communities abroad. Among the countries represented are the United States (a piece inspired by Revelation 12:1–2), Canada (a fine terracotta), England, and Australia. Particularly interesting are the Madonna and Child gifts from Japan (made with gold leaf and real pearls), Venezuela (a carved-wood statue), and Cameroon (a stylized painting in black, white, and brick red). In the courtyard, a glass-enclosed baptistery is built over what is thought to have been an ancient *mikveh,* a Jewish ritual immersion bath.

In the same complex as the Church of the Annunciation is the small **Church of St. Joseph,** just past Terra Sancta College, built over a complex of rock-hewn chambers traditionally identified as the workshop of Joseph the Carpenter. ⊠ *Casa Nova St.,* ☎ *06/657–2501.* 🎫 *Free.* ☉ *Apr.–Sept., Mon.–Sat. 8:30–11:45 and 2–5:45, Sun. 2–5:30; Oct.–Mar., Mon.–Sat. 8:30–11:45 and 2–4:30, Sun. 2–4:30.*

The **souk,** which you enter a few yards down Casa Nova Street from the exit of the Church of the Annunciation, is full of kitchenware, live chickens, and cassette tapes of Egyptian pop singer Oum Kultom (not religious souvenirs and ethnic trinkets, which you'll find around the lower part of Casa Nova Street and on Paulus VI Street, where the tour buses park). It's fun to poke around; one person's kitchenware is another's curio. The souk has been significantly renovated, and is now clean and attractive; but the city fathers' vow to create a real, bazaar-type tourist attraction in time for the year 2000—and the presumed influx of pilgrims celebrating Christianity's bimillennium—has yet to be realized.

Pilgrims occasionally seek the so-called **Synagogue Church,** clearly marked on the right side of the souk's main thoroughfare. The site belongs to the Melkites (Greek Catholics), who, the Franciscans complain, took it by force in the 18th century. The building, though old, was never a synagogue but rather a church built on the traditional site of the synagogue to which Jesus came "on the Sabbath day. And he stood up to read; and here was given to him the book of the prophet Isaiah" (Luke 4). Jesus selected a prophetic passage that, according to Christian tradition, he himself was destined to fulfill. His rendition apparently pleased his listeners, but his interpretation did not, and they drove him out of town. If the building is locked, ask for the key at the apartment upstairs (you'll be expected to leave something in the collection box).

NEED A
BREAK?

Try the Arab pastries at the **Mahroum** confectionery, at the corner of Casa Nova and Paulus VI streets. It's clean, has bathrooms, and serves wonderful *bourma,* a honey-soaked cylindrical pastry filled with whole pistachio nuts. Don't confuse this place with another one nearby: look for the Arab pastries, not the gooey Western imitations.

The Greek Orthodox **Church of St. Gabriel,** about 1 km (½ mi) north of the junction of Paulus VI and Casa Nova streets, contains a spring that the Greek Orthodox, citing the noncanonical Gospel of St. James, believe to be the site of the Annunciation. (At the bottom of the short approach to the church, on Paulus VI Street, is a round, white, stone structure marked MARY'S WELL—but this is merely a modern fountain.) One may question the validity of that tradition—though evidence of an earlier structure, perhaps a medieval church, suggests the tradition is not new—but one thing is certain: this is the only natural water source in Nazareth, and Mary must have come here almost daily to draw water.

The ornate church was built in 1750 and contains a fine carved-wood pulpit and iconostasis (chancel screen), with painted New Testament scenes and silver-haloed saints in the niches. The walls are adorned with frescoes of figures from the Bible and the Greek Orthodox hagiography. A tiny "well" stands over the running spring, and a modern aluminum cup on a cord gives a satisfying plop as it drops into the sacred water. (The water is pure spring water; the cup's sanitary condition is more suspicious.) The church's hours are flexible; sometimes you can enter during the midday break, sometimes in late afternoon. ⊠ *Off Paulus VI St.* ☎ *Small donation expected.* ☉ *Apr.–Sept., daily 8–11:45 and 3–6; Oct.–Mar., daily 8–11:45 and 3–5.*

Christianity speaks with many voices in Nazareth. The newly rebuilt **Baptist Church,** a few hundred yards north of the Church of St. Gabriel, along Paulus VI Street, is affiliated with the Southern Baptist Convention of the United States.

For unobstructed **panoramas** of the town, drive up to Upper Nazareth, on the eastern ridge, a Jewish town of about 35,000 founded as a separate municipal entity in the 1950s; or to the Salesian church on the western ridge (accessible from the police station at the town's northern exit, where the road heads for Tiberias).

### Dining and Lodging

Travelers tend to hit the sights in Nazareth and move on, and the result is a dearth of good restaurants. There is, however, a clutch of fairly decent little **Arab restaurants on Casa Nova and Paulus VI streets,** frequented mostly by locals. Dinner here means hummus, shish kebab, baklava, Turkish coffee, and the like. Decor is incidental, atmosphere a function of the clientele of the moment, and dinnertime early. Needless to say, reservations are not necessary, and dress is casual.

Roman Catholic **hospices** (hostelries) in Nazareth cater primarily to pilgrim groups, though some welcome individual travelers. Contact the Government Tourist Office (⊠ Casa Nova St., ☎ 06/657–3003) for listings of both hospices and other hotels.

## Cana

➓ *8 km (5 mi) north of Nazareth on Rte. 754, 1 km (½ mi) south of the junction of Rtes. 77 and 754; 50 km (31 mi) east of Haifa.*

According to the New Testament (John 2), it was here—in the Arab village of Kafr Kanna, the ancient Jewish village of Cana—that Jesus reluctantly performed his first miracle, turning water into wine at a wedding feast. He thus emerged from his "hidden years" to begin a three-year ministry in the Galilee. Approaching the town from Nazareth, the road winds down through typical Galilean countryside. The profusion of olive groves, pomegranates, grape vines, fig trees, and even the occasional date palm (unusual at this altitude) is a reminder of how much local scenery is described in the Bible. Even the clutter of modern buildings, power lines, and industrial debris cannot ruin the impression.

Within the village, red signs on the right lead to two rival churches—one Roman Catholic (Franciscan), the other Greek Orthodox—that enshrine the scriptural tradition. The alleyway to these churches is just barely passable for cars, and you can park in the courtyard of the souvenir store opposite the Franciscan **Cana Wedding Church** (☎ 06/651–7011). The present church, built in the 1880s, is worth a short visit. Admission is free, and you'll generally find it open weekdays 8–noon and 2–5 (until 6 April–September), Saturday 8–noon. From the vestibule, a few steps take you up to the main chapel, while another staircase descends into a grotto, believed by the Franciscans to be the very spot where the wedding took place. In the vestibule, look for an ancient mosaic with an Aramaic inscription (indicating the presence of a pre-Byzantine synagogue) and for the water trough in the grotto. The stone jar on display here is simply a reproduction of the kind mentioned in the gospel passage. The Greek Orthodox priests of St. Nathaniel, across the way, display two older jars, which their tradition suggests are original. Fine *authentic* examples of such water jars are on view in the Herodian mansions of Jerusalem's Jewish Quarter.

## Zippori

★ ⓫ *Village, 5 km (3 mi) west of Nazareth off Rte. 79; site, 4 km (2½ mi) farther; 47 km (29 mi) from Haifa.*

For years the main attraction of Zippori was its charming hilltop location, surrounded by planted pine and cypress woods, cultivated fields, and a fine view of the valley below. The site has been transformed into a national park, where archaeologists have unearthed much of the large and prosperous city of the Roman period, including a most impressive water system and a dozen mosaic floors of sometimes extraordinary fineness (at press time, only three were open to the public, though preparation of the others continues apace).

A Jewish town stood here from at least the 1st century BC through the early Middle Ages. Known also by its Greek name, Sepphoris, it is identified in some Christian traditions as the birthplace of the Virgin Mary. In the Great Revolt of the Jews against the Romans (AD 66–73), the citizens of Zippori opted out of the struggle and sued for peace with Vespasian, thus creating a serious gap in the rebel defenses in the Galilee and earning the ire of their compatriots but sparing their town the mortal fate of so many other Jewish towns.

In the late 2nd or early 3rd century AD, the legendary sage Rabbi Yehuda Hanassi (the Patriarch) moved here from Bet She'arim (☞ *above*) for health reasons. His enormous prestige and official status as the head of the Jewish community made the subsequent relocation of the Jewish high court, the Sanhedrin, to Zippori an obvious choice. It was apparently here (the sources are equivocal) that Rabbi Yehuda convened the greatest Jewish sages of the time and compiled the Mishnah, the codification of Oral Law. For centuries, rabbis had given learned responses to real-life questions of civil and religious law, basing their judgments on the do's, don'ts, and between-the-lines principles of the Torah (the biblical Five Books of Moses, and the foundation of Judaism). These rabbinic opinions had been transmitted orally from generation to generation and, like court decisions, had become legal precedents and the heart of Jewish jurisprudence. Further commentary was added to the Mishnah in later centuries to produce the Talmud, the primary guide to Orthodox Jewish practice to this day.

Zippori was clearly a town with a cosmopolitan soul, however. There is evidence that Jewish, Christian, and pagan communities coexisted for a while around the 3rd century AD. A relatively small **Roman the-**

ater—capacity about 4,000, its stone seats long since stolen by local villagers for their own building projects—tells mutely of the town's cultural life, and the mosaic floors bespeak the opulence that could support it. One mosaic is made up of Egyptian motifs, including the famous lighthouse at Alexandria and a mythological depiction of the source of the Nile River. Another mosaic, once a synagogue floor (not yet open to the public at press time), rather surprisingly depicts the signs of the zodiac, just like those found in Bet Alfa (☞ Jezreel and Jordan Valleys, *above*) and Hammat Tiberias (☞ Tiberias and the Sea of Galilee, *below*). The finest mosaic floor of all reveals a series of Dionysian drinking scenes as well as the exquisite face of a woman, dubbed "the Mona Lisa of the Galilee" by the popular press upon its discovery. Situated on the crest of the ridge, that floor must have been the centerpiece of the town's most prominent villa, perhaps the governor's residence. A reconstruction of the building has tastefully highlighted the mosaics and explained the various panels.

Alongside the villa is a **watchtower**, Zippori's landmark. The lower, Crusader part of the structure recycles Roman sarcophagi as cornerstones. The upper, Turkish levels have been renovated, and the roof offers superb views. Within the tower, a good video and, upstairs, a small museum that includes interactive CD-ROMs along with archaeological artifacts add extra dimension to your visit. East of the villa is an impressive Roman colonnaded street, possibly the *cardo maximus* (main thoroughfare) of the 3rd-century town.

One kilometer (⅔ mi) east of the main site—but still within the park—is a huge section of ancient Zippori's **water system,** fed by springs just north of Nazareth. The ancient aqueduct is in fact a deep, man-made, plastered canyon, and the effect is extraordinary. ✉ *Beyond the village of Zippori, off Rte. 79,* ☎ *06/656–8272.* ✆ *NIS 17 ($4.90).* ☉ *Sun.–Thurs., Sat., and holidays 8–4 (8–5 in summer), Fri. 8–3.*

### Donkey-Back Riding

You can rent a donkey or be guided on one in the Nazareth hills (☞ Guided Tours *in* Lower Galilee A to Z, *below*) from **Donkey Tracks,** in nearby Hoshaya (✉ Kfar Kedem, M.P. Hamovil 17915, ☎ 06/656–5511, ℻ 06/657–0378).

# Golani Junction

*6 km (3½ mi) east of Cana at intersection of Rtes. 77 and 65, 50 km (31 mi) from Haifa.*

One of the most important crossroads in the Lower Galilee, the Golani junction was captured by the Golani Brigade of the Israel Defense Forces in the War of Independence in 1948. A monument, a museum, and a McDonald's stand on the east side.

All around the Golani Junction are new groves of evergreens planted by visitors as part of the **Jewish National Fund's** (JNF) Plant a Tree with Your Own Hands. Over the last 90 years or so, the JNF has worked to redeem a land neglected for centuries. In an attempt to restore the forests that once covered the hills of Israel, more than 200 million trees have been planted nationwide. Jewish tradition elevates the act of planting a tree to the level of a mitzvah, a good deed given authority by the Bible. If you want to leave something living behind you, drop into the JNF offices (open Sunday–Thursday), to the left of Afula Road (Route 65), a few hundred yards from the junction. For NIS 37 ($10) you can pick out a sapling, dedicate it to someone if you wish, and plant it yourself.

At the **Horns of Hattin,** a small double hill that is an extinct volcano, Saladin crushed the Crusader army in 1187, finishing off the Latin Kingdom of Jerusalem. Richard the Lionhearted's Third Crusade, a few years later, restored some parts of the country to Christian control, but the power and glory of the Latin Kingdom were gone forever. The hill is just beyond Lavi Kibbutz ☞ Dining and Lodging, *below*), about 2½ km (1½ mi) east of the Golani Junction on Route 77.

## Dining and Lodging

**$–$$**    ✕ **Younes.** Don't look for elegant decor and ambience: Younes is a place for eating, not dining. This popular watering hole for locals and Israelis on the road serves up excellent Arab fare, including tasty Middle Eastern salads, shishlik, and grilled lamb chops. Big windows provide some fair views and an airy feeling, and you can sit outside when the weather is right. ⊠ *Rte. 77 at gas station, 1 km (½ mi) west of Golani Junction,* ☎ *06/676–7343. Reservations not accepted. No credit cards.*

**$$–$$$**    ▥ **Lavi Kibbutz Hotel.** The guest house at Kibbutz Lavi is designed like a hotel, with all the units in one building. The community is Jewish Orthodox, so there is no vehicular traffic into or out of the village (and thus no check-ins or checkouts) on the Sabbath, from sunset on Friday until sundown on Saturday. Schedule aside, the atmosphere at the kibbutz is warm and welcoming, and many Christian pilgrim groups make it their Galilee base. The rooms are comfortable and the food decent, but neither is out of the ordinary. Still, the experience of waking to rural surroundings has much to recommend it, and you're only 15 minutes from Tiberias. ⊠ *Rte. 77, 11 km (7 mi) west of Tiberias, Lower Galilee 15267,* ☎ *06/679–9450,* 𝔽𝔸𝕏 *06/679–9399. 112 rooms with bath, 12 with shower. Restaurant, pool, 2 tennis courts. AE, DC, MC, V.*

*En Route*    South of the Golani Junction, Route 65 passes through beautiful, undulating green countryside. Ilaniya, still known by its old Arabic name of **Sejera,** is the first village on the right. At the beginning of the century, it was a training farm for young Jewish pioneers, among them a certain David Ben-Gurion, who would become Israel's first prime minister.

# Mt. Tabor

★ ⑫   *16 km (10 mi) south of the Golani Junction off Rte. 7266, 17 km (10½ mi) northeast of Afula.*

Mt. Tabor and the nearby areas are rich with biblical associations and history. The large village of **Kfar Tavor,** a veteran pioneering community from the late 19th century, is dominated to the west by the domed mountain that gave it its name.

The modern kibbutz of **Ein Dor**—2 km (1½ mi) past Kfar Tavor, east on Route 7276—is the biblical Endor of I Samuel 28. Three thousand years ago King Saul communed here with the spirit of the prophet Samuel before his fateful battle against the Philistines. Saul got little consolation. "The Lord has torn the kingdom out of your hand, and given it to your neighbor, David," cried Samuel, "and tomorrow, you and your sons shall be with me. . . ." At the subsequent battle on Mt. Gilboa (☞ Jezreel and Jordan Valleys, *above*), Saul and his three sons were killed and the Israelite army was routed. "How are the mighty fallen . . .," lamented David when the news reached him.

**Shibli,** on Route 7266, is a village of Bedouin who abandoned their nomadic life a few generations ago and became farmers. The narrow switchback road up Mt. Tabor begins from a clearing beyond Shibli and between Shibli and the next village of Dabouriya. A Nazareth-based taxi is usually waiting at the bottom of the mountain to provide shuttle service to the top.

As far back as the Byzantine period, Christian tradition has identified Mt. Tabor as the "high mountain apart" that Jesus ascended with his disciples Peter, James, and John. "And he was transfigured before them, and his garments became white as light. And behold there appeared to them Moses and Elijah, talking with him" (Matthew 17). Early churches on the mountain were designed to represent the three tabernacles Peter had suggested to Jesus that they build, one for Moses, one for Elijah, and one for Jesus himself. The altar of the present **Church of the Transfiguration** (☏ 06/676–7489), which was consecrated in 1924, represents the tabernacle of Jesus; those of Moses and Elijah are represented as chapels at the back of the church. The church is open Sunday–Friday, 8–noon and 2–5; admission is free.

Thirty-two centuries ago, somewhere near the foot of the mountain, the Israelite conscripts of the prophetess-judge Deborah and her general, Barak, routed the Canaanite chariot army. From the terrace of the Franciscan hospice next to the church, you see the Jezreel Valley to the west and south; and from a platform on the Byzantine and Crusader ruins to the left of the modern church (watch your step), there is a panorama east and north over the Galilean hills. No wonder the Jewish general Yosef Ben Matityahu (Josephus Flavius) fortified the hill in the 1st century AD during the Great Revolt against the Romans.

NEED A BREAK? The **Dovrat Inn** (✉ Rte. 65, ☏ 06/659–9520) is a rather good cafeteria, now part of the Mövenpick chain, offering a wide range of attractively presented food. It's at the gas station, about 5 km (3 mi) from the Shibli turnoff (Route 7266), toward Afula.

## Dining

**$$$** ✕ **Tzela Hatavor.** This restaurant lies "in the shadow of Mt. Tabor"
★ (a fair translation of the name), but it's not a roadside diner. Split-pane arched windows and solid wood tables create a fashionably rustic ambience. The menu is wide-ranging—soups, salads, pastas, fish, fine steaks, and a kids' meal—and the creativity of chef-owner Ruti, especially in the subtle but flavorful sauces, is always evident. The best appetizers are mallard in orange sauce (also available as a main dish); lightly fried goose liver in a herb sauce; and "Aronchik's eggplant," a vertical skewer of eggplant, sun-dried tomatoes, red peppers, goat cheese, and herbs. If you decide on steak, have the Dijon-mustard sauce. For dessert, try the white-chocolate parfait swimming in caramel sauce. ✉ *Rte. 65 (next to gas station), Kfar Tavor,* ☏ *06/676–9966. Reservations essential on weekends and holidays. AE, DC, MC, V.*

*En Route* If you're heading to the Sea of Galilee, take Route 767, which breaks off Route 65 at Kfar Tavor. It's a beautiful drive of about 25 minutes. The first village, **Kafr Kamma,** is one of two in Israel of the Circassian (*Cherkessi*) community, Muslims from the Russian steppes who were settled here by the Ottoman Turks in the 19th century. The decorative mosque is just one element of the tradition they continue to preserve.

On the descent to the lake, there is a parking area precisely at sea level. The Sea of Galilee is still more than 700 ft below you, and the view is superb, especially in the afternoon. You meet Route 90 at the bottom of the road.

# TIBERIAS AND THE SEA OF GALILEE

The great American writer and humorist Mark Twain was unimpressed by the Sea of Galilee region. He passed through in 1867 in the company of a group of pilgrims and Arab dragomans (interpreters) on horseback and found "an unobtrusive basin of water, some mountainous desolation, and one tree." He would scarcely recognize it now. Modern agriculture and afforestation projects have made the plains and hills green; the handful of "squalid" and "reeking" villages of his day have been supplanted by a string of thriving and well-landscaped kibbutzim; and the "unobtrusive basin of water" has become a lively resort.

The Sea of Galilee is in fact a freshwater lake, 21 km (13 mi) long from north to south and 12 km (7½ mi) wide from east to west. The Jordan River feeds the lake from the north, then leaves it from the south to meander to the Dead Sea. Almost completely ringed by cliffs and steep hills, the lake lies in a hollow about 700 ft below sea level, which accounts for its warm climate and subtropical vegetation.

The city of Tiberias provides a sort of anchor for the region and the logical starting point for exploration. Thereafter, we describe sights in sequence as you circumvent the Sea of Galilee clockwise (via Routes 90, 87, 92, and 98), ending at Hammat Tiberias, at the city's southern edge. It's worth crossing the lake by boat if you have someone to bring your car around. Note that several of the Christian sites demand modest dress.

## Tiberias

★ ⑬ *38 km (23½ mi) north of Bet She'an, 36 km (23 mi) east of Nazareth, 70 km (43 mi) from Haifa.*

As the only town on the Sea of Galilee, Tiberias has become the natural center of the region. It is not a town with class, however; almost 2,000 years old, Tiberias still has the atmosphere of a community yet to come of age. It is at once brash and sleepy, a provincial town where falafel is far more popular than foie gras, where a few pubs with loud recorded music constitute the entertainment menu most nights. Its reputation as a resort town is based more on its great location and some decent hotels than on the town's own attractions.

Today's Tiberias, with a population of 40,000, spreads all the way up the slope behind it, from about 700 ft below sea level, at the lake, to 800 ft above sea level, in its highest hilltop neighborhoods—a difference big enough to create a serious temperature differential in midsummer. Tiberias itself is not lovely; it deserved better than the sort of development it has experienced. Most travelers, however, see little of the town proper and confine themselves to the lakeshore district, where most of the hotels and all of the pubs and restaurants are clustered. Tourism, as much Israeli as foreign, is one of the mainstays of the town's economy—you can eat well here, boogie a bit, and drink late along an incomparable subtropical lake.

Tiberias has an almost invisible history. Much has happened here, but you'll find few footprints of the past. Part of the black-basalt medieval city wall crosses Habanim Street just south of the Radisson Moriah Plaza Hotel; the Tourist Information Office, on Habanim Street opposite the hotel, is framed by restored Crusader arches; and massive Crusader towers and ramparts behind the Scottish Centre dominate Dona Gracia and Gedud Barak streets. Near the Promenade, between the Radisson Moriah and Caesar hotels, is a cluster of old basalt synagogues and mosques and a 19th-century church (some of the synagogues date from the Aboulafia period of the 18th century). The Franciscan Church of St. Peter commemorates the events described in John 21, in which Jesus entrusts Peter with the continuation of his ministry ("Feed my sheep").

In AD 18, the town was completed by Herod Antipas, son of the notorious Herod the Great, and dedicated to Tiberius, emperor of Rome at the time. Although Antipas, with the title of tetrarch, was able to surround himself with ambitious courtiers and functionaries, many common folk shunned the new town because it had been built on an old cemetery and was therefore considered unclean.

Rich men make poor rebels, and the Tiberians seem to have had little stomach for the Jewish war against Rome that broke out in AD 66. They surrendered to the Romans in 67, thus saving themselves from the vengeful destruction visited on so many other Galilean towns. In the 2nd century, the revered Rabbi Shimon Bar Yochai ceremonially purified Tiberias, opening the way for a wave of settlement and development that transformed the city. Jerusalem, devastated by Titus's legions in AD 70, lay in ruins, the Jews banished from the city; and the center of Jewish life in Israel gradually gravitated to the Galilee. By the 4th century, the Sanhedrin had established itself in Tiberias. It was here, around AD 400, that the Jewish Oral Law was finally compiled into what became known as the Jerusalem Talmud.

This was something of a golden era in Tiberias, assuring it a place among Judaism's holy cities in the Land of Israel (together with Jerusalem, Hebron, and Zfat). The community knew hard times under the Byzantines, stabilized under more-tolerant Muslim dynasties (the Arabs conquered the region in the 7th century), and declined again under the hostile Crusaders, who made Tiberias the capital of their Principality of Galilee. The Arab Saladin besieged the city in 1187, and, at the nearby Horns of Hattin, routed the Crusader army that was on its way to relieve it. Crusader fortifications remain a prominent feature of the cityscape.

Tiberias's decline was almost total after the debacle at Hattin. It was not until 1562, when the Ottoman sultan Suleiman the Magnificent gave the town to the Jewish nobleman Don Joseph Nasi, that an attempt was made to revive the community. Don Joseph resettled the town and planted mulberry trees in the hope—the vain hope, as it turned out—of developing a silkworm industry.

In the 18th century, Tiberias was expanded and fortified by renegade Bedouin governor Dahr el-Omar, who invited a group of Jews from Izmir, in Turkey, to settle it. In conflict with the Ottomans, and unable to trust his own subjects, this cunning ruler decided to populate his capital city with a citizenry loyal to him personally. The leader of the new settlers was Isaac Aboulafia, perhaps still the best-known family name in Tiberias today. The Jewish community swelled further with the arrival in 1777 of a group of Hasidim, members of a devout, charismatic sect from Eastern Europe.

In 1833 the Egyptian nationalist leader Ibrahim Pasha, enjoying his short-lived independence from Turkey, built the town up further, but a cataclysmic earthquake just four years later left Tiberias in ruins and (it is said) 1,000 dead.

Relations between Jewish and Arab Tiberians were generally cordial until the Arab riots of 1936, in which some 30 Jews were massacred. Confrontation during the 1948 War of Independence had a different consequence. An attack by local Arabs in anticipation of an imminent Syrian invasion brought a counterattack from Haganah forces (the Jewish underground army before Israeli statehood), and the Arab population abandoned the town.

Among the wealth of tombs in Tiberias is that of its most famous denizen, the great 12th-century sage Moses Maimonides (1135–1204). To get to the **tomb of Moses Maimonides** from the tourist office, walk north up Habanim Street and take a left at Hayarden Street. Walk two blocks, and then turn right onto Ben Zakkai Street. A short way up, you'll see the tomb on your right.

Born in Córdoba, Spain, Maimonides won renown as a philosopher, as the physician to the royal court of Saladin in Egypt, and, in the Jewish world, as the greatest religious scholar and spiritual authority since the Talmudic period of the 4th and 5th centuries AD. To his profound knowledge of the Talmud, Maimonides brought an incisive intellect honed by his study of Aristotelian philosophy and the physical sciences. The result was a rationalism unusual in Jewish scholarship and a lucidity of analysis and style admired by Jewish and non-Jewish scholars alike.

After his death, in Egypt, Maimonides' remains were interred in Tiberias, one of four Jewish holy cities (although he never lived here). His whitewashed tomb has become a shrine, dripping with candle wax and tears. Marble plaques on either side of the path approaching the tomb recall the many disciplines in which Maimonides distinguished himself. Less tasteful is the stall at the entrance selling cheap religious trinkets. ⊠ *Ben Zakkai St.* ✉ *Free.* ☉ *Sun.–Thurs. daylight hrs, Fri. and holiday eves until 2.*

On Derech Hagevura, in the uptown area, is the traditional **tomb of Rabbi Akiva,** the spiritual leader of the Bar Kochba Revolt against Rome (AD 132–135), who was captured and then tortured to death in Caesarea.

## Dining and Lodging

Tiberias and the Sea of Galilee are a much livelier proposition than other parts of Lower Galilee. Because most travelers to this region actually stay overnight here, there are some good restaurants. Most are in Tiberias proper, but a few of the daytime watering holes on the lake stay open into the evening. The local specialty is St. Peter's fish (*tilapia*), which is native to the Sea of Galilee, but demand far outstrips supply, so the fish most restaurants serve is pond-bred. Meat dishes tend to be more Middle Eastern: shishlik and kebabs accompanied by hummus, pickles, and the ubiquitous french fries. A string of virtually indistinguishable restaurants with this menu lines the Promenade.

At a right angle to the Promenade is the *midrachov* (pedestrian mall), between the Radisson Moriah Plaza and Caesar hotels, with a wide range of affordable eating options: hamburger joints, pizzerias, ice cream parlors, and restaurants serving light meals. Among the latter is a member of the nationwide Kapulsky chain, known for its sinfully rich cakes. Perhaps because of the competition, the "regular" restaurants, with their fish, grills, schnitzel, and *shwarma* (slices of spit-grilled meat served in a pita with salads and condiments), have kept their prices down; if you're not looking for a gourmet experience, you can eat quite well for $10 or less. Another genre that has gained popularity is the pub, with wood-paneled rooms and smoky atmosphere, and meals to mitigate the effect of the excellent local Goldstar draft. Try Big Ben, on the mall, and Le Pirate Pub, below the Caesar Hotel.

If you have a hankering for falafel, that classic Middle Eastern fast food (deep-fried chickpea balls and salad in pita bread), rub shoulders with the locals on Hagalil Street. In fact, if you're into local color, look for the tiny, modest restaurants (where English really *is* a foreign language) on Hagalil Street and in the little streets that connect it to Habanim Street. The menus predictably emphasize fish and Middle Eastern salads and meat dishes. It's possible to strike culinary gold here, often at very reasonable prices. A good bet is the small, pedestrian-only Kishon Street, opposite the Carmel Jordan River Hotel, which houses the well-considered El Gaucho, part of a national chain of Argentinian grill restaurants; the vegetarian A Taste of Life (run by former Americans), with veg-based shwarma and homemade non-dairy ice cream; and several fish-meat establishments popular with the locals.

Local authorities have developed a series of free or cheap lakeside campsites south of Tiberias, but the facilities are spartan.

$$$ ✕ **Decks.** Built right on a pier, Decks is at its best in fine weather. Begin with a (shared) focaccia. The kitchen specializes in good meat—steak, or long skewers of veal and vegetables—grilled slowly over hickory wood. Fish and large salads make good herbivorous alternatives. A crepe flamed at your table—a sort of suzette-plus—is the dessert of choice. ✉ *Lido complex, Rte. 90, at the exit from Tiberias north,* ☏ *06/672–1538. AE, DC, MC, V. Closed Fri. No lunch Sat.*

$$–$$$ ✕ **Ha'Italkia.** The menu at "the Italian" is more eclectic than the name suggests. The salmon fettuccine wins approval from locals and Israeli vacationers, and the pizzas are many and varied. The steaks and fish (especially trout) have earned something of a local reputation. The listed salads are entrée-size, but an unlisted smaller, chopped green salad makes a good side dish. Red-and-white checkered tablecloths add an Italian air, and the old-style wood windowpanes and outside greenery allow you to forget how close you are to the main street. ✉ *Corner of Hagalil and Habanim Sts.,* ☏ *06/672–3150. AE, DC, MC, V.*

$$–$$$ ✕ **Pagoda and The House.** These Chinese-Thai restaurants (under one
★ management) are part of the Lido Beach complex, which includes other eateries and a small harbor. Pagoda, in a faux Chinese temple with wraparound windows, is spacious, with a generous patio for outdoor dining overlooking the lake. The House, across the road, has a maze of smaller, more intimate rooms entered through a delightful garden. The restaurants have identical menus, with one difference: Pagoda is kosher and is closed on the Sabbath and on Jewish religious holidays. The House is open only when Pagoda is not. Neither serves pork or shrimp. The food is in general exceptionally good. Try the spicy Thai soups (coconut-based, or hot-and-sour), the (lamb) spareribs, and strips of beef sautéed in satay (peanut) sauce. ✉ *Gedud Barak St. (Rte. 90),* ☏ *06/672–4488 or 06/679–2564. Reservations essential. AE, DC, MC, V. The House: closed Sun.–Thurs. and no lunch Fri.; Pagoda: no dinner Fri. or lunch Sat.*

$–$$$ ✕🏨 **YMCA Peniel-by-Galilee.** One of the area's more unusual hostel-
★ ries, Peniel-by-Galilee was built as a retreat in the late 1930s by Archibald Harte, founder of the famous Jerusalem YMCA. It occupies a low cliff just north of Tiberias, where you can enjoy unobstructed lake views and a pebbly but clean beach. The common room is lined with 180-year-old Damascene wood and inlaid panels. The guest rooms and family-size apartments are less inspiring, though spacious and comfortable enough; apartments have kitchen facilities. Most units have views of the lake. Dinner is served only when there's group demand (at least eight people; call ahead to verify), and it's worth trying to round up the quota. The excellence of the lake-caught St. Peter's fish is matched by the other entrées, which might include grilled steak or lamb chops, roast chicken, and hamburgers. ✉ *Off Rte. 90, 3 km (2 mi) north of Tiberias, Box 192, Tiberias 14101,* ☏ *06/672–0685,*

FAX *06/672–5943. 12 rooms and 3 apartments with bath. Dining room, beach, playground. V.*

**$$$$** ⌂ **Caesar.** Part of a small national chain, the Caesar faces the lake, with views from all rooms. The public areas are all white marble and polished brass; the guest rooms have tasteful, if unexceptional, furnishings. Every suite has a whirlpool bath. There's a large outdoor swimming pool and an adjacent children's pool, but the area would have been enhanced by more grass and less concrete. The dining room does a very respectable job. ⌂ *The Promenade, Box 275, 14102,* ☎ *06/672–3333,* FAX *06/679–1013. 227 rooms with bath. Bar, coffee shop, dining room, 2 pools, sauna, exercise room, windsurfing, boating, waterskiing. AE, DC, MC, V.*

**$$$$** ⌂ **Gai Beach.** Many regard the Gai Beach as the current leader among Tiberias's upscale hotels. Its rare lakeshore location is a big plus, and many enjoy its distance from the noisy downtown promenade. The marble lobby is large, with comfortable armchairs for a touch of intimacy. Guest rooms are well designed and tastefully furnished, if smallish; some face the lake. The hotel owns the adjacent water park, with its beach, water slides, and wave pool, and all are free to guests. The attractions are undeniable, though the rates are a bit high for a hotel of this class. ⌂ *Rte. 90, Box 274, 14102,* ☎ *06/679–0790,* FAX *06/679–2776. 2 suites, 196 rooms with bath. Restaurant, bar, pool. AE, DC, MC, V.*

**$$$$** ⌂ **Howard Johnson Plaza Galei Kinneret.** Built in 1943—note the Bauhaus-style facade—the grande dame of Tiberias hotels was a favorite retreat of David Ben-Gurion's. The Galei Kinneret's most attractive feature is its lakeside location (most of its rivals only overlook the lake), slightly removed from the raucous hotel-and-pub strip, with lawns and eucalyptus-shaded patios right on the water. Renovations have improved the rooms and spruced up the lounge area, if in somewhat brassy style. ⌂ *1 Kaplan St., 14100,* ☎ *06/672–8888,* FAX *06/679–0260. 123 rooms with bath. 2 restaurants, bar, pool, exercise room, boating, waterskiing. AE, DC, MC, V.*

**$$$$** ⌂ **Radisson Moriah Plaza.** The lobby and bar of this modern hotel are bright, comfortable places to relax. Rooms are comfortable but fairly ordinary, with darkish furnishings that only emphasize the relative lack of space. The service is generally professional and accommodating, but there are occasional lapses in maintenance, such as faulty appliances. The hotel overlooks the lake but does not have lake frontage. The Texas restaurant and bar imports a touch of the American West in both its grill menu and its decor. ⌂ *Just off Habanim St., 14103,* ☎ *06/679–2233,* FAX *06/679–2320. 272 rooms with bath. 3 restaurants, bar, pool, beauty salon, hot tub, sauna, exercise room. AE, DC, MC, V.*

**$$$** ⌂ **Four Points Tiberias.** Lording it high above the city, this Sheraton
★ property compensates for its distance from the town center with a quiet location and superb lake views from every room. The guest rooms are fairly spacious, though the bathrooms are small; half the rooms have balconies. The Lodge Bar, with its wide picture windows, is a cozy evening hangout despite some bizarre touches of decor. A children's club, with diversions and scheduled activities, is staffed daily 9 AM–10 PM. ⌂ *18 Hashomer St., 14102,* ☎ *06/679–1484. 218 rooms with bath. 2 restaurants, bar, pool, hot tub, 2 saunas, exercise room, children's programs. AE, DC, MC, V.*

**$$** ⌂ **Astoria.** One of Tiberias's better moderately priced hotels, the Astoria is set away from the lake, halfway uptown, with few views from guest rooms; but what it lacks in aesthetics it makes up for in quality. It's comfortable, clean, and family-run, and it recently expanded, adding new furnishings in attractive pastels. Large family rooms are available. Prices jump in August and during the main Jewish holidays. ⌂ *13 Ohel Ya'akov St., 14223,* ☎ *06/672–2351,* FAX *06/672–5108.*

*88 rooms with bath. Restaurant, bar, coffee shop, pool. AE, DC, MC, V.*

$$ ⚷ **Church of Scotland Centre.** Built in 1893 as a hospital of the Free
★ Church of Scotland, this building was ultimately converted into a pilgrim hospice. Today it welcomes all visitors, professing a commitment "to build bridges of trust and respect among our neighbors, whoever they are and wherever they come from." The two-story stone buildings, with their deep porches and high-ceilinged rooms, are a pleasant change from the sterility of many modern hotels. The rambling, slightly wild gardens make a challenging adventureland for kids and a pastoral refuge for their elders. The outer gate is closed at 7 PM, but your key lets you in at your convenience, as well as providing access to the private beach across the road. The location could not be more central. ⊠ *Gedud Barak and Hayarden Sts., Box 104, 14100,* ☎ *06/672–3769 or 06/672–1165,* ℻ *06/679–0145. 48 rooms with bath. Beach. AE, DC, MC, V.*

$$ ⚷ **Ron Beach.** The last hotel in Tiberias on Route 90 north, the family-
★ run Ron Beach has rare private frontage on the lake. The amenities—high-quality mattresses, TVs, and hair dryers—are impressive in this price category. In addition to the main building, two rows of 27 rooms each open onto the lawn and the beach; those at ground level have their own patio. There are several enormous family rooms. All in all, it's a great value. ⊠ *Gedud Barak St. (Rte. 90 N), 14101,* ☎ *06/679–1350,* ℻ *06/679–1351. 74 rooms with bath. Restaurant, pool, beach. AE, DC, MC, V.*

$ ⚷ **Berger Hotel.** Run by the family of that name, this two-wing hotel
★ has spacious, well-furnished rooms, each with a balcony. It's uptown, and more convenient if you have a car, but buses to the downtown area are frequent (except on weekends). Meals are not served, but the supermarket across the road makes it easy to stock your kitchenette. Renovated sections, and new frills such as cable TV, have lifted the hotel's quality above its price category. The management is quick to upgrade you to a larger room at the same price when rooms are available and offers a further discount if you produce your Fodor's guide. ⊠ *27 Neiberg St., Box 535, 14105,* ☎ *06/671–5151,* ℻ *06/679–1514. 2 apartments, 24 rooms with bath, 21 rooms with shower. Kitchenettes. AE, DC, MC, V.*

$ ⚷ **Meyouhas Youth Hostel.** This large basalt building fronted by a lawn and trees is in the heart of downtown Tiberias, a minute's walk from the lake, the Promenade, and the mall. The term "youth" is inaccurate: the hostel is open to all, and at press time it was completing a massive renovation to bring it to the level of a guest house, with ensuite facilities and new pine furniture. Meals are cheap. Frills are few, but it's an excellent value for the budget-conscious. ⊠ *Corner of Gedud Barak and Hayarden Sts., Box 81, 14100,* ☎ *06/672–1775 or 06/679–0350,* ℻ *06/672–0372. 50 rooms, some double, some family, all with private showers and toilets. Restaurant. AE, DC, MC, V.*

## Nightlife and the Arts

As you might expect in a resort area, entertainment is more plentiful than culture. Much of it, especially in the larger hotels in Tiberias, is of the live-lounge-music variety: piano bars, dance bands, and crooners ("Sing along, folks!"). Thursday and Friday are "nightclub" nights at some hotels, with dance music for the weekend crowds. The clientele tends to be a bit older. Generally speaking, the younger set wouldn't be caught dead here, preferring to hang out at the pubs along the midrachov and the Promenade, where the recorded rock music is good and loud and the beer is on tap.

Some boat operators use their larger boats as floating dance clubs in the summer, usually departing from the piers at the Promenade for 45-minute cruises. The cost is NIS 15–NIS 20 ($4.30–$5.70). **Lido** also occasionally offers a two-hour dinner-and-disco cruise for about NIS 105 ($30); for details call **Lido Kinneret** (☎ 06/672–1538 or 06/679–2564) or **Kinneret Sailing** (Aug. only, disco only: ☎ 06/675–8008 or 06/675–8009).

The Ministry of Tourism sometimes sponsors a free **Israeli folklore evening** at one of the major hotels; call the tourist-information number (☎ 06/672–5666) for schedules. Sometimes a classier act comes through, often performing on one of the local kibbutzim, and if it's not too language-specific (a Hebrew comedian, for example), the performance can be a tasty slice of Israeli culture.

The **Galilee Experience,** a 27-projector, 38-minute audiovisual presentation, gives a good historical overview of the Galilee from a distinctly Christian viewpoint. ⊠ *Marina, southern end of Promenade,* ☎ *06/672–3620.* ⌸ *NIS 28 ($8).* ☉ *Screenings in English throughout the day and evening, some only when a group has reserved ahead; call for details.*

## Outdoor Activities and Sports

### SWIMMING

There's good swimming at a number of beaches near Tiberias.

**Blue Beach** (⊠ Rte. 90 at northern exit from Tiberias), **Sironit** (⊠ Rte. 90 at southern exit from Tiberias), and **Gai Beach** (⊠ next to Sironit) are all options.

### WALKING AND JOGGING

A promenade follows the lakeshore for about 5 km (3 mi) to the south of Tiberias.

### WATER SPORTS

For waterskiing, inquire at **Lido** (☎ 06/672–1538).

Water slides are available at the **Sironit and Gai beaches,** south of Tiberias.

## Shopping

Tiberias relies heavily on tourism, but despite its developing infrastructure, it has little in the way of shopping. The exceptions are jewelry, and, of course, souvenirs.

Two large, established **diamond factories** have outlets here, showing a video about the industry before releasing you into their showrooms: **Adipaz-Golan** (⊠ Rte. 90, just south of Tiberias, opposite Tiberias Hot Springs, ☎ 06/672–6930 or 06/671–6262) and the larger **Caprice** (⊠ Tabor St., ☎ 06/679–2616), which also gives a tour of its workshops and small museum. There are a few smaller **jewelry stores** near the intersection of Habanim and Yarden streets and in some of the better hotels.

*En Route*   North of Tiberias, the road to Metulla (Route 90) hugs the steep hillside, leaving only a few rocky beaches between it and the Sea of Galilee. About 5 km (3 mi) from the town, the shore widens. Among the trees and holiday bungalows is an enclosure with a small, unimposing cluster of black basalt ruins: this is all that remains of ancient **Magdala,** a Jewish town of the Second Temple period and the probable home of Mary Magdalene. The Galileans spearheaded the Great Revolt of the Jews against Rome in AD 66, but courage alone could not defeat the disciplined Roman legions. Magdala—called Tarichaeae by the Romans—saw one of the bloodiest battles of the campaign (AD 67). In a chilling passage, contemporary Jewish historian Flavius Josephus describes "the entire lake stained with blood and crammed with corpses; for there was not a single survivor."

## Ginosar

🔼 *10 km (6 mi) north of Tiberias.*

Perhaps the site of the New Testament's Gennesaret, Ginosar is now a veteran kibbutz in a glorious lakeside location. Many Israelis know it as the home of the late Yigal Allon (1918–80), commander of the crack Palmach battalions in the War of Independence and deputy prime minister in the 1970s under Golda Meir and Yitzhak Rabin. The settlement's favorite son is immortalized in **Bet Allon** (Allon House), a basalt-and-concrete eyesore of a building that houses a museum of the region's natural and human history. It's a good rainy-day option.

For the traveler, however, the site is intriguing for the brilliant archaeological find made on its shore: a 2,000-year-old wooden boat, the most complete boat of this age ever found in an inland lake. In January 1986, after three years of poor rainfall had lowered the level of the lake, fishermen from the adjacent kibbutz spotted the boat's prow in the mud. Excavated in a frenetic 11 days, the 28-ft-long boat became an instant media sensation. Considering its age (it dates from the 1st century AD) and the frequency of nautical references in the New Testament stories that took place around here, the popular press immediately dubbed it "the Jesus Boat." For a reader of the Gospels, it's a startlingly vivid relic.

The ancient boat was amazingly intact but extremely fragile, its timbers sodden like wet cardboard. To move it, experts sprayed the vessel inside and out with a Styrofoam mixture, giving it a buoyant "straitjacket." It was then towed a few hundred yards by rowboat and lifted by crane to its current home, a small building between the lake and the museum of Bet Allon. For almost a decade, it lay in a specially constructed bath filled with a wax-based preservative solution, an experiment that seems to have succeeded in its aim to displace the water molecules in the wood. Today the boat is dry and can be seen in all of its modest but remarkably evocative glory. Bet Allon screens an excellent video, filmed during the excavation, that explains the boat's unique features. The long-term plan is to build a special permanent pavilion to display the boat with the pride it deserves. ⊠ *Rte. 90,* ☎ *06/672–2905.* ⌧ *Museum and boat NIS 15 ($4.30); boat only (including video) NIS 9 ($2.60).* ⊙ *Sat.–Thurs. 8:30–5, Fri. and holiday eves 8:30–1 (boat only, 8:30–4). Last entry to museum 1 hr before closing; last entry to boat 30 min before closing.*

### Lodging

$$$ 🏨 **Nof Ginosar Guest House.** This is one of the largest and best established of the Galilee's kibbutz guest houses. Its location—right on the Sea of Galilee, with a private beach—makes Nof Ginosar especially popular. There are evening lectures on kibbutz life and a morning tour. Also on the grounds are a spectacular, 2,000-year-old fishing boat; the small natural-history and anthropological museum at Bet Allon; and kayak, pedal-boat, and rowboat rentals. The decor is rustic-resort, with good motel-like accommodations. Rooms are comfortable and airy, if not overly spacious; all have TVs. The large dining-room buffet alternates between decent meat-based meals and meatless offerings, which include tasty salads, hot fish, and outstanding blintzes with sweetened cheese. ⊠ *Rte. 90, M.P. Jordan Valley 14980,* ☎ *06/679–2161,* ⌨ *06/679–2170. 170 rooms with bath. Restaurant, bar, coffee shop, pool, beach. AE, DC, MC, V.*

## Outdoor Activities and Sports

There's a pleasant beach at **Nof Ginosar** (☞ Lodging, *above*), where you can also rent kayaks, pedal boats, and rowboats.

*En Route*    Just north of Ginosar, on Route 90 on your right, is an electric substation that powers huge water pumps buried in the hill behind it. The Sea of Galilee is Israel's primary freshwater reservoir and the beginning of the National Water Carrier, a network of canals and pipelines that integrates the country's water sources and distribution lines. On the hill above this is the small tel of the Old Testament city of **Kinneret,** which dominated the main highway of the ancient Near East, the so-called Via Maris (Way of the Sea). Scholars assume that the Hebrew name for the lake—Kinneret—comes from that of the most important city on its shores in antiquity. Romantics contend that the name derives from the lake's shape, which resembles the biblical *kinnor,* or lyre.

# Mount of Beatitudes

🔵 *8 km (5 mi) north of Ginosar; 3 km (2 mi) north of Capernaum Junction, where Rtes. 90 and 87 meet.*

Well-tended gardens and spreading ficus trees make a tranquil setting for contemplating the Sermon on the Mount, with which this hill is identified. "And seeing the multitudes, he went up into a mountain; and when he was set, his disciples came unto him. And he opened his mouth, and taught them, saying: 'Blessed are the poor in spirit, for theirs is the kingdom of Heaven . . .' " Thus the Gospel of Matthew (5:1–7:29) begins the record of Jesus' most extensive teaching.

The domed **Roman Catholic church** (of the Italian Franciscan Sisters), built by the famous architect Barluzzi, was completed in 1937. The marble walls carry quotations from the Beatitudes, the initial "Blessed are they . . ." verses from the Sermon on the Mount. The church is surrounded by a terrace and well-tended gardens, offering a superb view of the Sea of Galilee (best in the afternoon, when the diffused western sun softens the light and heightens colors). In keeping with the spirit of the place, this is one of the few Christian holy sites in the country where Catholics and Protestants seem to feel equally at ease. ⊠ *Rte. 8177 off Rte. 90.* ⊙ *Daily 8–noon and 2:30–5.*

# Tabgha

🔵 *14 km (8 mi) north of Tiberias, at Capernaum Junction (Rtes. 90 and 87).*

Greenery drapes the antiquities and frames the Roman Catholic churches at the two neighboring sights here. Tabgha is an Arabic corruption of the earlier Greek name Heptapegon (Seven Springs).

The German Benedictine **Church of the Multiplication,** a large building on the west side of Tabgha, is identified by Christian tradition with the "desert[ed] place" of Matthew 14. Here, toward evening, the gospel relates, Jesus miraculously "multiplied" two fish and five loaves of bread to feed the crowds that followed him. "And they did all eat, and were filled. . . . And they that had eaten were about 5,000 men, beside women and children." This event is known as the miracle of the Multiplication of the Loaves and Fishes.

The church, dedicated in 1981, is built in the Byzantine-basilica style—it's an airy limestone building with a wooden truss ceiling—and incorporates some remains of its 5th-century predecessor. Most impressive is the beautifully wrought Byzantine mosaic floor depicting flora and birds, and curiously including Egyptian motifs such as the Nilometer, a graded column once used to measure the water level of the Nile. In front of the altar is the small and simple *Loaves and Fishes,* perhaps the most famous mosaic in Israel. ⊠ *Rte. 87.* ⊙ *Mon.–Sat. 8:30–5, Sun. 10–5.*

The austere, basalt **Church of the Primacy of St. Peter,** 200 yards east of the Church of the Multiplication, is built on the water's edge, over a flat rock known as Mensa Domini (the Lord's Table) or Mensa Christi (the Table of Christ). After his resurrection, says the New Testament (John 21), Jesus appeared to his disciples by the Sea of Galilee and breakfasted on a miraculous catch of fish. Three times Jesus asked the disciple Peter if he loved him, and after Peter's reply of "You know that I love you," Jesus commanded him to "Feed my sheep." Some scholars see this affirmation as Peter's atonement for having thrice denied Jesus in Jerusalem after Jesus' arrest. The episode is seen as establishing Peter's "primacy" and, in the Roman Catholic tradition, that of his spiritual descendants, the bishops of Rome. Part of the Franciscan "Custody of the Holy Land," the site was included in the itinerary of Pope Paul VI in 1964. ⊠ *Rte. 87.* ⊙ *Daily 8–11:50 and 2–4:50.*

## Capernaum

**17** *3 km (2 mi) east of Tabgha and the Capernaum Junction, 17 km (10½ mi) northeast of Tiberias.*

Capernaum (Kfar Nahum in Hebrew) was once a thriving town of merchants, farmers, and fishermen; today it contains an archaeological site and two monasteries. The easterly one, distinguished by its red-domed, whitewashed church, is Greek Orthodox and is seldom visited, since its own antiquities have not been developed for tourists. The westerly, Franciscan (Roman Catholic) one, at the first turnoff after Tabgha, is what you come to see, along with the nearby excavations.

The prosperity of this ancient Jewish community is immediately apparent from the remains of its synagogue. Excavations by the Franciscan friars in the early 20th century exposed a large lakeside town that had thrived from the Second Temple/Early Roman period (about the 1st century BC) to the Byzantine period (5th–6th centuries AD). It was here that Jesus established his base for the three years of his ministry in the Galilee. Here, the New Testament relates, he called many of his disciples ("Follow me, and I will make you fishers of men"), healed the afflicted, taught in the synagogue. . . and ultimately cursed the city for not heeding his message.

To the right of the cashier as you enter the site is a display of finely carved stones showing the typical range of Jewish artistic motifs of the time, including the native fruits of the land: grapes, pomegranates, figs, dates, and olives. A dedication to a donor of the synagogue's building fund, one "Alpheus the son of Zebedah the son of John," is in Aramaic, the language spoken by Jews in the region at the time (compare the Gospel of Mark 15:34) and strong proof that this was a Jewish community. A horizontal stone—a lintel—shows an artist's depiction of the biblical Ark of the Covenant, typically carried by hand in Old Testament times but here shown on wheels, perhaps a reference to the two such instances recorded (I Samuel 6 and II Samuel 6).

Immediately before you is a modern church, suspended from its outer support pillars over the scanty remains of Capernaum's central Christian shrine, the **House of St. Peter.** The church follows the octagonal outline of the Byzantine basilica that once encompassed the house Jesus is supposed to have visited.

The partly restored **synagogue** dominates the complex. The ancient Jewish community went to the expense of transporting white limestone blocks from afar to set the synagogue off from the town's crudely built black-basalt houses. Stone benches line the inside walls, recalling the building's original, primary function as a place of assembly where the Torah was read and explained on Sabbaths and holidays. (The fixed synagogue liturgy used today was a later development.)

The age of the Capernaum synagogue is still contested—it's thought to date from sometime between the 2nd and 5th centuries AD—but one thing is certain: this is not the actual synagogue of Mark 1 where Jesus taught. Nevertheless, consecrated ground was often reused, so the small structure in the excavation pit in the southeastern corner of the present building may be the remains of that 1st-century synagogue.

Near the deep shade of the ficus trees, look for the remains of a fine olive-oil press and some small hand mills made from hard and durable volcanic basalt. Basalt's advantages over the limestone found in the rest of Israel gave the Sea of Galilee region the raw material for an important export commodity in ancient times: agricultural equipment. Such mills have been found as far afield as Masada, Jerusalem, and the Mediterranean coast. To the right of the olive-oil press is the capital of a column with Jewish symbols in relief—a seven-branched menorah, a shofar (ram's horn), and an incense shovel—to preserve the memory of the Temple, with which they were associated. A small 1st-century mosaic from Magdala shows a contemporary boat, complete with oars and sails—a dramatic illustration of the many New Testament and Jewish references to traffic and fishing on the lake. ⊠ *Rte. 87,* ☎ *06/ 672–1059.* 🔊 *NIS 2 (60¢).* 🕑 *Daily 8:30–4.*

*En Route*    Route 87 continues east past Capernaum and crosses the **Jordan River**—somewhat muddy at this point—at the Arik Bridge. Those raised on spirituals extolling the Jordan's width and depth are often surprised to find how small a stream it really is. Seldom more than 30 ft wide, it's often shallow enough to wade in. (Record-breaking rains in the winter of 1991–92 did swell the river, flooding fields and threatening homes farther south.) The Jordan enters the Sea of Galilee just a few hundred yards to your right. In this wetland part of the Jordan Delta, archaeologists have finally identified and begun exploring the elusive site of the ancient Jewish town of Bethsaida, Peter's birthplace, according to the New Testament.

# Kursi and the Eastern Shore

**⓲**    *Kursi is 17 km (10½ mi) from Capernaum, and 5 km (3 mi) north of Ein Gev.*

Route 92 skirts the lake's eastern edge under the imposing cliffs of the southern Golan Heights, stringing together a series of beaches, water parks, picnic spots, campgrounds, lodgings, a restaurant, and a few historical sites. Route 87 continues east, climbing to Katzrin and the central Golan Heights.

Kursi, at the junction with Route 789, is linked with the New Testament, which tells the story of a man from Gadara who was possessed by demons (Matthew 8; Mark 5, and Luke 8 have him from Gerasa). Jesus miraculously exorcised the evil spirits, causing them to enter a herd of swine grazing nearby, which then "ran violently down a steep place into the lake, and were choked." Fifth-century Byzantine Christians identified the event with this spot, at the foot of the steep Golan Heights, and built a monastery here. Those were days of frequent pilgrimage to holy places, and the monastery prospered from the gifts of the devout. The partly restored ruins of a fine Byzantine church are a classic example of the basilica style common at the time; the remains of the monastery are perched higher up the hillside behind it. ⊠ *Rte. 92,* ☎ *06/673–1983.* ☜ *NIS 8 ($2.30).* ☉ *Apr.–Sept., Sat.–Thurs. 8–5, Fri. and holiday eves 8–4; Oct.–Mar., Sat.–Thurs. 8–4, Fri. and holiday eves 8–3.*

## Dining and Lodging

If you're interested in **camping,** this area has two campgrounds with full cooking and washing facilities, beach access, and stores: **Ein Gev** (⊠ Ein Gev 14940, ☎ 06/665–8199) and **Ha'on** (⊠ M.P. Jordan Valley 15170, ☎ 06/665–6555).

$$ ✕ **Ein Gev Fish Restaurant.** This lunch institution on the eastern shore now serves dinner year-round. Known for its St. Peter's fish (pay the higher price for a large fish to ensure moist meatiness), it also serves alternative, light entrées such as pizza, pasta, salads, and omelets. The outdoor patio has a view of Tiberias, whose lights twinkle across the lake. ⊠ *Kibbutz Ein Gev,* ☎ *06/665–8035 or 06/665–8036.* AE, DC, MC, V.

$$$ ⌖ **Ramot Resort Hotel.** High up in the foothills of the Golan Heights, this hotel is still just a 10-minute drive from the excellent Golan and Lunagal beaches (the latter with a water park) and has fabulous views of the Sea of Galilee region. Its main building has well-designed, comfortable, and air-conditioned guest rooms, each with a very private balcony and a lake view. The cottages, which are less expensive but older, are not as well endowed and are a bit run-down, but their wooden paneling and shutters and green surroundings give them some charm. Guided tours of the area are available in summer. ⊠ *E. of Rte. 92, 12490,* ☎ *06/673–2636,* ⒻⒶⓍ *06/679–3590. 123 rooms with bath, 19 cottages. Bar, coffee shop, pool.* AE, DC, MC, V.

$$ ⌖ **Ein Gev Holiday Village.** The kibbutz at Ein Gev has been in the tourism business for many years and is best known for its fish restaurant (☞ *above*), cruise boats, campground, and air-conditioned caravans. Better-class guest rooms with patios have been added to the motel-style building, all on a palm-shaded lakeside stretch with lawns and beach. Rates go up 25% on weekends and Jewish holidays. ⊠ *Rte. 92, 12 km (7½ mi) from Tzemach Junction, Post Office Ein Gev, 14940,* ☎ *06/665–9800,* ⒻⒶⓍ *06/665–9818. 144 rooms with bath. Restaurant, miniature golf, boating.* AE, DC, MC, V.

$$ ⌖ **Ma'agan.** This kibbutz on the southern tip of the Sea of Galilee, 12 ★ km (7½ mi) from Tiberias, has abandoned its old campsite-and-bungalow image for a more upmarket one. The lodgings are now proper guest rooms, plus spacious and well-outfitted suites that include a living room (with a lake-view picture window), two small bedrooms, bathroom, a kitchenette, a patio, and barbecue facilities. The kibbutz's sandy beach, swimming pool, and extensive lawns among the palms and eucalypti make it the best deal in the area. Kids have two smaller pools, a play area, and a menagerie. ⊠ *Rte. 92, 1 km (½ mi) east of Tzemach Junction, M.P. Jordan Valley 15160,* ☎ *06/675–3753,* ⒻⒶⓍ *06/675–3707. 24 rooms with bath, 100 1-bedroom suites. Restaurant, coffee shop, 3 pools, windsurfing, boating.* AE, DC, MC, V.

## Nightlife and the Arts

The **Ein Gev Spring Festival** (☎ 06/665–8030, ⒻⒶⓍ 06/665–9800), a music festival held within Kibbutz Ein Gev during Passover, celebrated its 55th anniversary in 1998. The festival once hosted the likes of Bernstein and Rampal, Dietrich and Sinatra, but its direction today is Israeli music, from traditional to contemporary. Call ahead for dates.

## Outdoor Activities and Sports

SWIMMING

**Ma'agan** (☞ Dining and Lodging, *above*) has a shaded lawn and picnic facilities as well as a beach. **Ein Gev, Golan Beach** (parking fee), and **Lunagal** (parking fee) are good swimming spots on the eastern shore; all are along Route 92.

WATER SPORTS

**Golan Beach** (☎ 06/673–1750) has a wide range of attractions, including power-boat, rowboat, kayak, and pedal-boat rentals; waterskiing; and the inflatable, power-towed "banana." The on-shore **Lunagal** has pools, water slides, and other diversions for kids. Open April through mid-October, the water park has late evening hours Monday and Thursday in July and August.

# Hammat Gader

⑲ *10 km (6 mi) east of Zemach Junction, 22 km (14 mi) southeast of Tiberias, 36 km (22½ mi) northeast of Bet She'an.*

Named for its patron city, Gadara, high up the southern bank of the Yarmuk, Hammat Gader was in its heyday the second-largest spa in the Roman Empire (after Baiae, near Naples). The drive to the site is an absorbing experience in itself. The road clings to the gorge of the Yarmuk River, crossed here and there by defunct railway bridges that once carried the narrow-gauge Valley Railroad trains from Haifa via Bet She'an to Damascus. On the opposite bank is biblical Gilead, now part of Jordan. Just before the descent to Hammat Gader, Route 98 climbs to the southern Golan Heights in a series of heart-stopping switchbacks.

Built around three hot springs, Hammat Gader's impressive complex of baths and pools attests to the opulence that once attracted voluptuaries and invalids alike. In its time, the entrance corridor was kept dimly lighted to dramatize the effect of the fine ornamental pool beyond—well lighted, in contrast, by high, glass-paned windows. Niches overlooking the pool are believed to have contained statues of Asclepius, the god of healing, and of Eros, the god of love, representing the site's two distinct attractions.

The large number of ancient clay oil lamps found in one small pool is proof of nighttime bathing and a hint that this area might have been set aside for lepers, to keep them out of sight. The original "hot tub"— test the water!—is fed by a spring at a temperature of 54°C (129°F). A large, cool pool, once adorned with water-spouting gargoyles, has been partly restored.

Hammat Gader is immensely popular among the locals, who tend to make a day of it, picnicking amid the lawns and large trees near the outdoor warm pool. Also on hand are a freshwater pool, changing facilities, trampolines and other kids' attractions, an alligator farm, a cafeteria, and a Thai restaurant. It's delightful as a leisurely visit but pricey if seeing the antiquities is your only purpose. ⊠ Rte. 98, ☎ 06/665– 9999. ☞ NIS 40 ($11.50) Sun.–Fri., NIS 45 ($12.90) Sat. and holidays; NIS 33 ($9.50) after 6 PM (diners at Siam need not buy admission to the whole park). ⊙ Sun. 7–4:30, Mon.–Sat. 7 AM–11 PM. Children's attractions close at 5 PM, alligator farm and antiquities at dusk. Entrance up to 1 hr before closing.

## Dining

$$–$$$   ✕ **Siam.** The all-wood interior, ornamented with Thai artifacts, creates a cool, exotic haven in the warm-spring park. The Thai cooks work under the direction of an Israeli chef, who, through frequent visits to

Thailand, has honed his culinary skills in a cuisine he has learned to love. For starters, try one of the excellent soups—tom ka kai (a chicken soup based on coconut milk) or tom yum (a spicy, clear chicken soup made with lemon grass)—or the slightly unusual egg rolls. Delicious main courses include *nua pad ka po*, stir-fried beef with basil leaves and garlic; *pla rad prik*, pink St. Peter's fish with a spicy sweet-and-sour sauce; and *kai yang*, boned chicken legs in various Thai sauces. The vegetarian options are also good. Pork and shellfish are not served. Dessert—not entirely traditional in the Far East—comes as a very pleasant surprise. ⊠ *Within park at Hammat Gader,* ☎ *06/665–9922 or 06/665–9933. Reservations essential. AE, DC, MC, V.*

## Degania Alef

 *10 km (6 mi) south of Tiberias.*

The collective village of Degania Alef (alef is the *a* of the Hebrew alphabet)—not to be confused with its younger neighbor Degania Bet (for Hebrew's letter *b*)—on the banks of the Jordan River, is distinguished as the world's first kibbutz, founded in 1909 by Jewish pioneers from Eastern Europe and established here on its permanent site the following year. The kibbutz idea—there are now some 280 kibbutzim in Israel—is based on the principle of "from each according to his ability, to each according to his need." Israel's early pioneers needed a unified communal structure to cope with the forbidding terrain and a hostile neighborhood; but more than that, they were seeking the perfect society, based on absolute equality and the subordination of individual desires to the needs of the community.

The principles of the founders remained remarkably resilient for years, but the dream has begun to fade a bit; commitment to the old ideals has become more tenuous and less relevant for a new, more materialistic generation. Still, about 2.5% of the general population live on kibbutzim, the swampland and rocky soil have become fields and plantations, and light industry and tourism are significant additions to the communities' economic profiles.

Near the entrance to Degania Alef is a small Syrian tank of World War II vintage. On May 15, 1948, the day after Israel declared its independence, the fledgling state was invaded from all sides by Arab armies. Syrian forces came down the Yarmuk Valley from the east, overran two other kibbutzim en route, and were only stopped here, at the gates of Degania, by a teenager with a Molotov cocktail.

Within restored stone buildings of the early kibbutz is the museum of **Bet Gordon** (A. D. Gordon House), named for the white-bearded spiritual mentor of the early pioneers. It houses two fascinating collections: one devoted to the natural history of the region, with a renowned collection of stuffed birds, the other examining the history and archaeology of human settlement in the surrounding valleys. Among the prehistoric sites represented is Ubeidiya, just south of the kibbutz and Israel's oldest human settlement, now dated by scholars to 1.25 million years ago. Another **museum** (☎ 06/675–8111), also on Degania Alef, tells the story of the kibbutz; admission is free. There are no English labels here, but the bilingual curator is usually on hand to explain, and the traveler with a taste for modern history and a desire to get off the tourist trail might pass a pleasurable hour here. ⊠ *Near Rte. 90,* ☎ *06/675–0040.* ▣ *Bet Gordon NIS 6 ($2).* ☉ *Sun.–Thurs. 9:30–4, Fri. and holiday eves 8:30–noon, Sat. and holidays 9:30–noon.*

### Nightlife and the Arts

A welcome new addition to the region is **Bet Gabriel** cultural center (☎ 06/675–1175, 🆇 06/675–1187), on the southern shores of the Sea of Galilee near Degania Alef. Its fine architecture, beautiful garden setting, and state-of-the-art concert facilities have already established it as a magnet, a 10-minute drive from Tiberias.

Tiberias's **Tourist Information Office** (☎ 06/672–5666) and all major hotels carry information on that month's performances and art exhibits.

## Kinneret

> 2 km (1 mi) from Degania Alef, 10 km (6 mi) south of Tiberias.

Kinneret, a kibbutz just across the Jordan to the north of Degania, was founded in 1911 and named for the lake nearby. Two places in the immediate vicinity are of interest to travelers. On a picturesque stretch of the Jordan, where huge eucalyptus trees droop into the quiet water, is **Yardenit,** developed in recent years as a baptism site for Christian pilgrims. Although the baptism of Jesus by John the Baptist (Matthew 3) is traditionally identified with the southern reaches of the Jordan River, near Jericho, that area became a hostile frontier between Israel and Jordan in 1949, and pilgrims began to seek out accessible spots near the Sea of Galilee. Here at Yardenit, groups of white-robed pilgrims are often immersed in the Jordan, accompanied by prayers, hymns, and expressions of joy. There are showers and changing facilities, towels and robes for rent in the souvenir shop, and, at press time, an imminent cafeteria. ⊠ Off Rte. 90, ☎ 06/675–9141. ☉ Mar.–Nov., Sat.–Thurs. 8–5, Fri. and holiday eves 8–4; Dec.–Feb. daily 8–4.

The serene and somewhat enchanted **cemetery of Kibbutz Kinneret,** barely 1 km (½ mi) north of the Jordan River bridge at a bend in Route 90, holds the grave of Rachel Hameshoreret (Rachel the Poetess), which has become a virtual shrine for many Israelis. An opening in the low stone wall on the right leads by shaded paths to the shore of the Sea of Galilee, with a superb view of the Golan Heights and, rarely, of majestic Mt. Hermon, to the north. Among the other distinguished denizens of this ground are some early philosophers and pioneer leaders of the Zionist movement—Borochov, Hess, Syrkin, Katznelson. A few steps down from the clearing to the next path brings you to Rachel's grave.

The large number of pebbles left on her grave by visitors (a token of respect in the Jewish tradition) is a tribute to Rachel's renown and to the romantic hold she has on the national imagination. Born in Russia, Rachel immigrated to Eretz Yisrael (the Land of Israel) in 1909 at the age of 19, lived in Degania and Kinneret, and was in France studying agriculture when World War I broke out. Unable to get back into Ottoman Turkish Palestine because of her Russian citizenship, she spent the war years working with refugee children in Russia, where she contracted the tuberculosis that eventually took her life. She returned to her beloved lake, but she never regained her health and died in 1931.

Rachel became a poet of national stature in Hebrew, her third language. The modern flavor and immediacy of her poems made them natural lyrics for a whole genre of modern Israeli folk songs. Rachel wrote with great sensitivity of the beauty of this region, and with passion—knowing that her end was near—of her frustrated dream of raising a family. Her tombstone is eloquently devoid of biographical information; it carries the only name by which she is known, Rachel, and four lines from one of her poems: "Spread out your hands, look yonder:/nothing comes./Each man has his Nebo/in the great expanse." (It was from Mt. Nebo that Moses looked into the promised land that *he* knew he would never enter.) In a recess in the stone seat by the grave site is a weatherproof canister containing a complete volume (in Hebrew) of Rachel's poems, just a few steps from the spot where many were written. ✉ *Off Rte. 90, 600 yards south of the junction with Rte. 767.*

## Hammat Tiberias

★ ❷ *7 km (4 mi) north of Kinneret, 2 km (1 mi) south of Tiberias.*

Here you'll find Israel's hottest spring, gushing out of the earth at 60°C (140°F). The healing properties of its mineral-rich waters were already recognized in antiquity, as evidenced by the ruins of ancient towns—including an exquisite 4th-century AD mosaic floor of a synagogue. Legend says that Solomon, the great king of Israel, wanted a hot bath and used his awesome authority to force some young devils below ground to heat the water. The fame of the salubrious springs spread far and wide, bringing the afflicted to seek relief. Seeing such gladness among his subjects, Solomon worried about what would happen when he died and the devils stopped their labors. In a flash of the wisdom for which he was renowned, Solomon made the hapless devils deaf. To this day, they have not heard of the king's demise and so continue to heat the water for fear of his wrath.

The scientific explanation is almost tame by comparison. This and other hot mineral springs in Israel (Hammat Gader, Ein Gedi) were created by massive upheavals along the Great Syrian-African Rift, the world's longest fault line. Cracks in the earth's crust allow mineral-rich water to boil to the surface.

By the end of the Second Temple period (the 1st century AD), when settlement in the Sea of Galilee region was at its height, a Jewish town called Hammat (Hot Springs) stood here. With time, Hammat was overshadowed by its newer neighbor Tiberias and became known as Hammat Tiberias (Tiberias Hot Springs). The benefits of the mineral hot springs were already legendary: a coin minted in Tiberias during the rule of Emperor Trajan, around AD 100, shows Hygeia, the goddess of health, sitting on a rock with a spring gushing out beneath it.

Parts of ancient Hammat have been uncovered by archaeologists on the mountain side of the road, bringing to light a number of ruined synagogues built one upon the other. The most dramatic dates from the 4th century AD, with an elaborate mosaic floor that uses motifs almost identical to those at Bet Alfa: classical Jewish symbols, human figures representing the four seasons and the signs of the zodiac, and the Greek god Helios at the center (☞ *Bet Alfa in* Jezreel and Jordan Valleys, *above*). The childlike art of Bet Alfa has its charm, to be sure, but the mosaics of Hammat Tiberias are among the finest ever found in Israel. Later cultures exploited the hot springs, too, as the small adjacent Turkish bath attests. ✉ *Rte. 90,* ☎ *06/672–5287.* ✑ *NIS 8 ($2.30).* ☉ *Apr.–Sept., Sat.–Thurs. 8–5, Fri. and holiday eves 8–4; Oct.–Mar., Sat.–Thurs. 8–4, Fri. and holiday eves 8–3.*

Behind Hammat Tiberias, a turquoise dome marks the **tomb of Rabbi Meir Ba'al Ha-Nes**, the "Miracle Worker," a legendary personality who supposedly took a vow that he would not lie down until the Messiah came—and was therefore buried in an upright position. His name has become a sort of emblem for charitable organizations, and many a miracle has been attributed to the power of prayer at his tomb.

NEED A
BREAK?

**Tiberias Hot Springs,** on the lake side of the road, is one of the two modern spa facilities fed by the mineral spring (the other, on the mountain side of the road, is for medical use exclusively). In addition to sophisticated therapeutic services and facilities, it has a large, pampering, warm indoor mineral pool (35°C, or 95°F) and a small outdoor one right near the lake's edge. The restaurant serves lunch. ⊠ *Rte. 90,* ☎ *06/672–8500.* ⊞ *Pools NIS 48 ($13.70), extra for massages and therapies, 20% discount for weekday entry after 4 PM. Lockers NIS 5 ($1.50). Robe rental NIS 18 ($5) plus deposit of NIS 100 ($28.60).* ☉ *Sun.–Mon., Wed., and Sat. 8–7:30; Tues. and Thurs. 8 AM–10:30 PM; Fri. 8–4:30 (inquire about later summer hrs).*

# LOWER GALILEE A TO Z

## Arriving and Departing

### By Bus

The **Egged** bus cooperative provides frequent service from Jerusalem, Tel Aviv, and Haifa to Bet She'an, Afula, Nazareth, and Tiberias. There is no direct service from Ben-Gurion International Airport; change in Tel Aviv. From Tel Aviv, Buses 824 and 823 run to Afula and Nazareth several times a day; the ride takes 1½ hours to Afula, another 20 minutes to Nazareth. Bus 830 runs from Tel Aviv to Tiberias about every hour; the ride takes 2½ hours. To get from Haifa to Tiberias, take Bus 430, which leaves hourly; the ride is about one hour. From Haifa, take Bus 301 or 302 to Afula (about every 30 minutes); change in Afula for Nazareth or Bet She'an. Buses from Jerusalem to Bet She'an and Tiberias (Buses 961 and 963) depart roughly hourly. The ride to Bet She'an is about two hours, to Tiberias another 25 minutes. Buses 355, 823, and 824 make the 20-minute run between Afula and Nazareth.

### By Car

From Tel Aviv, the Lower Galilee can be reached by taking Route 2 north (the Tel Aviv–Haifa Highway) and then heading northeast along one of two regional roads: Route 65 (near Caesarea), emerging into the Jezreel Valley at Megiddo (80 km, or 50 mi; a 1¼-hour drive); or Route 70 (near Zichron Ya'akov), emerging at Yokne'am (90 km, or 57 mi; a 1½-hour drive). Avoid driving north out of Tel Aviv midday Friday and returning south to Tel Aviv Saturday afternoon and early evening. Access from Haifa is on Route 75 east to Bet She'arim and Nazareth (35 km, or 22 mi; a 45-minute drive to Nazareth); or from Route 75 onto Routes 70 and 66 south to Megiddo (34 km, or 22 mi; a 40-minute drive). The best route from Jerusalem is Route 1 east, then Route 90 north to Bet She'an (124 km, or 78 mi; a two-hour drive).

## Getting Around

### By Boat

The Ein Gev–based boat company **Kinneret Sailing** (⊠ Rte. 92, Kibbutz Ein Gev, ☎ 06/675–8008 or 06/675–8009) makes regularly scheduled morning, noon, and afternoon runs on the Sea of Galilee between Tiberias (western shore) and Ein Gev (eastern shore) in August and during the Jewish holiday seasons (Passover in the spring, Sukkoth/Tabernacles in the autumn). At other times, you can often join a chartered cruise; call close to the time you want to go (office open 8–4:30). The boats are large (100–170 passengers), and the 45-minute crossings are comfortable in almost all weather. Fares are about NIS 28 ($8) for the round trip, NIS 18 ($5.20) one-way. You'll probably have time to eat a fish lunch at Ein Gev before sailing back to Tiberias.

**Lido Kinneret** (✉ Gedud Barak St., ☎ 06/672–1538 or 06/679–2564) specializes in group charters, especially (but not exclusively) between Tiberias and Kibbutz Ginosar or Capernaum.

## By Bus

The most important sites in the region are accessible by bus, but the sometimes infrequent local service and transfers can make bus travel a time-consuming exercise. Bet She'an, Nazareth, Tiberias, and Tabgha are on the main routes; other places, such as Megiddo, the Mount of Beatitudes, and Bet She'arim, are a bit of a walk from a nearby junction—or even a good, long hike, as in the case of Capernaum and Mt. Tabor. Mt. Gilboa and Belvoir are essentially inaccessible without a car.

## By Car

Driving is the best way to explore this region. The main roads are fairly good—some newer four-lane highways are excellent—but some smaller roads are narrow and in great need of repair. Signposting is generally good (and in English), with route numbers clearly marked. Ask directions by destination, because most Israelis are not yet familiar with the relatively recent innovation of route numbers. Most sights and accommodations are indicated by brown signs. You'll find gas stations and refreshment stands all over.

## By Guide-Driven Limo-Van

Although not cheap for a couple, guide-driven vans can be very efficient and, for a larger party, cost-effective as well. Most people traveling this way reach the region in the company of their Jerusalem- or Tel Aviv–based guide; few guides are actually based in Galilee.

## By Taxi

This is generally an expensive and uninspiring way to travel. For sightseeing you're often much better off hiring a private guide with a car or limousine (☞ *above*). Some of the area's main taxi companies include the following:

AFULA
**Yizre'el,** ☎ 06/652–3111.

NAZARETH
**Abu el-Assal,** ☎ 06/655–4745; **Diana,** ☎ 06/655–5554; **Hashalom,** ☎ 06/657–2858.

TIBERIAS
**Hagalil,** ☎ 06/672–0353; **Ha'emek,** ☎ 06/672–0131.

# Contacts and Resources

## Car Rentals

Agencies close early Friday afternoon and are closed on Saturday (except in Nazareth).

In Tiberias, companies include **Avis** (✉ Central Bus Station, ☎ 06/672–2766); **Budget** (✉ Opposite Carmel Jordan River Hotel, Habanim St., ☎ 06/672–0864); **Eldan** (✉ In Carmel Jordan River Hotel, Habanim St., ☎ 06/672–2831); **Europcar** (National) (✉ Sonol Garage, Alhadeff St., ☎ 06/672–2777); **Hertz** (✉ In Jordan River Hotel, Habanim St., ☎ 06/672–3939); **Reliable** (✉ 9 Alhadeff St., ☎ 06/672–3464).

## Emergencies

**Ambulance service** (☎ 101). **First aid** (☎ 101). **Pharmacies** with late-night service (☎ 101). **Police** in the Lower Galilee (☎ 100).

## Guided Tours

A free walking tour of Tiberias leaves from the **Radisson Moriah Plaza Hotel** (⊠ Habanim St., ☎ 06/679–2233) on Saturday at 10 AM. Call ahead to verify.

Few bus tours actually originate in the Lower Galilee; they start instead from Jerusalem, Tel Aviv, Haifa, and Netanya. Most hotels can book a tour for you, and all buses will pick you up and drop you off at your hotel.

Both Egged Tours and United Tours conduct one- and two-day trips from Jerusalem, Tel Aviv, Haifa, and Netanya several times a week. Itineraries include (in different combinations) Megiddo, Nazareth, Zippori, Bet She'an, Hammat Gader, Tiberias, Tabgha, Capernaum, and a boat ride on the Sea of Galilee. Many two-day tours include the Upper Galilee and Golan Heights. Prices range from $54 to $60 for a day trip to $187 (including overnight lodging and dinner) for two days. For reservations, contact one of the following:

**Egged Tours,** in Jerusalem (⊠ 8 Shlomzion Hamalka St., ☎ 02/622–1999); Tel Aviv (⊠ 59 Ben Yehuda St., ☎ 03/527–1212 or 03/527–1215); Haifa (⊠ 300 Bar Yehuda St., ☎ 04/820–2838 or 04/820–2737); and Netanya (⊠ Central Bus Station, ☎ 09/860–6206 or 09/860–6207). For reservations with **United Tours,** call Jerusalem (⊠ King David Hotel annex, ☎ 02/625–2187 or 02/625–2188) or Tel Aviv (⊠ 113 Hayarkon St., ☎ 03/693–3412 or 03/522–2008).

For the more active or adventurous traveler, the nonprofit **Society for the Protection of Nature in Israel** does things differently. The group's three-day Galilee tour includes hiking and some Lower Galilee sights. For information call the society in Jerusalem (⊠ 13 Helene Hamalka St., ☎ 02/624–4605) or Tel Aviv (⊠ 19 Hasharon St., ☎ 03/638–8674).

**Vered Hagalil,** at Korazim Junction, is an Israeli version of a dude ranch, offering comfortable accommodations and a good restaurant on top of short and long horseback tours above and around the Sea of Galilee. For more information contact Vered Hagalil (⊠ Rte. 90, M.P. Korazim, ☎ 06/693–5785, ⅎ 06/693–4964).

Donkey rides, a revival of an ancient tradition, are singularly appropriate in the hills of Nazareth and the Lower Galilee. **Donkey Tracks** conducts fully guided group tours (call ahead to see what's available), or you can rent a donkey on your own for NIS 50 ($14.30) an hour, complete with map, directions, and safety instructions. Discounts are available if you reserve through certain B&Bs. For more information, contact Kfar Kedem (⊠ Hoshaya, M.P. Hamovil 17915, ☎ 06/656–5511, ⅎ 06/657–0378).

## Nightlife and the Arts

By far the best source of information on cultural life in the Lower Galilee is the tourist office on Habanim Street in Tiberias (☎ 06/672–5666), between the Radisson Moriah Plaza and Carmel Jordan River hotels.

Local kibbutzim periodically host theater troupes, dancers, and musicians on tour from the "big cities" to the south; inquire at your hotel or a tourist office for schedules.

## Outdoor Activities and Sports

BICYCLING

There is a **bicycle marathon** around the Sea of Galilee at the end of October or the beginning November, with both popular and competitive categories. There are three distances: 12 km (7½ mi), 25 km (15½ mi), and a complete 64-km (40-mi) ring around the Sea of Galilee. All end at the Tzemach Junction. For details contact the Sports Department of the Jordan Valley Regional Council (✉ Tzemach Junction 15132, ☎ 06/675–7630 or 06/675–7631, FAX 06/675–7641).

HIKING

For information on trails and organized hikes in the Jezreel and Jordan valleys, contact the SPNI's **Alon-Tavor Field Study Center** (✉ M.P. Lower Galilee 14101, ☎ 06/676–7798). The center also has hostel-type accommodations.

HORSEBACK RIDING

The **Vered Hagalil** ranch (✉ Rte. 90, M.P. Korazim, ☎ 06/693–5785, FAX 06/693–4964), on Route 90 north of the Sea of Galilee at Korazim Junction, conducts horseback tours (☞ Guided Tours, *above*).

SWIMMING

Thousands of swimmers take part in the **Kinneret Swim** in September, a tradition since 1953. Traditionally a 4-km (2½-mi) race, the event has now gained recognition as an international swim meet, and the toughest swimmers cover distances of up to 10 km (6 mi). Most, of course, are amateurs just out for fun. For details, contact the Jordan Valley Regional Council (✉ Tzemach Junction 15132, ☎ 06/675–7630 or 06/675–7631, FAX 06/675–7641).

WALKING AND RUNNING

The annual **Big Walk** (Hatza'adah in Hebrew), which takes place in March or April over a 11-km (7-mi) route along the Sea of Galilee shore, attracts participants from all over the country. For details contact the Jordan Valley Regional Council (✉ Tzemach Junction 15132, ☎ 06/ 675–7630 or 06/675–7631, FAX 06/675–7641).

Dedicated runners might want to participate in the **Sea of Galilee Marathon and Half-Marathon,** which take place in December or January. There's a triathlon at the beginning of May. For details contact the Sports Department of the Jordan Valley Regional Council (✉ Tzemach Junction 15132, ☎ 06/675–7630 or 06/675–7631, FAX 06/ 675–7641).

WATER SPORTS

The so-called kayaks of **Abukayak** (☎ 06/692–2245 or 06/692– 1078) are really inflated rubber canoes. Based inside the **Jordan River Park** (✉ Rte. 888, just north of the Sea of Galilee), Abukayak suggests a delightfully serene one-hour route (decidedly not white water!) down the lower Jordan River. Life jackets are provided, and the trip is entirely appropriate for young children.

For serious kayaking, look into the annual **international kayaking competition** held each March. Contact the Sports Department of the Jordan Valley Regional Council (✉ Tzemach Junction 15132, ☎ 06/ 675–7630 or 06/675–7631, FAX 06/675–7641).

## Visitor Information

There are **Tourist Information Offices** in Nazareth (✉ GTIO, Casa Nova St., ☎ 06/657–3003 or 06/657–0555) and Tiberias (✉ Habanim St., between the Carmel Jordan River and Radisson Moriah Plaza hotels, ☎ 06/672–5666).

# 7 Upper Galilee and the Golan

*Including Zfat (Safed)*

*With something for everyone, this area draws pilgrims and vacationers, serious hikers and bon vivants. You can walk around Zfat, the mystical hillside city, or kayak near a kibbutz guest house. Despite the political heat that pervades the region—the Golan Heights in particular—this is the part of Israel that best represents cool, comfortable relaxation. The area's history dates back a million years, but today its culture is geared to the modern traveler, with both traditional and trendy diversions.*

By Lisa Perlman

**I**SRAELIS CALL IT THE SWITZERLAND OF ISRAEL. The undulating hills of Western Galilee roll into sharper, more rugged limestone and basalt formations, bordered on the north by Lebanon and on the east by the volcanic, mountainous Golan Heights, beyond which lies Syria. The dominant feature of the Upper Galilee and the Golan is Mt. Hermon—the highest mountain in Israel, one of the highest in the Middle East, and the home of Israel's sole ski resort.

Most Israelis come here to get away from it all, indulging in everything from hiking and bird-watching to kayaking and wine tasting. The nature trails, the rustic restaurants, and the kibbutz guest houses make it easy to steer clear of the region's four cities; in fact, two of these—Kiryat Shmona and Ma'alot, both of which began life as development towns designed to absorb Jewish refugees, mainly from Arab countries—are of little interest to the traveler. The other two—Zfat (Safed) and Katzrin—have unique personalities, the first the result of a long history of Jewish religious mysticism and the second the result of a hard-headed determination to secure Israel's border with Syria.

Towering more than 9,000 ft, Mt. Hermon is Israel's "sponge" as well as its ski slope: huge volumes of water from snow and rain are absorbed into the ancient limestone rock, emerging at the base of the mountain in a series of gorgeous springs and feeding the Jordan River and its tributaries. Indeed, these rivers, all flowing through the region's Hula Valley, provide half of Israel's water supply. The abundant water sustains gazelles, wildcats, hyraxes and hares, hundreds of species of birds, and lush, verdant foliage that thrives year-round.

More than anything else, it is this water that has been the source of political contention since time immemorial. (In second place is the hilltop view, a key factor in the strategic value of the Golan Heights, officially annexed by Israel in 1981.) This region has been a center of human settlement for a million years. In earliest times, people hunted the rhinos, elephants, and fallow deer that have since roamed to other parts. Later they learned to farm—and to trade, for the Galilee was smack-dab on the Western world's first major trade route, the Via Maris, stretching from Egypt to Mesopotamia.

Consequently, the rivals for this prime real estate were many. In ancient times, Egyptians, Canaanites, Israelites, Romans, Ottomans, and Crusaders locked horns in various configurations; in the 20th century, the borders have been played with by Russia, Britain, France, and, of course, Israel and Syria.

In addition to the Jewish and Arab population, there has always been a small Druze presence here, particularly in the Golan Heights (home to about 17,000 Arabic-speaking Druze). After the Six-Day War in 1967, five Druze villages found themselves no longer in Lebanese or Syrian territory, but in Israel.

Borders are not the only things that have shifted here. A geological fault line, the Syrian-African Rift, cuts straight through the 30-km-long (19-mi-long) Hula Valley. Many symmetrical volcanic cones, hundreds of thousands of years old, daub the Golan; and in 1837 Zfat and Tiberias were razed in an earthquake, though no significant rumbles have been heard since.

With plenty of water and rich fertile soil, the Upper Galilee and the Golan have always been centers of agriculture. Since Jewish development of the area resumed a century ago, orange and apple orchards, fish-cultivation ponds, cotton fields, and vineyards have become common sights. These are closely intertwined with the region's other main industry: tourism. Travelers come to see and stay at the many successful communal settlements—the *kibbutzim* and *moshavim*—that dot the area. They also come to roam the nature reserves, most of which hug the rivers and springs; to witness the seasonal migration of birds that flit between Africa and Europe; and to taste the local wine.

Proximity to Lebanon and Syria does not deter people from visiting the Upper Galilee and the Golan. On the contrary, the so-called Good Fence, at the Israeli-Lebanese border crossing in Israel's northernmost town of Metulla, draws curious onlookers from all over the world.

Whether the status of the Golan Heights will change as a result of the on-again, off-again peace negotiations between Israel and Lebanon remains unknown. Since their arrival at the turn of the century, the Jews have fought malaria and other diseases, defended themselves against Arab armies and terror bands, and confronted a host of other hardships and hurdles. Yet the tenacious Galilean will still tell you there's no better place. Whether he's a kibbutznik or a town dweller, whether she was born here or chose this corner of the world, the Galilean's pride is palpable and transcends politics. It's amazing that despite the embattled past and uncertain future, Galileans remain largely laid-back and friendly. Only four hours' drive from hectic, humid Tel Aviv and visceral Jerusalem, this truly is another world.

## Pleasures and Pastimes

### Dining
Only a few years ago, one hand had too many fingers to count the number of good restaurants in this region. Decent light food, such as falafel in pita bread, is never far away, but the concept of real meals in real restaurants with real atmosphere is relatively new to Israel. The Upper Galilee and the Golan have inherent attractions for diners: with verdant hills, old stone dwellings, and crisp, appetite-whetting air, the landscape serves as an exquisite backdrop for a savory meal. Today many restaurants make the best of this environment. You can tuck into hearty steaks in the middle of the forest; fresh grilled Dan River trout in shady groves on the river's banks, Middle Eastern fare prepared by Druze villagers; and simple, home-style Jewish cooking in the heart of the holy city of Zfat. The excellent local wines from Katzrin enhance any meal; try the Mt. Hermon red, Gamla cabernet sauvignon, and Yarden cabernet blanc and merlot. Most restaurants are open every day except Yom Kippur; in a few places, however (Zfat, for example), it's hard to find one on Shabbat (Friday afternoon until Saturday sundown). Attire is always informal, but it's best to dress modestly in Zfat.

| CATEGORY | COST* |
|---|---|
| **$$$$** | over $30 |
| **$$$** | $22–$30 |
| **$$** | $12–$22 |
| **$** | under $12 |

*per person for a three-course meal, excluding drinks and service*

### Hiking
Superbly maintained nature reserves and national parks make this region an obvious destination for hikers. Most trails are well marked and not too challenging; stick to the tracks to avoid any trouble. Always carry water, and wear a hat, especially in summer; wear comfortable shoes as well. You may want to take an extra pair of shoes in case you get wet—there's an abundance of water in these parts.

## Horseback Riding

Horseback riding—on both long and short trails—has really taken off in the Upper Galilee. It's an excellent way to see and appreciate Israel's beautiful northern landscape.

## Jeep Tours

Jeep tours are very popular here. Needless to say, jeeps can cover more distance in less time than your legs or a horse's, and they add a dash of excitement.

## Kayaking and Rafting

One of the more adventurous local sports, and one that's enormously enjoyable for all ages, is skimming the Jordan River in a kayak, raft, or inner tube. Countless companies rent the necessary equipment. Novices needn't worry—this is not white-water territory.

## Lodging

There are no grand hotels here, but the ample selection of guest houses and inns ranges from ranch-style to home-style. As the local tourist industry has developed, many settlements, especially kibbutzim and moshavim, have added hotels (or just wings attached to homes) and an extensive range of amenities, including activities for children. Although most guest houses remain independent of the community's other industries, they sometimes offer lectures and tours of the settlement. In addition to providing meals, many also arrange kayaking and rafting, horseback riding, jeep tours, and other sports and services for both guests and the general public. The choice can be difficult, as all are in pretty settings and have well-maintained grounds.

| CATEGORY | COST* |
| --- | --- |
| $$$$ | over $120 |
| $$$ | $80–$120 |
| $$ | $55–$80 |
| $ | under $55 |

*All prices are for two people in a standard double room, including breakfast and 15% service charge.

# Exploring Upper Galilee and the Golan

The northern Jordan Valley serves as the border between these two regions, with the hilly Upper Galilee lying to the west and the Golan, a basalt plateau, to the east. Together, however, they are still small enough to be combined in a weekend trip.

## Great Itineraries

Tel Avivians do it. Jerusalemites do it. But cramming the Upper Galilee and the Golan into a day trip is far from ideal for the first-time visitor. Although brief visits are certainly possible (a day trip to the Golan Heights from Tiberias, for example), a several-day sojourn here can be as leisurely or as hectic as you wish. In three or four days, you can learn about Israel's military history, taste a bit of wine, hike a little piece of wilderness, relax over a hearty country meal, try your hand at kayaking, or just kick back in a room with a view.

Distances in this region are short—even shorter than elsewhere in Israel. Still, the more time you have here, the better; there's something about the soft gurgling of the brooks, the lush foliage of the forests, and the crisp mountain air of the Golan Heights that slows the pace. The ideal way to see this area is by car, but local buses will get you almost anywhere you want to go. Towns and sights in this chapter are arranged as in the order you would most likely visit them by road, either from Tel Aviv or from Tiberias.

# Upper Galilee and the Golan

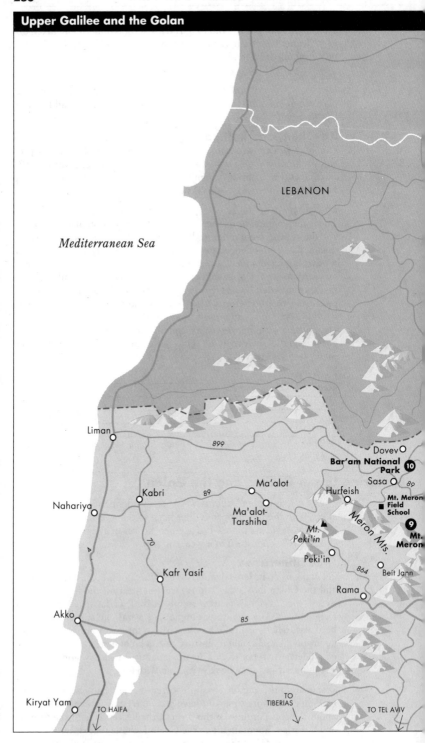

Mediterranean Sea

LEBANON

Liman

899

Dovev

**Bar'am National Park** ⑩

Sasa

89

Kabri

89

Ma'alot

Hurfeish

Mt. Meron Field School

Nahariya

Ma'alot-Tarshiha

Mt. Peki'in

Meron Mts.

⑨ **Mt. Meron**

70

Peki'in

864

Beit Jann

Kafr Yasif

4

Rama

Akko

85

Kiryat Yam

TO HAIFA

TO TIBERIAS

TO TEL AVIV

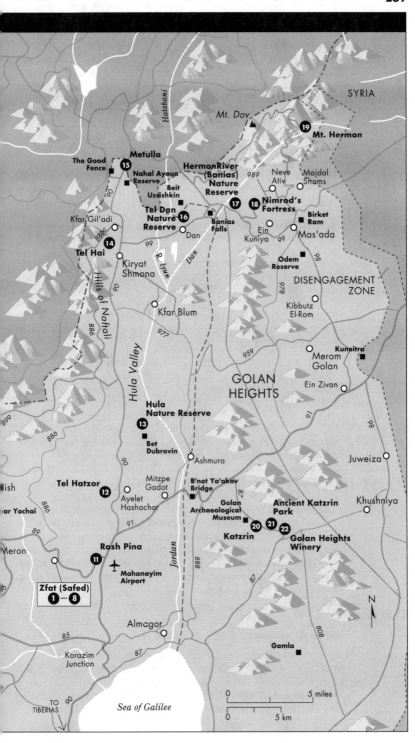

SYRIA

Mt. Dov

**19** Mt. Hermon

Hatzbani

The Good Fence

**15** Metulla

Nahal Ayoun Reserve

Beit Ussishkin

Hermon River (Banias) Nature Reserve

989

Neve Ativ

Majdal Shams

Kfar Gil'adi

**16** Tel Dan Nature Reserve

**17**

**18** Nimrod's Fortress

Birket Ram

886

Dan

Banias Falls

Ein Kuniya

Mas'ada

**14** Tel Hai

R. Iyun

99

Kiryat Shmona

Dan

98

**Odem Reserve**

Hills of Naftali

Kfar Blum

DISENGAGEMENT ZONE

886

977

978

Kibbutz El-Rom

GOLAN HEIGHTS

Merom Golan

Kuneitra

899

Hula Valley

959

Ein Zivan

886

Hula Nature Reserve

**13**

91

Bet Dubrovin

Ashmura

98

Juweiza

Tel Hatzor

Mitzpe Gadot

B'not Ya'akov Bridge

Ancient Katzrin Park

Khushniya

**12**

Ayelet Hashachar

87

Golan Archaeological Museum

**20** **21** **22**

ar Yochai

886

91

Katzrin

Golan Heights Winery

Rosh Pina

**11**

Jordan

Meron

89

Mahanayim Airport

888

87

Zfat (Safed)

**1** — **8**

Almagor

808

N

85

Gamla

Korazim Junction

87

TO TIBERIAS

90

*Sea of Galilee*

0      5 miles

0     5 km

Note: touring in the Upper Galilee and the Golan is perfectly safe. If, however, security demands unusual caution, certain areas may be temporarily inaccessible to visitors.

*Numbers in the text correspond to numbers in the margin and on the Upper Galilee and the Golan map and the Zfat (Safed) map.*

IF YOU HAVE 1 DAY

If your base is Tiberias or elsewhere in the Lower Galilee (or Western Galilee), spend your day trip in the northernmost part of the country, starting with a walk through the **Tel Dan** ⑯ or **Hermon River (Banias)** ⑰ nature reserve, and lunching on a Dan River trout. You can then either tackle **Nimrod's Fortress** ⑱ or, in spring and summer, take a chairlift to the top of **Mt. Hermon** ⑲. In winter, try wine tasting in **Katzrin** ⑳–㉒. Or spend the morning strolling through the Old City in **Zfat** ①–⑧ and the afternoon kayaking on the Jordan River.

IF YOU HAVE 2–3 DAYS

A few days give you a few different options. Tiberias is a good starting point; either spend a morning by the Sea of Galilee or head for **Zfat** ①–⑧ and take a walk through the Old City. Stop in **Rosh Pina** ⑪ for a cup of coffee and a break, and then check out the swampy **Hula Nature Reserve** ⑬. Spend the night in a kibbutz guest house; the next day, head for the Golan Heights via Route 98, which overlooks the Disengagement Zone between Israel and Syria. The third day is well spent outdoors—horseback riding, kayaking or rafting on the Jordan River, or jeep touring.

## When to Tour the Upper Galilee and the Golan

The Upper Galilee and the Golan are best in spring and fall. If you're a flora fan, the range of full-bloom colors is wondrous in late winter and spring. In the summer, days can be hot, but the region doesn't suffer the humidity of other parts of Israel. In the winter, you can expect some rain. Note, however, that Zfat comes alive from July through September, when more galleries are open. There are more activities for travelers then, but also more crowds.

# ZFAT (SAFED) AND ENVIRONS

In the southern part of the Upper Galilee, attractions range from the narrow streets and historic synagogues of the Old City of Zfat to the wilderness of the Hula Nature Reserve. Other nature reserves, such as Mt. Meron, have both scenic appeal and spiritual importance. At Rosh Pina you can see where the Galilee's first Zionist pioneers settled. And if you just want to relax at an inn or a kibbutz guest house and enjoy the wooded scenery, you can do that, too.

## Zfat (Safed)

*33 km (20 mi) north of Tiberias, 72 km (45 mi) northeast of Haifa.*

At 3,000 ft above sea level, Zfat (commonly translated as Safed) is Israel's highest city. Perhaps this proximity to the heavens accounts for its reputation as the center of Jewish mysticism (Kabbala). For although it is one of several holy cities in Israel—along with Jerusalem, Tiberias, and Hebron—Zfat has a spiritual dimension found nowhere else.

The Crusaders built a fortress here, and a thriving Jewish settlement grew up in the shadow of the castle walls. Although it declined with the eclipse of the Crusader presence in the Galilee, the town survived rule by the Ottomans, who retained Zfat as their capital through the 16th century. Soon after their expulsion in 1492, Jews from Spain started streaming in, among them respected rabbis and other spiritual leaders, intellectuals, and poets who gravitated to Zfat as a center of the revival of Kabbala study.

The Kabbala—whose oral tradition dates to ancient times but gained popularity starting in the 12th century, possibly as a reaction against formal rabbinical Judaism—is about reading between, behind, and all around the lines: each and every letter and accent of every word in the holy books has a numerical value with specific significance, offering added meaning to the literal word. Zfat was the heart of the Kabbala, the great rabbis its soul; under their tutelage, religious and mystical schools and meeting places mushroomed here. Some of these leaders would leave their mark on the age, on the generations to follow, and, of course, on Zfat itself.

For most of the year, Zfat can be something of an enigma to the traveler: it hibernates from October through June. The city's noted artists move to warmer parts of the country, opening their galleries in Zfat only infrequently, and other sites may also be closed. This does not mean you should leave Zfat off your itinerary during those months; there is enough to occupy the curious wanderer for at least a few hours, and much of it is free. In the summer, especially the school holidays (July and August), Zfat is abuzz with activity: galleries and shops stay open late, klezmer music dances around corners, and the city extends a warm welcome to everyone. Moreover, everyone comes—so avoid Zfat at this time if you don't like crowds.

It doesn't take long to walk all around Zfat's labyrinthine Old City and get a feel for it. Take time to poke around the little cobbled passages that seem to lead nowhere, or linger over some minute architectural detail on a structure from another time. And don't worry if you get lost; you're never far from the center. Yerushalayim (Jerusalem) Street runs through the heart of the Old City, encircling the Citadel, in its center; from here there is easy access to the two main areas of interest, the Old Jewish Quarter and the Artists' Colony. There is no getting around Zfat's hilly topography, so wear comfortable walking shoes. As the town is largely orthodox, modest dress is recommended.

## A Good Walk

Begin by exploring the **Park of the Citadel** ①, site of what was the largest Christian fortress in the Middle East. (You can leave your car here.) As you enter the park, on Hativat Yiftah Street, take in the sight of the old houses below and the undulating pastoral scene beyond. This image has inspired many of the paintings and drawings that have emerged from Zfat since time immemorial, and you'll no doubt see numerous modern interpretations of these at the General Exhibition (☞ *below*) and in the rooms of almost every Zfat hotel.

Turn right and walk about 300 ft to the remains of the Citadel tower. It was destroyed over the years, mainly by earthquakes, most recently and devastatingly in 1837. A little farther along on the right is the **Israel Bible Museum,** with its impressive arched entrance.

Walk down the steps and cross Yerushalayim Street. Near No. 24, more steps lead to the parallel Bar Yochai Street. You are now entering the Ashkenazi (Eastern European Jewish) section of the Old Jewish Quarter, distinguished from the Sephardic (Middle Eastern Jewish) section by its wider streets and more subtly colored buildings. Turn left and walk to **Kikar Hameginim** ②. Standing on the square, you'll notice through the arch a stepped street leading down and to the right. This draws you into the 16th century and the Ashkenazi **Ha'Ari Synagogue** ③, with its impressive olive-wood holy ark.

Leaving the synagogue, go down the steps, turn left at cobbled Alka-betz Street, and go down again at the first set of steps. Walk under the dome, and you'll soon notice blue window frames and a door next to a little alley. You are now in the heart of Sephardic Zfat. If you haven't found the sign marking the spot, just ask for the **Abouhav Synagogue** ④, whose elements reflect Sephardic traditions. Head back under the arch and up the stairs to Caro Street, with its *souk*-style souvenir stores, and the compact **Caro Synagogue** ⑤, arguably the most charming in the quarter.

A little farther ahead you'll find yourself in the middle of a stairway called **Ma'alot Olei Hagardom.** At this point, you have two options: you can take the stairs down, turn right at the bottom, and follow the road to the **cemetery** ⑥, with its intriguing gravestones old and new. En route you'll pass Hameiri House, a museum devoted to Zfat's history, especially the last 100 years. The other choice is to continue straight ahead, crossing over the stairway to the **Artists' Colony.** You should make your first stop the **General Exhibition** ⑦, a selection of works by resident artists. A walk down Tet-vav Street brings you to one of the colony's curiosities, the **Museum of Printing Art** ⑧.

## Sights to See

❹ **Abouhav Synagogue.** This large Sephardic synagogue is named in honor of a 14th-century Spanish scribe, one of whose Torah scrolls found its way here with the Spanish Jewish exiles 200 years later. A look around reveals a number of differences between this synagogue and its Ashkenazi counterparts, such as the Ha'Ari (☞ *below*); the walls are painted a lively blue and are richly decorated with religious motifs, the benches run along the walls instead of in rows (so that no man turns his back on his neighbor), and the dome-shape roof rests on four pillars.

Every detail is loaded with significance: There are three arks—for the three forefathers, Abraham, Isaac, and Jacob (the one on the right is said to be the Abouhav original)—and 10 windows in the dome, referring to the Commandments. The charmingly naive illustrations on the squinches include a depiction of the Dome of the Rock (referring to the destruction of the Second Temple) and pomegranate trees, whose 613 seeds are equal in number to the Torah's commandments. The original building was destroyed in the 1837 earthquake, but locals still swear that the southern wall—in which the Torah scroll penned by Abouhav is set—was spared. This scroll is taken out only on Rosh Hashanah, Yom Kippur, and Shavuot (Pentecost). ⊠ *Abouhav St.* ۞ *No set visiting hrs.*

**Artists' Colony.** The colony, set in Zfat's old Arab Quarter, was established in 1951 by six Israeli artists who saw the promise beyond Zfat's war-torn and dilapidated condition; for them, the old buildings, the fertile landscape, and the cool mountain air fused to form a veritable magic that would help them create. Others soon followed until, at its peak, the colony was home to more than 50 artists, some of whom are exhibited internationally. The numbers have since dwindled somewhat, and gallery opening hours are unpredictable, especially in winter, when Zfat's artists tend to hibernate. In summer, however (July–September), things really come alive as the artists open their doors and display—or work on—their latest pots, paintings, and sculptures.

❺ **Caro Synagogue.** Rabbi Yosef Caro arrived in Zfat in 1535 and led its Jewish community for years. He is the author of the Shulchan Aruch, the code of law that remains a foundation of Jewish religious interpretation to the present day; and this synagogue is said to have been Caro's study hall. It was destroyed in the great earthquake of 1837

# Zfat (Safed)

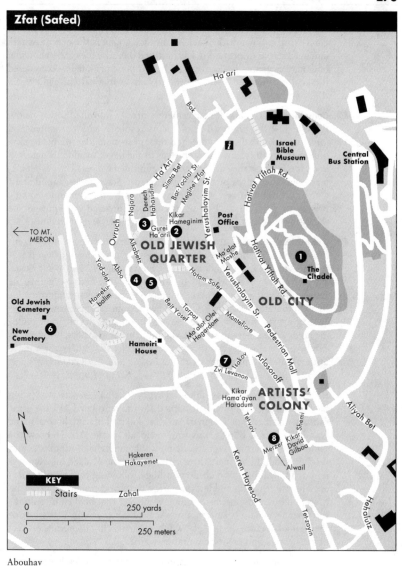

TO MT. MERON →

Ha'ari

Bak

Israel Bible Museum

Central Bus Station

Hativat Yiftah Rd.

Ha'Ari

Simta Bet

Bar-Yochai St.

Meginei Zfar

Yerushalayim St.

Najara

Derech Hahasidim

Kikar Hameginim

Post Office

Ovruch

Alkabetz

Abbo

Yodalei-batim

Hamekubalim

OLD JEWISH QUARTER

Gurei Ha'aril

Ma'alot Moshe

Hativat Yiftah Rd.

The Citadel

OLD CITY

Hotam Sofer

Tarpat

Beit Yosef

Ma'alot Olei Hagardom

Montefiore

Yerushalayim St.

Arlosoroff

Pedestrian Mall

Old Jewish Cemetery

New Cemetery

Hameiri House

Zvi Levanon

Kikar Hama'ayan Haradum

ARTISTS' COLONY

Telvav

Keren Hayesod

Metzer

Kikar David Gilboa

Alwail

Aliyah Bet

Hehalutz

Ter-zoyin

Hakeren Hakayemet

N

**KEY**

Stairs

Zahal

0    250 yards

0    250 meters

and rebuilt in the mid-19th century. If you ask, you can open the ark containing the Torah scrolls, one of which is at least 400 years old. A glass-faced cabinet at the back of the synagogue is the *geniza*, where damaged scrolls or prayer books are stored (because they carry the name of God, they cannot be destroyed). The turquoise paint here—considered the "color of heaven"—is believed to help keep away the evil eye. ⊠ *Alkabetz St.* ⊘ *No set visiting hrs.*

**❻ Cemetery.** An old and a new cemetery are set into the hillside below the Old Jewish Quarter. The old plots resonate with the names and fame of the Kabbalists of yore, and their graves are identifiable by sky-blue markers. It is said that if the legs of the devout suddenly get tired here, it is because they are walking over hidden graves. The new cemetery holds the graves of members of the pre-State underground Stern Gang and Irgun forces, who were executed by the British in Akko's prison (☞ Chapter 5). In a separate plot, bordered by cypresses, lie the 24 teenage victims of the 1974 terrorist massacre at Ma'alot.

**❼ General Exhibition.** The works inside this large space are a representative sample of the work of Zfat's artists, ranging from oils and watercolors to silk screens and sculptures, both traditional and avant-garde. The permission of the Muslim authorities was required to organize the Exhibition, as it is housed in the old mosque, easily identified from afar by its minaret. The Artists' Colony has recognized the growing presence of artists from the former Soviet Union, and the adjacent building holds the **Immigrant Artists' Exhibition.** In either facility, if any works catch your fancy, just ask directions to the artist's gallery for a more in-depth look at his or her work. ⊠ *Isakov and Zvi Levanon Sts.,* ☎ *06/692–0087.* ⬛ *Free.* ⊘ *Sun.–Fri. 9–5, Sat. and holidays 10–2.*

**❽ Ha'Ari Synagogue.** This Ashkenazi synagogue has associations going back to the 16th century. It is named for the renowned Ari, the great rabbi who left an indelible mark on Zfat and on Judaism; his real name was Isaac Luria, but he was known to all as the Ari, Hebrew for "lion" and an acronym for Adoneinu Rabbeinu Itzhak (our master and teacher Isaac). In his mere three years in Zfat, he evolved his own system of the Kabbala, which drew a huge following that would influence Jewish teaching and interpretation the world over, right up to the present day. Even more astounding is the fact that he died in his mid-thirties; it is generally said that one should not even consider study of the Kabbala before the age of 40, when one reaches the requisite level of intellectual and emotional maturity.

The synagogue itself is not outstanding but is typically Ashkenazi, with its pale colors and minimally decorated walls. The olive-wood holy ark, however, is a dazzling tour de force of carving, with two tiers of spiral columns and seemingly live plant reliefs. The synagogue was built after Luria's death, on the spot where the Ari is said to have come with his students on a Friday evening to welcome the Sabbath. It was leveled by the 1837 earthquake and rebuilt in 1857. (The Sephardic Ari Synagogue, where the rabbi prayed, is farther down the quarter, by the cemetery. The oldest of Zfat's synagogues, this 16th-century structure has especially fine carved wooden doors.) ⊠ *Ha'Ari St.* ⊘ *No set visiting hrs.*

**Israel Bible Museum.** This stone mansion was once the home of the Ottoman governor. Today it houses the somewhat dramatic paintings and sculptures of artist Phillip Ratner, all inspired by the Bible. ⊠ *Hativat Yiftah St.,* ☎ *06/699–9972.* ⬛ *Free.* ⊘ *May–Sept., Sun.–Thurs. 10–4, Fri. 10–1; Oct.–Dec. and Feb.–Apr., Sun.–Thurs. 10–2.*

❷ **Kikar Hameginim.** Defenders' Square is the main square of the Old Jewish Quarter and was once its social and economic heart. A sign points to a two-story house that served as the command post of the neighborhood's defense in 1948—hence the plaza's name.

**Ma'alot Olei Hagardom.** Part of Zfat's charm is its setting, on the slope of a hill. This stairway, which extends all the way down from Yerushalayim Street, forms the boundary between the Old Jewish Quarter and the Artists' Colony (formerly the Arab Quarter).

❽ **Museum of Printing Art.** The small but rich collection here spans the history of printing in Israel. On display are the first Hebrew press (operated in Zfat, in 1576), the first Hebrew book (which rolled off press a year later), the first newspaper printed in Israel (1863), and a copy of the May 16, 1948, *Palestine Post* declaring the birth of the State of Israel. ✉ *Merzer and Alwail Sts.,* ☎ *06/692-0947.* 🎟 *Free.* 🕐 *Sun.–Thurs. 10–noon and 4–6, Fri.–Sat. 10–noon.*

❶ **Park of the Citadel.** In Talmudic times, 1,600 years ago, hilltop bonfires here served as a massive beacon for surrounding communities to herald the lunar month, the basis for the Jewish calendar. In the 12th century, the Crusaders immediately grasped the strategic value of this setting and built the Citadel, only scattered sections of which remain. The Muslim ruler Saladin wrenched it from them in 1188, following his victory at the Horns of Hattin, but half a century later the Crusaders repossessed it, and the Order of the Templars turned it into the most massive Christian fortress in the East. For decades the Crusaders kept the aggressive Mamluk sultan Baybars at bay, but his army eventually besieged the Citadel in 1266. Having already destroyed many of the cities on the coast, Baybars decided to move his capital from Akko to Zfat. This marked the beginning of the end of the Crusader empire.

The Jewish settlements outside the castle walls grew and prospered during and after the Crusader era, with the city becoming a center of Kabbala studies. Zfat remained predominantly Jewish until a devastating earthquake in 1837 razed the town, leaving few survivors. In 1929, Arab riots drove most of these away, and by 1948, only 1,500 Jewish residents remained. The departing British army left the town's key strategic positions to the Arab forces, which set about besieging the Old Jewish Quarter. A handful of Palmach fighters (part of the Jewish clandestine army during the British Mandate) penetrated enemy lines and helped the quarter's (mostly elderly) devout Jews successfully resist the offense in what became known as the Miracle of Zfat. Once again, with its sweeping views and slopes in the heart of Zfat, the Citadel was the focal point of battle. ✉ *Old City.*

## Dining and Lodging

$$$ ✗ **Bat Ya'ar.** It takes a little determination to find the place through the winding roads behind Zfat and into the Birya Forest, but this timbered, pub-style restaurant in the middle of nowhere serves tasty steaks and salads and excellent chicken with rosemary, all enhanced by the pine-wood mountaintop setting. You can work up an appetite on one of Bat Ya'ar's horseback-riding or jeep tours. Outside the restaurant is a play area for children; they'll love the pony rides. ✉ *Birya Forest, 5 km (3 mi) from Zfat,* ☎ *06/692-1788. Reservations essential on weekends. AE, MC, V.*

$$ ✗ **Ein Camonim.** The Galilee Hills make perfect pastureland for livestock—in this case, goats—and in here you can taste the fresh output of Ein Camonim's dairy every day. The fixed menu contains a platter of goat cheeses, home-baked bread, a wicker basket of raw garden vegetables, a small carafe of local wine, coffee, and dessert. There's a half-

price menu for children 12 and under. The retail shop next door sells the cheeses, which are very good but not very cheap. ⊠ *Rte. 85, 20 km (12½ mi) southwest of Zfat, 5 km (3 mi) west of Kadarim Junction (north of highway),* ☎ *06/698–9894. AE, DC, MC, V.*

$$ ✕ **Gan Eden.** The setting, an old stone house, lends great atmosphere to this family-run vegetarian eatery. Taking in the view of Mount Meron (the restaurant's name means "paradise"), try the eggplant stuffed with creamed champignons, savory blintzes, or vine leaves, followed by one of the homemade cakes. The bar in the garden, called the Last Temptation, stays open into the wee hours. This is one of Zfat's few restaurants open on Saturday. ⊠ *Mount Canaan Promenade,* ☎ *06/697–2434. AE, DC, MC, V.*

$$ ✕ **Habayit Bik'tse Hanof.** The "House at the View's Edge," perched high in the Birya Forest with a stunning vista of the surrounding hills, is run as a holistic center. In addition to a café serving light dairy and fish meals, there is a gallery–gift shop with everything from natural soaps to furniture, and four guest rooms for those seeking the holistic experience. Shiatsu, reflexology, and other treatments are available. ⊠ *Birya Forest before Amuka, 7 km (4 mi) from Zfat,* ☎ *06/692–3737. AE, DC, MC, V.*

$$ ✕ **Hamifgash.** One of the institutions on pedestrian-only Yerushalayim Street, Hamifgash (which means "meeting place") has a wide range of options for light meals—soups, salads, snacks, and substantial meat dishes. There's self-service upstairs and table service downstairs. ⊠ *75 Yerushalayim St.,* ☎ *06/692–0510. AE, DC, MC, V. No dinner Fri., no lunch Sat.*

$$ ✕ **Pinati.** What do goulash and Elvis Presley have in common? They're both drawing cards to Pinati. Images of Elvis cover the walls, and though nobody can explain his connection to the Polish–Middle Eastern cuisine, the heavy volume of customers proves the success of this idiosyncratic formula. The kitchen serves up good, wholesome food and has awards to show for it. ⊠ *81 Yerushalayim St.,* ☎ *06/692–0855. AE, DC, MC, V. Closed Sat.*

$$$$ ▦ **Howard Johnson Plaza Ruth–Rimonim.** Two hundred years ago, when
★ the Turks were in charge, this gracious old building was the local post office. Rooms were added later, and it became a *khan,* or inn. It opened as the Rimonim in 1961 and has enjoyed a reputation for charm and excellence ever since. The stone-walled rooms have a rustic feel and are tastefully decorated with local art; the former stables serve as the dining room. Half the rooms have views over the mountain and gorges. ⊠ *Artists' Quarter, Box 1011, Zfat 13110,* ☎ *06/699–4666,* ℻ *06/692–0456. 76 rooms (50 in new wing), most with bath. 2 restaurants, bar, pool, exercise room, children's programs in summer. AE, DC, MC, V.*

$$$$ ▦ **Ron.** This pleasant but unassuming hotel has a good restaurant with an eclectic menu of European and Middle Eastern dishes. Rooms are spacious, clean, and light-filled, and half have mountain views. ⊠ *Near Metzuda Park, Hativat Yiftah, Box 22, Zfat 13214,* ☎ *06/697–2590,* ℻ *06/697–2363. 50 rooms with bath. Restaurant, bar, pool. AE, DC, MC, V.*

$$$$ ▦ **Sea View (Mitzpe Hayamim).** Halfway between Zfat and Rosh Pina, with a splendid view of the Sea of Galilee, is this serene (if snobby) spot dedicated to the pampering of both body and soul. The hotel specializes in packages of up to a week that include a medical checkup and diet (vegetarian), massage, reflexology, shiatsu, a pedicure, a manicure, and hairdressing—as well as full board. For the hale and hearty, there is a guided walk at 7 every morning. Some rooms have been individually decorated (all share a ban on smoking) to enhance the sense of luxury; a few have whirlpool baths. The lobby has a "tea corner," with a full range of herbal teas served 'round the clock.

A gallery exhibits Israeli works with extremely high prices, and a gift shop sells homemade breads, cheeses, and other local products. ✉ *Box 27, Rosh Pina 12000,* ☎ *06/699–9666,* ℻ *06/699–9555. 81 rooms with bath. Restaurant, pool, beauty salon, hot tub, massage, sauna, exercise room. AE, DC, MC, V.*

$$$$ ★ 🏨 **Vered Hagalil.** Stone and wood cottages, each with a front porch, create a sense of privacy, yet the extremely popular restaurant and stables on this guest farm are only steps away. Owners Yehuda and Yona Avni haven't lost their almost chauvinistic enthusiasm for the Galilee, which drew them here decades ago (he's from the United States, she's from Jerusalem), and it's reflected in the excellent maintenance of Vered Hagalil. Accommodations range from cottage apartments with bedroom, living room, and kitchenette to studios and smaller cabins. All are ranchlike in decoration—earth tones, exposed wood, and stone walls, and big picture windows for Sea-gazing. Trail-riding packages of up to three days are a specialty. Overnight guests enjoy 10% off riding and meals in the hotel restaurant. ✉ *Rte. 90, 15 km (9 mi) south of Zfat, next to Korazim, M.P. Korazim 12385,* ☎ *06/693–5785,* ℻ *06/693–4964. 17 units with bath (2 for people with disabilities). Restaurant, bar, pool, horseback riding. AE, DC, MC, V.*

$$ 🏨 **Joseph's Well.** Rooms here are like cozy studio apartments, with pine furniture, coordinated tablecloths and sheets, and chintz curtains—each has a coffee corner, with an electric kettle, cups, and tea and coffee. They're all on the ground floor, in clusters of three with a shared patio. The kibbutz dining room—Joseph's Well is on Kibbutz Amiad, 10 km (6 mi) south of Zfat—doubles as the restaurant. Unlike the bigger kibbutz hotels, Joseph's Well offers little to do; guests are here strictly to sleep. Amiad's main industry is wine, which it produces from unusual fruits such as kiwi and sells in a shop on the premises, which also peddles a range of local and imported products. ✉ *M.P. Upper Galilee 12335,* ☎ *06/693–3829,* ℻ *06/690–9307. 24 rooms with bath. Dining room, pool, horseback riding. AE, DC, MC, V.*

### Nightlife and the Arts

Zfat hosts a **klezmer festival** every summer, and indeed there could be no better setting for three days of "Jewish soul music" than this mystical city, with its labyrinthine cobblestone lanes. The roots of klezmer are Hasidic, making it almost prayerlike in tone, especially with its emphasis on wind instruments. Many events are street performances and therefore free. Keep in mind, though, that Zfat bursts at the seams at this time, with revelers both religious and secular. The festival is usually held in July; contact the **Zfat Tourist Information Office** (✉ 50 Yerushalayim St., Box 227, Zfat 13010, ☎ 06/692–7474) for details.

### Outdoor Activities and Sports

**Bat Ya'ar** (☎ 06/692–1788), in the Birya Forest 5 km (3 mi) from Zfat, is a steak house that doubles as a sort of ranch, with pony rides for kids and horseback riding for all. *See* Dining and Lodging, *above.*

**Vered Hagalil** (☎ 06/693–5785), a guest ranch at the Korazim Junction at Route 90 (☞ Dining and Lodging, *above*), offers a variety of horseback tours up to three days long, with a specialty in Western riding. Pony rides are available for kids. Prices for guided rides range from NIS 89 ($25.40) for an hour to NIS 310 ($88) for a day.

## Mt. Meron

❾ *21 km (13 mi) west of Zfat on Rte. 89.*

The spiritual importance of Zfat extends beyond the city limits to Mt. Meron and its environs, a pilgrimage site for both ultra-Orthodox Hasidic Jews and nature lovers.

Remote as it may seem, the village of Meron has for centuries drawn thousands upon thousands of Orthodox Jews to pay homage to several of the great rabbis of the Roman era who are buried at the eastern foot of the mount. The most important site—and one of the holiest places in Israel—is the **tomb of Rabbi Shimon Bar Yochai**, a survivor of the Bar Kochba Revolt of almost 2,000 years ago and a leading exponent of the Talmud. Refusing to kowtow to the Romans after they succeeded in taking Jerusalem, Bar Yochai is said to have fled with his son Elazar to a cave at Peki'in, not far from here, where he remained for 13 years. It is believed by the faithful, beginning with the 16th-century mystics who settled in Zfat, that while holed up in the cave, Bar Yochai penned the Zohar (the Book of Splendor), his commentary on the Pentateuch, or the Five Books of Moses, the first five books of the Old Testament. Opponents of this theory claim that the Zohar dates from 13th-century Spain, not 2nd-century Meron, but Hasidic pilgrims continue their annual visits to the great rabbi's tomb. Pieces of cloth and scraps of paper (inscribed with prayers) that hang from trees around the tomb are evidence of the pilgrims' devotion.

The pilgrimage is still celebrated en masse on Lag Ba'Omer, the festive 33rd day of the seven solemn weeks that begin with Passover and end with Shavuot (Pentecost). Mt. Meron comes alive as a grand procession of Hasidic Jews arrive on foot from Zfat, carrying Torah scrolls and singing fervently. Bonfires are lighted, and barbecues follow. Many ultra-Orthodox still uphold the tradition of bringing their three-year-old sons here on Lag Ba'Omer for their first haircuts.

Mt. Meron itself, at 3,926 ft, is the highest mountain in the Galilee and the largest **nature reserve** in northern Israel, with 24,700 acres of preserved slopes. A good road past the Society for the Protection of Nature (SPNI) field-study center takes you almost to the top (the actual summit is occupied by the Israeli army).

A 1½-km (1-mi) nature trail begins near the study center, with red markings guiding the walker all the way. The trail offers breathtaking views in all directions: the Druze villages of Western Galilee, Zfat, the Sea of Galilee, and, on a clear day, the Golan Heights, Hula Valley, and mountains of Lebanon. You can also spot the ugly scars of bushfires. The blackened tree "skeletons" date to the summer of 1978, when fire destroyed a significant chunk of this reserve. Much of the rich and varied flora on Mt. Meron has since regenerated—if you're here in autumn, you'll be dazzled by the glowing yellow of the sunflowers—but reminders of the fire remain.

Nor has fire been the only misfortune. Not so long ago, bears, antelope, and even leopards were hunted to extinction here. Today, Israel's hunting laws protect the wild boar, marten, polecat, and other fauna that still call the reserve home.

### Lodging

$$$ ◫ **Amirim Holiday Village.** The moshav (communal settlement) of Amirim offers something a little different: almost all of its 300 members are vegetarians. This is a real get-away-from-it-all kind of place, set on top of a hill overlooking Mt. Meron and the Sea of Galilee. Guests have a choice of health and beauty treatments. The lodging units have one or several rooms and are run by different families. Each has a kitchenette, but there is no shortage of external dining options: there are numerous family-run restaurants and café-cum-galleries on site, with a range of vegetarian fare. Especially good is Hase'uda Ha'aharona—even if the name means "the Last Supper." ⊠ *Moshav Amirim, near Mt. Meron, M.P. Carmiel, 20115,* ☎ *06/698–9571,* FAX *06/698–7824.*

*100 units with bath. 6 restaurants, kitchenettes, pool, children's pro-grams. No credit cards. No Sat. checkout in Aug.*

*En Route*  The Arab village of **Jish,** between Mt. Meron and Bar'am off Route 89, was called Gush Halav during the Second Temple period. In those days, it was renowned both for its exceptional olive oil and for the milk from its cattle. Gush Halav translates as "milk bloc," but it's unclear whether the name derived from the famous milk or from the whiteness of the chalky limestone that's used in the foundations of local buildings.

## Bar'am National Park

**10** *15 km (9 mi) from Meron, 40 km (25 mi) northwest of Zfat.*

In an otherwise deserted spot lie the **ruins of Bar'am,** one of the best-preserved ancient synagogues anywhere. Although Bar'am is less grand than the synagogue at Capernaum, on the Sea of Galilee (☞ Chapter 6), the community that built it must have devoted considerable funds and energy to their most important building. Like most synagogues uncovered in this area, it faces south, toward Jerusalem; unlike any other, how-ever, this one has lavish architectural elements, such as an entrance with a segmental pediment, and freestanding giant columns on the exterior.

The interior, which resembles other Galilean synagogues of the period, is in a worse state of repair than the facade. Rows of pillars in the prayer hall apparently served as supports for the ceiling, and the building may have had a second story. A section of the facade's lintel, now in the Louvre in Paris, contains the Hebrew inscription "May there be peace in this place, and in all the places of Israel. This lintel was made by Jose the Levite. Blessings upon his works. Shalom." ⊠ *Rte. 899,* ☎ *06/698–9301.* ⊡ *NIS 8 ($2.30).* ☉ *Apr.–Sept., daily 8–4; Oct.–Mar., daily 8–3.*

### Lodging

**$$**  ⊡ **Einat.** Although some distance off the main sightseeing tracks, this Romanian restaurant is worth the journey. Owner Moishe smokes his own meats with excellent results; the thick (roughly one-pound) steaks and kebabs are also excellent. The meats are enhanced by a range of traditional salads, several of them eggplant-based, and pickled vegetables. ⊠ *1 Klil Hahoresh (off Rte. 89, next to football field),* ☎ *04/957–0520. AE, DC, MC, V. Closed Tues.*

**$$**  ⊡ **Jascala.** Departing from the usual Middle Eastern plate of hummus and pita with chips, Jascala offers flavors of Lebanon, cooked up with the assistance of the owner's mother. The vine leaves come with or with-out meat; the fried *kube* is filled with either meat or hummus; and the pita baked with meat, onion, and hot pepper delivers a kick. ⊠ *Jish,* ☎ *06/698–7762. AE, DC, MC, V.*

## Rosh Pina

**11** *10 km (6 mi) east of Zfat, 25 km (15½ mi) north of Tiberias.*

Rosh Pina—literally, "headstone of the corner"—gets its name from the Bible: "The stone that the builder hath rejected hath become the headstone of the corner" (Psalm 118). This verse inspired the Galilee's first Zionist pioneers, who came from Romania in 1882, determined to build a village. They bought this land, 1,500 ft above sea level at the foot of the mountain ridge east of Zfat, and arrived with all they needed for their new home, right down to the timber for construction. Ironically, the boat that brought them to the Holy Land was called the *Titus,* the name of the Roman general whose destruction of Jerusalem forced the exile of Jews from that city in AD 70.

The Romanians' derived their main livelihood at Rosh Pina from the production of silk by silkworms; this industry was encouraged by the great philanthropist Baron Edmond de Rothschild, who gave them the fruit trees they needed for the project. Despite grand efforts, however, the desired results were elusive: residents walked around in silk scarves and socks but had nothing to eat. Slowly, family by family, the immigrants moved away to other settlements, leaving only squatters for decades to follow.

The little village has now been restored, and although it has not been developed as a tourist attraction, it warrants a brief visit simply for its cobblestone charm. To get here, walk for 10 minutes up the path from the modern township of Rosh Pina. The two-story **Schwartz Hotel,** on Ha'elyon Street, built in 1890, was the first rest house in the Galilee. Today it is a mere skeleton of the original, but try to imagine what it was like to check in here after a long, tiring journey on foot and enjoy the tranquil view of the Sea of Galilee below and white-capped Mt. Hermon to the north.

The **synagogue** (⊠ Ha'elyon St.) is usually locked. However, someone in the office of Old Rosh Pina (☎ 06/693–6603), a development company, next door to the restaurant at the bottom of Ha'elyon Street, may be able to open it. The interior of the no-longer-functioning synagogue remains as it was when it was built in the mid-1880s; the dark pews and holy ark made of the timber brought from Romania have aged gracefully. Look at the ceiling; the depictions of palm trees and biblical motifs are painted in rich colors.

The **Old Rosh Pina office,** which oversees the restoration and maintenance of Old Rosh Pina, occupies the house that belonged to Professor Gideon Mer, a leading expert on malaria in the 1930s. Legend has it that Mer used to inject his wife and children with experimental remedies in his efforts to combat malaria in this region. (All survived.) The British were so impressed with Mer's work that they sent him to Burma to fight malaria epidemics there.

Old Rosh Pina is populated today by some 60 artists, although, unlike their counterparts in the artists' village of Ein Hod (☞ The Rothschild Wine Country and Mt. Carmel *in* Chapter 5), they do not usually open their homes to visitors. There are, however, a few **galleries** displaying local creations.

## Dining and Lodging

Rosh Pina is a budding center of tourism for this region, and many residents are now opening their homes as bed-and-breakfasts. There is no central reservation center, but the various tourist-information centers (☞ Visitor Information *in* Upper Galilee and the Golan A to Z, *below*) can help you find simple, pleasant accommodations. There are family rooms at the small (100-bed) youth hostel (☎ 06/693–7086).

**$$$–$$$$**   ✕ **Babayit Shel Rafa ("Rafa's").** This inviting stone house in the century-old upper reaches of rustic Rosh Pina once belonged to the venerable Dr. Mer. Owner and chef Rafa infuses the menu with gastronomic memories of his native Argentina, and good service enhances the already comfortable atmosphere. (The restaurant's full name, Babayit Shel Rafa, means "Rafa's House.") The best starters are the pickled tongue and two kinds of empanadas. Entrées include steaks, chicken, and a choice of fish, but the house specialty is casseroles, hefty meals-in-a-pot with a salad on the side. Try the lamb casserole with celery, rosemary, lemon, potatoes, and sweet potatoes; or the piquant beef and chorizo *asado* (roasted). Vegetarians will enjoy the rich vegetable, mozzarella, prune, and almond combination, served with polenta. ⊠

*Old Rosh Pina restoration site,* ☎ *06/693–6192. AE, DC, MC, V. Reservations essential Fri. dinner and Sat. lunch.*

$$$ ✕ **Black Steer.** This red-roofed steak house is part of a South African chain that has only just arrived in Israel. (True, this seems a strange location for one of a few flagships.) The house specialty is spareribs. Outdoor dining is especially pleasant here, as the garden is leafy and surprisingly private; and the location is handy for those on the move. ⊠ *Opposite police station on west side of Rte. 90, at bottom of Rosh Pina,* ☎ *06/693–6250. AE, DC, MC, V.*

$$$ ✕ **Ja'uni.** Ja'uni is housed in a century-old structure built by Baron Rothschild, used by the British as a post office and, later, an arms hideout. The menu is seasonal and eclectic, with such options as roast peppers, zucchini in tahine, and a variation on the Spanish tapas. Good service and the separate room for nonsmokers earn extra points. ⊠ *30 David Shub St. (next to Beit Ha'am building),* ☎ *06/693–1881. AE, DC, MC, V.*

$$ ✕ **Indigo.** This easygoing café offers another angle on the changing face of Rosh Pina: youth. With wholesome salads and vegetarian pies, it's a good place to take a break before or after a walk around Old Rosh Pina, farther up the hill. ⊠ *30 Hechalutzim St.,* ☎ *06/693–5333. AE, DC, MC, V. Closed Mon.*

$$$$ ✕🏠 **Auberge Shulamit.** Opened in 1996 by veteran Galilee restaura-
★ teurs, this charming inn takes its name from the original Hotel Shulamit, where the 1948 Armistice Treaty was signed. Among the menu's delectables—along with home-smoked meats—are chestnut soup (in season), salmon fillet in crabmeat sauce, and shrimp in Gorgonzola sauce with wild rice. In addition to the restaurant, there are four French country–style guest rooms for those who really want to indulge for a day or two. ⊠ *David Shub St., Box 259, Yesod Hama'ala 12105,* ☎ *06/693–1494, 06/693–1495, or 06/693–1485,* 🖷 *06/693–1495. Reservations essential. AE, DC, MC, V.*

$$ 🏠 **Village Inn.** These accommodations at Kfar Hanassi give you a *real* taste of kibbutz life. The one- and two-room units look out onto a garden, each has a barbecue set, and some share a kitchenette. The decor is bright, with boldly colored sheets and cotton dhurrie rugs; all facilities are spotlessly clean. Meals are in the kibbutz's communal dining room. Amenities that will appeal to kids include a minizoo, picnic grounds, and a pagoda with a grand view of the Golan and Mt. Hermon. Several artists live and work at Kfar Hanassi, and you're welcome to visit their studios. ⊠ *Near Mahanayim Airport (10 km, or 6 mi, from Rosh Pina), M.P. Upper Galilee 12305,* ☎ *06/691–4870,* 🖷 *06/691–4077. 28 units with bath. Dining room, kitchenettes, pool, massage, miniature golf, 2 tennis courts, basketball, boating, travel services. AE, DC, MC, V.*

### Kayaking and Rafting

**Kibbutz Kfar Hanassi** (☎ 06/691–4870; ☞ Dining and Lodging, *above*) rents lightweight paddleboats called catarafts.

## Tel Hatzor

⓬ *8 km (5 mi) north of Rosh Pina.*

The large mound of Tel Hatzor, site of the ancient city of Hazor, is a good stop for archaeology buffs. Over a period of thousands of years, the city was built and rebuilt a total of 21 times, allowing latter-day diggers to slice off layer after layer of differing lifestyles spanning the ages. Situated on the Via Maris—the most important trade route in antiquity, since it linked Egypt and Mesopotamia—Hatzor is first referred to in Mesopotamian documents of the 2nd millennium BC; an ambassador from Hammurabi's court resided here.

The Book of Joshua (Joshua 11:13) mentions ancient Hatzor as "the head of all those kingdoms," although Joshua himself destroyed Canaanite Hatzor in the 13th century BC, and Israelites resettled it. Its next heyday came three centuries later, when King Solomon decided it would serve him well as one of his great regional military and administrative centers, like Megiddo and Gezer. In 732 BC, Hatzor met its end when invading Assyrian king Tiglath Pileser III conquered the Galilee and forced its Israelite inhabitants off the land in chains and into exile. The city would never regain its former glory.

This site was first identified as the ancient Hatzor in 1928, but the archaeologist who put it squarely on the modern map, between 1955 and 1959, was the renowned Dr. Yigal Yadin, best known for his excavations at Masada.

The huge site is divided into two areas: the *tel,* or **Upper City,** which comprised the oldest settlements, and the **Lower City,** first settled in the 18th century BC. Only the tel, covering less than a fifth of the total excavation site, is open to the public. The **Hatzor Museum** (on the grounds of Kibbutz Ayelet Hashachar, across the highway) houses many of the figurines, weapons, stone pots, and other artifacts unearthed in the two areas; still others are at the Israel Museum in Jerusalem. ⊠ *Tel Hatzor National Park, off Rte. 90,* ☎ *06/693–4855.* 🎫 *NIS 13 ($3.50).* ☿ *Park and museum Apr.–Sept., Sat.–Thurs. 8–5, Fri. 8–4; Oct.–Mar., Sat.–Thurs. 8–4, Fri. 8–3.*

### Lodging

$$$$ 🏨 **Ayelet Hashachar Kibbutz Guest House.** The first kibbutz to open a hotel, Ayelet Hashachar stands in a pastoral setting but is run with the efficiency and thoroughness of any urban hotel. The guest quarters, next door to the Tel Hatzor Museum, resemble apartments, with rooms in two-story buildings surrounded by lawn and flower beds. Timber-framed windows add a soft touch. Facilities are available for people with disabilities. Jeep tours and guided tours of the kibbutz can be arranged; Ayelet Hashachar is one of Israel's biggest honey producers. ⊠ *M.P. Korazim 12200,* ☎ *06/693–2611,* 📠 *06/693–4777. 144 rooms with bath. Cafeteria, dining room, pool, horseback riding, travel services. MC, V.*

## Hula Nature Reserve

★ ⑬   *8 km (5 mi) north of Tel Hatzor.*

The Hula Nature Reserve contains the last of Israel's swamplands and one of its last vestiges of wilderness. This is no accident: in the first half of the 20th century, British rulers under the Mandate (like the Ottomans before them) repeatedly refused Jewish settlers' requests to drain the swampland, a practice common in other parts of the tiny country as the need for arable land grew. After independence, the Israeli authorities eagerly approved the project almost as soon as they could.

Throughout much of the 1950s, the Hula Valley was drained and dredged again and again, until it was discovered that this was doing grave and irreversible harm to the ecosystem, particularly to the hundreds of thousands of migratory birds that stopped here on their biannual flights between Europe and Africa. This crisis led the International Union for the Conservation of Nature (IUCN) to declare the Hula Valley a reserve of world importance, which it has remained since the early 1970s.

Pelicans, wild geese, storks, plovers, and a host of exotic birds once again have their sanctuary, but they would not be here were it not also for the swampy waters that abound with carp, catfish, and perch, and a reed habitat boasting rare thickets of papyrus through which you might see a water buffalo or two. Less recognized is the topminnow, an American fish that lives on mosquito eggs and has played a big part in helping rid this region of malaria. The visitor center has complete information about the 800-acre reserve, an observation tower, and a snack bar. Hunting and fishing are strictly forbidden. ⊠ *East of Rte. 90,* ☎ *06/693–7069.* 🖃 *NIS 15 ($4.30).* ☉ *Daily 8–4.*

<table>
<tr><td>NEED A<br>BREAK?</td><td>For a rest stop with a bit of history, try **Bet Dubrovin** (⊠ Yesod Hama'ala, ☎ 06/693–7371), near the entrance to the Hula Nature Reserve. This reconstructed farmhouse-cum-museum was once owned by the Dubrovins, immigrant converts from Russia, part of a movement of Christian Russians who converted to Judaism and moved to the Holy Land. Old man Dubrovin brought his family to the swamps of the Hula in 1904, and, despite the hardships, these pioneers set up a model farm on their 173-acre estate, even winning first prize—for cattle in 1922 and for chickpeas in 1927—in the annual agricultural exhibitions in Rosh Pina. The property was eventually donated to the Jewish National Fund and was opened to the public in 1986.

The estate consists of a series of stone buildings built on a square, surrounding a courtyard that holds some old farming equipment and even a few farm animals. An exhibit in the building where the family lived gives a history of both the family and local area. There is also a ceramics store selling locally made pieces, and a restaurant. The museum entrance fee (NIS 8, or $2.30) is deducted from the price of a main course at the restaurant and also gets you a 20% discount at the nature reserve, so hang on to your ticket.</td></tr>
</table>

### Outdoor Activities and Sports

**Baba Yona's Ranch** (⊠ Yesod Hama'ala Junction, ☎ 06/693–8773), near the Hula Nature Reserve, offers adventure packages that combine horseback riding, canoeing, and jeep touring.

# UPPER HULA VALLEY

The sights that hug the border with Lebanon show different sides of Israel. The towns of Kiryat Shmona and Metulla bear eloquent witness to the varying fortunes of Israel's relationships with its Arab neighbors. Tel Dan Nature Reserve, on the other hand, draws visitors with its huge trees, surging river, and wild beauty.

## Kiryat Shmona

*45 km (28 mi) north of Tiberias, 30 km (19 mi) north of Zfat.*

The only urban center in the otherwise agrarian Upper Hula Valley, **Kiryat Shmona** in itself has little to offer travelers aside from burger joints and other fast-food stands in the shopping center on Route 90, and a new cable car that journeys between the town and Kibbutz Manara. Like Ma'alot, farther west, Kiryat Shmona made the headlines in 1974 when Arabs infiltrated Israel from Lebanon one night, came down the mountain behind the town, broke into an apartment at dawn, and massacred an entire family. By 1982 the spate of terrorist attacks had reached such proportions that Israel responded by invading Lebanon, the first stage of what would become the war with Lebanon. Kiryat Shmona was again in the news in 1996 when Hezbollah terrorists launched a focused and continued attack on the town and its environs using katyusha rockets. The Israel Defense Forces responded by targeting Hezbollah's bases in southern Lebanon in a campaign that became known as the Grapes of Wrath.

The Kiryat Shmona–Kibbutz Manara **cable car** runs regularly from 8 AM to midnight daily and costs NIS 30 ($8.60). There is one station midway on the 1,890-yard trip, where the adventurous can step out and do some rappelling ("snappelling" in Hebrew) and dry-sliding. If you opt to remain in the cable car, the trip takes eight minutes each way, overlooking cliffs and green hills from a height of some 850 yards.

**⑭** Perched on the northern edge of Kiryat Shmona is **Tel Hai,** meaning "hill of life" in Hebrew. In a sense, the hill did become a monument to life after a memorable battle in 1920. In the years immediately following World War I, while Britain and France bickered over who should have final control of the upper Hula Valley, bands of Arabs and Bedouins roamed the region, harassing and plundering the tiny Jewish farming settlements. They destroyed one such settlement completely, overran the communal settlement of Tel Hai, and caused the temporary abandonment of the veteran village of Metulla; only Kibbutz Kfar Giladi was successful in defending itself, and it has since gone on to become one of the largest and most prosperous of kibbutzim (☞ Dining and Lodging, *below*).

In the wake of the Tel Hai terror, in which two settlement members were killed, Josef Trumpeldor and seven comrades were called on to defend the place. Trumpeldor had served in the czar's army in his native Russia, and though he had lost an arm fighting, he had already won a reputation as a leader. Fired by Zionist ideals, he moved to Palestine in 1912 at the age of 32 with a group of followers in tow. Soon after, he was fighting with the British against the Turks at the ill-fated battle of Gallipoli. Upon his return to Palestine, he moved to Kibbutz Tel Hai, became its commander, and, like all the other Jewish settlers, was constantly on the alert for Arab terrorist bands.

In 1920 the final battle came. Trumpeldor and seven others were slaughtered on the kibbutz grounds, and it is for them that Kiryat Shmona—City of the Eight—is named. It is said that Trumpeldor's last words were "It is good to die for our country." Trumpeldor subsequently became not only a national hero but an inspiration, and he is still referred to with reverence. He is buried here, beneath the stone statue of a roaring lion on the hill behind the museum, once the stockade of Tel Hai. The heroic stand at Tel Hai came to have two important consequences for the area: it was the first modern instance of Jewish armed self-defense, and it did much to change the local image of the Jew as timid and defenseless. Moreover, the survival of at least two of the Jewish settlements this far north determined that when the final borders were drawn by the League of Nations in 1922, these settlements would be included in the British-mandated territory of Palestine and thus, after 1948, in the State of Israel.

The **museum** displays agricultural equipment and tools used in Trumpeldor's time. Some of the implements are still put to use (especially during school holidays); you may be able to catch, for example, an old-style pita-making demonstration. ⊠ *Off Rte. 886,* ☎ *06/695–1333.* ▨ *NIS 13 ($3.60).* ☉ *Sun.–Thurs. 8–4, Fri. and holiday eves 8–1, Sat. 10–5 (later in Aug.).*

## Dining and Lodging

In addition to the guest houses here, there is a large (200-bed) **youth hostel** in Tel Hai (⊠ Mobile Post, Upper Galilee 12210, ☎ 06/694–0043, ☒ 06/694–1743). For camping or bungalows, head for the **Hurshat Tal National Park** (⊠ East of Hagoshrim on Rte. 99, 8 km/5 mi east of Kiryat Shmona, ☎ 06/694–2360), opposite Kibbutz Dafna, but remember that it gets pretty cold here at night once summer is over.

**$$$** ✕ **Dag al Hadan.** Fresh trout and a cool glass of wine in a shady woodlet by the gurgling Dan River—it's as good as it sounds, except on crowded weekends. This was the first restaurant in the region to specialize in the fish the Dan yields in abundance; you can see the trout ponds in a small installation on the grounds. The same management runs a café next door. The restaurant is tucked away behind the main road, but it's large and well signposted. ⊠ *Off Rte. 99 near Kiryat Shmona, opposite Kibbutz Hagoshrim,* ☎ *06/695–0225. Reservations essential on weekends. AE, DC, MC, V.*

**$$$** ✕⊞ **Jordan Pagoda.** This is an unlikely place for a Chinese-Thai restaurant, perhaps, but somehow sitting in the timber pagoda (imported from Thailand, according to the owners) and eating South Asian delights on the banks of the Jordan River works. The restaurant is part of the Jordan's Source complex, which has 10 very reasonably priced wooden cabins. The complex is on the grounds of Kibbutz Sde Nechemia. ⊠ *Kibbutz Sde Nechemia (8 km, or 5 mi, from Kiryat Shmona), Rte. 918,* ☎ *06/694–7447. AE, DC, MC, V.*

**$$$** ⊞ **Hagoshrim Kibbutz Hotel.** The waters of the Hermon River flow right through Haoshrim, creating a uniquely natural setting that the residents have wisely exploited in their "pub in nature" (open May to October). Tractor rides are one of the hotel's more unusual activities. Hagoshrim had an impact on women the world over when it invented the Epilady, a revolutionary depilatory appliance that has won the kibbutz kudos for technological initiative. ⊠ *Rte. 99, east of Kiryat Shmona, Upper Galilee 12225,* ☎ *06/695–6231,* 𝔽𝔸𝕏 *06/695–6234. 121 rooms with bath. Restaurant, cafeteria, pub, pool, tennis court. AE, DC, MC, V.*

**$$$** ⊞ **Kfar Blum Guest House.** Tucked in the northern Hula Valley, Kfar
★ Blum enjoys a reputation for attentive service that surpasses many of its rivals'. The home-style hospitality is enhanced by the garden setting, and period photographs in the rooms depict kibbutz life as it's meant to be. Most members of Kfar Blum hail from English-speaking countries, so there are no language barriers here. One of the kibbutz's major attractions is its collection of kayaks—what better way to experience the Jordan River? Kfar Blum hosts an annual chamber-music festival in summer (☞ The Arts, *below*). ⊠ *North of Rte. 977, near Kiryat Shmona, Upper Galilee 12150,* ☎ *06/694–3666,* 𝔽𝔸𝕏 *06/694–8555. 108 rooms with bath. Restaurant, bar, pool, sauna, tennis courts, boating, travel services. AE, DC, MC, V.*

**$$$** ⊞ **Kibbutz Hotel Kfar Giladi.** Atop a hill behind Tel Hai overlooking the Hula Valley, this is one of the oldest and largest kibbutz hotels in Israel. It's run very efficiently, but it still retains a homey atmosphere. The lovely woods nearby make for great walks, and the kibbutz grounds contain the Bet Hashomer Museum, which explores the pre-State history of the kibbutz and the vicinity. Kfar Giladi produces sunglasses, which you can buy in the hotel. ⊠ *Rte. 886, Upper Galilee 12210,* ☎ *06/690–0000,* 𝔽𝔸𝕏 *06/690–0069. 180 rooms with bath. Snack bar, pool, tennis court, health club. AE, DC, MC, V.*

## The Arts

For the classically minded, Kibbutz Kfar Blum (⊠ Upper Galilee 12150, ☎ 06/694–3666) hosts **Chamber Music Days** each year in late July and early August, a nationally renowned festival of chamber music in a pastoral setting.

## Outdoor Activities and Sports

A plethora of outfits organize water-sport trips in this region, and almost all hotels can make reservations for you. The minimum age for kayaks and other water "vehicles" is usually six.

KAYAKING

**Hagoshrim Kayaks** (☎ 06/681–6034; ☞ Dining and Lodging, *above*) has a 5-km (3-mi) "family" course that lasts 1½ hours and a 6-km (4-mi) "stormy" course that expands on the family course to last almost two hours. The family course costs NIS 45 ($12.85) per person, the stormy course NIS 55 ($15.70) per person,.

**Kibbutz Kfar Blum** (☎ 06/694–8755; ☞ Dining and Lodging, *above*) rents two-person rubber kayaks for 1½-hour or two-hour runs and transports you back to the kibbutz at the end of your run. The cost is NIS 45 ($12.85) per person for the short course, NIS 75 ($21.40) per person for the long course. Kayaks are available from March through October; call ahead to inquire at other times of the year.

TUBING

**Sde Nechemia** (✉ Kibbutz Huliot, ☎ 06/694–6010), near Kiryat Shmona along Route 99, rents inner tubes at NIS 40 ($11.40) for an hour or so.

## Metulla

**15** *7 km (4 mi) north of Kiryat Shmona.*

Israel's northernmost town, Metulla, is so picturesque that it's hard to believe this tranquil spot is just a stone's throw from a foe, Lebanon. And the happy story of cooperation between the Israelis and the Lebanese at the so-called Good Fence here draws visitors from all over the world.

Metulla was founded as a farming settlement in 1896 with the aid of Baron Edmond de Rothschild, and in the century since then its residents have shown such tenacity and determination that it has not only survived but thrived. Essentially, it has one thoroughfare, Harishonim Street (though this can hardly be called a main street), where hotels and restaurants are clustered. Somehow the tensions of the Middle East dissipate here, at least briefly; one- and two-story limestone buildings in European-styles line the street, and the Continental atmosphere is enhanced by the numerous signs offering ZIMMER (German for "room") for rent. Even the weather is decidedly un-Mediterranean, with refreshingly cool mountain breezes in summer and snow in winter. Yet the cypresses and cedars provide a whiff of Lebanon.

The **Good Fence** is just a three-minute drive from the town center. Although you're greeted by little more than a thoroughly touristy kiosk and souvenir shop, there's a certain thrill to standing on the border of a country that has long been hostile to Israel. There's a twist, though: this segment of the Israel-Lebanon border has enjoyed its nickname since June 1976, when Israel first sent medical and other aid to residents of southern Lebanon. In one version of the story, Israeli soldiers noticed a Lebanese woman in labor at the border crossing. They rushed her to an Israeli hospital, where she delivered a healthy baby, and within days there were several very pregnant women waiting at the Good Fence. The peaceful interaction between the two sides has developed ever since: first Lebanese citizens with relatives in Israel were allowed to come over to visit, then summer camps were organized (and still are) for Lebanese schoolchildren and their Israeli counterparts, and today hundreds of southern-Lebanese workers commute across the border to their jobs in the Galilee.

| NEED A BREAK? | Take a picnic down to the streams and waterfalls that flow year-round in the lush **Nahal Ayoun Nature Reserve,** just south of Metulla next to Route 90. |

## Outdoor Activities and Sports

The multistory, multipurpose **Canada Centre** (☎ 06/695–0370), at the top of the hill, has just about everything a sports complex can offer. For the price of admission—NIS 40 ($11.40)—you can spend the whole day here, playing basketball, ice-skating, working out, swimming, zooming down the water slide, or taking aim on the shooting range. If it gets to be too much, just repair to the sauna or hot tub. The complex is open daily 10–10 and contains a restaurant in case you're afraid you burned too many calories.

The ice-skating rink is one of only two in the Middle East; the other is in Saudi Arabia. But what the Saudis cannot boast are world-class former Soviet skaters, several of whom now live in Metulla and teach the sport at the center. If you're lucky, you might catch a demonstration of their dazzling skills.

# Tel Dan Nature Reserve

**⑯** *25 km (15½ mi) from Metulla, 15 km (9 mi) from Kiryat Shmona.*

Tel Dan is hard to beat for sheer natural beauty. A river surges through it, and large, luxuriant trees, including majestic Mt. Tabor oaks, provide shade over wide paths. A host of small mammals live here, many partial to water, such as the otter and the mongoose. This is also the home of Israel's largest rodent, the nocturnal Indian crested porcupine, and its smallest predator, the marbled polecat, recognizable by its bushy tail, which accounts for about half the creature's 1-ft length. There are wildcats in these parts, too, though you'll rarely see them by day. The reserve has several hiking trails.

A rather majestic city occupied this land in biblical times; Dan was an urban center second only to Hatzor in importance in northern Palestine. According to Genesis, when Abraham "heard that his brother had been taken captive [by the four kings of the north] he armed his trained servants, born in his own house, three hundred and eighteen, and pursued them up to Dan." Five centuries later, when Canaan extended from Dan (then called Laish), in the north, to Beersheva, in the south, Joshua led the Israelites through the area to victory.

Fine ruins from several epochs lie here. The Canaanite city of Laish existed here 5,000 years ago; its name was changed when the Israelite tribe of Dan captured the tel, sometime in the period of Judges, and it became the northernmost point of the kingdom of Israel. When the kingdom was divvied up, the secessionist King Jeroboam I built a religious center here (and another at Bethel) and erected a cultic golden calf. Among the finds archaeologists have turned up are the city gate and a 9th-century BC paved plaza that was probably the town center.

Tel Dan is particularly noteworthy among nature reserves for its wheelchair-accessibility: there are no steps, and separate wheelchair paths ease the way when necessary. It also has a pleasant cafeteria-style restaurant, Dan-Eden (☎ 06/695–3826), operated by Kibbutz Dan. ⊠ *North of Rte. 99,* ☎ *06/695–1579.* 🎫 *NIS 15 ($4.30).* ☉ *Daily 8–4.*

# Kibbutz Dan

*1 km (⅔ mi) from Tel Dan Nature Reserve.*

🐣 Adjacent to the Tel Dan Nature Reserve, this kibbutz has an attraction that can really enhance a trip to this area. The **Bet Ussishkin Museum** was founded in 1955 by the Jewish National Fund and is now operated jointly by Kibbutz Dan and the Society for the Protection of

Nature in Israel (SPNI). Children will appreciate the displays here, which document the wildlife and natural phenomena found around the Hula Valley, the Golan Heights, and the Jordan River. The audiovisual presentations are concise and informative. ⊠ *Off Rte. 99,* ☎ *06/694–1704.* ☎ *NIS 12 ($3.40).* ☉ *Sun.–Thurs. 8:30–4:30, Fri. and holiday eves 8:30–3:30, Sat. 9:30–4:30.*

# GOLAN HEIGHTS

Geologically distinct from the limestone massif of Mt. Hermon, to its north, the basalt slopes of the Golan Heights extend about 60 km (37 mi) from north to south and between 15 km and 25 km (between 9 mi and 15½ mi) across. The whole region was volcanic in the not-so-distant past, and many symmetrical volcanic cones and pronounced reliefs still dominate the landscape, particularly in the upper Golan. Where the dark basalt rock has weathered or been cleared, the mineral-rich soil supports a wide variety of crops. The Golan's gentle terrain and climate have generally attracted far more settlement than the less hospitable northern Upper Galilee. In spring the region, already greened by winter rains, comes alive with wildflowers; but when the summer heat has frizzled everything to a uniform yellow-brown, it seems a land of desolation. Sights here range from nature reserves, in the north, to a winery and archaeological sites near Katzrin, in the south.

## Hermon River (Banias) Nature Reserve

★ ⑰ *20 km (12½ mi) from Kiryat Shmona.*

One of the most stunning corners of Israel, this reserve contains gushing waterfalls, dense foliage along riverbanks, and remains of a temple dedicated to the god Pan. There are two entrances, each with a parking lot: the first is indicated on a sign as "Banias Waterfall"; the other is 1 km (⅔ mi) farther along the same road and marked "Banias." A circular walking trail connects the two. It's an easy walk, but if time is short (the trail takes about two hours), you may prefer to take a short walk to the falls, return to your car, then drive on to the second entrance to see the caves and the spring where the Hermon River originates. The cost of admission covers entry to both sites.

At the lookout near the **Banias Waterfall,** maps point out the principal mountains and other features on the horizon. The approach to the waterfall, marked by a signpost, is enhanced by huge carob trees, maidenhair ferns, brier ivy, laurel (bay leaf) bushes, and other shrubs. Swimming at the waterfall is prohibited, but don't be surprised to see groups of Israelis splashing around and scrambling to photograph each other against it. There's a tremendous reverence for these unusual 33 ft of cascading water, and people come from all over the country to see them, especially in the rainless summer months.

Backtrack to the signpost and head in the other direction, passing walnut trees, willows, and lemon and fig trees as you head for the riverside walk to the spring and caves. Along the way, the trail passes two abandoned flour mills, and at times you'll be walking on aqueducts that once brought water to these mills. About 1 km (⅔ mi) from the waterfall, a sign points to **hreichat haketzinim** (Officers' Pool), a pool built around the spring by Syrians for the use of their officers (swimming is now prohibited).

NEED A
BREAK?

A few minutes' walk beyond the Officers' Pool is a little **stall,** where you can buy Druze-style pita (bigger and flatter than the commercial version) not only baked on the premises but also milled here. The ancient flour mill is still powered by water from an aqueduct as it was in days of yore. In fact, until only a few years ago this was where local Druze villagers milled their flour. Now the mill and "bakery" service hungry hikers. Pull up a rock, and for a few shekels you'll be served a large rolled-up pita with *labane* (white goat's cheese) and Turkish coffee.

The remainder of the trail (about 600 ft) follows and crosses the river before reaching the spring. Note the pungent aroma of mint. There are blackberry bushes here, too, their fruit particularly sweet at the end of summer.

**Banias Spring** emanates at the foot of mostly limestone Mt. Hermon, just where it meets the basalt layers of the Golan Heights. When it rains, or as the snow on the mountain melts, water seeps through the Hermon's crannies and gushes forth at the foot of what is called Pan's Cave.

The name *Banias* is an Arabic corruption of the Greek *Panias*, the original name given to what became a cult center dedicated to the colorful Greek god Pan. (Arabic has no *p* sound, hence the modification.) Pan (son of Hermes), the god of herdsmen, music, and wild nature, and patron of homosexuals and nymphs, was too hedonistic even for the ancient Greeks. In their attempts to keep him at some distance, they eventually built the half man–half goat a temple in this succulent corner of the world.

Take the path that crosses the spring and proceed toward **Banias Cave,** easily identified by the sturdy fig tree at its entrance. Note the five niches hewed out of the rock to the right of the cave; these are what remain of the Hellenistic temple, and probably once held statues. Three of the niches bear inscriptions in Greek mentioning Pan, the lover of tunes; Echo, the mountain nymph; and Galerius, one of Pan's priests. Archaeologists are only in the early stages of excavation, but they have already turned up what they believe are the remains of a second temple as well. All early references to the cave identify it as the source of the spring, but earthquakes over the years have changed its formations, forcing the water to emerge at the foot of the cave rather than from within it. (For those in a hiking mood, a long, very steep trail leads from here through the oak and thorny broom forest up to Nimrod's Fortress [☞ *below*], a 40- to 60-minute climb.)

The path continues up to the whitewashed **tomb of Nebi Khader** (Arabic for "the prophet Elijah"), built on a ledge of the cliff. The tomb is closed, but from here you have a terrific view of the Hula Valley and the Hermon River. A little farther along are the remains of an ancient wall with a ceramic inlay that archaeologists believe was part of the white marble temple that Herod built as a tribute to Caesar Augustus, who had given him the Hula Valley and Panias in 26 BC.

Herod's son Philip inherited this part of his father's kingdom, and when he made Panias his capital, he changed its name to Caesarea Philippi, to distinguish it from the Caesarea his father had founded on the Mediterranean coast. It was in Caesarea Philippi that Jesus changed Peter's name from Simon and gave him "the keys to the kingdom of heaven" after Peter declared him the Messiah for the first time: "Jesus came here and asked his disciples, 'Who do you say that I am?' and Peter replied, 'You are Christ, the son of the living god,' to which Jesus responded, 'Blessed are you, Simon, son of Jonah. And I tell you, you are Peter [*petros* means "rock" in Greek], and on this rock I will build my church and the powers of death shall not prevail against it' " (Matthew 16:13–20). Some scholars think Christ may have deliberately selected the heartland of paganism for this great declaration of faith. The small Greek Orthodox church nearby (now closed) was built to commemorate the site.

Though Roman rule in this part of the kingdom would not last another generation past Philip, Panias continued to flourish for more than 1,000 years—and its original name, with only slight modification, has endured.

In the early 12th century, Banias was held by Crusaders, and just outside the second entrance to the reserve (marked BANIAS) are the ruins of what is thought to have been the marketplace of the day: a string of single "rooms" along a well-preserved section of wall might well have been shops. The archaeologist leading the excavations here, Vassilos Tsaferis, believed that more of the city might lie under the parking lot, and in mid-1994 his team unearthed within the reserve a Roman-era health and leisure center for tired soldiers. The luxurious 1,613-square-ft facility dates from the 1st century; it had marble floors, mosaics, and a series of subterranean (*under*-underground, if you will) passages. ⊠ *Off Rte. 99,* ☎ *06/695–0272.* ⊠ *NIS 15 ($4.30).* ⊙ *Daily 8–4.*

<hr>

OFF THE
BEATEN PATH

**TEL FAHER –** The large number of monuments to fallen soldiers in the Golan is a reminder of the region's strategic importance—and the price paid to attain it. Among the easily accessible sites, where old Syrian bunkers give a gunner's-eye view of the valley below, is Tel Faher, in the northern Golan (⊠ Off Rte. 99; turn right just above Banias). At Tel Faher—also known as Mitzpe Golani, for the elite Golani Brigade soldiers who died here in 1967—children can climb onto the tank that now sits passively. **Caution:** These sites are safe, but beyond the fences and clearly marked paths are old Syrian minefields that have not been completely detonated.

<hr>

# Nimrod's Fortress

★ ⑱ *5 km (3 mi) from Hermon River (Banias) Nature Reserve.*

The history of Nimrod's Fortress (Kal'at Namrud), the huge, burly limestone fortress perched above Banias, is still vociferously debated. It was built around 1100, but by whom? Muslims? Crusaders? Academic controversy aside, a visit to the fortress is a real treat. Overgrown with scruffy shrubbery, it blends in with the stony mountain terrain and commands superb vistas, especially through the frames of its arched windows or the narrow archers' slits in its walls.

What *is* known about the fortress is that it guarded the vital route from Damascus via the Golan and Banias to Lebanon and to the Mediterranean coast. Although Muslim legend says it was first built by Arabs, it is widely believed to have been a Crusader structure later modified by the Arabs. In any event, it changed hands between Muslims and Christians in the centuries to follow as both vied for control of the region. During one of its more curious periods, from 1126 to 1129, Nimrod's Fortress was occupied by a fanatical sect of Muslims famous as murderers. Before heading out to track down their enemies, the cutthroats would indulge in huge quantities of hashish, thus earning the nickname *hashashin* (hashish users), from which the word *assassin* is derived. Nimrod functioned as a prison during the Mamluk period and was abandoned in the 16th century. Between 1948 and 1967 Syria used it to observe Israeli troop movements.

You enter the fortress through a breach in its western wall. There are several large vaulted cisterns here, which were particularly crucial during a siege: they could store enough water for 500 people for three years. Follow the path through the citadel ruins to the donjon, or keep, the fortress's central tower. You may notice that it faces east—the Crusaders expected attacks from this direction. It's possible to climb the donjon, 100 ft above the surrounding castle; this is where the feudal lord would have lived. It forms a kind of fortress within a fortress; the outer wall on the east and south sides is well protected by protruding towers, also equipped with slits. ⊠ *Nimrod's Fortress National Park, Rte. 989 (off Rte. 99),* ☎ *06/698–4316.* ☎ *NIS 13 ($3.70).* ☉ *Daily 8–4.*

# Mt. Hermon

**⑲** *12 km (7½ mi) from Nimrod's Fortress, 25 km (15½ mi) from Kiryat Shmona.*

The summit of Mt. Hermon—famous as Israel's highest mountain, at 9,232 ft above sea level—is actually in Syrian territory. Its lower slopes attract Israelis to the country's only ski resort, but the fun is significantly chilled by the high prices (☞ Skiing, *below*). In fact, summer is arguably the most interesting time on the Hermon: after the winter snows melt, hikers can discover chasms and hidden valleys here, the long-term result of extremes in temperature. Moreover, a powerful array of colors and scents emerges from the earth as cockscomb, chamomile, and scores of other flowers and wild herbs are drawn out by the summer sun. Approaching from Nimrod's Fortress, you'll pass the Jewish township of **Neve Ativ,** designed to look like a little piece of the Alps in the Middle East, replete with A-frame chalet-style houses, a handful of which have guest rooms. (The residents of Neve Ativ operate the ski slopes.) You'll also go by the old Druze village of **Majdal Shams,** with a number of good eateries.

## Skiing

Don't compare the slopes of **Mt. Hermon** (☎ 06/698–1337) with those in Europe or the Americas. For Israelis, there is a certain thrill to having a ski resort in a hot Mediterranean country—and it's a bargain compared with flying to the Alps (figure about NIS 26, or $90, per day for admission to the site, lift tickets, and equipment rental). Frankly, though, Mt. Hermon has little to offer the serious, or even the novice, skier. The chairlifts and cafeterias run year-round, the better to enjoy the place in summer, when it's bursting with wildflowers.

*En Route* **Ein Kuniya,** which appears across a valley on your left as you head east into the Golan on Route 99, is the most picturesque of the several Druze villages here. The houses are built of the black basalt so prevalent in the Golan.

# Merom Golan

*20 km (12½ mi) from Mt. Hermon.*

Kibbutz Merom Golan was the first settlement built in the Golan after the Six-Day War. Its fields and orchards are typical of local kibbutzim. Apples are especially good in these parts, but man cannot live by apples alone, so Merom Golan runs Cowboys' Restaurant (☞ *below*), with good, reasonably priced steaks.

## Dining

**$$** ✕ **Cowboys' Restaurant.** Here's the best corral this side of the Israel-Syria Disengagement Zone. Saddle-shape stools at the bar and cattle hides on the walls contribute to the frontier atmosphere. But it's the grub—specifically the hearty steaks and other meat—that packs 'em in. ⊠ *Kibbutz Merom Golan, off Rte. 959,* ☎ *06/696–0206. AE, DC, MC, V.*

## Kuneitra/The Disengagement Zone

*3 km (2 mi) from Merom Golan.*

Syria is not far away now. The ruined town of Kuneitra was captured by Israel in 1967, lost and regained in the 1973 Yom Kippur War, and returned to Syria in the Disengagement Agreement that followed. It is now a demilitarized zone, and Syria has made no effort to rebuild it. The cluster of white buildings next door houses the United Nations Disengagement Observer Force. ⊠ *Near Rte. 98.*

## Katzrin

**20** *20 km (12½ mi) from Merom Golan, 38 km (23½ mi) from Tiberias, 35 km (22 mi) from Zfat.*

The "capital" of the Golan Heights, Katzrin (Qazrin) was founded in 1977 on the site of a 2nd-century town of the same name. It is the administrative center of the Golan and one of the most appealing residential areas in the north. To get here from the northern Golan, take Route 91 west, and then go south on Route 87.

Katzrin has a homey, suburban feel, despite its strategic location and attendant sensitivity. It's not unusual to see bomb shelters decorated and converted into recreation centers, or into Hebrew classrooms for Russian immigrants. The water here is very soft: straight from the basalt bedrock, it's delicious to drink and makes your skin feel like silk.

Commercial Katzrin has general services—a café (open during the day), a pizzeria (open at night), a gift store, a minimart, and a library. There's also a doll museum (☎ 06/696–2982), where some 1,000 handmade dolls serve as the narrators of Jewish history from biblical times until the signing of the Israeli-Jordanian peace treaty. The museum is open Sunday through Thursday from 9 to 5 and Friday from 9 to 2; admission is NIS 14 ($4).

The **Golan Archaeological Museum,** though small, has a comprehensive collection of animal bones, stones, and artifacts that put the region into historical and geographical perspective. Among the exhibits is a Copper Age dwelling reconstructed from materials excavated close by. One room is devoted to the story of Gamla, the "Masada of the North" (☞ *below*), and includes an excellent audiovisual presentation on Gamla's history during the Great Revolt against the Romans (AD 66) and the discovery of the ancient site by archaeologists exactly 1,900 years later. The museum is run in conjunction with the Ancient Katzrin Park (☞ *below*). ⊠ *Katzrin commercial center,* ☎ *06/696–1350.* ◻ *NIS 13 ($3.70), including Ancient Katzrin Park.* ☉ *Sun.–Thurs. 8–5, Fri. and holiday eves 8–3, Sat. 10–4.*

**21** **Ancient Katzrin Park,** 2 km (1¼ mi) east of Katzrin's business center, is an excavation-in-progress of a Jewish village, possibly from the 3rd century, whose economy was based on the production of olive oil. In all such villages (some say there were once 27 in the vicinity) the synagogue was the focus of community activities. Its importance was reflected in the abundance and complexity of ornamentation. The Katzrin Temple, a contemporary of those at Bar'am and Capernaum, has decorative architectural details, such as a mosaic pavement and a wreath of pomegranates and amphorae in relief on the lintel above the entrance. Built of basalt, the synagogue was used for 400 years until it was partly destroyed, possibly by an earthquake, in 747.

Since 1967, when the excavations at Katzrin began, 10% of the ancient Jewish village has been uncovered. The park's two reconstructed buildings, the so-called House of Uzi and House of Rabbi Abun (presumably a Talmudic sage), are attractively decorated with rope baskets, weavings, baking vessels, and pottery (based on remnants of the originals) and lighted with little clay oil lamps. ⊠ *Rte. 87,* ☎ *06/696–2412.* ☞ *NIS 13 ($3.70), including Golan Archaeological Museum.* ☉ *Sun.–Thurs. 8–5, Fri. and holiday eves 8–3, Sat. 10–4.*

**㉒** The **Golan Heights Winery,** in Katzrin's industrial zone, is one of Israel's top businesses—it launched the country into the international wine-making arena with its Yarden and Gamla labels. (A third label is called, predictably, Golan.) The area's unique volcanic soil, cold winters and cool summers, and state-of-the-art vinifying techniques have proven a recipe for success. Wine-tasting tours are generally available if reserved in advance. The shop sells the full line of wines, including the Katzrin chardonnay, the Yarden Gewürtztraminer, and the Gamla Muscat Canelli, as well as sophisticated accessories for the oenophile. If you don't feel like buying here (and you may find the wines a tad less expensive in urban liquor stores), the winery can give you the business cards of their distributors around the world. ⊠ *Rte. 87 (east of town center),* ☎ *06/696–2001, 06/696–1646 for tours.* ☞ *Tour and tasting NIS 12 ($3.40).* ☉ *Sun.–Thurs. 9–5, Fri. 9–2.*

### Nightlife

Within Katzrin Park, there's a **pub** (☎ 06/696–2521) in a century-old Syrian dwelling. The sheer experience of having a drink among the ancient ruins is worth a detour if you're lodging in this area.

OFF THE BEATEN PATH    **MITZPE GADOT –** If you continued northwest on Route 87 from Katzrin and then west on Route 91, you would pass this tall, triangular concrete monument to fallen Israeli soldiers. It's just above the B'not Ya'akov Bridge and is named after the kibbutz it overlooks. **Caution:** The site is safe, but don't explore beyond any marked paths, because there may be undetonated Syrian minefields.

## Gamla Nature Reserve

*20 km (12 mi) southeast of Katzrin; take Rte. 87 to Rte. 808 and watch for Gamla signpost.*

Aside from having a fascinating history of determination, struggle, and death, the "Masada of the North" is truly inspiring in its beauty. Gamla's rugged, hilly terrain is softened in late winter and spring by the greenery and wildflowers that follow the rains. A collection of predatory birds returns here twice a year between migrations, and their nests are clearly visible from the Vultures' Lookout. You can also keep your eyes peeled for gazelles, porcupines, and foxes.

Digs have turned up a fortified town dating from the early Bronze Age, but the main story of the camel-shape Gamla (the name *Gamla* is probably related to *gamal,* the Hebrew word for "camel") goes back 2,000 years. Those were the days when Herod was encouraging Jews to settle here in order to populate the frontiers of his kingdom. By AD 66, the Jews of Gamla had joined the Great Revolt against Rome. Herod's great-grandson Agrippa II, of Banias, sided with the Romans and challenged the zealous rebels. When he failed to overpower them, Rome dispatched the general Vespasian with three legions in tow. In AD 67, the Romans launched a bloody attack here that ended seven months later, when the 9,000 surviving Jews flung themselves to their deaths in the abyss below the town.

Flavius Josephus told the story of Gamla in *The Jewish War,* and vivid descriptions from this tome are engraved in stones along the trails throughout the site. "Sloping down from a towering peak is a spur like a long shaggy neck, behind which rides a symmetrical hump, so that the outline resembles that of a camel. . . . On the face of both sides it is cut off by impassable ravines. Near the tail it is rather more accessible where it is detached from the hill. . . . Built against the almost vertical flank, the town seemed to be hung in the air . . . ." Indeed, this dramatic image is precisely the first one you have as you approach Gamla from the hilltop entrance to the reserve.

It was this steep terrain that almost caused Vespasian's three legions of Roman soldiers to fail in their siege. No sooner had the Romans succeeded in reaching the town than the defenders swung around and counterattacked; the Romans were, Josephus wrote, "swept down the slope and trapped in the narrow alleys." Rallied by Vespasian, the Romans were able to drive the last defenders to the summit. Seeing no escape, the survivors opted for mass suicide.

The town subsequently fell into ruin and oblivion, but this turned out to be a boon for visitors 1,900 years later. Because it was never rebuilt, Gamla is the only example of a Roman battlefield whose relics match the vivid stories from the past; among the finds are 2,000 "missile stones" and arrowheads. Moreover, there are about 200 **dolmens** scattered in the area—strange stone structures shaped like the Greek letter pi. The effort required to erect these large basalt burial monuments, probably during the 2nd millennium BC, indicates the importance of death and burial rituals at that time.

The site has three walking trails. There is an excellent short film on the story of Gamla at the Golan Archaeological Museum in Katzrin (☞ *above*). ⊠ *Off Rte. 808,* ☎ *050–509930.* ☑ *NIS 13 ($3.70).* ☉ *Daily 8–4.*

# UPPER GALILEE AND THE GOLAN A TO Z

## Arriving and Departing

### By Bus
**Egged** buses (☎ 03/694–8888) run daily from Tel Aviv to Kiryat Shmona (Buses 842 and 845) and to Zfat (Bus 846); from Jerusalem to Kiryat Shmona (Bus 963) and to Zfat (Bus 964); from Haifa to Kiryat Shmona (Buses 501 and 502) and to Zfat (Buses 331 and 362); and to both cities from Tiberias (Bus 459).

### By Car
Driving is unquestionably the best way to see the Upper Galilee and the Golan. It takes three hours to make the 180-km (112-mi) drive from Tel Aviv; 1½ hours of driving from both Akko and Nahariya, about 60 km (37 mi) away; and four hours from Jerusalem, which is 200 km (124 mi) to the south. There are numerous ways to approach the area. From Tiberias and the Sea of Galilee, Route 90 runs due north between the Hula Valley, on the east, and the hills of Naftali, on the west. The more rugged Route 98 runs from the eastern side of the Sea of Galilee up through the Golan Heights to Mt. Hermon. Near the top of Route 98 you can pick up Route 91, which heads west into the Upper Galilee.

From the Mediterranean coast there are several options, but the main one is Route 85 from Akko. Route 89 runs parallel to Route 85 a little farther north, from Nahariya, and has some gorgeous scenery. From Haifa take Route 75 to Route 77, turning onto Route 90 at Tiberias, or Route 70 north onto Route 85 east. If you're starting from

Tel Aviv, drive north on Route 4 or 2 to Hadera; from there you'll head northwest on Route 65, exiting onto Route 85 east.

### By Plane

**Arkia Israeli Airlines** (☎ 1800/444888) and **IsraAir** (☎ 03/613–6564) operate several daily flights from Sde Dov Airport in Tel Aviv to the small Galilee airport of Mahanayim (☎ 06/693–5301), part of the township of Rosh Pina. From the airport it is 10 km (6 mi) to Zfat and 30 km (19 mi) to Kiryat Shmona. Arkia also flies from Jerusalem several times a week.

## Getting Around

### By Bus

Local buses stop at all major sights in this region (there is always a kibbutz, a town, or some other small residential settlement nearby), but you should avoid buses if you're on a tight schedule, as they tend to be infrequent. Call **Egged** (☎ 03/694–8888) for schedules. If you have trouble getting through to Egged, you can try the **local depots**: Kiryat Shmona (☎ 06/694–0740), Tiberias (☎ 06/672–9222), and Zfat (☎ 06/692–1122).

### By Car

The state of Israel's **roads** is changing from bad-to-fair to fair-to-good. In the Upper Galilee in particular, the government is making an effort to improve them, but don't expect wide, even highways. Sometimes the roads are paved, and sometimes, well, they just aren't. This is especially true in the Golan. It's tremendously important to drive cautiously. Try to avoid driving during peak hours, which are usually late Saturday afternoons, when city folk crowd the roads back to Jerusalem and Tel Aviv after a day out in the country.

The main north–south roads in the region are Route 90, which goes all the way up to Metulla at the Lebanese border; the Tiberias–Metulla Road; and the less- traveled Route 98, which runs from the eastern side of the Sea of Galilee through the Golan Heights (along the Disengagement Zone) to Mt. Hermon. The main west–east highways are Route 85, which runs from Akko to Korazim, and Route 89, which connects Nahariya and Zfat.

**Gas stations** are easy to find along Route 90 and in the towns, such as Katzrin (Route 87) and Zfat (Route 89). Most are open daily but close by 9 PM, so it's best to fill up during the day.

## Contacts and Resources

### Car Rental

It's much easier to rent a car in Tiberias (☞ Lower Galilee A to Z *in* Chapter 6), Tel Aviv, Jerusalem, or Haifa than to search for a dependable rental agency in the tiny towns of the Upper Galilee. For those flying to the Galilee (☞ Arriving and Departing, *above*), **Arkia Israeli Airlines** (☎ 1800/444888 in Tel Aviv) can arrange for a rental car to be waiting at Mahanayim Airport, outside Rosh Pina.

### Emergencies

**Police** (☎ 100). **Ambulance** (☎ 101). **Fire** (☎ 102). Emergency calls from public phones do not require tokens or telecards.

The main **police station** in the Upper Galilee is in Kiryat Shmona (⌧ 1 Salinger St., ☎ 06/694–3444 or 06/694–3445).

The **Magen David Adom** station in Kiryat Shmona (⌧ 3 Tchernichovsky St., ☎ 06/694–4334 or 06/694–9401), near the central bus station, handles medical and dental emergencies 24 hours a day

## Guided Tours

### GENERAL INTEREST

Both of Israel's major bus companies, **Egged Tlalim** (⊠ 59 Ben Yehuda St., Tel Aviv, ☎ 03/527–1212; ⊠ 8 Shlomzion Hamalka St., Jerusalem, ☎ 02/622–1999; ⊠ Zfat Bus Station, Zfat, ☎ 06/692–1122) and **United Tours** (⊠ 113 Hayarkon St., Tel Aviv, ☎ 03/522–2008 or 03/6933412; ⊠ King David Hotel Annex, Jerusalem, ☎ 02/625–2187) offer one- and two-day guided tours of this region, departing from Tel Aviv and Jerusalem. Both offer a 10% discount to children under 12.

### SPECIAL INTEREST

The **Society for the Protection of Nature in Israel** (SPNI; ⊠ 4 Hashfela St., Tel Aviv 66183, ☎ 03/638–8666) sponsors excellent hikes and walking tours in this area. The tours are usually aimed at all ages, so Olympic-level fitness is not required; hikes that require serious physical exertion are clearly described as such.

## Hospital

The largest hospital in the north outside Haifa is the **Rivka Sieff General Hospital,** in Zfat (⊠ Harambam Rd., ☎ 06/697–8811). Bus 6 from the Zfat bus station stops here.

## Kayaking and Rafting

**Whitewater Rafting** (⊠ Rte. 91, not far from Mahanayim Junction, ☎ 06/693–6867 or 06/693–4622) operates professionally guided rafting trips through the rapids of the Jordan.

## Lodging

Rooms in kibbutz guest houses can be reserved directly or through **Kibbutz Hotels Chain,** a central reservation service based in Tel Aviv (⊠ 90 Ben Yehuda St., ☎ 03/524–6161, FAX 03/527–8088), although not all the kibbutzim are represented. **Moshav Beit Hillel** (⊠ M.P. Upper Galilee 12255, ☎ 06/695–1806 or 06/693–5016, FAX 06/695–9861) also makes kibbutz and bed-and-breakfast reservations.

## Visitor Information

All hotels and kibbutz guest houses can provide tourist information, and many will arrange tours as well.

The Tourist Information Office (TIO) in **Tiberias** (⊠ Habanim St., ☎ 06/672–5666) can furnish information on the entire region. The Municipal Tourist Information Office in **Zfat** (⊠ 50 Yerushalayim St., Box 227, Zfat 13010, ☎ 06/692–0961) is useful for regional information and has a list of licensed guides in the city. **Tourist Information Center– Upper Galilee,** a small office, is at the Mahanayim Junction, next to the gas station (⊠ Kibbutz Mahanayim, M.P. Hevel Korazim 12315, ☎ 06/693–6945) but has little printed information in English. **Bet Us-sishkin Museum** (⊠ Kibbutz Dan, M.P. Upper Galilee 12245, ☎ 06/694–1704) has information on the Upper Galilee's nature reserves, natural history, and bird-watching.

# 8 Eilat and the Negev

*In the sun-drenched city of Eilat, you can get to know the Red Sea by snorkeling through tropical reefs or just reclining on sandy beaches. To the north, in the Negev Desert—the biblical "southland"—you can explore the quiet vastness of the landscape and the civilizations that have made it bloom. And to the east, at Ein Bokek, on the Dead Sea, you can take the famed waters at one of the area's many spas.*

**T**HE NEGEV IS ISRAEL'S southernmost region, an upside-down triangle that constitutes about half the country's land mass, though only about 6% of the population lives here. The Negev's northern border, the base of the triangle, lies about 27 km (17 mi) north of Beersheva, known as the capital of the Negev and the only large city within its borders. The Jordanian and Egyptian borders mark its eastern and western limits, respectively, and Eilat, on the Gulf of Eilat at the gateway to the Red Sea, is at its southernmost tip.

By Judy Stacey
Goldman

The Negev may well have changed more since the foundation of the modern state of Israel than in the entire period since the end of the Roman Empire. The region's first kibbutzim were established in the early 1940s, with new immigrants sent south after the War of Independence, in 1948. Two years later, people started trickling into Eilat, which was nothing but a few rickety huts. Arad put down its roots in 1961. The desert itself was pushed back, and the semi-arid areas between Tel Aviv and Beersheva became fertile farmland. Today, agricultural settlements in the scorching Arava Valley make use of brackish water to raise flowers, vegetables, and dates that are sent to winter markets in Europe. (The cultivation of the desert is most evident when you fly over the Negev and see the patches of deep, rich green below you.)

The army has been deployed over a large part of the Negev since the Sinai was handed over to Egypt in 1982. You'll feel a military presence at roadside diners, where soldiers stop to eat; at bus stations, where they're in transit; and at tent-filled compounds here and there. Signs declaring FIRING ZONES indicate areas that the public may not enter, and checkpoints—where a smile and a wave-through are the order of the day—are scattered throughout.

The area has a long and varied human history. The ancient Israelites had fortifications here, as did the Nabateans and the Romans after them. These early settlers developed irrigation techniques that were remarkably sophisticated, even by modern standards. Throughout these periods of permanent settlement, the entire area was home to Bedouins, whose distinctive way of desert life, developed thousands of years ago, can still be seen today.

Despite its rapid development, the Negev remains Israel's Wild West. It takes a certain kind of person to live and work here, someone who relishes the challenge of turning the hot, bone-dry desert into a hospitable place to live. The Negev draws those who have been seduced by the beauty of great canyons and cliffs spilling over with color at dawn and dusk; by the thousands of migrating birds who fill the skies twice a year; by the endless expanses of still, rocky terrain where the only movement might be a stone clattering down a hillside as an ibex makes a leap; by the sound of the wind coming up at the end of a dusty day; and by the pleasure of bright flowers carpeting the hills in winter.

The Negev contains some of Israel's most fascinating and dramatic scenery, from gigantic *makhteshim* (erosion craters) and the moonscape of the Dead Sea to carved-out *wadis* (ancient dry riverbeds), the red granite mountains around Eilat, and long cliff faces along the Arava Valley. You can visit the kibbutz home and grave of Israel's first prime minister—David Ben-Gurion, the man who first dreamed of settling the desert—and the millennia-old ruins at Tel Beer Sheva, visited by the biblical patriarch Abraham. The Hai Bar Nature Reserve, farther south, is home to animals described in the Bible, and the Timna Valley Park is a wonderland of unusually colored rock formations. At the port city of Eilat you can snorkel past Technicolor tropical fish and coral formations, and in both Eilat and Ein Bokek you can indulge in pampering treatments at a spa.

# Pleasures and Pastimes

## Adventure Tours

A thrilling way to see the Negev is by jeep or camel, in the company of an expert guide who is not only familiar with every facet of desert life but who also knows how to prepare open-air meals and brew tea from desert plants (your guide might live in a desert settlement). If you have time, take a several-day trek in the desert, an unforgettable experience; tour outfits provide the camping equipment. Some desert expeditions combine hiking, camel riding, and rappelling. (For more details, *see* Hiking *under* Guided Tours *in* Eilat and the Negev A to Z, *below*.) It's wise to reserve in advance, and you can often do so through a travel agency or your hotel. Note that some tours close down for the summer, when it's very hot.

## Dining

If the word *dining* conjures up starched and draped tablecloths, gliding waiters, and gleaming silver, and if that's what your heart is set on, head for the upscale restaurants and luxury hotels of Eilat and Ein Bokek. Despite the fact that Eilat is at the southern tip of a desert, it's got all the essentials—including Ben & Jerry's. If you like fish, you'll be especially happy in Eilat, as specialty fish restaurants abound—a rarity elsewhere in Israel. Excellent sea fish, such as those raised in ponds around Eilat, and delicacies, such as *denise* (sea bream) and the Israeli specialty *furel,* salmon-trout bred in the Dan River up north, make wonderful meals. And fresh fruits and vegetables are flown in from afar—Italian, Indian, French, Argentinian, Yemenite.

In the rest of the Negev, with the notable exception of the Mitzpe Ramon Inn, plan to dine in humble surroundings—typically a roadside diner—on meals that are apt to reflect the cook's ethnic background. You might find Tunisian carrot salad, Moroccan *cigarim* (flaky pastry with a meat or potato filling), or standard Middle Eastern fare: hummus, pita, grilled meat, french fries (known here as chips), chopped or shredded vegetable salads (*salatim*), strong coffee in small cups, and a dessert such as fruit or chocolate mousse. Keep in mind that outside Eilat restaurants close early on Friday, and the main meal of the day is served at noon in the desert, so lunch may be history if you arrive after 1:30.

If people are dressed up anywhere, it will be at the better restaurants (and nightclubs and discos) in Eilat and Ein Bokek, though ties are never required. Everywhere else, the finest attire you'll see is a clean T-shirt. Keep in mind, too, that it's always a good idea to make reservations at Eilat and Ein Bokek restaurants, especially on Friday and Saturday night.

| CATEGORY | COST* |
|---|---|
| **$$$$** | over $35 |
| **$$$** | $22–$35 |
| **$$** | $12–$22 |
| **$** | under $12 |

*per person for three-course meal, excluding drinks and service charge*

## Hiking

Hiking the splendid scenery, rugged heights, and steep cliff faces of the Negev requires knowledge and skill. In summer the heat is extreme, and in winter the danger of floods is ever present. Hiking on your own is not recommended unless you're well versed in the art of reading topographical maps. The best way to hike the Negev is to join one of several excellent organizations (☞ Hiking *under* Guided Tours *in* Eilat and the Negev A to Z, *below*). If you do venture out without a guide, be sure to give the details to someone who is staying behind—where you're headed, the route you plan to follow, and when you expect to be back. Always follow the desert guidelines for water consumption (☞ Desert Precautions, *below*).

## Lodging

Hotels in sunny Eilat and Ein Bokek (Dead Sea) run from compact and family-style to huge, lush, and luxurious. Pleasure comes first: you'd be hard pressed to find business facilities in any but a few hotels, whereas a beautiful and up-to-the-minute spa is an important feature of each large hotel. Even the smallest hostelry is proud of its spa. Hotels are constantly updating these facilities; most of their treatments incorporate the therapeutic properties of the Dead Sea.

Keep in mind that prices rise during high season and holidays. High season is Hanukkah/Christmas, Passover/Easter, and July and August, when Israelis take a break. At Ein Bokek, high season is mid-March to mid-June and mid-September to the end of November. Eilat's hotels are crowded with Europeans from October until April. Be sure to reserve well in advance at any time of year.

| CATEGORY | EILAT AND EIN BOKEK* | OTHER AREAS* |
|---|---|---|
| $$$$ | over $164 | over $99 |
| $$$ | $125–$164 | $70–$99 |
| $$ | $75–$125 | $40–$70 |
| $ | under $75 | under $40 |

*All prices are for a standard double room, including breakfast for two but excluding 15% service charge.*

## Natural Wonders

The star of the Negev is the Makhtesh Ramon (Ramon Crater), one of a group of geological formations found only in Israel. But knockout views abound throughout the area: the changing colors of the Wilderness of Zin as the day progresses; the sunsets that stain Eilat's waters a deep red; the snow-white blocks of salt clumped on the surface of the Dead Sea; and the erosion sculptures surrounded by brooding mountains in Timna Valley Park.

## Scuba Diving

Eilat is at the gateway to the Red Sea, one of the best dive sites in the world. After the Six-Day War, in 1967, Israeli divers opened facilities along the Sinai coast south of Eilat, and although the Sinai Peninsula was returned to Egypt more than a decade ago, Eilat's dive centers still run regular dive safaris over the border. Amazing coral formations, underwater tropical plants, and a dazzling array of fish live in waters that stay warm year-round (22°C, or 72°F, in winter). The reefs are a mere 10 yards offshore, with an immediate deep drop, so a dive is just a walk away. Divers should bring their license, insurance certification, and appropriate footwear—the sea floor is rough, and so are the sea urchins. Top-level diving courses are widely available.

# Exploring Eilat and the Negev

Our peregrinations cover three basic areas in the inverted triangle of the Negev. The first is the heart of the Negev, with sites such as David Ben-Gurion's home and grave, the ancient Nabatean-Roman-Byzantine ruins at Tel Avdat, and the amazing Ramon Crater. The second includes the capital city of Beersheva, the spa-resort town of Ein Bokek at the Dead Sea, the ancient city of Tel Arad, and the modern city of Arad. The southern tip of the triangle encompasses carefree Eilat, the

Underwater Observatory at Coral Beach, and Timna Valley Park. Eilat is also the jumping-off point for day or longer trips to Jordan (ancient Petra) or Egypt (the Sinai Peninsula); *see* Chapter 9 if these interest you.

As you travel through the Negev, you'll pass stretches of flat, uninhabited countryside under hot, blue skies, punctuated by the odd acacia tree, twisting wadi, or craggy mountain. In winter you'll see delicate desert flowers along the road. If you want to skip the desert-driving experience, you might limit your trip here to Eilat or Ein Bokek. In Eilat you can stay at a luxurious hotel, relax on the sunny shore, and dive or snorkel. In Ein Bokek you can settle into one of the numerous spas that make use of the Dead Sea waters and medicinal mud.

## Great Itineraries

The following itineraries cover the major (and some off-the-beaten-path) Negev sights for travelers who are driving and have a limited amount of time. All assume that you're coming from Tel Aviv or Jerusalem. You can reach a few of these places by bus, but this is definitely not the most comfortable way to get around. You might consider combining one of our suggested itineraries with a short guided tour (☞ Guided Tours *in* Eilat and the Negev A to Z, *below*).

Although Beersheva is considered the capital of the Negev, it is not included in the two-day or five-day itinerary because it is not of major importance, nor does it have many good hotels. You might want to stop there briefly for a snack or gas.

*Numbers in the text correspond to numbers in the margin and on the Eilat and the Negev map.*

### IF YOU HAVE 1 OR 2 DAYS

You can cram a lot of Negev sights into a day or two; just get an early start from Jerusalem or Tel Aviv: You can either stop at the **Bedouin Heritage Center** ① or drive straight to Beersheva on your way to **Mitzpe Revivim** ② to see the reconstruction of a 1943 military desert outpost. Next, visit renowned prime minister **David Ben-Gurion's desert home** ③ and **grave** ④, overlooking the Wilderness of Zin. Head down the twisting road near the grave site to get to **Ein Avdat** ⑤, a welcome respite of splashing waterfalls in the blazing summer and a green and picturesque sight in winter. It's a short drive from Ein Avdat to the 2,000-year-old Nabatean hilltop stronghold of **Avdat** ⑥, which you can explore on foot. If you have only one day, skip Ein Avdat and Avdat and drive straight to the visitor center at **Mitzpe Ramon** ⑦ to see the **Makhtesh Ramon** ⑦. If you have two days, spend the night in Mitzpe Ramon and explore the immense crater the next morning. (If you've brought children, they'll appreciate a visit to the **Alpaca Farm,** just outside town.) Your return trip brings you back to **Beersheva** ⑨, where you can choose between visiting **Tel Beer Sheva** ⑪ and the possible site of Abraham's Well and stopping at the **Israel Air Force Museum** ⑩, in Hatzerim, to see a field full of planes.

### IF YOU HAVE 5 DAYS

Start at the **Museum of Bedouin Culture** ⑧ for a look at the lifestyle of Israel's nomads. The sandy landscape along Route 31 takes you through ancient **Tel Arad** ⑫ and modern **Arad** ⑬. From Arad drive the dramatic 24-km (15-mi) descent on sharply curving Route 31 to the Dead Sea, the lowest point on earth. Stay overnight in 🏨 **Ein Bokek** ⑭. Devote the next morning to floating in the Dead Sea and enjoying your hotel's spa facilities. By afternoon you'll be well relaxed and ready to drive south to 🏨 **Eilat** ⑮ and spend two more days relaxing in an entirely different setting. Back on the road on the fourth day, going north, drive through the **Makhtesh Ramon** ⑦ to reach 🏨 **Mitzpe Ramon** ⑦, on the

# Eilat and the Negev

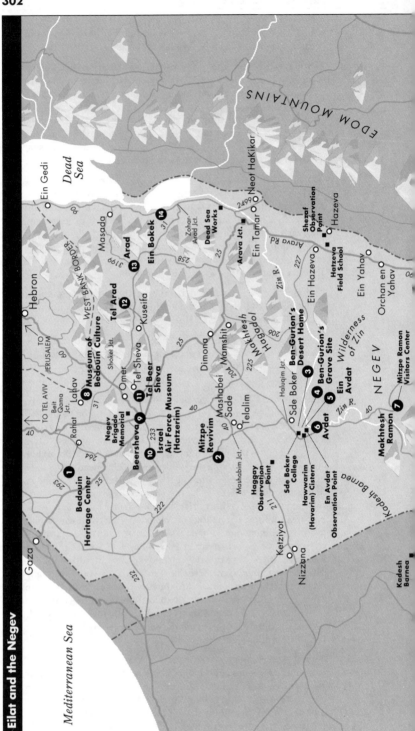

Mediterranean Sea

Gaza

Bedouin Heritage Center **1**

Rahat

Beit Qama Jct.

TO TEL AVIV

Hebron

TO JERUSALEM

WEST BANK BORDER

Lahav

Museum of Bedouin Culture **8**

Shoket Jct.

Omer

Negev Brigade Memorial

Beersheva **9**

Tel-Beer Sheva **11**

Tel Sheva

Israel Air Force Museum (Hatzerim) **10**

Mitzpe Revivim **2**

Mashabei Sade

Telalim

Dimona

Mamshit

Makhtesh Hagadol

Kuseifa

Tel Arad **12**

Arad **13**

Ein Bokek **14**

Masada

Zohar-Arad Jct.

Dead Sea Works

Arava Jct.

Ein Tamar

Neot HaKikar

Shezaf Observation Point

Hazeva

Hatzeva Field School

Ein Hazeva

Ein Yahav

Orchan en Yahav

Ein Gedi

Dead Sea

EDOM MOUNTAINS

Ben-Gurion's Desert Home **3**

Ben-Gurion's Grave Site **4**

Sde Boker

Haluqim Jct.

Zin R.

Ein Avdat **5**

Ein Wilderness of Zin

Avdat **6**

NEGEV

Mitzpe Ramon Visitors Center **7**

Makhtesh Ramon

Mashabim Jct.

Haggay Observation Point

Sde Boker College

Hawwarim (Havarim) Cistern

En Avdat Observation Point

Ketziyot

Nizzana

Kadesh Barnea

Kadesh Barnea

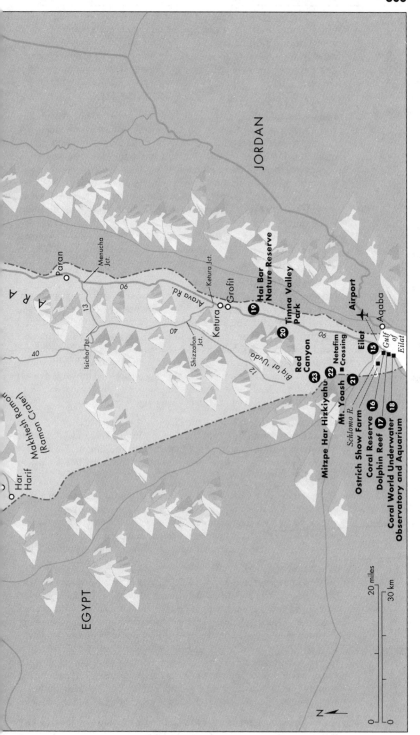

EGYPT

JORDAN

Har
Harif

Makhtesh Ramon
(Ramon Crater)

A R A V A

Paran

Menucha
Jct.

Isichor Jct.

40

13

90

Shizzafon
Jct.

40

Arava Rd

Ketura Jct.

12

Bi'al ta'Uvda

Ketura

Grofit

**19** Hai Bar
Nature Reserve

**20** Timna Valley
Park

90

Red
Canyon

Mitzpe Har Hizkiyahu

**23**

**22** Netafim
Crossing

Mt. Yoash

Schlomo R.

**21**

**16** Ostrich Show Farm

**17** Coral Reserve

Dolphin Reef

**18** Coral World Underwater
Observatory and Aquarium

**15** Eilat

Gulf
of
Eilat

Airport

Aqaba

N

0
0

20 miles

30 km

crater's edge; spend the night there. You might have time to go to the visitor center or at least enjoy the cliffside Promenade before dark. On your last day head back to Tel Aviv or Jerusalem, stopping at either **Arad** ⑬, **Ben-Gurion's desert home** ③, **Ben-Gurion's grave** ④, **Mitzpe Revivim** ②, or the **Israel Air Force Museum** ⑩ (you won't have time to see them all).

IF YOU HAVE 9 DAYS
Follow the first three days of the itinerary above, spending the third and fourth nights in **Eilat** ⑮. On the fourth and fifth days, kick back, learn to dive, swim with dolphins, bird-watch, hike, or take a guided tour of the Eilat area. On Day 6 drive north to the **Makhtesh Ramon** ⑦. Stay overnight in 🏨 **Mitzpe Ramon** ⑦. On Day 7 you might take a jeep tour, and perhaps visit the Alpaca Farm. Heading north on Route 40 on Day 8, visit ancient **Avdat** ⑥, **Ben-Gurion's home** ③, **Ben-Gurion's grave** ④, or **Ein Avdat** ⑤ on your way to 🏨 **Beersheva** ⑨ for the night. If your last day (spent in Beersheva) is a Thursday, you can get an early start at the **Bedouin market** or visit **Tel Beer Sheva** ⑪—or the **Israel Air Force Museum** ⑩, or **Mitzpe Revivim** ②—on your way to Tel Aviv or Jerusalem.

## When to Tour the Negev

October through May is the best time to explore the Negev. In January and February it's dry and cold. Scorching-hot conditions prevail from June through late September (though it's very dry), so your best bet then is to stay by the water, in Eilat. Ein Bokek, with its unique Dead Sea properties, attracts visitors even in the wildly hot summer. In early March, you'll be treated to the sight of scarlet, bright yellow, white, and hot pink desert flowers bursting out against the brown desert earth; March is also when Eilat's International Bird-watchers' Festival takes place. In August, Eilat hosts a jazz festival.

Negev sites open at 8:30 AM and close by 4 PM in winter and 5 PM in summer. Restaurants (except for those in Ein Bokek and Eilat) serve their main meal of the day (hot food) at noon and often close by early evening. Most places close early on Friday; roadside diners close at around 1:30 PM.

Try to get an early start; plan to be inside or resting at midday in summer; and make every effort to reach your destinations by nightfall. If you're traveling a long distance, stay alert and awake. Lock your car at all times, take your valuables when you leave it, and keep your bags where they're not visible from the outside. Women should not hitchhike.

DESERT PRECAUTIONS
To remain comfortable, happy, and *safe,* you must observe certain rules of the desert. You should drink 2 quarts of water a day in the winter, and, if you're active, 1 quart per hour in the summer; dehydration sets in quickly in the desert. Keep a jerrican (which holds 5 gallons) of water in your car, plus extra bottles. You'll find water fountains along the way, but they don't always function. Wear sunblock, sunglasses, protective lip balm, and a hat (a must year-round). (You'll forget personal vanity when you see *everyone* wearing hats, some that you thought you wouldn't be caught dead in.) Light hiking shoes and a small knapsack are indispensable for walks and hikes, as are bug spray and a flashlight.

Although it may seem incongruous in the desert, road flooding is a very real danger from September through March, especially the day after a rainfall farther north. In the spring, low-pressure systems from the Red Sea can bring torrential rains. If it's raining or has recently rained, call the police (☎ 100) or the Society for the Protection of Nature in Israel (SPNI; ☎ 03/638–8696) and ask if the road you intend to take is in passable condition. If you're already in the Negev, contact the local tourist office (☞ Visitor Information *in* Eilat and the Negev A to Z, *below*) for an update. If, while traveling, you see even a small amount of water flowing across the road in front of you, stop and wait, even if it takes a while for the water to subside. Water on the road is a warning of possible imminent flooding. When hiking, do not enter canyons or dry riverbeds on rainy days, or days when it has just rained farther north.

# THE HEART OF THE NEGEV

The area extending from the Negev Highlands to Eilat has a whole range of sights: the Bedouin Heritage Center, in the village of Rahat; Mitzpe Revivim, a reconstructed desert outpost; David Ben-Gurion's kibbutz home and grave site; an icy desert pool at Ein Avdat; the 2,000-year-old Nabatean hilltop stronghold of Avdat; and the immense Makhtesh Ramon (Ramon Crater).

## Bedouin Heritage Center

🐫 **❶** *110 km (66 mi) south of Tel Aviv, 15 km (9 mi) north of Beersheva. After the sign for Rahat, drive 2 km (1¼ mi); the Bedouin Heritage Center is opposite the gas station.*

You can meet the Negev's indigenous people, the Bedouin, at the Bedouin Heritage Center, a large black tent and fieldstone building in the village of Rahat. (Notice the cemetery on your way in from the road; each grave has both a headstone and a footstone.) Rahat is a 23-year-old Bedouin village with modern villas, schools, and a community center—and resident Salem Abu Siam's authentic tent. Seated inside, Bedouin hosts welcome you by performing the traditional coffee ceremony: roasting the beans over a fire and rhythmically pounding them (to let neighbors know that guests have arrived) in a wooden container using a wooden pestle. You'll sit on rugs around the fire and drink coffee from small cups. Singing, playing the *rababa* (Bedouin violin), and storytelling (as it has been done for centuries) are part of the visit. You can watch demonstrations of rug-making on a loom in a nearby tent and purchase Bedouin crafts, such as rugs and embroidery. Children will especially enjoy the short camel and donkey rides. ⊠ *Rte. 264, 27 km (17 mi) from Kiryat Gat,* ☎ *07/991–8263 or 07/991–8656.* 🎫 *NIS 12 ($3.40).* ☉ *Sun.–Fri. 8:30–8, Sat. 11:30–5.*

*En Route* On your way south from the Bedouin Heritage Center, you'll drive through **Beersheva** (☞ *below*), where you might want to stop for gas or a snack. Watch for the rectangular tents and huts sprawling over the low hills on the outskirts of town. This is a settlement of the Azazme, a Bedouin tribe. Although Bedouin traditionally live in black goat-hair tents, the Azazme, like many other modern Bedouin, are leaving behind their nomadic way of life and settling down. What you see is a step in the modern-day transition from tents to hutlike structures to concrete homes in permanent villages (it's not unusual to see tents interspersed with these modern houses). But these traditionally desert nomads still depend on their flocks for sustenance, much as their ancestors did. As you drive, you'll see Bedouin women, their faces covered and their embroidered black dresses flying in the wind, tending sheep and goats. Alongside the road (and all over the Negev), you'll also see the occasional isolated, often oval-shape cluster of eucalyptus and tamarisk trees. Called a *liman* (Greek for a small port or haven), each of these is the result of Jewish National Fund desert afforestation efforts, in which trees are sown in depressions to catch even the smallest amount of runoff water. Keep an eye out for donkey and sheep crossings!

# Mitzpe Revivim

❷ *36 km (22¼ mi) southeast of Beersheva.*

Mitzpe Revivim is the site of an early desert outpost. In 1943, in a desolate and empty Negev, three such outposts were set up to gauge the feasibility of Jewish settlement in the southernmost part of the country; one of these was Mitzpe Revivim (*mitzpe* means "lookout," *revivim* means "showers"). Revivim's very presence, along with a handful of other Negev settlements, influenced the U.N.'s decision to include the Negev as part of the State of Israel in the 1947 partition plan. During the War of Independence, isolated Mitzpe Revivim was besieged by Egyptian soldiers, and a hard battle was won by a small band of pioneers and Palmach soldiers. The defenders' fort and living quarters have been preserved: The radio room, ammunition room, kitchen, and engineers' quarters contain their original equipment. Outside are a cave—actually a Byzantine-period cistern—where a medical clinic was set up, and two airplanes, which were used to bring supplies and evacuate the wounded. The kibbutz members who maintain the place act as guides, and a small restaurant offers snacks and hot food. ⊠ *Rte. 222,* ☏ *07/656–2570.* ⊡ *NIS 10 ($2.85).* ⊙ *Sun.–Thurs. 9–3, Fri. 9–1, Sat. 10–4, holidays and holiday eves 9–5.*

*En Route*   Proceed south along Route 40 and you'll come to the gas station at **Mashabim Junction,** which also serves as a roadside café (good for stocking up on bottled water) and a tourist-information kiosk. Continue on Route 40 for 2 km (1¼ mi) past the station and make a left at the sign for Mitzpe Ramon, at Telalim Junction. Heading southwest along this stretch of road, you'll pass through areas where signs announce FIRING ZONE. The signs indicate closed military areas, which you may not enter without proper authorization. It's perfectly safe to travel on the main roads; just don't wander off them.

Continuing along Route 40, you'll see a sign on the right for the **Haggay Observation Point.** The parking lot is on the opposite side of the highway at a curve in the road. After parking the car, carefully cross the road to the observation point for a glorious first view of the **Wilderness of Zin**—stark, flat, beige terrain—and **Kibbutz Sde Boker.** Except for the greenery of the kibbutz, the area looks just as it did to the wandering Children of Israel making their way from Egypt to the Land of Canaan more than 3,000 years ago, no doubt muttering gripes about the lack of figs, vines, and water.

# Ben-Gurion's Desert Home

❸ *24 km (15 mi) south of Mitzpe Revivim. Sign for Ben-Gurion's home is just after Kibbutz Sde Boker.*

Thousands of people make their way to this pilgrimage site every year. Ben-Gurion himself hoped that tens of thousands would settle in the Negev, though his dream has not come true; he was passionate about the Negev, and the entrance path to his home is lined with stones bearing his now-famous sentiments. A new outdoor exhibit narrates the great leader's life story on large signboards; early photos and a map show how the Negev looked in 1953, when Ben-Gurion and his wife moved here. Inside the small hut are more descriptions and various personal effects, including the fez Ben-Gurion wore as a law student in Istanbul.

Amid the waving eucalyptus trees is David Ben-Gurion's simple dwelling. Ben-Gurion (1886–1973), Israel's first prime minister, was one of the great statesmen of the 20th century, yet his small Negev home is commonly known as "the hut" because of its humble ambience. It's not actually a hut but a one-story wooden home with a small kitchen, an eating corner with a table and two chairs, and simple furniture throughout. Visitors such as Dag Hammarskjöld, secretary-general of the United Nations, drank tea with Ben-Gurion in the living room, with its miniature version of Michelangelo's *Moses* on a side table and a picture of Abraham Lincoln on the wall. Ben-Gurion's library shelves contain 5,000 books (there are 20,000 more in his Tel Aviv home)—in fact, most of the space in the "hut" is taken up by the Old Man's (as he was locally known) books. On Ben-Gurion's desk are the papers on which he copied out sentences from the Old Testament: "I will even make a way in the wilderness, and rivers in the desert. . . . I give waters in the wilderness, and rivers in the desert, to give drink to my people, my chosen" (Isaiah 43). His bedroom, with its single picture of Mahatma Gandhi, holds the iron cot on which he slept (only three hours a night) and his slippers on the floor beside it. The house is as Ben-Gurion left it, with only a porch added to exhibit memorabilia, such as gifts from world leaders.

When Ben-Gurion resigned from government in 1953 (later to return), he and his wife, Paula, moved to the isolated, brand-new **Kibbutz Sde Boker** to provide an example for others. "Neither money nor propaganda builds a country," he announced. "Only the man who lives and creates in the country can build it." This said, the George Washington of Israel—whose interests were history, philosophy, and politics, as the artifacts in his home indicate—took up his new role in the kibbutz fold. In February 1955 he became prime minister once more and spent only holidays and weekends at the kibbutz; he returned here to live when he retired in 1970. (He returned to his Tel Aviv residence some months before his death in 1973.) ☎ 07/655–8444. ☒ *Free.* ☉ *Sun.–Thurs. 8:30–4, Fri. and holiday eves 8:30–2, Sat. and holidays 9–2:30.*

### Dining

$  ✕ **Sde Boker Inn.** At this cozy eatery under the trees, kibbutz members dish up homemade hot meals, plus salads and sandwiches, for breakfast and lunch. They'll also pack box lunches for the road. Bags of kibbutz-grown pistachio nuts are a delicious treat, and the shop next door sells kibbutz-made handicrafts, including jewelry. ☒ *Next door to Ben-Gurion's home,* ☎ *07/656–0379. AE, D, MC, V. No dinner.*

## Ben-Gurion's Grave

❹ *3 km (2 mi) southwest of Ben-Gurion's home, to the right of the main gate for Sde Boker College.*

Ben-Gurion's grave is not far from his former home. Walk through the beautiful garden until you reach the quiet, windswept plaza, in the center of which are the simple raised stone slabs marking the graves of David and Paula Ben-Gurion (she died five years before her husband). The couple's final resting place—selected by Ben-Gurion himself—overlooks Zin Valley's geological finery: a vast, undulating drape of velvety-looking stone in shades of cream, ivory, coffee, and soft brown that slowly changes hue as the day goes on. The cluster of greenery and palm trees to the right on the valley floor indicates Ein Avdat (Avdat Spring; ☞ *below*).

## Sde Boker College

*Enter through the gate with the traffic arm, next to Ben-Gurion's grave.*

Ben-Gurion envisioned a place of learning in the desert. This campus became part of Ben-Gurion University of the Negev, whose main campus is in Beersheva. Although there isn't much to see here, the **National Solar Energy Center,** where a research program investigates new ideas for the harnessing of solar energy, is interesting. For the traveler, the college is primarily a good place to eat and spend the night. In the middle of the campus, under a peaked roof, the **commercial center** has a restaurant, a supermarket open until 8 PM, a post office, and the field school of the SPNI (☎ 07/653–2016).

### Dining and Lodging

$ ✕ **Zin Inn.** As hot a spot as you'll find in the middle of the desert, the Zin Inn is where everyone hangs out—desert researchers from overseas, soldiers from the nearby base, visiting schoolchildren from all over the country, and field-school guides. The menu is the usual desert-restaurant fare: soup, schnitzel (breaded and fried chicken cutlets), french fries, salad, ice cream, coffee, and soft drinks. ⊠ *Sde Boker campus,* ☎ *07/653–2811. No credit cards. Closed Sat. and after 2 PM Fri.*

$$ 🏨 **Desert Research Institute Guest House.** If you'd like the Wilderness of Zin as your backyard, consider this place. A university-run facility for visiting scientists, the guest house sometimes has rooms available for travelers seeking the simple life. It's quiet and rather remote, situated on a winding path at the edge of a beautiful canyon, with superb views. Each room has two beds (you can add as many as three cots if necessary) and an alcove with a small refrigerator, a teakettle, and a few dishes. Towels are provided. There is a small TV lounge, a communal kitchen for light cooking (you can stock up at the nearby supermarket), and a restaurant in the commercial center. There are no phones in the rooms, but there is a pay phone in the commercial center. ⊠ *Ben-Gurion University of the Negev, Sde Boker campus, 84990,* ☎ *07/659–6711,* ℻ *07/659–6704. 14 rooms with bath. Air-conditioning. No credit cards.*

$ 🏨 **SPNI Field School Hostel.** A short walk from the commercial center, this hostel is a cut above. Each of the octagonal units has a large room with a skylight, two bunk beds, two twin beds, a small desk, and a private bathroom (bring your own towel). You can use the large kitchen to prepare meals, and there's always hot water in the urn for coffee. ⊠ *Sde Boker campus,* ☎ *07/653–2016,* ℻ *07/653–2721. No credit cards.*

---

## Ein Avdat

🕐 ❺ *3 km (2 mi) south of Ben-Gurion's grave and Sde Boker College.*

Ein Avdat (Avdat Spring) lies at the foot of the canyon that divides the plateau between the ancient Nabatean city of Avdat and Kibbutz Sde Boker, in **Ein Avdat National Park.** To get to the spring from Ben-Gurion's grave, head down the curving road to a clump of palm trees and the admission booth. Ask for the explanatory leaflet when you pay. Lock the car, taking valuables with you. Walk toward the thickets of rushes, and about five minutes later you'll see on the left, against the white-chalk cliff, a lone, ancient atlantica pistachio tree, the first of many reminders of a time when there was more water, and thus more vegetation, here. Look for ibex tracks on the ground, made with hoofs that enable these agile creatures to climb sheer rock faces. Try to spot the ibex, barely discernible against the cliff's rocks—they even have striped markings on their coats that resemble the rock's many strata. Rock pigeons, Egyptian vultures (black-and-white feathers, bright yellow beak, and long, pinkish legs), and sooty falcons nest in the natural holes in the soft rock and in cliff ledges.

The big surprise at Ein Avdat is the pool of ice-cold spring-fed water, complete with splashing waterfall. To reach this cool oasis, shaded by the surrounding cliffs, walk carefully along the spring and across the dam toward the waterfall. Swimming and drinking the water are not allowed (you'll not be *sorely* tempted, though—the water is swarming with tadpoles), but relaxing and enjoying the sight and sound of cold water in the arid Negev certainly are. You will see that the trail continues up the cliffside (using ladders and stone steps), but you can't follow it unless your party has two cars and leaves one at the destination, the Observation Point—the descent is considered too dangerous and is prohibited. ⊠ *Ein Avdat National Park,* ☎ *07/655–5684.* 🚗 *Parking NIS 12 ($3.40).* ⊗ *Apr.–Sept., Sun.–Thurs. 8–5, Fri. and holiday eves 8–4; Oct.–Mar., Sun.–Thurs. 8–4, Fri. and holiday eves 8–3.*

*En Route*   For an eagle's-eye view of the waterfall and spring below, turn off Route 40 at the orange sign for Ein Avdat to get to the **Ein Avdat Observation Point.** Below you is the white canyon carved out by the Zin River, with its waterfall (most of the year) tumbling into the pool, surrounded by greenery. From the lookout, a path leads around the top of the cliff (be very careful, especially with children), enabling you to see the rope marks in the rock; these have been created over the years by Bedouin pulling up water buckets. (For information on the hike from here to ancient Avdat, consult the SPNI Field School at Sde Boker College, *above*.)

## Avdat

★ ❻   *About 20 km (12 mi) south of Ben-Gurion's desert home and grave.*

The Nabatean city of Avdat, a 12-acre acropolis, looms on a hilltop. Here you can see the ancient stronghold and urban ruins of three peoples who have left their mark all over the Negev: the Nabateans, the Romans, and the Byzantines.

The Nabateans were seminomadic pagans who came here from northern Arabia in the 3rd century BC. Establishing prosperous caravan routes connecting the desert hinterland with the port city of Gaza, on the Mediterranean coast, they soon rose to glory with a vast kingdom whose capital was Petra (in present-day Jordan), a city cut entirely out of rock. Strongholds to protect the caravans, which carried gold, precious stones, and spices, were established along these routes, usually a day's journey apart.

The name Avdat is the Hebrew version of Oboda (30 BC–9 BC), a deified king who may have been buried here. Another king of Avdat, Aretas, is mentioned in the New Testament. The prominent local dynasty intermarried with the family of Herod the Great, and the Nabatean kingdom was finally abolished by the Romans in AD 106, when it became a Roman province. Most of the remains on the acropolis date from the 3rd, 4th, and 5th centuries—the Byzantine period, when the Nabateans adopted Christianity. The city was sacked by the Persians in AD 620 and was only rediscovered in the 20th century.

Start at the visitor center, where you can learn about the desert-trader Nabateans in a 10-minute video, see examples of what they actually transported across the desert, and examine archaeological artifacts found in the excavations. The shop sells copies of the original Nabatean jewelry. Be sure to pick up the National Parks Authority's excellent leaflet and map. Drive up the road (save your energy for walking around the site itself) and take the right turn at the sign for the **Roman burial cave.** Park and walk the 300 ft for a quick peek. The 20 burial niches cut into the rock date from the 3rd century BC.

Back in your car, drive up a little farther to the **lookout point** at the restored **Roman building.** The cultivated fields below were re-created in 1959 by Professor M. Even-Ari of Hebrew University, who wanted to see if the ancient Nabatean and Byzantine methods of conserving the meager rainfall (measured in millimeters) for desert farming would still work. The proof is in the cultivated crops and orchards before you. Runoff water was collected and distributed using a clever system of catchment areas, conduit walls, dams, and cisterns. Barren slopes around Nabatean sites all over the Negev were put to use in this way. Groups (with a minimum of 10 people) may call ahead to arrange a tour of the farm (☎ 07/656–5741 or 07/655–8462) for a small fee.

With the help of the National Parks Authority's map, you can trace the resourcefulness of the former locals at sites such as a reconstructed three-story Roman tower (there are good views from the tower corner of the 4th-century AD fortress walls); a rare Nabatean pottery workshop, where you might just find some eggshell-thin shards; a winepress (indicating that grapes were grown here, a testament to the Nabatean genius for conserving water); cisterns; two Byzantine churches; and a large baptismal font (to accommodate the converted). Near the baptismal font you can walk down the steps on the eastern slope to see the 6th-century AD Byzantine dwellings, each consisting of a cave (possibly used as a wine cellar) with a stone house in front of it. At the bottom of the hill, north of the gas station, is a well-preserved Byzantine bathhouse. ⊠ *Rte. 40,* ☎ *07/658–6391.* ⌑ *NIS 17 ($4.85) for all sights.* ⊙ *Apr.–Sept., Sat.–Thurs. 8–5, Fri. and holiday eves 8–4; Oct.–Mar., Sat.–Thurs. 8–4, Fri. and holiday eves 8–3.*

## Makhtesh Ramon and Mitzpe Ramon

**❼** *21 km (13 mi) south of Avdat, 80 km (50 mi) south of Beersheva.*

Makhtesh Ramon (the Ramon Crater) is Israel's most spectacular natural sight, an immense depression 40 km (25 mi) long, 10 km (6¼ mi) wide, and 1,320 ft deep. Because it's a phenomenon known only in this country (there are three others in the Negev), the Hebrew term *makhtesh*—meaning mortar, as in mortar and pestle—is now accepted usage. By definition, a makhtesh is an erosion valley walled with steep cliffs on all sides and drained by a single watercourse.

Mitzpe Ramon is a tiny town on the edge of the crater. The populace numbers 5,500 people, including recently arrived Russian immigrants. The town has one hotel, one swimming pool, one small shopping area, and no theater except its own raison d'être, the greatest show in the whole Negev—the giant crater. A promenade winds along its edge, a sculpture garden sits on its rim, outdoor enthusiasts head straight for its cliff walls, and the local main road runs through it.

Bear in mind that the four-year-old Ramon Inn is the only hotel in town. If rooms are unavailable and you're continuing south to Eilat, you can still see the crater, as Route 40 goes right through it; just try to plan your day so that you won't be driving to Eilat after dark. There are no gas stations between Mitzpe Roman and Yotvata, a distance of more than 100 km (62 mi).

The impressive **visitor center,** at the very edge of the makhtesh, is built in the shape of an ammonite fossil (a spiral-shape sea creature that lived here when everything was under water, millions of years ago). The helpful staff are rangers with the Israel Nature Reserve Authority. Guided tours of the center are available by advance request.

As you stand behind the glass, you peer out at a world formed millions of years ago. The crater's walls are made of layer upon layer of different-colored rock beds containing fossils of shells, plants, and trees. The makhtesh floor is covered with nature's creations: heaps of black basalt formed by volcanic activity, the peaks of ancient volcanoes themselves, jagged chunks of quartzite, huge blocks of overturned rock, and beds of multicolored clays used by potters today.

For a clear understanding of the makhtesh phenomenon (including a world-class view of it), the center offers an explanatory audiovisual presentation; a large, walk-around model of the makhtesh; and wall-to-wall, backlighted transparencies of geological points of interest. On the way to the top-floor lookout are informative panels describing the makhtesh's geological makeup, ecology, vegetation, and settlement. ⊠ *On the main road in Mitzpe Ramon,* ☎ *07/658–8691 or 07/658–8620.* ☑ *NIS 15 ($4.30).* ☉ *Sun.–Thurs. 9–5, Fri. 9–4, Sat. 9–5; winter Sun.–Thurs. 9–3, Fri. 9–1, Sat. 9–4.*

You may be inspired to take a walk (about 1 km, or ⅔ mi) along the **Albert Promenade,** which winds east to west along the edge of the crater from the visitor center to the camel-shape Mt. Gamal. This is not the time to run out of film—the view is overwhelming. If it's late afternoon, you may see ibex along the cliffs and raptors wheeling overhead. The promenade is fashioned from local stone, as is the huge sculpture by Israel Hadani, the back of which faces town and represents the crater's geological layers.

With the crater as a magnificent backdrop, the **Desert Sculpture Park** exhibits a far-flung collection of huge stone sculptures. The park took shape in 1962 with the work of a group of Israeli and foreign sculptors under the direction of Negev artist Ezra Orion. Their idea was to add to the natural stone "sculptures" with geometrical rock formations of similar design. The sculptors, each allocated a space on the cliff's edge, brought their chosen rocks and formed their desert works of art with minimal hand-shaping. ⊠ *Turn off near gas station on main road at sign marked* MA'ALE NOAH.

For a look at just one of the crater's geological sub-phenomena, drive to the **Carpentry.** A path goes up to a wooden walkway, built to protect nature's artwork from travelers' feet. Long ago, the sandstone was probably hardened and slightly warmed by volcanic steam, and the rocks split into prisms, due either to cooling joints or to another unknown process. The formations look like wooden chips piled up in a carpentry shop and have a lustrous patina caused by a chemical reaction brought on by climatic conditions. ⊠ *Along Rte. 40, going south.*

Another of nature's works is the **Ammonite Wall,** which is on the right as you drive through the crater. A sign indicates a distance of 5 km (3 mi), which applies to the marked hike in the crater (for fit walkers only—take water). The rock face contains hundreds of ammonite fossils, which look like ram's horns and are indeed named for the Egyptian god Ammon, who had the head of a ram.

☾ Just outside town is the **Alpaca Farm,** with its hundreds of sweet-faced alpacas and llamas. Young and old get a kick out of feeding the animals, even if they receive the occasional spit in the face from these long-eyelashed, gentle-looking animals. Children can take a llama ride. ⊠ *Turn off the main road opposite the gas station,* ☎ *07/658–8047.* ☑ *NIS 18 ($5).* ☉ *Daily 9–6; call about shorter hrs in winter.*

*En Route*    As you drive through the Ramon Crater, the wadis of the Negev increase in size from their source, in the Sinai, and cut through the Negev on their way to the Arava Valley, to the east. The sight of the Edom Mountains on the eastern horizon is beautiful, especially in the light of late afternoon. After the Tsichor Junction with Route 13 (which connects with the nearby north–south highway Route 90), you'll see lime-stone strata that have "folded" over the millennia. After the Ketura Junction (where Route 40 ends), there are breathtaking views of the Arava Valley (on your left), which marks the Israel-Jordan border and is part of the Great Syrian-African Rift, a fault line formed millions of years ago. From here, Route 90 leads straight to Eilat (52 km, or 33 mi). It's not advisable to take Route 12 to Eilat if you're finishing this tour after a long day's drive or toward dark, when Route 90 is the better and safer road.

## Dining and Lodging

**$$**  ✕ **The Ramon Inn.** The dearth of restaurants at the spectacular Ramon
★   Crater is more than made up for by the dining room at the Inn, conveniently located near the visitor center. It's cheerful and bright, and the hearty buffet meals are enlivened by jams, pickles, and other condiments made by local cooks. Desert life moves in mysterious ways, so lunch is not always served; it's a good idea to call ahead. ⊠ *Mitzpe Ramon,* ☎ *07/658–8822. Reservations essential. AE, DC, MC, V.*

**$$**  ✕ **Tsukit.** If you're lucky enough to get a window table at Tsukit ("little cliff"), you'll be sitting right on the edge of the crater, and the scenery will outshine whatever's on your plate. Choose either self- or waiter service for standard fare including beef, chicken, schnitzel, pasta, hummus, and stuffed vegetables. ⊠ *Beside Mitzpe Ramon Visitors Center,* ☎ *07/658–6079. Reservations not accepted. DC, MC, V. No dinner.*

**$**  ✕ **Misedet Hanna.** A cheerful roadside-diner atmosphere—dark-red ta-
★   bles and chairs and the enchanting spell cast by fluorescent lighting—prevails in this gas station–cum–restaurant opposite the Mitzpe Ramon Visitors Center. The owner, who seems to know everyone here and who talks warmly to all of them at the same time, says the food comes from "mother's kitchen." She does a fine job with both the food and the prices: a hearty breakfast of vegetable salad, *havita* (a crisp, plain omelet), cheese, bread, jam, and coffee costs only NIS 20 ($5.70). Breakfast starts at 8 AM. Lunch offerings include soups, salads (a round tray with six small, fresh vegetable dishes), oven-broiled ribs, schnitzel, chicken, fish, spaghetti, rice, and fries. ⊠ *Paz gas station,* ☎ *07/658–8158. Reservations not accepted. No credit cards. No dinner Fri.–Sat., no lunch Sat.*

**$$**  🏨 **The Ramon Inn.** There's nothing draconian about a stay at this
★   desert hotel, on the cliff of the crater. The four-story building has no elevator, but the accommodations are entirely comfortable. Stay in a pastel-and-white studio apartment (for one or two) or a two- or three-room apartment (for four to six people), the latter equipped with kitchenettes. The lobby has an open fireplace for chilly winter nights. The homey atmosphere extends to the dining room, where the condiments served are made by town residents. A swimming pool is scheduled to open in August 1999. The front desk can arrange camel and jeep trips. ⊠ *Mitzpe Ramon, Box 318, 80600,* ☎ *07/658–8822,* FAX *07/658–8151. 96 rooms with bath. Restaurant, lobby lounge, kitchenettes, coin laundry. AE, DC, MC, V.*

**$$**  🏨 **Sukkah in the Desert.** Deep in the Negev, Rachel Bat Adam, Ph.D., has created an out-of-the-ordinary encampment of sukkahs, the portable dwellings used by the Children of Israel when they wandered in this very same desert. You arrive in the middle of nowhere, and there on the rocky hillside are six small, isolated dwellings, each made of stone with a palm-frond roof. You can congregate and prepare your own meals in the central sukkah. It's an appealing combination: the starkness and purity of the desert and some modern amenities. Each sukkah has a carpet on its earthen floor and a mattress with cozy blankets; household essentials include a gas hot plate for cooking, a solar heater, and a clay water jar and copper bowls for ablutions. You use the great outdoors for anything else. ✉ *On road to Alpaca Farm, 7 km (4½ mi) west of Mitzpe Ramon, Box 272, 80600,* ☎ *07/658–6280. 6 units that sleep 2; shared bath. No credit cards.*

$$ ⌂ **Youth Hostel.** Famed in Israel for its high standards, and fairly luxurious as hostels go, this one has to be booked well in advance (June and September are busiest). Fine for families, the place is done in bright colors, with a plant-filled lobby and a cheerfully decorated dining room. Most rooms have three to four beds, but there are also four double rooms. Food is inexpensive and plentiful, and you can order box lunches; nonguests must reserve for dinner. ✉ *Opposite Mitzpe Ramon Visitors Center, 80600,* ☎ *07/658–8443,* FAX *07/658–8074. 164 beds, 4 double rooms with bath. Dining room, snack bar, dance club. DC, MC, V.*

## Nightlife and the Arts

You have two options once night falls in Mitzpe Ramon: gaze at the stars or have a drink in the lobby of the **Ramon Inn** (☞ Dining and Lodging, *above*).

## Outdoor Activities and Sports

### ADVENTURE TRIPS

If you want to include a **camel or jeep trip** in your Negev experience, the well-established desert-tour company **Desert Shade Eco Tourism** (reserve through Tel Aviv; ☎ 03/575–6885, FAX 03/613–0160) offers a variety of jeep trips (☞ Guided Tours *in* Eilat and the Negev A to Z, *below*). Desert Shade also rents **mountain bikes** for NIS 40 ($11.40) a day and takes people **rappelling** down the spectacular cliffs of the Ramon Crater.

The new and professional **Ramon Desert Tours** (☎ 07/658–8125, 052/703451 or 050/308272), based near the Ramon Inn, leads jeep trips and hikes, and rents mountain bikes.

### HIKING

The staff at the **visitor center** (☎ 07/658–8691) in Mitzpe Ramon can help you plan a short local hike, though the explanatory maps are in Hebrew (☞ Desert Precautions, *above,* for planning information). The **Society for the Protection of Nature in Israel** (☎ 03/638–8673 or 03/638–8677) often includes the Negev heartland in its trips.

### SWIMMING

The only body of water in town (and for miles around) is the **municipal pool** (✉ at the entrance to town, near the shopping center, opposite the gas station, ☎ 07/995–7702). Call for hours and admission fees.

## Shopping

The **Amonit Gallery** at the visitor center has a varied and rather unusual selection: jewelry and batiks made by the owner, water pipes, Bedouin drums, Armenian pottery, hats, T-shirts, and small, framed sketches of the area. Both the Amonit Gallery and the **Alpaca Farm** (☎ 07/658–8047) sell skeins of alpaca wool—light as a feather, soft as down, and warm as toast. It comes in natural shades of white, gray, and brown.

# BEERSHEVA TO EIN BOKEK

This area stretches east from Beersheva, known as the capital of the Negev, to the resort town of Ein Bokek, on the Dead Sea. In between are ancient Tel Arad and modern Arad. Between Beersheva and Arad you'll encounter scenes that look strikingly biblical—black tents,

Bedouin shepherds with robes flying, and sheep and goats bumbling around. And after several twists of the road from Arad, you'll come to the shores of the Dead Sea, the lowest point on earth.

## Museum of Bedouin Culture

☚ ❽ *95 km (57 mi) south of Tel Aviv, 24 km (14 mi) north of Beersheva.*

This one-of-a-kind museum features the Bedouin who have long populated the Negev. The folklore center, anticipated by an orange sign, is named for the late Colonel Joe Alon, a pilot who took a great interest in this area and its people. Housed in a circular, tentlike building, the museum creates an authentic look at the rapidly changing lifestyle of the Bedouin using various tableaux containing life-size mannequins. The tableaux are grouped by subject: wool-spinning and carpet-weaving, bread-baking, the Bedouin coffee ceremony, wedding finery (including a camel elaborately decorated for the event and bearing nuptial gifts), donkeys and camels at work, and toys made from found objects such as pieces of wire and wood. The tools and artifacts—most handmade, and many already out of use in modern Bedouin life—form an outstanding collection. The film about Bedouin life in the Negev is a nice touch. Admission includes a cup of thick coffee in a Bedouin tent, where the sheikh performs the coffee ceremony over an open fire. ⊠ *Rte. 325, off Rte. 40,* ☎ *07/991–8597 or 07/991–3322.* ☑ *NIS 12 ($3.40).* ☉ *Sun.–Thurs. 9–4, Fri. 9–2, Sat. 9–4.*

## Beersheva

❾ *24 km (14 mi) south of Museum of Bedouin Culture, 113 km (70 mi) southeast of Tel Aviv.*

Beersheva's emblem consists of a tamarisk tree, representing the biblical past, and a pipe through which water flows, symbolizing the city's modern revival. It was here that the patriarch Abraham constructed his well (*be'er* in Hebrew) and swore an oath (*shevua* in Hebrew) over seven (*sheva* in Hebrew) ewes with the king of Gerar, who vowed to prevent his men from seizing the well. And it was here that Abraham planted a grove of tamarisk trees. The Book of Genesis describes other patriarchal figures who lived in this area as well, wandering the hills with their flocks. It's easy to envision these scenes today thanks to the cloaked figures of Bedouin shepherds with their sheep and goats in the surrounding hillsides.

Tel Beer Sheva (☞ *below*), just outside the city, is the site of the biblical Beersheva and could easily be the site of Abraham's well. An expression from the Book of Judges, "from Dan to Beersheva," once set the northern and southern boundaries of the Land of Israel; in biblical times, living farther south of the city meant living a true desert (nomadic) life.

Romans and Byzantines built garrisons in Beersheva, but the city was later abandoned. In 1900 the Ottoman Turks, who had ruled Palestine since 1517, rebuilt Beersheva as their Negev district center (the present Old City). They set aside an area for a Bedouin market, which still takes place every Thursday (☞ Shopping, *below*). During World War I, the British took Beersheva from the Turks after a difficult battle. During the War of Independence the town became an Egyptian base, and in 1948 it was conquered by the Israelis.

Beersheva is now the the fourth-largest city in Israel, with its own university—named after David Ben-Gurion, who envisioned a flourishing Negev—and a regional hospital that serves Bedouin shepherds, kibbutzniks, and other desert dwellers. The city's population of 170,000 now boasts a symphony orchestra and a light-opera company, both nationally respected. Largely blue-collar, Beersheva is struggling to provide housing for thousands of recent immigrants, many from Ethiopia and the former Soviet Union.

Nowhere is the saying "Israel's national bird is the crane" more apt than in boomtown Beersheva. The city is blossoming: workers toil to build the municipal buildings, all of which will be concentrated in the center of town, near the Hilton Hotel; entire new neighborhoods sit neatly under the sun. The Turkish-built Old City is being spruced up; there's already a wine shop and a charming wine bar with an exceedingly good list; and a tour bus with explanations and entertainment is in the works.

The famed Bedouin Market, once a treasure trove of some of Israel's best ethnic handicrafts, has been hit by modern times (items from the Far East) and isn't what it used to be. But it finally has a permanent location, and it's interesting to visit with the hope that you'll find something authentic. Most authentic are the Bedouin themselves, wearing desert clothing and presiding over goods spread out on the ground.

The city is a good starting point for Negev travel, though it has been rather neglected by tourists. Main roads branch out from here, and buses from the south depart from here as well. An overnight stay in Beersheva will give you a glimpse of a growing desert city bustling with immigrants from all over the world, plus proximity to several unique sights.

## Dining and Lodging

$$ ✕ **Bulgarit.** Bulgarit ("Bulgarian"), on the pedestrian mall in the Old City, has been in business for 48 years; the third generation is now at the helm. The owner sits with his cronies at a corner table under a fancy silver sconce and reels off the selections from his "international" menu: roast lamb and grilled meats, oven-baked meats (the lamb is very good), baked fish, moussaka, vegetables stuffed with meat and rice, *gvetch* (an assortment of vegetables cooked together), and chocolate mousse. If you speak Bulgarian, your meal comes with stories of pioneer days; if not, you still get friendly, efficient service. ⊠ *K.K. le Israel St.,* ☎ *07/623–8505. Reservations not accepted. DC, MC, V. Closed Fri.*

$$ ✕ **Ilie's.** It's not much to look at from the outside, but this Old City eatery does offer the novelty of choosing your own piece of meat and watching it cook over the charcoal grill. The emphasis is definitely on meat, with various cuts of steak topping the menu. The tasty lamb chops and the fresh fish (from Beersheva's daily outdoor market) are also fine choices. Seasonal fruit salad complements the main course, and there's baklava for dessert. ⊠ *21 Herzl St.,* ☎ *07/627–8685. Reservations not accepted. AE, DC, MC, V. No dinner Fri., no lunch Sat.*

$$ ✕ **Pitput.** The name means "gossip" in Hebrew, and it's probably flying around in this restaurant, which has been smartly redecorated with blond-wood chairs and washed blue and yellow walls. The young staff here is congenial and the food beautifully served. Sitting outside on the busy street or inside listening to recorded jazz or blues, desert diners have a range of selections, including salads, omelets, blintzes ranging from cheese to salmon, pasta, and grilled fish with grilled vegetables. Cheese sandwiches are made on seeded rolls called *begeles*. Half bottles of Yarden wine may be ordered. You can't go wrong with homemade hot pecan pie or cheesecake with fresh fruit. ⊠ *122 Herzl St.,* ☎ *07/623–7708. Reservations not accepted. AE, DC, MC, V.*

$$ ⊞ **Beersheva Hilton.** This three-year-old hotel is changing travel in the Negev by providing up-to-date lodgings in the desert's urban gateway. The pink-tinged brown stone of the 15-story building reflects its desert surroundings, and arched windows soften the city's square look. Guest rooms are comfortably outfitted with wicker chairs, and the curtains and bedspreads form a snappy color scheme of red, green, and butterscotch. Good reading lights are a welcome touch. The cool, outdoor patio, complete with bubbling fountains, is a lovely place to relax in the desert climate. ⊠ *Henrietta Szold St., near City Hall, 84100,* ☎ *07/640–5444,* ℻ *07/640–5445. 264 rooms with bath. 2 restaurants, lobby lounge, pool, health club. AE, DC, MC, V.*

$$ ⊞ **Desert Inn.** Established 35 years ago and still run reflecting a down-to-earth manner, this friendly, small-town hotel is on the edge of Beersheva in a huge garden. (Use the hotel's Hebrew name, Neot Midbar, when asking directions.) The staff, made up largely of Russian immigrants, is attentive. Renovations have spruced things up considerably: the lobby now sports contemporary blue, orange, and lime-green chairs, and the modern poolside changing room has individual showers and dressing rooms plus a sauna and hot tub. Also new is the center for alternative medicine, which includes massage treatments and dietary advice. Kids will enjoy the well-equipped playground. ⊠ *Sderot Tuviyahu, 84100,* ☎ *07/642–4922 or 07/641–2772,* ℻ *07/641–2772. 165 rooms with bath. 3 restaurants, piano bar, 3 pools, hot tub, massage, sauna, tennis court, basketball, exercise room, Ping-Pong, playground. AE, DC, MC, V.*

## Nightlife and the Arts

Both the **Beersheva Sinfionetta** (☎ 07/623–1616) and the **Beersheva Music Conservatory Chamber Orchestra** (☎ 07/627–6019) are well regarded. Once a year, in March or April, the **Light Opera Group of the Negev** presents two performances of Gilbert and Sullivan here, in English; contact the tourist office in Beersheva for details.

Beersheva's yuppies congregate for après-theater food and drink at the **Othello** (☎ 07/623–2230), in the Beersheva Theater Building.

Savor a long, leisurely evening of wine and tapas at the **Hatzer Hayain Wine Bar** (☎ 07/623–8135), in the Artists' Quarter. Proprietor, wine expert, and congenial host Michael will guide you through the intricacies of Israeli and other wines.

## Shopping

The Negev is still the home of the Bedouin, but today's Bedouin women are less interested than yesterday's in staying home all day to weave and embroider. That's why you need the eye of an eagle and the patience of a saint to search through the bundles and stacks of rather ordinary stuff at the **Bedouin market** to find articles made by Bedouin grandmothers. The market, which starts at daybreak each Thursday and lasts until early afternoon, is on the eastern side of the huge outdoor market site near the bridge, at Derech Eilat and Derech Hebron streets. (Men conduct a goat and sheep market on the other side.) The best time to be there is 6 AM, an hour or so later in winter. For sale, if you can find them, are wonderful embroidered dresses, yokes, and side panels from dresses; woven camel bags; rugs; earrings, bracelets, amulets, and nose rings; decorative beads and beaded bags; coin headbands (used as dowry gifts); tassels; copperware; and *finjans* (Bedouin coffee utensils). An inexpensive necklace of simple beads and cloves, used to ward off evil spirits, also makes a pleasing purchase.

"The older, the better" is the rule of thumb here; only the old work is handmade. Be warned that prices are high for articles of good quality.

Bargaining over prices is part of the Arab culture, but you need your wits about you to succeed—and ideally a local to act as a gladiator! You should ultimately pay 20%–30% less than the original asking price. If you want to take photographs here, bear in mind that Bedouin men usually don't mind being snapped, but women often do.

Convenient and cool in summertime, Beersheva's modern mall, **Kanionit** (⊠ HaNesiim Blvd. and Eilat St.), has an underground parking garage that leads to an entire floor of fast-food restaurants. The other floor, reached by a glass elevator, has a drugstore and a number of shops selling Israeli-made American-style clothes and accessories (lots of jeans and sunglasses).

Even more conveniently located, right in the Hilton Hotel, is **Dalia Schen's Gift Shop** (☎ 07/628–2785 or 050/622363). An expert in Israeli handicrafts, Dalia seeks out the unusual and offers a small but careful selection of weavings, artifacts, Ethiopian crafts, modern Yemenite and Bedouin jewelry, locally made rugs, and other pieces by local artists. Ask to see her unusual T-shirts and blouses decorated with old Bedouin embroidery.

An elegant wine shop in the desert? You'll be impressed with the state-of-the-art design, large stock of imported and local wines, and well-informed staff at **Aninei Hayain** (⊠ 117 Trumpeldor St., ☎ 07/628–9444).

*En Route*  On Route 40 northeast from Beersheva to Arad is the large and impressive **Negev Brigade Memorial,** designed and built by Israeli artist Danny Karavan. The monument's 15 symbolic parts and Hebrew text tell the story of the battle of the Palmach's Negev Brigade against the Egyptians after the birth of the State of Israel. The tower, representing a Negev settlement water tower, offers a great view of Beersheva and the surrounding desert. **Kafriat Shoket** is a kibbutz-run way station at the intersection of Route 31 and Route 60. Its large cafeteria serves hot food, sandwiches, salads, cakes, and drinks; especially recommended are the apple turnovers and raisin Danish pastries. Snack inside at the long wooden tables or outside under the tamarisk trees. The on-site minimart sells bottled water. ⊠ *Intersection of Rtes. 31 and 60,* ☎ *07/646–9421.* ☉ *Sun.–Thurs. 6 AM–11 PM, Fri. 6–6, Sat. 8 AM–11 PM.*

Continuing east along Route 31 toward Arad, you can see Bedouin encampments along the way. The slow transition from a nomadic lifestyle to a more rooted one is demonstrated by the Bedouin village of **Kuseifa,** already more than 10 years old.

## Israel Air Force Museum

🐾 ❿  *7 km (4½ mi) west of Beersheva.*

For plane lovers, this is a field of dreams. The open-air Israel Air Force Museum (also known as Hatzerim, for the nearby kibbutz) is a gigantic concrete field with 90 airplanes parked in rows. The fighter, transport, and training (plus a few enemy) aircraft tell the story of Israel's aeronautic history, from the Messerschmitt—obtained in 1948 from Czechoslovakia, and one of four such planes to help halt the Egyptian advance in the War of Independence—to the *Kfir,* Israel's first fighter plane. The young air-force personnel who staff the museum lead tours that take about 2½ hours and include a movie about this branch of the military. (The movie theater is an air-conditioned Boeing 707 that was used in the 1977 rescue of Israeli passengers held hostage in a hijacked Air France plane forced to fly to Entebbe, Uganda.) Another attention-getting display is a shiny, black Supermarine Spitfire with a red lightning bolt on its side. It was flown by Ezer Weizmann, the IAF's first pilot, who became defense minister and is now the president of Israel. Be sure to wear a hat to protect against the sun. ⊠ *Rte. 233,* ☎ *07/990–6855 or 07/990–6890.* ☎ *NIS 22 ($6.25).* ☉ *Sun.–Thurs. 8–5, Fri. 8–noon.*

## Tel Beer Sheva

⓫   *2 km (1¼ mi) east of Beersheva.*

Tel Beer Sheva, biblical Beersheva—traditionally associated with the patriarch Abraham—is an artificial *tel* (mound) created by nine successive settlements between 3500 BC and 600 BC. The tel is a recent addition to the roster of the National Parks Authority; ask for the excellent explanatory leaflet.

At the top of the tel is the only planned Israelite city uncovered in its entirety. Most of the visible remains date from the 10th to 7th centuries BC. A fine example of a circular layout typical of the Iron Age, the city is believed to have been destroyed around 706 BC by Sennacherib of Assyria. In the northeast, outside the 3,000-year-old city gate, is a huge well more than 6 ft in diameter, which apparently once reached groundwater 90 ft below (it has not been completely excavated). This ancient well served the city from its earliest times, and scholars speculate that it could be the well that is documented in the Old Testament as Abraham's Well (Genesis 21:22–32). The observation tower is rather ugly, but it affords some beautiful views. ⊠ *Rte. 60,* ☎ *07/646–7286.* ☎ *NIS 8 ($2.30).* ☉ *Apr.–Sept., Sun.–Thurs. 8–5, Fri. and holiday eves 8–3; Oct.–Mar., Sun.–Thurs. 8–4, Fri. and holiday eves 8–2, Sat. 8–4.*

## Tel Arad

⓬   *38 km (23 mi) east of Beersheva, 8 km (5 mi) west of Arad.*

Approaching Tel Arad, the 25-acre site of the biblical city of Arad, from the west takes you through flat fields of the low shrub called *rotem* (white broom). At the new information center, you can pick up the National Parks Authority's pamphlet, which explains the ongoing excavations, and purchase (for NIS 8, or $2.30) the plan of the early Canaanite city of Arad, with a map, recommended walking tour, and diagrams of the typical Arad house. (The center also has a souvenir shop and a snack bar.)

Arad was first settled during the Chalcolithic period (4000–3000 BC) by seminomadic pastoralists who lived and traveled together, herding and farming. It was they who first developed bronze. Arad was continually occupied until the end of the Early Bronze Age (3500–3200 BC), but the city you see most clearly here is from the Early Bronze Age II (2950–2650 BC). Here you can walk around a walled urban community and enter the carefully reconstructed one-room **Arad houses.**

After the Early Bronze Age II, Arad was abandoned and hidden beneath the light loessial soil for nearly 2,000 years, until the 10th century BC, when a **fortress**—one of many in the Negev (the first may have been built by Solomon)—was built on the site's highest point. It's worth the trek up the somewhat steep path. Take a moment to appreciate the view as you take your leave of the Early Bronze Age; at the top, you step into the Iron Age (10th–6th centuries BC). The small, square fortress served the area intermittently until Roman times; most of the visible remains date from the end of the First Temple period (935–586 BC). Note the small Israelite temple sanctuary, with its two standing stones (these are replicas—the originals are in the Israel Museum, in

Jerusalem) and sacrificial altar of unhewn stone. In the 7th century BC, the southern part of the Israelite kingdom of Judah reached as far as today's Eilat. Artifacts found at the tel are on display at the visitor center in Arad (☞ *below*). ✉ *Off Rte. 31,* ☎ *07/995–7690.* 🎟 *NIS 8 ($2.30).* ☉ *Sun.–Thurs. 8–5 (until 4 in winter), Fri. and holiday eves 8–4 (until 3 in winter).*

## Arad

**❶❸** *46 km (28½ mi) east of Beersheva, 8 km (5 mi) east of Tel Arad.*

The modern town of Arad was established as a planned community in 1961. Arad's population of nearly 25,000 now includes immigrants from Russia and Ethiopia; writer Amos Oz is its most famous resident. Breathe deeply: the town sits 2,000 ft above sea level and is famous for its dry, pollution-free air and mild climate. Arad has made a particular name for itself as a healthy home for asthma sufferers. Industrial waste and the planting of trees and bushes are government-controlled to keep pollution and pollen at bay. Arad is a popular base for excursions to sites in the Dead Sea area, notably to Masada (☞ Guided Tours *under* Around Jerusalem A to Z *in* Chapter 3), and is the only approach (via Route 31) to Masada's sound-and-light show.

In the middle of town is the **Arad Museum and Visitors Center,** whose helpful staff dispenses maps, brochures, and hiking information. Its innovative "Meet the Israeli" program arranges for travelers to have coffee and a chat with locals. The 20-minute audiovisual presentation gives a general sense of the desert, explains the causes and effects of floods, shows how animals adapt to a wilderness diet, and explores other Negev issues. The small museum displays the work of local artists as well as archaeological discoveries from nearby Tel Arad. You can see replicas of the so-called "Arad letters" (the originals are in the Israel Museum, in Jerusalem), 2,500-year-old inscribed potsherds in ancient Hebrew script, some written by the fortress commander Eliashiv, concerning provisions of flour and wine for the soldiers. One has the name Arad inscribed on it seven times. ✉ *28 Ben Yair St.,* ☎ *07/995–4409.* 🎟 *NIS 15 ($4.30).* ☉ *Sun.–Thurs. 9–5, Fri. and holiday eves 9–2, Sat. 9–5.*

### Dining and Lodging

**$$** ✕ **Pundak Alon.** On Route 31 at the entrance to Arad, next to the gas station, this roadside eatery changed hands a few years ago and has been completely refurbished. Mr. Steiner, the original owner, who had served local faithfuls and travelers since 1965, used to say that "people come to visit this restaurant as though it's a historical site." The cook is the same, but the bar is new, and the wood paneling lends a country air. You can order soups, 12 different meat dishes, and a variety of fish. The apple strudel is known far and wide. ✉ *Rte. 31,* ☎ *07/995–3328. Reservations not accepted. AE, D, MC, V. Closed Sat.*

**$$$** 🏨 **Margoa.** Well known for its asthma clinic and two-day packages, the seven-story Margoa carries on a 29-year tradition of pleasing its guests. Room furnishings are simple and subdued in hue; those on the south side have a desert view that stretches to the mountains of Moab. The 48 newer rooms, on the ground level around the garden, have spacious, modern bathrooms and are connected to the pool area by an open walkway. The terrace is particularly pleasant. The brand-new spa (with massage, Dead Sea mud treatments, skin treatments, and reflexology) is on the top floor, providing a wide-angle desert view. ✉ *Moab St., Box 20, 80700,* ☎ *07/995–1222,* FAX *07/995–7778. 165 rooms with bath. Restaurant, lobby lounge, pool, hot tub, sauna, spa, nightclub. AE, D, MC, V.*

# The Road to the Dead Sea

*The steep, 24-km (15-mi) descent to the Dead Sea on Rte. 31 has one sharp curve after another. Watch for the sign on the right indicating that you've reached sea level.*

The drama of this drive is enhanced by the stunning canyons and clefts that unfold on every side. Two observation points soon appear on the left. You can't cross to the first—**Metsad Zohar**—from your side of the road. The second—**Nahal Zohar**—looks down on the light marl of the ancient, dry riverbed of Zohar, the last vestige of an eons-old body of water that once covered this area. The Dead Sea lies directly east, with the Edom Mountains of Jordan on the other side. To the right (south) is Mt. Sodom. You can walk back to the left to Metsad Zohar to see the Roman-built Zohar fort.

You'll soon see, from above, the southern end of the Dead Sea, sectioned off into the huge evaporation pools of the Dead Sea Works, where potash and salts such as bromine and magnesium are extracted. It's common to see row after row of plastic "tunnels," which act as hothouses for fruit (often tomatoes and melons) that is sold to Europe in winter.

Two roads lead from Route 90 to the Ein Bokek hotel area, and when you get there you're at *the bottom of the world*: 1,292 ft below sea level. Although the Dead Sea (☞ Dead Sea Region *in* Chapter 3) can be as deep as 1,320 ft, it's much shallower at this end—only about 6½ ft deep. This area is now an artificial basin that serves the resort at Ein Bokek and provides an abundance of minerals for local use and for export.

## Dining

**$$** ✕ **Grill Michel.** A prime example of the Negev's gas-station eateries, Grill Michel is a minimally decorated (just a few posters), *Baghdad Cafe*–style diner on the road to the Zohar-Arad junction. It's run by a desert-hardened but friendly proprietor who's usually surrounded by regular customers and friends. Truck drivers, Dead Sea Works employees, and other locals come as much for the conversation and laughter as for the grub, which features simple grilled meats, french fries, hummus, fresh chopped-vegetable salads, and good, strong coffee. ⊠ *At gas station north of Rte. 31, 10 km (6 mi) from observation points. No credit cards.*

# Ein Bokek

**⓮** *8 km (5 mi) north of Zohar–Arad Junction on Rte. 90.*

The rather startling sight, in this bare landscape, of multilevel, hot-white modern hotels surrounded by waving palm trees signals your arrival at the Ein Bokek spa. According to the Bible, it was along these shores that the Lord rained fire and brimstone on the people of Sodom and Gomorrah (Genesis 19:24) and later turned Lot's wife into a pillar of salt (Genesis 26). The hot, sulfur-pungent air hangs heavy, the odd cry of the indigenous grackle bird is heard, and there is often a haze over the Dead Sea itself. The temperature of the oily water, where you cannot sink, is 30°C (88°F) from July through September; it's coldest in February, when the temperature gets as low as 19°C (66°F).

The legendary Dead Sea, whose rare physical properties attracted glitterati such as King Herod and Cleopatra in their day, retains its unusual attractions. Its salt content (six times denser than that of the Mediterranean), high content of special minerals (bromine, for example, which has a calming effect on the nervous system), and thick, black mud are sought out for their curative and beautifying properties. They are found nowhere else in the world.

Ein Bokek, at the southern tip of the Dead Sea, is the site of sulfur-rich hot springs with a temperature of 31°C (88°F). This water is used along with Dead Sea water and mud to treat rheumatic and arthritic problems—even tennis elbow or a sore back. The combination of sunshine (it's sunny 320 days a year), Dead Sea water, and mineral-rich mud seems to work wonders on psoriasis and other skin problems. (So positive are the results that German and Austrian health plans cover treatments here.) Harmful sun rays are filtered out by the haze that floats over the Dead Sea, so you can even tan more healthfully.

The resort hugs the shore. It comprises a collection of impressive hotels (each with its own state-of-the-art spa), a small commercial center, and a public solarium-spa, all linked by a palm-fringed promenade. It's a 30-minute drive from Masada and a 45-minute drive from Ein Gedi. You can explore interesting local sights, such as the nearby white-marl **Flour Cave** (from which you emerge dusted with white powder), with a guide, arranged through your hotel concierge.

## Dining and Lodging

$$$ ✕ **Hordus.** Named for Herod the Great, who built Masada (just up the road) in 36 BC, Hordus is somewhat less awesome than its namesake and his creations. But diners actually get lockers, so they can dip right into the Dead Sea at the beach outside. The sprawling cafeteria serves sandwiches, hot meals, fresh fruit (including local dates), baklava, and beer until 7:30 PM on weekdays (until 4:30 on Friday, until 6:30 on Saturday). There's a large gift shop inside and a falafel stand outside. ⊠ *Rte. 90, opposite Galei Zohar Hotel, Masada,* ☎ *07/658–4636. Reservations not accepted. AE, DC, MC, V.*

$$$ ✕ **Kapulsky.** This airy cafeteria in the middle of the hotel area has large windows all around, the better to gaze at banana trees and the Dead Sea. It's best known for luscious cakes and good coffee, but the hot meals are also very good. Choose from fresh salads, blintzes, sandwiches, pizza, and St. Peter's fish, plus beer and wine (meat is not served). Changing rooms and lockers are free to customers, and the place is open every day from 8 AM to 4 AM. ⊠ *Next to Kanionit shopping center,* ☎ *07/ 658–4382. Reservations not accepted. AE, DC, MC.*

$$$$ ☷ **Caesar.** Brand-new and gleaming white, both inside and out, the terraced, nine-story, stone Caesar is just right across the road from the beach. Two 6-ft-high silver urns furnish the soaring lobby, and the glass elevator adds to the airy feel. The eighth floor is designed for business travelers, and one floor is designated nonsmoking. Each room has a balcony and is decorated with bedspreads and curtains of green, beige, and brown crewelwork. Suites have balconies with whirlpool baths. The huge wooden wall at the entrance to the dining room is carved in a distinctive bas-relief with date palms, fish, flowers, and fruit. The gracious, ultra-equipped spa features a bath for two with an aromatic-oil massage done in the water, while each treatment room (from mud and aloe-vera massage to body peeling) has its own shower. The Dead Sea–water pool starts inside the hotel and ends outside. ⊠ *M.P. Dead Sea 86980,* ☎ *07/668–9666,* FAX *07/652–0303. 298 rooms with bath. Restaurant, lobby lounge, 3 pools, playground, children's programs. AE, DC, MC, V.*

$$$$ ☷ **Carlton Galei Zohar.** The Carlton was established in 1971, when the vision of spas in the desert was considered a mirage. It consists of two buildings, one a seven-story wing in which all rooms have kitchenettes. The modern spa is thoroughly modern and offers medical and beauty treatments. ⊠ *M.P. Dead Sea 86930,* ☎ *07/658–4311 or 07/*

658–4422, FAX 07/658–4503. *250 rooms with bath. Restaurant, bar, pool, sauna, exercise room, nightclub, baby-sitting, travel services. AE, DC, MC, V.*

$$$$  🏨 **Grand Nirvana Resort and Spa.** At press time the Grand Nirvana was both renovating and adding an entire new wing, which will bring its number of rooms to an impressive 400. Plans are creative indeed: one of the coming improvements is a heliport serving Jerusalem, Tel Aviv, and Eilat. The massive dining room has already been refurbished and looks over the Dead Sea through angled windows from blond-wood chairs with turquoise upholstery. The huge, outdoor pool is shaped like a dolphin; another pool is under construction; and the private, sandy beach is part of the Nirvana's own lagoon. The present accommodations are comfortable, and the staff is cooperative. ✉ *M.P. Dead Sea 84960,* ☎ *07/658–4614,* FAX *07/658–4620. 207 rooms with bath. 3 restaurants, bar, pool, beauty salon, hot tub, mineral baths, sauna, spa, exercise room, beach, dance club, car rental. AE, DC, MC, V.*

$$$$  🏨 **Hyatt Regency Dead Sea Resort and Spa.** Opened in September 1996,
★     this lavish, white, ultramodern, 17-story hotel is said to contain the largest spa in the region—20 rooms devoted to beauty, fitness, and recreation. Treatments include the use of therapeutic mud and two Dead Sea–water pools, one indoors and one outdoors. The medical center offers various services including sports medicine, postsurgery recovery, and alternative medical treatments. An extensive and interesting collection of Israeli paintings and sculptures decorates the public spaces. One restaurant serves Italian and fish specialties; the other mixes Caribbean, European, Far Eastern, and Middle Eastern fare. ✉ *M.P. Dead Sea 86980,* ☎ *07/659–1234,* FAX *07/659–1235. 600 rooms with bath. 2 restaurants, bar, 1 indoor and 1 outdoor pool, spa, 2 tennis courts, squash court, dance club. AE, DC, MC, V.*

$$$  🏨 **Hod.** There's a lot of traffic in the lobby—German travelers consider this a home away from home—but the feeling at the 10-year-old Hod remains one of homey comfort in a cheerful, friendly atmosphere. Room decor is modern, with multicolor checkered bedspreads and lots of pale wood. A walkway leads to the hotel's private beach, where the typical pebbled shore of the Dead Sea has been covered over with fine sand. Spa facilities include hot Dead Sea–mud treatments as well as the Stauffer diet and relaxation system. The dining room looks onto the water. ✉ *M.P. Dead Sea 86930,* ☎ *07/658–4644,* FAX *07/658–4606. 205 rooms with bath. Restaurant, lobby lounge, pool, massage, sauna, exercise room, Ping-Pong, beach, dance club, playground. AE, DC, MC, V.*

$$$  🏨 **Radisson Moriah Plaza Dead Sea.** A venerable beachside member
★     of the Moriah chain, this hotel keeps up with the times by constantly maintaining and refurbishing its modern and well-equipped spa. Week-long package options focus on beauty, relaxation, and rheumatic treatment. The always busy but cozy lobby overlooks the outdoor pool. Rooms are decorated in pastels, and their balconies have been thoughtfully walled for privacy and lovely views of the pool or the Dead Sea. ✉ *M.P. Dead Sea 86910,* ☎ *07/659–1591,* FAX *07/658–4238. 225 rooms with bath. 2 restaurants, piano bar, snack bar, 2 pools, beauty salon, hot tub, massage, mineral baths, sauna, spa, tennis court, basketball, exercise room, health club, beach. AE, DC, MC, V.*

## Nightlife and the Arts

**Kapulsky** (✉ Next to Kanionit shopping center, ☎ 07/658–4382), open until 11 PM, is *the* place to go at night—literally. There's nowhere else to go.

## Outdoor Activities

BEACHES

Although pebbles line much of the shore of the Dead Sea at Ein Bokek, the Tamar Local Council has beautified two public beaches by bringing in desert sand and planting palm trees. These beaches lie between the Nirvana and Moriah Plaza Dead Sea hotels and the cluster of hotels about 2 km (1¼ mi) north; they're free to the public and are usually fairly crowded. Facilities include changing rooms, rest rooms, and chair rental, and there's a lifeguard on duty from mid-March through November. There is ample parking alongside the promenade. Although there are no food stands on the beaches, Ein Bokek's two shopping areas have eateries, and there are two restaurants on the promenade, Kapulsky and Hordus, both of which offer their customers changing rooms.

A nice sandy beach with all facilities is **Hammei Zohar** (sign in Hebrew only, "Pundak HaDekel"; ☎ 07/658–4101), at the southern end of Ein Bokek near the Moriah Plaza hotel. It's open 24 hours a day from April through November; it closes at 4 PM in winter. Amenities include changing rooms, showers, big shade umbrellas, and a kiosk serving sandwiches, ice cream, beer, and coffee. You can whip up your own meals on the resident barbecues and even pitch a tent. It's very crowded on Saturday and holidays.

The only water sport in the Dead Sea is floating.

SPAS

Spas are an understood feature of Ein Bokek's hotels, but note that you must reserve treatments in advance and pay extra for them. Make arrangements with your hotel upon arrival. You can still sample the sybaritic delights if you're in Ein Bokek only for a day; again, just reserve a treatment in advance. Each spa is under medical supervision and has an indoor Dead Sea–water pool, a sauna, and a hot tub and offers a range of beauty and health treatments. Sample prices for individual treatments are as follows: NIS 85 ($24) for a half-hour massage, NIS 48 ($13) for a sulfur bath, NIS 66 ($18) for a mud treatment. Hotel guests pay lower fees. Other facilities and services often include fitness rooms, private solariums, and cosmeticians. Some hotels offer one- or two-week spa packages.

## Shopping

Several companies manufacture excellent **Dead Sea bath and beauty products** made from mud, salts, and minerals; the actual mud is sold in squishy, leak-proof packages. Ahava, DSD, and Jericho are three popular brands whose products are sold at Kapulsky and most hotel shops.

**Danny's** (✉ Kanionit shopping center, ☎ 07/658–4435) has a wide selection of gold, silver, diamond, and Eilat stone jewelry and a workshop on the premises. It's open Sunday–Thursday 10–10 and Friday 9–3. There are satellite branches in the Moriah Gardens Dead Sea Hotel and the Moriah Plaza Dead Sea Hotel.

# Arava Road

*North–south from Ein Bokek to Eilat.*

Arava Road (Route 90) traverses Arava Valley from Ein Bokek and to Eilat and parallels the Jordanian border, almost touching it at some points. To the east you'll see the spiky, red-brown mountains of Moab, in Jordan. There is no obvious military presence, but you can be sure it's here.

Arava Road follows an ancient route mentioned in biblical descriptions of the journeys of the Children of Israel. The Arava (meaning "valley") is part of the Syrian-African Rift, that great crack in the earth stretching from Turkey to East Africa, the result of an ancient shift of land masses. Along the road are several agricultural settlements, as the extremely hot climate is ideal for growing fruit, flowers, and vegetables year-round.

You'll pass signs for the settlements Neot HaKikar and Ein Tamar, whose date palms draw water from underground springs rather than irrigation. This area also has a number of commercial fishponds that breed gray mullet, St. Peter's, and other varieties plus fish to stock aquariums. Neot HaKikar's perimeter fence practically touches the border with Jordan.

With the Edom Mountains rising in the east (to your left), the road continues along the southern Dead Sea Valley. You'll cross one of the largest dry riverbeds in the Negev, Nahal Zin. It's hard to believe that the large valley to the right can fill with water during the winter months (mid-December to early April), causing flash floods dangerous to both hikers and drivers (☞ Desert Precautions, *above*). The landscape is dotted with acacia, the tree used by the wandering Children of Israel to build the Ark of the Covenant, which held the tablets given to Moses at Mt. Sinai; today the acacia is a source of food for grazing goats and camels. On your left at one point, you'll see an experimental farming station's greenhouses, used for research and development by local flower and vegetable growers.

An orange sign points to the **Shezaf Nature Reserve,** where the **Shezaf Observation Point** looks out over the reddish-orange sandstone hills, to the south, and the Edom Mountains and Arava Valley, to the east, roughly the Israel-Jordan border.

| | |
|---|---|
| NEED A<br>BREAK? | About halfway between Ein Bokek and Eilat is **Kushi Rimon** (Km 101). Named for the eccentric Shimon Rimon (whose nickname is Kushi) and the legendary army unit in which he served, this is a particularly offbeat Negev road stop. The place is huge and is landscaped with lots of palm trees and large, metal-and-wire sculptures. Peacocks and ducks wander about, and cages house a monkey and a tiger (the latter with a quotation from Jeremiah affixed to its quarters). Inside is a cafeteria with all manner of hot food, a bar stocked with every liquor imaginable, and a minimart. You'll also find a game room with a billiards table, other games, and a TV. ✉ Km 101 on Arava Rd., ☎ 07/658-1609. ☉ Daily 24 hrs except Yom Kippur. |

# EILAT AND ENVIRONS

The Arava Plain comes to an abrupt end where it meets the Bay of Eilat, site of the country's southernmost town: the sun-drenched resort town of Eilat. The Gulf of Eilat gives way to the Red Sea, which lies between the Sinai Mountains, to the west, and Jordan's Edom Mountains, to the east. The Jordanian port of Aqaba is directly across the bay—Eilat residents will eagerly point out the Jordanian royals' yacht and vacation villa—and to the southeast is Saudi Arabia. The Sinai Desert is just over the Egyptian border.

Most travelers fly into or whiz down to Eilat to flop down on its beaches and snorkel or scuba-dive among its tropical reefs. But if you have time, give yourself a chance to see the vast desert landscape to the north of Eilat. You'll find cliffs, canyons, and unique formations at the Timna Valley Park and indigenous animals at the Hai Bar Nature Reserve. Both make good side trips from Eilat; just leave time for a sunset stop at Mt. Yoash or Mitzpe Har Hizkiyahu.

# Eilat

**⓯** *307 km (190 mi) from Jerusalem, 356 km (221 mi) from Tel Aviv.*

Eilat's strategic location as a crossroads between Asia and Africa dictated its place in history. The Children of Israel stopped here as they fled from Egypt into the Promised Land, and it was long thought that King Solomon kept his fleet in the area between Aqaba and Eilat: "And King Solomon made a navy of ships in Ezion-geber, which is beside Eloth, on the shore of the Red Sea. . . ." Later, because of its position on a main trade and travel route, Eilat was conquered by every major power: the Romans, Byzantines, Arabs, Crusaders, Mamluks, Ottoman Turks, and, most recently, the British, whose isolated police station (headquarters of their camel corps) was taken by the Israelis in March 1949. Called Umm Rash Rash, this was the first building in modern-day Eilat, a town founded in 1951 and developed as a port in 1956 after the Egyptian blockade of the Tiran Straits was lifted.

A legend says that after the Creation, the angels painted the earth. When they got tired, they spilled their paints: the blue became the waters of Eilat, and the other colors became its fish and the corals. Add to this rainbow Eilat's year-round warm weather, its superb natural surroundings of sculptural red-orange mountains, and its situation on the sparkling Red Sea—whose coral reefs attract divers from all over the world—and you've got a first-rate resort. Fittingly or ironically, depending on your view, Eilat is the sister city of Los Angeles.

Most travelers decide that Eilat's natural assets more than make up for undistinguished architecture and overdevelopment. For wherever you are in Eilat, a glance eastward presents you with the dramatic sight of the granite mountain range of Edom, whose predominant shades of red intensify and fade with the light of day, culminating in a red-gold sunset blaze over the Red Sea. This incongruous name for a body of water that's brilliantly turquoise along the shore is the result of a 17th-century typographical error by an English printer: in setting the type for an English translation of a Latin version of the Bible, the printer left out an *e,* and thus "Reed Sea" became "Red Sea." The name was easily accepted because of the sea's red appearance at sunset.

With an average rainfall of about 7½ inches and an average winter temperature of 21°C (70°F), Eilat is a haven from the cold winter of Israel's north. Eilat's high season is mid-October to April, but the city is also crowded during Jewish and Christian holidays. It's hottest here in July and August—many travel agencies close their doors, and jeep trips and hikes are curtailed. The burning summer heat is a dry heat, though, without any mugginess. The wind picks up in late afternoon, and beaches, hotel terraces, and outdoor cafés fill up with loungers sitting, sipping, and watching the Edom Mountains turn red and the Saudi Arabian hills go purple. Summer walking in Eilat is pleasant in the early morning and the late afternoon; save indoor attractions, shopping, and siestas for midday, when the heat can be still and stifling.

Arava Road (Route 90) runs north–south through the town, bordered by the airport on the east side. The main intersection just south of the airport is Durban Road, site of the tourist office (behind the Burger Ranch). The section of Eilat called the North Beach includes the Promenade south to the main marina and past the lagoon and contains many of the town's luxury hotels, restaurants, and boutiques. Eilat's residential area and the Central Bus Station are in the foothills of the Eilat Mountains, which rise west of Route 90.

South of Eilat, Route 90 (now called Eilat–Taba Road) continues past the port and navy base to Coral Beach; then passes Coral Reserve, Dolphin Reef, and the Coral World Underwater Observatory and Aquarium; and finally reaches the Taba border crossing to the Sinai, in Egypt. To reach sights south of Eilat, take Bus 15 (from the hotel area; the Central Bus Station, on HaTmarim Boulevard; or Arava Road) or grab a taxi. Although the sights are close enough together that you can walk from one to the next, the inexpensive taxis are a good alternative when the afternoon sun is searing.

Start exploring Eilat with a walk along the **Promenade,** beginning at the Dan Hotel, near the Jordanian border. The 3-km (2-mi) promenade is also known as the Peace Walk, since it is hoped that one day it will continue to Aqaba, Jordan. Purple and pink bougainvillea pour down from the Royal Beach hotel's terrace, above, and you can top off your stroll with an ice cream (say, mango) from one of the stands. If you're here at sunset, this is the place to sit and savor the show-stopping view of the Red Sea turning red, with the dark, reddish-gray shapes of the Edom Mountains to the east and the rugged Eilat Mountains to the west. On a clear day, you can see as far as Saudi Arabia and Egypt. A quick walk brings you to the **Dutch Bridge,** which opens for tall-masted vessels. One one side is the **lagoon,** where yachts are anchored and various small craft are for hire; on the other is the **marina,** where cruise boats of all types wait to sally forth. The Promenade winds past swank hotels and beaches covered with folks reddening in the sun. The scene includes sophisticated strollers, the backpack crowd, artists doing quick portraits, and vendors selling earrings, all accompanied by strolling street musicians. You'll continue past the new Sea Gate Mall and alongside the water until you reach a palm-filled plaza with a tiny, cement block–shaped building with a statue of four fighters boosting a comrade aloft while a flag "flies" above. This is Umm Rash Rash, where the Israelis first took control of the Gulf of Eilat in March 1949, as determined by the U.N.'s Partition Plan. The small building—the only one in existence then—is a far cry from today's superstructures.

NEED A BREAK?    At the western end of the Promenade, at the intersection of Durban and Arava, is the new **Sea Gate Shopping Mall,** identifiable by the seahorse over its entrance. Outside, facing the water, is the outdoor **Mul HaYam** café, which feeds the crowd with ice cream, sweet drinks, and good coffee. Locals turn out in force here to sip, chat, and watch the tourists go by.

**16** Less than 1 km (⅔ mi) south of Eilat, the **Coral Reserve** is one of the finest such protected areas in the world. Close to the shoreline, its coral reef is 1¼ km (¾ mi) long and is zealously protected by the Nature Reserves Authority. Divers (☞ Outdoor Activities and Sports, *below*) will enjoy the especially beautiful Japanese Gardens, so named for the way in which the closely packed, multicolored corals overlap each other. You can rent masks, fins, and snorkels, and perhaps try snuba, a form of diving in which you breathe through tubes connected to tanks carried in a boat on the surface. Landlubbers can see the reef by crossing the beach into the shallow water; just be sure to wear water-resistant shoes to protect your feet from the rough seabed and spiny sea urchins. If you do have a brush with an urchin, don't pull out the stingers, as doing so may cause infection; they dissolve in a day or two. There are hot showers and a snack bar on the premises. ⊠ *Rte. 90 (Eilat–Taba Rd.),* ☎ *07/637–6829.* ☑ *NIS 15 ($4.30).* ☉ *Nov.–Mar., daily 9–5; Apr.–Oct., daily 9–6.*

**17** **Dolphin Reef,** 1 km (⅔ mi) south of Eilat, was developed for the study of marine mammals, specifically dolphins, in their natural habitat. (Only a flexible net separates them from the open sea.) Dolphin Reef allows you the novel experience of meeting bottle-nosed dolphins face-to-face: you can actually swim, snorkel, or scuba-dive with them, or join in on their training. The guide who introduces you to these friendly creatures is there to protect them from people, not the other way around. Dolphins are trained daily at 10, noon, 2, and 4. Facilities include a dive center (☞ Outdoor Activities and Sports, *below*), snorkel rental, and a photo shop with on-the-spot film and video developing. After you frolic, unwind in a serious way under the palm-frond umbrellas on the pretty beach, or at the Reef Bar, a thatched-roof pub and restaurant serving tasty seafood. Eilatis come here on Friday afternoons to "welcome" Shabbat (☞ Nightlife and the Arts, *below*). Note that you must reserve a specific time to swim or dive with the dolphins; it's best to call in advance. ⊠ *Rte. 90 (Eilat–Taba Rd.),* ☎ *07/637–1846.* ☑ *NIS 32 ($9.15).* ☉ *Daily 9–5.*

⓲ The **Coral World Underwater Observatory and Aquarium,** one of Eilat's star attractions, is recognizable by the tall space-needle structure that floats offshore. A highlight of the complex is the onshore **Red Sea Reef** (the building with stones piled around it), a circular aquarium surrounded by a coral reef. The aquarium's 12 windows provide views of rare fish so magnificent and so Day-Glo colorful that it's hard to believe they're real. The **Aquarium** offers a look at fish from other parts of the world—there's an unlighted room where phosphorescent fish and other sea creatures glow in the dark, and nearby a stingray and sea-turtle pool (one turtle is 250 years old) and shark pools. The newest attraction is the **Oceanarium,** an audiovisual show in a simulated-motion theater where you sit on a moving chair and journey through the wonders of the sea.

The **Underwater Observatory** is reached by a 110-yard wooden bridge. You might notice a yellow submarine docked to the right; it submerges several times a day to show passengers the coral reefs. Once inside the circular building, you'll find yourself in an attractive bar and restaurant, with generous picture windows for drinking in the lovely view. Head down the spiral staircase and into the sea. You are now 15 ft underwater, in a round, glass-windowed room, looking at a coral reef. Swimming in and out of the reef are thousands of exotic tropical fish often in colors and shapes you might have thought only Walt Disney could have created. The **Observatory Tower**—reached by elevator or stairs—is 70 ft above sea level, allowing certain views of Israel's neighboring countries. There's a café up here. ⊠ *Rte. 90 (Eilat–Taba Rd.),* ☎ *07/637–6666.* ☑ *NIS 49 ($14).* ☉ *Sat.–Thurs. 8:30–4:30, Fri. and holiday eves 8:30–3.*

## Dining

Eilat has so many restaurants that you can dine at a different one each night over a long holiday. Savor the finest local seafood and fresh fish; charcoal-grilled meats of every kind; Chinese, Indian, Thai, Italian, and California cuisine; and ethnic meals reflecting Israel's most recent waves of immigration. Many restaurants provide outdoor seating, often near the water or amid pots of pink bougainvillea. The luxury hotels serve lavish meals in highly designed surroundings. On the other end, fast food, such as crunchy falafel, abounds on HaTmarim Boulevard between the Central Bus Station and Hativat HaNegev Street, and at the Pninat Eilat shopping area, on the North Beach Promenade. Outdoor cafés are a way of life in Eilat—business deals are made over café *hafuch* (strong coffee with a frothy, hot-milk topping), and others come just to see and be seen—and several cafés face the water from the new Sea Gate Mall. They serve light food, such as cheese toast (grilled-cheese sandwiches) and salads, as well as rich cakes, ice cream, iced drinks, and various coffees.

$$$ ✗ **Au Bistrot.** In this informal town, it's fun to sit at a white-napped
★ table, with a small lamp gleaming on your gold-rimmed plate. This bistro only serves dinner, and it will not disappoint. The extensive menu—there's a separate one for dessert—includes Emperor fillet with goose liver and morel sauce (the house specialty); frogs' legs in butter and wine; fresh shrimp in Grand Marnier sauce; and lamb chops with tomato-and-basil sauce. The Moroccan chef studied in Belgium and returns yearly to hone his skills and collect recipes. Top-of-the-line Israeli and French wines are available. ⊠ *3 Elot St.,* ☏ *07/637–4333. Reservations essential. AE, DC, MC, V.*

$$$ ✗ **Blue Fish.** A fixture on the Eilat dining scene for the past 32 years, the Blue Fish has a relatively new location. It's not pretentious: pink walls with the odd plastic starfish form a simple background for green tablecloths and dark-turquoise chairs. Charcoal-grilled fish and seafood are the house specialties, but if you prefer meat, try a carefully prepared grilled steak. The crème caramel makes a tasty, light dessert. The wine list is lengthy. ⊠ *Across from entrance to Moriah Hotel (on land side),* ☏ *07/633–7450. Reservations essential. AE, DC, MC, V.*

$$$ ✗ **Eddie's Hideaway.** As the name implies, Eddie's is slightly hard to
★ find. But the way affable Eddie prepares food makes it easy to understand why his place receives such rave reviews, especially for the delicious steaks. Eddie's devotees also appreciate his shrimp and fish dishes. Starters such as Buffalo chicken wings and pâté *maison* can be followed by steak Eilat (with mushrooms, mustard, cream, and brandy) or Shanghai fish with hot soybean paste. For the grand finale, try lime divine or pecan pie. ⊠ *68 Almogim St. (enter from Elot St.),* ☏ *07/ 637–1137. Reservations essential. AE, DC, MC, V. No lunch.*

$$$ ✗ **El Gaucho.** Just north of Eilat—a five-minute taxi ride—this restaurant is preceded by a larger-than-life figure of an Argentine cowboy. It's a good clue to what you'll be eating inside—beef. The owners proudly explain that their meat is cut on the premises and seasoned with special herbs and spices; the steaks, cooked on a charcoal grill that occupies one side of the restaurant, are then brought to your table on minigrills. Consistent with this two-fisted approach to eating, drinks are served in glasses 14 inches tall. The empanadas are homemade, and the chorizo is excellent. ⊠ *Arava Rd. (Rte. 90) at entrance to Eilat,* ☏ *07/633–1549. Reservations essential. AE, DC, MC, V.*

$$$ ✗ **The Last Refuge.** This fine seafood and fish restaurant beside a
★ Coral Beach marina is highly regarded by Eilatis, who take their guests from "up north" here. The dining room is large, with dark wooden paneling and predictable nautical motifs. Presented with a flourish are just-caught Red Sea fish, such as arichola and drumfish; calamari; creamed seafood served in a seashell; and fish, crab, or lobster soup. Also delicious are the charcoal-grilled lobster, jumbo shrimps, and salmon fillet. The salads are enormous. The staff is harried but professional and eager to please. ⊠ *Rte. 90 near overhead bridge, Coral Beach,* ☏ *07/637–3627. Reservations essential. DC, MC, V. Closed 4–6 daily.*

$$$ ✗ **La Trattoria.** *Bella*—and the food's good, too. Against a calm background of cream-color walls, beige-and-white furnishings, sheer white curtains, and soft Italian music, you can sample the works of an Israeli-born, Italian-trained chef. His specialty is spaghetti with baby zucchini and dill in butter sauce, but he also offers fried mozzarella, sautéed forest mushrooms, 10 kinds of pizza, 10 types of fish, and four house pastas with 15 different sauces. Wines include some Italians and some Galilees. ⊠ *Radisson Moriah Plaza Hotel, North Beach,* ☏ *07/636– 1111. Reservations essential. AE, DC, MC. No lunch.*

**$$$** ✕ **Mandy's.** The first Chinese restaurant in Eilat, Mandy's opened in 1976 with the late prime minister Yitzhak Rabin in attendance. It's in a quiet area 5 km (3 mi) south of Eilat and has a sea view. The steady stream of customers still likes the original decor, which includes seven large Chinese-style paintings; and many appreciate the nonsmoking room, a rarity in Israel. The Szechuan cook comes up with tasty dishes such as pork in oyster sauce, fish in hot garlic sauce, steamed fish with ginger, spare ribs Szechuan-style, crispy duck, and the house special, Shrimp Kon Po. A business lunch costs NIS 50 ($14). Israeli and French wines are available. ⌧ *Arava Rd., Coral Beach,* ☎ *07/637–2238. Reservations essential. AE, DC, MC, V. Closed 3–6:30 Sun.–Fri. (open all day Sat.).*

**$$$** ✕ **Salsa.** New, hot, designed by well-known Israeli architect Adam Tihani, and dramatically sited, Salsa serves an esoteric mélange of Californian–Mexican–New Orleans cuisine. The doors open onto a huge, curvy bar made of wood stained blue, red, and mustard, while the dining room itself is a series of soaring beams and arcs colored dark blue, coral, and pink. A guitarist strolls across the stone floor playing (quiet) Mexican songs. Upstairs, wrought-iron squiggles lie on top of the dividing wall, then spill onto the walls, whose lights are set in free-form shapes of hammered copper. The innovative menu beckons, beginning with a house salad of tomatoes, salted cheese, beans, peppers, and deep-fried Cajun onions, or layers of fresh sea bream with an orange, lime, and chili dressing. For the main course, you can tuck into roast leg of lamb for two (takes 45 minutes); breast of chicken marinated in Cajun spices with sweet potatoes and crème fraîche; fajitas; tacos; saddle of lamb; fish of the day; or pasta shells stuffed with calamari. Forest-fruit soup is all one can stuff in for dessert. The wine list is international. ⌧ *Promenade, near Dan Hotel,* ☎ *07/636–2295. Reservations essential. AE, D, MC, V.*

**$$$** ✕ **Tandoori.** Indian cuisine of the first order is graciously presented amid
★  embroidered wall hangings, authentic Indian wood carvings, and brass table appointments. The food is prepared to order; while you wait, sip a *lassi* (a refreshing Indian drink of yogurt, fruit, and saffron) or one of the many cocktails on the menu. House specialties are various succulent meats cooked in a tandoor (a charcoal-fired clay oven), curries, and a selection of vegetarian dishes. Indian musicians and dancers perform at night. If you can't afford dinner here, try the moderately priced business lunch (NIS 42, or $12). ⌧ *King's Wharf at the Lagoon (below Lagoona Hotel),* ☎ *07/633–3879. Reservations essential. AE, DC, MC, V.*

**$$** ✕ **Mai Tai.** This small and serene restaurant serves authentic Thai food, not the more common Israelized Asian cuisine. Thai cooking is popular in Eilat, and Mai Tai is often singled out by selective diners. The fixed menu of soup, egg roll, main course, rice, tea, and dessert comes to a moderate NIS 40 ($11.40), and there's an à la carte menu as well. The lamp shades made of Thai food baskets and rice-paper umbrellas are a nice touch. ⌧ *Yotam St.,* ☎ *07/637–2517. Reservations essential. DC, MC, V. Closed 3:30–6.*

**$$** ✕ **Shauli and Guy.** Two brothers and their dad run this place, inviting you to feast on special Algerian-Tripolitan–style grilled meats such as veal chops, lamb chops, and skewers of lamb (there's fish, too). These guys know what they're about: three generations of butchers work in the family-run butcher shop next door. Start with a plate of hummus and mushrooms, and try to make room for the first-rate chips (french fries). The grilled goose liver here is sublime. The plain and simple setting is both spotless and homey—a Coke cooler looms large over the white-Formica tables and chairs, and the kitchen forms one end of the room. Wine and beer are available. It's in the middle of the Industrial

Zone, so you can't walk here; but taxi drivers know this place well. ⊠ *"Azore Hatassia" (Industrial Zone),* ☎ *07/633–1930. Reservations not accepted. AE, DC, MC, V. No dinner Fri., no lunch Sat.*

$$ ✕ **Spring Onion.** Vegetarians, front and center! Here's the place to get
★ garden-fresh salads dressed with interesting toppings, as well as carefully cooked fresh fish, vegetable quiches, blintzes, and surprisingly authentic pizzas. There's also a selection of what's known as cheese toast in Israel: a grilled-cheese sandwich with tuna, tomato, or egg. Portions are large, but if you have room left over, try a layer cake or a cream cake. Beer and wine are available. The two dining rooms are always crowded (and the top floor is nonsmoking), but there's plenty of outdoor seating. ⊠ *Bridge House, near bridge over marina,* ☎ *07/637–7434. MC, V.*

## Lodging

$$$$ 🏨 **Ambassador.** This spiffy hotel shares its grounds and facilities with
★ the Red Sea Sports Club Hotel (☞ *below*), which caters to divers, so you'll see lots of wet suits making their way through the splashily decorated lobby. (Ambassador guests get a discount at the Dive Club.) The hotel's entrance, facing the Eilat Mountains, is up a palm-lined lane; inside, the decor is ultramodern. Rooms face the pool and the sea and have light-blue carpeting, wood furniture, and sea-green bedspreads. Every room has a coffee corner, with a small refrigerator, coffeemaker, and cups. ⊠ *Rte. 90 (Eilat–Taba Rd.), 88000,* ☎ *07/638–2222,* 🆁🅰🆇 *07/638–2200. 170 rooms with bath. Restaurant, 2 pools (1 for water games), wading pool, sauna, dive shop, children's programs. AE, DC, MC, V.*

$$$$ 🏨 **Club-In Villa Resort.** This resort is a two-level arrangement of con-
★ nected, self-contained "villas" set into the mountainside opposite the Coral Beach Reserve. Each unit has two bedrooms, a kitchenette with a microwave (there's a minimart on the premises), a balcony, and a living room with a TV. Picking up on the desert colors outside, rooms are beige with sky-blue ceilings and cacti painted on some walls. Front units face the pool; those in the rear have mountain views. If you don't want to prepare your own meals, just present yourself in the dining room. ⊠ *Rte. 90 (Eilat–Taba Rd.), Box 1505, Coral Beach 88000,* ☎ *07/633–4555,* 🆁🅰🆇 *07/633–4519. 168 villa units with bath. Restaurant, bar, grocery, pool, wading pool, tennis court, exercise room, dance club, children's programs, coin laundry. AE, DC, MC, V*

$$$$ 🏨 **Dan Eilat.** The 14-floor, U-shape Dan is on the North Beach Prom-
★ enade near the Jordanian border. The decor, designed by Israeli architect Adam Tihani, is nothing short of stunning, effectively combining high style with comfort. The two connecting two-story lobbies feature a winding glass stairway (as scary as it sounds), craggy rock walls with a water cascade, floating ceiling sculptures, a huge aviary, a rock pool with iguanas, and creative Italian furniture such as bright-red chairs on green roller-skate wheels. The larger-than-usual blue and terracotta rooms have blond furnishings and lack for nothing—the dresser mirror, for example, can be adjusted to reflect the sea. The large, lush pool-and-beach area features a 20-meter pool for serious swimmers, a children's pool, a special pool with waterfalls and a slide, and a shaded hot tub. One of the three restaurants serves Lebanese and Mediterranean food, another French, and the third a meat buffet. ⊠ *Promenade, North Beach,* ☎ *07/636–2222,* 🆁🅰🆇 *07/636–2333 or –2444. 374 rooms with bath. 3 restaurants, bar, pool, hot tub, sauna, spa, Turkish bath, health club, squash, video games, children's programs. AE, DC, MC, V.*

$$$$ 🏨 **Howard Johnson Plaza Neptune.** Well located opposite the shore, on the Promenade near the marina, this airy, modern hotel has a certain elegance. The lobby, with its potted plants and large wicker chairs,

is especially appealing. Rooms, overlooking the pool with views of the marina or the sea, are decorated in blue, green, and rose, complemented by striking, angular furniture. The pool area is replete with flower beds, palm trees, and potted plants. The hotel maintains the stretch of public beach in front, with thatched umbrellas and sunbeds. ⊠ *Promenade, North Beach, Box 259, 88000, ☎ 07/636–9369, ℻ 07/633–4389. 279 rooms with bath. 3 restaurants, snack bar, pool, beauty salon, hot tub, massage, exercise room, dance club, nightclub, children's programs. AE, DC, MC, V.*

$$$$ 🏨 **King Solomon's Palace.** Solomon's entire court could have been accommodated at this hotel, a senior member of the Isrotel chain and one of several members grouped around the Lagoon. It's huge and comfortably utilitarian, with an expansive lobby furnished in dark wicker. The staff attends to your every need, and everything runs like clockwork. Floor-by-floor renovations are in progress; the health club has already been completely redone. The large dining room is divided into three small restaurants (Continental, Chinese, and Italian); for breakfast, there is a vast buffet with fresh-cooked pancakes and croissants. The palm-fringed pool overlooks the Lagoon. The garden-terrace suites have their own hot tubs. ⊠ *Promenade, North Beach, 88000, ☎ 07/633–3444, ℻ 07/633–4189. 420 rooms with bath. 3 restaurants, piano bar, 2 pools, hot tub, massage, sauna, 2 tennis courts, health club, dance club, playground. AE, DC, MC, V.*

$$$$ 🏨 **Orchid.** This reproduction Thai village is perched on the craggy mountainside amid greenery and palm trees. Only the arrangement is faux, though: everything here—from the teak furniture and ceiling beams to the decorative statuary—was brought from Thailand. Individual cottages are connected by steep, winding pathways; you can be driven around in a special, golf cart–like vehicle to get from place to place. Each cottage has one bedroom downstairs, a sleeping loft for two under the pointed roof, and a balcony. The restaurant, overlooking the pool, serves delicious Thai food. ⊠ *Rte. 90 (Eilat–Taba Rd.) Box 994, 88000, ☎ 07/636–0360, ℻ 07/637–5323. 135 units with bath. Restaurant, piano bar, pub, pool, beach. AE, DC, MC, V.*

$$$$ 🏨 **Princess.** Geographically the last hotel in Israel (it's five minutes from ★ the Egyptian border), the Princess is also the last word in sumptuous lodging. The lobby faces a two-story sheer rock cliff through a glass wall. The public spaces are dazzlingly white with gold trim, and six of the suites are done in themes, such as Chinese, Moroccan, and Indian. The various dining rooms serve various cuisines, including Japanese, Cantonese, and French, and are decorated to reflect them. The pool area is a country club in itself, with squiggle-shape pools connected by bridges. Down at the beach, two jetties lead to the water, and sunbeds beckon. The spa in this self-contained world is ultramodern; and other amenities include a shuttle into town. ⊠ *Rte. 90 (Eilat–Taba Rd.), Box 2323, 88000, ☎ 07/636–5555, ℻ 07/637–6333. 418 rooms with bath. 4 restaurants, pub, 2 pools, beauty salon, spa, health club, dance club, children's programs. AE, DC, MC, V.*

$$$$ 🏨 **Radisson Moriah Plaza.** Facing the beach from the Promenade, ★ near the marina, this pleasing, six-floor hotel could not have a better location; everything you'll want is within walking distance. The eye-catching lobby has a slanted glass roof, trees decorated with tiny white lights, and a cut-glass wall that separates it from the dining room. Rooms, most of which have sea views, are nicely designed with color-stained pieces setting off the other, blond-wood furniture. The fourth-floor business lounge has fax and e-mail facilities. Three pool areas ensure your rest and relaxation. The Moriah manages the beach out front. ⊠ *Promenade, Box 135, Eilat 88000, ☎ 07/636–1111, ℻ 07/633–*

*4158. 306 rooms with bath. 3 restaurants, 3 pools, beauty salon, health club, beach, business services. AE, DC, MC, V.*

**$$$$** ☎ **Riviera Apartment Hotel.** Apartment hotels are prone to an institutional air, but the Riviera escapes. It has a lively atmosphere and a fresh, turquoise-and-white color scheme to match. Units sleep two to six people and have fully equipped kitchenettes; many have living rooms, and the premium ones have a small garden and patio and are set back from the pool. The green and flowery grounds are very nicely kept. There's no dining room, but the on-site minimart carries a reasonably varied stock, from baked goods to canned tuna. Three movies are shown every day; the beach is 165 yards away; and guests can use the myriad facilities of the Country Club (at the nearby Sport Hotel) at a reduced rate. All in all, it's a good choice for families. ⊠ *North Beach, Box 1738,* ☎ *07/633–3944,* FAX *07/633–3939. 172 units with bath. Grocery, snack bar, kitchenettes, 2 pools, Ping-Pong, children's programs. AE, DC, MC, V.*

**$$$$** ☎ **Royal Beach.** Isrotel's latest addition to its Eilat collection, Royal Beach is the jewel in the company's crown. It's not glitzy (though there is a glass elevator), but the Royal holds its own in the glamour department. Opened in spring 1994, this beachfront property is well known for its interesting collection of paintings and sculptures by 26 Israeli artists. The oversize terrace, filled with purple pansies, faces the Bay of Eilat, a stunning view at sundown. Rooms are decorated in warm blue and rose; all have comfortable sofas and chairs and a coffee corner, and the 22 suites come with whirlpool tubs. Two rooms are equipped for those with hearing impairments. There's a beautiful, fully equipped spa on the premises, and you're welcome to the facilities at the neighboring Sport Hotel at reduced rates. ⊠ *North Beach,* ☎ *07/636–8888,* FAX *636–8811. 363 rooms with bath. 5 restaurants, bar, pub, 4 pools, massage, hot tubs, sauna, spa, children's programs. AE, DC, MC, V.*

**$$$** ☎ **Crowne Plaza.** You can count on competent service here. The well-designed public areas are decorated in cool white and beige; the entrance features a glass-domed ceiling. Rooms, all with air-conditioning, have tasteful, light-wood furniture and bedspreads of coral, pink, and blue. The entire fifth floor is no-smoking. ⊠ *Lagoon, North Beach, 88101,* ☎ *07/636–7777,* FAX *07/633–0821. 202 rooms with bath. Air-conditioning, pool, hot tub, health club, children's programs. AE, DC, MC, V.*

**$$$** ☎ **Moon Valley.** Laid-back, lively, and friendly, Moon Valley is perfect for families and popular with Europeans. Each pastel-color unit sleeps three and has air-conditioning and TV; the units are grouped closely on one level around the pool. Kids like the palm tree that grows in the dining room, complete with a few birds. And everyone likes "New York, New York," the American-style burger-and-steak joint next door. ⊠ *North Beach, Box 1135, 88100,* ☎ *07/633–3888,* FAX *07/633–4110. 182 rooms with bath. Piano bar, air-conditioning, pool. AE, DC, MC, V.*

**$$$** ☎ **Red Sea Sports Club Hotel.** Attention, divers! Billed as the first hotel
★ in Israel for divers and adventurers, this white, three-story hostelry houses the Manta Club—a fully equipped diving center with five-star PADI training center, qualified diving instructors, air-conditioned classrooms, personal lockers, a dive shop, rinsing pools, and a sauna. The staff can arrange diving trips to the Sinai. Rooms, each with a balcony, have modern furnishings accented with sea hues of green and bright blue. Guests share all facilities with the Ambassador Hotel (☞ *above*). A fun-loving atmosphere prevails, with dancing at night in the courtyard under the stars. It's a good value in this price category. ⊠ *Rte. 90 (Eilat–Taba Rd.), Box 390, 88000,* ☎ *07/638–2222,* FAX *07/637–4083. 86 rooms*

*with bath. Restaurant, cafeteria, bar, sauna, pool, dive shop. AE, DC, MC, V.*

**$$$** 🏨 **Sport Hotel.** The name says it all: this Isrotel hotel offers a full range of facilities for the active guest. These include tennis, squash, racquetball, and basketball courts; a fitness center with the latest equipment and a trainer; and a sauna and hot tub. (A small fee is charged for equipment rental.) Having just been renovated in spring 1998, the hotel is looking particularly snazzy at the moment; the lobby is loaded with palms and accented with blue and butter yellow, with woven-leather backs on the dark-blue armchairs. The rooms have green and soft-turquoise bedcovers and green- and rose-striped curtains. Those in the newer wing look out on the Gulf of Eilat. ⊠ *North Beach 88000,* ☎ *07/630–3333,* 𝔽𝔸𝕏 *07/633–2766. 327 rooms with bath. 2 restaurants, bar, 2 pools, massage, sauna, hot tub, 5 tennis courts, basketball, exercise room, racquetball, squash, dance club, children's programs. AE, DC, MC, V.*

**$$$** 🏨 **Taba Hilton.** If you want to avoid the hubbub, you'll appreciate the
★ isolation of the Taba, which is just over the Egyptian border in the Sinai, 11 km (7 mi) south of Eilat. The fine service and excellent cuisine (Italian and Middle Eastern) put the Taba on a par with Israel's top hotels. Most rooms have balconies overlooking the pool or the sea; and in case you don't feel like leaving the premises, there's a three-story gambling casino on-site. The two large pools (one seawater, one fresh water) have only one drawback: no lifeguard. The hotel's beach (also unguarded) has a dive center and water-sport facility, sunshades, a snack bar, and a playground. Nelson Village, a new extension of the Taba Hilton, is an 84-room, three-level, stone and wood building on the beach; it's named after the late bohemian Rafi Nelson, a bearded local character and tourist attraction who set up his own "village" right here. ⊠ *Taba Beach, Egypt (mailing address: Box 892, Eilat 88107),* ☎ *02/ 763677 in Egypt, 07/632–6222 in Israel;* 𝔽𝔸𝕏 *02/747044 in Egypt, 07/ 632–6660 in Israel. 326 rooms with bath. 5 restaurants, 3 bars, 5 tennis courts, health club, beach, dive shop, boating, waterskiing, nightclub, children's programs, travel services. AE, DC, MC, V.*

**$$** 🏨 **Reef.** This modest, stucco beachfront hotel occupies a quieter spot, away from the clutch of hotels farther north. A corresponding perk is your direct access to the beach from the Reef's wooden sundeck and pool area. Water-sports outfits, including a dive center, are but a splash away. The modern rooms are in soothing light green and mauve; all balconies face the sea. There are rooms around the pool on the ground level. The newly redecorated dining room is fresh and lively. ⊠ *Rte. 90 (Eilat–Taba Rd.), Box 3367, 88100,* ☎ *07/636–4444,* 𝔽𝔸𝕏 *07/ 636–4488. 80 rooms with bath. Piano bar, pool, bicycles AE, DC, MC, V.*

**$$** 🏨 **Topaz.** A new tourist area has sprouted along the main road into Eilat, near the central bus station. One of several hotels in this pleasant area, the two- year-old Topaz attracts those who want good value for their money. It has 30 four-person suites and 50 large studios decorated in blue and beige, with curtains and bedspreads in a seashell design. Every unit has a kitchenette and dinette, and the complex has a central, fresh-looking dining room, with a nice selection of artwork on the walls. ⊠ *Shfifon Street, Box 609, 88103,* ☎ *07/636–2111,* 𝔽𝔸𝕏 *07/636–2121. Restaurant, lobby lounge, pool, wading pool, children's programs. AE, DC, MC, V.*

**$** 🏨 **Eilat Youth Hostel & Guest House.** The word *hostel* takes on new
★ meaning here: each room is air-conditioned and has its own bathroom. Rooms are simply furnished and sleep two to six. A mere 10-minute walk from the central bus station and right across the highway from the beach at the Red Rock Hotel, this hostel is a popular place, so make

reservations well ahead of time. The dining room serves three meals a day and snacks between mealtimes. Bed linen and towels are provided. ⊠ *HaArava Rd., Box 152, 88101,* ☎ *07/637–0088,* FAX *07/637– 5835. 80 rooms with bath. Dining room, air-conditioning, dance club, coin laundry. AE, DC, MC, V.*

## Nightlife and the Arts

For an overview of local events, pick up a copy of the detailed leaflet "Events and Places of Interest," available at the tourist office. For the coming week's arts and entertainment information, check out Friday's *Jerusalem Post,* which carries listings for the entire country.

### BARS AND CLUBS

Most hotels in Eilat have a piano bar (some with space for cutting loose), and many have dance clubs; all are open to the public. Pubs also abound, though not quite in the same form as those in Great Britain or Ireland. In Israel, a "pub" is almost any place where people come to hang out and drink (even a restaurant or café during the day); at many you can even get a decent meal.

**Dolphin Reef** (⊠ Eilat–Taba Rd., ☎ 07/637–1846) is a good example of a bar-pub-restaurant. Eilatis have a soft spot for **Teddy's** (⊠ Ophira Park, ☎ 07/637–3949), which has a long wooden bar and a restaurant. For traditionalists, the nautically decorated **Yacht Pub** (⊠ King's Wharf, ☎ 07/633–4111) is the real McCoy: it was transported from England.

**King's** (⊠ Eilat–Taba Rd., ☎ 07/636–5555), at the Princess Hotel, tops the disco bill, with mirrored walls, fluted columns, and a checkered dance floor. **Platinum** (⊠ Promenade, ☎ 07/633–4111), at the King Solomon Hotel, has laser light shows. **Yekev** (⊠ Industrial Area, ☎ 07/633–4343), where the noise can't disturb anyone, hosts Israeli music and dancing on the tables; take a taxi there. Other dancing options are **beach parties,** where bronzed bodies groove to recorded music all night long; keep an eye out in town for English-language posters listing times and places. Admission is free.

For a taste of the nautical nightlife, consider dining and dancing under moonlit Red Sea skies while bobbing in a boat. **Eilat Cruises** (⊠ At the marina, ☎ 07/633–3351) runs evening trips with live music for NIS 66 ($18.80). The **Red Sea Sports Club** (⊠ King's Wharf, ☎ 07/637– 9685) also has night cruises.

### CONCERTS

One of Israel's biggest arts events is the **Red Sea Jazz Festival,** a stop on the international jazz circuit. It's held during the last four days of August in the unusual setting of Eilat's port, later spilling indoors to hotel lobbies for jam sessions that continue till dawn. Past acts have included Wayne Shorter, Diana Krall, and James Moody, as well as excellent local talent. For more information, contact the tourist office in Eilat or Multi Media, in Tel Aviv (⊠ 20 Amzaleg St., Tel Aviv 65148, ☎ 03/528–8989). **Music by the Red Sea,** a festival featuring chamber-music concerts and workshops, takes place in December and January; inquire at the tourist office. The **Philip Murray Cultural Center** (⊠ HaTmarim Blvd., ☎ 07/637–2257) hosts classical music, art exhibits, and other cultural events year-round.

### FOLK EVENINGS

From October to mid-April, Saturday nights bring Israeli folk dance and entertainment to **Kibbutz Elot,** 5 km (3 mi) north of Eilat. Tickets, which include transportation and a buffet dinner, are NIS 108 ($30); they're available through your hotel or the **Municipal Information Office** (☎ 07/637–2111).

Also on Saturday, you can be a Bedouin for a night: enjoy traditional desert hospitality at a festive dinner in a sheikh's tent, and listen to stories under the stars. Including pickup at your hotel, the price of the **Desert Shade** (☎ 07/633–5377) outing is NIS 120 ($34).

### LOCAL HOSPITALITY

Another way to spend an evening (or an afternoon) soaking up some culture is to join an Israeli family in their home. For information and arrangements, call Mrs. Morris (☎ 07/637–2344).

## Outdoor Activities and Sports

Many of the activities outlined below can be arranged through your hotel or a travel agency. Several tour operators maintain desks in hotel lobbies and will take reservations there. For more information on guided activities, *see* Guided Tours *in* Eilat and the Negev A to Z, *below.*

### BEACHES

Eilat's beachfront—the North Beach and the South Beach—is unusual in that none of it is private; rather, the municipality grants licenses to individuals to run certain sections. In turn, the beach managers must ensure the cleanliness of their section and provide open-air showers and deck chairs. The Tourist Patrol makes sure that standards are maintained, and can also be called on for assistance. Most of the beaches are free and have a clublike atmosphere, with thatched-roof restaurants and pubs, beach chairs, contemporary music, and dancing day and night. The beach at the Plaza Neptune hotel is particularly pleasant. Although topless bathing is against the law, you'll often see European women indulging, mostly on the southern beaches.

Young people tend to hang out at the southernmost beaches, where the dive centers are, while families favor North Beach, which runs northeast from the intersection of Durban and Arava streets to the clean and sandy stretch near the Royal Beach and Dan hotels. North Beach is always full of action—you can go paragliding or rent paddle boats or a "banana" (a plastic boat towed by a motor boat), and dancing goes on in the pubs until the wee hours. Sleeping on the beach is permitted (in sleeping bags, not tents). The southern beaches (south of the port, along the Eilat–Taba Road) share the coast with the Underwater Observatory, Dolphin Reef, and the Coral Reserve.

### BIKING

Rent mountain bikes at **Red Sea Sports** (⌧ King's Wharf, ☎ 07/637–9685; ⌧ Coral Beach ☎ 07/637–6569), where the staff will help you plan routes to places such as the bird-watching area and the Dolphin Reef.

### BIRD-WATCHING

The **International Birdwatching Center** (⌧ Entrance to Eilat, near gas station, ☎ 07/633–5339) conducts daily demonstrations during the migrating seasons at the Ringing Station, about a 20-minute walk from most hotels. It also organizes jeep bird-watching tours (☞ Guided Tours *in* Eilat and the Negev A to Z, *below*).

### BOATING

There are boat-rental and water-sports facilities at both Eilat's marina and Coral Beach, the area south of the port on the Eilat–Taba Road (Route 90). The **Red Sea Sports Club** (☎ 07/637–9685), at King's Wharf on the Lagoon, rents paddleboats, canoes, and mini-speedboats. You can also charter a 115-horsepower speedboat piloted by a water-ski instructor for NIS 420 ($120) per hour.

### DEEP-SEA FISHING

The **Red Sea Sports Club** (⊠ King's Wharf, ☎ 07/637–9685) takes six people out for six hours on a chartered motor yacht. The price for catching, say, a tuna or the rare barracuda is NIS 1,468 ($410) for six people, including lunch and the use of fishing gear. Each additional person pays NIS 54 ($15).

### HEALTH CLUBS

The state-of-the-art fitness center at the **Sport Hotel Country Club** (⊠ North Beach, ☎ 07/633–3333) is open to the public for NIS 35 ($10); use of the sauna and hot tub costs an additional NIS 18 ($5).

### HORSEBACK RIDING

**Texas Ranch** (⊠ Rte. 90, ☎ 07/637–6663 or 07/637–8638), in Coral Beach, takes riders on trails through Wadi Shlomo (Solomon's River) and into the desert. The sunset rides are particularly popular. The cost is about NIS 107 ($30); call ahead to reserve a horse. Children over 11 who know how to ride are welcome on the trails, and younger children may ride in the ring for NIS 25 ($7) per 10 minutes.

### PARASAILING

**Red Sea Sports Club** (⊠ King's Wharf, ☎ 07/637–9685) will give you a bird's-eye view of all those beach loafers for NIS 126 ($34) per 10 minutes.

### RAPPELLING

It's actually called "snappelling" in Israel. **Jeep See** (⊠ Bridge House, near the marina, ☎ 07/633–0133, FAX 07/633–0134) runs trips for both novices and more experienced rappellers. Call to reserve in advance; trips depart only in groups.

### SCOOTERS

See the sights on a Piaggio scooter, available from **Doobie** (⊠ North Beach, ☎ 07/633–6557), at the Dan Eilat hotel. Depending on the type of scooter, the price for half a day ranges from NIS 42 ($12) to NIS 66 ($18). Double those amounts for a whole day.

### SCUBA DIVING AND SNORKELING

Divers have excellent facilities at the marina in North Beach and at Coral Beach, offering diving courses, introductory dives for the whole family, and night dives. Equipment is available for rental or purchase.

The **Aqua Sport International Red Sea Diving Center Ltd.** (⊠ Coral Beach, ☎ 07/633–4404, FAX 07/633–3771) was the first diving center established in the Middle East. Aqua Sport offers one-day dive cruises with lunch (NIS 270, or $77, per person) plus weekly diving safaris that run from one to five days. You'll take a jeep to the most exotic dive locations, such as the famous Blue Hole and Ras-Nasrani at Sharm-el-Sheikh, in the Sinai. **Lucky Divers** (⊠ Promenade, ☎ 07/633–5990), at the Galei Eilat Hotel, operates a top-quality, full-service dive center. **Manta Diving Club** (⊠ Eilat–Taba Rd., Coral Beach, ☎ 07/637–6569), at the Red Sea Sports Club Hotel, is also excellent.

The **Coral Reserve** (⊠ Eilat–Taba Rd., Coral Beach, ☎ 07/637–6829, FAX 07/637–5776), open daily 8–6 (8–5 in winter), is a great place to observe the fabulous fish and corals. Qualified divers, in limited numbers, can explore the unique coral formations of the so-called Japanese Gardens. Call ahead to reserve a time. You can't rent diving equipment here, but snorkeling equipment is available. Masks rent for NIS 6 ($1.70), snorkels for NIS 6 ($1.70), and fins for NIS 9 ($2.50). Admission to the Coral Reserve is NIS 15 ($4.50). Be sure to wear protective footgear. Facilities include hot showers, lockers, and a small restaurant.

Families (children must be over 10) will have fun snuba-diving at the **Caves Reef,** south of the Underwater Observatory. In this snorkeling-diving hybrid, you breathe through tubes connected to tanks carried in a rubber boat. The price, NIS 120 ($34.40) per person, includes instruction, a practice session in shallow water, and a guided underwater tour that goes no deeper than 20 ft. Reserve in advance (☎ 07/637–2722).

At **Dolphin Reef** (⊠ Eilat–Taba Rd., Coral Beach, ☎ 07/637–5935 or 637–1846), you can "dive with dolphins" using snorkel equipment (NIS 150, or $42.80, for half an hour), and preserve the experience on video for posterity (for an extra charge). Be sure to call ahead for a reservation. Dolphin Reef also runs a professional dive center.

### SKI-DIVING

Fly high—from 10,000 ft—and free-fall for 40 seconds at more than 320 mph. Pull the cord and you slow to a six-minute ride over the water with your instructor. Call 052/629004 or 07/637–2745 for this big thrill, available on Fridays and Saturdays. The cost is a hefty NIS 875 ($250).

### SPAS

The **Princess Hotel** (☎ 07/637–0195), the **Royal Beach Hotel** (☎ 07/636–8860), and the **Dan Eilat** (☎ 07/636–2222) all have state-of-the-art spas.

### SWIMMING

Most hotels have outdoor pools, but you can also go to the **public pool** (⊠ Hativat HaNegev St., ☎ 07/636–7233). Call for hours and admission fees.

### TENNIS AND SQUASH

Most hotels have floodlit tennis courts. At the **Sport Hotel Country Club** (⊠ North Beach, ☎ 07/630–3333) tennis courts are available at the hourly rate of NIS 35 ($10) in the morning, NIS 45 ($12.80) in the evening; the price includes racquet and balls. Squash courts go for NIS 30 ($8.60) an hour; racquet rental is NIS 6 ($1.70).

### WINDSURFING AND WATERSKIING

At the **Red Sea Sports Club** (⊠ King's Wharf, ☎ 07/637–9685) water-skiers can rent equipment and boats for NIS 105 ($30) for 15 minutes. Windsurfing equipment and lessons are also available at the **Aqua Sport International Red Sea Diving Center Ltd.** (⊠ Coral Beach, ☎ 07/633–4404); one hour on the board costs NIS 70 ($20). **Mistral** (⊠ Coral Beach, ☎ 07/637–6416), at the Reef Hotel, also rents Windsurfers.

## Shopping

Eilat is a tax-free zone, meaning that all items are exempt from VAT (Value-Added Tax) and/or purchase tax. Articles such as bathing suits and jewelry sold in chain stores are less expensive in Eilat branches. Items that are price-controlled, such as gas, beer, cigarettes, and alcohol, are also cheaper.

The city's two shopping malls, **Kanion Adom and Shalom Plaza** (⊠ HaTmarim Blvd.), connected by a café-filled passage, sell similar merchandise. You'll find camera and music stores here but a notable absence of souvenir and gift shops.

**Le Drugstore** (⊠ North Beach Promenade, ☎ 07/636–6667) and **Boutique Carnaval** (⊠ North Beach Promenade, ☎ 07/633–4111) are large stores housing mini-boutiques with everything from clothes to locally made gifts to baby clothes and newspapers. The WIZO counter in Boutique Carnaval sells modern and traditional handicrafts and religious items.

Order custom-made wet suits from **Frog** (⌧ New Industrial Zone, ☏ 07/637–7465), where they also make repairs and sell accessories.

Israel has an international reputation for creative jewelrymaking, and although the Negev is not a center for this particular craft, certain stores in Eilat carry good examples of what Israel's jewelers are producing, most of it contemporary in style. Diamonds—one of Israel's most important exports, in cut and polished form—are put to imaginative use. The indigenous "Eilat stone," malachite (turquoise streaked with various shades of green), mined near Eilat in ancient times, is also a good choice. In close proximity at the entrance to town are two good outlets for diamonds, gold, pearls, and Eilat stone jewelry: **Cadurit** (⌧ Eilat–Taba Rd., ☏ 07/637–8551) and **Eilat Stone Mines** (⌧ Eilat–Taba Rd., ☏ 07/633–6363). Both companies are open daily and will pick you up at your hotel.

**Jerusalem of Gold** (⌧ King's Wharf) and **H. Stern** (☏ 07/637–1706 or 07/637–2898), in the King Solomon, Plaza Neptune, Royal Beach, Dan, and other hotels, are tried-and-true firms with merchandise of reliable quality. Another well-known store is **Malkit** (⌧ HaDekel neighborhood, ☏ 07/637–3372), which houses a workshop where indigenous Eilat stones are cut, polished, and set in a whole line of jewelry designed in-house; it's open Sunday–Thursday 8–7, Friday 8–1. In case you forgot your watch, **Padani** (⌧ Royal Beach hotel, ☏ 07/637–6287) sells Breitling timepieces.

## Hai Bar Nature Reserve

**⑲** *35 km (21½ mi) north of Eilat on Rte. 90. Look for the sign for Hai Bar and Predator Center, opposite entrance to Kibbutz Samar. Drive 1½ km (1 mi) to entrance.*

The Hai Bar Nature Reserve makes a good day trip from Eilat and can be combined with a visit to the Timna Valley Park (☞ *below*) and a refreshing stop at the Ye'elim pool (☞ *below*). Try to see Hai Bar in the morning, when the animals are most active; excellent, 1½-hour guided tours leave the entrance daily between 9 and 2. Timna Valley Park is especially beguiling at sunset. In very hot weather, plan to see one of the two sights in the early morning and spend midday at the pool. If you're continuing north rather than returning to Eilat, you may want to visit Timna Valley Park first and then Hai Bar, with a stop at Ye'elim pool in-between.

The Nature Reserve consists of both a large natural habitat for biblical-era animals and birds, and the Predator Center. The reserve was created not only as a refuge for animals that were almost extinct in the region but also as a breeding place; the animals are then set free to re-populate other parts of the Negev. Opened to the public in 1977, the 12-square-km (4½-square-mi) area re-creates the ancient savanna landscape, with lots of acacia trees; roaming around are the striped-legged wild ass, onagers (another species of wild ass), addaxes, gazelles and ibex, and white oryx. Ostriches come prancing over, ready to stick their heads into the van windows.

The 20-square-km (7¾-square-mi) **Predator Center** is where local birds and beasts of prey are raised and displayed. An audiovisual presentation introduces both history and wildlife. You can observe the animals without disturbing them because the glass you stand behind is one-way and soundproof. As you watch the hyena feed, notice that his front legs are stronger than his rear legs, enabling him to carry his heavy prey a long distance. (The meat fed to these animals comes from hit-and-run victims and sometimes animals that die of old age in local kibbutzim.)

The birds of prey hang out in gigantic cages, where you'll see, among other species, the only lappet-faced vultures left in Israel, with average wingspans of about 10 ft. ⊠ *Rte. 90, 35 km (21½ mi) north of Eilat,* ☎ *07/637–3057.* 🗳 *NIS 26 ($7.30), including tour; Predator Center only NIS 14 ($4).* ⊙ *Sun.–Thurs. 8:30–5, Fri.–Sat. 8:30–3:30.*

NEED A BREAK? The **Ye'elim Restaurant, Swimming Pool, and Water Slide,** on Route 90, is a good place to stop for lunch and cool off. The large, spic-and-span cafeteria-style restaurant serves hot meals (a variety of meats, rice, and vegetables), plus soup-and-salad plates. The pool area, lined with palm trees and equipped with changing rooms and showers (but no lockers), has children's play equipment and a water slide, and you can arrange poolside service for light meals. (Entrance to the pool is occasionally free if you order a full meal at the restaurant.) ⊠ *Rte. 90,* ☎ *07/637–3086.* 🗳 *Pool NIS ($5.70).* ⊙ *Restaurant daily 7 AM–9 AM, noon–4 PM, and 7 PM–8:30 PM; pool daily 10–7.*

# Timna Valley Park

★ ⑳ *From Hai Bar Nature Reserve, return to Rte. 90 south toward Eilat. Turn right after 15 km (9 mi) at sign for Timna Park and Timna Lake. A 3-km (2-mi) access road (which passes Kibbutz Elifaz) leads to entrance booth.*

When you arrive, ask for the explanatory pamphlet, which shows the driving route in red. Because of the park's size (60 square km, or 23 square mi), we suggest driving from sight to sight, each of which can then be explored on foot (some of the sights are several miles apart). A small building just inside the entrance screens a video detailing humanity's 6,000-year-old relationship with the Timna area and its precious copper ore, mined well before Solomon's time by the Egyptians. Wall panels explain the valley's fascinating geological makeup. Experienced hikers can pick up a map, or consult the wall map, which marks trails for experienced hikers; hikes here are from three to seven hours long and are best done in winter (the heat in summer is scorching). Watch out for old mine shafts, take lots of water, and let the person at the gate know you are going and approximately when you'll be back.

The Timna Mountains (whose highest peak is 2,550 ft) surround a spectacular collection of cliffs, canyons, and rock formations. Millions of years of erosion have sculpted shapes of amazing beauty, such as the red-hued **Solomon's Pillars** (created by nature, *not* by the biblical king) and the 20-ft-high freestanding **Mushroom.**

People have also left their mark here. You'll soon come to an ancient smelting camp, with living quarters for the copper miners. Near the Pillars are the remains of a small **temple** built by Egyptians who worked the mines 3,400 years ago, during the Egyptian New Kingdom (the time of Moses); the temple was dedicated to the cow-eared goddess Hathor. Archaeologists discovered in the temple a snake made of copper (*nehushtan* in Hebrew)—according to Numbers 21:4–9, Moses made a serpent in the wilderness to heal people suffering from snake bites, and the snake remains a symbol of healing to this day (in, for example, the caduceus). The snake at Timna bears a resemblance to a votive copper snake made by the people who followed the Egyptians in this area, the Midianites (Moses' father, Jethro, was a Midianite), now in the collection of the Eretz Israel Museum, in Tel Aviv. Near the temple, a path and stairway lead up to the observation platform overlooking the valley. Above the platform is a rock-cut inscription whose hieroglyph you can see clearly with the aid of a sighting tube—it shows Ramses III offering a sacrifice to Hathor. ⊠ *Rte. 90*, ☎ *07/635–6215*. 💳 *NIS 24 ($6.80)*. ☉ *Daily 7:30–5, except Yom Yippur.*

| | |
|---|---|
| NEED A BREAK? | Here's a surprise in the desert landscape, right in the park: a lake (man-made), and on its shore the roomy, air-conditioned **Timna Oasis Restaurant.** Built of local stone and decorated in desert colors, this self-service eatery serves hot dishes such as chicken schnitzel, dairy meals (cheeses and salads), sandwiches, hummus, and ice cream. Although swimming is not permitted, you can enjoy the lake from picnic tables in shaded areas on the shore. From January through March, a 20-minute demonstration of ancient copper-mining and -smelting techniques is held on Sunday, Monday, and Thursday at 11 and 1; the staff will narrate in English upon request. ⊠ *Timna Valley Park*, ☎ *07/637-4937*. ☉ *Daily 11–5.* |

## Mt. Yoash

**㉑** *Leave Eilat from junction of Rte. 90 (Arava Rd.) and Yotam Blvd., traveling west on Yotam (which becomes Rte. 12), with New Tourist Center on the left.*

This fine lookout along the border road with Egypt is an easy trip from Eilat. Notice the huge tanks as you drive along Route 12; they belong to the Eilat–Ashkelon oil pipeline. After you pass the tanks, you enter the Eilat Mountains Nature Reserve, with Nahal Shlomo, a dry riverbed, on your left. Drive in 12 km (7½ mi) and turn left at the orange sign for Mt. Yoash; then drive another 1 km (⅔ mi), bearing right up a rough, steep, and winding stone road. Park and prepare yourself for knock-out views of the alternating light and dark ridges of the Eilat Mountains; Eilat and Aqaba; the mountains of Edom, behind Aqaba; the start of the Saudi Arabian coastline and the Nahal Geshron gorge, emptying into the Red Sea at Taba; and the plain of Moon Valley and the mountains of Sinai, in Egypt.

*En Route*    From Mt. Yoash, take Route 12 and drive north; look for a green sign labeled NATAFIM CROSSING. The Israeli flag flies over the checkpoint at **Natafim Crossing,** where there are usually two soldiers. Nearby is a "base," with two prefab buildings—one on either side of the fence—one flying the Egyptian flag, the other, the Israeli flag. The low fence is the border between the two countries. From this vantage point, looking toward Egypt, you can often see an Egyptian patrol, either walking or riding camels.

## Mitzpe Har Hizkiyahu

**㉒** *5 km (3 mi) from Natafim Crossing on Rte. 12; look for green sign for Mitzpe Har Hizkiyahu.*

As you drive along Route 12, you'll see an Israeli flag flying, and you'll be looking at Moon Valley, where the wadi Nahal Paran starts. There are two lookouts here, each with an excellent etched plan. From one, you can see a base for the MFO (Multinational Force of Observers), a UN-sponsored international organization formed to supervise the Egypt-Israel peace accords of 1978; and an Egyptian military post that guards the border between the two countries. From the other, you can see Aqaba in Jordan, the salt ponds of Eilat, Aqaba's airport, and the Gulf of Eilat.

# Red Canyon

**㉓** *From Mitzpe Har Hizkiyahu lookout, drive 4 km (2½ mi) to orange sign for Red Canyon (Canyon Adom), on right. Immediately turn left at another small sign. Drive 2 km (1¼ mi) on packed gravel road, park, and lock the car.*

At Red Canyon, you can absorb the dazzling panoramas you've just seen from Mitzpe Har Hizkiyahu (☞ *above*) on a nature walk that takes no longer than an hour. The combination of the two vantage points makes a great side trip from Eilat. At the beginning of the walk, the ancient riverbed is made up of conglomerate (cemented silt and stones) that settled when the onetime river was much wider; you can see stones just sticking out, as though deliberately placed there. Walking along on the stony ground, you'll find yourself in a narrow part of the canyon—about 2 yards wide—where the colors have abruptly changed to the reddish hue of the sandstone walls, a startling sight. Follow the canyon's wadi, a small part of Nahal Shani. When you meet the main course of Nahal Shani, follow the trail marked in green to a descent with metal handrails; descend in a sitting position. You'll then climb down a ladder, and shortly afterward you'll come to the end of the narrow gorge. Here, on the right, is a sign reading TO THE CARPARK, still on the green trail. You will now retrace your route, except that now you're *above* the canyon rather than inside it. Once on top, walk on the edge of the canyon (watch your footing and keep an eye on your children) until you reach the parking lot. Note that although the hike is not very difficult, it's not suitable for the very young or very old.

# EILAT AND THE NEGEV A TO Z

## Arriving and Departing

### By Bus

The national bus company, **Egged** (☎ 03/694–8888)—open Sunday–Thursday 6:30 AM–11 PM, Friday and holiday eves 6:30 AM–3 PM, and Saturday 4 PM–11 PM—provides frequent daily bus service (except Sat.) to Beersheva from Tel Aviv's Central Bus Station (⊠ Levinsky St.) and Arlozoroff Station (⊠ Arlozoroff St. and Haifa Rd.) and from Jerusalem's Central Bus Station (Jaffa Rd.); the trip takes 1½ hours. From the Beersheva Central Bus Station (Ben Zvi St., ☎ 07/629–4311) buses depart four times a day for Arad, Avdat, Ein Bokek, Mitzpe Ramon, and Sde Boker. For Ein Bokek, there's a daily 8:30 AM bus from Tel Aviv's Central Bus Station, and several buses from Jerusalem's Central Bus Station. Most buses do not run on Saturday, though some routes do resume in the early evening.

At one time, *sherut* (shared) taxis ran between Jerusalem, Tel Aviv, and Eilat, but now that this service has stopped, the buses are more crowded than ever, especially on Friday and Sunday (return trips). You cannot buy tickets *or* reserve seats by phone; you have to go to the Central Bus Station. Once you've done that, it's wise to be at the bus station early. The bus to and from Eilat stops midway for refreshments.

Egged buses run from Tel Aviv to Eilat at least four times a day and twice at night. A round-trip ticket costs NIS 100 ($28.40). Buses from Jerusalem to Eilat leave during daylight hours from the Central Bus Station; the trip takes about 5½ hours and costs NIS 91 ($26) round-trip. It's important to buy tickets two days in advance at the Central Bus Station to ensure a seat. Be sure to reserve your seat for the return trip at Eilat's Central Bus Station.

### By Car

Beersheva is 113 km (70 mi) southeast of Tel Aviv. The drive from either Tel Aviv or Jerusalem takes about 1½ hours. To drive from Tel Aviv to Beersheva, take Route 2 (the Ayalon Highway) south until the turnoff marked BEERSHEVA–ASHDOD. After this you'll be on Route 41, which runs into Route 40 after 6 km (4 mi). Continue on 40 to Beersheva; there are clear signs all the way.

To reach Beersheva from Jerusalem, take Route 1 west to the Sha'ar Hagai Junction. Turn left (south) and follow Route 38, then Route 32, which turns into Route 35, to Kiryat Gat. Here you can pick up Route 40 south to Beersheva.

To drive to Ein Bokek from Tel Aviv, leave Tel Aviv via the Ayalon Highway (Route 2) south and join Route 1, following signs to AIRPORT–JERUSALEM. As you approach Jerusalem, stay left, on Route 1, which is marked JERICHO–DEAD SEA. Continue 30 km (18½ mi) to the unmarked Almog Junction (where Route 1 meets Route 90; there is a turnoff on the left, heading north, marked JERICHO). Stay on the same road, now Route 90, for 10 km (6 mi) to the Dead Sea. Bear right (due south) and follow Route 90 along the coast, passing Qumran, Ein Gedi, and Masada, until you reach Ein Bokek. To get to Eilat, continue south along Route 90 (Arava Rd.) for another 177 km (111 mi). The trip to Ein Bokek takes about an hour and a half.

The most direct way from Tel Aviv to Eilat is Route 40 south to Beersheva. Leave Beersheva via Route 25 (marked DIMONA–EILAT), driving 69 km (43 mi) to the Arava Junction. Turn right (south) onto Route 90 (Arava Road), and travel straight to Eilat. The trip takes about five hours.

### By Plane

Keep in mind that flights to the Negev are not always on schedule, so call ahead for the status of your flight and arrive at the airport early (a shuttle runs from Jerusalem to the airport). Regularly scheduled flights to and from Eilat use the **Eilat Airport,** in the middle of the city a five-minute cab ride from hotels and a two-minute walk to the center of town. Charter flights from Europe arrive at **Ovda Airport** (also known as Eilat West), 60 km (37 mi) north of Eilat; transportation to Eilat is arranged by the travel agents who book the flights.

**Arkia Israel Airlines** (☎ 03/523–3285) serves Eilat from **Sde Dov Airport** (☎ 03/690–3333), in north Tel Aviv; from **Atarot Airport** (☎ 02/583–3677), 10 km (6¼ mi) north of Jerusalem; and from **Haifa Airport** (☎ 04/847–6165), with a stop in Tel Aviv or Jerusalem. The 55-minute flight to Eilat leaves Tel Aviv every 1½ hours Sunday–Thursday 6:30 AM–10 PM, Friday 6:30 AM–4 PM, and Saturday 3 PM–10 PM. From Jerusalem, Arkia flies to Eilat three times daily, twice on Friday; there are no flights on Saturday. The flight takes about 45 minutes. Flights from Haifa, which take about 1½ hours, depart three times a day; there are no flights on Saturday. For reservations from anywhere in Israel, call 177/022–4888.

### By Train

There is one train, and one train only, from the north to the Negev, and that's from Tel Aviv's Arlozoroff Station (☎ 03/693–7515) to Beersheva. Hop aboard at 5 PM any day except Friday or Saturday; the fare is NIS 21 ($6).

## Getting Around

### By Bus

You *can* explore the Negev independently by bus, but you'll waste a lot of time waiting for connections, and the heat can make standing at a bus stop in the middle of nowhere very uncomfortable. Moreover, the buses don't go everywhere. However, Egged (☞ *above*) connects Beersheva (the transfer point for buses from Tel Aviv and Jerusalem) with all major Negev towns.

In Eilat, Buses 1 and 2 travel through the hotel area to town every 30 minutes. Bus 15 goes along Arava Road (Eilat–Taba Road) to the Egyptian border (Taba crossing), stopping at such attractions as the Underwater Observatory, Coral Beach, and the dive centers.

In Ein Bokek, a shuttle bus links all hotels to each other and the center of town.

### By Car

The only way to see the Negev Desert comfortably and efficiently is to drive (air-conditioning in summer is a must). All roads have two lanes. The conditions of secondary roads vary; only those in good condition are mentioned here. Roads marked in Hebrew only are not for public travel. To avoid dangerous wintertime floods, proceed with caution when there is any indication of rain (☞ Desert Precautions *in* Exploring Eilat and the Negev, *above*). Driving at night in the Negev is not recommended; plan to reach your destination by 5 in winter and by 8 in summer.

Apart from those in towns and cities, there are gas stations at Tel Avdat (near Sde Boker), Ketziyot (near Nizzana), Mashabei Sade Junction (40 km, or 25 mi, south of Beersheva), Zohar–Arad Junction (near Ein Bokek), Ramat Hovev, and Shoket Junction (on the way to Arad). You'll find gas stations on Route 90 (Arava Road) at Ein Hazeva, Ein Yahav, Ketura (tires fixed here), and Yotvata. There's a tire-repair shop in the industrial area just before the entrance to Mitzpe Ramon. Most gas stations share space with a roadside café, and a majority are open 24 hours a day.

The following are the main roads in the Negev: Route 40 goes through the Negev highlands to Eilat via Sde Boker, Mitzpe Ramon, and Makhtesh Ramon; Route 90 (called Arava Road in the Negev), which starts in Metulla near the Lebanese border, runs through Ein Bokek and along the Jordanian border and ends in Eilat; and Route 31 runs from Beersheva to the Shoket Junction, Arad, and Ein Bokek. Most of your driving will be along stretches of straight road; the exceptions are the winding (and in some parts rough and ill-maintained) road through Makhtesh Ramon, and the steep road between Arad and Ein Bokek (one hairpin turn after another). Beersheva is 45 km (28 mi) from Arad, 80 km (50 mi) from Mitzpe Ramon, and 241 km (151 mi) from Eilat. Mitzpe Ramon is 148 km (93 mi) from Eilat. Ein Bokek is 177 km (111 mi) from Eilat.

### By Taxi

In Eilat, the preferred (and air-conditioned) way of hopping from one place to another is by taxi. Rides don't usually cost much more than NIS 25 ($7); you can hail a taxi on the street or order one from **Arava** (☎ 07/637–4141) or **Taba** (☎ 07/633–3339). In Beersheva, **Netz Taxis** (☎ 07/627–0888) operates seven days a week. Taxis are not necessary in Ein Bokek or Mitzpe Ramon.

# Contacts and Resources

## Car Rental
**Beersheva: Avis**, ☒ 11 Derech Hanessiim, ☎ 07/627–1777; **Eldan**, ☒ 100 Tuviahu St., ☎ 07/643–0344; **Hertz**, ☒ 5 Ben Zvi St., ☎ 07/627–3878; **Reliable**, ☒ 1 HaAtzmaut St., ☎ 07/623–7123.

**Eilat: Avis**, ☒ Eilat Airport, ☎ 07/637–3164; **Budget**, ☒ Shalom Center, ☎ 07/637–4124 or 07/637–4125; **Eldan**, ☒ 143 Shalom Center, ☎ 07/637–4027; **Hertz**, ☒ Red Kanion Shopping Center, ☎ 07/637–6682; **Reliable**, ☒ Hofit Center, Binyamin St., ☎ 07/637–4126.

**Ein Bokek: Hertz**, ☒ Galei Zohar Hotel, ☎ 07/658–4530.

## Consulates
In Eilat, all English-speakers may contact the honorary consul of the United Kingdom, Fay Morris (☎ 07/637–2344), for assistance.

## Emergencies
**Police:** ☎ 100.

**Ambulance:** ☎ 101 (☎ 911, for English-speaking operator).

**Hospitals:** Beersheva: **Soroka Hospital** (☒ Hanessi'im St., ☎ 07/640–0111); Eilat: **Yoseftal Hospital** (☒ Yotam St., ☎ 07/640–0111).

**Fire:** ☎ 102.

### PHARMACIES
Call the **Magen David Adom Medical Service** (☎ 100), the Red Cross of Israel, for assistance with emergency prescriptions. In Eilat, the **Michlin Pharmacy** (☒ Opposite Central Bus Station, ☎ 07/637–2434) is open Sunday–Thursday 8–2 and 4–8:30, Friday 8–3. Michlin will deliver to your hotel if necessary. In the Negev, there are pharmacies in Arad, Beersheva, Eilat, and Mitzpe Ramon.

## Guided Tours
### AIRPLANE TOURS
From Sde Dov Airport in Tel Aviv, **Ayt Aviation & Tourism Ltd.** (☎ 03/699–0185) will take you for a two-hour flight over the Negev's *makhteshim* (canyonlike craters), the spring and waterfall of Ein Avdat, and the Dead Sea; the cost is NIS 910 ($260) per person.

### BEDOUIN LIFE
For a complete day in the desert, **United Tours** (07/637–1720; in Tel Aviv, 03/693–3412; in Jerusalem, 02/625–2187) starts you off with a two-hour camel ride along the ancient Nabatean trade route and a look at the natural phenomenon of the Makhtesh Gadol (Big Crater). The day winds down at a Bedouin encampment, with traditional hospitality and a meal. The cost is NIS 220 ($66) per person.

Spend Wednesday evening in a **Bedouin tent** enjoying a Middle Eastern dinner and stories of the desert, for NIS 120 ($34). For reservations call 07/637–3565.

### BIRD-WATCHING TOURS
Every spring and fall, millions of birds fly over **Eilat** on their long journey between winter grounds in Africa and summer breeding grounds in Eurasia. Migration takes place between mid-February and early June, and between mid-August and the end of September, although the **International Birdwatching Center,** just north of Eilat (☒ Main highway, near Dor gas station, Box 774, 88106, ☎ 07/633–5339, ℻ 07/637–6922), is aflutter year-round; it's open Sunday, Tuesday, and Wednesday 9–4; Monday and Thursday 9–1 and 5–7; and Friday 9–1. The center conducts half- and full-day trips to bird-watching hot spots in

the vicinity of Eilat. You'll see the ringing station, and you can plant a tree at the bird sanctuary, created on a landfill. The center provides binoculars for better views of birds of prey, waterfowl, and songbirds, among others. Based on a minimum of four people, prices range from $25 to $50 per person per trip.

### BOAT TOURS

Take in the spectacular underwater phenomena near Eilat—unusual coral, tropical plant life, and colorful fish of all sizes and shapes—from one of the glass-bottom boats that depart from Eilat's marina. The **Jules Verne Explorer** (☎ 07/637–7702 or 07/633–4668; reservations suggested), a mobile underwater observatory with two upper decks and a glass-sided underwater section, takes a two-hour trip past the Coral Reserve three times daily. The cost is NIS 63 ($18).

If you really want to see the fish and coral from down under, take a ride on **Yellow Submarine**'s 72-ft-long *Jacqueline*, which leaves three to four times daily from Coral World Underwater Observatory (☎ 07/636–4222), on the Eilat–Taba Road in Coral Beach. The sub—which really *is* yellow—dives deep beneath the surface to the renowned reefs of the Coral Reserve. A camera is mounted outside so that you can see the water closing around you as you descend. Reservations are required; the sub runs every day except Sunday. The 40-minute guided trip costs NIS 222 ($63) and includes entrance to the observatory.

Take a daylong cruise in the Gulf of Eilat (Aqaba) on one of the many boats anchored in the marina, among them the **Orionia** (⊠ Red Sea Sports Club, ☎ 07/637–9685), a classic Spanish-built sailing yacht whose skipper explains what's to see at sea; it's wise to reserve ahead. **Holiday Charter** (⊠ Marina, ☎ 07/633–1717, ℻ 07/633–3351) offers a barbecue lunch cruise on an Old World–style sailboat to Coral Island, 17 km (10 mi) south of Eilat, with time to explore its Crusader fortress—all for NIS 171 ($49). In addition, there's a five-hour cruise on an all-wood, Cutty Sark–style schooner that anchors at the Lighthouse, near Taba, and costs NIS 115 ($33). Service boats come along while you're out there, offering (for an additional fee) to take you parasailing or waterskiing or for an introductory scuba dive.

If you're itching for more-active sailing, the operators of the 47-ft ketch **Shooneet** (☎ 050/286334), in the marina, offer various trips—including an overnight sail for NIS 140 ($40) and a 24-hour sail for NIS 315 ($90)—in which guests can take the helm and hoist the sails. The skipper gives short explanations of the surroundings.

If you can't stay down south overnight, one-day jaunts from Jerusalem or Tel Aviv combine the Dead Sea (from Jerusalem or Tel Aviv); a hike in the Ein Gedi nature reserve, where David fled from Saul; and a visit to a desert kibbutz with a botanical garden. After lunch at the kibbutz, step aboard *Lot's Wife* for a boat ride on the Dead Sea. The cost is a very reasonable NIS 72 ($20) per person.

### CAMEL TOURS

Once you're in Mitzpe Ramon, bite the bullet and wake up early for a breathtaking view of the awakening desert. The "Morning Tour" led by **Desert Shade Eco Tourism** (reserve through Tel Aviv, ☎ 03/575–6885, ℻ 03/613–0160) starts at 6:30, lasts an hour and a half, costs NIS 105 ($30), and obligingly includes coffee; children must be over 5. There's also a two-day trip (weekly; minimum six people) following the ancient Spice Route, with a sleep-out under the stars.

Based in the heart of the mountains near Eilat, **Camel Riders** runs adventure-filled desert crossings. The two-day "Smugglers' Route" trek sets out from the Shacharut Desert Adventure Center (☎ 07/637–3218), 60 km (37 mi) north of Eilat. It crosses the Negev Highlands, through remote corners of the desert, on the route taken by smugglers in centuries past. The trip leaves on Friday (though usually stops for the summer) and costs NIS 525 ($150). The **Camel Ranch** (☎ 07/637–0022, 07/637–8638 evenings), at the Texas Ranch in Coral Beach, takes you into the desert mountains and canyons around Eilat; a half-day excursion (the sunset trip is smashing) costs NIS 157 ($45).

### DIGS

If you fancy working all day in the dust under a blazing sun with the hope of finding Abraham's tent peg (and perhaps contributing to Holy Land archaeology and meeting interesting people), zap this Web site for the latest information on digs that need volunteers: www.israel-mfa.gov.il/archdigs. (It's so popular that they'll no longer give out their phone number!)

### GENERAL INTEREST

Several Tel Aviv– and Jerusalem-based tour companies, including **Egged Tours** (✉ 59 Ben Yehuda St., Tel Aviv, ☎ 03/527–1212; ✉ 8 Shlomzion HaMalka, Jerusalem, ☎ 02/622–1999 or 622–2929) and **United Tours** (✉ 113 Hayarkon St., Tel Aviv, ☎ 03/522–2008 or 03/693–3412; ✉ King David Hotel Annex, 23 King David St., Jerusalem, ☎ 02/625–2187 or 02/625–2189), offer two-day air-conditioned bus tours to Eilat. Both companies will pick you up at your hotel, including those in Herzliya and Netanya. Among the highlights covered are David Ben-Gurion's home at Sde Boker, the Ramon Crater, and attractions in and around Eilat. For an extra fee, you can arrange to make the return trip by air. The trip costs NIS 787 ($225), with a small surcharge during peak season. Egged and United also organize half-day trips from Eilat to Timna Park, the Hai Bar Wildlife Reserve, and Kibbutz Yotvata.

**Yoel Tours** (✉ Carlton Hotel, ☎ 07/658–4311), in Ein Bokek, operates a half-day minibus tour to the Bedouin market in Beersheva, followed by a cup of coffee with a Bedouin family in their tent. The trip costs NIS 122 ($35) and runs every Thursday. Yoel also runs a one-day trip to Eilat, which includes the Underwater Observatory and a swim in the Red Sea; and a yacht trip, which includes snorkeling.

From Eilat, the **Timna Express** (☎ 07/637–4741) leads a detailed exploration of Timna Park, with hotel pickups at 8 AM. The price of NIS 210 ($48) includes lunch at a kibbutz; you'll be back around 2 PM.

**Amiel Tours** (✉ Khan Center, ☎ 07/637–6308) takes travelers north from Eilat to visit Timna Park and a kibbutz; the trip lasts half a day and costs NIS 136 ($39).

### HIKING TOURS

A safer—and probably more interesting—alternative to venturing out on your own is an off-the-beaten-track hike led by professional guides from the **SPNI** (Society for the Protection of Nature in Israel; 13 Hashfela St., Tel Aviv 66183, 03/638–8674 or 03/638–8677; 13 Helene Hamalka St., Jerusalem 96101, 02/625–2357 or 02/624–4605). Although some one-day hikes are conducted in English, don't dismiss hikes conducted in Hebrew; English-speakers in the group are often glad to translate, and the outings are a good way to get to know nature-loving Israelis. SPNI day trips are planned only a short time in advance, so call to see what's happening.

The expert guides at **Ramon Desert Tours** (☎ 07/658–8125, 052/703451, or 050/308272) take hikers down and around the phenomenal Ramon Crater.

For the ecology-minded, half-day tours around Eilat (the Sunset Hike is especially pleasant) are offered by **Nature's Way** (⊠ 257/4 Tsukim, in the residential area, ☎ 07/633–0057). The company also gives out free information about hiking on your own.

The **Eilat Field School** (a branch of the Society for the Protection of Nature in Israel, or SPNI) leads light three-hour hikes into the "untouched" desert, with views of the Sinai. All ages are welcome; the hikes leave Monday, Tuesday, and Friday and cost NIS 60 ($17) per person, with all profits going to conservation efforts. Call 07/637–2021 for details.

### JEEP TOURS

From Eilat, the well-established **Red Sea Sports Club** (⊠ King Solomon Hotel, King's Wharf, ☎ 07/637–9685) leads jeep trips through the Granite Mountains around Eilat to lookout points above Moon Valley, and sometimes also to the Red Canyon for a hike. The cost is NIS 122 ($35) per person for half a day, NIS 171 ($49) per person, including picnic lunch, for a full day.

If you're over 23 and would like to try your hand at driving a jeep, contact **Johnny Tours** (☎ 07/631–6215), in Eilat. Johnny also offers hardtop desert vehicles—not as romantic as jeeps, which are open to the sky, but air-conditioning has its appeal. Routes include Amram's Pillars, Timna Park, and the desert oasis of Ein Evrona. The half-day trip costs NIS 119 ($34); the full-day trip is $44–$55, including lunch.

**Avi Desert Tours** (⊠ Moshav Givat Yeshayahu 16, Jerusalem 99825, ☎ 02/991–8855; in Eilat, ☎ 07/653–2004) leads carefully planned jeep and four-wheel-drive expeditions from Beersheva, Eilat, and Ein Bokek. From Eilat, **Jeep See** (⊠ Bridge House, near marina, Box 4188, 88100, ☎ 07/633–0133) offers a half-day trip to the red-sand Hidden Canyon for NIS 122 ($35) and a 2½-hour trip to the Lost Valley and Black Canyon for NIS 98 ($28). Jeep See also runs full-day trips complete with picnic lunch, Bedouin tales, and a great sunset view for NIS 175 ($50).

From Mitzpe Ramon, **Desert Shade Eco Tourism** (⊠ Box 238, Tel Aviv 80600, ☎ 03/575–6885) leads a tour of the Ramon Crater, including a desert-style lunch, a camel ride, and a visit to the Alpaca Farm. Tours run on Sunday from February to April; the cost is NIS 308 ($88).

**Ramon Desert Tours** (☎ 77/658–8125 or 07/659–5106) creates personalized jeep tours of Mitzpe Ramon, the Ramon Crater, and the Negev Highlands.

### SHOOTING

You don't need experience or a license to be a quick draw at **Red Sea Sports Club** advanced shooting range at the Ambassador Hotel (☎ 07/638–2243), using live-fire video simulators. Qualified instructors are on hand for lessons.

## Hiking

Throughout Negev parklands and reserves, hiking trails have been marked by the SPNI, the National Parks Authority, and the Nature Reserves Authority. The **SPNI** publishes topographical maps (in Hebrew) on which the trails are color-coded to match the markings on the trails themselves. The trail markers have three short stripes: white/color/white, with the color either red, green, blue, or black. Yellow indicates military areas. Maps are available at SPNI headquarters in Tel Aviv and Jerusalem, and at its field study centers in Sde Boker (☎ 07/656–5016), Eilat (⊠ Rte. 90, Coral Beach, ☎ 07/637–2021), Beersheva (⊠ Meshachrerim St. at Tuviyahu Blvd., ☎ 07/623–8527), and Har Hanegev

(⊠ Mitzpe Ramon, ☎ 07/658–8616). Keep in mind that at least 60% of the Negev is occupied by the military, and you are forbidden to enter these areas. Firing zones and mines are marked in yellow on SPNI maps.

The **Nature and National Parks Protection Authority** (⊠ 78 Yirmiyahu St., Jerusalem 94467, ☎ 02/500–5444) is expertly represented at the Mitzpe Ramon visitor center (☎ 07/658–8691) and at the Coral Reserve in Eilat (Rte. 90, ☎ 07/637–3988). The rangers are experienced and knowledgeable and will help you get your hike off the ground.

## Travel Agencies

There are a host of travel offices in **Eilat** around the Central Bus Station, in the Khan Center, and at Bridge House, near the marina. Well-established Negev agencies include **Galilee Tours** in Eilat (⊠ Under the Howard Johnson Plaza Neptune, ☎ 07/633–5131), **Amiel Tours** in Ein Bokek (⊠ Shopping center, ☎ 07/623–2988), and **Lahish Tours** in Beersheva (⊠ 79 Herzl St., ☎ 07/628–1057). Note that some agencies close in July and August.

## Visitor Information

There are general tourist offices in **Beersheva** (⊠ 6 Ben Zvi St., opposite Central Bus Station, Box 591, 84104, ☎ 07/623–6001 or 07/623–6002) and **Eilat** (⊠ Tourist Information Office, Arava Rd. at Yotam St., Box 14, 88100, ☎ 07/637–2111). Especially useful in Eilat is the detail-filled leaflet called "Events and Places of Interest." Eilat's **Tourist Patrol** (⊠ Tourist Information Office, ☞ *above*, ☎ 07/636–7269 or 636–7209), a sort of tourist police, is open from 8:30 to 4 daily.

There are visitor centers in **Arad** (⊠ 28 Ben Yair St., Box 824, 80700, ☎ 07/995–4409) and **Mitzpe Ramon** (⊠ Top of main street, Box 340, 80600, ☎ 07/658–8691 or 07/658–8620).

# 9 Side Trips to the Sinai and Petra

Egypt's Sinai Peninsula attracts adventurous travelers to trek in its granite mountains or dive in the magnificent coral reefs along its coast. The area also draws pilgrims with such sights as St. Catherine's Monastery and Mt. Sinai. Travelers to Jordan are flocking to Petra, the rose-red remains of an ancient Nabatean city carved into sandstone, whose gigantic monuments and royal tombs are treasures even in a region filled with antiquities.

**F**ROM ISRAEL, YOU CAN EASILY pop into Egypt or Jordan if you want to broaden your sense of the Middle Eastern region or pursue a particular passion. The Sinai Peninsula's location along the ancient trading route linking Africa and Asia has made it a meeting place of cultures since time immemorial. People from all over the world are still drawn to this pristinely beautiful part of Egypt, and the Sinai coast is a world-class diving attraction, with its year-round sunshine and dramatic granite mountains set against a teal-cobalt sea.

Petra, in Jordan, combines awesome scenery with another element: artifacts of the mysterious and ancient culture of the Nabatean people. The Nabateans controlled the famed spice route stretching from Arabia to the Mediterranean, and Petra became both their financial center and their royal necropolis. Hidden from Western eyes until they were first excavated in the early 19th century, Petra's tombs, carved out of the rust-hued sandstone cliffs of the biblical region of Edom, have gigantic proportions and intricately carved facades. Its Roman remains are a window on the culture that ruled the world 2,000 years ago. In a region studded with antiquities, Petra is still a crown jewel for students of ancient history.

# THE SINAI

By Judy Stacey Goldman

Updated by Nora El Samahy and Magda Abdou

Today the Sinai is nothing less than a paradise for adventurers. Its interior seems untouched and even forbidding, and its coast is famous for its marvelous coral reefs. Jeep and hiking trails beg to be explored, and at the end of every day the weary traveler is within a few hours of beautiful hotels and resorts.

The Sinai is a 61,000-square-km (37,820-square-mi) triangular peninsula, bounded on the east by the Gulf of Eilat (also called the Gulf of Aqaba) and on the west by the Gulf of Suez. The apex of the triangle, pointing down toward the Red Sea, was the main route to the East for the traders of antiquity. Many legends of ancient Egypt are set in the Sinai: the goddess Isis came here to search for the body of her murdered husband, and the goddess Hathor, patroness of the Sinai's copper mines and known to the pharaohs as "Our Lady of Sinai," also sanctified the area. And, of course, biblical references to the Sinai are numerous. Pilgrims have long been drawn to the scene of the wanderings of the ancient Israelites.

The Sinai's vastness can mislead the uninitiated into regarding it as one geographical unit. In fact, the peninsula can be divided into three major subsections, each very different from the other. The plains of the northern Sinai are bounded on their southern edge by Darb el-Haj, the Muslim pilgrim's route connecting Egypt to Aqaba and, finally, to Mecca. The immense limestone massif of the Tih Desert, whose western reaches are rich in water sources and dramatic canyons, dominates the central Sinai. The word Tih, translated by some as "wanderers," has led some scholars to identify this wilderness with the wanderings of the Children of Israel. The southern Sinai is the most traveled part of the peninsula, as it is home to the traditional Mt. Sinai and, along the coast, some of the best diving in the world.

Most travelers to the southern Sinai, the area covered in this trip, follow a route leading from Eilat to St. Catherine's Monastery at the foot of Mt. Sinai. The simplest way to do this is by organized bus trip. This may not sound madly adventurous, but it offers the security of know-

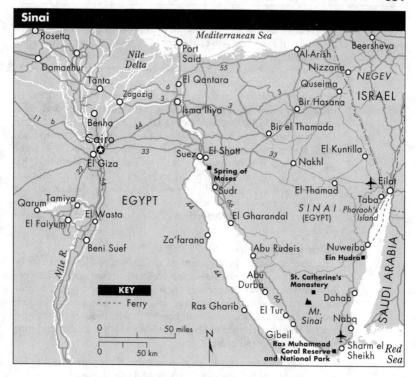

Sinai

ing that everything from start to finish is taken care of and the freedom to do nothing but gaze at the wonderful scenery. A whirlwind tour of the Sinai coast and a visit to St. Catherine's Monastery can be accomplished in one day. Longer tours, of two days or more, allow for swimming or snorkeling stops and visits to additional sights.

Independent travelers can see the region's highlights in a three-day driving trip. The road passes along the eastern coast, where the town of Nuweiba is both a crossroads to the interior and a vacation center. Nuweiba's beautiful beach has some of the best diving and snorkeling in the Sinai, and it can serve as a stopover on the road west to Sinai's interior and St. Catherine's Monastery, or on the way south to the coral reefs of Dahab and Ras Muhammad (near the town of Sharm el Sheikh), at the peninsula's southernmost tip.

## Pleasures and Pastimes

### Dining

While the Sinai's location on the coast ensures a number of fish restaurants, proprietors come and go, and so does the level of hygiene. Keep an ear to the ground, gleaning information from fellow travelers about the latest gems. Otherwise, count on having your best meals in the resort hotels, and leave your exploring for the scenery. The most notable restaurants are in Sharm el Sheikh, where you can sample an array of good European and Eastern cuisines at reasonable prices.

| CATEGORY | COST* |
| --- | --- |
| **$$$** | over $30 |
| **$$** | $15–$30 |
| **$** | under $15 |

*per person for a three-course meal, excluding drinks and service charge

## Diving

The Gulf of Eilat is an extension of the Indian Ocean, linked to it by the straits of Tiran and Bab el Mandeb. The water temperature reaches about 25°C (77°F) in the summer and drops to 19°C (66°F) in the winter. This tropical sea is poor in plankton—a fact that accounts for the striking clarity of its waters—but rich in algae, which live in symbiosis with the coral around them. The result of this symbiosis is nature's most magnificent regional work of art: the Sinai coast coral reefs, home to some 1,000 species of fish and more than 137 species of coral. Diving safaris are organized at several points along the eastern Sinai coast, and nondivers can often rent snorkeling equipment there. Some well-known dive sites are Ras-a-Sitan, 54 km (33 mi) south of Taba, and Ras-Abu Gulum, an unspoiled reef about 50 km (31 mi) south of Nuweiba and accessible only by Jeep. From Dahab, the Canyon and Blue Hole are two favorite sites; from Sharm el Sheikh, the most popular spots are in the Ras Muhammad National Park and the straits of Tiran.

## Hiking and Trekking

The southern Sinai's landscape of gorges and valleys, towered over by multicolored granite mountains, provides virtually unlimited hiking opportunities. A few of the routes are well traveled, and you can enjoy them even if you only have a short time. The area around St. Catherine's Monastery has several trails besides the strenuous but not-to-be-missed hike up to the top of Mt. Sinai. Other widely available exploring options are Jeep and camel tours.

Experienced hikers can trek to remote parts of the Sinai, like the Tih Desert or Mt. Sirbal, though they should do so only with the leadership of experienced guides. Trails in the Sinai are largely unmarked, and attempting even the shortest ones without exact directions from experts can be risky.

## Lodging

Travelers can choose from luxury hotels and resorts and medium- and low-price hotels at Nuweiba, Dahab, and Sharm el Sheikh. Campsites also abound and are well advertised, although some may not be very clean.

| CATEGORY | COST* |
| --- | --- |
| $$$ | over $130 |
| $$ | $45–$130 |
| $ | under $45 |

*All prices are for a standard double room, including tax.*

# Gateway to Egypt

Once you leave Eilat and border formalities behind, you'll sense the freedom of the magnificent scenery that lies ahead. The turquoise waters of the Gulf of Eilat sparkle in the sunlight against the backdrop of the red and black mountains that nearly touch the water in many places. This is the landscape that will accompany you as you move down the eastern coast of the Sinai. The slopes are dotted with acacia trees, and wooden fishing boats bob offshore in the gulf waters.

# Pharaoh's Island

*17 km (11 mi) south of Eilat, 38 km (24 mi) north of Wadi Malkha.*

With its ruined Crusader castle and Ottoman additions, Pharaoh's Island (also known as Coral Island) attracts many a roadside photographer. The island's recorded history begins during the reign of Pharaoh Ramses III, who reigned from 1198 to 1166 BC and was probably the source of the island's name—in Arabic, Jezirat Phar'un, or Pharaoh's Island. A document from this period relates that workers sent to mine copper from Timna, north of present-day Eilat, found shelter here. The island next served as a port for the region's rulers during the Byzantine period, when busy shipping lanes connected India with the Land of Israel via the Gulf of Suez and the Gulf of Eilat.

The best-known period in the island's occupation is marked by the dramatic remains visible from shore. These are the ruined walls of the **Crusader outpost** created here in 1115 by Baldwin I. For 55 years, the Crusaders controlled both the trade and pilgrimage routes that passed this way from the safety of the island. But in 1171, shortly after coming to power in Egypt, Saladin attacked the fortress by surprise, transporting his dismantled ships secretly through the Sinai on camelback. Despite repeated attempts, the Crusaders never again regained control of the island. Most of what now remains dates from the Mamluk period (14th century).

If you're intrigued enough by the ruins to make this a full-blown stop, you can cross the 250 yards from the shore to the island in a boat that leaves from the Saladin Motel every 15 minutes from 9 to 5; a round-trip ticket costs about L.E. 24 ($7).

Just a few miles south of the island, take the time to stop at the fjord, an impressively beautiful inlet, for another great photo op.

*En Route*  At Wadi Malkha-Sheikh Suleiman Junction (38 km, or 24 mi, south of Pharaoh's Island; 10 km, or 6 mi, north of Nuweiba), there is a Bedouin-run kiosk that rents camels and guides and sells food and water for trips to some of the natural attractions inaccessible by car. Hour-long jaunts are an option.

## Nuweiba

*48 km (30 mi) south of Coral Island, 125 km (78 mi) northeast of St. Catherine's Monastery.*

Nuweiba is one of the eastern Sinai's several growing resort towns. Its name means "bubbling springs," and Nuweiba has long been an important oasis for Muslim pilgrims en route to Mecca. Lovely, sandy beaches and colorful coral reefs accessible from the shore have earned it a reputation as the perfect place for a resort-style vacation, and it's an excellent starting point for tours to the Sinai's interior.

Now a city of about 3,000, Nuweiba is the center for two tribes. Their members, once the outstanding fishermen of the Sinai coast, still inhabit the area in two villages: Nuweiba el Muzeina, south of Nuweiba city, and Nuweiba Tarabin, to the north. Nuweiba city also has a touristy center, with a Bedouin bazaar and a few shops and restaurants. But you'll probably spend most of your time enjoying the beach, its coffeehouses, and the outstanding scenery.

One unusual attraction in Nuweiba el Muzeina is Holly, a solitary dolphin. Scientists are still studying solitary dolphins, loving and sociable creatures that sometimes break away from their pod and "move in" near human habitations. Holly has been a dockside resident of Nuweiba el Muzeina since 1994 and will often allow visiting swimmers to approach her and engage her in play.

From Nuweiba a car-and-passenger ferry runs daily to Aqaba, Jordan. It's the way the locals make the crossing, but it's slow going at 3½ hours' duration. A good alternative for travelers is the high-speed catamaran that makes the trip in 45 minutes, part of a package assembled by the Nuweiba Hilton Coral Resort (☞ Lodging, *below*), which makes a one-day round-trip to Petra, Jordan, every Friday at 6 AM.

### Lodging

**$$$** 🏨 **Nuweiba Hilton Coral Resort.** This resort is a five-minute taxi ride away from Nuweiba's port and thus ideally situated for trips into the Sinai's interior as well as across the Gulf of Aqaba to Jordan. The hotel's public areas—restaurants, disco, and poolside—have a distinct shell motif. The rooms are decorated simply, with basic white tiles, wooden furniture, underwater photography, and large balconies. With an eye toward ecological friendliness, the hotel asks that you limit your use of water to what's necessary and insert a power card to activate your room's electricity. ⊠ *Nuweiba port,* ☏ *062/520320 or 062/520321,* ☏ *800/445–8667 in the U.S.;* FAX *062/520327 or 062/520423. 100 rooms with bath. 2 restaurants, 2 bars, 2 pools, tennis court, horseback riding, squash, beach. AE, DC, MC, V.*

**$$** 🏨 **El Salam.** This hotel has air-conditioned rooms with minibars; a swimming pool; and a private beach. ⊠ *Nuweiba Tarabin,* ☏ *062/500441,* FAX *062/500440. 100 rooms with bath. No credit cards.*

**$–$$** 🏨 **Helnan.** The Helnan, in Nuweiba city near the bus station, has air-conditioned rooms and a private beach. Helnan Camping, on the hotel grounds, has bungalow accommodations in the $ category. ⊠ *Nuweiba,* ☏ *062/50040, 062/500402, 062/500403, or 062/500404;* FAX *062/500407. 117 rooms with bath. AE, MC, V.*

*En Route* About 10 km (6 mi) past the junction of the Nuweiba–St. Catherine's road, you'll see a Bedouin hut by the roadside. Stop here to walk (about 20–30 minutes) to the point where you have a view of an emerald-green oasis, Ein Hudra, believed by some scholars to be the biblical site of Hatzeroth (Numbers 11:35). On the way, you can see a stone burial structure of the type known as *nawamis,* one of several in the vicinity; it dates from the Chalcolithic period. There are also rock inscriptions along the path, carved by shepherds and pilgrims over the ages in Greek, Armenian, and Hebrew. Make sure you get walking directions from the Bedouin, or, better yet, rent a camel here. As well known as these attractions are, they are not carefully signposted, and it's easy to get lost.

## St. Catherine's Monastery

★ *125 km (78 mi) southwest of Nuweiba.*

The sight of St. Catherine's Monastery, utterly isolated in a valley surrounded by great, craggy mountains, is extraordinary. One of the most sacred monasteries in the world, it was constructed by the emperor Justinian in AD 530. But one look at the looming, fortresslike complex is enough to realize that religious fervor was not the emperor's only incentive. Right on the main caravan route carrying goods across the Sinai from Africa to Asia, the monastery no doubt served the emperor's soldiers as a base of operations against the bandits who plagued this route. It is surrounded by sites immortalizing various biblical stories, including what is said to be the exact location where the Israelites worshiped the Golden Calf.

The monastery comprises several buildings, each built or expanded at different times over the centuries. Among them are a church, several chapels, and a library (closed to the public) containing thousands of rare books, including a copy of the Codex Sinaiticus (the 3rd-century AD Greek translation by Jewish scholars of the Hebrew Bible), one of

50 copies commissioned by Constantine the Great in 331. Within the complex are also the monks' living quarters, an ancient refectory, and a white mosque with a minaret built in 1106 (not in use). All of this is encircled by high stone walls. Originally named after Mary, the monastery was later named for St. Catherine, martyred in Alexandria in the 4th century (the round firework called a Catherine wheel is named for the form of torture to which she was submitted); the faithful believe that her bones were carried here by angels. About 12 Greek Orthodox monks currently live and work here; the archbishop, who resides in Cairo, visits at Easter and other important holidays. Outside and around the monastery live the Christian Bedouin of the Jabaliyeh tribe, who have long served the monks by working in the gardens and orchards.

Inside the **Church of the Transfiguration,** the apse is decorated with an ancient mosaic of the Transfiguration of Jesus, with Moses and Elijah. Oil lamps and decorated eggs hang from the ceiling, and some of the monastery's unique collection of icons adorn the walls. All around you are old and treasured works of art—inscriptions, wall coverings, inlaid metalwork, stone reliefs and other carvings, and chandeliers (some of which are lighted on religious holidays). The doors to the church itself date from the 6th century, and the outer doors were built in the 11th century; the bell tower, a gift from Czar Nicholas II of Russia, was built in 1897.

The **chapel** behind the church is the most sacred part of the monastery. Unfortunately, it's not always open to the public. Dating from the 4th century AD, the chapel is the oldest part of the church, and its walls are covered with icons, of which the monastery itself has 2,000. (You can see yet more icons in the hall next to the library; the rest are kept in secured rooms, closed to the public.) One icon, portraying the Sacrifice of Isaac, was painted in the 7th century. Outside the chapel, you can see the bush where, according to tradition, God spoke to Moses.

Many visitors are intrigued by the **Room of the Skulls,** a chamber to which the bones of deceased monks are transferred from the cemetery after five years of internment. (Their burial plot is very small.) The skulls number 1,500 and are lined up neatly in rows.

Above St. Catherine's Monastery looms the multipeaked summit of **Jabal Musa,** 6,855 ft above sea level. This, your local guide will tell you, is Mt. Sinai, where Moses received the Ten Commandments as the Israelites waited impatiently below. But how reliable is this designation? Scholars have wrestled with this question for years, with no solution in sight. Most sites mentioned in the Bible are "internal"—they were named for events that happened to the Israelites but are not noted in external sources. Other locations have been suggested for the biblical Mt. Sinai, but Jabal Musa has been the most enduring conjecture, probably because of its situation on the main trade route. Pilgrims' journals, the main guidebooks of earlier periods, passed the legend of Jabal Musa's holiness from one generation to the next.

Viewing Jabal Musa even from afar is an awe-inspiring experience. If you can climb to the summit in time for a sunrise, the sweeping view of the granite peaks from one end of the horizon to the other will probably convince you that no place could serve better as the site of Moses' epiphany. The climb to Jabal Musa takes 2½ to 3 hours, including 700 steps to the very top. There is a 3,000-step descent back down to the monastery. ☎ 062/470346. 🎫 Free. ⊙ Monastery Mon.–Thurs. and Sat. 9–noon; closed Greek Orthodox Christmas (Jan. 7) and Easter.

If you have a day to spare, you may want to go back to the coast and on to bohemian **Dahab,** another oasis and resort, 130 km (81 mi) east of St. Catherine's Monastery.

## Lodging

**$$$** ⊡ **El Raha.** The price for a double in this simple hotel includes dinner and breakfast. ⊠ *Village of St. Catherine,* ☎ *062/470333,* FAX *062/ 470323. 124 rooms with bath. No credit cards.*

**$$** ⊡ **Daniela Village.** This is a compound of double-bedded, air-conditioned bungalows. Its restaurant, the Hala, serves Middle Eastern as well as international specialties. ⊠ *Near the Santa village square,* ☎ *202/470379 (Cairo),* FAX *202/360–7750; or write* ⊠ *c/o 18 Shehab St., Monahdessin, Cairo. 54 rooms with bath. No credit cards.*

**$** ⊡ **Morganland Village.** In high season, rooms are $45 per person, including dinner; hostel accommodations are $20 per person, including dinner. ⊠ *3 km (2 mi) from the monastery, just east of St. Catherine Rd., near the Zeituna area,* ☎ *202/356–2437 (Cairo),* FAX *202/356– 4104. 70 rooms with bath. No credit cards.*

# Sharm el Sheikh

*240 km (150 mi) southeast of St. Catherine's Monastery.*

Thirteen years ago Sharm el Sheikh, at the Sinai's southern tip, consisted of one hotel, two dive centers, and a snack bar. Today this bustling little town has more than 40 hotels, with respective dive centers, malls, casinos, and restaurants—and more on the way. Sharm, as it's lovingly called, has inexhaustible activities for divers, loungers, and everyone in-between, and there's plenty of nightlife to chase it—after a day of diving, snorkeling, or water-skiing you can knock back a pint of Guinness at the Pirate's Bar, go dancing at the Bus Stop, or just hang out on the outdoor patio at the Sanafir hotel.

Ras Muhammad National Park, at the southernmost tip of the Sinai Peninsula, is considered one of the best dive sites in the world. Most of the dives south of Sharm el Sheikh are wall dives—some reaching depths of over 1,600 ft—rich in fan, fire, and plate coral, napoleon fish, puffer fish, barracudas, and not without the occasional shark (usually in slumber). With great beaches and over 10 reefs, Ras Muhammad is a great place for both shore and boat diving. The yellow starkness of the desert contrasts wonderfully with the explosion of life and color under the water. The most popular boat dives include Shark's Reef and Yolanda Reef, where you'll see hordes of great fish, beautiful coral, and some toilets and sinks. For more information, call the Aquamarine Diving Center, run by Diver's International, in Na'ama Bay (☎ 062/600276).

## Dining and Lodging

**$$** ✕ **Kokai.** The kitschy decor (fake plants, red lanterns, and Stella beer bottles plastered onto the wall) is a bit much, but the food at this centrally located Asian restaurant is excellent. The menu is an array of Polynesian and Japanese cuisine, with everything from vegetable spring rolls with a tasty sweet-and-sour sauce to Teppan-Yaki. Dinner here is a good time: a Japanese chef smacks noodle dough against a table while an Egyptian chef chops fixings for omelets at supersonic speed. From your situation on the boardwalk, you have a view of the sea as well as those strolling along it. Come with an appetite—portions are generous. ⊠ *Ghazala Hotel, Na'ama Bay,* ☎ *062/600150. AE, MC, V.*

**$** ✕ **TamTam.** Authentic Egyptian food is often hard to come by in a resort town, but TamTam fills the bill. The facade is decorated with the leftovers of other building projects, and the furniture inside is basic—wooden, cafeteria-like tables and chairs. Upstairs is an open-roof deck, perfect for keeping an eye on the boardwalk. Enjoy a fresh falafel sandwich in the locally made pita bread, or a *foul* sandwich. The typical Egyptian dish, foul is based on fava beans that have been cooked overnight and then flavored with olive oil, cumin, salt, pepper, and lemon. It's healthy and full of protein and packs a burst of energy; Egyptians eat it for breakfast, lunch, or dinner. If you want carbohydrates, order *koshary,* a mixture of rice, macaroni, lentils, and tomato sauce sprinkled with browned onions. ⊠ *Ghazala Hotel, Na'ama Bay,* ☎ *062/ 600150. AE, MC, V.*

**$$$** 🖭 **Sofitel Sharm el Sheikh Coralia.** This fully equipped five-star hotel is perched on the northeastern tip of Sharm el Sheikh's famous cove, Na'ama Bay. The Arabesque theme gives it the desired Mediterranean effect—a stark, white, Moorish exterior; brass chandeliers; and Arab tilework, all tastefully executed. Your private terrace looks onto the Red Sea and is perfect for watching the sun set. Four of the rooms are specially equipped for people with disabilities, including both bath and shower. ⊠ *Na'ama Bay,* ☎ *062/600080,* ℻ *062/600085. 340 rooms, 11 suites. 7 restaurants, 4 bars, minibars, room service, pool, hot tub, massage, sauna, steam room, 2 tennis courts, exercise room, racquetball, squash, dive shop, waterskiing, billiards. AE, DC, MC, V.*

**$$** 🖭 **Sanafir.** Sanafir's prime location and relaxed atmosphere have made it a longtime hub and meeting place for those staying in Na'ama Bay. The rooms are basic and clean, with few accessories; two narrow beds, with a dome above the head of each; and a view of the pool at best. Sanafir is not about service or decor; it's about nocturnal activities. The nearby Bus Stop dance club, pseudo Bedouin Tent, and three on-site restaurants are the main draws. ⊠ *Na'ama Bay,* ☎ *062/600197,* ℻ *062/600196. 47 rooms, 22 suites. 3 restaurants, bar, pool. DC, MC, V.*

# The Sinai A to Z

## Before You Go

### BORDERS

The border crossing at Taba, just over the Egyptian border from Eilat, is open 24 hours a day, seven days a week, except for the Jewish holiday of Yom Kippur and the Muslim holiday of Id el Adkha. There is a tax of NIS 45 ($15) on the Israeli side and a tax of L.E. 20 ($6) on the Egyptian side. The phone number for the border crossing is 07/ 637–2104. Crossing the border on either side can take anywhere from five minutes to five hours, so arrive with plenty of patience!

### CLOTHING

Although it's very hot during the day in the Sinai, temperatures dip at night. Even in summer it's wise to pack a jacket and socks. Winter days are generally warm and sunny, but the mountains around St. Catherine's are known for their freezing nights, including bouts of frost and snow. Modest dress is required in the monastery.

### CURRENCY

Egyptian currency is calculated in pounds (L.E.) and piasters. The exchange rate at press time was approximately L.E. 3.38 to the U.S. dollar, L.E. 2.53 to the Canadian dollar, and L.E. 5.66 to the British pound.

Visitors to Egypt must convert currency at authorized exchange points, such as those found in major hotels and banks. Convenient places to do this are the exchange office at the border and the bank in the Taba Hilton, which is usually open all day, every day.

PASSPORTS AND VISAS

Both adults and children need valid passports to enter Egypt. If a child shares a parent's passport, the parent cannot enter Egypt *without* the child, even for a one-day visit. You can obtain visas at the border, or through Egyptian consulates in Israel. Egyptian consulates are in northern Tel Aviv (⊠ 54 Basle St., ☎ 03/546–4151 or 03/546–4152) and Eilat (⊠ 68 Avrony St., ☎ 07/637–6882). U.S. citizens do not need visas to visit Nuweiba, Dahab, St. Catherine's, or Sharm el Sheikh, although they may be necessary for other destinations in Egypt.

## Arriving and Departing

BY BUS

In Eilat, board Egged Bus 15 at the Central Bus Station. At Taba you'll switch to an Egyptian bus, which provides scheduled daily service to Nuweiba, Dahab, St. Catherine's, and Sharm el Sheikh. Be patient; punctuality is optional here.

BY CAR

Only cars registered in their drivers' names may be driven into Egypt. For more information on driving into the Sinai from Israel, contact MEMSI, the Israeli branch of the AAA, with an office in Tel Aviv (☎ 03/564–1122).

BY FOOT

You may walk across the border from Eilat to the Taba Hilton Hotel in Egypt. A hotel representative has an office at the border crossing and will arrange transport to the hotel if you request it. If you're unencumbered by luggage, however, it's an easy walk.

BY PLANE

Arkia (⊠ Red Canyon shopping center, Eilat, ☎ 07/637–6102; ⊠ 11 Frishman St., Tel Aviv, ☎ 03/523–3285) and Air Sinai (⊠ Migdalor Bldg., 1 Ben Yehuda St., 13th floor, Tel Aviv, ☎ 03/510–2481) have biweekly flights to Sharm el Sheikh on Monday and Friday mornings. They operate jointly on this route, so you can make reservations by calling either company. A one-way ticket costs about $110.

## Getting Around

BY CAR

For information on entering Egypt by car, *see* Arriving and Departing, *above.* Unleaded fuel is not available in the Sinai. Drive with extreme caution on Sinai roads; there are an inordinate number of accidents, and emergency medical care is not always available.

BY TAXI

A popular means of transportation to Nuweiba, Dahab, and Sharm el Sheikh are Bedouin taxis, which you can pick up just across the Egyptian border or at the Taba Hilton. It's advisable to use the buddy system—at least two to a car—and negotiate the fare in advance, bargaining down if it sounds exorbitant (the taxis don't have meters). Typical fares from the Taba Hilton are Taba to Nuweiba, L.E. 130 ($38); Taba to Dahab, L.E. 250 ($74); Taba to Sharm el Sheikh, L.E. 350 ($104). Bedouin Jeep drivers are available for hire at the various tourist centers.

## Contacts and Resources

CAR RENTALS

Europcar rents cars at the Taba Hilton Hotel (☎ 07/637–9222) and has offices in Nuweiba, Dahab, and Sharm el Sheikh hotels as well. It's open daily 8–1 and 5–8. You can also arrange to rent a car with a driver.

GUIDED TOURS

Reliable tour operators with day trips to St. Catherine's Monastery include **Geographical Tours Ltd.** (✉ Neptune Hotel, North Beach, Eilat, ☎ 07/637–3410; ✉ 37 Bograshov St., Tel Aviv, ☎ 03/528–4113); **Johnny Desert Tours** (✉ Shalom Center, opposite the airport, Eilat, ☎ 07/637–2608); **Mazada Tours** (✉ 141 Ibn Gvirol St., Tel Aviv, ☎ 03/544–4454; ✉ 24 Ben Sira St., Jerusalem, ☎ 02/625–5453, ℻ 02/625–5454; Paul VI St., Nazareth, ☎ 06/656–5937); and **Neot Hakikar** (main office: ✉ 67 Ben Yehuda St., Tel Aviv, ☎ 03/520–5858, ℻ 03/522–1020; ✉ Khan Center, Eilat, ☎ 07/632–6281).

Information on diving in the Sinai, as well as diving safaris of varying durations and locations, is offered by several diving clubs in Eilat: **Aqua Sport** (✉ Box 300, Coral Beach, ☎ 07/633–4404, ℻ 07/633–3771), the **Dolphin Reef Diving Center** (✉ Box 104, Southern Beach, ☎ 07/637–5935, ℻ 07/637–5921), and the **Red Sea Sports Club** (✉ Kings Wharf, ☎ 07/637–9685).

The **Green Club** (J.E.T. Travel and Tours, ✉ 3 Ben Sira St., Jerusalem, ☎ 02/623–5535, ℻ 02/624–7270) offers a special five-day tour of the Sinai with specially equipped four-wheel-drive vehicles, at a cost of $445 per person. **Mazada Tours** (☞ *above*) has Sinai safaris from two to five days long at a cost of per person, depending on trip length. The Sinai Department of the **Society for the Protection of Nature in Israel (SPNI)** (✉ 3 Hashefela St., Tel Aviv, ☎ 03/638–8675; ✉ 13 Helene Hamalka St., Jerusalem, ☎ 02/625–2357) has a well-earned reputation for expert, off-the-beaten-track nature tours; its four- and seven-day trips cost $380 and $525 per person, respectively. The **Red Sea Sports Club,** in Eilat (✉ Kings Wharf, ☎ 07/637–9685), has hiking and combination camel-hiking and Jeep–water sports trips. Choices include a minisafari day trip from Eilat ($85 per person), a two-day tour to St. Catherine's Monastery ($125–$165 per person, depending on accommodations), and an eight-day Sinai dive safari ($749 per person, including accommodations).

In Egypt, **Abanoub Travel Agency** (☎ 062/500140, ℻ 062/520206), at the new commercial center in Nuweiba, runs camel, Jeep, and trekking tours of varying durations to all parts of the Sinai. The **Aquamarine Dive Center,** in Sharm el Sheikh, leads daily boat trips to nearby dive sites, including Ras Muhammed and Tiran, and a snorkeling trip on the sensational sailboat *Henry de Monfried* (✉ Novotel Aquamarine Hotel, Na'ama Bay, ☎ 062/600276, ℻ 062/600176). **Divers' International,** in Dahab, offers daily Jeep trips to nearby dive sites, including the popular Canyon and Blue Hole (✉ Ganet Sinai Hotel, ☎ 062/640415).

MEDICAL CARE

Medical care is available at Nuweiba, Sharm el Sheikh, Dahab, and El Tur, but the hospitals are very basic. In a serious medical emergency, a person would need to be evacuated from the region by helicopter. The hospital in Sharm el Sheikh has a decompression chamber for divers. There is a private pharmacy in Nuweiba and a hospital pharmacy at St. Catherine's. A doctor is in residence at the Nuweiba Hilton, available 24 hours a day.

TELEPHONES

When calling Sinai listings from Israel, add the prefix 002. The country code for Egypt is 20; the area code for the Sinai is 062.

VISITOR INFORMATION

In Israel, you can contact the Sinai Department of the **Society for the Protection of Nature in Israel** in Tel Aviv (☞ Guided Tours, *above*). In

Egypt, the **Abanoub Travel Agency** (☞ Guided Tours, *above*) can be helpful.

# PETRA

By Miriam
Feinberg
Vamosh

Updated by
Nora El
Samahy and
Magda Abdou

Poet Dean Burger described Petra as the "rose-red city, half as old as time." Petra's boulevards, temples, theater, and splendid royal and noble tombs, secreted among the high cliffs, have an incomparable mystery and grandeur. Once inaccessible to all but an intrepid few, Petra's magnificent ruins were the epitome of romance. They're still romantic, but, happily, they're now easy to reach.

Overnight trips to Petra to explore the ruins have been increasingly popular since the Israel-Jordan border was opened in 1994. The jaunt is unforgettable, both for the antiquities and breathtaking scenery and for the sense of being a part of recent history. What was a distant dream only a few years ago—crossing a peaceful border here—is now a reality.

Petra lies in the biblical region of Edom, southeast of the Dead Sea in modern-day Jordan. According to the Book of Genesis, the Edomites were descendants of Esau, Jacob's brother and rival. When Moses led the Israelites into the promised land, he asked the Edomites permission to pass through their land and was refused. The water sources and agriculture of this highland region were probably considered too precious to share with these newcomers from the wilderness (Numbers 20:14–21).

Edom's fertile land was a magnet that desert dwellers could not ignore, however, and the Israelites were not the last to appear there. By the 4th century BC, a new group had arrived from the wilderness to take advantage of the riches of the highlands of Edom: the Nabateans. It is their spectacular tombs and urban monuments that draw travelers to Petra today.

Little is certain about the origins of the Nabateans; historians assume they were nomads from Arabia. One rare source is an early 4th-century BC record kept by one of the officers of Alexander the Great, in which the writer describes the Nabateans as shepherds who wandered the wilderness. Later historical sources describe them as traders in frankincense and myrrh, the most valuable of biblical spices. They were also mentioned as highway robbers and even as pirates. When Alexander the Great died, his empire was divided between the Seleucids, in the north, and the Ptolomies, in the south. The Nabateans eventually won independence from the Seleucids, and historical and archaeological sources hint that they gradually abandoned their nomadic lifestyle and became the wealthy masters of the region's trade routes.

Aretas, who may have been the first Nabatean king, is mentioned briefly in the Book of Maccabees. According to the New Testament (I Corinthians 11:32), one of his descendants, also named Aretas, ruled in Damascus. In his book *The Jewish War,* the 1st-century AD Roman Jewish historian Josephus mentions "Petra, capital of Arabia," and writes of both a succession of Nabatean kings who ruled Petra and a Nabatean bowman who served with the Roman army in quelling the Jewish revolt of AD 66–70.

Most of Petra's famous tombs were carved during this period. Although the combination of a necropolis and a capital city may seem strange today, this custom was common among the ancients, who established cemeteries at the entrance to many of their capitals, including Rome itself. The presence of the tombs of Petra's rich and powerful near the city's major monuments seems to have been part of a cult of the dead. When traders and travelers came to visit the marvels of the capital, they would leave offerings at the tombs to ensure the success of their journeys.

When the Nabateans emerged from the desert, they brought with them a faith in the deities who had protected them both as nomads and as traders. In the wetter, northern regions, they met people whose deities protected their crops and cities. The principal deity of the Nabateans had been Dusares, whose name means "Lord of Sarat"; near Petra, the Nabateans found an area called Shara, and Dusares easily changed his name to Dushara, "Lord of Shara." As Egyptian and Greek influences crept in, Dushara became associated with the chief male gods of those pantheons. The chief Nabatean goddess was al-Uzza, who reigned with her sisters Allat and Manat. She, too, took on Greek and Egyptian attributes, and her cult was eventually identified with Aphrodite, the Greek goddess of love; Tyche, goddess of fortune and protector of cities; and the Egyptian Isis. Almost all of the shrines in Petra were dedicated to Dushara and al-Uzza.

In AD 106, during the reign of Trajan, the Romans annexed the Nabatean Kingdom into their new province of Arabia. Hadrian visited Petra in 130, after which it was renamed in his honor—Petra Hadriane. With the completion of the main north–south artery of the eastern Roman empire, the Via Nova Triana, Petra flourished as the region remained a prime trading conduit.

A unique combination of talents made the Nabateans the unchallenged masters of this route. Though they eventually abandoned their nomadic way of life, they did not forget its survival secrets. Into the rocky wilderness they carved cisterns, into which they channeled every drop of precious water that condensed on the desert floor or fell in rare rainstorms. Control over water enabled Nabatean caravans to cross vast expanses efficiently, and their cargo—frankincense, myrrh, and other spices—was worth its weight in gold.

The spices had their origin in what is now Yemen, and the caravan road stretched from Arabia to Petra before continuing across the Arava Valley to the Negev highlands of what is now Israel, and eventually reaching the Mediterranean port of Gaza. Another branch of the road continued north from Petra to Damascus and to the ports of Lebanon. According to Roman historian Pliny the Elder, the journey from Arabia to Gaza took 65 days. Each night the caravan would put in at a Nabatean trading post, and the caravan masters would handsomely reward their hosts for their hospitality.

After the arrival of Christianity in the early 4th century, churches were built in Petra, and the new faith gradually replaced the old one. Bishops from Petra appear in ecclesiastical records as participants in the ecumenical councils that decided the doctrinal issues of the early Church. By this time, Petra was far past its prime as a trade center; the ancient traders had learned that they could use the prevailing winds to hasten ships across the sea. Some Arabian goods thus began to come to Egypt and its Mediterranean ports via the Red Sea. The overland route that passed through Petra was still used, but to a lesser extent. Furthermore, a series of earthquakes left a ruinous mark on the city.

After Petra was captured by the Muslims in 633, both strategic alliances and crossroads changed course, and the world lost interest in the area. Capitalizing on the region's ancient strategic value, the Crusaders built fortifications among the old ruins in the 11th century, but in 1189 they surrendered to the Muslim warrior Saladin. After that, Petra sank into oblivion, and it remained there for more than 500 years, most knowledge of it confined to a few references in history books. It was not until 1812 that Swiss explorer Johann Ludwig Burckhardt (who had converted to Islam to facilitate his travels through the unknown area) penetrated Petra on the pretext of offering a sacrifice at the traditional tomb of Aaron. It was Burckhardt who provided the Western world with its first contemporary description of the marvels of the ancient city.

A two-day trip to Petra from Eilat will allow you to move beyond the city's highlights. Crossing the border early in the morning should put you in Petra around noon. Drop your things off at your hotel, put on comfortable walking shoes, and spend the rest of the day touring the major monuments. The next day, you can go back for a second look; then choose one or two hikes off the main route to round out your experience. Petra is open daily from 7 AM to sunset; the city is gated and has an entrance fee of about 21 JD ($30).

## Pleasures and Pastimes

### Dining
Hotel restaurants and food stands constitute Petra's limited range of dining choices. At the Taybet Zeman Hotel, a rich buffet offers dozens of salads in the Middle Eastern tradition and main courses leaning more toward European tastes; it's worth the trip to the village of Taybeh. The Petra Forum Hotel also has a very good buffet and runs a cafeteria-style restaurant in the museum building. Not far from there, stands sell sandwiches and other snacks. Some fast-food chains now operate in the village of Wadi Musa.

### Hiking
Of several short hikes within Petra's immediate vicinity, one leads to the High Place of Sacrifice, another to the monument on the mountaintop known as Jabal a-Deir. A third hike leads to Little Petra, to the north of the village of Wadi Musa. The first two involve strenuous climbs, but the views and the antiquities at the top are well worth the effort for those in good physical condition. The trip to Little Petra is usually made by car, with a short walk to the sights.

### Lodging
New hotels are springing up in Petra. The ones closest to the site obviously provide the most convenient access, but except for the Movenpick you may find that they're not worth the money. Several hotels are in Wadi Musa, adjacent to the site. Taybet Zeman, in the village of Taybeh 9 km (5½ mi) from Petra, is the farthest from the site, but its authentic flavor is well worth the small expense of the ride. All rooms have a private bath unless otherwise indicated.

| CATEGORY | COST* |
| --- | --- |
| $$$$ | over $160 |
| $$$ | $100–$160 |
| $$ | $50–$100 |
| $ | under $50 |

*All prices are for two people in a standard double room, including taxes.*

### Shopping
You'll find "sand artists"—artisans who fill bottles with sand in a variety of designs—lined up in a row in the area known as the Open Siq. They can customize your purchase by writing a name in sand; you place your order in the morning and pick it up that the afternoon. Part of the fun is watching the artist at work.

# Exploring Petra

The walk that follows will take you through Petra's main sights. You can also hike to the High Place of Sacrifice and make a side trip to Little Petra.

*Numbers in the text correspond to numbers in the margin and on the Petra map.*

## A Good Walk

After paying your entrance fee, you'll see the **Horse Square** ①, with lean-tos where you can rent horses. After that, on the right of the path about 1,485 ft past the entrance, you'll come to the large **Djinn Blocks** ②. On the other side of the path is the **Snake Tomb** ③; step in and you'll see why it's so named. Back on the path, you'll see a large two-story tomb on your left. The lower story is called the Triclinium Tomb; the upper story is the **Obelisk Tomb** ④ and Bas-a-Siq Triclinium. From **Bab a-Siq** ⑤, a 1¼-km (¾-mi) walk brings you to the main ruins of Petra; from here you can see the remains of a Nabatean water tunnel.

Nineteenth-century travelers described a **triumphal arch** ⑥ that spanned the road at this point. As you traverse the narrow canyon of the **Siq** ⑦, nothing prepares you for the overwhelming first glimpse of the light at the end of the passage. The first burial monument is the magnificent **Khazneh** ⑧, or Treasury, adorned with figures from mythology. As you face the Khazneh, the Siq widens and soon makes a sharp turn to the right. It's here, in the area called the **Outer Siq** ⑨, that you'll meet the sand artists. On the right is **Uneishu's Tomb** ⑩. Across from the tomb, a flight of stairs leads to the path to the High Place of Sacrifice and the other tombs of **Wadi Farasa** ⑪–⑰, south and west of the main street of antiquities (☞ Another Good Walk, below).

Continuing down this street brings you to Petra's **theater** ⑱, a sign of Roman influence. Continuing straight ahead, you'll see four elevated tombs on your right. The **Urn Tomb** ⑲ is the first in a series of some of the finest tombs in Petra, which also include the **Silk Tomb** ⑳, the **Corinthian Tomb** ㉑, and the **Palace Tomb** ㉒. No one really knows anything about those who were buried here, but the tombs' grandeur certainly suggests royal occupants. You can study them from the path or walk up and enter them. Northeast of the four tombs is a road leading toward the **Tomb of Sextius Florentinus** ㉓. The **House of Dorotheos** ㉔ is next, in an area where tombs were later reused for storage and habitation.

Returning to the main path in the city center, you'll come to the **Nymphaeum** ㉕, one of the most important monuments in Petra. The ancient main street, known as the **Colonnaded Street** ㉖, was built by the Romans; on the slope to its north are the poorly preserved remains of a **Byzantine church** ㉗. Nearby is one of the city's most elaborate temples, the **Temple of the Winged Lions** ㉘. At the western end of the Colonnaded Street stood a monumental gateway to Petra's *temenos,* or sacred precinct; here you can see the remains of statues of deities, including Hermes and Tyche. The temenos leads you to a well-preserved temple, **Qasr al-Bint** ㉙. You can end your visit at Petra's **museum** ㉚.

TIMING

Plan to spend about six hours to see the highlights of Petra. It takes about 45 minutes to walk through the Siq to the main sights; if you want to hike to Jabal a-Deir, give yourself half a day. In summer, this area is very hot—protect yourself from the sun, and carry water.

364

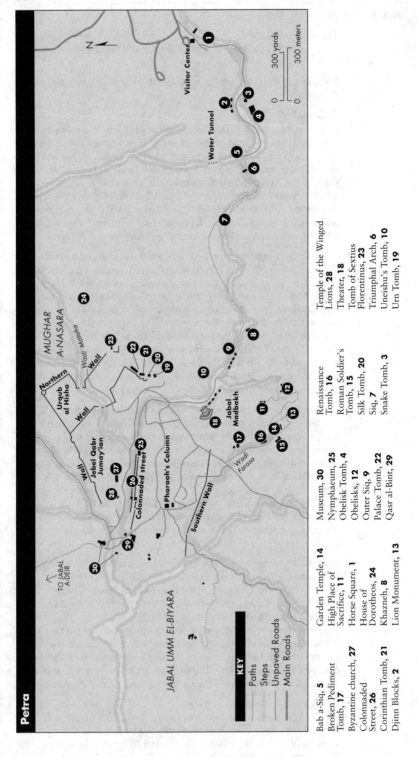

**Petra**

**KEY**

Paths
Steps
Unpaved Roads
Main Roads

Bab a-Siq, **5**
Broken Pediment Tomb, **17**
Byzantine church, **27**
Colonnaded Street, **26**
Corinthian Tomb, **21**
Djinn Blocks, **2**

Garden Temple, **14**
High Place of Sacrifice, **11**
Horse Square, **1**
House of Dorotheos, **24**
Khazneh, **8**
Lion Monument, **13**

Museum, **30**
Nymphaeum, **25**
Obelisk Tomb, **4**
Obelisks, **12**
Outer Siq, **9**
Palace Tomb, **22**
Qasr al-Bint, **29**

Renaissance Tomb, **16**
Roman Soldier's Tomb, **15**
Silk Tomb, **20**
Siq, **7**
Snake Tomb, **3**

Temple of the Winged Lions, **28**
Theater, **18**
Tomb of Sextrius Florentinus, **23**
Triumphal Arch, **6**
Uneishu's Tomb, **10**
Urn Tomb, **19**

## Sights to See

**⑤ Bab a-Siq.** The Gate of the Cleft is near the Siq, the canyon-lined passageway leading to the main sights. From here you can spot the remains of a Nabatean water tunnel, built to divert flood waters from coursing through the narrow cleft and flooding the necropolis. A dam, constructed for the same purpose in the second half of the 1st century AD, was restored by the Jordanians after particularly serious flooding some years ago.

**㉗ Byzantine church.** Richly decorated with mosaics in the style of the period, this church appears to have been destroyed by fire soon after its construction, perhaps in a severe earthquake that took place in AD 551. Unfortunately the remains are now closed to visitors.

**㉖ Colonnaded Street.** The Romans built the main street of Petra over earlier remains in the early 1st century BC. In typical Roman style, it became the city's major thoroughfare, suitable for both commerce and grand ceremonial processions. After the Roman annexation of the Nabatean kingdom, the street was restored, as noted in an inscription dated AD 114 and dedicated to Emperor Trajan. In 363 an earthquake devastated Petra and the entire surrounding region; the city's inhabitants dug themselves out, but the street never attained its former glory. You can still see the remains of the columns that lined it in antiquity.

**㉑ Corinthian Tomb.** Set among some of Petra's finest tombs is one named for the large number of Corinthian capitals, now badly deteriorated, that once decorated its facade.

**❷ Djinn Blocks.** The function of these large structures is unclear; they may have been connected to Nabatean worship, perhaps symbolizing one of their deities. In Arabic, *djinn* means "spirits," a common theme in Arab folklore.

**❶ Horse Square.** Horses used to be the conveyance of choice for the approximately 1-km (½-mi) trip to Petra's main antiquities. The growing number of visitors has made this mode impractical, but you can still hire horses for the first 800 yards, before the path narrows to become the Siq (☞ *below*). Carriages ply the route for those with difficulty walking. 🕿 *Horse or carriage hire approximately 7 JD ($10), not including the expected tip of about 1 JD, or $1.*

**㉔ House of Dorotheos.** The words THE HOUSE OF DOROTHEOS were found in this tomb in two Greek inscriptions. The area to the north of the tomb is called Mughar a-Nasara, meaning "caves of the Christians," and crosses carved on monuments here indicate their adaptation for Christian use.

**★ ❽ Khazneh.** Petra's most famous monument, this 130-ft-high structure has a splendid frontage graced by a number of mythological figures adopted by the Nabateans from Greek and Roman worship. Castor and Pollux (who after their death became the two brightest stars in the constellation Gemini), Amazons, Gorgons, eagles, and other creatures march across the Khazneh's rosy facade. Between the columns of the *tholos* (the rounded section above the tympanum) are the remains of a female deity holding a cornucopia; she is believed to be al-Uzza, the patroness of Petra and the Nabatean version of Aphrodite, goddess of love.

The Arabic name for this monument means "treasury"—its full name is Khaznet Fara'un, the Pharaoh's Treasury. Legends of treasures allegedly secreted within have led grave robbers here for centuries. The urn carved at the top of the tholos was thought to be the hiding place for the hoard. The Bedouin have been taking potshots at it for generations in the hopes of dislodging its contents, a practice whose results are still visible. The structure's true function is unclear, but like most of the other large monuments at Petra, the Khazneh is assumed to have been a tomb, built during the first century.

**㉚ Museum.** Petra's museum is in the same building as the Petra Forum restaurant, as well as rest rooms; another section is in a nearby tomb. Displays include a small number of Nabatean artifacts, such as jewelry and pottery.

OFF THE
BEATEN PATH

**JABAL A-DEIR –** Beginning near the museum, a strenuous, 45-minute climb up a steep path takes you to the summit of Jabal a-Deir, one of the most scenic points in Petra. The Mount of the Monastery takes its name from the crosses carved into the rock of the giant monument at its summit by monks who lived here in the 4th and 5th centuries. The monument's similarity to the Khazneh is remarkable, although this one is much larger; and its relatively remote location may suggest greater sanctity—the monument bears an inscription referring to the god Obodas. Nabatean king Obodas I is remembered for his triumph over both the Hasmonean ruler Alexander Jannaeus and the Seleucid king of Syria Antiochus XII. Obodas died in 86 BC in the Negev and was deified shortly thereafter; he is buried somewhere in the ruins of the Nabatean city of Obodat (Avdat in Hebrew), in the Negev. This site was probably a shrine constructed in his honor, where supplicants gathered to perform rituals.

A clamber up the hill to the east of the monument affords a view of epic proportions: west of Petra, the highest peak in the region is the 4,455-ft-high sacred spot of Jabal Haroun, the traditional burial place of Aaron, brother of Moses. Beyond lies the wide expanse of the Arava Valley and, to the west, Israel's Negev Plateau.

**㉕ Nymphaeum.** Dedicated to the water nymphs, this fountain was used for both refreshment and worship. The fountains of the two-story structure were fed by a water channel that continued along Petra's main street.

**❹ Obelisk Tomb.** This upper story of a two-story tomb is named for the four free-standing obelisks that decorate its facade. The lower story, the Triclinium Tomb, was so named because three walls of the empty room are lined with triclinia, a Latin word for this kind of bench. In other settings, diners would recline on these.

**❾ Outer Siq.** As you cross the area also known as Facade Street, you'll see several tombs with variations on Nabatean architectural themes, including repeated triangular step patterns and pilasters topped with Nabatean or more classical capitals. Water pipes set into channels along the facades of the last tombs on the right-hand side were the continuation of the system that brought water from the Siq to the city beyond.

**㉒ Palace Tomb.** This unfinished tomb is one of the few in Petra not carved entirely out of the rock. Many of the tomb's constructed segments have fallen away, so it's hard to ascertain its original dimensions. At the base of the Palace Tomb are the remains of the northern city wall, built after the 1st century BC.

**㉙ Qasr al-Bint.** This structure's full name, which translates as the "Palace of the Daughter of Pharaoh," stems from a legend that the pharaoh's daughter promised she would marry the man who could channel water to the city where she lived. When she had to choose between two winners, she asked each how he had managed his appointed task. The one whose answer she preferred won her hand. In fact, the structure is a temple, built in the early 1st century AD. Its interior was approached through areas of gradually increasing sanctity. As in the Temple of the Winged Lions, the identity of the deity worshiped here is not known, but a statue depicting him or her—perhaps Dushara, the greatest deity of the Nabatean pantheon—certainly stood in the temple's inner sanctum.

⓴ **Silk Tomb.** The striations of natural color in the rock of the Silk Tomb make it one of Petra's finest, and certainly aid in identification. They flow across the facade like a multicolor silk scarf blowing gently in the wind.

❼ **Siq.** The Siq (meaning "cleft"), a rocky passage between towering walls of stone, leads visitors to the main ruins. The colors of the rock are astounding, varying in hues of red and purple. Nabatean paving is still visible in two locations along the way. Niches, some of which contain inscriptions dating from the 2nd and 3rd centuries AD, show that this road was as much a ceremonial path as a passageway. One niche is carved into a small outcropping of rock near one of the paved patches; it's unusual in that it faces away from the approach, and may have been designed to bestow a blessing on those leaving the city. Film buffs may recall Harrison Ford riding through this area in some of the concluding scenes of *Indiana Jones and the Last Crusade.*

❸ **Snake Tomb.** No outward decoration marks this tomb, but 12 burial niches are carved into the floor inside. The name comes from a wall relief that shows two snakes attacking what may be a dog.

㉘ **Temple of the Winged Lions.** This impressive building takes its name from the sculptures that serve as capitals for its columns. The identity of the deity worshiped within is unknown, but figurines suggest that it may have been Isis, Egyptian goddess of the heavens and patroness of fertility. An inscription dates the construction of the temple to around AD 27.

⓲ **Theater.** This semicircular hallmark of Roman culture is a clear sign of the extent to which the Nabateans, like most other peoples of this region, had adopted the Roman way of life. The Nabateans apparently had no qualms about building a theater in a cemetery; their stone masons even cut into some of the existing tombs (the remains of which you can see at the back of the rock-cut theater) to do so. The capacity of the theater has been estimated at 10,000.

㉓ **Tomb of Sextius Florentinus.** The name of this Roman governor of Arabia appears in the tomb's inscription. Historical records indicate that he died in office in AD 128.

❻ **Triumphal arch.** Today, all that's left of this arch near the Siq are niches with the remains of statues that decorated the point where the springers of the arch were built. The arch collapsed in 1895.

⓾ **Uneishu's Tomb.** This tomb in the Outer Siq got its name from an inscription discovered within that read UNEISHU, BROTHER OF SHAQILATH, QUEEN OF THE NABATEANS.

⓳ **Urn Tomb.** Named for the vaselike decoration at the top of its pediment, this tomb is supported by a series of vaults at its lower level, dubbed *al makhamah* (the law court) by the locals for some long-forgotten reason; the upper level was called *a-sijn* (the prison). According to an inscription within, Petra's Byzantine Christians turned the Urn Tomb into a church in AD 446.

## Another Good Walk

The path to the Nabatean shrine known as the **High Place of Sacrifice** ⑪ branches off from the main path through the city between the end of Facade Street and the theater. On a flat protrusion below the High Place are two **obelisks** ⑫ carved from the mountain. The curving path continues past the **Lion Monument** ⑬, a fountain. About 400 yards beyond, you'll see the tomb known as the **Garden Temple** ⑭. A short distance ahead lies the **Roman Soldier's Tomb** ⑮, an eclectic creation. Farther along are the **Renaissance Tomb** ⑯, named for its graceful facade, and the **Broken Pediment Tomb** ⑰. The relatively easy-to-follow path continues through Wadi Farasa and ends at the monument known as Pharaoh's Column, not far from the Colonnaded Street. From here you can continue on to the museum if you wish.

TIMING

The hike to the High Place of Sacrifice takes approximately three hours from the beginning of the ascent to the museum and its restaurant. To ascend to the High Place and then return to the main street of antiquities takes about 1½ hours.

## Sights to See

⑰ **Broken Pediment Tomb.** This tomb is characterized by the broken-off gable of its roof, supported by four pilasters topped with capitals in the unique Nabatean style.

⑭ **Garden Temple.** To the right, above this tomb (which also served as a temple), a wall closes off a cleft in the rock; it acted as a dam for water that flowed from a small spring south of the village of Wadi Musa. Two more channels also reached this point, bringing runoff from the area of the High Place of Sacrifice.

★ ⑪ **High Place of Sacrifice.** An ancient flight of stairs—restored in recent years by the Jordanian Department of Antiquities—leads to the top of Jabal Madhbah, the Mount of the Altar. At its peak is a rectangular court surrounded on three sides by benches in the triclinium style of the Roman dining room; in the center of the court is a raised block of stone, on which the priest may have stood. To the west are two altars accessed by steps, in front of which is a channel into which the blood of the sacrificial animal may have pooled. The presence of a triclinium may indicate that one of the rituals involved a ceremonial meal. The small jumble of ruined walls near the High Place of Sacrifice may have served the Nabateans as a fort; the site's location, overlooking Petra's main thoroughfare, had clear strategic value.

⑬ **Lion Monument.** Surface runoff fed this fountain via a channel leading to the lion's mouth, from which water once streamed.

⑫ **Obelisks.** These two 20-ft-tall obelisks are examples of a common method of representing deities in the ancient Near East. Some scholars believe them to be representations of Dushara and al-Uzza; others believe they are simply the remains of quarrying activity.

⑯ **Renaissance Tomb.** This tomb bears a resemblance to the Tomb of Sextius Florentinus (☞ A Good Walk, *above*), in the main part of the city. It may have been created around the same time, the first third of the 1st century AD.

⑮ **Roman Soldier's Tomb.** The figure in the niche of this tomb's facade is dressed in typical Roman military garb, while the friezes and capitals appear more typical of Nabatean architecture before the Roman annexation. Directly opposite the Roman Soldier's Tomb is a triclinium; the rubble in between was probably once a courtyard connecting the two edifices.

## Side Trip to Little Petra

*3 km (2 mi) north of the village of Wadi Musa.*

Little Petra was the region's main commercial center in Nabatean times. To reach it, leave Petra and drive north, passing through Wadi Musa and continuing along the narrow blacktop. You'll soon see a collection of ruins on a rocky outcropping on the left; this is all that remains of the **Crusader castle of al-Wu'eira,** built by Baldwin I in 1100. The first Crusader fortification east of the Jordan River, it was one of several strategic castles that protected the Crusader kingdom on its sensitive eastern flank. The castle also ensured the Crusaders revenue from the major trade route from Cairo to Damascus. In 1189, al-Wu'eira became the last Crusader fortress east of the Jordan to surrender to the Muslim warrior Saladin.

Next you'll come to the village of **Umm Saihun,** whose residents are Bdhoul Bedouin, the main tribe of the Petra region. A 15-minute drive north will lead you to **al Beidha,** whose name—Arabic for "the white"— refers to the color of the sandstone formations along the way. Excavations here have uncovered the remains of an 11,000-year-old settlement from the Neolithic era, whose people were hunter-gatherers but also farmers and traders. Thousands of years after that culture became extinct, the Nabateans took over the same site and built agricultural terraces, remains of which are still visible.

When you come to a T junction, turn left onto the dirt road. You'll soon arrive at **Siq al-Barid,** a cleft in the rock that will remind you of the Siq at Petra except that it's much shorter and the sun does not penetrate it (hence the meaning of its Arabic name, "the cold cleft"). A walk through this passage brings you to Little Petra. This, rather than the city of Petra itself, was the staging area for the thousands of camels that would have arrived with each caravan. Merchants conducted business in Little Petra's rock-cut courtyard, but evidence shows that they made time for diversion as well. One room off the courtyard is a dining room, the ceiling of which was once richly painted; another is a theater. ✉ *Admission included in Petra entrance fee; keep ticket.* ☉ *Daily, dawn to dusk.*

## Lodging

**$$$$** 🏨 **Petra Movenpick.** This is Petra's finest hotel. Beyond its excellent location, right by the city gates, the Movenpick has plenty of its own draws—first and foremost its staff, who are markedly cordial, helpful, and accommodating. Public spaces are beautifully decorated in an Asian theme: the lobby has a Moroccan tiled fountain and wooden furniture decorated with mother-of-pearl in an Islamic design, and the hand-carved wooden screens in Al'Maqa'ad (Bar) are intricately inlaid with turquoise and gold leaves. The rooms are simply and elegantly done in soft colors and have exceptionally comfortable beds. Moreover, the Movenpick is known for its food; the buffet features a different theme every night, and you're bound to make full use of the option for seconds. ✉ *Box 214, Wadi Musa 718101,* ☎ *03/215–7111 or 800/344–6835 in the U.S.,* 📠 *03/215–7112. 156 rooms, 28 suites. 2 restaurants, bar, minibars, no-smoking rooms, pool, sauna, exercise room, library. AE, DC, MC, V.*

**$$$** 🏨 **Petra Forum.** The Forum is at the entrance to Petra, on the outskirts of the village of Wadi Musa. Its restaurant, Aretas, serves Middle Eastern and European food and will prepare box lunches. Two of the rooms are wheelchair-accessible. ✉ *Box 30, Wadi Musa,* ☎ *03/215–6266,* 📠 *03/215–6977. 147 rooms. Restaurant, pool, car rental. AE, D, MC, V.*

**$$$**   🔝 **Taybet Zeman.** Nine kilometers (5½ miles) from Petra, on the outskirts of the town of Taybeh, this unique lodging was once a Bedouin village. Abandoned for years, it was eventually revamped into a lovely hotel with a spectacular view of the mountains of Edom. The central courtyard has a spice garden, and its yields are served in the excellent restaurant—the menu mixes Eastern and Western favorites, and the buffet, about 18 JD ($25) per person, is worth a trip in itself. ⊠ *Box 2, Wadi Musa,* ☎ *03/215–0111,* 📠 *03/215–0101. 106 rooms. Restaurant, sauna. AE, D, MC, V.*

**$$**   🔝 **Kings Way Inn.** The Kings Way is in the village of Wadi Musa, 4 km (2½ mi) from Petra, across from the Ein Musa Spring. ⊠ *Box 71, Wadi Musa,* ☎ *03/215–6799,* 📠 *03/215–6796. 81 rooms. AE, D, MC, V.*

**$$**   🔝 **Petra Palace.** The relatively new Palace is only 250 yards from Petra's entrance, and the rate includes breakfast. ⊠ *Box 70, Wadi Musa,* ☎ *03/215–6723,* 📠 *03/215–6724. 83 rooms. Restaurant, bar, pool. MC, V.*

**$$**   🔝 **Petra Rest House.** This option is near Petra's entrance. ⊠ *Wadi Musa,* ☎ *03/215–6246,* 📠 *03/215–6977. 72 rooms. Restaurant. MC, V.*

**$$**   🔝 **Treasury.** This hotel is by the traffic circle in the center of Wadi Musa. ⊠ *Box 5, Wadi Musa,* ☎ *03/215–72741. 72 rooms. MC, V.*

**$**   🔝 **Amra.** A budget option, the Amra is in the center of Wadi Musa. ⊠ *Box 124, Wadi Musa,* ☎ *03/551–0001,* 📠 *03/551–0003. 48 rooms. No credit cards.*

**$**   🔝 **Candles.** The Candles Hotel is 660 ft from the entrance to Petra. ⊠ *Box 149, Wadi Musa,* ☎ 📠 *03/215–6954. 31 rooms. AE, MC, V.*

# Petra A to Z

## Before You Go

### BORDERS

The Arava border crossing, just north of Eilat in Israel, is open Sunday–Thursday 6:30 AM–10 PM, Friday–Saturday 8–8. The crossing is closed on the religious holidays Yom Kippur and Id el Fitr. There is a border tax of NIS 56 ($16) on the Israeli side.

Two other border crossings might be convenient under certain circumstances. The Allenby Bridge crossing (four hours' drive from Petra) is about 45 minutes from Jerusalem. If you plan to enter Jordan here, you'll need to obtain your visa ahead of time at the Jordanian Embassy in Tel Aviv (☞ Passports and Visas, *below*) or in your country of origin. The Beit She'an border crossing (five hours' drive from Petra) is approximately 40 minutes from Tiberias.

### CURRENCY

The Jordanian unit of currency is the dinar, indicated by the suffix JD. The exchange rate at press time was approximately .708 JD to the U.S. dollar, .53 JD to the Canadian dollar, and 1.18 JD to the British pound.

### PASSPORTS AND VISAS

You need a valid passport to enter Jordan. Holders of non-Israeli passports can obtain visas on the spot after crossing into Jordan (except at the Allenby Bridge crossing; ☞ Borders, *above*) or through the Jordanian Embassy (⊠ 14 Abba Hillel St., Tel Aviv, ☎ 03/751–7722). A visa costs the equivalent of $21.

## Arriving and Departing

### BY BUS

There are only two buses per day from the Jordanian side of the Arava crossing to Aqaba, one at 7:30 AM and one at 8 PM. Taxis are far more convenient.

### BY CAR

Only cars registered to their drivers can be driven into Jordan (☞ Car Rentals *in* Contacts and Resources, *below*). Note that unleaded fuel is not sold in Jordan.

### BY PLANE

El Al and Royal Jordanian Airlines fly to Amman, Jordan's capital, from Tel Aviv's Ben-Gurion Airport. This option has limited appeal, as you must be at the airport two hours before flight time for the 15-minute flight, then drive three hours from Amman to Petra.

### BY TAXI

Taxis are available on the Jordanian side of the Arava border to take you into Aqaba, where you can rent a car. A shared taxi to Aqaba costs about $1.50 per person, a private taxi about 4 JD ($5.60).

## Getting Around

### BY CAR

Driving the narrow, winding Aqaba–Petra Highway is an experience. Remember to stay well to the right, but bear in mind that the driver coming from the opposite direction may not be so inclined.

## Contacts and Resources

### CAR RENTALS

The **Petra Travel and Tourism Company** (☞ Guided Tours, *below*) is the local agent for Hertz, Avis, and other companies. If you reserve in advance, the car will be waiting for you at the Arava border crossing; otherwise, you'll pick up and drop off the car at the agency's offices in Aqaba.

### GUIDED TOURS

A number of operators run tours to Petra that you can reserve in advance. These are a good option if you want to see the highlights without having to worry about logistics.

**Galilee Tours** (⊠ 42 Ben Yehuda St., Tel Aviv, ☎ 03/525–2888, FAX 03/525–2999; ⊠ Neptune Hotel, Eilat, ☎ 07/633–5145, FAX 07/633–5121) runs a two-day tour to Wadi Rum (including a Jeep tour of the beautiful sandstone landscapes) and Petra, with an overnight in Petra. The price is $219 per person, including admission fees, horses in Petra, and Jeeps in Wadi Rum.

**Neot Hakikar** (⊠ 67 Ben Yehuda St., Tel Aviv, ☎ 03/522–8161, FAX 03/522–1020; ⊠ Khan Amiel Center, Eilat, ☎ 07/633–0426) has a two-day trip to Petra, including a stop at Wadi Rum for a Jeep tour. The $169 fee does not include admission to Petra.

**Petra Travel and Tourism Company** (Headquarters: ⊠ Aqaba Gulf Hotel, Box 1312, Aqaba, Jordan, ☎ 03/201–6636, FAX 03/201–8246) offers a full-day tour of Petra with a driver-guide for 50 JD ($70) a day. You can also hire a private guide to join *your* car for 25 JD–35 JD ($35–$50) per day, depending on the season.

### MEDICAL CARE

There is a doctor at the **clinic** in the tourist compound near the Petra Forum Hotel, at the entrance to Petra. The closest **hospital** is in Ma'an (☎ 03/213–2222), about 40 km (25 mi) away.

### TELEPHONES

When dialing from Israel, dial 00–962 and the area code 3 before numbers in Petra; for Amman, use 00–962 and the area code 6. When dialing within Jordan, add a 0 before the area code. The international country code for Jordan is 962.

### VISITOR INFORMATION

Petra's **visitor center** (☎ 03/215–6020) has brochures.

# 10 Chronology and Further Reading

# ISRAEL AT A GLANCE: A CHRONOLOGY

As the only land bridge between Africa and Asia, Israel has always been a thoroughfare, a distinction that has made it desirable to foreign powers and often turned it into a battleground. Moreover, the country's position between the desert and the Mediterranean Sea has determined its climate and economy and, by extension, the character of those who conquered the land and settled here.

Israel was once called Canaan, then the Land of Israel (Eretz Yisrael, in Hebrew), then Israel. Later, the name Israel came to represent only the northern Israelite kingdom, including Samaria and Galilee, while the southern kingdom was called Judah. Judah became the Greek "Judea," first applied only to a small part of the country centered on Jerusalem but later to a much larger territory. After the Bar Kochba Revolt (2nd century AD), the Roman emperor Hadrian changed the name Judea to Palaestina (after the long-gone Philistines) in order to dissociate the country from its Jewish identity. Palestine later became the name of this tiny district in the huge Muslim empires of the Middle Ages. To Christians it was always the Holy Land; to Jews, Eretz Yisrael. The use of the name Israel in the following chronology does not always imply any specific set of borders, past or present, but the country as a whole, the ancient Land of Israel.

## Prehistoric Israel

**ca. 1.2 million years ago** Earliest known human habitation in Israel (Lower Paleolithic Period), at Ubeidiya, in Jordan Valley.

**ca. 7800 BC** The establishment of Jericho (Neolithic Pre-Pottery Period), the oldest walled town ever found.

## Canaanite Period (Bronze Age) ca. 3200 BC–1250 BC

**ca. 3200–2150** Writing is developed in Mesopotamia; beginning of recorded history. Early Canaanite/Bronze Age in Israel. Major cities are built: Jerusalem, Megiddo, and Hazor.

**ca. 2150–1550** Age of the Patriarchs: Abraham, Isaac, and Jacob. Middle Canaanite/Bronze Age.

**ca. 1550–1250** Time of Hebrews' enslavement in Egypt. Decline of Egyptian power. Moses leads Hebrews in exodus from Egypt. Late Canaanite/Bronze Age: Israel divided into city-kingdoms.

**ca. 1290** The Hebrews—the "Children of Israel"—receive the Torah (the Law) at Mt. Sinai. The nation of Israel is formed, the basis of its religion established, and its relationship with the one God defined. Forty years of desert wandering separate the nation from its Promised Land.

## First Temple—Old Testament Period (Iron Age) ca. 1250 BC–586 BC

**ca. 1250** Moses dies within sight of the Promised Land. Joshua leads the nation across the Jordan River and embarks on the conquest of Canaan, beginning with Jericho.

**ca. 1200–1025** Period of the Judges (e.g., Deborah, Gideon, Samson), charismatic regional leaders.

**ca. 1150** The Philistines invade from the west and establish a league of five city-states. Israelites appeal to the prophet Samuel for a king.

**1025** Saul, of humble origin, is the first King of Israel.

**1006** Saul and three sons, including Jonathan, are killed fighting the Philistines. David rules Judah.

**1000** David conquers Jerusalem, a Jebusite enclave, and makes it the national capital of unified Israel. Having brought the sacred Ark of the Covenant to Jerusalem, he establishes the city as the new religious center.

**968** Solomon becomes king, consolidates David's kingdom, and in 950 builds the First Temple to the Lord, in Jerusalem.

**928** Division of the monarchy after death of Solomon. The northern Tribes of Israel, under Jeroboam, break away to form the Kingdom of Israel. The southern Tribes, now known as the Kingdom of Judah, with its capital at Jerusalem, are ruled by Rehoboam, Solomon's weak son.

**ca. 865** Ahab rules as King of Israel (871–851) and Jehosophat as King of Judah (867–843). Peace between the two kingdoms. Ahab's wife, Jezebel, reintroduces pagan idol-worship.

**721** Kingdom of Israel destroyed by the Assyrians (now the region's superpower) and exile of its population (the "Ten Lost Tribes"). Kingdom of Judah comes under the Assyrian yoke.

**701** Hezekiah, King of Judah, revolts against Assyria. Assyrians lay siege to Jerusalem. With new fortifications, a superb water system, and the inspiration of the prophet Isaiah, the city withstands the siege.

**609** Josiah, last great king of Judah (640–609) and important religious reformer, is killed trying to block Egyptian advance. Jeremiah prophesies national catastrophe.

**586** Assyrians defeated by new power, the Babylonians, whose king, Nebuchadnezzar, conquers Judah and destroys Jerusalem and the First Temple. Of those who survive, large numbers are exiled to the "rivers of Babylon."

## Second Temple Period, 538 BC–AD 70

During this period the Babylonians are defeated, the Temple in Jerusalem is rebuilt, and the sacrificial rites are restored, but the Land of Israel must still share its preeminence with important Jewish centers in Babylon, Egypt, and elsewhere. Starting in the 3rd century BC, deep divisions appear within the Jewish nation over theological issues and the seductive Hellenistic culture, introduced to the region by Alexander the Great. The Sadducees, which draw their strength from the upper classes, take a literal, Bible-based view and are willing to accommodate elements of Hellenism. The Pharisees, a Jewish group of the common people, add the Oral Law (the unwritten rabbinic interpretation of the Torah) to the authority of the Scriptures; they reject accommodation of the pagan world and spin off groups like the ascetic Essenes and the militant Zealots.

**538** Cyrus, King of Persia, conquers Babylon and allows the Jewish exiles to return home. In Jerusalem, the returnees rebuild the Temple (completed ca. 516). In Babylon, the synagogue, a communal place of assembly with an emphasis on the reading of the Bible and (eventually) on prayer, develops.

**445** Nehemiah, a Jewish nobleman, is sent by the Persian king with the authority to rebuild Jerusalem's walls and rule the district.

**333** Persian Empire is defeated by Alexander the Great, and the entire Near East comes under Hellenistic sway.

**323** Death of Alexander and struggle for control of his empire. Ptolemy rules in Egypt; Seleucus in Syria and Mesopotamia.

**301** Ptolemy establishes control over Judea (as Judah is now called) and Samaria and the Galilee (an area once known as Israel), to the north of it. Egypt's now Greek-speaking Jewish population burgeons. The Bible is translated into Greek and called the Septuagint.

**198** The Syrian Seleucids defeat the Egyptian Ptolemies at Banias, the headwaters of the Jordan, annex Judea, and establish good relations with the Jewish community.

**167** The Seleucid king Antiochus IV outlaws all Jewish religious practices. Beginning of the Maccabean Revolt.

**165** After four decisive victories over Hellenistic armies, Judah the Maccabee (Judas Maccabeus) enters the desecrated Temple in Jerusalem, purifying and rededicating it.

**142** Simon, brother of Judah the Maccabee, achieves independence for Judea and establishes the Hasmonean dynasty.

**63** Pompey, the Roman general, enters the country to settle a civil war between the last Hasmonean princes and annexes it as a Roman province.

**48** The influential royal counselor Antipater, a Jewish convert, appoints his sons, among them Herod, to key administrative positions.

**40** Mark Antony appoints Herod as king of the Jews.

**37** After fighting his way through the country, Herod claims his throne in Jerusalem. Hated by the Jews, he seeks to legitimize his reign by marrying a Hasmonean princess (whom he later murders).

**31** Antony is defeated by Octavian, now the emperor Caesar Augustus. Herod pays homage to Augustus in Rome and is confirmed in his titles and territories, then rebuilds the Second Temple in Jerusalem on a grand scale, winning great esteem.

**ca. 5** Birth of Jesus in Bethlehem.

**4** Death of Herod, called by history "the Great." His kingdom is divided among three sons: Archelaus rules in Jerusalem (and is exiled 10 years later, replaced by the direct Roman rule of Judea by procurators based in Caesarea); Herod Antipas rules the Galilee and Perea (east of the Jordan River); and Philip controls Golan, Bashan, and the sources of the Jordan River.

**ca. AD 27** Beginning of Jesus' Galilean ministry. He calls the disciples, heals and performs miracles, teaches, and preaches, mostly around the Sea of Galilee.

**ca. 29** Jesus and his disciples celebrate Passover in Jerusalem. Arrest, trial, and crucifixion of Jesus by the Romans on orders of the Roman governor, Pontius Pilate. For the Romans, the claim of Jesus as the Messiah (Hebrew for "the anointed one"), with its implication of kingship, is tantamount to high treason. The New Testament relates that Jesus' death and resurrection were divinely determined, an expiation for the sins of humanity. Identification with this event as the way to personal salvation becomes the basis for the community of faith that is Christianity.

**66** Start of Great Revolt against Roman oppression. Jews briefly reassert their political independence.

**67** Galilee falls to the Romans. The Jewish commander defects to the enemy.

Romanizing his name to Josephus Flavius, he follows the Roman campaigns, eventually recording them in *The Jewish War*.

**69**  Before the fall of Jerusalem, the sage Yochanan Ben Zakkai leaves the city, settling with his disciples in the town of Yavneh in the coastal plain, by grant of Roman general and caesar-elect Vespasian.

**70**  Jerusalem, torn by internal faction fighting, falls to the Roman general Titus after long siege. The Second Temple is destroyed. Slaughter and slavery of Jews follow. The revolt is officially at an end.

**73**  The last Jewish stronghold, at Masada, falls. Its defenders take their own lives rather than surrender. With the destruction of Jerusalem and the Temple, Yavneh becomes the seat of the Sanhedrin, the Jewish High Court. Its sages find religious responses to the new reality of Judaism without the Temple, and the spiritual and legal authority of Yavneh is established.

# Late Roman and Byzantine Period, 73–640

**132**  When the Roman emperor Hadrian threatens to rebuild Jerusalem as a pagan city, another Jewish revolt breaks out, led by Bar Kochba and supported by Rabbi Akiva. Secret preparations and a strong unified command lead to spectacular initial successes.

**135**  Death of Bar Kochba. The revolt is brutally suppressed, but only after severe Roman losses. Hadrian plows over Jerusalem and builds in its place Aelia Capitolina, a pagan city off-limits to Jews; the name of the country is changed to Palaestina, and Jewish religious practice is outlawed. The Sanhedrin relocates to the Lower Galilee.

**ca. 200**  At Zippori or Sepphoris, in the Galilee, Judah the Nasi (patriarch), spiritual and political head of the Jewish community, compiles the Mishnah, the summary of the Oral Law, which is the basis of Jewish jurisprudence. Period of peace and prosperity under the tolerant Severan emperors.

**325**  Emperor Constantine the Great makes Christianity the imperial religion and eventually converts to the faith. His mother, Helena, comes to the Holy Land in 326 and initiates the building of major churches—the Holy Sepulcher in Jerusalem and the Nativity in Bethlehem.

**330**  Constantine transfers his capital from Rome to Byzantium, now renamed Constantinople. Beginning of the Byzantine Period. Judaism is on the defensive.

**351**  Jewish revolt, primarily in the Galilee, against the Roman ruler Gallus is brutally suppressed.

**361**  Emperor Julian the Apostate (r. 361–363) tries to reintroduce pagan cults.

**ca. 400**  Final codification of the so-called Jerusalem Talmud, the result of years of rabbinic elaboration of the Mishnah. (The Babylonian Talmud, codified a century later, is regarded as more authoritative.)

**527–565**  Reign of Emperor Justinian. Many important churches built or rebuilt, among them the present Church of the Nativity in Bethlehem. Vibrant Jewish community despite persecution.

**614**  Persian invasion, with destruction of churches and monasteries.

**622**  Muhammad's "flight" (*hejira*) from Mecca to Medina in Arabia; beginnings of Islam.

**628**  Persians defeated and Byzantine rule restored in Israel.

**632** Death of Muhammad. His followers, ruled by a series of caliphs, burst out of Arabia and create a Muslim empire that within a century would extend from India to Spain.

**636** Arab invasion of the country and, in 638, the fall of Byzantine Jerusalem to the caliph Omar (r. 634–644).

# Medieval Period, 640–1516

**691** Caliph Abd al-Malik builds the Dome of the Rock in Jerusalem.

**1099** Sworn to wrest Christian holy places from Muslim control, the European armies of the First Crusade reach the Holy Land. Jerusalem is taken, and most of its population, Muslim and Jew alike, is massacred.

**1100** Establishment of the Latin Kingdom of Jerusalem, with Baldwin I at its head. Chronic shortage of manpower puts the burden of defense on the monastic orders—the Hospitallers and Templars, for example—who build castles (among them Belvoir, in the Lower Galilee, and the underground quarter in Akko).

**1110** Most coastal cities in Crusader hands.

**1187** Crusader armies decimated by the Arab ruler Saladin. Crusaders expelled from the country.

**1191** The Third Crusade arrives, led by Richard the Lionhearted of England and Philip II (Augustus) of France. The Latin Kingdom of Jerusalem never regains its former size and glory—and except for a very brief time, the holy city itself—and the Crusaders content themselves with the coast from Tyre to Jaffa and the Galilee. Acre (Akko) becomes the royal capital.

**1228** The Crusaders gain Jerusalem by treaty but lose the city again in 1244.

**1250** The militant Mamluk class seizes power in Egypt. The Crusade of King Louis IX (St-Louis) against Egypt fails. He is captured but comes to the Holy Land after his release.

**1260** The Mamluks check the Mongol invasion at Ayn Jalout (Ein Harod), in the Jezreel Valley.

**1265** Muslim reconquest of the land begins under the Mamluk sultan Baybars.

**1291** Fall of Akko and end of Crusader kingdom. Commerce and trade decline with destruction of coastal cities. Beginning of period of outstanding architecture, especially in Jerusalem's Temple Mount (Haram esh-Sharif) and Muslim Quarter and in the Cave of Machpelah in Hebron.

**1492** Expulsion of the Jewish community from Spain. Many of these Sephardic Jews later immigrate to Israel.

# The Modern Period, 1516–Present

**1516** Mamluk armies defeated in Syria by the Ottoman Turks, who extend control over the land of Israel (Palestine) as well. Jewish community throughout the country grows. Zfat is center of Kabbalah.

**1520–1566** Suleiman the Magnificent reigns. His many projects include rebuilding Jerusalem's walls.

**1700** Large numbers of Ashkenazi (Eastern European) Jews arrive.

**1799** Invasion by Napoléon Bonaparte founders at Akko.

**1832** Egyptian nationalists under Muhammad Ali and Ibrahim Pasha take control of Israel. They are expelled in 1840 with the help of European nations.

**1853**   The Crimean War breaks out in Europe against the background of conflict between Catholic France and Orthodox Russia over the custody of holy places in Israel.

**1882**   First Aliyah (wave of Jewish immigration), mostly idealistic Eastern Europeans. Baron Edmond de Rothschild establishes new villages and wineries in the coastal plain and the Galilee.

**1897**   First World Zionist Conference, organized by Theodore Herzl in Basel, Switzerland, gives great impetus to the idea of a "Jewish national home."

**1906**   The Second Aliyah, or wave of immigration, of young Jewish idealists from Russia and Poland, including David Ben-Gurion, who would become Israel's first prime minister.

**1909**   Tel Aviv founded. Degania, the first kibbutz, established on the southern shore of the Sea of Galilee.

**1917**   British government issues Balfour Declaration expressing support for a "Jewish national home" in Palestine. General Edmund Allenby captures Jerusalem.

**1918**   Ottoman Turkey, which had sided with Germany during World War I, abandons Palestine.

**1920–1939**   As Arab nationalism rises in the post-Ottoman Middle East, tensions increase between Jews and Arabs in Palestine, peaking in the massacres of Jews in 1920, 1929, and 1936. Jewish militias form to counter the violence. Substantial immigration of European Jews, who come with growing urgency, as Nazis take power in Germany.

**1921**   Transjordan is separated from Palestine.

**1922**   The newly formed League of Nations confirms the Mandate entrusting the rule of Palestine to Great Britain and incorporating the text of the Balfour Declaration.

**1939**   British Government issues white paper restricting Jewish immigration to Israel and Jewish purchase of land there in an attempt to secure Arab goodwill in the coming war. In World War II, Jews enlist on Allied side. "We shall fight the war as if there were no white paper," said Palestinian Jewish leader David Ben-Gurion, "but we shall fight the white paper as if there were no war."

**1945**   End of World War II, in which one-third of Jewish people were annihilated by the Nazis. When British policy does not change, underground movements challenge British authority. Illegal immigrants, many of them Holocaust survivors, are brought in on ships; many don't get through British blockade. Clashes with Arabs increase.

**1947**   United Nations Special Commission on Palestine recommends plan to partition the country into a Jewish state and an Arab state (three disconnected territorial segments in each) and to internationalize Jerusalem and Bethlehem. Jewish euphoria, Arab rejection. Beginning of Israel's War of Independence. Discovery of the first Dead Sea Scrolls at Qumran.

**1948**   May 14: Last British forces depart, ending British Mandate. David Ben-Gurion declares Israel an independent state. The new state survives invasion by the armies of seven Arab countries.

**1949**   End of fighting in January. UN-supervised cease-fire agreements signed. Transjordan annexes the West Bank (of the Jordan River) and East Jerusalem, which it captured in the war, and changes the country's name to the Hashemite Kingdom of Jordan. Egypt annexes the Gaza Strip along the southern Mediterranean coast. Palestinian Arabs who fled during the conflict are housed in refugee camps in neighboring countries; those who remain behind become citizens of Israel. First elections to the Knesset, Israel's parliament. David Ben-Gurion is elected prime minister; Dr. Chaim Weizmann, first president.

**1949–1952** Israel absorbs great numbers of Jewish refugees, trebling its Jewish population by the end of the decade.

**1950** The Knesset enacts the Law of Return, giving any Jew the right to Israeli citizenship.

**1956** Sinai Campaign, in which British, French, and Israeli forces oppose Egyptian nationalization of the Suez Canal. Fedayeen terrorist attacks from Egyptian-controlled Gaza Strip become less frequent, but sporadic Syrian shelling of Israeli villages below the Golan Heights is a major security issue into the 1960s.

**1964** Formation of the Palestine Liberation Organization (PLO). Seeks independent state for Palestinians and refuses to recognize the legitimacy of the State of Israel.

**1967** June: Outbreak of Six-Day War. Egypt, Jordan, and Syria are routed; Israel occupies the Sinai Peninsula, Gaza Strip, West Bank, East Jerusalem, and the Golan Heights and finds itself in control of almost 1 million Palestinian Arabs. Some Jewish settlements are established in the West Bank and Golan Heights.

**1973** Egypt and Syria attack Israel on the holiest Jewish holiday, the Day of Atonement (hence, the name Yom Kippur War). Israel beats off the invasion but is sobered.

**1974–1975** Signing of Disengagement Agreement on the Golan with Syria and the Interim Agreement with Egypt.

**1976** Dramatic Israeli commando raid frees Air France passengers taken hostage in Entebbe, Uganda, by Palestinian hijackers.

**1977** Menachem Begin's Likud Party comes to power in May, ending almost four decades of Labor domination of Israeli politics. Egyptian president Anwar Sadat visits Israel.

**1978** Camp David Accords give direction to Egypt-Israel peace talks and produce guidelines for a solution to the Palestinian problem.

**1979** Israel-Egypt peace agreement signed.

**1980** Israeli prime minister Menachem Begin and Egyptian president Anwar Sadat share the Nobel Peace Prize.

**1982** Israeli forces cross into southern Lebanon in pursuit of Palestinians shelling civilian settlements in Israel. This escalates into the Lebanon War (1982–85), with unprecedented opposition from Israelis.

**1987** A road accident in the Gaza Strip triggers the beginning of the *intifada*, sustained Palestinian Arab street violence, demonstrations, strikes, and sporadic terrorist activity.

**1989–1992** Israel absorbs more than 500,000 Soviet Jewish immigrants.

**1991** Persian Gulf War; Israel under constant attack but restrained from retaliating. June: 14,500 Ethiopian Jews airlifted to Israel. December: Peace talks in Madrid between Israel and Jordan, Syria, Lebanon, and the Palestinians.

**1992** In June the Labor Party under Yitzhak Rabin, vowing to step up the peace process and halt Israeli "political" settlements in West Bank, is voted in after 15 years out of office.

**1993–1994**  The Oslo Accords provide for mutual recognition of Israel and the PLO, as well as Palestinian autonomy in the Gaza Strip and Jericho. Nobel Peace Prize shared by Yitzhak Rabin, Shimon Peres, and Yasir Arafat.

**1995**  Prime minister Yitzhak Rabin assassinated in November by an Israeli, a tragic climax to a year of rancorous national debate on the "territory for peace" concept. Six more Palestinian Arab West Bank cities are given autonomy.

**1996**  New law for direct election of the prime minister brings Likud's Binyamin Netanyahu to power by a margin of less than 1%. Contrary to expectations, the major parties lose much strength, with the religious parties—now powerful partners in the new, far more conservative government—the big winners.

**1997**  Israel and the Palestinians sign the Hebron Agreement.

**1998**  Israel celebrates its 50th anniversary.

# FURTHER READING

## History and Biography

If you haven't opened the Bible in a while, this is a good time to review biblical narratives; better yet, bring it along on your trip. For a modern look at the Bible, take a look at *Genesis and the Big Bang*, by Gerald Schroeder (Bantam). *Heritage, Civilization and the Jews*, by Abba Eban (Steimatzky), is a pictorial survey illustrating 5,000 years of Jewish civilization. *Jews, God and History*, by Max I. Dimont (Signet), is an old but very readable history of the Jewish people (and very portable for traveling). Karen Armstrong's *Jerusalem: One City, Three Faiths* (Alfred A. Knopf) traces the city's physical history and spiritual meaning from its beginning to the present day. *Understanding the Dead Sea Scrolls*, edited by Hershel Shanks (Random House), is a selection of essays by leading scholars; it provides numerous insights into that important discovery. Last, but far from least, is Flavius Josephus's *The Jewish War*. The Jewish commander who defected to the Romans during the Great Revolt wrote a still-fascinating account of the Roman campaigns.

To better understand some of the leading players in Israel's modern history, try: *The Life of Moshe Dayan,* by Robert Slater (St. Martin's Press); *Ben-Gurion,* by Shabtai Teveth (Houghton Mifflin); *The Revolt,* by Menachem Begin (Steimatzky), the former prime minister's account of the fighting unit he headed; and *My Life,* by Golda Meir (Weidenfeld and Nicolson). *O Jerusalem,* by Larry Collins and Dominique Lapierre (Simon and Schuster), is a dramatic account of the establishment of the Israeli state.

*The Book of Our Heritage,* by Eliayahv Kitov (Feldheim), is a superb guide to Jewish holidays and traditions.

## Fiction and Poetry

*Exodus,* a novel by Leon Uris (Doubleday), deals with the founding of the State of Israel. *The Source,* by James Michener (Fawcett), is the novelist's vivid look at Israel's early history. *Closing the Sea,* by Yehudit Katzir (Harcourt, Brace, Jovanovich), is a book of short stories set in Israel. *The Black Box,* by Amos Oz (Flamingo), is a modern love story. *Saturday Morning Murder,* by Batya Gur (Harper Collins), is a psychological mystery. Among the works of poet Yehuda Amichai is *Poems of Jerusalem.* Other contemporary Israeli writers worth looking out for are A. B. Yehoshua, Meir Shalev, David Grossman, and Irit Linor.

## Modern Israel

*To Jerusalem and Back,* by Saul Bellow (Avon), conveys the flavor of modern Israeli life through the impressions of the Nobel Prize–winning author. *In the Land of Israel,* by Amos Oz (Chatto and Windus), is a series of articles depicting various settlements and towns and conversations with local people. In *Arab and Jew* (Times Books), David K. Shipler, a former *New York Times* correspondent, takes a contemporary look at the relationship. *Intifada,* by Zeev Schiff and Ehud Yaari (Touchstone), gives background and analysis of the Arab unrest in the late 1980s and early '90s. In *My Enemy, Myself* (Penguin), Yoram Binur, a journalist, imagines himself a Palestinian. Thomas Friedman looks at modern events and politics in the Middle East in *From Beirut to Jerusalem* (Farrar, Straus & Giroux). And try *Jerusalem, City of Mirrors,* by Amos Elon (Fontana), and *Safed, the Mystical City,* by David Rossoff (Feldheim Publishers).

# INDEX

# NOTES

# NOTES

# NOTES

With guidebooks for every kind of travel—from weekend getaways to island hopping to adventures abroad—it's easy to understand why smart travelers go with **Fodor's**.

At bookstores everywhere.
**www.fodors.com**

# Fodor's Travel Publications

*Available at bookstores everywhere. For descriptions of all our titles and a key to Fodor's guidebook series, visit http://www.fodors.com/books/*

## Gold Guides
### U.S.

Alaska

Arizona

Boston

California

Cape Cod, Martha's Vineyard, Nantucket

The Carolinas & Georgia

Chicago

Colorado

Florida

Hawai'i

Las Vegas, Reno, Tahoe

Los Angeles

Maine, Vermont, New Hampshire

Maui & Lāna'i

Miami & the Keys

New England

New Orleans

New York City

Oregon

Pacific North Coast

Philadelphia & the Pennsylvania Dutch Country

The Rockies

San Diego

San Francisco

Santa Fe, Taos, Albuquerque

Seattle & Vancouver

The South

U.S. & British Virgin Islands

USA

Virginia & Maryland

Washington, D.C.

### Foreign

Australia

Austria

The Bahamas

Belize & Guatemala

Bermuda

Canada

Cancún, Cozumel, Yucatán Peninsula

Caribbean

China

Costa Rica

Cuba

The Czech Republic & Slovakia

Denmark

Eastern & Central Europe

Europe

Florence, Tuscany & Umbria

France

Germany

Great Britain

Greece

Hong Kong

India

Ireland

Israel

Italy

Japan

London

Madrid & Barcelona

Mexico

Montréal & Québec City

Moscow, St. Petersburg, Kiev

The Netherlands, Belgium & Luxembourg

New Zealand

Norway

Nova Scotia, New Brunswick, Prince Edward Island

Paris

Portugal

Provence & the Riviera

Scandinavia

Scotland

Singapore

South Africa

South America

Southeast Asia

Spain

Sweden

Switzerland

Thailand

Toronto

Turkey

Vienna & the Danube Valley

Vietnam

### Special-Interest Guides

Adventures to Imagine

Alaska Ports of Call

Ballpark Vacations

The Best Cruises

Caribbean Ports of Call

The Complete Guide to America's National Parks

Europe Ports of Call

Family Adventures

Fodor's Gay Guide to the USA

Fodor's How to Pack

Great American Learning Vacations

Great American Sports & Adventure Vacations

Great American Vacations

Great American Vacations for Travelers with Disabilities

Halliday's New Orleans Food Explorer

Healthy Escapes

Kodak Guide to Shooting Great Travel Pictures

National Parks and Seashores of the East

National Parks of the West

Nights to Imagine

Orlando Like a Pro

Rock & Roll Traveler Great Britain and Ireland

Rock & Roll Traveler USA

Sunday in San Francisco

Walt Disney World for Adults

Weekends in New York

Wendy Perrin's Secrets Every Smart Traveler Should Know

Worlds to Imagine

# WHEREVER YOU TRAVEL, *H*ELP IS NEVER FAR AWAY.

From planning your trip to providing travel assistance along the way, American Express® Travel Service Offices are always there to help you do more.

---

## *Israel*

---

**Haifa**
American Express Travel Service (R)
6 Derech Hayam Street
(972)(4) 8362696

**Haifa**
American Express Travel Service (R)
2 Kikar Khayat
(972)(4) 8642266

**Jerusalem**
American Express Travel Service (R)
19 Hilel Street
(972)(2) 6240830

**Kiriat Bialik**
American Express Travel Service (R)
9 Jerusalem Boulevard
(972)(4) 8418466/8421898

**Ramat Gan**
American Express Travel Service (R)
47 Bialik Street
(972)(3) 6721343

**Rishon Le Zion**
American Express Travel Service (R)
95 Rothschild Street
(972)(3) 9662050

**Tel Aviv**
American Express Travel Service (R)
El Al Building
32 Ben Yehuda Street
(972)(3) 5268888

**Yessod Hamaala**
American Express Travel Service (R)
Commercial Center
Upper Galilee
(972)(6) 6930481

do more AMERICAN EXPRESS
**Travel**

www.americanexpress.com/travel